Boston
June '94

L. A. O'Mama

Fodor's 94
Florida

D0675299

Fodor's Travel Publications, Inc.
New York • Toronto • London • Sydney • Auckland

Copyright © 1993
by Fodor's Travel Publications, Inc.

ISBN 0-679-02515-4

Grateful acknowledgement is made to Alfred A. Knopf, Inc., for permission to reprint excerpts from *Tropical Splendor: An Architectural History of Florida*, by Hap Hatton. Copyright © 1987 by Hap Hatton. Reprinted by permission of Alfred A. Knopf, Inc.

Fodor's Florida

Editor: Holly Hughes
Area Editor: Herb Hiller
Editorial Contributors: April Athey, Al Burt, Natalie Fairhead, Catherine Fredman, Barbara Freitag, Janet and Gordon Groene, Ann Hughes, George and Rosalie Leposkey, Peter Oliver, Marcy Pritchard, Linda K. Schmidt, G. Stuart Smith, Karen Feldman Smith.
Creative Director: Fabrizio La Rocca
Cartographer: David Lindroth
Illustrator: Karl Tanner
Cover Photograph: Edward Slater/Southern Stock Photos
Design: Vignelli Associates

Special Sales

MANUFACTURED IN THE UNITED STATES OF AMERICA
10 9 8 7 6 5 4 3 2 1

Contents

Maps

Foreword

Florida is one of the world's most popular tourist destinations. Visitors from far and near are attracted to the state's sandy beaches, warm and sunny climate, and theme parks such as Walt Disney World. Travelers find Florida rich in historic sites, vast stretches of wildlife preserves, recreational trails, fine restaurants, accommodations to suit every budget, and shopping. Our Florida writers have put together information on the widest possible range of activities, and within that range present you with selections of events and places that will be safe, worthwhile, and of good value. The descriptions we provide are just enough for you to make your own informed choices from among our selections.

We wish to express our gratitude to those who have helped with this guide, including the Florida Division of Tourism, especially Dean Sullivan and Rosetta Stone Land; the Florida Department of Natural Resources, especially Mary Ann Koos; the Greater Fort Lauderdale Convention and Visitors Bureau, in particular Francine Mason; Timothy P. Brigham at the Greater Miami Convention and Visitors Bureau; Jennifer Clark at the Palm Beach County Convention and Visitors Bureau; Warren Zeiller and Nita Jensen at the South Dade Visitors Information Center; Mary Lou Reoch with the Tampa/Hillsborough Convention & Visitors Association; G. Lee Daniel with the Pinellas Suncoast Convention and Visitor Bureau; Stuart Newman and Associates; Geiger & Associates; Delta Airlines, particularly Dean Breest; and Joan and Peter Jefferson in Stuart, Florida.

While every care has been taken to assure the accuracy of the information in this guide, the passage of time will always bring change, and, consequently, the publisher cannot accept responsibility for errors that may occur.

All prices and opening times quoted here are based on information available to us at press time. Hours and admission fees may change, however, and the prudent traveler will avoid inconvenience by calling ahead.

Fodor's wants to hear about your travel experiences, both pleasant and unpleasant. When a hotel or restaurant fails to live up to its billing, let us know, and we will investigate.

Send your letters to the editors of Fodor's Travel Publications, 201 E. 50th St., New York, NY 10022.

Highlights'94 and Fodor's Choice

Highlights '94

Miami By the end of 1993, the effects of 1992's devastating **Hurricane Andrew** were largely limited to the slow revival of activity on Key Biscayne—no hotels were opened by mid-1993—and the popular Bill Baggs Cape Florida Park remained closed.

Two new **major-league franchises** began full schedules of play in 1993: the Florida Marlins of the National Baseball League, and the Florida Panthers of the National Hockey League. The two teams bring to six the major-league franchises in Florida.

Fort Lauderdale Florida's first **velodrome**, for competitive cycling and roller skating, opened in 1993 at Brian Piccolo Park, just off I–595 in western Broward County. The velodrome makes it possible for south Florida to host world-class sporting events such as the Inter-American Games or Olympic Games.

Palm Beach Donald Trump was expected to begin work in 1994 on converting the 17-acre **Mar-A-Lago waterfront estate** to a private social club. In its heyday as home of Marjorie Merriweather Post, Mar-A-Lago had 58 bedrooms and 33 bathrooms. Trump's plans call for a par-three, nine-hole golf course and a spa.

Everglades Agreement between the state of Florida and agricultural interests was expected before the end of 1993 on a plan to clean pollutants from waters drawn from **Lake Okeechobee** that flow through the Everglades and into Florida Bay. If satisfactorily concluded, the agreement will signify a landmark in the state's shift of priorities—away from serving farming interests and toward balancing environmental and economic needs.

Florida Keys Two high-priority environmental problems affecting the Florida Keys show that the commitment of Florida's business community to environmental protection is still lukewarm. A coalition of business and environmental interests wishes to halt the deterioration of Florida Bay and take decisive steps to replenish its freshwater flows from the Everglades. The bay's over-salinization has been aggravated by a lethal mix of chemical fertilizer and other runoffs from Florida's west coast. The results are the death of the bay's grasses and mangroves, and vastly reduced numbers of young sea creatures. Devastating algae flourish and are swept through channels between the Keys and onto coral reefs. But despite consensus that bay waters must be improved, hotel and fishing interests resist efforts to complete a plan for the new **Florida Keys National Marine Sanctuary**. The plan should be issued by the end of 1993; backers hope it will include provisions that set aside portions of the reef and adjacent waters as non-use zones, allowing sea life to replenish itself.

Tampa At the Garrison Seaport Center on Tampa's downtown waterfront, the new $84 million **Florida Aquarium** is under construction and is scheduled to open in April 1995. Under its seashell-shape glass roof the aquarium will tell the story of Florida's diverse water habitats, from stream and swamp to coast and open sea. Another attraction, the *Whydah* **Pirate Complex,** focusing on the history of the 18th-century shipwrecked pirate vessel *Whydah*, is also expected to open on a site nearby, during the Gasparilla Festival in February 1995.

St. Petersburg– The first 35 miles of the **Pinellas Trail,** a multi-use recrea-
Pinellas County tional corridor that replaces an abandoned rail line through Florida's most populous county, were expected to be complete by the end of 1993.

The **Stouffer Vinoy Resort** has opened in St. Petersburg, returning to public use one of Florida's legendary resort properties. After a $93 million restoration, the hotel, which opened as the Vinoy Park Hotel in 1925 and has been closed for 18 years, has helped rejuvenate St. Petersburg's boomera downtown. The hotel has 360 rooms and suites, including a new 102-room guest tower. The Vinoy joins the Breakers in Palm Beach, the Boca Raton Hotel, the Marriott Casa Marina in Key West, the Belleview-Mido in Clearwater, and the Don Cesar in St. Petersburg Beach as one of Florida's landmark historic hotels.

Orlando Area A milestone cooperative effort by private industry, the state, and conservation interests has resulted in preservation of an 8,500-acre wilderness area in Kissimmee. The property was purchased by the Walt Disney Company and given to the state for management by the Nature Conservancy, to mitigate environmental effects of the expansion of Walt Disney World. Formerly known as the Walker Ranch, the property will henceforth be known as the **Disney Wilderness Preserve.** It's in the upper Kissimmee River watershed, on the north shore of Lake Hatchineha. As part of the three-way agreement, Disney set aside another 8,350 acres on its property through a conservation easement held by the state and the South Florida Water Management District. The preserve has the greatest concentration of active bald-eagle nests in the southeastern United States.

World Cup soccer games will take place in Orlando in June and July 1994.

The Panhandle Another 124 acres of **Topsail Hill** land near Destin has been bought by the state of Florida and added to this pristine beachfront area, one of Florida's finest.

Fodor's Choice

No two people will agree on what makes a perfect vacation, but it's fun and helpful to know what others think. We hope you'll have a chance to experience some of Fodor's Choices yourself while visiting Florida. For detailed information about each entry, refer to the appropriate chapter in this guidebook.

View to Remember

The Gulf of Mexico at sunset, particularly at Mallory Square in Key West, where sunset watching is an evening ritual

Art Deco District in Miami Beach

Downtown Miami from the elevated Metromovers

The new Riverwalk cultural facilities and oceanfront aesthetics in Fort Lauderdale

The main span of Sunshine Skyway Bridge, St. Petersburg

IlluminNations in Walt Disney World's Epcot Center, Orlando

Historic Sites

San Agustin Antiguo, a restored Spanish colonial village in St. Augustine

Fort Caroline National Historic Monument, Jacksonville

Edison's and Ford's homes, with adjoining museum displaying many of their inventions, Fort Myers

Whitehall, the Flagler museum in Palm Beach

The Vizcaya Museum and Gardens in Miami

Theme Parks and Attractions

Walt Disney World, Orlando

Universal Studios Florida, Orlando

Busch Gardens, Tampa

Miami Seaquarium, Miami

Spaceport USA, Cocoa Beach

Hotels

The Breakers, Palm Beach (*Very Expensive*)

Cheeca Lodge, Islamorada (*Very Expensive*)

South Seas Plantation, Captiva Island (*Very Expensive*)

Amelia Island Plantation, Amelia Island (*Expensive–Very Expensive*)

Peabody Orlando, Orlando (*Expensive–Very Expensive*)

Sandestin Beach Resort, Destin (*Expensive–Very Expensive*)

Caribbean Beach Resort, Walt Disney World (*Moderate*)

Miami River Inn, Miami (*Moderate*)

Casa Rosa Inn, Kissimmee (*Inexpensive*)

Restaurants

Louie's Back Yard, Key West (*Very Expensive*)

Mark's Place, North Miami Beach (*Very Expensive*)

Bern's Steak House, Tampa (*Expensive*)

Chalet Suzanne, Orlando (*Expensive*)

Jamie's, Pensacola (*Moderate*)

Topaz Cafe, Flagler Beach (*Moderate*)

Homestead, Jacksonville (*Inexpensive*)

Romeros, Orlando (*Inexpensive*)

Beaches

Fort Pickens area of Gulf Islands National Seashore

Grayton Beach, near Destin

John U. Lloyd Beach State Recreation Area, Dania

Sarasota County beaches

Delnor-Wiggins Pass State Recreation Area, Naples

Events

Gasparilla Festival, Tampa

The ground shaking underfoot as a rocket soars spaceward from Cape Canaveral

Carnaval Miami, including the *Calle Oche* Open House, in early March in the Little Havana district of Miami

Coconut Grove and Winter Park arts festivals

Sports

Walking, jogging, or cycling on the new, largely complete 35-mile Pinellas Trail that runs through the heart of urban Tarpon Springs, Dunedin, Clearwater, and St. Petersburg

Fishing from the Redington Long Pier, or game fishing for the big ones off the Florida Keys

A jai alai game at any of the many frontons throughout the state

The Orange Bowl Classic football game and its preceding King Orange Jamboree Parade, Miami

After Hours

For local color, a drink at Captain Tony's, the original Sloppy Joe's, Hemingway's favorite bar in Key West

Comedy Corner, Palm Beach

Musicians Exchange, Fort Lauderdale

Ragtime Tavern for Dixieland and classic jazz, Atlantic Beach

Tobacco Road bar and restaurant, Miami

Sliders, Fernandina Beach

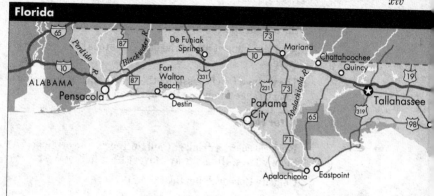

Florida

ALABAMA

Pensacola

Perdido R.

Blackwater R.

De Funiak Springs

Fort Walton Beach

Destin

Panama City

Mariana

Chattahoochee

Quincy

Apalachicola R.

Tallahassee

Apalachicola

Eastpoint

Gulf of Mexico

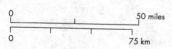

0   50 miles

0   75 km

The United States

500 miles

800 km

N

World Time Zones

Numbers below vertical bands relate each zone to Greenwich Mean Time (0 hrs.).
Local times frequently differ from these general indications,
as indicated by light-face numbers on map.

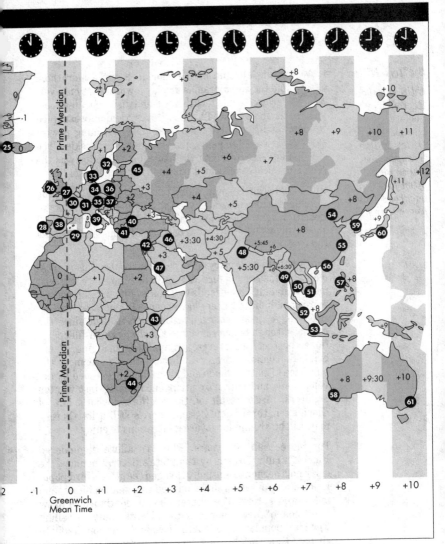

Mecca, **47**
Mexico City, **12**
Miami, **18**
Montréal, **15**
Moscow, **45**
Nairobi, **43**
New Orleans, **11**
New York City, **16**

Ottawa, **14**
Paris, **30**
Perth, **58**
Reykjavík, **25**
Rio de Janeiro, **23**
Rome, **39**
Saigon (Ho Chi Minh City), **51**

San Francisco, **5**
Santiago, **21**
Seoul, **59**
Shanghai, **55**
Singapore, **52**
Stockholm, **32**
Sydney, **61**
Tokyo, **60**

Toronto, **13**
Vancouver, **4**
Vienna, **35**
Warsaw, **36**
Washington, D.C., **17**
Yangon, **49**
Zürich, **31**

Introduction

By Herb Hiller

Editor of the Ecotourism Society Newsletter, Herb *Hiller is also a freelance writer whose pieces often focus on backroad travel and cycling.*

At the Museum of the Florida Keys in Marathon, photos and dioramas display a world that only yesterday teemed with bird and fish life, deer and gators, scrub flats laced by mangroves, randomly canopied by palm and hardwood hammocks. Over all hung pewter skies of dawn, blue skies, purple skies, storm skies, red skies of sunset. Rimming the shore for 220 miles was the reef, a magical other world spangled beneath the sea.

But outside the museum, along the Overseas Highway, the splendor is elbowed aside by urban hustle—motels, gas stations, RV parks, fast-food chains, convenience stores, shell shops, dive shops, dives. A barrage of come-ons assaults the land.

Florida these days is trying to redress a century of environmental disasters, before it's too late. The state has lost more than half its wetlands and much of its upland forests, more than half its waters have been contaminated, and its coasts have been cankered with concrete. But since the mid-'80s, tough policies now restrict dredge-and-fill operations, protect mangroves, prohibit the bridging of unbridged islands, preserve beach dunes, finance the purchase of critical lands and riverfront threatened by development, and authorize stringent fines against wanton polluters. As a result of these efforts, what's left of Florida's natural beauty—and there's still a lot there—may still be around for future generations to enjoy.

For more than 100 years, Florida's allure engendered Florida's ruin. Drawn by the state's natural bounty, the early northerners eventually ravaged the state's bird populations, tore out its orchids, burned tree snail habitats, and massacred gators. The winter climate continues to draw hundreds of new year-round residents daily—swelling Florida's population to fourth place in the nation, likely to surpass New York by the turn of the century.

Juan Ponce de Leon was only the first European to stumble upon the bounty. Long before the Spanish invasion, Native Americans had already discovered the area's restorative springs, the fishing and hunting grounds along both coasts, and along the lakes and rivers. Spain named the land for its conspicuous feature. They called the place *Florida,* land of flowers. But the Spanish never stopped to smell the fragrance: Florida dissappointed them. Gold was what they were after and Florida produced none of that.

None of the Europeans made much of Florida. The land was too wet, and the Indians, tricked and harassed, constantly fought back. Even after acquisition by the United States in

1821 and following statehood in 1845, Florida attracted few permanent settlers. Except for railroaders who linked Atlantic and Gulf ports to facilitate commerce in cotton and timber, settlement of the state had to await the end of the Civil War.

Even then, epidemics of malaria and yellow fever swept the state. Lurid reports described brigands, and worse, snakes and alligators that imperiled homesteads and carried off dogs and children.

In an attempt to recast Florida's reputation, railroaders cleverly enlisted poet Sidney Lanier to counter the scary reports by composing flowery tracts about Florida's charms. Responding to the writer's prose, the curious began arriving, but inadequate transportation made the trip arduous and long. No wonder once they arrived they stayed the winter!

But in the last two decades of the 19th century, Florida began to come into its own. One of the early visionaries was Ralph Middleton Munroe, a sailboat designer from Staten Island, who shared Ralph Waldo Emerson's idea that man had gotten the civilizing process wrong and should start over again in the wilderness. Finding his own piece of wilderness, Munroe settled at Jack's Bight, where he formed the community of Coconut Grove. He convinced early Grove settlers Charles and Isabella Peacock to open an inn, which in the winter of 1882–83, became the first lodging along Florida's lower east coast. When the inn was later closed, Munroe himself began putting up winter guests. His Camp Biscayne for years drew an intellectually prominent clientele, attracted by the clean bay waters and hospitality. Coconut Grove, when annexed years later in 1925, would become the oldest district in the city of Miami, and even today, though burdened by trendy excess, it remains a sanctuary of some vital Florida spirit.

But Munroe's thoughtful style of development was the exception rather than the rule. The state government, eager to get ahead, usually cast its lot with entrepreneurial monopolists eager to exploit the resources. Chief among them were the two Henrys: railroaders Henry Plant and Henry Flagler. Plant heaped sophistications on a barely civilized Gulf Coast; Flagler more opulently tamed the east.

By the time of his first Florida visit in 1878, Flagler—the partner of John D. Rockefeller in Standard Oil—was one of the richest men in America, and notorious for his ruthless and sometimes corrupt methods. When his sickly wife needed a winter in the sun, he brought her to Florida, but he encountered horrible transportation and a depressingly sick winter crowd in St. Augustine. In 1882, widowed, he returned to St. Augustine, and again two years later (now remarried to his deceased wife's former nurse). Flagler engaged a pair of New York architects to design for St. Augustine the grandest hotel Florida had ever seen: the Ponce de Leon Hotel, opened in 1888. Henry Plant did much the same thing for the west coast when he opened his $3 million Tampa Bay Hotel in 1891.

Moving down the coast, Flagler bought an entire island, burned out the inhabitants, and created the opulent new American Riviera he called Palm Beach. His magnificent Royal Poinciana Hotel opened in 1894, and The Breakers— another of his great creations—remains, rebuilt, among Florida's finest accommodations.

Now that healthy, vigorous people were coming to enjoy the climate, sports and outdoor activities began to become a vital component of a Florida vacation. Flagler indulged winter colonists with imaginative forms of recreation. Laborers pedaled wicker rickshaws called Afromobiles; and sportier types amused themselves as they raced their new motorcars on the hard-packed sand. Henry Plant, meanwhile, at another of his west-coast resorts, paved the first asphalt track for the newly popular sport of racing bicycles, and lavished an entire golf course—the first in Florida conceived as a resort amenity—on his immense Belleview Hotel, as popular today as ever, on the bluffs of Clearwater Bay.

In 1896, Flagler brought the railroad to Miami (until then an Indian trading post), then, at the turn of the century, seized by his own manifest destiny, he began the overseas extension of his railroad to Key West. He proceeded unmindful of the havoc construction caused to fisheries of Florida Bay, denied responsibility for slavelike treatment of workers, and left his workers unprepared for the 1906 hurricane that was to kill 200 of them. His railroad reached Key West six years later—and Flagler was hailed as one of history's great engineers. He died within the year.

Meanwhile, Florida everywhere was being massively altered. Citrus planters extended cultivation from along the lower St. Johns south into the lakes district, and fouled the water with pesticides. Phosphate mining lowered the water table and reduced to trickles the flows of springs which for years had supported the state's spa resorts.

Not only Flagler and Plant but all Florida's captains of enterprise have claimed partiality to tourism. They saw themselves as imperial hosts, without whom Florida would have remained beyond the pale of development: They portrayed themselves as sympathetic to what remained of the state's natural beauty, so that Florida could continue to attract northern dreamers.

Almost 100 years after Flagler, Walt Disney, trading on his own enormous reputation, created the ultimate empire: Walt Disney World, the ultimate realm of tourism. Florida granted Disney extraordinary tax breaks and near-sovereign control over rule-making throughout his fiefdom. Typically, a compliant Orlando newspaper remained silent when it learned about Disney's plans in the early '60s, thus making possible Disney's quiet acquisition of 28,000 acres for $5.5 million. But recently, even Disney has had to pay fines for disrupting the natural environment. And Orlando's Lake Eola Park, with its mile-round jogging path, in the late '80s was reclaimed from vagrants and remade the healthy heart of the city with a $900,000 amphitheater, swan boats, night-lit fountain, and landscaping—reasserting that there *is* more to Orlando than just theme parks.

As Florida has grown disenthralled with its potentates, citizens have become more aware of the problems the state faces. In addition to green legislation, Floridians supported financing for new cultural institutions and increased parks and trails. Florida has been lucky enough to nab several of the new major league sports franchises—the Miami Heat and Orlando Magic basketball teams, the Tampa Bay Buccaneers in football, the Florida Marlins in baseball, and the Florida Panthers and Tampa Bay Lightning hockey teams. Such facilities improve the quality of life for residents as well as for tourists.

But Florida still lives or dies by tourism, and despite the fact that the state has a tourist "season"—winter for most of the peninsula, summer for the Panhandle—the action really goes on all year round, and it draws not just other Americans but visitors from around the globe. Bahamians, who make up Florida's largest contingent of overseas visitors, fly over early each June to celebrate with mainland kin the annual Bahamian heritage festival called Goombay. In February, Latins come from around the Americas for Carnaval Miami and its hip-swiveling finale, the salsa-spiced Calle Ocho Festival. The annual Miami Book Fair—now the largest book event in America—attracts bibliophiles from around the hemisphere each November.

Sportsmen come for special events: the Breeders Cup at Gulfstream Track in Fort Lauderdale each October and the winter polo season at the Palm Beach Polo and Country Club. Speed Weeks and the biannual summer seasons of the London Philharmonic Orchestra have become major draws for Daytona Beach, while as many as can find a room anywhere within 50 miles pack Key West for the annual Hallowe'en Fantasy Fest.

No city in Florida more decisively ties quality of life to tourism than Fort Lauderdale. The 1¼-mile Riverwalk, downtown, has become a magical setting for shaded promenades and al fresco entertainment. New performing-arts and fine-arts venues are enabling residents and visitors to enjoy year-round cultural entertainment. Along the beachfront—for years infamous for spring break debauchery—2½ miles of shore road attest to the good life by the sea. Farther up the east coast, the rich and famous of Palm

Beach County and the Treasure Coast willingly pay higher taxes to support and patronize its arts and recreational facilities, which are unequaled in the state.

Miami—the big bad boy of Florida cities, its image tarbrushed by the TV crime-fighter series "Miami Vice"—has cleaned up its act somewhat, too. In south Miami Beach the Art Deco District, once a seedy retirement strip, sparkles as Florida's top people attraction, where café society and day-trippers ogle the lollipop-colored deco hotels and the broad beach across Ocean Drive. In Coconut Grove, the new Cocowalk shops, cinemas, and smart bistros have renewed that sense of life-as-art that dates from Munroe's earliest indulgence of bohemian society.

Along the lower west coast, Naples to the far south boasts the best environmental planning in Florida. Even the grandest hotels—the Ritz-Carlton and the Registry Resort—as well as baronial new residential estates lie to the back or to the side of coastal wetlands. Today marshes front the posh new communities, linked only by boardwalks to the beach. Lee County, farther north, stands out for its nature preserves, shelling beaches, and unbridged barrier islands. Since 1988 the county has collected ⅓¢ of its tourist-development tax solely to buy, protect, and improve beaches and parks.

Florida's environmental turn shows best where tourism has been slow to take hold—mainly where beaches are few or where railroaders never laid track. In late 1991 nine counties along the mid-Gulf Coast north of Tampa Bay banded together as "The Nature Coast," to flaunt their lakes and bubbling springs, hilly inland stretches, and marshes. In the upper mid-state, known as the Big Scrub, Paynes Prairie provides habitat for sandhill cranes and bison, and Cross Creek—where Marjorie Kinnan Rawlings wrote *The Yearling*—in 1990 gained protection from quick-buck promoters who were about to erect the usual mishmash to cash in on the publicity from the film version of Rawlings' *Cross Creek*. At the Devil's Millhopper you can descend a 221-foot walkway to the bottom of a 120-foot deep sinkhole, and at O'Leno State Park watch the Santa Fe River swirl underground. At Ichetucknee State Park you can tube the mighty "Itch." Nearby you can dive a dozen or more pellucid springs.

Florida's Panhandle, wherein lie many of the state's most beautiful parks—Florida Caverns, Falling Waters, Natural Bridge, Eden State Gardens, Maclay State Gardens, and Torreya State Park—has Florida's finest beaches, including Grayton in south Walton County. And nearby, beside another white beach, is Seaside, perhaps America's most acclaimed new resort. With its shell- and picket-lined lanes too narrow for automobiles, it harks back to early 20th-century town planning, trying to recapture that old-fashioned sense of community, leisure pace, and human scale. It's just one of the answers that Florida has found for its problems.

By early 1993 Florida Bay, where the Everglades meets the Gulf, was dying, just as Lake Apopka died two decades before, and Lake Okeechobee continues to be threatened. A University of Georgia report in 1991 forecast the death of the reefs off the Florida Keys by the turn of the century. New, stronger coalitions have formed among hoteliers, fisherfolk, and environmentalists that may forestall disaster. Yet these same groups fight among themsevles over a management plan, due by the end of 1993, for the new Florida Keys National Marine Sanctuary.

Tourism has long been more of a problem than a solution for Florida's environmental distress. Tourism promoters increasingly aim to attract visitors to natural resources—state parks, beaches, nature preserves, rivers—with the hope that politicans will pay more attention to preserving these resources. Although the answers to Florida's future are still out, there's still plenty of natural beauty there—enjoy it while you can.

1 Essential Information

Before You Go

Visitor Information

Contact the **Florida Division of Tourism** (126 Van Buren St., Tallahassee 32399, tel. 904/487–1462 or 904/487–1463) for information on tourist attractions and answers to questions about traveling in the state. Canadian travelers can get assistance from U.S. Travel in Toronto, tel. 416/595–0335.

For additional information, contact the regional tourist bureaus and chambers of commerce in the areas you wish to visit (*see* individual chapters for listings).

Tours and Packages

Should you buy your travel arrangements to Florida packaged or do it yourself? There are advantages either way. Buying packaged arrangements saves you money, particularly if you can find a program that includes exactly the features you want. You also get a pretty good idea of what your trip will cost from the outset. In Florida, you have two options: fully escorted tours and independent packages. Escorted tours are most often via motorcoach, with a tour director in charge. Your baggage is handled, your time rigorously scheduled, and most meals planned. Escorted tours are therefore the most hassle-free way to see Florida, as well as generally the least expensive. Independent packages—usually fly/drive programs here—allow plenty of flexibility. They generally include airline travel, hotels, and rental car, plus certain other options such as sightseeing and excursions. Independent packages are usually more expensive than escorted tours, but your time is your own.

Travel agents are your best source of recommendations for both tours and packages. They will have the largest selection, and the cost to you is the same as buying direct. Whatever program you ultimately choose, be sure to find out exactly what is included: taxes, tips, transfers, meals, baggage handling, ground transportation, entertainment, excursions, sports or recreation (and rental equipment for any sports you may pursue). Ask about the level of hotel used, its location, the size of its rooms, the kind of beds, and its amenities, such as pool, room service, or programs for children, if they're important to you. Another important point: If the beach is the centerpiece of your vacation, ask exactly where your hotel is located: The words "beach nearby" can have many meanings.

Find out the operator's cancellation penalties. Nearly everyone charges them, and the only way to avoid them is to buy trip-cancellation insurance (*see* Trip Insurance, *below*). Also ask about the single supplement, a surcharge assessed to solo travelers. Some operators do not make you pay it if you agree to be matched up with a roommate of the same sex, even if one is not found by departure time. Remember that a program that has features you won't use may not be your most cost-wise choice.

Fully Escorted Tours Escorted tours are usually sold in three categories: deluxe, first-class, and tourist or budget class. The most important differences are the price, of course, and the level of accommodations. Some operators specialize in one category, while others offer a range. One deluxe operator is **Tauck Tours** (11 Wilton

Rd., Westport, CT 06881, tel. 800/468–2825). However, most Florida programs are in the first-class category, including **Domenico Tours** (751 Broadway, Bayonne, NJ 07002, tel. 800/554–8687), **Gadabout Tours** (700 E. Tahquitz Way, Palm Springs, CA 92262-6761, tel. 800/952–5068), and **Globus-Gateway** (5301 S. Federal Circle, Littleton, CO 80123, tel. 303/797-2800 or 800/221–0090). **Cosmos**, Globus' sister company, sells similar programs at lower prices.

Most itineraries are jam-packed with sightseeing, so you see a lot in a short amount of time (usually one place per day). To judge just how fast-paced the tour is, review the itinerary carefully. If you are in a different hotel each night, you will be getting up early each day to head out, travel to your next destination, do some sightseeing, have dinner, and go to bed, then you'll start all over again. If you want some free time, make sure it's mentioned in the tour brochure; if you want to be escorted to every meal, confirm that any tour you consider does that. Also, when comparing programs, be sure to find out if the motorcoach is air-conditioned and has a restroom on board. Make your selection based on price and stops on the itinerary.

Note that many of the motorcoach tours to Florida include a stop at Walt Disney World, but for just one day.

Independent Packages Independent packages are offered by airlines, tour operators who may also do escorted programs, and any number of other companies from large, established firms to small, new entrepreneurs. Airline operators include **American Fly AAway Vacations** (tel. 800/321–2121), **Continental Airlines' Grand Destinations** (tel. 800/634–5555), **Delta Dream Vacations** (tel. 800/872–7786), and **United Airlines' Vacation Planning Center** (tel. 800/328–6877); all have packages that include admission to Walt Disney World theme parks. **American Express Vacations** (300 Pinnacle Way, Norcross, GA 30093, tel. 800/241–1700 or 800/421–5785) has a big selection of destinations and prices.

These programs come in a wide range of prices based on levels of luxury and options. Note that when pricing different packages, it sometimes pays to purchase the same arrangements separately, as when a rock-bottom promotional airfare is being offered, for example. Again, base your choice on what's available at your budget for the destinations you want to visit. Note that if you plan to visit Walt Disney World, many package operators can get you rooms on Disney property even when the Disney organization itself tells you all rooms are booked.

Special-interest Travel Special-interest programs may be fully escorted or independent. Some require a certain amount of expertise, but most are for the average traveler with an interest and are usually hosted by experts in the subject matter. When the program is escorted, it enjoys the advantages and disadvantages of all escorted programs; because your fellow travelers are apt to be passionate or knowledgeable about the subject, they can prove as enjoyable a part of your travel experience as the destination itself. The cost is usually higher—sometimes a lot higher—than for ordinary escorted tours and packages, because of the expert guiding and special activities.

Adventure and Nature **Oceanic Society Expeditions** (Fort Mason Center, Building E, San Francisco, CA 94123, tel. 800/326–7491) offers a "Swim with the Manatees" program under the guidance of an experienced manatee biologist. **Wilderness Southeast** (711 Sandtown

Rd., Savannah, GA 31410, tel. 912/897–5108) offers trips
through the Everglades and in Central Florida. Also contact
Smithsonian Associates Travel Program (1100 Jefferson Dr.,
SW, Washington, DC 20560, tel. 202/357–4700).

Tips for British Travelers

**Government
Tourist Offices**
Contact the **United States Travel and Tourism Administration**
(Box 1EN, London W1A 1EN, tel. 071/495–4466).

**Passports
and Visas**
British citizens need a valid 10-year passport.

A visa is not necessary unless 1) you are planning to stay more
than 90 days; 2) your trip is for purposes other than vacation;
3) you have at some time been refused a visa, or refused admission to the United States, or have been required to leave by the
U.S. Immigration and Naturalization Services; or 4) you do not
have a return or onward ticket. You will need to fill out the Visa
Waiver Form, 1–94W, supplied by the airline.

To apply for a visa or for more information, call the U.S.
Embassy's Visa Information Line (tel. 0891/200-290; calls cost
48p per minute or 36p per minute cheap rate). If you qualify for
visa-free travel but want a visa anyway, you must apply in
writing, enclosing an SAE, to the U.S. Embassy's Visa Branch
(5 Upper Grosvenor St., London W1A 2JB), or, for residents of
Northern Ireland, to the U.S. Consulate General (Queen's
House, Queen St., Belfast BTI 6EO). Submit a completed
Nonimmigrant Visa Application (Form 156), a valid passport, a
photograph, and evidence of your intended departure from the
United States after a temporary visit. If you require a visa, call
0891/234224 to schedule an interview.

Customs
Bristish visitors age 21 or over may import the following into
the United States: 200 cigarettes or 50 cigars or 2 kilograms of
tobacco; one liter of alcohol; gifts to the value of $100. Re-
stricted items include meat products, seeds, plants, and fruits.
Never carry illegal drugs.

Insurance
Most tour operators, travel agents, and insurance agents sell
specialized policies covering accident, medical expenses, personal liability, trip cancellation, and loss or theft of personal
property. Some policies include coverage for delayed departure and legal expenses, winter-sports, accidents, or motoring
abroad. You can also purchase an annual travel-insurance policy valid for every trip you make during the year in which it's
purchased (usually only trips of less than 90 days). Before you
leave, make sure you will be covered if you have a pre-existing
medical condition or are pregnant; your insurers may not pay
for routine or continuing treatment, or may require a note from
your doctor certifying your fitness to travel.

The **Association of British Insurers,** a trade association representing 450 insurance companies, advises extra medical coverage for visitors to the United States.

For advice by phone or a free booklet, "Holiday Insurance,"
contact the Association of British Insurers (51 Gresham St.,
London EC2V 7HQ, tel. 071/600–3333; 30 Gordon St., Glasgow
G1 3PU, tel. 041/226–3905; Scottish Provincial Bldg., Donegall

Sq. W, Belfast BT1 6JE, tel. 0232/249176; call for other locations).

Tour Operators Tour operators offering packages to Florida include **Albany Travel (Manchester) Ltd.** (Royal London House, 196 Deansgate, Manchester M3 3NF, tel. 061/833–0202); **British Airways Holidays** (Atlantic House, Hazelwick Ave., Three Bridges, Crawley, W. Sussex RH10 1NP, tel. 0293/518022); **Jetsave Travel Ltd.** (Sussex House, London Rd., East Grinstead, West Sussex RH19 1LD, tel. 0342/312033); **Key to America** (15 Feltham Rd., Ashford Middx. TW15 1DQ tel. 0784/248777).

Airfares Fares vary enormously. Fares from consolidators are usually the cheapest, followed by promotional fares such as APEX. A few phone calls should give you the current picture. When comparing fares, don't forget to figure airport taxes and weekend supplements. Once you know which airline is going your way at the right time for the least money, book immediately, since seats at the lowest prices often sell out quickly. Travel agents will generally hold a reservation for up to 5 days, especially if you give a credit card number.

Some travel agencies that offer cheap fares to Florida include **Trailfinders** (42–50 Earl's Court Rd., London W8 6EJ, tel. 071/937–5400), specialists in Round-The-World fares and independent travel; **Travel Cuts** (295a Regent St., London W1R 7YA, tel. 071/637–3161), the Canadian Students' travel service; **Flightfile** (49 Tottenham Court Rd., London W1P 9RE, tel. 071/700–2722), a flight-only agency.

Car Rental Make the arrangements from home to avoid inconvenience, save money, and guarantee yourself a vehicle. Major firms include **Alamo** (tel. 0800/272–2000), **Budget** (tel. 0800/181181), **EuroDollar** (tel. 0895/233300), **Europcar** (tel. 081/950–5050), and **Hertz** (tel. 081/679–1799).

In the United States you must be 21 to rent a car; rates may be higher for those under 25. Extra costs cover child seats, compulsory for under-5s (about $3 per day); additional drivers (around $1.50 per day); and the all-but-compulsory Collision Damage Waiver (*see* Car Rentals, *below*). To pick up your reserved car, you will need the reservation voucher, a passport, a U.K. driver's license, and a travel policy covering each driver.

For Travelers with Disabilities Main information sources include the **Royal Association for Disability and Rehabilitation** (RADAR, 25 Mortimer St., London W1N 8AB, tel. 071/637–5400), which publishes travel information for the disabled in Britain, and **Mobility International** (228 Borough High St., London SE1 1JX, tel. 071/403–5688), the headquarters of an international membership organization that serves as a clearinghouse of travel information for people with disabilities.

When to Go

Florida is a state for all seasons, although most visitors prefer October–April, particularly in southern Florida.

Winter is the height of the tourist season, when southern Florida is crowded with "snowbirds" fleeing the cold weather in the North. Hotels, bars, discos, restaurants, shops, and attractions are all crowded. Hollywood and Broadway celebrities appear in sophisticated supper clubs, and other performing artists hold the stage at ballets, operas, concerts, and theaters. From mid-December through January 2, Walt Disney World's Magic Kingdom is lavishly decorated, and there are daily parades and other extravaganzas, as well as overwhelming crowds. In the Panhandle, winter is the low season, so it's an excellent bargain.

For the college crowd, **spring** vacation is still the time to congregate in Florida, especially in Panama City Beach and the Daytona Beach area; Fort Lauderdale, which city officials are making an effort to refashion more as a family resort, no longer indulges young revelers, so is much less popular with college students than it once was.

Summer in Florida, as smart budget-minded visitors have discovered, is often hot and very humid, but ocean breezes make the season bearable along the coast. Besides, many hotels lower their prices considerably during summer. In the Panhandle, though, summer is the peak season. Walt Disney World and other Orlando attractions draw crowds in summer—but fewer during the week when children return to school in September.

For senior citizens, **fall** is the time for discounts to many attractions and hotels in Orlando and along the Pinellas Suncoast in the Tampa Bay area.

Climate   What follows are average daily maximum and minimum temperatures for major cities in Florida.

Key West (The Keys)	Jan.	76F	24C	May	85F	29C	Sept.	90F	32C
		65	18		74	23		77	25
	Feb.	76F	24C	June	88F	31C	Oct.	83F	28C
		67	19		77	25		76	24
	Mar.	79F	26C	July	90F	32C	Nov.	79F	26C
		68	20		79	26		70	21
	Apr.	81F	27C	Aug.	90F	32C	Dec.	76F	24C
		72	22		79	26		67	19

Miami	Jan.	74F	23C	May	83F	28C	Sept.	86F	30C
		63	17		72	22		76	24
	Feb.	76F	24C	June	85F	29C	Oct.	83F	28C
		63	17		76	24		72	22
	Mar.	77F	25C	July	88F	31C	Nov.	79F	26C
		65	18		76	24		67	19
	Apr.	79F	26C	Aug.	88F	31C	Dec.	76F	26C
		68	20		77	25		63	17

Orlando	Jan.	70F	21C	May	88F	31C	Sept.	88F	31C
		49	9		67	19		74	23
	Feb.	72F	22C	June	90F	32C	Oct.	83F	28C
		54	12		72	22		67	19
	Mar.	76F	24C	July	90F	32C	Nov.	76F	24C
		56	13		74	23		58	14
	Apr.	81F	27C	Aug.	90F	32C	Dec.	70F	21C
		63	17		74	23		52	11

Information Sources   For current weather conditions for cities in the United States and abroad, plus the local time and helpful travel tips, call the

Weather Channel Connection (tel. 900/WEATHER; 95¢ per minute) from a touch-tone phone.

Festivals and Seasonal Events

For exact dates and details about the following events, call the listed numbers or inquire from local chambers of commerce.

Winter **Early Jan.: Polo Season** opens at the Palm Beach Polo and Country Club (13420 South Shore Blvd., West Palm Beach 33414, tel. 407/793–1440).

Jan. 6: Greek Epiphany Day includes religious celebrations, parades, music, dancing, and feasting at the St. Nicholas Greek Orthodox Cathedral (Box 248, Tarpon Springs 34689, tel. 813/937–6109).

Mid-Jan.: Art Deco Weekend spotlights Miami Beach's historic district with an Art Deco street fair, a 1930s-style Moon Over Miami Ball, and live entertainment (1244 Ocean Dr., Miami Beach 33119, tel. 305/672–2014).

Mid-Jan.: Taste of the Grove Food and Music Festival is a popular fund-raiser put on in Coconut Grove's Peacock Park by area restaurants (tel. 305/442–2001).

Mid-Jan.: Martin Luther King, Jr., Festivals are celebrated in Miami and Tampa (7225 S.W. 24th St., Miami 33155; and 1420 N. Tampa St., Tampa 33602, tel. 813/223–8615).

Late Jan.: Miami Rivers Blues Festival takes place on the south bank of the river next to Tobacco Road (626 S. Miami Ave., Miami 33130, tel. 305/374–1198).

Feb.: Gasparilla Festival celebrates the legendary pirate's invasion of Tampa with street parades, an art festival, and music (111 Madison St., Suite 1010, Tampa 33602, tel. 813/223–1111).

Feb.: Florida Strawberry Festival in Plant City celebrates its winter harvest for two weeks, with country music stars, rides, exhibits, and strawberry delicacies (tel. 813/752–9194).

Feb.: Olustee Battle Festival in Lake City, the second largest Civil War reenactment in the nation after Gettysburg, features a memorial service, crafts and food festival, 10K run, and parade (Box 1847, Lake City 32056, tel. 904/755–5666).

Early Feb.–late Feb.: Speed Weeks is a three-week celebration of auto racing that culminates in the famous Daytona 500 in Daytona Beach (Daytona International Speedway, Drawer S, Daytona Beach 32015, tel. 904/254–2700).

Feb.–Mar.: Winter Equestrian Festival includes more than 1,000 horses and three grand-prix equestrian events at the Palm Beach Polo and Country Club in West Palm Beach (tel. 407/798–7000).

First weekend in Feb.: Sarasota Classic is a major event on the LPGA tour (Classic, Box 2199, Sarasota 33578).

Mid-Feb.: Florida State Fair includes carnival rides and 4-H competitions in Tampa (Box 11766, Tampa 33680, tel. 813/621–7821).

Mid-Feb.: Miami Film Festival is 10 days of international, domestic, and local films sponsored by the Film Society of America (444 Brickell Ave., Suite 229, Miami 33131, tel. 305/377–FILM).

Mid-Feb.: Florida Manatee Festival in Crystal River focuses on both the river and the endangered manatee (tel. 904/795–3149).

Mid-Feb.: Florida Citrus Festival and Polk County Fair in Winter Haven showcases the citrus harvest with displays and entertainment (Box 9229, Winter Haven 33883, tel. 813/293–3175).

Mid-Feb.: Coconut Grove Art Festival is the state's largest (tel. 305/447–0401).

Last full weekend in Feb.: Labelle Swamp Cabbage Festival is a salute to the state tree, the cabbage palm (tel. 813/675–0125).

First weekend in Mar.: Sanibel Shell Fair is the largest event of the year on Sanibel Island (tel. 813/472–2155 or 813/472–4709).

Early Mar.: Azalea Festival is a beauty pageant, arts and crafts show, and parade held in downtown Palatka and Riverfront Park (tel. 904/328–1503).

Early Mar.: Carnaval Miami is a carnival celebration staged by the Little Havana Tourist Authority (970 S.W. First St., Miami 33130, tel. 305/836–5223).

Spring **Mid-Mar. and early July: Arcadia All-Florida Championship Rodeo** is professional rodeo at its best (Rodeo, Box 1266, Arcadia 33821, tel. 813/494–3773).

Mid-Mar.–early May: Springtime Tallahassee is a major cultural, sporting, and culinary event in the capital (tel. 904/224–5012).

Apr.: Arts in April presents a series of visual and performing arts events produced by local independent arts organizations (Elizabeth Kurz, Office of the Mayor, 1 City Commons, 400 S. Orange Ave., Orlando 32801, tel. 407/246–2221).

Early Apr.: Delray Affair is the biggest event in the area and features arts, crafts, and food.

Early Apr.–late May: Addison Mizner Festival in Boca Raton celebrates the 1920s in Palm Beach County (tel. 800/242–1774).

Palm Sunday: Blessing of the Fleet is held on the bay front in St. Augustine (tel. 904/829–5681).

Mid-Apr.: Cedar Key Sidewalk Arts Festival is celebrated in one of the state's most historic towns (tel. 904/543–5600).

Late Apr.: River Cities Festival is a three-day event in Miami Springs and Hialeah that focuses attention on the Miami River and the need to keep it clean (tel. 305/887–1515).

Late Apr.–early May: Sun 'n' Fun Festival includes a bathtub regatta, golf tournament, and nighttime parade in Clearwater (tel. 813/462–6531 or 813/461–0011).

Late Apr.–early May: Conch Republic Celebration in Key West honors the founding fathers of the Conch Republic, "the small island nation of Key West" (tel. 305/294–4440).

First weekend in May: Sunfest includes a wide variety of cultural and sporting events in West Palm Beach (tel. 407/659–5980).

Mid-May: Arabian Nights Festival in Opa-locka is a mix of contemporary and fantasy-inspired entertainment (tel. 305/953–2821).

Mid-May: Tropicool Fest for two weeks draws thousands to more than 30 concerts as well as arts and sports events all around town (Kris Paradis, 362 U.S. 41 N, Naples 33940, tel. 813/262–6141).

Mid-June: Fiesta of Five Flags in Pensacola celebrates de Luna's landing with dancing and reenactments of the event (tel. 904/433–6512).

First weekend in June: Miami-Bahamas Goombay Festival in Miami's Coconut Grove, celebrates the city's Bahamian heritage (tel. 305/443–7928).

Early–mid-June: Billy Bowlegs Festival in Fort Walton Beach is a week of entertaining activities in memory of a pirate who ruled the area in the late 1700s (tel. 904/267–1216).

Summer   **July 4: Firecracker Festival** in Melbourne is one of the state's most colorful Independence Day celebrations (tel. 407/724–5400).
Mid-July: Hemingway Days Festival in Key West includes plays, short-story competitions, and a Hemingway look-alike contest (tel. 305/294–4440).
Labor Day: Worm Fiddler's Day is the biggest day of the year in Caryville (tel. 904/548–5571).
Early Sept.: Anniversary of the Founding of St. Augustine is held on the grounds of the Mission of Nombre de Dios (tel. 904/247–4242).

Autumn   **Oct.: Jacksonville Jazz Festival** is a three-day event featuring jazz superstars, performances, arts and crafts, food, and the Great American Jazz Piano Competition (tel. 904/353–7770).
Oct.: Destin Seafood Festival is a two-day affair where you can sample smoked amberjack, fried mullet, or shark kabobs (tel. 904/837–6241).
Mid-Oct.: Florida State Chili Cookoff Championship at Port of the Islands Resort in the Everglades means all the chili you can eat (25000 Tamiami Trail E, Naples 33961, tel. 800/237–4173).
Late Oct.: Boggy Bayou Mullet Festival is a three-day hoedown in celebration of the "Twin Cities," Valparaiso/Niceville, and the famed scavenger fish, the mullet (tel. 904/678–5077).
Late Oct.: Fantasy Fest in Key West is an unrestrained Halloween costume party, parade, and town fair (tel. 305/296–1817).
Early Nov.: Light Up Orlando is a street celebration of bands, international foods, and the Queen Kumquat Sashay Parade (tel. 407/363–5800).
Early Nov.: Florida Seafood Festival is Apalachicola's celebration of its seafood staple with oyster-shucking-and-consumption contests and parades (tel. 904/653–8051.)
Mid-Dec.: Walt Disney World's Very Merry Christmas Parade in the Magic Kingdom celebrates the season at the Magic Kingdom (Walt Disney World, Box 10000, Lake Buena Vista 32830–1000).
Mid-Dec.: Grand Illumination is a colorful display in St. Augustine (tel. 904/829–5681).
Late Dec.: Coconut Grove King Mango Strut is a parody of the Orange Bowl Parade (tel. 305/858–6253).

What to Pack

Clothing   The northern part of the state is much cooler in winter than the southern part. Winters are mild in the Orlando area, with daytime temperatures in the 70s and low 80s. But the temperature can dip to the 50s, even in the Keys, so take a sweater or jacket, just in case. Farther north, in the Panhandle area, winters are cool and there's often frost at night.

The Miami area and the Tampa/St. Petersburg area are warm year-round and often extremely humid during the summer months. Be prepared for sudden summer storms, but don't wear plastic raincoats—they're uncomfortable in the high humidity.

Dress is casual throughout the state, with sundresses, jeans, or walking shorts appropriate during the day. A pair of comfortable walking shoes or sneakers is a must for the major theme parks. A few of the better restaurants request that men wear jackets and ties, but most do not. Be prepared for air-conditioning working in overdrive.

You can swim in most of peninsular Florida year-round. Be sure to take a sun hat and a good sunscreen because the sun can be fierce, even in winter.

Luggage   Free baggage allowances on an airline depend on the airline,
Regulations   the route, and the class of your ticket. In general, on domestic flights and on international flights between the United States and foreign destinations, you are entitled to check two bags—neither exceeding 62 inches, or 158 centimeters (length + width + height), or weighing more than 70 pounds (32 kilograms). A third piece may be brought aboard as a carryon; its total dimensions are generally limited to less than 45 inches (114 centimeters), so it will fit easily under the seat in front of you or in the overhead compartment. There are variations, so ask in advance. Charges for excess, oversize, or overweight pieces vary, so inquire before you pack.

Safeguarding Your   Before leaving home, itemize your bags' contents and their
Luggage   worth; this list will help you estimate the extent of your loss if your bags go astray. To minimize that risk, tag them inside and out with your name, address, and phone number. (If you use your home address, cover it so that potential thieves can't see it.) At check-in, make sure that the tag attached by baggage handlers bears the correct three-letter code for your destination. If your bags do not arrive with you, or if you detect damage, do not leave the airport until you've filed a written report with the airline.

Miscellaneous   An extra pair of glasses, contact lenses, or prescription sunglasses is always a good idea. If you have a health problem that may require you to purchase a prescription drug, take enough to last the duration of the trip. And don't forget to pack a list of the addresses of offices that supply refunds for lost or stolen traveler's checks.

Cash Machines

Automated-teller machines (ATMs) are proliferating; many are tied to international networks such as **Cirrus** and **Plus.** You can use your bank card at ATMs away from home to withdraw money from your checking account and get cash advances on a credit-card account (providing your card has been programmed with a personal identification number, or PIN). Check in advance on limits on withdrawals and cash advances within specified periods. Remember that finance charges apply on credit-card cash advances from ATMs as well as on those from tellers. And note that transaction fees for ATM withdrawals outside your home turf will probably be higher than for withdrawals at home.

For specific Cirrus locations in the United States and Canada, call 800/424–7787 (for U.S. Plus locations, 800/843–7587), and press the area code and first three digits of the number you're calling from (or the calling area where you want an ATM).

Traveling with Cameras, Camcorders, and Laptops

About Film and   If your camera is new or if you haven't used it for a while, shoot
Cameras   and develop a few rolls of film before leaving home. Pack some

lens tissue and an extra battery for your built-in light meter, and invest in an inexpensive skylight filter, to both protect your lens and provide some definition in hazy shots. Store film in a cool, dry place—never in the car's glove compartment or on the shelf under the rear window.

Films above ISO 400 are more sensitive to damage from airport security X-rays than others; very high speed films, ISO 1,000 and above, are exceedingly vulnerable. To protect your film, don't put it in checked luggage; carry it with you in a plastic bag and ask for a hand inspection. Such requests are honored at American airports. Don't depend on a lead-lined bag to protect film in checked luggage—the airline may very well turn up the dosage of radiation to see what you've got in there. Airport metal detectors do not harm film, although you'll set off the alarm if you walk through one with a roll in your pocket. Call the Kodak Information Center (tel. 800/242–2424) for details.

About Camcorders and Videotape Before your trip, put new or long-unused camcorders through their paces, and practice panning and zooming. Invest in a skylight filter to protect the lens, and check the lithium battery that lights up the LCD (liquid crystal display) modes. As for the rechargeable nickel-cadmium batteries that are the camera's power source, take along an extra pair, so while you're using your camcorder you'll have one battery ready and another recharging.

Unlike still-camera film, videotape is not damaged by X-rays. However, it may well be harmed by the magnetic field of a walk-through metal detector. Airport security personnel may want you to turn the camcorder on to prove that that's what it is, so make sure the battery is charged when you get to the airport.

About Laptops Security X-rays do not harm hard-disk or floppy-disk storage. Most airlines allow you to use your laptop aloft but request that you turn it off during takeoff and landing so as not to interfere with navigation equipment. Make sure the battery is charged when you arrive at the airport, because you may be asked to turn on the computer at security checkpoints to prove that it is what it appears to be. If you're a heavy computer user, consider traveling with a backup battery.

Car Rentals

Florida is a car renter's bazaar, with more discount companies offering more bargains—and more fine print—than any other state in the nation. Shop around for the best combination rate for car and airfare. Jacksonville, for example, is often somewhat cheaper to fly into than Miami, but Miami's car-rental rates are usually lower than Jacksonville's.

Firms Avis (tel. 800/831–2847), **Budget** (tel. 800/527–0700), **Dollar** (tel. 800/800–4000), **Hertz** (tel. 800/654–3131), **National** (tel. 800/227–7368), Sears (tel. 800/527–0700), and **Thrifty** (tel. 800/367–2277) maintain airport and city locations throughout much of Florida. So do **Alamo** (tel. 800/327–9633) and **General** (tel. 800/327–7607), which offer some of the state's lowest rates. **Rent-A-Wreck** (tel. 800/535–1391) and **Ugly Duckling** (tel. 800/843–3825) rent used cars throughout the state, usually with more stringent mileage restrictions. Rent-A-Wreck, however, has no location in Orlando.

Besides the national rental companies, several regional and local firms offer good deals in major Florida cities. These include **Payless** (tel. 800/237–2804), **USA** (tel. 800/872–2277), and **Value** (tel. 800/468–2583). In Fort Lauderdale, local companies include **Aapex Thompson** (tel. 305/566–8663) and **Florida Auto Rental** (tel. 305/764–1008). In Orlando, try **InterAmerican Car Rental** (tel. 407/859–0414) and **Snappy Car Rental** (tel. 407/859–8808). In Tampa–St. Petersburg call **A-Plus Car Rentals** (tel. 813/289–4301). In Miami, **Superior Rent-A-Car** (tel. 305/649–7012) is a local budget company, as are **Pass** (tel. 305/444–3923) and **InterAmerican Car Rental** (tel. 305/871–3030). Down in Key West, try **Tropical Rent-a-Car** (tel. 305/294–8136).

Rates In major Florida cities, peak-season rates for a subcompact average around $120 a week, often with unlimited mileage. Some companies advertise peak-season promotional rates as low as $69 a week with unlimited mileage, but only a few cars are available at this rate, and you may have to pay twice as much if you keep the car less than seven days! Some of these companies require you to keep the car in the state and are quick to charge for an extra day when you return a vehicle late.

Extra Charges Picking up the car in one city or country and leaving it in another may entail drop-off charges or one-way service fees, which can be substantial. The cost of a collision or loss-damage waiver (*see below*) can be high, also.

Cutting Costs If you know you will want a car for more than a day or two, you can save by planning ahead. Major international companies have programs that discount their standard rates by 15%–30% if you make the reservation before departure (anywhere from two to 14 days), rent for a minimum number of days (typically three or four), and prepay the rental. Ask about these advance-purchase schemes when you call for information. More economical rentals are those that come as part of fly/drive or other packages, even those as bare-bones as the rental plus an airline ticket (*see* Tours and Packages, *above*).

Other sources of savings are the several companies that operate as wholesalers—companies that do not own their own fleets but rent in bulk from those that do and offer advantageous rates to their customers. Rentals through such companies must be arranged and paid for in advance. Among them is **Auto Europe** (Box 1097, Camden, ME 04843, tel. 207/236–8235 or 800/223–5555, 800/458–9503 in Canada). You won't see these wholesalers' deals advertised; they're even better in summer, when business travel is down. Always ask if unlimited mileage is available. Find out about any required deposits, cancellation penalties, and drop-off charges, and confirm the cost of the CDW.

One last tip: Remember to fill the tank when you turn in the vehicle, to avoid being charged for refueling at what you'll swear is the most expensive pump in town.

Insurance and Collision Damage Waiver The standard rental contract includes liability coverage (for damage to public property, injury to pedestrians, etc.) and coverage for the car against fire, theft, and collision damage with a deductible—most commonly $2,000–$3,000, occasionally more. In the case of an accident, you are responsible for the deductible amount unless you've purchased the collision damage waiver (CDW), which costs an average $12 a day, although this varies depending on what you've rented, where, and from whom.

Because this adds up quickly, you may be inclined to say "no thanks"—and that's certainly your option, although the rental agent may not tell you so. Planning ahead will help you make the right decision. By all means, find out if your own insurance covers damage to a rental car while traveling (not simply a car to drive when yours is in for repairs). And check whether charging car rentals to any of your credit cards will get you a CDW at no charge. Note before you decline that deductibles are occasionally high enough that totaling a car would make you responsible for its full value. In many states, laws mandate that renters be told what the CDW costs, that it's optional, and that their own auto insurance may provide the same protection.

Traveling with Children

Publications *Family Travel Times,* published 10 times a year by Travel With
Newsletter Your Children (TWYCH, 45 W. 18th St., 7th Floor Tower, New York, NY 10011, tel. 212/206–0688; annual subscription $55), covers destinations, types of vacations, and modes of travel; an airline issue comes out every other year (the last one, February/March 1993, is sold to nonsubscribers for $10). On Wednesday, the staff answers subscribers' questions on specific destinations.

Periodicals for parents that are filled with listings of events, resources, and advice are available free at such places as libraries, supermarkets, and museums; *Florida Parent* (Box 2321, Boca Raton 33427, tel. 407/750–7765), a monthly, covers Palm Beach, Broward, and Dade counties.

Books *Great Vacations with Your Kids,* by Dorothy Jordan and Marjorie Cohen ($13; Penguin USA, 120 Woodbine St., Bergenfield, NJ 07621, tel. 800/253–6476) and *Traveling with Children—And Enjoying It,* by Arlene K. Butler ($11.95 plus $3 shipping per book; Globe Pequot Press, Box 833, Old Saybrook, CT 06475, tel. 800/243–0495, or 800/962–0973 in CT) help you plan your trip with children, from toddlers to teens. Also from Globe Pequot Press is *Recommended Family Resorts in the United States, Canada, and the Caribbean,* by Jane Wilford with Janet Tice ($12.95).

Tour Operators **GrandTravel** (6900 Wisconsin Ave., Suite 706, Chevy Chase, MD 20815, tel. 301/986–0790 or 800/247–7651) offers international and domestic tours for grandparents traveling with their grandchildren. The catalogue, as charmingly written and illustrated as a children's book, positively invites armchair traveling with lap-sitters aboard. **Rascals in Paradise** (650 5th St., Suite 505, San Francisco, CA 94107, tel. 415/978–9800 or 800/872–7225) specializes in programs for families.

Getting There On domestic flights, children under 2 not occupying a seat travel free, and older children currently travel on the "lowest applicable" adult fare.

Safety Seats The FAA recommends the use of safety seats aloft and details approved models in the free leaflet "**Child/Infant Safety Seats Recommended for Use in Aircraft**" (available from the Federal Aviation Administration, APA–200, 800 Independence Ave. SW, Washington, DC 20591, tel. 202/267–3479). Airline policy varies. U.S. carriers must allow FAA-approved models, but because these seats are strapped into a regular passenger seat, they may require that parents buy a ticket even for an infant under 2 who would otherwise ride free.

Facilities Aloft   Airlines do provide other facilities and services for children, such as children's meals and freestanding bassinets (to those sitting in seats on the bulkhead, where there's enough legroom to accommodate them). Make your request when reserving. The annual February/March issue of *Family Travel Times* gives details of the children's services of dozens of airlines (*see below*). "Kids and Teens in Flight" (free from the U.S. Department of Transportation, tel. 202/366–2220) offers tips for children flying alone.

Lodging   Florida may have the highest concentration of hotels with organized children's programs in the United States; sometimes they are complimentary and sometimes there's a charge. Not all accept children who are still in diapers. The following list gives only a few representative examples of what's available. Many hotels allow children under a certain age to stay in their parents' room at no extra charge, while others charge them as extra adults; be sure to ask about the cut-off age.

Orlando Area   Look into the **Sonesta Villa Resort Orlando** (tel. 800/766–3782); Camp Gator for children 5–12 at the **Hyatt Regency Grand Cypress** (1 Grand Cypress Blvd., Orlando 32819, tel. 407/239–1234 or 800/228–9000); Wally's Kids Club at **Delta Orlando Resort** (5715 Major Blvd., Orlando 32819, tel. 407/351–3340); Shamu's Playhouse at the **Stouffer Orlando Resort** (6677 Sea Harbor Dr., Orlando 32821, tel. 407/351–5555 or 800/468–3571); and the programs at **Holiday Inn Main Gate East** at Walt Disney World (5678 Space Coast Hwy., Kissimmee 32741, tel. 407/396–4488 or 800/465–4329) and **Holiday Inn Lake Buena Vista** (13351 S.R. 535, Lake Buena Vista 32830, tel. 800/366–6299).

Miami Area   Contact the **Sonesta Beach Hotel Key Biscayne** (tel. 800/766–3782).

Fort Lauderdale   Look into the **Guest Quarters Suite Hotels** (2670 E. Sunrise Blvd., Fort Lauderdale, 33304, tel. 800/424–2900) and **Marriott's Harbor Beach Resort** (3030 Holiday Dr., Fort Lauderdale 33316, tel. 305/525–4000 or 800/228–9290).

Palm Beach and the Treasure Coast   **Club Med** (40 W. 57th St., New York, NY 10019, tel. 800/CLUB–MED) operates the Sandpiper resort village in Port St. Lucie; there's a "Baby Club" (4–23 months), "Mini Club" (2 years and up), and "Kids Club" (8 years and up).

The Keys   A good starting point is **La Concha Holiday Inn** (430 Duval St., Key West 33040, tel. 305/296–2991 or 800/227–6151).

Northeast Florida   **Amelia Island Plantation Resort** (Rte. A1A, Amelia Island 32034, tel. 904/261–6161) is wonderful for families.

Fort Myers/Naples   Look for children's programs at **Marriott's Marco Island Resort** (400 S. Collier Blvd., Marco Island 33937, tel. 813/394–2511 or 800/228–9290); and the Marco Munchkins program for ages 3–6 and Radisson Rascals for 7–12 at **Radisson Suite Beach Resort in Marco Island** (600 S. Collier Blvd., Marco Island 33937, tel. 813/394–4100 or 800/333–3333).

Hints for Travelers with Disabilities

Organizations Several organizations provide travel information for people with disabilities, usually for a membership fee, and some publish newsletters and bulletins. Among them are the **Information Center for Individuals with Disabilities** (Fort Point Pl., 27–43 Wormwood St., Boston, MA 02210, tel. 617/727–5540 or 800/462–5015 in MA between 11 and 4, or leave message; TDD/TTY tel. 617/345–9743); **Mobility International USA** (Box 3551, Eugene, OR 97403, voice and TDD tel. 503/343–1284), the U.S. branch of an international organization based in Britain and present in 30 countries; **MossRehab Hospital Travel Information Service** (1200 W. Tabor Rd., Philadelphia, PA 19141, tel. 215/456–9603, TDD tel. 215/456–9602); The **Society for the Advancement of Travel for the Handicapped** (SATH, 347 5th Ave., Suite 610, New York, NY 10016, tel. 212/447–7284, fax 212/725–8253); **Travel Industry and Disabled Exchange** (TIDE, 5435 Donna Ave., Tarzana, CA 91356, tel. 818/368–5648); and **Travelin' Talk** (Box 3534, Clarksville, TN 37043, tel. 615/552–6670).

Travel Agencies and Tour Operators **Directions Unlimited** (720 N. Bedford Rd., Bedford Hills, NY 10507, tel. 914/241–1700), a travel agency, has expertise in tours and cruises for the disabled. **Evergreen Travel Service** (4114 198th St. SW, Suite 13, Lynnwood, WA 98036, tel. 206/776–1184 or 800/435–2288) operates Wings on Wheels Tours for those in wheelchairs, White Cane Tours for the blind, and tours for the deaf; it also makes group and independent arrangements for travelers with any disability. **Flying Wheels Travel** (143 W. Bridge St., Box 382, Owatonna, MN 55060, tel. 800/535–6790 or 800/722–9351 in MN), a tour operator and travel agency, arranges international tours, cruises, and independent travel itineraries for people with mobility disabilities. **Nautilus**, at the same address as TIDE (*see above*), packages tours for the disabled internationally.

Publications Several free publications are available from the **Consumer Information Center** (Pueblo, CO 81009): "New Horizons for the Air Traveler with a Disability," a U.S. Department of Transportation booklet describing changes resulting from the 1986 Air Carrier Access Act and those still to come from the 1990 Americans with Disabilities Act (include Department 608Y in the address), and the Airport Operators Council's *Access Travel: Airports* (Dept. 5804), which describes facilities and services for the disabled at more than 500 airports worldwide.

Twin Peaks Press (Box 129, Vancouver, WA 98666, tel. 206/694–2462 or 800/637–2256) publishes the *Directory of Travel Agencies for the Disabled* ($19.95), listing more than 370 agencies worldwide; *Travel for the Disabled* ($19.95), listing some 500 access guides and accessible places worldwide; the *Directory of Accessible Van Rentals* ($9.95) for campers and RV travelers worldwide; and *Wheelchair Vagabond* ($14.95), a collection of personal travel tips. Add $2 per book for shipping. The Sierra Club publishes *Easy Access to National Parks* ($16 plus $3 shipping; 730 Polk St., San Francisco, CA 94109, tel. 415/776–2211).

Hints for Older Travelers

Although Florida probably attracts more elderly people than any other state, the state publishes no booklet addressed directly to senior citizens.

Senior-citizen discounts are common throughout Florida, but there are no set standards. Some discounts, like those for prescriptions at the Eckerd Drug chain, require that you fill out a card and register. The best bet is simply to ask whether there is a senior-citizen discount available on your purchase, meal, or hotel stay.

Organizations The **American Association of Retired Persons** (AARP, 601 E St. NW, Washington, DC 20049, tel. 202/434–2277) provides independent travelers the Purchase Privilege Program, which offers discounts on hotels, car rentals, and sightseeing, and the AARP Motoring Plan, provided by Amoco, which furnishes domestic trip-routing information and emergency road-service aid for an annual fee of $39.95 per person or couple ($59.95 for a premium version). AARP also arranges group tours, cruises, and apartment living through AARP Travel Experience from American Express (400 Pinnacle Way, Suite 450, Norcross, GA 30071, tel. 800/927–0111); these can be booked through travel agents, except for the cruises, which must be booked directly (tel. 800/745–4567). AARP membership is open to those 50 and over; annual dues are $8 per person or couple.

Two other membership organizations offer discounts on lodgings, car rentals, and other travel products, along with such nontravel perks as magazines and newsletters. The **National Council of Senior Citizens** (1331 F St. NW, Washington, DC 20004, tel. 202/347–8800) is a nonprofit advocacy group with some 5,000 local clubs across the United States; membership costs $12 per person or couple annually. **Mature Outlook** (6001 N. Clark St., Chicago, IL 60660, tel. 800/336–6330), a Sears Roebuck & Co. subsidiary with 800,000 members, charges $9.95 for an annual membership.

Note: When using any senior-citizen identification card for reduced hotel rates, mention it when booking, not when checking out. At restaurants, show your card before you're seated; discounts may be limited to certain menus, days, or hours. If you are renting a car, ask about promotional rates that might improve on your senior-citizen discount.

Educational Travel **Elderhostel** (75 Federal St., 3rd Floor, Boston, MA 02110, tel. 617/426–7788) is a nonprofit organization that has inexpensive study programs for people 60 and older since 1975. Programs take place at more than 1,800 educational institutions in the United States, Canada, and 45 countries overseas, and courses cover everything from marine science to Greek myths and cowboy poetry. Participants generally attend lectures in the morning and spend the afternoon sightseeing or on field trips; they live in dorms on the host campuses. Fees for programs in the United States and Canada, which usually last one week, run about $300, not including transportation.

Tour Operators **Saga International Holidays** (222 Berkeley St., Boston, MA 02116, tel. 800/343–0273), which specializes in group travel for people over 60, offers a selection of variously priced tours and cruises covering five continents. If you want to take your grandchildren, look into GrandTravel (*see* Traveling with Children, *above*).

Further Reading

Suspense novels that are rich in details about Florida include Clifford Irving's *Final Argument,* Elmore Leonard's *La Brava,* John D. MacDonald's *The Empty Copper Sea,* Joan Higgins's *A Little Death Music,* and Charles Willeford's *Miami Blues.* Pat Frank's *Alas Babylon* describes a fictional nuclear disaster in Florida. *Under Cover of Daylight* and *Tropical Freeze,* by James W. Hall, chronicle the adventures of a Key Largo fisherman-avenger by the name of Thorn.

Marjorie K. Rawlings's classic, *The Yearling,* poignantly portrays life in the brush country, and her *Cross Creek* re-creates the memorable people the author knew in her 13 years of living at Cross Creek. Peter Matthiessen's *Killing Mister Watson* re-creates turn-of-the-century lower southwest Florida of the Ten Thousand Islands in a tale about a prosperous killer in an Everglades settlement of hardscrabble pioneers.

Look for *Princess of the Everglades,* a novel about the 1926 hurricane by Charles Mink, and *Snow White and Rose Red* and *Jack and the Beanstalk,* Ed McBain's novels about Matthew Hope, an attorney who practices law in a Florida gulf city. *The Tourist Season* is Carl Hiaasen's immensely funny declaration of war against the state's environment-despoiling hordes; he has also written *Double Whammy, Skin Tight,* and *Native Tongue.* Other recent titles include Pat Booth's *Miami,* Sam Harrison's *Birdsong Ascending,* T.D. Allman's *Miami,* and Alice Hoffman's *Turtle Moon.*

Other recommended novels include *Florida Straits,* by Laurence Shames; Evelyn Mayerson's *No Enemy But Time; To Have and Have Not,* by Ernest Hemingway; *The Day of the Dolphin,* by Robert Merle; and *Their Eyes Were Watching God,* by Zora Neale Hurston.

Among the recommended nonfiction books are *Key West Writers and Their Homes,* Lynn Kaufelt's tour of homes of Hemingway, Wallace Stevens, Tennessee Williams, and others; *The Everglades: River of Grass,* by Marjory S. Douglas; *Florida,* by Gloria Jahoda, published as part of the Bicentennial observance; *Miami Alive,* by Ethel Blum; and *Florida's Sandy Beaches,* University Press of Florida. Mark Derr's *Some Kind of Paradise* is an excellent review of the state's environmental follies; John Rothchild's *Up for Grabs,* equally good, is about Florida's commercial lunacy. Alex Shoumatoff's 20-year-old *Florida Ramble* is still in print, as is Stetson Kennedy's *Palmetto Country,* written in 1942. Good anthologies include *The Florida Reader: Visions of Paradise* (Maurice O'Sullivan and Jack Lane, eds.); *The Rivers of Florida* (Del and Marty Marth, eds.), and *Subtropical Speculations: An Anthology of Florida Science Fiction* (Richard Mathews and Rick Wilber, eds.).

Arriving and Departing

By Plane

Flights are either nonstop, direct, or connecting. A **nonstop** flight requires no change of plane and makes no stops. A **direct** flight stops at least once and can involve a change of plane, although the flight number remains the same; if the first leg is late, the second waits. This is not the case with a **connecting** flight, which involves a different plane and a different flight number.

Airports and Airlines Most major U.S. airlines schedule regular flights into Florida, and some, such as Delta and USAir, serve Florida airports extensively.

Delta (and its commuter affiliate, Comair) and USAir have regular service into Jacksonville, Daytona Beach, Orlando, Melbourne, West Palm Beach, Fort Lauderdale, Miami, Fort Myers, Tampa, Tallahassee, Gainesville, and Key West. Delta also flies into Sarasota, Naples, Panama City, and Pensacola.

Other major airlines that serve the Florida airports include American, American Trans Air, Continental, Northwest, TWA, and United. Many foreign airlines also fly into some of the major airports in Florida; the smaller, out-of-the-way airports are usually accessible through the commuter flights of major domestic carriers.

Packages that combine airfare and vacation activities at special rates are often available through the airlines. For example, Delta (tel. 800/872-7786) offers travel packages to Disney World in Orlando (*see* Independent Packages in Before You Go), and USAir ties in with Universal Studios.

Smoking Since February 1990, smoking has been banned on all domestic flights of less than six hours duration; the ban also applies to domestic segments of international flights aboard U.S. and foreign carriers. On U.S. carriers flying overseas, a seat in a no-smoking section must be provided for every passenger who requests one, and the section must be enlarged to accommodate such passengers, as long as they have complied with the airline's deadline for check-in and seat assignment. If smoking bothers you, request a seat far from the smoking section.

By Car

Three major interstates lead to Florida from various parts of the country. I-95 begins in Maine, runs south through New England and the Mid-Atlantic states, and enters Florida just north of Jacksonville. It continues south past Daytona Beach, the Space Coast, Vero Beach, Palm Beach, and Fort Lauderdale, eventually ending in Miami.

I-75 begins at the Canadian border in Michigan and runs south through Ohio, Kentucky, Tennessee, and Georgia before entering Florida. The interstate moves through the center of the state before veering west into Tampa. It follows the west coast south to Naples, then crosses the state and ends in Miami.

California and all the most southern states are connected to Florida by I-10. This interstate originates in Los Angeles and moves east through Arizona, New Mexico, Texas, Louisiana, Mississippi, and Alabama before entering Florida at Pensacola on the west coast. I–10 continues straight across the northern part of the state until it terminates in Jacksonville.

Travelers heading from the Midwest or other points west for the lower east coast of Florida will want to use Florida's Turnpike from Wildwood, which crosses the state for 321 miles and goes as far as Florida City. Coin service plazas have replaced the use of toll cards in the southern part of this road. For current information on tolls and other services, try the Florida Turnpike public information number (tel. 800/749–7453), but it's not always answered.

Speed Limits In Florida the speed limits are 55 mph on the state highways, 30 mph within city limits and residential areas, and 55–65 mph on the interstates and on Florida's Turnpike. These limits may vary, so be sure to watch road signs for any changes.

By Train

Amtrak (tel. 800/USA–RAIL) provides north–south service on two routes to the major cities of Jacksonville, Orlando, Tampa, West Palm Beach, Fort Lauderdale, and Miami, and, since 1993, east–west service through Jacksonville, Tallahassee, and Pensacola, with many stops in between on all routes.

By Bus

Greyhound Lines passes through practically every major city in Florida, including Jacksonville, Daytona, Orlando, West Palm Beach, Fort Lauderdale, Miami, Sarasota, Tampa, Tallahassee, and Key West. For information about bus schedules and fares, contact your local Greyhound Information Center.

Staying in Florida

Visitor Information

The **Florida Division of Tourism** operates **welcome centers** on I–10, I–75, I–95, U.S. 231 (near Graceville), and in the lobby of the new Capitol in Tallahassee (Department of Commerce, 126 Van Buren St., Tallahassee 32399, tel. 904/487–1462).

Shopping

Malls in Florida are full of nationally franchised shops, major department-store chains, and one-of-a-kind shops catering to a mass audience. Small shops in out-of-the-way places, however, often have the best souvenirs and most special gift items.

Indian Artifacts Native American crafts are abundant, particularly in the southern part of the state, where you'll find billowing dresses and shirts, hand-sewn in striking colors and designs. At the Miccosukee Indian Village, 25 miles west of Miami on the Tamiami Trail (U.S. 41), as well as at the Seminole and Miccosukee reservations in the Everglades, you can also find handcrafted dolls and beaded belts.

Seashells The best shelling in Florida is on the beaches of Sanibel Island off Fort Myers. Shell shops, selling mostly kitsch items, abound throughout Florida. The largest such establishment is The Shell Factory near Fort Myers (*see* Shopping in Chapter 11). The coral and other shells sold in shops in the Florida Keys have been imported for sale because of restrictions on harvesting these materials.

Citrus Fruit Fresh citrus is available most of the year, except in summer. Two kinds of citrus grow in Florida: the sweeter and more costly Indian River fruit from a thin ribbon of groves along the east coast, and the less-costly fruit from the interior, south and west of Lake Okeechobee.

Citrus is sold in ¼, ½, ¾, and full bushels. Many shippers offer special gift packages with several varieties of fruit, jellies, and other food items. Some prices include U.S. postage, others may not. Shipping may exceed the cost of the fruit. If you have a choice of citrus packaged in boxes or bags, take the boxes. They are easier to label, and harder to squash than the bags.

Antiques Antiques lovers should explore Micanopy, south of Gainesville off I–75; the Antiques Mall in St. Augustine's Lightner Museum; on U.S. 1 north of Dania Beach Boulevard in Dania; and S.W. 28th Lane and Unity Boulevard in Miami (near the Coconut Grove Metrorail station).

Beaches

No point in Florida is more than 60 miles from saltwater. This long, lean peninsula is bordered by a 526-mile Atlantic coast from Fernandina Beach to Key West and a 792-mile coast along the Gulf of Mexico and Florida Bay from Pensacola to Key West. If you were to stretch Florida's convoluted coast in a straight line, it would extend for about 1,800 miles. What's more, if you add in the perimeter of every island surrounded by saltwater, Florida has about 8,500 miles of tidal shoreline— more than any other state except Alaska. Florida's coastline comprises about 1,016 miles of sand beaches.

Visitors unaccustomed to strong subtropical sun run a risk of sunburn and heat prostration on Florida beaches, even in winter. The natives go to the beach early in the day or in the late afternoon. If they must be out in direct sun at midday, they limit their sun exposure and strenuous exercise, drink plenty of liquids, and wear hats. Wherever you plan to swim, ask if the water has a dangerous undertow.

The state owns all beaches below the mean high-tide line, even in front of hotels and private resorts, but gaining access to the public beach can be a problem along much of Florida's coastline. You must pay to enter and/or park at most state, county, and local beachfront parks. Where hotels dominate the beach frontage, public parking may be limited or nonexistent.

Along the Atlantic Coast from the Georgia border south through the Daytona Beach area the beaches are broad and firm. In Daytona Beach you can drive on them. Some beachfront communities in this area charge for the privilege; others provide free beach access for vehicles.

From the Treasure Coast south, erosion has affected the beaches. Major beach rehabilitation projects have been completed in Fort Lauderdale, the Sunny Isles area of north Dade County, Miami Beach, and Key Biscayne.

In the Florida Keys, coral reefs and prevailing currents prevent sand from building up to form beaches. The few Keys beaches are small, narrow, and generally have little or no sandy bottom.

The waters of the Gulf of Mexico are somewhat murky, and Tampa Bay is heavily polluted, but the Gulf Coast beaches are beautiful. The Panhandle is known for its sugarlike white sand; around Sarasota the sand is soft and white. The barrier islands around Naples are known for the excellent shelling on their beaches, particularly on Sanibel Island.

Sports and Outdoor Activities

The **Governor's Council on Physical Fitness and Sports** (1330 N.W. 6th St., Suite D, Gainesville 32601, tel. 904/336–2120) puts on the annual Sunshine State Games in July each year in a different part of the state, and promotes the business of sports. Call for information on events. The **Florida Sports Foundation** (107 W. Gaines St., Suite 342, Tallahassee 32399–2000, tel. 904/488–8347) publishes a number of Florida sports guides.

Bicycling Bicycling is popular throughout Florida. The terrain is flat in the south and gently rolling along the central ridge and in much of the Panhandle. Most cities of any size have bike-rental shops, which are good sources of information on local bike paths.

Florida's Department of Natural Resources (Div. of Recreation and Parks, Mail Station 585, 3900 Commonwealth Blvd., Tallahassee 32399–3000, tel. 904/487–4784) is developing three overnight bicycle tours of different areas of the state. The tours will vary in length between 100 and 450 miles (for 2–6 days of cycling), and will use state parks for rest stops and overnight camping.

Florida's Department of Transportation (DOT) publishes free bicycle trail guides, which you can request from the state bicycle–pedestrian coordinator (605 Suwannee St., Mail Station 82, Tallahassee 32399-0450, tel. 904/487–1200); you can also request a free touring information packet. Also contact the DOT for names of bike coordinators around the state. In Greater Miami, contact Dade County's bicycle–pedestrian coordinator (Office of County Manager, Metro-Dade Government Center, 111 N.W. 1st St., Suite 910, Miami 33128, tel. 305/375–4507).

For information on local biking events and clubs, contact **Florida Bicycle Association** (Box 16652, Tampa 33687–6652, tel. 800/FOR–BIKE).

Canoeing The best time to canoe in Florida is winter, the dry season, when you're less likely to get caught in a torrential downpour or be eaten alive by mosquitoes.

The Everglades has areas suitable for flat-water wilderness canoeing that are comparable to spots in the Boundary Waters region of Minnesota. Other popular canoeing rivers include the Blackwater, Juniper, Loxahatchee, Peace, Oklawaha, Suwannee, St. Marys, and Santa Fe. A free guide issued by the Florida Department of Natural Resources (DNR), *Florida Recreational Trails System Canoe Trails,* describes nearly 950 miles of designated canoe trails and support services along 36 Florida creeks, rivers, and springs (Div. of Recreation and

Parks, Bureau of Local Recreation Services, MS 585, 3900 Commonwealth Blvd., Tallahassee 32399–3000, tel. 904/488–7896, fax 904/488–3665). Two additional guides include *Canoe Liveries and Outfitters Directory*, which lists organizations that offer livery and rental services for canoe trails in the system, and *Canoe Information Resources Guide*, which lists canoe clubs and organizations and gives a bibliography of maps, books, films, etc., about canoeing. Contact individual national forests, parks, monuments, reserves, and seashores for information on their canoe trails. Local chambers of commerce have information on canoe trails in county parks.

Two Florida canoe-outfitter organizations publish free lists of canoe outfitters who organize canoe trips, rent canoes and canoeing equipment, and help shuttle canoeists' boats and cars. **"Canoe Outpost System"** is a brochure listing six independent outfitters serving 11 Florida rivers (Rte. 7, Box 301, Arcadia 33821, tel. 813/494–1215). The **Florida Association of Canoe Liveries and Outfitters (FACLO)** publishes a free list of 33 canoe outfitters who organize trips on 28 creeks and rivers (Box 1764, Arcadia 33821).

Fishing In Atlantic and Gulf waters, fishing seasons and other regulations vary by location, and by the number and size of fish of various species that you may catch and retain. For a free copy of the annual *Florida Fishing Handbook,* write to the Florida Game and Fresh Water Fish Commission (620 S. Meridian St., Tallahassee 32399–1600, tel. 904/488–1960).

Opportunities for saltwater fishing abound from the Keys all the way up the Atlantic Coast to Georgia and up the Gulf Coast to Alabama. Many seaside communities have fishing piers that charge admission to anglers (and usually a lower rate to watchers). These piers usually have a bait-and-tackle shop. Write the **Florida Sea Grant Extension Program** for a free list of Florida fishing piers (Rm. G-022, McCarty Hall, University of Florida, Gainesville 32611, tel. 904/392–1771).

Inland, there are more than 7,000 freshwater lakes to choose from. The largest—448,000-acre **Lake Okeechobee,** the fourth-largest natural lake in the United States—is home to bass, bluegill, speckled perch, and succulent catfish (which the locals call "sharpies"). In addition to the state's many natural freshwater rivers, South Florida also has an extensive system of flood-control canals. In 1989 scientists found high mercury levels in largemouth bass and warmouth caught in parts of the Everglades in Palm Beach, Broward, and Dade counties, and warned against eating fish from those areas. Warnings have since been extended to parts of northern Florida.

It's easy to find a boat-charter service that will take you out into deep water. Some of the best are found in the Panhandle, where Destin and Fort Walton Beach have huge fleets. The Keys, too, are dotted with charter services, and Key West has an extensive sportfishing and shrimping fleet. Depending on your taste, budget, and needs, you can charter anything from an old wooden craft to a luxurious, waterborne palace with state-of-the-art amenities.

Licenses are required for both freshwater and saltwater fishing. The fees for a saltwater fishing license are $30 for nonresidents and $12 for residents. A nonresident seven-day saltwater license is $15. Nonresidents can purchase freshwater fishing licenses good for 10 days ($15) or for one year ($30); residents pay $12 for an annual license. Combined annual freshwater fishing and hunting licenses are also available at $22 for residents.

Golf Except in the heart of the Everglades, you'll never be far from one of Florida's more than 1,050 golf courses. Palm Beach County, the state's leading golf locale with 130 golf courses, also houses the home offices of the National Golf Foundation and the Professional Golfers Association of America. Many of the best golf courses in Florida allow visitors to play without being members or hotel guests. *See* Chapter 3, The Florida Fifty, for details on the state's best courses.

Especially in winter, you should reserve tee-off times in advance. Ask about golf reservations when you make your lodging reservations.

Horseback Riding Trail and endurance riding are popular throughout the state, with seven state parks providing overnight camping with stables, facilities, and 14 parks with trails and campgrounds for horses. Amelia Island offers horseback riding on the beach. Spring and fall meetings for riders are held. In the fall they meet in Altoona in the Ocala National Forest; in the spring, in a different location. For more information, contact **AHOOF** (Affiliated Horse Organization of Florida, Box 448, Laurel 34272, tel. 813/484–6449).

Hunting Hunters in Florida stalk a wide variety of resident game animals and birds, including deer, wild hog, wild turkey, bobwhite quail, ducks, and coots. A plain hunting license costs $11 for Florida residents, $150 for nonresidents, except nonresidents from Alabama who pay $100. Nonresidents can get a 10-day hunting license for $25, except for nonresidents from Georgia, who pay $121.

Each year in June, the **Florida Game and Fresh Water Fish Commission** announces the dates and hours of the fall hunting seasons for public and private wildlife-management areas. Hunting seasons vary across the state. Where hunting is allowed, you need the landowner's written permission—and you must carry that letter with your hunting license in the field. Trespassing with a weapon is a felony. For a free copy of the annual *Florida Hunting Handbook,* contact the game commission (620 Meridian St., Tallahassee 32399–1600, tel. 904/488–4676).

Jogging, Running, and Walking All over Florida, you'll find joggers, runners, and walkers on bike paths and city streets—primarily in the early morning and after working hours in the evening. Some Florida hotels have set up their own running trails; others provide guests with information on measured trails in the vicinity. The first time you run in Florida, be prepared to go a shorter distance than normal because of higher heat and humidity.

Two major Florida festivals include important running races. Each year in December the **Capital Bank Orange Bowl 10K,** one of the state's best-known running events, brings world-class runners to Miami. In April, as part of the Florida Keys annual Conch Republic Days, runners congregate near Marathon on one of the world's most spectacular courses for the **Seven Mile Bridge Run.**

Local running clubs all over the state sponsor weekly public events for joggers, runners, and walkers. For a list of local clubs and events throughout the state, call or send a self-addressed stamped envelope to the **Florida Athletics Congress** (1330 N.W. 6th St., Gainesville 32601, tel. 904/378–6805). For information about events in south Florida contact the 1,500-member **Miami Runners Club** (7900 S.W. 40th St., Miami 33155, tel. 305/227–1500).

Scuba Diving and Snorkeling South Florida and the Keys attract most of the divers and snorkelers, but the more than 300 dive shops throughout the state schedule drift-, reef-, and wreck-diving trips for scuba divers all along Florida's Atlantic and Gulf coasts. The low-tech pleasures of snorkeling can be enjoyed all along the Overseas Highway in the Keys and elsewhere where shallow reefs hug the shore.

Inland in north and central Florida divers explore more than 100 grottoes, rivers, sinkholes, and springs. In some locations, you can swim with manatees ("sea cows"), which migrate in from the sea to congregate around warm springs during the cool winter months. Ginnie Springs (Rte. 1, Box 153, High Springs 32643, tel. 904/454–2202 or 800/874–8571), near Branford, is one of Florida's most famous springs. Crystal Lodge Dive Center in the Econo Lodge (525 N.W. 7th Ave., Crystal River 32629, tel. 904/795–6798) is a popular gateway to river-diving in the Crystal River in central Florida.

Contact the **Dive Industry Association** for lists of advertisers who provide services for boaters, divers, and fisherfolk. The Keys packet is $6.95. An all-inclusive Florida state packet is no longer sold, but you can inquire about individual Florida charts (Teall's Inc., 111 Saguaro La., Marathon 33050, tel. 305/743–3942).

PADI recommends that you not scuba dive and fly within a 24-hour period.

Tennis Many Florida hotels have a resident tennis pro and offer special tennis packages with lessons. Many local park and recreation departments throughout Florida operate modern tennis centers like those at country clubs, and most such centers welcome nonresidents, for a fee. For general information and schedules for amateur tournaments, contact the **Florida Tennis Association** (801 N.E. 167th St., Suite 301, North Miami Beach 33162, tel. 305/652–2866).

National and State Parks

Although Florida is the fourth-most-populous state in the nation, there are 9,711,043 acres of public and private recreation facilities set aside in national forests, parks, monuments, reserves, and seashores; state forests and parks; county parks; and nature preserves owned and managed by private conservation groups.

On holidays and weekends, crowds flock to Florida's most popular parks—even to some on islands that are accessible only by boat. Come early or risk being turned away. In winter, northern migratory birds descend on the state. Many resident species breed in the warm summer months, but others (such as the wood stork) time their breeding cycle to the winter dry season. In summer, mosquitoes are voracious and daily afternoon thundershowers add to the state's humidity, but this is when the sea turtles come ashore to lay their eggs and when you're most likely to see frigate birds and other tropical species.

National Parks The federal government maintains no centralized information service for its natural and historic sites in Florida. You must contact each site directly for information on current recreational facilities and hours. To obtain a copy of **Guide and Map of National Parks of the U.S.**, which provides park addresses and facilities lists, write to U.S. Government Printing Office, Washington, DC 20402. GPO No. 024005008527. Cost: $1.25 (no tax or postage).

In 1993 **Fort Jefferson National Monument** in the Dry Tortugas was declared a national park. **Everglades National Park** was established in 1947. Other natural and historic sites in Florida under federal management include **Big Cypress National Preserve** and **Biscayne National Park** in the Everglades, **Canaveral National Seashore** in central Florida, **Castillo De San Marcos National Monument** in north Florida, **De Soto National Monument** in Bradenton, the 130-acre **Fort Caroline National Memorial** on the St. Johns River in Jacksonville, **Fort Matanzas National Monument** south of St. Augustine, and **Gulf Islands National Seashore** in north Florida.

The federal government operates three national forests in Florida. The **Apalachicola National Forest** encompasses 557,000 acres of pine and hardwoods across the northern coastal plain. The 336,000-acre **Ocala National Forest** includes the sandhills of the Big Scrub (*see* the essay in Chapter 2). Cypress swamps and numerous sinkhole lakes dot the 157,000-acre **Osceola National Forest.**

National wildlife refuges in Florida include the **Great White Heron National Wildlife Refuge** in the Keys, Pelican Island National Wildlife Refuge (America's first) in Indian River County, **Loxahatchee National Wildlife Refuge** near Palm Beach, **J. N. "Ding" Darling National Wildlife Refuge** in southwest Florida, and **Merritt Island National Wildlife Refuge.** The federal government also operates the **Key Largo National Marine Sanctuary, Looe Key National Marine Sanctuary,** and the **Florida Keys National Marine Sanctuary,** largest in the national system.

State Parks The **Florida Department of Natural Resources** is responsible for hundreds of historic buildings, landmarks, nature preserves, and an expanding state park system. When you request a free copy of the *Florida State Park Guide,* mention which parts of the state you plan to visit. For information on camping facilities at the state parks, ask for the free **"Florida State Parks, Fees and Facilities"** and **"Florida State Parks Camping Reservation Procedures"** brochures (Marjory Stoneman Douglas Bldg., MS 535, 3900 Commonwealth Blvd., Tallahassee 32399–3000, tel. 904/488–7872, fax 904/488–3947). Delivery takes 10–14 days.

Private Nature Preserves Wood storks nest at the National Audubon Society's **Corkscrew Swamp Sanctuary** near Naples; on Big Pine Key, there's the **National Key Deer Refuge.** Audubon also controls more than 65 other Florida properties, including islands, prairies, forests, and swamps. Visitation at these sites is limited. For information, contact **National Audubon Society,** Sanctuary Director (Miles Wildlife Sanctuary, RR 1, Box 294, W. Cornwall Rd., Sharon, CT 06069, tel. 203/364–0048).

The Nature Conservancy admits the public to five of its preserves: the 6,267–acre **Apalachicola Bluffs & Ravines Preserve** in Liberty County, **Blowing Rocks Preserve** with its unique anastasia limestone rock formations, the 970–acre **Cummer Sanctuary** in Levy County, **Tiger Creek Preserve** near Lake Wales in Polk County, and the 150–acre **Spruce Creek Preserve** with its restored historic buildings in Volusia County. For information about self–guided walks and access to preserves, contact the **Florida Chapter of The Nature Conservancy** (2699 Lee Rd., Ste. 500, Winter Park 32789, tel. 407/628–5887). Visitors are welcome at the Winter Park office and at offices in Tequesta (250 Tequesta Drive, Suite 301, Tequesta 33469, tel. 407/575–2297), Key West (201 Front St., Key West 33041, tel. 305/292–1763), Lake Wales (225 E. Stuart Ave., Lake Wales 33859, tel. 813/678–1551), Tallahassee (625 N. Adams St., Tallahassee 32301, tel. 904/222–0199), and West Palm Beach (Comeau Building, 319 Clematis St., West Palm Beach 33401, tel. 407/833–4226). All offices are open weekdays 9–5.

Dining

Florida regional cuisine changes as you move across the state, based on who settled the area and who now operates the restaurants. But always you can expect seafood to be a staple on nearly every menu. Look for Minorcan cuisine in St. Augustine, and the traditional Miccosukee and Seminole Indian fried bread, catfish, and frogs' legs at tribe-owned restaurants in the Everglades. South Florida's diverse assortment of Latin American restaurants offers the distinctive national fare of Argentina, Brazil, Colombia, Cuba, El Salvador, Mexico, Nicaragua, and Puerto Rico as well as West Indian delicacies from the Bahamas, Haiti, and Jamaica, and an acclaimed new tropical-Continental-nouvelle fusion that originated in Miami. The influence of earlier Hispanic settlements remains in Key West and Tampa's Ybor City.

All over Florida, Asian cuisine no longer means just Chinese. Indian, Japanese, Pakistani, Thai, and Vietnamese specialties are now available. Continental cuisine (French, German, Italian, Spanish, and Swiss) is also well represented all over Florida.

Every Florida restaurant claims to make the best Key lime pie. Pastry chefs and restaurant managers take the matter very seriously—they discuss the problems of getting good lime juice and maintaining top quality every day. Traditional Key lime pie is yellow, not green, with an old-fashioned Graham cracker crust and meringue top. The filling should be tart, and chilled but not frozen. Some restaurants serve their Key lime pie with a pastry crust; most substitute whipped cream for the more temperamental meringue. Each pie will be a little different. Try several, and make your own choice.

Price Categories

Category	Cost*
Very Expensive	over $50
Expensive	$35–$50

Moderate	$20–$35
Inexpensive	under $20

*per person, excluding drinks, service, and 6% sales tax

Lodging

Hotels and Motels Florida, with 40 million visitors a year, has every conceivable type of lodging for visitors, everything from tree houses to penthouses, from mansions for hire to hostels. Recession in the early 1990s discouraged investors from adding to Florida's hotel-room supply, but with occupancy rates hovering around 70 percent, there are always rooms for the night, except maybe during Christmas and other winter holiday weekends. Even the most glittery resort towns have affordable lodgings, typically motel rooms that may cost as little as $20–$25 a night—not in the best part of town, mind you, but not in the worst, either, perhaps along busy highways where you'll need the roar of the air-conditioning to drown out the traffic. Beachfront properties are always more expensive than comparable properties off the beach, yet many beachfront properties are surprisingly affordable, too.

Travelers who favor vintage hotels can find them everywhere. The classics include The Breakers and the Boca Raton Hotel and Country Club, both in Boca Raton; the Biltmore in Coral Gables; and the Casa Marina in Key West. Florida also has more than 200 historic inns, from the Miami River Inn in downtown Miami to the Governors Inn in Tallahassee and the New World Landing Inn in Pensacola.

Often the best bet for traveling with children is to book space that comes with a kitchen and more than one bedroom. Such properties are especially plentiful around Orlando, where hoteliers expect steady family trade. Children are welcome generally everywhere in Florida. Pets are another matter, so if you're bringing an animal with you, inquire ahead of time.

Reserving ahead always makes sense for the top properties in the busy seasons—over Christmas, from late January through Easter, and during holiday weekends in summer. St. Augustine stays busy all summer because of its historic flavor. Key West is jam-packed for Fantasy Fest at Halloween. If you're not booking through a travel agent, call the visitors bureau or the chamber of commerce in the area where you're going to check whether any special event is scheduled for when you plan to arrive. If demand isn't especially high for the time you have in mind, you can often save by showing up at a lodging in mid- to late afternoon—desk clerks are typically willing to negotiate with travelers in order to fill those rooms late in the day.

The Florida Hotel & Motel Association (FH&MA) publishes an *Annual Travel Directory* which you can obtain without charge from the **Florida Division of Tourism** (Department of Commerce, 126 Van Buren St., Tallahassee 32399, tel. 904/487-1462). You can also order it from the FH&MA if you send a stamped, addressed No. 10 envelope and $1 for handling (200 W. College Ave., Box 1529, Tallahassee 32301–1529, tel. 904/224–2888).

Price Categories Category	Cost*
Very Expensive	over $150
Expensive	$90–$150
Moderate	$60–$90
Inexpensive	under $60

*All prices are for a standard double room, excluding 6% state sales tax (some counties also have a local sales tax) and 1%–4% tourist tax.

Inns and B&Bs Small inns and guest houses are becoming increasingly numerous and popular in Florida. Many offer the convenience of bed-and-breakfast accommodations in a homelike setting; many, in fact, are in private homes, and the owners treat you almost like a member of the family. **Inn Route, Inc.** (9660 E. Bay Harbor Drive, Bay Harbor Islands, FL 33154, tel. 305/868–4141 or 800/524–1880) a statewide association of small, architecturally distinctive historic inns, will send you a free brochure.

Bed-and-breakfast referral and reservation agencies in Florida include: **Bed & Breakfast Co., Tropical Florida** (Box 262, Miami 33243, tel. 305/661–3270), **Bed & Breakfast East Coast** (Box 1373, Marathon 33050, tel. 305/743–4118), **Bed & Breakfast Scenic Florida** (Box 3385, Tallahassee 32315–3385, tel. 904/386–8196), **Open House Bed & Breakfast,** (Box 3025, Palm Beach 33480, tel. 407/842–5190), **RSVP Florida & St. Augustine** (Box 3603, St. Augustine 32085, tel. 904/826–4266), **Southern Comfort Reservation & Referral Service** (8021 S.E. Helen Terr., Hobe Sound 33455, tel. 407/546–6743), and **Suncoast Accommodations of Florida** (8690 Gulf Blvd., St. Petersburg Beach 33706, tel. 813/360–1753).

Home Exchange This is obviously an inexpensive solution to the lodging problem, because house-swapping means living rent-free. You find a house, apartment, or other vacation property to exchange for your own by becoming a member of a home-exchange organization, which then sends you its annual directories listing available exchanges and includes your own listing in at least one of them. Arrangements for the actual exchange are made by the two parties to it, not by the organization. Principal clearinghouses include **Intervac U.S./International Home Exchange** (Box 590504, San Francisco, CA 94159, tel. 415/435–3497), the oldest, with thousands of foreign and domestic homes for exchange in its three annual directories; membership is $62, or $72 if you want to receive the directories but remain unlisted. The **Vacation Exchange Club** (Box 650, Key West, FL 33041, tel. 800/638–3841), also with thousands of foreign and domestic listings, publishes four annual directories plus updates; the $50 membership includes your listing in one book. **Loan-a-Home** (2 Park La., Apt. 6E, Mount Vernon, NY 10552, tel. 914/664–7640) specializes in long-term exchanges; there is no charge to list your home, but the directories cost $35 or $45 depending on the number you receive.

Apartment, Villa, and Condo Rentals If you want a home base that's roomy enough for a family and comes with cooking facilities, a furnished rental may be the solution. It's generally cost-wise, too, although not always: some rentals are luxury properties (economical only when your party is large). Home-exchange directories do list rentals—often second homes owned by prospective house swappers— and there are services that can not only look for a house or apartment for you (even a castle if that's your fancy) but also handle the paperwork. Some send an illustrated catalogue and others send photographs of specific properties, sometimes at a charge; up-front registration fees may apply.

Among the companies are **Interhome Inc.** (124 Little Falls Rd., Fairfield, NJ 07004, tel. 201/882–6864); **Overseas Connection** (31 North Harbor Dr., Sag Harbor, NY 11963, tel. 516/725–9308); **Rent a Home International** (7200 34th Ave. NW, Seattle, WA 98117, tel. 206/789–9377 or 800/488–7368); **Vacation Home Rentals Worldwide** (235 Kensington Ave., Norwood, NJ 07648, tel. 201/767–9393 or 800/633–3284). **Hideaways International** (15 Goldsmith St., Box 1270, Littleton, MA 01460, tel. 508/486–8955 or 800/843–4433) functions as a travel club. Membership ($79 yearly per person or family at the same address) includes two annual guides plus quarterly newsletters; rentals are arranged directly between members, not by the club staff.

See also *The Condo Lux Vacationer's Guide to Condominium Rentals in the Southeast* by Jill Little (Vintage Books/Random House, New York; $9.95).

Camping and RV Facilities   Contact the national parks and forests you plan to visit directly for information on camping facilities (*see* National Parks, *above*). For information on camping facilities in state parks, contact the Florida Department of Natural Resources (*see* State Parks, *above*).

The free annual *Florida Camping Directory* lists 200 commercial campgrounds in Florida with 50,000 sites. It's available at Florida welcome centers, from the Florida Division of Tourism, and from the **Florida Campground Association** (1638 N. Plaza Dr., Tallahassee 32308–5364, tel. 904/656–8878).

Vacation Ownership Resorts   Vacation ownership resorts sell hotel rooms, condominium apartments, or villas in weekly, monthly, or quarterly increments. The weekly arrangement is most popular; it's often referred to as "interval ownership" or "time sharing." Of more than 2,500 vacation ownership resorts around the world, some 400 are in Florida, with the heaviest concentration in the Disney World/Orlando area. Most vacation ownership resorts are affiliated with one of two major exchange organizations—**Interval International** (6262 Sunset Dr., Penthouse One, S. Miami 33143, tel. 305/666–1861 or 800/828–8200) or **Resort Condominiums International** (3502 Woodview Trace, Indianapolis, IN 46268–3131, tel. 317/876–8899 or 800/338–7777). As an owner, you can join your resort's exchange organization and swap your interval for another someplace else in any year when you want a change of scene. Even if you don't own an interval, you can rent at many vacation ownership resorts where unsold intervals remain and/or owners have placed their intervals in a rental program. For rental information, contact the exchange organizations (Worldex, tel. 800/235–4000; Resort Condominiums International, tel. 800/338–7777), the individual resort, or a local real estate broker in the area where you want to rent.

Credit Cards

Throughout the book credit card abbreviations refer to the following: AE, American Express; D, Discover; DC, Diners Club; MC, MasterCard; and V, Visa.

2 Portraits of Florida

In Search of the Real Florida

By April Athey

A free-lance writer based in Tallahassee, April Athey has been writing about her home state for magazines and newspapers since 1977. Her work has appeared in many publications, including the New York Times, Chicago Tribune, Christian Science Monitor, Frequent Flyer, *and* Gulf-shore Life.

It's hard to imagine a Florida without a magic kingdom, a spaceport to the stars, interstate highways, or high-rise beachfront hotels. But such a Florida exists, and to-day the state's natural and historical treasures are being imitated, refurbished, restored, and recognized for their lasting appeal.

There are those who recall the day when Walt Disney World's fantasy lands and futuristic hotels opened in 1971, setting a technological standard in entertainment that may still be unrivaled. The owners of natural attractions like Silver Springs, Weeki Wachee, and Homosassa Springs struggled to keep the attention of technology-hungry Americans. The lush jungle-lined rivers, exotic wildlife, and crystal-clear spring waters somehow paled in contrast to the make-believe, never-a-dull-moment amusements for which the Disney corporation had become famous. The convenience of a one-stop, no-surprise vacation apparently made real wilderness cruises, beaches, wildlife, and historical attractions passé.

To see and appreciate the real thing, one had to leave the interstate highways and brave a few side roads. Because not many tourists cared to take the road less traveled, many owners of natural attractions were forced to expand their offerings with man-made amusements. If budgets weren't sweet enough to permit this sort of commercialization, the attractions (usually the lesser-known botanical gardens, great homes, and wildlife reserves) saw lean years.

Fortunately, the cycle is coming full circle. Technology-harassed Americans are now looking for the good old days, and Florida is obliging them.

Today, developers of new resorts are focusing attention on the Florida of the 19th century. New resorts not only imitate Old Florida architecture but also, through their land-scaping, recall when the only silhouettes scraping Florida's sky were of stout cabbage palms, mossy oaks, towering cypress, and hardy evergreens.

Maintaining the ecological integrity of the land and its often-endangered inhabitants has become an increasing concern of developers. The Grand Cypress Resort in Orlando was designed to be complemented by a stand of native cypress, and the Registry Resort in Naples nestles at the edge of a 1,000-acre nature preserve, through which a $1-million boardwalk was built to provide access to the beach and protection for the delicate sand dunes.

St. Augustine is the oldest permanent European settlement in the United States—with an extensive historic district to prove it—and was the first Florida resort popularized by Henry Flagler when he brought his Florida East Coast Railroad and friends south for the winter. Key West was the last resort Flagler helped build. His Casa Marina hotel still stands, having been restored and expanded under management by Marriott. The island's "conch houses" also are being restored, and many have been converted into guest houses and restaurants. Flagler also put Palm Beach and its sister, West Palm Beach, on the map. Though his original wooden hotels burned to the ground, his private estate is now the Flagler Museum.

Sharing space with the glinting glass of skyscrapers are the castlelike villas and Old Florida–style homes of former Florida residents. You can tour Ca'd'Zan, the bay-side villa that John Ringling and his wife Mable built, which now is part of the Ringling Museums Complex in Sarasota. Like an oasis in the middle of Miami's asphalt-and-concrete desert, the palatial bay-front estate of John Deering, with its formal gardens and surrounding natural jungles (Vizcaya Museum and Gardens), may be toured daily. Visit Thomas Edison's Winter Home in Fort Myers, and dine out on Cabbage Key, the tiny island accessible by boat (offshore from Captiva)—the retreat of mystery writer Mary Roberts Rinehart. Ormond Beach has reminders of its heyday, when John D. Rockefeller and friends made the riverfront Ormond Hotel a world-renowned wintering spot. Rockefeller eventually built his winter home, The Casements, across the street from the hotel, and both still stand proudly by the shores of the Halifax River, just north of Daytona Beach. The Casements is now an art museum and site of an annual antique-auto show.

Fort Jefferson, the Civil War island fortress on which Samuel Mudd—the physician who treated Lincoln's assassin—was imprisoned, is only a seaplane flight away from tropical Key West. On Key West are the 19th-century fortifications—East and West Martello Towers—one now home to the city's historical museum, and the other the setting of the garden club. Recently excavated and open to the public on Key West is Fort Zachary Taylor. Living-history interpretations are conducted daily at Fort Clinch, a Civil War fortress in Fernandina Beach, and at Fort Foster in Hillsborough State Park, just west of Tampa. Speaking of Tampa, the next time you order a rum and Coke, remember that the concoction was invented there by Teddy Roosevelt's Rough Riders.

In addition to the monuments of recent history, there are the archaeological reminders of Florida's first residents, the aboriginal Indians who greeted European explorers and expatriates. Several state parks preserve treasured archaeological sites, like Hontoon Island on the St. Johns

River, Tomoka River State Park, near Daytona Beach (both sites of Timucuan Indian settlements), and Jonathan Dickinson State Park, near the Palm Beaches (site of a Quaker shipwreck and their subsequent imprisonment by Jaega Indians).

These and later Indians left their place names as a lasting legacy—names like Ichetucknee (now a tubing river north of Gainesville), Pensacola, Apalachicola, Tequesta, Kissimmee, Chassahowitzka (a national wildlife refuge near Homosassa Springs), Okeechobee (a 590-square-mile inland lake), Ocala, and Tallahassee (the state capital).

Victorian homes with gingerbread-trimmed wraparound verandas, shaded by sloping tin roofs, are being restored and operated as bed-and-breakfast inns or chic restaurants. Florida's B&Bs have increased from an estimated five in 1980 to more than 50 in 1988.

Main Street programs are flourishing throughout the state, revitalizing the business/entertainment districts of towns like Winter Park, Orlando, DeLand, and Quincy (in northwest Florida).

Historic hotels and inns, once threatened by wrecking crews, are living new lives. Check out the Heritage in St. Petersburg, a restored, 60-year-old hotel (the original Florida "cracker" home in the backyard now serves as an atrium-greenhouse bar); or book a weekend at Apalachicola's 100-year-old Gibson Inn.

Waterfront redevelopment projects like Miami's Bayside and Jacksonville Landing (Rouse Marketplace developments) are focusing fresh attention on the inlets and bays that once harbored renegade pirates and adventurous pioneers.

Quiet waterfront hamlets, built during the boom in steamboat travel—Sanford and Crescent City are good examples—are beginning to blossom again with the reemergence of riverboat cruising.

Oddly enough, it may be easier to find an Old Florida vacation experience now than it was 20 years ago. Washed by both the Gulf of Mexico and the Atlantic Ocean, Florida seems to be more water than land. Underground freshwater rivers course through the limestone bedrock of its north and central highlands, often boiling to the surface and flowing overland to the sea. A bird's-eye view reveals a peninsula whose upper reaches are dotted and crisscrossed by hundreds of lakes and streams and whose ragged southern borders are home to a vast, shallow river of grass called the Everglades and a maze of mangrove clumps called the Ten Thousand Islands. From the town of Everglades City, on Florida's southwest tip, sightseeing boats meander through the maze of islands, and just off the Tamiami Trail (U.S. 41), on the north-central boundary of Everglades National Park, you can climb the observation deck at Shark Valley Overlook for a good look at the river of grass.

This view, perhaps more than anything, helps to remind people of what Floridians are trying to recapture.

The Florida Scrub

By Al Burt

A roving writer-columnist for The Miami Herald for the past 15 years, Al Burt specializes in Florida's history, natural habitat, and future. He has written two books on the state—Becalmed in the Mullet Latitudes and Florida: A Place in the Sun. In 1974, Burt left Miami's city life to make his base in his beloved Scrub Country, near Melrose in north Florida.

Understanding Florida requires at least some knowledge of the historic Scrub Country, the oldest, the driest, the harshest, and, in some ways, the most delicate part of the state. In water-loving Florida, the Scrub struggles to remain a desert outlaw.

If you have ever walked a beach and observed how the tides and the wind have rolled the sterile sands into a long, graceful dune on which grow a few scraggly, scratchy plants, you may have gotten some idea about Florida's unique Scrub Country and its peculiar beauty.

The Scrub, which once covered most of Florida with bone-dry sandhills, is the legitimate kin to a desert, and it's full of puzzles. The life forms there are persistent, thrifty, and fragile. Once, you could look across the low profile of its vegetation and see odd "islands" of fertility, little oases of tall trees and green life, while all around was the stunted, prickly, vulnerable Scrub growth. They were like oddly matched siblings of nature, growing up side by side, but, by freakish accident, one had been denied its vitamins.

The name came from an early and natural lack of appreciation. It was scrubby country, not like the scenic Florida of the travel books. Except in those "islands," it lacked the towering slash pines and the comfortable shade of large-crowned live oaks and the open landscapes beneath. The Scrub was a place unto itself, with few easy pleasures, and it was not good for conventional farming.

Loving the Scrub came easiest if you grew up with it, if it came naturally to you. Sometimes it became a fierce, protective thing, like a stubbornly loyal Cracker Mama who adored the scrawniest of her children most because it was the misfit.

Flooding rains leached quickly through Scrub sands and left them dry as ever. Rosemary bushes, prickly pears, saw palmettos, sand pines, sandburs, gnarled dwarf oaks, and other scraggly little trees commonly grew there.

The deep sand made it difficult to walk with shoes on. The sands in summer burned the soles of bare feet with temperatures of 135–140 degrees. Everything in the Scrub seemed to scratch and claw at you, fighting for life.

Rattlesnakes loved it. Exotic little creatures (in addition to raccoons, bobcats, and deer), some of them now rare and endangered, made it home—scrub jays, lizards, skinks, gopher frogs and gopher tortoises, exotic mice, red widow spiders, and such.

For years, big patches of the Scrub Country, especially if they were inland and off the main tracks, lay abandoned. If they attracted anyone, it was likely to be the young, who sometimes found the sandhills great places for exploring or play, sliding down them, burrowing into them, and holding beer parties and buggy chases on the tricky sand.

The Scrub did not rebound easily from such use, but nobody cared. The track of a jeep across virgin scrub vegetation might take unaided nature years to erase. That was minor compared with what else happened in the history of the Scrub.

I t began when Florida began. The Scrub probably was the first part of Florida to emerge from the ocean, geologists say. Its dunes or sandhills formed under pressures of wind and tides as the ocean levels rose and fell during the ice ages. Great, irregular ridges took shape, almost like terraces. Time altered them into graceful sandhills.

The original Scrub Country became the Central Highlands of Florida, which stretches from east of Gainesville in the north-central part of the state south for some 200 miles and flatten out into the prairies of Lake Okeechobee. In places, the elevation reaches 300 feet.

For Florida, those great sandhills became Sierra Citrus, center of one of its greatest trademark industries. The well-drained Scrub lands were easily cleared and were perfect for oranges—once the growers added fertilizers and artificial irrigation.

You can ride that ridge today in one of the state's most scenic inland drives and imagine the beginning. U.S. 27, a fine highway, rolls up and down those great sandhills, past a series of lakes, along the fringes of Disney World country, and through miles and miles of green and seasonally fragrant citrus groves. (Even though the freezes of recent winters blighted many of them, the scene remains impressive.)

Like smaller versions of the Central Highlands, lesser dunes trailed away to the ocean. All had similar characteristics, but closer to the coast there were subtle changes, particularly if they were close enough to get the windblown ocean spray.

The dunes and the life on them also differed in their northern stretches, where the climate was temperate and subject to more seasonal changes than in southern Florida. In the south, the influence of the Gulf Stream and the more prominent crosswinds from the gulf and the ocean produced an exotic subtropical climate.

Scrub Country was high ground. Water did not collect there, but in strategic or special places development did, especially along the coast. Around the turn of the century, Henry Flagler built his pioneering railroad partially on a high dune ridge running down the east coast. Then he opened up cities like Palm Beach, Miami, and eventually Key West to tourists and development.

For the most part, the Scrub Country was an ugly duckling among Florida real estate developers. Many wanted to use it as raw material or take advantage of its special location, but few perceived it as anything that was uniquely beautiful or valuable in itself. As a result, 90% or more of this original Florida scene no longer exists.

The sand, some of it as fine as sugar, was mined for construction materials. Great areas were leveled for shopping centers and other development. Subdivisions turned dune ripples into square blocks of cottages. Water was piped in, and developers covered these desert sands with St. Augustine grass.

Except for exploiters, the Scrub Country had few advocates. The most notable of them was the writer, Marjorie Kinnan Rawlings, an easterner. Rawlings's work elevated one area of the Scrub into legend.

In 1928, Rawlings fled the rigors of newspaper life in Rochester, NY, and settled in an old Cracker house by an orange grove in an unlikely little village oasis called Cross Creek. She sought inspiration in isolation and frontier surroundings. The creek (between Ocala and Gainesville) was a lane of water connecting two large lakes in north-central Florida.

Her love of the creek and its people expanded to the areas nearby, which included a significant piece of Scrub Country known locally as the Big Scrub. To enrich her knowledge of it, she lived for a while with a family in the Scrub, hunted there, and befriended the Crackers who chose it as a place to live.

Rawlings's novels, particularly *The Yearling*, which won the Pulitzer Prize and then was made into a popular movie, realistically acknowledged but nevertheless romanticized the Big Scrub. She depicted the impoverished Crackers as primitives who lived by their own code—a code that she clearly thought had a noble base.

Rawlings gave the Big Scrub and Florida's Scrub Country a national identity. Within the past few years, her book of essays on Cross Creek and a short story entitled "Gal Young 'Un" also were made into well-received movies. Those films renewed and enlarged Rawlings's loving images of the Cross Creek area and the Big Scrub. Since then, the importance of the Scrub as a unique plant and animal habitat has been recognized. Scientists and conservationists have dedicated themselves to its study and preservation.

Rawlings's books became especially significant because the largest remaining area of Scrub left in Florida, modified though it may be, is the one she idealized. It lies in the cen-

One good thing to remember is that, globally, Florida lies in the zone of the great deserts, including the Sahara, so the Scrub is not out of character. Florida began with those ocean sands that bleached into dunes and sandhills and then into the variety that visitors enjoy today.

Remembering the past explains a lot about the true nature of Florida, no matter how wet it looks right now. The Scrub Country reminds us that the makings of a desert are still there, waiting.

tral and western portions of the 380,000-acre Ocala Nati
al Forest (a multiple-use forest that permits hunting
camping) and still is called the Big Scrub.

The Big Scrub contains the world's largest stand of s
pines. Many of them occur naturally, but, because in so
areas the pines were planted in rows so neat that the na
ral poetry of the forest is altered, some have criticized it
a sand-pine plantation. In either case, both the pines
the patches of dunes, as close as the road shoulders, are
ible from the car during a drive through the forest. The a
illustrates how sand pines and other scrub vegetation, o
time, tend to close and fill in an area, giving it a cano
above and a soil below slowly being altered by collections
natural forest debris, especially leaves, fallen limbs, a
root systems. This cycle can change the natural charact
istics of the Scrubs, unless fire (the sand pine is highly fla
mable) or timbering activities interfere. Even so, the Scr
retains its mysteries. Even the foresters cannot alwa
predict with certainty that the Scrub cycle will begin ag
after a fire.

Most of Florida's Scrub Country is now scattered in b
and pieces around the state. You have to search and gue
and inquire locally. Aside from the Ocala forest, a visit
can see examples of it in the Jonathan Dickinson Sta
Park, 13 miles south of Stuart on U.S. 1.

In that same area, you may see from the highway a ty
cal patch of surviving Scrub—a high roadside du
topped by a windswept sand pine, so stressed tha
seems picturesquely oriental. The same sand pine, see
the Ocala Forest, may grow bushy and erect and look lik
ideal Christmas tree.

Finding examples of the Scrub elsewhere becomes a m
of travel and identification, of looking for inland dun
untouched by development. Where there is a low, san
there could be scrub. You can find areas of it down t
coast, from St. Augustine to West Palm Beach, in no
Florida near the coast and along Rte. A1A, and th
some that sweep back off the Panhandle beaches i
west Florida. Little of the scrub, however—excep
public parks—has tourist convenience for study a
ment. Even in the state and national forests, t
footing, the heat, and the numerous insects disc
but the most hardy explorers.

At least two large tracts are being maintained fo
research. The University of Florida owns sever
acres of Scrub east of Gainesville, and the Arch
ical Station (established in 1941) has 3,800 acre
tive Scrub near Lake Placid on the southern
Central Highlands. These are not open for pul
however.

Miami Beach Art Deco

By Hap Hatton

Born and raised in Florida, Hap Hatton now lives in New York City, where he is in charge of still photography for PBS station WNET 13. His previous books include The Tent Book *and* The Virgin Homeowner's Handbook.

By 1910 Miami Beach had failed first as a coconut plantation, then as an avocado farm. Now it was being tried as a residential development. It took 10 years to create the present landmass. Carl Fisher, the Hoosier millionaire who financed much of the dredging and land-clearing, envisioned the area as a playground for the wealthy. Interspersed between his opulent hotels were huge estates on lots running 400 feet in from Biscayne Bay. Meanwhile, the southern portion of the barrier island was developed by the Lummus brothers, who plotted smaller lots for a middle-class resort. Scarcely had the dredging begun than the Lummus brothers in 1912 opened the Ocean Beach Realty Company, the first real estate office on the beach. Steady growth was interrupted by World War I, but then Miami Beach took off—until the collapse of the Florida real estate boom and the ensuing Depression.

By 1936, assisted by an expanding tourist industry, south Florida had emerged from the Depression. Hundreds of small hotels and apartment buildings were constructed on the small Lummus lots at the rate of 100 a year until 1941, making Miami Beach one of the few cities in the United States to have a building boom during the Depression. Ernest Hemingway's brother Leicester, also a writer, explains the phenomenon:

During the Depression, people needed to let go. . . . They became wild on Miami Beach. . . . They didn't watch their nickels. . . . [Architects] were determined not to use any older styles like the Spanish. . . . They wanted something modern, so they smoothed out all the Spanish things. They smoothed everything until you got the feeling that life was smooth. The buildings made you feel all clean and new and excited and happy to be there.

The style that prevailed in South Miami Beach was a zesty, crowd-pleasing Art Deco built by a handful of architects and contractors. Many of the architects were not formally trained but freely adapted national design trends to this tropical setting, creating a uniformity in style and scale rarely found in an urban setting. Called Miami Beach Art Deco (the name Tropical Deco has also been applied to the style), this brand of Art Deco was both relatively inexpensive to construct and offered a slick, dramatic, fashionable appearance, while its strong visual tropical symbols—

From Tropical Splendor: An Architectural History of Florida *by Hap Hatton. Copyright 1987 by Hap Hatton. Reprinted by permission of Alfred A. Knopf, Inc.*

"Floridiana"—impressed upon visitors the unique charms of the area.

Florida didn't invent the decorative vegetative and animal motifs that dominated the more ornate Miami Beach Art Deco buildings, but it raised them to new stylistic heights with facade bas-reliefs of cast or dyed stone, etched windows, and decorative metalwork on doors and porches.

Flowers, especially voluptuous gladiolus, alluded to the fecund floral paradise. Nymphs and nudes hedonistically stressed sensuous youth and romance. Fountains as well as sunbursts and symbolic zigzag equivalents of rays conjured up the life-renewing natural properties of the climate. Animals such as peacocks, flamingos, greyhounds, herons, and pelicans were chosen for their romantic associations, arabesque shapes, and exaggerated proportions. Originally, most of the buildings were stark white, with trims of azure blue, ocean turquoise, blazing yellow, palm tree green, erotic pink, or purples and mauves that evoked tropical sunsets, bougainvillea, and feelings both sensuous and exotic.

The sense of place is strong among these Deco buildings, leaving no doubt that this is the tropics, far from the cold, gray, sooty, industrial North.

The variances in Miami Beach Art Deco reflected what was occurring economically and architecturally on the national scene. Among others, four prevalent Deco styles comprise Miami Beach Art Deco.

Art Deco. The earliest buildings adapted the original Art Deco style's sharply angular massing with shallow stepped-back facades. Ornate bas-relief panels often framed large central openings. The French love of luxurious, sensuous textures such as crystal, mother-of-pearl, and unusual woods translated into indigenous Florida oolitic limestone, etched glass, stucco, and terrazzo (a cast agglomerate of marble or granite particles in colored and polished cement).

Depression Moderne. By 1937 the mode had shifted to a Deco with the more austere look of the reigning International Style. Art Moderne's vertical stucco bands, flat roof with stepped parapet, and facade symmetry were still there, but with an increased horizontal emphasis that would later become dominant in streamlining. Depression Moderne was also readapted for government buildings such as the Miami Beach Post Office, and called PWA Moderne for the Public Works Administration.

Streamlined Moderne. By 1939, a full-blown aerodynamic Moderne featured curved forms, applied racing stripes that accentuated horizontal emphasis, and "eyebrow" shading of the windows with cantilevered slabs to reduce the angle of penetration of the sun. The continuously wrapped stucco surfaces expressed concepts associated with travel and speed. Here the angularity of the originally imported Art Moderne was entirely replaced by soft flowing masses accented with horizontal lines and rows of windows. This phase combined smooth, sweeping curves with straight lines of the machine age in simple, definite, contrasting shapes. Combinations of Cubism's suggestion of dimensionality, Futurism's romance with speed, and Surrealist fantasy are cited as sources of inspiration. This streamlining restored the fun and humor drained by Depression Moderne.

Mannerism. A final development of Miami Beach streamlining was called Resort Mannerism or Mannerist Moderne (from Mannerism, a late 16th-century reaction against the High Renaissance characterized by a deliberate distortion of the existing artistic and architectural repertoire; it gave way to the Baroque, and today the term is associated with the exaggeration and/or distortion of existing themes). Resort Mannerism included Nautical Moderne, with its exaggerated and literal invocations of ships at sea with porthole windows, decklike balconies, and flagstaffs. This mature Moderne emphasized sinuous curves, stylized directional ornament, and bold projections, marking a conscious search by architects both here and in Europe for a unique form to express contemporary modernity. Never a pure style, it even incorporated highlights from the Spanish Mediterranean, such as sloping tile roofs or colored ceramic tiles. The late 1930s film influence brought soaring "trylons" or space-age needles to roofs and facades. This Flash Gordon touch turned the buildings visually into spaceships with Hollywood stage-set lobbies that were also referred to as Cinema Style and Hollywood Style.

Larger Deco hotels did make their appearance, but, by and large, the area known as Old Miami Beach consists of two- and three-story hostelries small in scale and rich in expression. Deco architecture prevailed here later than anywhere else in the country, until World War II abruptly terminated construction. By 1941, most hotels were occupied by the military in training for the war effort. After the war, the area began to decline as Miami Beach continued its development northward.

In 1979, one square mile of Miami Beach became this country's first 20th-century national historic district. It reflects a trend in architecture that took place between the two world wars, when more than 500 Art Deco structures went up in one small area. It is not only the largest and most cohesive concentration of Art Deco buildings in the world but the first historic district that has registered buildings less than 50 years old. It sits on one of the best pieces of real estate in Florida, perhaps on the entire East Coast.

The fight for preservation of these landmarks has raged for years between developers who want to erect more profitable high-rise condominiums and the local Miami Design

Preservation League, founded by Barbara Baer Capitman. A former art historian and now president of the Art Deco Society of Miami, she held her first organizational meeting in 1976 with six people and spoke of the area's potential as "capital of the Art Deco world." Capitman attracted 100 volunteers to survey and research the locality. Then the battle was launched that resulted in tax and zoning incentives for the owners of Deco buildings who preserve their original structures.

By its nature, rehabilitation means modernization and deviation from original design schemes, and nowhere is this more apparent than in color restoration. The original white with vivid color accents has been rejected in favor of a palette of Post-Modern cake-icing pastels now associated with the former television series "Miami Vice." Leonard Horowitz, the designer who introduced these colors, rationalized that because the neighborhood had deteriorated and much of the original vegetation had died, there was justification for using a plethora of color. Finally, white is being reintroduced.

The buildings of the Miami Beach Historical District chronicle more than a decade of historic cultural change and served the emotional needs of the public in a time of national crisis. No orthodox academic style has accomplished this. Whatever their historical significance or their eventual evaluation as art, these Miami Art Deco habitations are built to the human scale where the desires of the people are met rather than dictated to by sociological or aesthetic theory. Such a value in buildings has generally been condescended to or given mere lip service by respected architects who consider the tastes of the public beneath contempt. Yet the art of living cannot be measured by formal architectural standards of purity or style, only by the pleasure of the time and place. Miami Beach Art Deco created this quality of life with consummate success.

Today, the buildings still hold magic for visitors and inhabitants. Although the romance is slightly tarnished by peeling facades, and idealistic dreams have succumbed to more jaded views, there is still a sense of desire and expectation in the air. There is a glamour about these buildings that invites thoughts of moonlit walks on sparkling beaches, movie-screen romances, dancing under starry skies. There is a sadness, too, of once-vital dreams lost, either demolished or covered over with gaudy wallpaper and wall-to-wall carpeting. But this special fantasy of Florida still twinkles seductively among the vast pile of urban mediocrity that threatens to engulf the Miami Beach Deco District.

3 The Florida Fifty

Golfing Throughout the State

By Peter Oliver

Updated by Ann Hughes

When it comes to golf, Florida is far and away the top dog among U.S. states. If you doubt it, the state can round up a host of statistics as evidence. More than one of every 10 rounds of golf played in the United States is played in Florida. The roughly 3 million golfers who visit Florida annually far exceeds the number of golfers who visit any other state. They bring their wallets with them, too, shelling out more than $1.5 billion directly on golf and $5 billion in related spending. Put in perspective, that combined figure exceeds the gross national product of more than half of the countries of the world.

Most significantly, Florida has more golf courses than any other state. Present count tallies more than 1,000, with about 100 other courses in either the planning stages or under construction. According to a National Golf Foundation estimate, the number of courses in Florida will approach 1,500 by the year 2000.

Many of these grounds, however, are (and will be) private. Still, at last count roughly two-thirds were either public courses, "semiprivate" courses, or private courses allowing limited access to the public (for example, courses extending privileges to guests of nearby hotels). So if you're on your way to Florida with a mind to play golf, you'll have more than 600 courses to choose from.

A big part of the appeal of Florida golf is its year-round availability. Although a few courses might close for a day or two in the fall to reseed greens, and a few in the north might delay morning tee times in winter because of occasional frost, it's still fair to say that you can golf in Florida 365 days a year. That's why a large number of touring professionals—players such as Jack Nicklaus and Greg Norman—have settled here.

What sort of play can golfers visiting Florida expect? It's no state secret that Florida is flat; with a highest elevation of 345 feet, Florida can't claim many naturally rolling courses. And the few that can be found are mostly in the northwest. Don't be deceived, though, into thinking that the natural flatness of the Florida landscape is an assurance of flat fairways or greens. The world's leading golf-course designers, including Tom Fazio, Jack Nicklaus, and Ed Seay, have compensated by creating lots of manmade rolls and undulations. No designer, however, has been more notable in this regard than Pete Dye, pioneer of the "stadium" style (courses designed to accommodate large tournament audiences) of golf-course construction.

The two characteristics most common to Florida play are water and sand. That shouldn't be a surprise in a flat state with a high water table; often, lakes and canals have to be carved out anyway, just to make fairways. Sand is also a natural part of the Florida environment, although many courses import special fine-grain sand to fill traps. Regardless of the sand's origin, it is plentiful; it isn't unusual to come across a hole in Florida with 10 or more traps, and several courses have more than 100 traps each. In some ways, however, Florida sand works to the golfer's advantage. The sandy soil drains well after rain and also provides a surface more forgiving in playing iron shots than denser, clay-rich soil more common elsewhere.

What this adds up to is a premium on accuracy when it comes to approach shots. While Florida fairways are characteristically wide, greens tend to be heavily bunkered or protected by water. A diabolically popular invention of Florida course builders is the island green, completely surrounded by water.

One other element that often comes into play in Florida is wind. This is particularly true at seaside courses, of which there are many in a state with more than 3,000 miles of coastline. But wind can also be a vexing factor inland, where it swirls and becomes unpredictable as it moves through tall pine and palm trees. If all of this sounds unfairly treacherous, golfers can take heart in the fact that deep rough is uncommon as a penalizing element in Florida play; short rough is especially prevalent during the winter.

Finally, keep in mind that for most of the year, Florida greens are seeded with Bermuda grass. Golfers used to putting on bent-grass greens found in other parts of the country might find that the speed (on the slow side) and grain of Bermuda greens takes time to get used to.

The Florida Fifty

In a state with more than 1,000 courses, coming up with only 50 recommended courses is no easy task. In creating a "Florida Fifty," some properties in the state are easily eliminated: those that are private or those with policies for public play that are unusually restrictive. Nine-hole and par-3 (sometimes called "executive") courses also have not been considered. That still leaves hundreds of courses from which to choose.

This list is a sampling of the broad range of what is available in Florida, from inexpensive municipal courses to luxurious resort courses. Compiled after consulting several experts on Florida golf as well as various golf magazines, books, and guides, this index includes those courses repeatedly cited as being among Florida's best. This does not, however, mean these are the only ones worth playing in the state. Also, although just one course has been highlighted at each of the multicourse resorts cited (for example, Doral, Grand Cypress, PGA National), other courses at these resorts may also be among Florida's best. For that reason, the *total* number of holes at any resort is listed, and the number includes the holes of the featured course.

Yardages included are of the featured course and are calculated from the championship, or blue, tees. The championship length represents a course at its most difficult; most golfers won't play any of the courses at anywhere near the listed length, but yardage is a useful indication of a course's length relative to other courses listed. Courses are typically 400–800 yards shorter from the regular men's tees and 1,000–1,500 yards shorter from the regular women's tees. With its large retirement population, Florida also has many facilities with "seniors" tees, usually in front of the women's tees and often designated as gold. A few designers—notably Jack Nicklaus—include five or more sets of tee boxes to make courses playable for varying golf abilities.

The USGA ratings are also from the championship tees and indicate a course's relative difficulty; the rating is the average a scratch (0-handicap) golfer should expect to score. Any course with a rating of two or more strokes higher than par is consid-

Florida Golf Courses

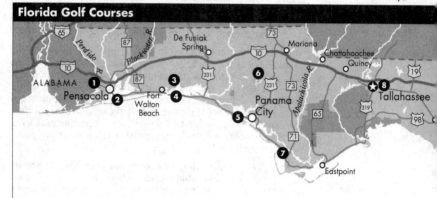

Gulf of Mexico

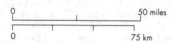

0   50 miles

0   75 km

Panhandle
Bay Point Yacht & Country Club, **5**
Bluewater Bay Resort, **3**
Perdido Bay Resort, **1**
St. Joseph's Bay Country Club, **7**
Sandestin Golf Club, **4**
Sunny Hills Country Club, **6**
Tiger Point Country Club, **2**

Northeast Florida
Amelia Island Plantation, **9**
Golden Ocala Golf Club, **16**
Indigo Lakes Resort, **15**
Killearn Inn & Golf Club, **8**
Marriott at Sawgrass, **10**
Ponce de Leon Golf Club, **13**
Ponte Vedra Inn & Club, **11**
Ravines Golf & Country Club, **12**
Sheraton Palm Coast, **14**

Orlando Area
Grand Cypress Golf Club, **19**
Grenelefe Resort, **21**
Mission Inn Golf & Tennis Resort, **17**
Timacuan Golf & Country Club, **18**
Walt Disney World Resort, **20**
Willowbrook Golf Club, **22**

Tampa Bay Area
Bloomingdale Golfers Club, **26**
Innisbrook Resort & Golf Club, **25**
Longboat Key, **27**
Plantation Golf & Country Club, **29**
Plantation Inn Golf Club, **23**
Saddlebrook Golf Club, **24**
Sun 'n Lakes Golf Club, **28**

Fort Myers/Naples
Cape Coral Golf & Tennis Resort, **30**
Eastwood Golf Club, **32**
Lely Flamingo Island Golf Club, **34**
Lochmoor Country Club, **31**
Naples Beach Hotel Golf Club, **35**
Pelican's Nest, **33**

Palm Beach
Boca Raton Resort & Club, **43**
Boynton Beach Municipal Golf Course, **42**
Breakers Hotel Golf Club, **39**
Emerald Dunes Golf Club, **40**
Indian River Plantation, **36**
Palm Beach Polo & Country Club, **41**
PGA National Golf Club, **37**
Royal Palm Beach Country Club, **38**

Fort Lauderdale
Bonaventure Resort & Spa, **45**
Colony West Country Club, **46**
The Oaks Golf & Racquet Club, **44**

Miami
Don Shula's Golf Club, **49**
Doral Hotel Golf Club, **48**
Key Biscayne Golf Club, **50**
Turnberry Isle Country Club, **47**

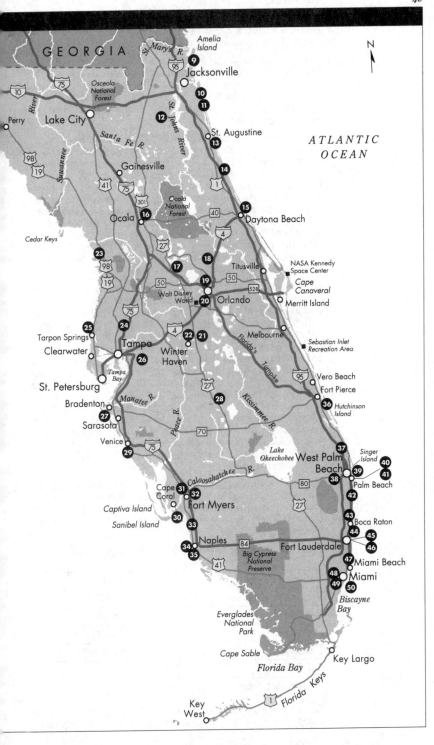

ered especially demanding and generally suitable only for experienced golfers. Courses with ratings below their par are usually better choices for less experienced golfers.

Keep in mind that a golf course tends to be a work-in-progress; holes are often lengthened or shortened, greens are rebuilt, traps added, and so forth. The statistics and descriptions here were accurate at the time of publication, but courses may have undergone changes—even major overhauls—by the time you end up playing them.

Because Florida courses tend to be flat, most are easy to walk, but unfortunately for people who enjoy walking, this is rarely a consideration any more in Florida. Except on public courses, carts are usually required throughout the state, though a few courses allow late-afternoon players to walk. The official reason is that carts help speed up play, which is generally true; however, operators concede that the cart concession also means extra revenue. A note for anyone interested in walking, when and where it is permitted: In Florida, where the "golf community" is a pervasive concept, walking distances *between* holes can be substantial, a real-estate ploy to allow more space for course-side homes and condos.

Greens fees are per person, regular-season rates, with mandatory cart fees (per person) included, where applicable. Note that greens fees, especially at resort courses, can be as much as 50% more during the high season, which runs generally from February to May, or substantially lower in slow summer months. Many resorts also offer golf packages, with greens fees included, which may represent a considerable savings. There are also companies that specialize in golf packages. Notable among these is **Golfpac Inc.** (Box 162366, Altamonte Springs, 32716, tel. 407/260–2288 or 800/327–0878). An invaluable resource for any golfer seeking a comprehensive listing of Florida courses is *The Official Florida Golf Guide*, available for free from the Florida Division of Tourism (Florida Sports Foundation, 107 W. Gaines St., Tallahassee, 32399). Note that many courses listed in this publication as "private" do allow nonmembers to play.

Most courses (even some municipal ones) have dress codes, the standard requiring shirts with collars and long pants (often no jeans) or Bermuda-length shorts. While many courses are less than militant in dress-code enforcement, come prepared to play by the rules.

Prices quoted in the following chart refer to greens fees:

Catagory	Cost
Very Expensive	over $75
Expensive	$50–$75
Moderate	$20–$50
Inexpensive	under $20

Northeast Florida

Amelia Island Plantation. The Tom Fazio–designed Long Point course is unusual for Florida: It features water on only three holes. Cedars, oaks, marshes, and ocean views make scenery a strong point. *Hwy. A1A S, Amelia Island 32034, tel. 904/261–6161 or 800/874–6878. Yardage: 6,775. Par: 72. USGA rating: 72.5. Total number of holes: 45. Greens fees: Very Expensive. Cart: mandatory. Special policies: must be a resort guest. Course facilities: restaurant, driving range, accommodations.*

Golden Ocala Golf Club. Ron Garl designed this course with several "replica" holes, including one of the famed, par-3 Postage Stamp hole at Royal Troon, Scotland; and also of the 12th and 13th holes at Augusta National, home of the Masters. *7300 U.S. 27 NW, Ocala 32675, tel. 904/622–0172. Yardage: 6,755. Par: 72. USGA rating: 72.2. Total number of holes: 18. Greens fees: Moderate. Cart: mandatory. Special policies: tee times available a week in advance for weekdays, 3 days in advance for weekends. Facilities: driving range.*

Indigo Lakes Resort. Headquarters of the Ladies Professional Golf Association, Indigo Lakes is distinguished by its oversize greens, each averaging more than 9,000 square feet. *2620 Volusia Ave., Daytona Beach 32020, tel. 904/258–6333 or 800/874–9918. Yardage: 7,123. Par: 72. USGA rating: 73.5. Total number of holes: 18. Greens fees: Moderate. Cart: mandatory. Special policies: public tee times up to a day in advance. Facilities: restaurant, driving range, accommodations.*

Killearn Inn & Golf Club. Gently rolling fairways and clusters of large oak trees give this course its distinctive character. The course hosts the Centel Classic, which in 1992 offered the largest prize purse on the Ladies Professional Golf Association tour. *100 Tyron Circle, Tallahassee 32308, tel. 904/893–2186 or 800/476–4101. Yardage: 7,025. Par: 72. USGA rating: 73.9. Total number of holes: 27. Greens fees: Moderate. Cart: optional. Special policies: must be a member or an inn guest. Facilities: restaurant, accommodations.*

Marriott at Sawgrass. With 99 holes, this is one of Florida's largest golfing compounds. The Pete Dye–designed TPC Stadium course—famed for its island 17th hole—vexes even top pros who compete in the Tournament Players Championship. *110 TPC Blvd., Ponte Vedra Beach 32082, tel. 904/273–3235. Yardage: 6,857. Par: 72. USGA rating: 74. Total number of holes: 99. Greens fees: Very Expensive. Cart: mandatory. Special policies: must be a hotel guest or the guest of a club member. Facilities: restaurant, driving range, accommodations.*

Ponce de Leon Golf Club. This is an older style Florida course, originally designed by Donald Ross. Here, marshland tends to be more of a backdrop to play than a hazard, as opposed to newer courses where marshy areas are more likely to have been converted into ponds or lakes that are very much in play. *4000 U.S. 1N, St. Augustine 32085, tel. 904/829–5314. Yardage: 6,878. Par: 72. USGA rating: 72.9. Total number of holes: 18. Greens fees: Moderate. Cart: mandatory. Special policies: tee times may be made one week in advance. Facilities: restaurant, driving range, accommodations.*

Ponte Vedra Inn & Club. Designed by Robert Trent Jones, Sr., the Ocean course features an island hole—the 147-yard 9th said to have inspired Pete Dye's design of the 17th at the nearby TPC Stadium course—and plays tough when the wind is up. *200 Ponte Vedra Blvd., Ponte Vedra Beach 32082, tel. 904/285–1111 or 800/234–7842. Yardage: 6,515. Par: 72. USGA rating: 70.9. Total number of holes: 36. Greens fees: Moderate. Cart: mandatory. Special policies: private course; must be an inn* guest or guest of a member. *Facilities: restaurant, driving range, accommodations.*

Ravines Golf & Country Club. Trees, rolling terrain, and deep ravines (hence the name) lend to a type of play atypical of Florida, where longer, flat courses with many water hazards are the norm. *2932 Ravines Rd., Middleburg 32068, tel. 904/282-7888. Yardage: 6,733. Par: 72. USGA rating: 72.7. Total number of holes: 18. Greens fees: Moderate. Cart: mandatory. Special policies: weekday reservations available a week in advance; 2 days in advance for weekends. Facilities: restaurant, driving range, accommodations.*

Sheraton Palm Coast. The Matanzas Woods course, one of four 18s open to resort guests, is an Arnold Palmer/Ed Seay design, featuring rolling fairways and large greens. *300 Clubhouse Dr., Palm Coast 32137, tel. 904/445-3000. Yardage: 6,985. Par: 72. USGA rating: 73.3. Total number of holes: 72. Greens fees: Moderate. Cart: mandatory. Special policies: none. Facilities: restaurant, driving range, accommodations.*

The Panhandle

Bay Point Yacht & Country Club. The Lagoon Legend course, used for the PGA Tour's qualifying school, is a watery monster, with the beast coming into play on 16 holes. Completed in 1986, the Lagoon Legend has been rated by magazines among the 1980s top new courses in the United States. *100 Delwood Beach Rd., Panama City Beach 32411, tel. 904/234-3307 or 800/874-7105. Yardage: 6,942. Par: 72. USGA rating: 73. Total number of holes: 36. Greens fees: Expensive. Cart: mandatory. Special policies: tee times available 2 months in advance; lower greens fees for resort guests. Facilities: restaurant, driving range, accommodations.*

Bluewater Bay Resort. Generally ranked among the top courses in the state's northwest by golf magazines, the Tom Fazio–designed layout features thick woods, water, and marshes on four 9-hole courses that combine to make six different 18-hole routes. *Box 247, 1950 Bluewater Blvd., Niceville 32578, tel. 904/897-3613 or 800/874-2128. Yardage: 6,803. Par: 72. USGA rating: 73.1. Total number of holes: 36. Greens fees: Moderate. Cart: optional after 1 PM. Special policies: none. Facilities: restaurant, driving range, accommodations.*

Perdido Bay Resort. This course demands accuracy: On the par-5 11th, for example, water lines both sides of the fairway and the front of the green. *1 Doug Ford Dr., Pensacola 32507, tel. 904/492-1223 or 800/874-5355. Yardage: 7,154. Par: 72. USGA rating: 73.8. Total number of holes: 18. Greens fees: Moderate. Cart: mandatory. Special policies: open to public; preferred tee times for club members and resort guests. Facilities: restaurant, driving range, accommodations.*

St. Joseph's Bay Country Club. Length is not a factor on this public course but water is: it winds around 16 ponds. *Rte. C-30 S, Port St. Joe 32456, tel. 904/227-1751. Yardage: 6,673. Par: 72. USGA rating: 71.8. Total number of holes: 18. Greens fees: Inexpensive. Cart: optional weekdays; $13 per cart. Special policies: carts required on weekends. Facilities: restaurant, driving range.*

Sandestin Golf Club. The Links course requires play around and across canals on most of its holes. After little water on the first three holes, the fourth—a par-5 of 501 yards and ranked as one of Florida's toughest—is flanked by a lagoon and marsh.

Emerald Coast Pwky., Destin 32541, tel. 904/267–8144 or 800/ 277–0800. Yardage: 6,710. Par: 72. USGA rating: 72.5. Total number of holes: 45. Greens fees: Expensive. Cart: mandatory on weekends. Special policies: tee time preference and reduced greens fees for resort guests. Facilities: restaurant, driving range, accommodations.

Sunny Hills Country Club. Typical of Florida, this course has plenty of sand, but atypically, only one hole features a water hazard. *1150 Country Club Blvd., Sunny Hills 32428, tel. 904/ 773–3619. Yardage: 6,832. Par: 72. USGA rating: 71.6. Total number of holes: 18. Greens fees: Inexpensive. Cart: optional after 11 AM; $7 per cart. Special policies: carts required for tee times before 11 AM except Tues. and Thurs.; tee times available up to 2 days in advance. Facilities: restaurant, driving range.*

Tiger Point Country Club. In the design of the East course, Jerry Pate and Ron Garl built many "spectator mounds," a relatively modern design feature that frames greens. *1255 Country Club Dr., Gulf Breeze 32561, tel. 904/932–1333. Yardage: 7,033. Par: 72. USGA rating: 73.9. Total number of holes: 36. Greens fees: Moderate. Cart: mandatory. Special policies: tee times available 4 days in advance. Facilities: restaurant, driving range.*

Orlando Area

Grand Cypress Golf Club. The New Course—a Jack Nicklaus re-creation of the famed Old Course in St. Andrews, Scotland—comes complete with hidden "pot" bunkers, deep enough to have stairs for entry and exit, in the fairways. *1 N. Jacaranda, Orlando 32836, tel. 407/239–4700. Yardage: 6,773. Par: 72. USGA rating: 72.1. Total number of holes: 45. Greens fees: Very Expensive. Cart: optional, with a $10 greens-fee reduction for walkers. Special policies: must be a resort guest; tee times available 2 months in advance. Facilities: restaurant, driving range, accommodations.*

Grenelefe Resort. Length is the key here: The West course, designed by Robert Trent Jones, Sr., plays to 7,325 yards from the championship tees. An absence of water hazards (there are just two ponds) softens the course somewhat. *3200 Rte. 546, Grenelefe 33844, tel. 813/422–7511 or 800/237–9549. Yardage: 7,325. Par: 72. USGA rating: 75. Total number of holes: 54. Greens fees: Expensive. Cart: mandatory. Special policies: tee times may be booked 90 days in advance. Facilities: restaurant, driving range, accommodations.*

Mission Inn Golf & Tennis Resort. Originally built 60 years ago, this course is a mixed bag, featuring island greens typical of Florida as well as elevated tees and tree-lined fairways more characterisic of courses in the Carolinas and the Northeast. *10400 C.R. 48, Howey-in-the-Hills 34737, tel. 904/324–3885 or 800/874–9053. Yardage: 6,770. Par: 72. USGA rating: 73.5. Total number of holes: 36. Greens fees: Expensive. Cart: mandatory. Special policies: open to public; tee times available a week in advance. Facilities: restaurant, accommodations.*

Timacuan Golf & Country Club. This is a two-part course designed by Ron Garl: Part I, the front nine, is open, with lots of sand; Part II, the back nine, is heavily wooded. *550 Timacuan Blvd., Lake Mary 32746, tel. 407/321–0010. Yardage: 7,019. Par: 72. USGA rating: 73.5. Total number of holes: 18. Greens fees: Moderate. Cart: mandatory. Special policies: reserved for members until noon on weekends and holidays; tee times* *available 3 days in advance. Facilities: restaurant, driving range.*

Walt Disney World Resort. Where else would you find a sand trap shaped like the head of a well-known mouse? The Magnolia course, played by the pros in the Walt Disney World Oldsmobile Golf Classic, is long but forgiving, with extra-wide fairways. The resort also features a "Wee Links" for preteen golfers. *1950 W. Magnolia Palm Dr., Lake Buena Vista 32830, tel. 407/ 824–2270. Yardage: 7,190. Par: 72. USGA rating: 73.9. Total number of holes: 99. Greens fees: Expensive. Cart: mandatory. Special policies: tee times 30 days in advance for resort guests; a week in advance for the public. Facilities: restaurant, driving range, accommodations.*

Willowbrook Golf Club. This is a relatively short municipal course, but lack of length is balanced by plenty of water, especially on the par-5 17th hole. *4200 Hwy. 544 N, Winter Haven 33881, tel. 813/299–7889. Yardage: 6,450. Par: 72. USGA rating: 70.6. Total number of holes: 18. Greens fees: Inexpensive. Cart: optional; $8 per cart. Special policies: tee times available 6 days in advance. Facilities: driving range, snack bar.*

Tampa Bay Area

Bloomingdale Golfers Club. Playing here can be like playing in an open-air aviary, because there are, reportedly, more than 60 bird species (including a bald eagle) in residence on the course. For golfers, however, birdies and eagles are hard to come by on this water- and tree-lined course. *1802 Natures Way Blvd., Valrico 33594, tel. 813/685–4105. Yardage: 7,165. Par: 72. USGA rating: 74.5. Total number of holes: 18. Greens fees: Moderate. Cart: mandatory. Special policies: club members only from 11:30 AM Fri.–Sun. Facilities: driving range, restaurant.*

Innisbrook Resort & Golf Club. Innisbrook's Copperhead course, generally ranked among Florida's toughest, has several long, dogleg par-4s. *U.S. 19, Tarpon Springs 34685, tel. 813/ 942–2000. Yardage: 7,087. Par: 71. USGA rating: 74.4. Total number of holes: 63. Greens fees: Very Expensive. Cart: mandatory. Special policies: must be a resort guest or a member of a U.S. or Canadian golf club. Facilities: restaurant, driving range, accommodations.*

Longboat Key. Water, water everywhere: Amid canals and lagoons, the Islandside course brings water into play on all but one hole, and play can be especially tough when the wind comes off Sarasota Bay or the Gulf of Mexico. *361 Gulf of Mexico Dr., Longboat Key 34228, tel. 813/383–8821. Yardage: 6,792. Par: 72. USGA rating: 74.2. Total number of holes: 45. Greens fees: Expensive. Cart: mandatory. Special policies: tee times required 3 days in advance. Facilities: restaurant, driving range, accommodations.*

Plantation Golf & Country Club. Local knowledge can be helpful on the Bobcat course: With water on 16 holes and greens not visible from the tee on 12 holes, shot placement and club selection are critical. *500 Rockley Blvd., Venice 34293, tel. 813/ 493–2000. Yardage: 6,862. Par: 72. USGA rating: 73.4. Total number of holes: 36. Greens fees: Moderate. Cart: mandatory. Special policies: tee times available 2 days in advance, Bobcat course open to members and resort guests only Jan.–Apr. Facilities: restaurant, driving range, accommodations.*

Plantation Inn Golf Club. The Championship course winds

through pines and natural lakes. An assortment of tee boxes makes the course playable for golfers of varying ability levels. *9301 W. Fort Island Trail, Crystal River 32629, tel. 904/795–7211 or 800/632–6262. Yardage: 6,654. Par: 72. USGA rating: 71.6. Total number of holes: 27. Greens fees: Moderate. Cart: optional off-season; $14. Special policies: tee times available 7 days in advance, 2 days in advance in Feb. and Mar.; walking restricted in peak season. Facilities: restaurant, driving range, accommodations.*

Saddlebrook Golf Club. The Saddlebrook course, designed by Arnold Palmer, is relatively short, but the premium is on accuracy, with lots of water to avoid, and large undulating greens make four-putting a constant concern. *5700 Saddlebrook Way, Wesley Chapel 33543, tel. 813/973–1111 or 800/729–8383. Yardage: 6,603. Par: 70. USGA rating: 72. Total number of holes: 36. Greens fees: Very Expensive. Cart: mandatory. Special policies: open to public, with tee time preference given to resort guests. Facilities: restaurant, driving range, accommodations.*

Sun 'n Lake Golf Club. The original 18-hole course has a "wilderness" reputation: deer are often spotted on the fairways, and playing from the rough can be like playing from a jungle. *5306 Columbus Circle, Sebring 33872, tel. 813/385–4830. Yardage: 6,731. Par: 72. USGA rating: 72. Total number of holes: 27. Greens fees: Moderate. Cart: mandatory. Special policies: tee times available a week in advance; Wed. afternoons, ladies only; Thurs. afternoons Jan.–Apr., men only. Facilities: restaurant, driving range, accommodations.*

Fort Myers/Naples

Cape Coral Golf & Tennis Resort. This course tests those who think themselves expert in sand play. Although not long and not difficult, the course is guarded by more than 100 bunkers. *4003 Palm Tree Blvd., Cape Coral 33904, tel. 813/542–7879. Yardage of the featured course: 6,649. Par: 72. USGA rating: 71.6. Total number of holes: 18. Greens fees: Inexpensive–Moderate. Cart: mandatory. Special policies: tee times available 3 days in advance. Facilities: restaurant, driving range, accommodations.*

Eastwood Golf Club. Included on many lists of America's best public courses, Eastwood demands accuracy, with tight fairways, water, and well-bunkered greens. *4600 Bruce Herd La., Fort Myers 33905, tel. 813/275–4848. Yardage: 6,772. Par: 72. USGA rating: 73.3. Total number of holes: 18. Greens fees: Inexpensive. Cart: mandatory before 3 PM in season; $12.50. Facilities: driving range.*

Lely Flamingo Island Club. This Robert Trent Jones course was completed in 1991 and was the first of a planned three at this resort-in-the-making. Multilevel greens are guarded by a fleet of greedy bunkers, but the wide, rolling fairways generally keep errant drives in play. *8004 Lely Resort Blvd., Naples 33962, tel. 813/793–2223. Yardage: 7,171. Par: 72. USGA rating: 73.9. Total number of holes: 36. Greens fees: Expensive–Very Expensive. Cart: mandatory. Special policies: tee times available 3 days in advance. Facilities: driving range, restaurant.*

Lochmoor Country Club. The course is well-maintained for a heavily played public links and winds around lakes and through tall palms and pine trees. *3911 Orange Grove Blvd., North Fort*

Myers 33903, tel. 813/995–0501. Yardage: 6,950. Par: 72.
USGA rating: 70.6. Total number of holes: 18. Greens fees:
Moderate. Cart: optional after 2 PM; $10. Special policies: carts
mandatory until 2 PM. Facilities: restaurant, driving range.

Naples Beach Hotel Golf Club. Originally built in 1930, this is one of Florida's oldest courses. Although the course is short and flat, the strategic bunkering can make for challenging play. *851 Gulf Shore Blvd. N, Naples 33940, tel. 813/261–2222. Yardage: 6,462. Par: 72. USGA rating: 70.6. Total number of holes: 18. Greens fees: Expensive. Cart: mandatory. Special policies: additional greens fees for non-hotel guests. Facilities: restaurant, driving range, accommodations.*

Pelican's Nest. A Tom Fazio design, the Seminole and Hurricane courses are lined with thick vegetation—cypress, pine, oak, and palm trees—and swampland. Recent renovations to the elegant and enormous clubhouse and meticulous groundskeeping make the Pelican's Nest a haven for guests of Naples's luxury resorts. *4450 Bay Creek Dr. SW, Bonita Springs 33923, tel. 813/947–4600. Yardage: 6,940. Par: 72. USGA rating: 70.8. Total number of holes: 27. Greens fees: Expensive–Very Expensive. Cart: mandatory. Special policies: public course, limited number of caddies in winter. Facilities: restaurant, driving range.*

Fort Lauderdale

Bonaventure Resort & Spa. Plenty of trees, water, and bunkers line the East course. The highlight hole is the par-3 third, with the green fronted by a waterfall. *250 Racquet Club Rd., Fort Lauderdale 33326, tel. 305/389–3300 or 800/327–8090. Yardage: 7,011. Par: 72. USGA rating: 71. Total number of holes: 36. Greens fees: Expensive. Cart: mandatory. Special policies: tee times available 3 days in advance. Facilities: restaurant, driving range, accommodations.*

Colony West Country Club. There is water on 14 of the Championship course's holes, with the most interesting hole the 12th, a par-4 through a cypress forest. *6800 N.W. 88th Ave., Tamarac 33321, tel. 305/726–8430. Yardage: 6,864. Par: 71. USGA rating: 73.9. Total number of holes: 36. Greens fees: Moderate. Cart: mandatory. Special policies: tee times available 3 days in advance. Facilities: restaurant.*

The Oaks Golf & Racquet Club. The Cypress, the more challenging of two courses, has familiar Florida features: lots of palms and greens well protected by sand and water. *3701 Oaks Clubhouse Dr., Pompano Beach 33069, tel. 305/978–1737. Yardage: 6,910. Par: 72. USGA rating: 73.3. Total number of holes: 36. Greens fees: Moderate. Cart: mandatory. Special policies: tee times a day in advance. Facilities: restaurant, driving range, accommodations.*

Miami

Don Shula's Golf Club. Large greens and elevated tees—unusual in south Florida—are features of the championship course. For golfers who can't get enough, there's also a lighted par-3 course at night. *7610 Miami Lakes Dr., Miami Lakes 33014, tel. 305/821–1150 or 800/247–4852. Yardage: 7,055. Par: 72. USGA rating: 73. Total number of holes: 18. Greens fees: Moderate. Cart: optional, $17. Special policies: open to public;*

reservations no more than 2 days in advance. Facilities: restaurant, driving range, accommodations.

Doral Hotel Golf Club. The 18th hole on the Blue course, nicknamed "the Blue Monster" and venue for the Doral Open, rates among the hardest finishing holes on the PGA Tour. Veteran pro Ray Floyd reportedly called it the toughest par-4 in the world. *4400 N.W. 87th Ave., Miami 33178, tel. 305/592–2000 or 800/327–6334. Yardage: 6,939. Par: 72. USGA rating: 72. Total number of holes: 99. Greens fees: Expensive–Very Expensive. Cart: mandatory. Special policies: open to public but tee time preference for hotel guests; extra greens fees for Blue course. Facilities: restaurant, driving range, accommodations.*

Key Biscayne Golf Club. Regularly rated highly among U.S. public courses, this one—the site of the Royal Caribbean Classic on the PGA Seniors Tour—is surrounded by mangrove swamps and inhabited by many bird species and alligators. *6700 Crandon Blvd., Key Biscayne 33149, tel. 305/361–9129 or 305/669–9500. Yardage: 7,070. Par: 72. USGA rating: 74. Total number of holes: 18. Greens fees: Moderate. Cart: optional after 1 PM, $14. Special policies: walking permitted after 1 PM; tee times available a day in advance. Facilities: restaurant, driving range.*

Turnberry Isle Country Club. The South course, which has hosted the PGA Senior Championship, is a Robert Trent Jones design that mixes old and new: a double green, similar to those at the Old Course at St. Andrews, Scotland, and an island green (on the 18th hole), a common feature of modern design. *199th St. and Biscayne Blvd., North Miami Beach 33180, tel. 305/932–6200 or 800/327–7028. Yardage: 7,200. Par: 72. USGA rating: 72.9. Total number of holes: 36. Greens fees: Expensive. Cart: mandatory. Special policies: open to hotel guests and club members only; tee times 2 days in advance. Facilities: restaurant, driving range, accommodations.*

Palm Beach

Boca Raton Resort & Club. It's not so much the resort course as the celebrity aura that serves as an attraction here. When you play this one, you follow in the footsteps (or cart tracks) of Frank Sinatra and Gerald Ford, among others. *501 E. Camino Real, Boca Raton 33432, tel. 407/395–3000 or 800/327–0101. Yardage: 6,732. Par: 71. USGA rating: 71.7. Total number of holes: 36. Greens fees: Expensive. Cart: mandatory. Special policies: open to resort guests and club members only; tee times up to 4 days in advance. Facilities: restaurant, driving range, accommodations.*

Boynton Beach Municipal Golf Course. The rolling terrain of this relatively short public course is unusual for the generally flat Palm Beach area. *8020 Jog Rd., Boynton Beach 33437, tel. 407/969–2200. Yardage: 6,340. Par: 71. USGA rating: 70.1. Total number of holes: 27. Greens fees: Inexpensive. Cart: mandatory until 3 PM. Special policies: none. Facilities: driving range, snack bar.*

Breakers Hotel Golf Club. The Ocean course, designed by Donald Ross and among Florida's oldest, compensates for its shortness with tight fairways and small greens. *1 S. County Rd., Palm Beach 33480, tel. 407/655–6611 or 800/833–3141. Yardage: 6,017. Par: 70. USGA rating: 69.3. Total number of holes: 36. Greens fees: Expensive. Cart: mandatory. Special policies: hotel guests and members only; free shuttle bus to*

West Course, 11 mi off-site. Facilities: restaurant, driving range, accommodations.

Emerald Dunes Golf Club. This Tom Fazio–designed course gets official credit as the 1,000th course to open in Florida and was considered one of the best new courses in the United States in 1990. *2100 Emerald Dunes Dr., West Palm Beach 33411, tel. 407/684–4653. Yardage: 7,006. Par: 72. USGA rating: 73.8. Total number of holes: 18. Greens fees: Expensive–Very Expensive. Cart: mandatory. Special policies: guaranteed tee times available 7 days in advance. Facilities: restaurant, driving range.*

Indian River Plantation. The course, a par-61, is classically Florida—flat, with lots of palms and bunkers, made tricky by ocean breezes. *555 N.E. Ocean Blvd., Stuart 33496, tel. 407/225–3700. Yardage: 4,042. Par: 61. USGA rating: 59.9. Total number of holes: 18. Greens fees: Moderate. Cart: mandatory; price included in greens fees. Special policies: open to resort guests and members only; resort guests can book one tee time up to 1 week in advance. Facilities: restaurant, driving range, accommodations.*

Palm Beach Polo & Country Club. The Dunes course—the resort's newest—is a Ron Garl/Jerry Pate design with Scottish touches such as pot bunkers and grass traps. *13198 Forest Hill Blvd., West Palm Beach 33414, tel. 407/798–7000 or 800/327–4204. Yardage: 7,050. Par: 72. USGA rating: 73.6. Total number of holes: 45. Greens fees: Very Expensive. Cart: mandatory. Special policies: open to resort guests and club members only; tee times up to 2 days in advance. Facilities: restaurant, driving range, accommodations.*

PGA National Golf Club. The Champion course, recently redesigned by Jack Nicklaus, demands length and accuracy, with more than 100 traps as well as water on 17 holes. It is the course used for the PGA Seniors Championship. *1000 Ave. of Champions, Palm Beach Gardens 33418, tel. 407/627–1800. Yardage: 7,022. Par: 72. USGA rating: 74.4. Total number of holes: 90. Greens fees: Expensive–Very Expensive. Cart: mandatory. Special policies: must be a resort guest, member, or golf pro; higher greens fees for the Champion course. Facilities: restaurant, driving range, accommodations.*

Royal Palm Beach Country Club. The course is longer than most public courses, but most holes are open, with few water hazards. *900 Royal Palm Beach Blvd., Royal Palm Beach 33411, tel. 407/798–6430. Yardage: 7,067. Par: 72. USGA rating: 72.5. Total number of holes: 18. Greens fees: Moderate. Cart: mandatory. Special policies: tee times available 3 days in advance. Facilities: restaurant, snack bar, driving range.*

4 Miami and Miami Beach

What they say about Miami is true. The city *is* different. Miami is different from what it once was, and it's different from other cities. Once a sleepy southern resort town, Miami today is a burgeoning giant of international commerce and finance as well as a place to find pleasure and relaxation. It now supports four major-league sports teams—the Miami Dolphins football team, the Florida Marlins baseball team, basketball's Miami Heat, and the National Hockey League's newest franchise. Like all big cities, Miami inspires the first-time visitor with hopes and dreams. Also as in other cities, many of these hopes and dreams can be sidetracked by crime and violence.

Miami's natural difference can be detected when you fly into the city. Clinging to a ribbon of dry land between the marshy Everglades and the Atlantic Ocean, Miami remains vulnerable to its perennial mosquitoes, periodic flooding, and potential devastation by hurricanes. When Hurricane Andrew swept through the city in 1992, it seemed that everybody's worst fears had been realized, although most of the serious damage turned out to be in South Dade County. The rest of the Miami area was soon back on its feet, despite the irreparable loss of some beautiful trees and other plantings.

Miami may be the wrong place for a city, but it's the right place for a crossroads. Long before Spain's gold-laden treasure ships passed offshore in the Gulf Stream, the Calusa Indians who lived here had begun to trade with their mainland neighbors to the north and their island brethren to the south. Repeating this prehistoric pattern, many U.S. and multinational companies now locate their Latin American headquarters in Greater Miami because no other city can match its airline connections to the Western Hemisphere and because no other city is so *sympatico*.

That same ease of access, coupled with a congenial climate, attracts hordes of Latin tourists—especially in Miami's steamy summer months (South America's winter), when domestic visitors from the northern United States are less in evidence. Access and climate also explain why Miami has become what *Newsweek* calls "America's Casablanca." Whenever a Latin American or Caribbean government erupts in revolution and economic chaos, the inevitable refugees flock inexorably to Miami (where they open restaurants).

Even without a revolution, Miami's cosmopolitan character and entrepreneurial spirit attract other immigrants from all over the world. The still relatively cheap U.S. dollar has lured European tourists and commercial interests as well, spurring a full complement of European air connections.

Today more than half of Greater Miami's population is Latin—the majority from Cuba, with significant populations from Colombia, El Salvador, Nicaragua, Panama, Puerto Rico, and Venezuela. About 150,000 French- and Creole-speaking Haitians also live in Greater Miami, as do Brazilians, Chinese, Germans, Greeks, Iranians, Israelis, Italians, Jamaicans, Lebanese, Malaysians, Russians, Swedes, and others—a veritable Babel of tongues. Most either know or are trying to learn English. You can help them by speaking slowly and distinctly.

Try not to think of Miami as a melting pot. Where ethnic and cultural diversity are the norm, there's less pressure to conform. Miamians practice matter-of-factly the customs they brought here—much to the consternation of other Miamians whose customs differ. The community wrestles constantly with these tensions and sensitivities.

As a big city, Miami has its share of crime, violence, and drug trafficking. The city led the nation in car thefts in 1992, and a number of criminal attacks on tourists drew much publicity in early 1993. Still, the Greater Miami Chamber of Commerce in 1993 stepped up its visitor-safety program by installing new highway direction signs, by removing items that make rental cars conspicuous to would-be criminals, and by distributing multilingual pamphlets with tips on how to avoid crime. The hope is that, more than ever, visitors will find in Miami a multicultural metropolis that works and plays with vigor and that welcomes everyone to share its celebration of diversity.

Essential Information

Important Addresses and Numbers

Tourist Information
Coconut Grove Chamber of Commerce (2820 McFarlane Rd., Coconut Grove 33133, tel. 305/444–7270).
Coral Gables Chamber of Commerce (50 Aragon Ave., Coral Gables 33134, tel. 305/446–1657).
Florida Gold Coast Chamber of Commerce (1100 Kane Concourse, Suite 210, Bay Harbor Islands 33154, tel. 305/866–6020) serves the beach communities of Bal Harbour, Bay Harbor Islands, Golden Beach, North Bay Village, Sunny Isles, and Surfside.
Greater Miami Chamber of Commerce (1601 Biscayne Blvd., Miami 33132, tel. 305/350–7700).
Greater Miami Convention and Visitors Bureau (701 Brickell Ave., Suite 2700, Miami 33131, tel. 305/539–3063 or 800/283–2707). Satellite tourist information centers are located at Bayside Marketplace (401 Biscayne Blvd., Miami, 33132, tel. 305/539–2980), in Miami Beach (Miami Beach Chamber of Commerce, 1920 Meridian Ave., Miami Beach 33139, tel. 305/672–1270), and in Homestead–Florida City (South Dade Visitors Information Center, 1160 U.S. 1, Florida City 33034, tel. 305/245–9180 or 800/852–8675).
Greater South Dade/South Miami Chamber of Commerce (6410 S.W. 80th St., South Miami 33143–4602, tel. 305/661–1621).
Key Biscayne Chamber of Commerce (Key Biscayne Bank Bldg., 95 W. McIntyre St., Key Biscayne 33149, tel. 305/361–5207).
Miami Beach Chamber of Commerce (1920 Meridian Ave., Miami Beach 33139, tel. 305/672–1270).
North Miami Chamber of Commerce (13100 W. Dixie Hwy., North Miami 33181, tel. 305/891–7811).
Surfside Tourist Board (9301 Collins Ave., Surfside 33154, tel. 305/864–0722).

Emergencies
Dial **911** for **police** and **ambulance.** You can dial free from pay phones.

Ambulance
Randle Eastern Ambulance Service Inc. (35 S.W. 27th Ave., Miami 33135, tel. 305/642–6400) is open 24 hours.

Hospitals
The following hospitals have 24-hour emergency rooms:

Miami Beach: *Mt. Sinai Medical Center* (off Julia Tuttle Causeway I–195, at 4300 Alton Rd., Miami Beach, tel. 305/674–2121; emergency room, tel. 305/674–2200; physician referral, tel. 305/674–2273), *Miami Beach Community Hospital* (250 W. 63rd St., near Collins Ave. and n. end of Alton Rd., Miami Beach, tel. 305/868–2700; emergency room, tel. 305/868–2770; physician referral, tel. 305/868–2728).

Central: *University of Miami/Jackson Memorial Medical Center* (near Dolphin Expressway, 1611 N.W. 12th Ave., Miami, tel. 305/325–7429; emergency room, tel. 305/585–6901; physician referral, tel. 305/547–5757), *Mercy Hospital* (3663 S. Miami Ave., Coconut Grove, tel. 305/854–4400; emergency center, tel. 305/285–2171; physician referral, tel. 305/285–2929), *Miami Children's Hospital* (6125 S.W. 31st St., Miami, tel. 305/666–6511; emergency room, ext. 2702; physician referral, ext. 2563).

South: *Baptist Hospital of Miami* (8900 N. Kendall Dr., Miami, tel. 305/596–1960; emergency center, tel. 305/ 596–6556; physician referral, tel. 305/596–6557).

24-Hour Pharmacies **Eckerd Drugs** (1825 Miami Gardens Dr. NE, at 185th St., North Miami Beach, tel. 305/932–5740; 9031 S.W. 107th Ave., Miami, tel. 305/274–6776).

Walgreens (500–B W. 49th St., Palm Springs Mall, Hialeah, tel. 305/557–5468; 12245 Biscayne Blvd., Miami, tel. 305/893–6860; 5731 Bird Rd., Miami, tel. 305/666–0757; 1845 Alton Rd., Miami Beach, tel. 305/531–8868).

Physician-Referral Services **Dade County Medical Association** (1501 N.W. North River Dr., Miami, tel. 305/324–8717) is open weekdays 9–5 for medical referral.

East Coast District Dental Society (420 S. Dixie Hwy., Suite 2E, Coral Gables, tel. 305/667–3647) is open weekdays 9–4:30 for dental referral. Services include general dentistry, endodontics, periodontics, and oral surgery.

Services for the Hearing Impaired **Fire, police, medical, rescue,** TDD tel. 305/595–4749.
Operator and directory assistance, TDD tel. 800/855–1155.
Deaf Services of Miami (9100 S. Dadeland Blvd., Suite 104, Miami 33156, voice tel. 305/444–2266) operates 24 hours but not on all holidays.
Florida Relay Service, voice tel. 800/955–8770, TDD tel. 800/955–8771.

Arriving and Departing by Plane

Airport and Airlines **Miami International Airport (MIA),** 6 miles west of downtown Miami, is Greater Miami's only commercial airport. With a daily average of 1,302 flights, MIA handles almost 30 million passengers each year, making it the nation's second-largest international airport for combined passenger and cargo operations, and the 10th or 11th busiest passenger airport in the world. MIA has 118 aircraft gates and seven concourses.

Anticipating continued growth, the airport has begun a $2 billion expansion program that will require much of the decade to complete; passengers will mainly notice expanded gates for American and United Airlines. The new 20-gate arrival-departure concourse A, now under construction, will probably be completed in 1995. Concourse F, where Pan Am used to operate, was rebuilt with expanded gates for United Airlines in 1993; Concourses C and H should be rebuilt by the end of 1994. A largely underused convenience for passengers who have to get from one concourse to another in this long, horseshoe-shape terminal is the cushioned Moving Walkway, one level up from the departure level, with access points at every concourse.

U. S. airlines that fly into MIA include **American** (tel. 800/433–7300), **American Eagle** (tel. 800/225–9920), **Chalk's International** (tel. 800/432–8807), **Comair** (tel. 800/354–9822), **Continental** (tel. 800/525–0280), **Delta** (tel. 800/221–1212), **Northwest** (tel. 800/225–2525), **Tower Air** (tel. 800/324–8693), **TWA** (tel. 800/221–2000), **United** (tel. 800/241–6522), **USAir** (tel. 800/842–5374), and **USAir Express** (tel. 800/842–5374). Among the international carriers serving the airport are **Aeroflot** (tel. 800/995–5555), **Aerolineas Argentinas** (tel. 800/333–0276), **Aeromexico** (tel. 800/237–6639), **Air Canada** (tel. 800/776–3000), **Air France** (tel. 800/237–2747), **Alitalia** (tel. 800/223–5730), **Avianca** (tel. 800/284–2622), **British Airways** (tel. 800/247–9297), **Continental** (tel. 800/231–0856), **El Al** (tel. 800/223–6700), **Iberia** (tel. 800/772–4642), **Lan Chile** (tel. 800/735–5526), **LTU** (tel. 800/888–0200), **Lufthansa** (tel. 800/645–3880), **Mexicana** (tel. 800/531–7921), **Varig** (tel. 800/468–2744), **Viasa** (tel. 800/468–4272), and **Virgin Atlantic** (tel. 800/862–8621).

When you fly out of MIA, plan to check in 55 minutes before departure for a domestic flight and 90 minutes before departure for an international flight. Services for international travelers include 24-hour multilingual information and paging phones and multiple-currency conversion booths throughout the terminal. There is an information booth with a multilingual staff and 24-hour currency exchange at Concourse E. Not widely known, except to frequent travelers, is the 263-room Miami International Airport Hotel (Concourse E, arrival level, tel. 305/871–4100), with its Top of the Port restaurant on the seventh floor and Port Lounge on the eighth.

Between the Airport and Center City By Bus The county's **Metrobus** system has one benefit—its modest $1.25 cost—if you're willing to put up with the inconveniences of infrequent service, scruffy equipment, and circuitous routes. From the airport you can take Bus 7 to downtown (operates weekdays every 40 minutes from 5:30 AM to 8:30 PM; weekends 7–7), Bus 37 South to Coral Gables and South Miami (operates every 30 minutes from 6 AM to 10 PM), Bus 37 North to Hialeah (operates every 30 minutes from 5:30 AM to 10:50 PM), Bus J to Coral Gables (operates every 30 minutes from 6 AM to 12:30 AM), Bus 42 to Coconut Grove (operates hourly from 5:40 AM to 6:30 PM), and Bus J east to Miami Beach (operates every 30 minutes from 5:30 AM to 11:30 PM). *Tel. 305/638–6700. Fare: $1.25 (exact change), transfer 25¢; 60¢ with 10¢ transfer for senior citizens and students.*

By Taxi For trips originating at MIA or the Port of Miami, a $1 toll is added to the meter fare—except for the flat-fare trips described below. You'll pay a $14 flat fare between MIA and the Port of Miami, in either direction. Other approximate fares from MIA include $10 to Coral Gables, $15 to downtown Miami, $25 to Miami Beach, and $30 to Key Biscayne.

For taxi service from the airport to destinations in the immediate vicinity, ask a uniformed county taxi dispatcher to call an

ARTS (Airport Region Taxi Service) cab for you. These special blue cabs offer a short-haul flat fare in two zones: an inner-city ride is $5; an outer-city fare is $8. The area of service is roughly as far north as Miami Springs, west to Red Road (57th Avenue), south to N.W. 12th Street, and east to Douglas Road (37th Avenue). Maps are posted in cab windows on both sides.

By Van **SuperShuttle** vans transport passengers between MIA and local hotels, the Port of Miami, and even individual residences, on a 24-hour basis. The company's service area extends from Palm Beach to Monroe County (including the Lower Keys). Drivers provide narration en route. It's best to make reservations 24 hours before departure, although the firm will try to arrange pickups within Dade County on as little as four hours' notice. *Information and reservations from inside MIA, tel. 305/871–8488. Reservations from outside MIA, tel. 305/871–2000 (Dade and Monroe counties) or 305/764–1700 (Broward and Palm Beach counties). Reservations outside FL, tel. 800/874–8885. Pet transport fee: $5. Lower rate for 2nd passenger in same party for many destinations. Children 3 and under ride free with parents. AE, DC, MC, V.*

By Limousine **Bayshore Limousine** offers chauffeur-driven four-door town cars and stretch limousines through a 24-hour reservation service. It serves Miami, Fort Lauderdale, Palm Beach, and the Keys. *Box 330093, Miami 33233, tel. 305/858–5888. MC, V.*

Rental Cars Six rental-car firms—**Avis Rent-a-Car** (tel. 800/331–1212), **Dollar Rent-a-Car** (tel. 800/800–4000), **General Rent-a-Car** (tel. 800/327–7607), **Hertz Rent-a-Car** (tel. 800/654–3131), **National Rent-a-Car** (tel. 800/328–4567), and **Value Rent-a-Car** (tel. 800/327–2501)—have booths near the baggage-claim area on MIA's lower level.

Arriving and Departing by Car, Train, and Bus

By Car The main highways into Greater Miami from the north are Florida's Turnpike (a toll road) and I–95. From the northwest take I–75 or U.S. 27 into town. From the Everglades to the west, use the Tamiami Trail (U.S. 41). From the south use U.S. 1 and the Homestead Extension of Florida's Turnpike. In late 1993 or early 1994 construction is expected to begin on U.S. 1 on the new Brickell Avenue bridge from the south into downtown, and drivers will have to use I–95. Further delays before the end of 1994 will occur when construction begins along I–95 between N.W. 58th and 95th streets and on new midtown ramps. On the other hand, look for easier driving across the newly widened MacArthur Causeway, which connects downtown with Miami Beach.

By Train **Amtrak** (tel. 800/USA–RAIL) runs two trains between Miami and New York City, the *Silver Meteor* and the *Silver Star*, which make different stops along the way. Each has a daily Miami arrival and departure. The Amtrak station is at 8303 N.W. 37th Avenue; for recorded arrival and departure information, call 305/835–1200.

The five-year-old **Tri-Rail** commuter train system connects Miami with Broward and Palm Beach daily. Call for a schedule and details on weekly and monthly passes. *Suite 200, 1 River Plaza, 305 S. Andrews Ave., Fort Lauderdale 33301, tel. 305/728–8445 or 800/TRI–RAIL.*

By Bus **Greyhound/Trailways** buses stop at five bus terminals in Greater Miami. *700 Biscayne Blvd., Miami, tel. 305/374-7222 (fares
and schedules only). No reservations.*

Getting Around Miami

Greater Miami resembles Los Angeles in its urban sprawl and
traffic congestion. You'll need a car to visit many of the attractions and points of interest listed in this book. Some are accessible via public transportation.

A department of the county government, the Metro-Dade
Transit Agency, runs the public transportation system. It consists of more than 540 **Metrobuses** on 71 routes, the 21-mile
Metrorail elevated rapid-transit system, and the **Metromover,**
an elevated light-rail system circling downtown Miami. Free
maps, schedules, and a "First-Time Rider's Kit" are available.
*Government Center Station, 111 N.W. 1st St., Miami 33128;
Maps by Mail, tel. 305/638-6137; route information, tel. 305/
638-6700 daily 6 AM-11 PM.*

By Train Elevated **Metrorail** trains run from downtown Miami north to
Hialeah and south along U.S. 1 to Dadeland, daily 5:30 AM–midnight. Trains runs every 7½ minutes in peak hours, every 15–20
minutes at other times. The fare is $1.25. Transfers, which cost
25¢, must be bought at the first station entered. Parking at train
stations costs $1.

Metromover has two loops that circle downtown Miami, linking
major hotels, office buildings, and shopping areas (*see* Tour 2:
Downtown Miami in Exploring Miami, *below*). The system is
currently 1.9 miles long, but it will expand to 4.4 miles with two
new extensions set to open by mid-1994—the 1.4-mile Omni extension, with six stations to the north, and the 1.1-mile Brickell
extension, with six stations to the south. Service runs daily every 90 seconds, 6 AM–midnight. The fare is 25¢.

By Bus **Metrobus** stops are marked by blue-and-green signs with a bus
logo and route information. The frequency of service varies
widely. Obtain specific schedule information (tel. 305/638-
6700) in advance for the routes you want to ride. The fare is
$1.25, transfers 25¢.

By Taxi It is recommended that you be on your guard when traveling by
cab in Miami, as some drivers are rude and unhelpful and have
been known to take advantage of visitors unfamiliar with their
destinations or the layout of the city. Some drivers don't know
their way around, either. If it's possible, avoid taking a cab; if
you must, try to be familiar with your route and destination.

Fares are $1.10 for the first ⅐ mile, 20¢ for each additional ⅐
mile; waiting time is 20¢ for each ⅖ minute. There is no additional charge for extra passengers, luggage, or tolls. Taxis can
be hailed on the street, although you may not always find one
when you need one—it's better to call for a dispatch taxi or
have a hotel doorman hail one for you. Taxi companies with dispatch service are **All American Taxi** (tel. 305/947-3333), **Central Taxicab Service** (tel. 305/534-0694), **Diamond Cab
Company** (tel. 305/545-7575), **Dolphin Cab** (tel. 305/948-6666),
Magic City Cab Company (tel. 305/757-5523), **Metro Taxicab
Company** (tel. 305/888-8888), **Miami-Dade Yellow Cab** (tel. 305/
633-0503), **Miami Springs Taxi** (tel. 305/888-8541), **Society Cab
Company** (tel. 305/757-5523), **Speedy Cab** (tel. 305/861-9999),

Super Yellow Cab Company (tel. 305/888–7777), **Tropical Taxicab Company** (tel. 305/945–1025), and **Yellow Cab Company** (tel. 305/444–4444). Many now accept credit cards; inquire when you call.

By Car In general, Miami traffic is the same as in any big city, with the same rush hours and the same likelihood that parking garages will be full at peak demand. The large immigrant population creates additional problems, however, introducing a different cultural attitude toward traffic laws. Many drivers who don't know their way around turn and stop suddenly, and you may often find drivers stopping where they shouldn't to drop off passengers. Some drivers are short-tempered and will assault any motorist who cuts them off or honks a horn at them. Be careful where you drive, and always keep your eyes open.

Guided Tours

Orientation **Old Town Trolley of Miami.** Ninety-minute narrated tours of Miami and 90-minute tours of Miami Beach leave Bayside Marketplace every half hour between 10 and 4. *Box 12985, Miami 33101, tel. 305/374–8687. Miami and Miami Beach tours: $16 adults, $7 children 5–12.*

Special-Interest **Air Tours of Miami.** One-hour sightseeing tours cover Miami,
Air Tours the Everglades, and nearby waters in a Piper Seneca II six-seater. *1470 N.E. 123rd St., Suite 602, Miami, tel. 305/893–5874. Tours depart from Opa-Locka Airport; ask for directions. Cost: $75 adults, $50 children, minimum of 3 adults. Reservations required.*
Chalk's International Airlines. Seaplane tours from Watson Island depart every Saturday at 1:45 and last 25 minutes. They include the Vizcaya Museum and Gardens, Miami Seaquarium, Fisher Island/Star Island, the Art Deco Disrict, and Orange Bowl Stadium. *1000 MacArthur Causeway, Miami, tel. 305/371–8628. Cost: $39.50 adults, $29.50 children 2–11.*
Gold Coast Helicopters. Tours in Bell 47 helicopters last eight minutes or longer. *15101 Biscayne Blvd., North Miami, tel. 305/940–1009. Cost: $60 for 1 or 2 people for 8 min.; longer rides cost more. Reservations advised.*

Boat Tours **Island Queen, Good Times Too, Island Lady,** and **Island Princess.** These 150-passenger double-decker tour boats dock at Bayside Marketplace (401 Biscayne Blvd.) and offer daily 90-minute narrated tours of the Port of Miami and Millionaires' Row. *Tel. 305/379–5119. Cost: $10 adults, $5 children.*
Nikko Gold Coast Cruises. Two 150-passenger boats based at Haulover Park Marina specialize in water tours to major Greater Miami attractions. *10800 Collins Ave., Miami Beach, tel. 305/945–5461. Tours include Bayside Marketplace ($9.59 adults, $5.33 children under 13), Seaquarium ($27.64/$18.06, including admission), Vizcaya ($18.11/$9.59, including admission), and 2-hr sightseeing trips at 10 AM and 2 PM ($7.99/$4.21).*

History Tours **Art Deco District Tour.** Operated by the Miami Design Preservation League, 90-minute guided walking tours leave at 10:30 AM Saturday and 5 PM Wednesday; there's also a bike tour at 10:30 AM Sunday. Tours depart from the league's welcome center at the Leslie Hotel. *1244 Ocean Dr., Miami Beach, tel. 305/672–2014. Cost: $6.*
Professor Paul George. A three-hour walking tour of downtown

is led by Paul George, a history professor at Miami-Dade Community College and past president of the Florida Historical Society. Tours are usually given Saturday at 10 AM, beginning either on the north bank of the Miami River behind the Hyatt Regency Hotel (400 S.E. 2nd Ave.), or at Bayside Marketplace (401 Biscayne Blvd.). George also leads a number of other tours by appointment. *1345 S.W. 14th St., Miami, tel. 305/858–6021, $10 adults, $7 children 7–14, under 7 free.*

Rickshaw Tours **Majestic Rickshaw.** Look for two-person rickshaws along Main Highway in Coconut Grove's Village Center, nightly 8 PM–2 AM. *75 N.E. 156 St., Biscayne Gardens, tel. 305/256–8833. Cost: $3 per person for 10-minute ride through Coconut Grove, $6 per person for 20-minute lovers' moonlight ride to Biscayne Bay.*

Self-Guided Tours The **Junior League of Miami** publishes five excellent self-guiding tours to architectural and historical landmarks in Coconut Grove, Coral Gables, downtown Miami, the northeast, and south Dade. *2325 Salzedo, Coral Gables 33134, tel. 305/443–0160. Cost: $3 per tour.*

The **Miami Design Preservation League**'s *Art Deco District Guide* is a book of six detailed walking or driving tours of the Art Deco District on Miami Beach. *Bin L, Miami Beach 33139, tel. 305/672–2014. Cost: $10.*

Exploring Miami

People don't necessarily come to Miami for sightseeing, but once here you'll probably want to do something besides lounge on the beach. The main attractions of the city are mostly located away from downtown, and visitors enjoy seeing the neighborhoods that over the years have revived—Coconut Grove, Little Havana, and the Art Deco District. Since everything worth seeing is spread out, and since public transportation isn't adequate, the default solution is driving yourself.

Finding your way around Greater Miami is easy if you know how the numbering system works. Miami is laid out on a grid with four quadrants—northeast, northwest, southeast, and southwest—which meet at Miami Avenue and Flagler Street. Miami Avenue separates east from west and Flagler Street separates north from south. Avenues and courts run north–south; streets, terraces, and ways run east–west. Roads run diagonally, northwest–southeast.

Many named streets also bear numbers. For example, Unity Boulevard is N.W. and S.W. 27th Avenue, and LeJeune Road is N.W. and S.W. 42nd Avenue. However, named streets that depart markedly from the grid, such as Biscayne Boulevard and Brickell Avenue, have no corresponding numerical designations. Dade County and most other municipalities follow the Miami numbering system.

In Miami Beach, avenues run north–south; streets, east–west. Numbers rise along the beach from south to north and from the Atlantic Ocean in the east to Biscayne Bay in the west.

In Coral Gables, all streets bear names. Coral Gables uses the Miami numbering system for north–south addresses but begins counting east–west addresses westward from Douglas Road (S.W. 37th Avenue).

Hialeah has its own grid. Palm Avenue separates east from west; Hialeah Drive separates north from south. Avenues run north–south and streets east–west. Numbered streets and avenues are designated west, east, or southeast.

Highlights For First-Time Visitors

Art Deco District (Tour 1: Miami Beach)
Bayside Marketplace (Tour 2: Downtown Miami)
Biltmore Hotel (Tour 4: Coral Gables and South Miami)
Lincoln Road Mall (Tour 1: Miami Beach)
Little Havana (Tour 3: Little Havana)
Metro-Dade Cultural Center (Tour 2: Downtown Miami)
Metromover (Tour 2: Downtown Miami)
Miami Seaquarium (Tour 6: Key Biscayne)
Village of Coconut Grove/Barnacle/Cocowalk (Tour 5: Coconut Grove)
Vizcaya (Tour 5: Coconut Grove)

Tour 1: Miami Beach

Numbers in the margin correspond to points of interest on the Tour 1: Miami Beach map.

Most visitors to the Greater Miami area don't realize that Miami and Miami Beach are separate cities. Miami, on the mainland, is southern Florida's commercial hub. Miami Beach, on 17 islands offshore in Biscayne Bay, is sometimes considered America's Riviera, luring refugees from winter to its warm sunshine, sandy beaches, and graceful palms.

In 1912 what would become Miami Beach was little more than a sand spit in the bay. Then Carl Graham Fisher, a millionaire promoter who built the Indianapolis Speedway, began to pour much of his fortune into developing the island city.

Ever since, Miami Beach has experienced successive waves of boom and bust—thriving in the early 1920s and the years just after World War II but enduring the devastating 1926 and 1992 hurricanes, the Great Depression, and travel restrictions during World War II. During the 1960s, jets full of onetime Beach winter vacationers began winging to the more reliably warm Caribbean, and the flow of summer family vacationers had been dammed midstate by Disneyworld.

Today a renaissance is under way as Miami Beach revels in the architectural heritage of its mile-square Art Deco District. About 650 significant buildings in the district are listed on the National Register of Historic Places. For detailed tours of the Art Deco District, contact the Miami Design Preservation League (*see* Guided Tours in Essential Information, *above*).

From the mainland, cross the **MacArthur Causeway** (Route 41), which spans Biscayne Bay, to reach Miami Beach. (To reach the causeway from downtown Miami, turn east off Biscayne Boulevard north of N.E. 11th Street. From I–95, turn east onto I–395. The eastbound Dolphin Expressway, Route 836, becomes I–395 east of the I–95 interchange.) As you approach the MacArthur Causeway bridge across the Intracoastal Waterway, the *Miami Herald* building looms above Biscayne Bay on your left.

❶ Cross the bridge to **Watson Island,** created by dredging in 1931. To your right is the seaplane base of **Chalk's International Airlines** (tel. 305/371–8628), the oldest scheduled international air carrier, founded in 1919. Today it operates seaplanes to Key West, Bimini, and Nassau.

East of Watson Island the causeway leaves Miami and enters **❷** Miami Beach. On the left you'll pass the bridge to **Palm** and **❸ ❹** **Hibiscus islands** and then the bridge to **Star Island.** Celebrities who have lived on these islands include Al Capone (93 Palm Ave., Palm Island), author Damon Runyon (271 Hibiscus Island), and actor Don Johnson (8 Star Island).

East of Star Island the causeway mounts a high bridge. Look **❺** left to see an island with an obelisk, the **Flagler Memorial Monument.** The memorial honors Henry M. Flagler, who built the Florida East Coast Railroad, which opened all of east coast Florida to tourism and commerce, reaching Miami in 1896 and Key West in 1912. Flagler's hotels set a new standard for opulent vacationing and ushered in a long train of imperial developers, the list crowned in our own time by Walt Disney.

Just beyond the bridge, turn right onto Alton Road past the **Miami Beach Marina** (300 Alton Rd., tel. 305/673–6000), where dive boats depart for artificial reefs offshore in the Atlantic Ocean. Continue to the foot of Alton Road, turn left on Biscayne Street, and then right at Washington Avenue to enter **❻** **South Pointe Park** (1 Washington Ave.). From the 50-yard Sunshine Pier, which adjoins the mile-long jetty at the mouth of Government Cut, you can fish while watching huge ships pass. No bait or tackle is available in the park. Other facilities include two observation towers, and volleyball courts.

Time Out   **Crawdaddy's Restaurant** (1 Washington Ave., tel. 305/673–1708) provides the catbird seat for enjoying a brew while watching the mammoth cruise ships sail out Government Cut from the Port of Miami.

Continue to the end of Alton Road, and turn left onto Ocean Drive. At 5th Street you'll start to see a line of pastel-hue Art Deco hotels on your left and palm-fringed **Lummus Park** and the beach on your right. This is the **Art Deco District,** a 10-block stretch that has become perhaps the most talked-about beachfront in America. Less than 10 years ago, the vintage hotels along Ocean Drive were badly run down, catering to infirm retired people. But a group of visionaries saw this collection of buildings as an architectural treasure, a peerless grouping of Art Deco modern architecture from the 1920s and 1930s. As you drive past, notice that the forms and decorative detail of these buildings are drawn from nature (including birds, butterflies, and flowers); from ancient Aztec, Maya, Babylonian, Chaldean, Egyptian, and Hebrew designs; and from the streamlined, aerodynamic shapes of modern transportation **❼** and industrial machinery. Drive up Ocean Avenue to the **Art Deco District Welcome Center** (1244 Ocean Dr., tel. 305/672–2014), open weekdays 11–6, Saturday 10–6. It is located in the **Leslie Hotel,** built in 1937. You may want to get out of your car to stroll around the district, but, from midmorning on, parking is scarce along Ocean Drive—you'll do better on Collins or Washington avenues, the next two streets paralleling Ocean Drive to the west.

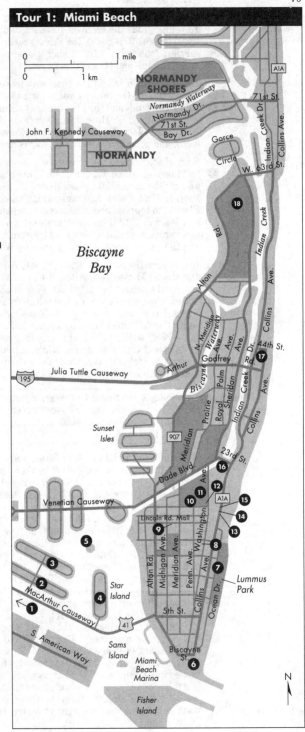

Tour 1: Miami Beach

In the early 1980s, investors started fixing up the interiors of these hotels and repainting their exteriors with vibrant colors. International bistro operators then moved in, sensing the potential for a new café society. The media took note, and celebrities came, among them singer Gloria Estefan, designer Gianni Versace, and record executive Chris Blackwell, who bought pieces of the action.

Now the place hums 24 hours a day, as fashion photographers pose beautiful models for shoots that make backdrops of the throngs of visitors. Pop singer and actress Madonna even photographed some of her controversial 1992 book *Sex* up and down the beach.

Turn left on 15th Street and left again at the next corner to cruise down **Collins Avenue.** Follow Collins south to 5th Street, and turn right. Turn right again at the next corner to go back north on **Washington Avenue,** a mix of chic restaurants, avant-garde shops, delicatessens, produce markets, and stores selling Jewish, Cuban, and Haitian religious books and artifacts. Most intriguing on the avenue is the eclectic **Botánica La Caridad** (651 Washington Ave., tel. 305/538–7961), selling various herbal and folkloric items from island religions.

Continue north on Washington Avenue to the new **Wolfsonian Foundation Gallery,** which will eventually display the 50,000-item collection of modern design and so-called propaganda arts amassed by Miami native Mitchell Wolfson, Jr., a world traveler and connoisseur. The gallery and its adjoining study center will open fully in 1995. *1001 Washington Ave., tel. 305/531–1001. Admission: $1 adults, 50¢ senior citizens and children. Open Mon.–Fri. 1–5.*

Time Out   Turn right on 12th Street to **Muff'n Man** (234 12th St., tel. 305/538–6833). Multiberry, apple, and cinnamon-raisin muffins and brownies and cookies are baked here daily. The interior is filled with Deco District photos and silk pillows.

Back on Washington Avenue, walk past 14th Street to ❽ **Espanola Way,** a narrow street of Mediterranean-revival buildings constructed in 1925 and frequented through the years by artists and writers. In the 1930s, Cuban bandleader Desi Arnaz performed in the Village Tavern, now part of the **Clay Hotel & AYH International Youth Hostel** (1438 Washington Ave., tel. 305/534–2988). For one block of Espanola Way, east of Washington Avenue to Drexel Avenue, the way for cars has been narrowed to a single lane, and Miami Beach's trademark pink sidewalks have been widened to accommodate new sidewalk cafés. As recently as 1990, this street was troubled by derelicts; now it has miraculously popped up clean, safe, and redeemed, chockablock with imaginative clothing, jewelry, and art shops.

Continue two blocks beyond Drexel to Meridian Avenue, and ❾ turn right. Three blocks north of Espanola Way is **Lincoln Road Mall.** Here you can expect throngs of new visitors promenading who up until 1990 wouldn't have been caught dead on the mall, which had turned into a sideshow of freaks and panhandlers. During its heyday in the 1950s, Lincoln Road was known as the Fifth Avenue of the South, but, like all of the beach, by the '60s it had been bypassed. It was closed to traffic and turned into a pedestrian mall between Washington Avenue and Alton Road, but that couldn't halt the decline. When rents bottomed out, however, artists and arts groups moved in and rehabilitated their buildings. Cafés and restaurants followed, and then retailers. Today the mall is thriving.

Park in the municipal lot ½ block north of the mall, between Washington and Meridian avenues, then either walk along the mall or catch one of the trams that shuttle shoppers. At 541–545 Lincoln Road you'll see a classical four-story Deco gem with its friezes repainted in wavy greens—this is where the **New World Symphony** (tel. 305/673–3331), a national advanced-training orchestra led by Michael Tilson Thomas, rehearses and performs. As you walk west, toward Biscayne Bay, the street is lined with chic food markets like **Lyon Freres** (600 Lincoln Rd., tel. 305/534–0600), with exotic new businesses like the **Mideastern Dance Exchange** (622 Lincoln Rd., tel. 305/538–1608), with artistic cafés like the **Beehive Diner** (630 Lincoln Rd., tel. 305/538–7484), and with brilliant boutiques like **Diamonds & Chicken Soup** (828 Lincoln Rd., tel. 305/532–7687). Go farther west, and you'll see the **South Florida Art Center** (924 Lincoln Rd., tel. 305/674–8278), one of the first arts groups to help resurrect the area. The building houses visual artists' studios and showrooms; they are open to the public, with no admission charge, weekdays 9–5. The 500-seat **Colony Theater** (1040 Lincoln Rd., tel. 305/674–1026), a black-and-white Deco movie house with a Mediterranean barrel-tile roof, has become a city-owned performing-arts center featuring dance, drama, music, and experimental cinema.

The first main street north of Lincoln Road Mall is 17th Street, named **Hank Meyer Boulevard** for the local publicist who persuaded the late comedian Jackie Gleason to broadcast his TV show from Miami Beach in the 1950s. East on 17th Street, be-
- ⑩ side the entrance to **Miami Beach City Hall** (1700 Convention Center Dr., tel. 305/673–7030), stands *Red Sea Road*, a huge
- ⑪ red sculpture by Barbara Neijna. Also to your left is the **Miami Beach Convention Center** (1901 Convention Center Dr., tel. 305/673–7311), a stucco 1960s-vintage building that gained its peach-tone, art-deco look in a 1990 renovation and expansion. It's the Miami area's largest convention space, with 1.1 million square feet. Behind the Convention Center, at the northwest end of the parking lot near Meridian Avenue, is the **Holocaust Memorial** (1933–1945 Meridian Ave., tel. 305/538–1663 or 305/538–1673), a monumental sculpture and a graphic record in memory of the 6 million Jewish victims of the Holocaust. Admission is free, but a small donation is requested for literature on the memorial. A garden conservatory (2000 Convention Center Dr., tel. 305/673–7256) next door is worth a visit but has limited public hours.

Just south of the convention center, at 17th Street and Washington Avenue, you'll see another large sculpture, *Mermaid*,
- ⑫ by Roy Lichtenstein, in front of the **Jackie Gleason Theater of the Performing Arts** (1700 Washington Ave., tel. 305/673–7300), where Gleason's TV show originated. Now the 3,000-seat theater hosts touring Broadway shows and classical-music concerts. Near the sculpture, performers who have appeared in the theater since 1984 have left their footprints and signatures in concrete. This **Walk of the Stars** includes George Abbott, Julie Andrews, Leslie Caron, Carol Channing, and Edward Villella.

Go one block east to Collins Avenue and turn right (south) toward three of the largest Art Deco hotels, all built in the 1940s. Their streamlined tower forms reflect the 20th century's transportation revolution. The round dome atop the 11-story **Hotel National** (1677 Collins Ave., tel. 305/532–2311) resembles a balloon. The tower at the 12-story **Delano Hotel** (1685 Collins Ave., tel. 305/538–7881) has fins suggesting the wings of an airplane or a Buck Rogers spaceship. The 11-story **Ritz Plaza** (1701 Collins Ave., tel. 305/534–3500) rises to a cylindrical tower resembling a periscope.

Go north on Collins Avenue. At 21st Street turn left beside the Miami Beach Public Library in Collins Park, go two blocks to Park Avenue, and turn right. You're approaching the **Bass Museum of Art,** which houses a diverse collection of European art, including *The Holy Family*, a painting by Peter Paul Rubens; *The Tournament*, a 16th-century Flemish tapestry; and works by Albrecht Dürer and Henri de Toulouse-Lautrec. Park behind the museum, and walk around to the entrance, past massive tropical baobab trees. *2121 Park Ave., tel. 305/673–7530. Admission: $5 adults, $4 students with ID and senior citizens, $3 children 13–17, $2 children 6–12, under 6 free; donations Tues. Some exhibitions may be more expensive. Open Tues.– Sat. 10–5, Sun. 1–5.*

Return on 21st or 22nd Street to Collins Avenue, and turn left. As you drive north a triumphal archway looms ahead, framing a majestic white building set in lush vegetation beside a waterfall and tropical lagoon. This vista is an illusion—a 13,000-square-foot outdoor mural on an exterior wall of the **Fontainebleau Hilton Resort and Spa** (4441 Collins Ave., tel. 305/538–2000). Artist Richard Haas designed the mural to illustrate how the hotel and its rock-grotto swimming pool would look behind the wall. Locals call the 1,206-room hotel Big Blue. It's the giant of Miami Beach.

Turn left on 65th Street, left again at the next corner onto Indian Creek Drive, and right at 63rd Street, which leads into **Alton Road,** a winding, landscaped boulevard of gracious homes styled along art-deco lines. You'll pass **La Gorce Country Club** (5685 Alton Rd., tel. 305/866–4421), which developer Carl Fisher built and named for his friend Oliver La Gorce, then president of the National Geographic Society.

To return to the mainland on the MacArthur Causeway stay on Alton Road south to 5th Street, then turn right.

Tour 2: Downtown Miami

Numbers in the margin correspond to points of interest on the Tour 2: Downtown Miami map.

From a distance you see downtown Miami's future—a 21st-century skyline already stroking the clouds with sleek fingers of steel and glass. By day this icon of commerce and technology sparkles in the strong subtropical sun; at night it basks in the man-made glow of floodlights.

Here staid, suited lawyers and bankers share the sidewalks with Latino merchants wearing open-neck, intricately embroidered shirts called *guayaberas*. Fruit merchants sell their wares from pushcarts. European youths with backpacks stroll the streets. Foreign businessmen haggle over prices in import-export shops. You hear Arabic, Chinese, Creole, French, German, Hebrew, Hindi, Japanese, Portuguese, Spanish, Swedish, Yiddish, and even a little English now and then.

Yet Miami's downtown is sorely neglected. Although office workers crowd the area by day, the city is deserted at night. Visitors to the city spend as little time there as possible, since most tourist attractions are in other neighborhoods. Miami's oldest downtown buildings date from the 1920s and 1930s—not very old compared to the historic districts of St. Augustine and Pensacola. What's best in downtown Miami today results from recent moves to bring people back. The following walking tour doesn't include many must-see sights, but it can help you really get to know the city.

Thanks to the Metromover, the light-rail mass-transit system that circles the heart of the city on twin elevated loops, this is the best part of Miami to see by rail. No part of this downtown tour is more than two blocks from a Metromover station. We've organized the tour around those stations, so you can ride Metromover directly to the attractions that interest you most. Parking downtown is inconvenient and expensive—if you're staying elsewhere in the area, leave your car at an outlying Metrorail station and take the train downtown.

Get off the Metrorail train at **Government Center Station,** where the Metromover connects with the 21-mile elevated Metrorail commuter system. Metromover has two loops through downtown, an inner and an outer loop; this tour approximately follows the outer loop.

As you leave the Government Center Metrorail station, notice
❶ the **Dade County Courthouse** (73 W. Flagler St.). It's the building to the east with a pyramid at its peak, where turkey vultures roost in winter. Built in 1928, it was once the tallest building south of Washington, D.C.

❷ Leaving the Metrorail station you'll enter **Metro-Dade Center,** the county government's sleek 30-story office building. Designed by architect Hugh Stubbins, it opened in 1985.

Across N.W. 1st Street from Metro-Dade Center stands the
❸ **Metro-Dade Cultural Center** (101 W. Flagler St.), one of the focal points of Miami's downtown. The city's main art museum, historical museum, and library are gathered here, in a 3.3-acre complex. Opened in 1983, the complex is a Mediterranean expression of architect Philip Johnson's postmodern style. An elevated plaza provides a serene haven from the city's pulsations and a superb setting for festivals and outdoor performances.

The **Center for the Fine Arts,** an art museum in the tradition of the European *Kunsthalle* (exhibition gallery), has no permanent collection, but it organizes and borrows temporary exhibitions on many themes. Shows scheduled for 1994 include "Portrait Drawings from the National Portrait Gallery in London," "18th Century Dutch Watercolors," "American History Paintings," and one-person exhibitions by Bill Viola, Jonathan Borofsky, Martin Johnson Heade, and Jim Dine. *Tel. 305/375–1700. Admission: $5 adults, $2 children 6–12, under 6 free; donations Tues. Open Tues.–Sat. 10–5, Thurs. 10–9, Sun. noon–5.*

The **Historical Museum of Southern Florida** is a regional museum that interprets the human experience in southern Florida

Tour 2: Downtown Miami

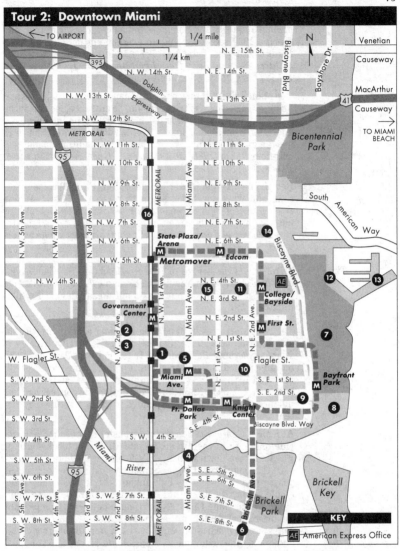

← TO AIRPORT

0   1/4 mile
0   1/4 km

METRORAIL

N. W. 15th St. N. E. 15th St. Venetian
N. W. 14th St. N. E. 14th St. Causeway
N. W. 13th St. N. E. 13th St. MacArthur
N. W. 12th St. Causeway
N. W. 11th St. N. E. 11th St. TO MIAMI BEACH
N. W. 10th St. N. E. 10th St.
N. W. 9th St. N. E. 9th St.
N. W. 8th St. N. E. 8th St.
N. W. 7th St. N. E. 7th St.
N. W. 6th St. N. E. 6th St.
N. W. 5th St.

Dolphin Expressway

Bicentennial Park

Biscayne Blvd.
Bayshore Dr.

South American Way

State Plaza/ Arena
Metromover Edcom
Government Center
College/ Bayside
First St.
Flagler St.
Bayfront Park
Miami Ave.
Ft. Dallas Park
Knight Center
Biscayne Blvd. Way

W. Flagler St.
S. W. 1st St.
S. W. 2nd St.
S. W. 3rd St.
S. W. 4th St.
S. W. 5th St.
S. W. 6th St.
S. W. 7th St.
S. W. 8th St.

N. E. 4th St.
N. E. 3rd St.
N. E. 2nd St.
N. E. 1st St.
S. E. 1st St.
S. E. 2nd St.

S. W. 4th St.
S. E. 4th St.
S. E. 5th St.
S. E. 6th St.
S. E. 7th St.
S. E. 8th St.

Miami River

Brickell Park

Brickell Key

Brickell Ave.

KEY
AE American Express Office

Bayfront Park, **7**
Bayside Marketplace, **12**
Brickell Avenue, **6**
Dade County Courthouse, **1**
Flagler Street, **5**
Freedom Tower, **14**

Gusman Center for the Performing Arts, **10**
Hotel Inter-Continental Miami, **8**
Metro-Dade Center, **2**
Metro-Dade Cultural Center, **3**
Miamarina, **13**

Miami Arena, **16**
Miami Ave. Bridge, **4**
Miami-Dade Community College, **11**
Southeast Financial Center, **9**
U.S. Courthouse, **15**

from prehistory to the present. Artifacts on permanent display include Tequesta and Seminole Indian ceramics, clothing, and tools; a 1920 streetcar; and an original edition of Audubon's *Birds of America. Tel. 305/375–1492. Admission: $4 adults, $2 children 6–12, under 6 free; donations Mon. Open Mon.–Sat. 10–5, Thurs. 10–9, Sun. noon–5.*

The **Main Public Library** has more than 3.5 million holdings and a computerized card catalog. Inside the entrance, look up at the rotunda mural, in which artist Edward Ruscha interpreted a quotation from Shakespeare: "Words without thought never to heaven go." You'll find art exhibits in the auditorium and second-floor lobby. *Tel. 305/375–2665. Open Mon.–Sat. 9–6, Thurs. 9–9, Sun. 1–5. Closed Sun. May–mid-Oct.*

Get off the Metromover at the next stop, **Ft. Dallas Park Station,** and walk one block south to reach the **Miami Avenue Bridge,** one of 11 bridges on the river that open to let ships pass. From the bridge approach, watch freighters, tugboats, research vessels, and luxury yachts ply this busy 5-mile waterway.

Time Out Stroll across the bridge to **Tobacco Road** (626 S. Miami Ave., tel. 305/374–1198) for a drink, snack, or meal. Built in 1912, this friendly neighborhood pub was a speakeasy during Prohibition.

The next Metromover stop, **Knight Center Station,** nestles inside **International Place** (100 S.E. 1st St.), a wedge-shape 47-story skyscraper designed by I. M. Pei and Partners. The building is brilliantly illuminated at night. Inside the tower follow signs to the **James L. Knight International Center** (400 S.E. 2nd Ave., tel. 305/372–0929), a convention and concert hall in a bulbous concrete building appended to the Hyatt Regency Hotel.

At Knight Center Station you can transfer to the inner loop and ride one stop to the **Miami Avenue Station,** a block south of **Flagler Street,** downtown Miami's commercial spine. Like most such thoroughfares, Flagler Street has lost business in recent years to suburban malls—but, unlike most, it found a new lease on life. Today the ½ mile of Flagler Street from Biscayne Boulevard to the Dade County Courthouse is the most important import-export center in the United States. Its stores and arcades supply much of the world with bargain automotive parts, audio and video equipment, medical equipment and supplies, photographic equipment, clothing, and jewelry.

Time Out Walk about 2½ blocks north of Flagler Street to **The Eating Place** (240 N. Miami Ave., tel. 305/375–0156), an open-air Jamaican restaurant as authentic as any in Kingston. The jukebox pours reggae onto Miami Avenue while waitresses pour Jamaican beer, Red Stripe, which goes well with the oxtail stew or curried goat.

From the Knight Center Station, as of mid-1994 you'll be able to get on the new Metromover spur that will link downtown with the Brickell District, just across the Miami River along **Brickell Avenue,** a southward extension of S.E. 2nd Avenue. Heading south on Brickell Avenue through a canyon of tall buildings, you'll pass the largest concentration of international banking offices in the United States. From the end of the Metromover line, you'll be able to look south to where several architecturally interesting condominiums rise between Brickell Avenue and Biscayne Bay. Israeli artist Yacov Agam painted the rainbow-hue exterior of **Villa Regina** (1581 Brickell Ave.). Arquitectonica, a nationally prominent architectural firm based in Miami, designed three of these buildings: **The Palace** (1541 Brickell Ave.), **The Imperial** (1627 Brickell Ave.), and **The Atlantis** (2025 Brickell Ave.).

The next station past Knight Center on the outer loop is **Bayfront Park Station,** opposite **Claude and Mildred Pepper Bayfront Park,** which extends east from busy, palm-lined Biscayne Boulevard to the edge of the bay. Japanese sculptor Isamu Noguchi redesigned the park just before his death in 1989; it now includes a memorial to the *Challenger* astronauts, an amphitheater, and a fountain honoring the late Florida congressman Claude Pepper and his wife. Just north on the boulevard a 2-mile beautification is to begin in fall 1993; new mosaic-tile sidewalks designed by Brazilian landscape architect Roberto Burle Marx will be installed.

Just south of Bayfront Park, the lobby of the **Hotel Inter-Continental Miami** (100 Chopin Plaza; *see* Lodging, *below)* contains *The Spindle*, a huge sculpture by Henry Moore. West of Bayfront Park Station stands the tallest building in Florida, the 55-story **Southeast Financial Center** (200 S. Biscayne Blvd.), with towering royal palms in its 1-acre Palm Court plaza beneath a steel-and-glass frame.

As you continue north on the Metromover, take in the fine view of Bayfront Park's greenery, the bay beyond, the Port of Miami in the bay, and Miami Beach across the water. The next Metromover stop, **First Street Station,** places you a block north of Flagler Street and the landmark **Gusman Center for the Performing Arts,** an ornate former movie palace restored as a concert hall. Gusman Center resembles a Moorish courtyard with twinkling stars in the sky. Performances here include the Miami City Ballet, directed by Edward Villella, and the New World Symphony, the advanced-training orchestra led by Michael Tilson Thomas. *174 E. Flagler St.; box office, tel. 305/ 372-0925; ballet, tel. 305/532-4880; symphony, tel. 305/673- 3330.*

The **College/Bayside Station** Metromover stop serves the downtown campus of **Miami-Dade Community College.** In Building 1, you can browse through two fine galleries: the **Centre Gallery** on the third floor and the **Frances Wolfson Art Gallery** on the fifth floor, which houses traveling exhibitions of contemporary art. *300 N.E. 2nd Ave., tel. 305/237-3278. Admission free. Both galleries open weekdays 9-5.*

College/Bayside Station is also the most convenient Metromover stop for **Bayside Marketplace,** a waterside entertainment-and-shopping center built by the Rouse Company between Bayfront Park and the entrance to the Port of Miami. After completing an $11 million renovation in 1992, Bayside at last is attracting crowds of locals and visitors, including cruise passengers who come over from the port for a few hours' shopping before their ships head for the Caribbean. Bayside's 235,000 square feet of retail space house 150 specialty shops, pushcarts in the center's Pier 5 area, outdoor cafés, a Hard

Rock Cafe, and an international food court where everyone's gone show biz—don't miss the acrobatic fudge-makers, who draw huge crowds. *401 Biscayne Blvd., tel. 305/577–3344. Open Mon.–Sat. 10–10, Sun. noon–8; extended hrs for restaurants and outdoor cafés.*

From the Bayside Marketplace you can stroll to the adjoining
❸ 145-slip **Miamarina,** where luxurious yachts are moored. Here you can take a ride in an authentic 36-foot-long Venetian gondola; or walk out on Pier 5, a fisherman's wharf, to buy fresh seafood; or sign on for a deep-sea or bay-fishing charter with any of 35 boats. Street performers entertain free throughout the day and evening, and live bands perform on the marina stage daily. *401 Biscayne Blvd., tel. 305/579–6955. Open daily 7 AM–11 PM.*

Look just north of Bayside to see a new twin-span bridge, which leads to the Port of Miami. More than 1.5 million cruise passengers a year go through this port; its 12 terminals are home base for 20 cruise liners. The first series of passenger "pods" were built in 1964 in concrete shapes sculpted in the form of wind scoops. Though the pods are now enclosed and climate-controlled, in midweek when there are few ships docked here you can still see the graceful wave-like pod shapes inside.

As Metromover rounds the curve after College/Bayside Sta-
❹ tion, look northeast to see **Freedom Tower** (600 Biscayne Blvd.), where the Cuban Refugee Center processed more than 500,000 Cubans who entered the United States to flee Fidel Castro's regime in the 1960s. Built in 1925 for the *Miami Daily News,* this imposing Spanish-baroque structure was inspired by the Giralda, an 800-year-old bell tower in Seville, Spain. After years in derelict condition, Freedom Tower was renovated in 1988 and opened for office use in 1990, although, oddly, it has remained untenanted. To see it up close, walk north from **Edcom Station** to N.E. 6th Street then two blocks east to Biscayne Boulevard.

A two-block walk south from Edcom Station will bring you to
❺ the **U.S. Courthouse,** a handsome building of coquina coral stone, erected in 1931 as Miami's main post office. In the second-floor central courtroom is *Law Guides Florida Progress,* a huge Depression-era mural by Denman Fink. Surrounding the central figure of a robed judge are several images that define the Florida of the 1930s: fish vendors, palm trees, beaches, and a Pan Am airplane winging off to Latin America. *300 N.E. 1st Ave. Building open weekdays 8:30–5; security guards open courtroom on request. No cameras or tape recorders allowed in building.*

As you round the northwest corner of the loop, at **State Plaza/**
❻ **Arena Station,** look two blocks north to see the **Miami Arena** (721 N.W. 1st Ave., tel. 305/530–4444), built in 1988 as a home for the Miami Heat, a National Basketball Association team. Round, squat, windowless, and pink, the arena hosts other sports and entertainment events when the basketball team isn't playing.

Tour 3: Little Havana

Numbers in the margin correspond to points of interest on the Tours 3–7: Miami, Coral Gables, and Key Biscayne map.

More than 30 years ago the tidal wave of Cubans fleeing the Castro regime flooded an older neighborhood just west of downtown Miami with refugees. This area became known as Little Havana. Today, with ½ million Cubans widely dispersed throughout Greater Miami, Little Havana remains a magnet for Cubans and Anglos alike. They come to experience the flavor of traditional Cuban culture. That culture, of course, functions in Spanish. Many Little Havana residents and shopkeepers speak almost no English.

From downtown go west on Flagler Street across the Miami River. Drive west on West Flagler Street to Teddy Roosevelt
❶ Avenue (S.W. 17th Avenue), and pause at **Plaza de la Cubanidad,** on the southwest corner. Redbrick sidewalks surround a fountain and monument with a quotation from José Martí, a leader in Cuba's struggle for independence from Spain: LAS PALMAS SON NOVIAS QUE ESPERAN (The palm trees are girlfriends who will wait.), counseling hope and fortitude to the Cubans.

Turn left at Douglas Road (S.W. 37th Avenue), drive south to
❷ **Calle Ocho** (the Spanish name for S.W. 8th Street), and turn left again. You are now on the main commercial thoroughfare of Little Havana.

Time Out For a total sensory experience, have a snack or meal at **Versailles** (3555 S.W. 8th St., tel. 305/445–7614), a popular Cuban restaurant. Etched-glass mirrors lining its walls amplify bright lights, and there's the roar of rapid-fire Spanish. Most of the servers don't speak English; you order by pointing to a number on the menu (choice of English or Spanish menus). Specialties include *palomilla* (beefsteak), *ropa vieja* (literally, "old clothes," a shredded-beef dish in tomato sauce), and *arroz con pollo* (chicken and yellow rice).

Drive east on Calle Ocho. After you cross Unity Boulevard (S.W. 27th Avenue), Calle Ocho becomes a one-way street eastbound through the heart of Little Havana, where every block deserves exploration. If your time is limited, we suggest the three-block stretch from S.W. 14th Avenue to S.W. 11th Avenue. Parking is more plentiful west of Ronald Reagan Avenue (S.W. 12th Avenue).

At Calle Ocho and Memorial Boulevard (S.W. 13th Avenue)
❸ stands the **Brigade 2506 Memorial,** commemorating the victims of the unsuccessful 1961 Bay of Pigs invasion of Cuba by an exile force. An eternal flame burns atop a simple stone monument with the inscription: CUBA—A LOS MARTIRES DE LA BRIGADA DE ASALTO ABRIL 17 DE 1961. The monument also bears a shield with the Brigade 2506 emblem, a Cuban flag superimposed on a cross. Walk a block south on Memorial Boulevard from the Brigade 2506 Memorial to see other monuments relevant to Cuban history, including a statue of José Martí.

❹ Drive five blocks south on Ronald Reagan Avenue to the **Cuban Museum of Arts and Culture.** Created by Cuban exiles to preserve and interpret the cultural heritage of their homeland, the museum has expanded its focus to embrace the entire Hispanic arts community and work produced by young local artists in general. In 1989 some artists who had previously exhibited in Havana were invited to show here. Because of United States–Cuba relations this event caused controversy for the museum.

Tours 3 – 7: Miami, Coral Gables, and Key Biscayne

81

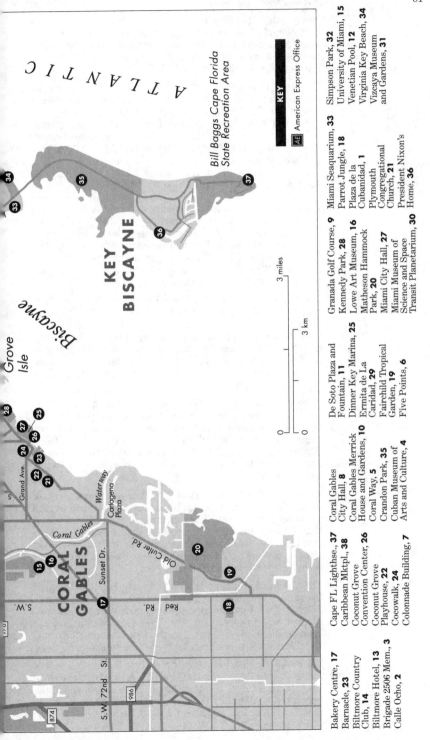

KEY

AE American Express Office

ATLANTIC

Bill Baggs Cape Florida State Recreation Area

KEY BISCAYNE

Biscayne

Grove Isle

Coral Gables

Cartagena Plaza

Waterway

Old Cutler Rd.

Sunset Dr.

Coral Way

Coral Gables

CORAL GABLES

S.W.

Red Rd.

Grand Ave.

S.W. 72nd St.

Bakery Centre, **37**
Barnacle, **23**
Biltmore Country Club, **14**
Biltmore Hotel, **13**
Brigade 2506 Mem., **3**
Calle Ocho, **2**

Cape FL Lighthse., **37**
Caribbean Mktpl., **38**
Coconut Grove Convention Center, **26**
Coconut Grove Playhouse, **22**
Cocowalk, **24**
Colonnade Building, **7**

Coral Gables City Hall, **8**
Coral Gables Merrick House and Gardens, **10**
Coral Way, **5**
Crandon Park, **35**
Cuban Museum of Arts and Culture, **4**

De Soto Plaza and Fountain, **11**
Dinner Key Marina, **25**
Ermita de La Caridad, **29**
Fairchild Tropical Garden, **19**
Five Points, **6**

Granada Golf Course, **9**
Kennedy Park, **28**
Lowe Art Museum, **16**
Matheson Hammock Park, **20**
Miami City Hall, **27**
Miami Museum of Science and Space Transit Planetarium, **30**

Miami Seaquarium, **33**
Parrot Jungle, **18**
Plaza de la Cubanidad, **1**
Plymouth Congregational Church, **21**
President Nixon's Home, **36**

Simpson Park, **32**
University of Miami, **15**
Venetian Pool, **12**
Virginia Key Beach, **34**
Vizcaya Museum and Gardens, **31**

Nevertheless the museum survives, including among its Cuban work the art of exiles and of artists who continue to work on the island. Other exhibits are drawn from the museum's small permanent collection. *1300 S.W. 12th Ave., tel. 305/858–8006. Donation requested. Open Wed.–Sun. 1–5.*

To return to downtown Miami take Ronald Reagan Avenue back north to S.W. 8th Street, turn right, drive east to Miami Avenue or Brickell Avenue, turn left, and continue north across the Miami River. To pick up the Coral Gables tour that follows, drive south to the end of Ronald Reagan Avenue, where it intersects with Coral Way; turn right onto Coral Way and head west.

Tour 4: Coral Gables and South Miami

Coral Gables, a planned community of broad boulevards and Spanish Mediterranean architecture, justifiably calls itself "The City Beautiful." Developer George E. Merrick began selling Coral Gables lots in 1921 and incorporated the city in 1925. He named most of the streets for Spanish explorers, cities, and provinces. Street names are at ground level beside each intersection on whitewashed concrete cornerstones.

The 1926 hurricane and the Great Depression prevented Merrick from fulfilling many aspects of his plan. The city languished until after World War II but then grew rapidly. Today Coral Gables has a population of about 41,000. In its bustling downtown more than 100 multinational companies maintain headquarters or regional offices. The University of Miami campus, in the south part of Coral Gables, brings a youthful vibrance to its corner of the area.

From downtown Miami drive south on S.E. 2nd Avenue across the Miami River, where the street becomes Brickell Avenue.
❺ One-half mile south of the river turn right onto **Coral Way,** which at this point is S.W. 13th Street. Within ½ mile, Coral Way doglegs left under I–95 and becomes S.W. 3rd Avenue. It
❻ continues another mile to a complex intersection, **Five Points,** and doglegs right to become S.W. 22nd Avenue.

Along the S.W. 3rd Avenue and S.W. 22nd Avenue segments of Coral Way, banyan trees planted in the median strip in 1929 arch over the roadway. The banyans end at the Miami–Coral Gables boundary, where **Miracle Mile** begins. Actually only ½ mile long, this four-block retailing stretch of Coral Way, from Douglas Road (37th Avenue) to Le Jeune Road (42nd Avenue) is the heart of downtown Coral Gables.

❼ The **Colonnade Building** (133–169 Miracle Mile) once housed the sales office for Coral Gables's original developer, George Merrick. Its rotunda bears an ornamental frieze and a Spanish-tile roof 75 feet above street level. The Colonnade Building has been restored and connected to the new 13-story Colonnade Hotel and an office building that echoes the rotunda's roofline.

❽ The ornate Spanish Renaissance structure facing Miracle Mile just west of Le Jeune Road is **Coral Gables City Hall,** opened in 1928. It has a three-tier tower topped with a clock and a 500-pound bell. A mural by Denman Fink inside the dome ceiling depicts the four seasons and can be seen from the second floor. *405 Biltmore Way, tel. 305/446–6800. Open weekdays 7:30–5.*

Proceeding west on Coral Way you'll pass on your right the

⑨ **Granada Golf Course** (2001 Granada Blvd., tel. 305/460–5367), one of two public courses in the midst of the largest historic district of Coral Gables.

One block west of the golf course turn right on Toledo Street to

⑩ park behind **Coral Gables Merrick House and Gardens,** George Merrick's boyhood home. The city acquired the dwelling in 1976 and restored it to its 1920s appearance. It contains Merrick family furnishings and artifacts. *907 Coral Way, tel. 305/460–5361. Admission: $2 adults, $1 children. Open Sun. and Wed. 1–4.*

Continue west on Coral Way to the first stoplight, and turn left. Now you're southbound on Granada Boulevard, approaching

⑪ **DeSoto Plaza and Fountain,** a classical column on a pedestal with water flowing from the mouths of four sculpted faces. The closed eyes of the face looking west symbolize the day's end. Denman Fink designed the fountain in the early 1920s.

Follow the traffic circle almost completely around the fountain to northeast-bound DeSoto Boulevard. On your right in the

⑫ next block is **Venetian Pool,** a unique municipal swimming pool transformed from a rock quarry. *2701 DeSoto Blvd., tel. 305/460–5356. Admission (nonresident): $4 adults, $3.50 teens, $1.60 children under 12. Free parking across DeSoto Blvd. Open summer, weekdays 11–7:30, weekends 10–4:30; winter, Tues.–Fri. 11–4:30, weekends 10–4:30.*

From the pool, go around the block, turning right three times, until you are on Sevilla Avenue. Return to the DeSoto Fountain, and follow DeSoto Boulevard southeast to emerge in front

⑬ of the **Biltmore Hotel** (1200 Anastasia Ave., tel. 305/445–1926). Like the Freedom Tower in downtown Miami, the Biltmore's 26-story tower is a replica of the Giralda Tower in Seville, Spain. After extensive renovations the hotel reopened in 1992, looking better than ever. The Biltmore Golf Course, known for its scenic layout, has been restored to its original Donald Ross design.

Just west of the Biltmore Hotel is a separate building, the

⑭ **Biltmore Country Club,** which the city restored in the late 1970s. It's a richly ornamented Beaux Arts–style structure with a superb colonnade and courtyard. On its ground floor are facilities for golfers. In the former club lounge, meeting rooms include one lofty space paneled with veneer from 60 species of trees. In 1989 the structure was reincorporated into the Biltmore Hotel, of which it was originally a part.

From the hotel, turn right on Anastasia Avenue, go east to Granada Boulevard, and turn right. Continue south on Granada Boulevard over a bridge across the **Coral Gables Waterway,** which connects the grounds of the Biltmore Hotel with Biscayne Bay. In the hotel's heyday, Venetian gondolas plied the waterway, bringing guests to a bayside beach.

At Ponce de León Boulevard turn right. On your left is Metrorail's Stonehenge-like concrete structure, and on your

⑮ right is the **University of Miami**'s 260-acre main campus. With more than 14,000 full-time, part-time, and noncredit students, UM is the largest private research university in the Southeast.

Turn right at the first stoplight to enter the campus, and park

⑯ in the lot on your right designated for visitors to UM's **Lowe Art**

Museum. The Lowe's permanent collection of 8,000 works includes Renaissance and Baroque art, American paintings, Latin American art, and Navajo and Pueblo Indian textiles and baskets. The museum also hosts traveling exhibitions. *1301 Stanford Dr.; recorded information, tel. 305/284–3535; museum office, 305/284–3536. Admission: $4 adults, $3 senior citizens, $2 students, under 6 free. Open Sun. noon–5, Tues.–Sat. 10–5.*

Exit the UM campus on Stanford Drive, pass under Metrorail, and cross Dixie Highway. Just beyond the Burger King on your right, bear right onto Maynada Street. Turn right at the next stoplight onto **Sunset Drive.** Fine old homes and mature trees line this city-designated "historic and scenic road." Sunset Drive leads to and through South Miami, a pioneer farming community that grew into a suburb but retains its small-town charm.

On the northwest corner of Sunset Drive and Red Road (57th Avenue), note the pink building with a mural in which an alligator seems ready to devour a horrified man. This trompe l'oeil fantasy, *South Florida Cascade*, by illusionary artist Richard Haas, highlights the main entrance to the **Bakery Centre** (5701 Sunset Dr., tel. 305/662–4155). This oversize shopping mall, constructed on the former site of the Holsum Bakery, has failed to attract the hoped-for hordes of shoppers.

On the third level of the Bakery Centre, the **Miami Youth Museum** features arts exhibits, hands-on displays, and activities to enhance children's creativity and inspire interest in artistic careers. *5701 Sunset Dr., tel. 305/661–2787. Admission: $3 adults and children, $2 senior citizens, under 1 free. Open Mon. and Fri. 10–5, Tues.–Thurs. 1–5, weekends 11–5. Closed Thanksgiving, Christmas, New Year's Day.*

Drive south on Red Road, and turn right just before Killian Drive (S.W. 112th Street) into the grounds of **Parrot Jungle,** where more than 1,100 exotic birds are on display. Many of the parrots, macaws, and cockatoos fly free, and they'll come to you for seeds, which you can purchase from old-fashioned gum-ball machines. Attend a trained-bird show, watch baby birds in training, and pose for photos with colorful macaws perched on your arms. The "jungle" is a natural hammock surrounding a sinkhole. Stroll among orchids and other flowering plants nestled among ferns, bald cypress, and massive live oaks. Other highlights include a primate show, small-wildlife shows, a children's playground, and a petting zoo. Also see the cactus garden and Flamingo Lake, with a breeding population of 75 Caribbean flamingos. Opened in 1936, Parrot Jungle is one of Greater Miami's oldest and most popular commercial tourist attractions. *11000 S.W. 57th Ave., tel. 305/666–7834. Admission: $10.50 adults, $7 children 3–12. Parrot Jungle open daily 9:30–6, café open daily 8–6.*

From Parrot Jungle follow Red Road ⅓ mile south, and turn left at Old Cutler Road, which curves north along the uplands of southern Florida's coastal ridge. Visit the 83-acre **Fairchild Tropical Garden,** the largest tropical botanical garden in the continental United States. Although the gardens lost most of their tropical foliage in the 1992 hurricane, the cycads survived, and the rare-plant house will be replaced by late 1993. Replanting has already brought back much of the tropical lushness. *10901 Old Cutler Rd., tel. 305/667–1651. Admission: $7 adults, under 13 free with parents. Tram ride: $1 adults; 50¢ under 13. Open daily 9:30–4:30. Closed Christmas. Tram runs hourly.*

North of the garden, Old Cutler Road traverses Dade County's oldest and most scenic park, **Matheson Hammock Park.** The Civilian Conservation Corps developed the 100-acre tract of upland and mangrove swamp in the 1930s on land donated by a local pioneer, Commodore J. W. Matheson. The park's most popular feature is a bathing beach, where the tide flushes a saltwater "atoll" pool through four gates. *9610 Old Cutler Rd., tel. 305/666–6979. Parking fee for beach and marina: $3 per car, $5 per car with trailer. Limited upland parking free. Park open daily 6 AM–sunset. Pool lifeguards on duty winter, daily 8:30–6; summer, daily 7:30–7.*

Continue north on Old Cutler Road to **Cartagena Plaza,** cross the bridge over the waterway onto Le Jeune Road, turn right on U.S. 1, and return to downtown Miami.

Tour 5: Coconut Grove

Coconut Grove is southern Florida's oldest settlement, inhabited as early as 1834 and established by 1873, two decades before Miami. Its early settlers included Bahamian blacks, "Conchs" from Key West, and New England intellectuals. They built a community that attracted artists, writers, and scientists to establish winter homes. By the end of World War I more people listed in *Who's Who* gave addresses in Coconut Grove than anyplace else.

To this day Coconut Grove reflects its pioneers' eclectic origins. Posh estates mingle with rustic cottages, modest frame homes, and starkly modern dwellings—often on the same block. To keep Coconut Grove a village in a jungle, residents lavish affection on exotic plantings while battling to protect remaining native vegetation.

The historic center of the village of Coconut Grove went through a hippie period in the 1960s, laid-back funkiness in the 1970s, and a teenybopper invasion in the early 1980s. Today the tone is upscale and urban, with a mix of galleries, boutiques, restaurants, bars, and sidewalk cafés. On weekends the Grove is jam-packed.

From downtown Miami follow U.S. 1 south to S.W. 27th Avenue (Grapeland Boulevard), turn left, and drive south to South Bayshore Drive. Turn right, and follow this road until it jogs right and becomes McFarlane Road. At the next intersection turn left onto Main Highway, which passes through the heart of the Village of Coconut Grove. Before you explore this trendy area, however, go on to Devon Road, and turn right in front of **Plymouth Congregational Church.** Opened in 1917, this handsome coral-rock structure resembles a Mexican mission church. The front door, of hand-carved walnut and oak with original wrought-iron fittings, came from an early 17th-century monastery in the Pyrenees. *3400 Devon Rd., tel. 305/444–6521. Call office 1 day in advance to see inside of church weekdays 9–4:30. Sun. service 10 AM.*

Return to Main Highway, and head northeast toward the historic **Village of Coconut Grove,** a trendy commercial district with redbrick sidewalks and more than 300 restaurants, stores, and art galleries. Parking can be a problem in the village—especially on weekend evenings, when police direct traffic and prohibit turns at some intersections to prevent gridlock. Be prepared to walk several blocks from the periphery into the heart of the Grove.

②② As you enter the village center, note the apricot-hue Spanish rococo **Coconut Grove Playhouse** to your left. Built in 1926 as a movie theater, it became a legitimate theater in 1956 and is now owned by the state of Florida. The playhouse presents Broadway-bound plays and musical revues and experimental productions in its 1,100-seat main theater and 100-seat cabaret-style Encore Room. *3500 Main Hwy.; box office, tel. 305/442–4000; administrative office, tel. 305/442–2662. Parking: $2 daytime, $4 evening.*

②③ Benches and a shelter opposite the playhouse mark the entrance to the **Barnacle**, a pioneer residence that is now a state historic site. Although damaged by the 1992 hurricane, the house should be reopened by the end of 1993. Commodore Ralph Munroe built the Barnacle in 1891. Its broad, sloping roof and deeply recessed verandas channel sea breezes into the house. A central stairwell and rooftop vent allow hot air to escape. Many furnishings are original. *3485 Main Hwy., tel. 305/448–9445. Admission: $2. Reservations required for groups of 8 or more; others meet ranger on porch. Open Thurs.–Mon. 9–4; tours 10, 11:30, 1, 2:30.*

Time Out   Turn left at the next street, Commodore Plaza, and pause. Cafés at both corners overflow the brick sidewalks. Try the **Green Streets Cafe** (3110 Commodore Plaza, tel. 305/567–0662) on the south side. This gourmet French café features, among other fare, breakfast all day and a superb Greek-style salad bulging with brine-soaked olives and feta.

②④ At the north end of Commodore Plaza is Grand Avenue, a major shopping street. **Cocowalk** (3015 Grand Ave.), a multilevel open mall of Mediterranean-style brick courtyards and terraces overflowing with people, opened early in 1991 and has revitalized Coconut Grove's nightlife. The mix of shops, restaurants, and theaters has renewed the Grove by creating a new circuit for promenading between these attractions and the historic heart of the Grove along Commodore Plaza. The area now teems with Manhattanlike crowds, especially on weekend evenings. Across Virginia Street is **Mayfair,** a more upscale version of people-friendly Cocowalk.

②⑤ Leaving the village center, follow McFarlane Road east from its intersection with Grand Avenue and Main Highway. **Peacock Park,** site of the first hotel in southeast Florida, is on your right. Ahead, seabirds soar and sailboats ride at anchor in **Dinner Key Marina** (3400 Pan American Dr., tel. 305/579–6980), named for a small island on which early settlers held picnics. With 581 moorings at nine piers, it's Greater Miami's largest marina.

②⑥ McFarlane Road turns left onto South Bayshore Drive. Turn right at the first stoplight (S.W. 27th Ave.), and drive east into a parking lot that serves the marina and the 150,000-square-foot **Coconut Grove Convention Center** (2700 S. Bayshore Dr., tel. 305/579–3310), where antiques, boat, and home-furnishings shows are held.

②⑦ At the northeast corner of the lot is **Miami City Hall,** built in 1934 as the terminal for the Pan American Airways seaplane base at Dinner Key. The building retains its nautical-style Art Deco trim. *3500 Pan American Dr., tel. 305/250–5400. Open weekdays 8–5.*

Return to South Bayshore Drive and turn right. Drive north **②⑧** past Kirk Street to **Kennedy Park,** where you can park your car and walk toward the water. From a footbridge over the mouth of a small tidal creek you'll enjoy an unobstructed view across Biscayne Bay to Key Biscayne. Film crews often use the park to make commercials and Italian westerns.

Drive north on South Bayshore Drive. At the entrance to Mercy Hospital, South Bayshore Drive becomes South Miami Avenue. At the next stoplight, turn right on a private road that **②⑨** passes St. Kieran's Church to **Ermita de La Caridad** (Our Lady of Charity Shrine), a conical building 90 feet high and 80 feet wide overlooking the bay so worshipers face toward Cuba. A mural above the shrine's altar depicts Cuba's history. *3609 S. Miami Ave., tel. 305/854–2405. Open daily 9–9.*

Another 3/10 mile up South Miami Avenue, turn left to the **③⓪ Miami Museum of Science and Space Transit Planetarium.** This is a participatory museum, chock-full of sound, gravity, and electricity displays for children and adults alike to manipulate and marvel at. A wildlife center houses native Florida snakes, turtles, tortoises, birds of prey, and large wading birds—175 live animals in all. *3280 S. Miami Ave., tel. 305/854–4247; 24-hr Cosmic Hotline for planetarium show times and prices, tel. 305/854–2222. Museum admission: $6 adults, $4 children 3–12. Planetarium show: $5 adults, $2.50 children and senior citizens. Laser-light show: $6 adults, $2.50 children and senior citizens. Open daily 10–6.*

③① Across South Miami Avenue is the entrance to **Vizcaya Museum and Gardens,** an estate with an Italian Renaissance–style villa built in 1912–16 as the winter residence of Chicago industrialist James Deering. The house and gardens overlook Biscayne Bay on a 30-acre tract that includes a native hammock and more than 10 acres of formal gardens and fountains. The house contains 70 rooms, with 34 rooms of paintings, sculpture, antique furniture, and other decorative arts, open to the public. These objects date from the 15th through the 19th centuries and represent the Renaissance, Baroque, Rococo, and Neoclassic styles. *3251 S. Miami Ave., tel. 305/579–2813. Admission: $8 adults, $4 children 6–12. Guided 45-min tours available, group tours by appointment. House and ticket booth open daily 9:30–4:30, garden daily 9:30–5. Closed Christmas.*

Continue north on South Miami Avenue to 17th Road, and turn **③②** left to **Simpson Park.** Enjoy a fragment of the dense tropical jungle—large gumbo-limbo trees, marlberry, banyans, and black calabash—that once covered the entire 5 miles from downtown Miami to Coconut Grove. You'll get a rare glimpse of how things were before the high rises towered. Avoid the park during summer, when mosquitoes whine as incessantly today as they did 100 years ago. You may follow South Miami Avenue the rest of the way downtown or go back two stoplights and turn left to the entrance to the Rickenbacker Causeway and Key Biscayne.

Tour 6: Virginia Key and Key Biscayne

Government Cut and the Port of Miami separate the dense urban fabric of Miami Beach from Greater Miami's playground islands, Virginia Key and Key Biscayne—the latter being the no-longer-laid-back village where Richard Nixon set up his presidential vacation compound. Parks occupy much of both keys, providing congenial upland with facilities for basking on the beach, golf, tennis, softball, and picnicking, plus uninviting but ecologically valuable stretches of dense mangrove swamp. Unfortunately, these islands were hit hard in 1992 by Hurricane Andrew, and, although most of the hotels should be reopened by the time you read this, the tourist attractions—many of which are outdoors and near the water—may take a long time to restore.

To reach Virginia Key and Key Biscayne, take the **Rickenbacker Causeway** (toll $1 per car) across Biscayne Bay from the mainland at Brickell Avenue and S.W. 26th Road, about 2 miles south of downtown Miami. The causeway links several islands in the bay.

The new high-level **William M. Powell Bridge** rises 75 feet above the water to eliminate the need for a draw span. The panoramic view from the top encompasses the bay, keys, port, and downtown skyscrapers, with Miami Beach and the Atlantic Ocean in the distance.

Just south of the Powell Bridge, the **Old Rickenbacker Causeway Bridge,** built in 1947, is now a fishing pier. At its western end, about a mile from the tollgate, is a stub of bridge where you can fish. Park near its entrance, and walk past anglers tending their lines to the gap where the center draw span across the Intracoastal Waterway was removed. There you can watch boat traffic pass through the channel, pelicans and other seabirds soar and dive, and porpoises cavort in the bay.

Next along the causeway, on Virginia Key, stands the 6,536-seat **Miami Marine Stadium** (3601 Rickenbacker Causeway, tel. 305/361–6732), site of summer pop concerts, occasional shows by name entertainers, and a spectacular Fourth of July fireworks display. You can join the audience on land in the stadium or on a boat anchored just offshore. Down the causeway from Marine Stadium is the **Miami Seaquarium,** a popular attraction that has reopened partially after severe hurricane damage. Daily performances feature sea lions, dolphins, and Lolita, a killer whale that cavorts in a huge tank. Exhibits include a shark pool, a 235,000-gallon tropical-reef aquarium, and manatees. *4400 Rickenbacker Causeway, tel. 305/361–5705. Admission: $17.95 adults, $14.95 senior citizens, $12.95 children 3–12. Open daily 9:30–6.*

Opposite the causeway from the Seaquarium, a road leads north to **Virginia Key Beach,** a City of Miami park with a 2-mile stretch of oceanfront, shelters, barbecue grills, ball fields, nature trails, and a fishing area. Ask for directions at the entrance gate. *Parking: $2 per car.*

In 1992 a 400-acre portion on the west side of this mangrove-edged island was dedicated as the **Virginia Key Critical Wildlife**

Area. Birds to be seen here include reddish egrets, black-bellied plovers, black skimmers, and roseate spoonbills—but only May through July. The area is left undisturbed the other nine months, to be more amenable to migratory shorebirds.

From Virginia Key the causeway crosses **Bear Cut** to the north end of Key Biscayne, where it becomes Crandon Boulevard.
㉟ The boulevard bisects 1,211-acre **Crandon Park,** which has a popular 3.3-mile Atlantic Ocean beach. Turnouts on your left lead to four parking lots and adjacent picnic areas. *Parking: $2 per car. Open daily 8 AM–sunset.*

Time Out Enjoy that rarity among Miami-area restaurants, a freestanding waterfront bar, at **Sundays on the Bay** (5420 Crandon Blvd., tel. 305/361–6777). A 60-item brunch is served Sunday 10:30–3:30, and lunch and dinner are served daily.

On your right are entrances to the **Key Biscayne Golf Course** and the **International Tennis Center,** where in 1992 a $16.5 million, 7,500-seat tennis stadium was constructed for the 1994 Lipton International Players Championships.

From the traffic circle at the south end of Crandon Park, Crandon Boulevard continues for 2 miles through the developed portion of Key Biscayne. You'll come back that way, but
㊱ first detour to the site of **President Nixon's home** (485 W. Matheson Dr.). Turn right at the first stoplight onto Harbor Drive, go about a mile, and turn right at Matheson Drive. A later owner enlarged and totally changed the house.

Continue south on Harbor Drive to Mashta Drive; turn left on Mashta Drive and return to Crandon Boulevard. Turn right to reach the entrance to **Bill Baggs Cape Florida State Recreation Area,** named for a crusading newspaper editor whose efforts prompted the state to create this 406-acre park. The park includes, a nature trail, 1¼ miles of beach, and a seawall along Biscayne Bay where anglers catch bonefish, grouper, jack, snapper, and snook. The park was devastated by Hurricane Andrew but was scheduled to reopen before spring 1994; plans were to replant it with native Florida plants instead of the exotics that had overtaken it. Also in the park is the oldest struc-
㊲ ture in southern Florida, the **Cape Florida Lighthouse,** erected in 1825 to help ships avoid the shallows and reefs offshore. In 1836 a band of Seminoles attacked the lighthouse and killed the keeper's helper. You can no longer climb the 122 steps to the top of the 95-foot-tall lighthouse because the structure needs repair. *1200 S. Crandon Blvd., tel. 305/361–5811. Admission to park: $3.25 per vehicle; to lighthouse and keeper's residence: $1 per person, under 6 free. Park open daily 8–sunset. Lighthouse tours Wed.–Mon. at 1, 2:30, 3:30.*

When you leave Cape Florida, follow Crandon Boulevard back to Crandon Park through Key Biscayne's commercial center, a mixture of posh shops and more prosaic stores catering to the needs of the neighborhood. On your way back to the mainland, pause as you approach the Powell Bridge to admire the downtown Miami skyline. At night the brightly lighted International Place looks from this angle like a clipper ship running under full sail before the breeze.

Tour 7: Little Haiti

Of the nearly 200,000 Haitians who have settled in Greater Miami, almost half live in Little Haiti, an area on Miami's northeast side covering some 200 city blocks. More than 400 small Haitian businesses operate in Little Haiti.

For many Haitians, English is a third language. French is Haiti's official language, but much day-to-day conversation takes place in Creole, a French-based patois.

From downtown Miami, follow Biscayne Boulevard north to N.E. 36th Street, turn left, and drive about ⁴⁄₁₀ mile west to North Miami Avenue. Turn right, and drive north through the **Miami Design District,** on the fringe of Little Haiti, where about 225 wholesale stores, showrooms, and galleries feature interior furnishings and decorative arts.

Little Haiti begins immediately north of the Design District in an area that contains some of Miami's oldest dwellings, dating from the dawn of the 20th century through the 1920s land-boom era. Drive the side streets to see elegant Mediterranean-style homes and bungalows with distinctive coral-rock trim.

Return to North Miami Avenue and drive north. A half block east on 54th Street is the tiny storefront office of the **Haitian Refugee Center** (119 N.E. 54th St., tel. 305/757–8538), a focal point of activity in the Haitian community. The building's facade is decorated by the painting of an uncomprehending Haitian standing in front of the Statue of Liberty, which denies him entry to America. Continue north on North Miami Avenue past the **former Cuban consulate** (5811 N. Miami Ave.), a pretentious Caribbean-Colonial mansion that is now the clinic of Haitian physician Lucien Albert.

North of 85th Street, cross the Little River Canal into **El Portal,** a tiny suburban village of modest homes, where more than a quarter of the property is now Haitian-owned. Turn right on N.E. 87th Street and right again on N.E. 2nd Avenue. You are now southbound on Little Haiti's tree-lined main commercial street.

Time Out   Stop for Haitian breads and cakes made with coconut and other tropical ingredients at **Baptiste Bakery** (7488 N.E. 2nd Ave., tel. 305/756–1119).

Along N.E. 2nd Avenue between 79th and 45th streets, rows of storefronts in faded pastels reflect a first effort by area merchants to dress up their neighborhood and attract outsiders.

More successful—aesthetically, if not yet commercially—is the **Caribbean Marketplace** (5927 N.E. 2nd Ave., tel. 305/758–8708), which the Haitian Task Force (an economic-development organization) opened in 1990. Its 10 or so merchants sell handmade baskets, Caribbean art and craft items, books, records, videos, and ice cream.

To return to downtown Miami follow N.E. 2nd Avenue south to N.E. 35th Street, turn left, drive east one block to Biscayne Boulevard, and turn right to go south.

Tour 8: South Dade

This tour directs you to major attractions in the suburbs southwest of Dade County's urban core—or what is left of them, after Hurricane Andrew devastated the area in fall 1992. Although the population was largely dislocated by the storm, little damage is evident today, and almost all of the attractions reopened in early 1993.

From downtown Miami follow the Dolphin Expressway (Route 836) west to the Palmetto Expressway (Route 826) southbound. Bear left south of Bird Road (S.W. 40th Street) onto the Don Shula Expressway (Route 874). Exit westbound onto Killian Drive (S.W. 104th Street), and drive west to Lindgren Road (S.W. 137th Avenue). Turn left, and drive south to S.W. 128th Street, the entrance to the Tamiami Airport and **Weeks Air Museum.** Destroyed by the hurricane, the air museum is rebuilding a space to display its aircraft, which include a World War I–vintage Sopwith Camel (of Snoopy fame) and a B–17 Flying Fortress bomber and P–51 Mustang from World War II. For the time being you can visit the collection in its temporary shed. *14710 S.W. 128th St., tel. 305/233–5197. Admission: $5 adults, $4 senior citizens, $3 children 12 and under. Open daily 10–5.*

Continue south on Lindgren Road to Coral Reef Drive (S.W. 152nd Street). Turn left, and drive east to **Metro Zoo,** a cageless 290-acre zoo where animals roam free on islands surrounded by moats. Devastated by the hurricane, the zoo has reopened but without its monorail or "Wings of Asia," a 1.5-acre aviary where hundreds of exotic birds from Southeast Asia fly through a rain forest beneath a protective net. Most of the animals are still there; the elephants, koalas, and flamingos were shipped to other zoos after the storm but may be back by the time you visit. "Paws," a petting zoo for children, features three shows daily. *12400 Coral Reef Dr. (S.W. 152nd St.); tel. 305/251–0401; recorded information, tel. 305/251–0400. Admission, including monorail tickets: $8.79 adults ($5 during rebuilding), $4.53 children 3–12 ($2.50 during rebuilding). Admission for FL residents with proof of citizenship, Mon.–Sat. 9:30 AM–11 AM only: $5.33 adults, $2.66 children. Open daily 9:30–5:30. Last admission at 4.*

Next to the zoo, the **Gold Coast Railroad Museum** displays a 1949 *Silver Crescent* dome car and the *Ferdinand Magellan,* the only Pullman car ever constructed specifically for U.S. presidents, used by Roosevelt, Truman, Eisenhower, and Reagan. The museum was damaged in the hurricane but should be open again by the end of 1993. *12450 Coral Reef Dr. (S.W. 152nd St.), tel. 305/253–0063. Weekday admission, including 20-min train ride: $3 adults, $2 children. Weekend admission: $5 adults, $3 children. Open weekdays 10–3, weekends 10–5. Train rides weekends, holidays.*

Drive south on the Homestead Extension of Florida's Turnpike, exit at Hainlin Mill Drive (S.W. 216th Street), and turn right. Cross South Dixie Highway (U.S. 1), drive 3 miles west, and turn right into **Monkey Jungle,** home to more than 400 monkeys representing 35 species—including orangutans from Borneo and Sumatra, golden lion tamarins from Brazil, and brown lemurs from Madagascar. Its rainforest trail, damaged in the hurricane, should reopen by the end of 1993. Performing-monkey shows begin at 10 and run continuously at 45-minute intervals. The walkways of this 30-acre attraction are caged; the monkeys roam free. *14805 Hainlin Mill Dr. (S.W. 216 St.), tel. 305/235–1611. Admission: $10.50 adults, $8.85 senior citizens, $5.35 children 4–12. Open daily 9:30–5.*

Continue west on Hainlin Mill Drive to Krome Avenue (S.W. 177th Avenue). Cross Krome to Redland Road (S.W. 187th Avenue), and turn left to Coconut Palm Drive (S.W. 248th Street). You are at the **Redland Fruit & Spice Park,** a Dade County treasure since 1944, when it was opened as a 20-acre showcase of tropical fruits and vegetables. Two of the park's three historic buildings were ruined by the hurricane, as well as about half of its trees and plants, but relandscaping has begun, and the park has reopened. More than 500 varieties of exotic fruits, herbs, spices, and nuts from throughout the world grow here, including poisonous plants. There are 50 varieties of bananas, 40 varieties of grapes, and 100 varieties of citrus. A gourmet-and-fruit shop offers many varieties of tropical-fruit products, jellies, seeds, aromatic teas, and reference books. *24801 S.W. 187th Ave. (Redland Rd.), tel. 305/247–5727. Admission: $1 adults, 50¢ children. Guided tour: $1.50 adults, $1 children. Open daily 10–5. Tours given weekends at 1 and 3.*

Drive east on Coconut Palm Drive (S.W. 248th Street) to Newton Road (S.W. 157th Avenue). Continue south on Newton Road to South Dixie Highway (U.S. 1), and turn left. Almost immediately you'll find **Coral Castle of Florida,** on your right. It was built by Edward Leedskalnin, a Latvian immigrant, between 1920 and 1940. The 3-acre castle has a 9-ton gate a child can open, an accurate working sundial, and a telescope of coral rock aimed at the North Star. *28655 South Dixie Hwy., tel. 305/248–6344. Admission: $7.75 adults, $4.50 children 6–12. Open daily 9–9.*

To return to downtown Miami after leaving Coral Castle, take South Dixie Highway to Biscayne Drive (S.W. 288th Street) and go east to the turnpike. Follow the turnpike back to the Don Shula Expressway (Route 874), which leads to the Palmetto Expressway (Route 826), which leads to the Dolphin Expressway (Route 836).

Miami for Free

Beaches The best free beaches are along Miami Beach and the neighboring communities of Surfside and Sunny Isles (*see* Beaches, *below*).

Concerts **Performing Arts for Community and Education** (PACE, tel. 305/681–1470; recorded information, tel. 305/237–1718) supports free concerts in parks and cultural and religious institutions throughout Greater Miami.

University of Miami School of Music (1314 Miller Dr., tel. 305/284–6477) offers many free concerts at the Coral Gables campus.

Museums There is no charge for admission to the **South Florida Art Center** (*see* Tour 1: Miami Beach, *above*) or the **Centre Gallery** and the **Frances Wolfson Art Gallery** (*see* Tour 2: Downtown Miami, *above*). Admission to the following museums is also free of charge:

The **Black Heritage Museum,** located on the upper level of the Miracle Center, a vertical shopping mall, has rotating exhibits and a 3,000-item permanent collection that includes carvings from Africa, artifacts of Black Americana, and vestiges and artifacts of local history. *Miracle Center, 3301 Coral Way, tel. 305/446-7304. Open daily 7-9.*

At the **North Miami Center of Contemporary Art,** rotating exhibits feature contemporary paintings, photographs, and Florida artworks. Avant-garde films are also screened. *12340 N.E. 8th Ave., tel. 305/893-6211. Open weekdays 10-4, Sat. 1-4.*

In the unusual, tiled Bacardi Imports building, the **Bacardi Art Gallery** exhibits works by local and international artists. Tours are available in English and Spanish if requested in advance. *2100 Biscayne Blvd., tel. 305/573-8511. Open weekdays 9-5. Enter through basement on 21st St., and obtain visitor pass.*

The **Bakehouse Art Complex,** a two-story masonry building built as the Flowers Bakery in the 1920s, was revived in 1987 as a gallery and studios for area artists. On the second Sunday of every month, from 1 to 5, artists meet with visitors. *561 N.W. 32nd St., tel. 305/576-2828. Open Tues.-Fri. 10-4.*

You can pay whatever amount you wish for admission to the **Cuban Museum of Arts and Culture** (*see* Tour 3: Little Havana, *above*). Admission is also by donation on Tuesday at the **Bass Museum of Art** (*see* Tour 1: Miami Beach, *above*) and the **Center for the Fine Arts** (*see* Tour 2: Downtown Miami, *above*) and on Monday at the **Historical Museum of Southern Florida** (*see* Tour 2: Downtown Miami, *above*).

What to See and Do with Children

Greater Miami is a family-oriented vacation destination. Most of the major hotels can provide access to baby-sitters for young children.

Beachgoing families often gravitate to the new children's play area in **Lummus Park,** between Ocean Drive and the beach at 5th and 14th streets.

The following sights are of particular interest to children:

American Police Hall of Fame and Museum exhibits more than 10,000 law enforcement–related items, including weapons, a jail cell, and an electric chair, as well as a 400-ton marble memorial listing the names of more than 3,000 police officers killed in the line of duty since 1960. *3801 Biscayne Blvd., tel. 305/891-1700. Open daily 10-5:30. Admission: $6 adults, $4 senior citizens, and $3 children under 12.*

The **Ancient Spanish Monastery** is the oldest building in the Western Hemisphere. It was built in 1141 in Segovia, Spain. Newspaper magnate William Randolph Hearst had it removed in pieces and stored it in California for 25 years. In 1954 Miami developers rebuilt it at its present site. *16711 W. Dixie Hwy., tel. 305/945-1461. Admission: $4 adults, $2.50 senior citizens, $1 children 7-12. Open Mon.-Sat. 10-4, Sun. noon-4.*

Coconut Grove Farmers Market (*see* Outdoor Markets in Shopping, *below*).

Coral Castle of Florida (*see* Tour 8: South Dade, *above*).

Fairchild Tropical Garden (*see* Tour 4: Coral Gables and South Miami, *above*).

Gold Coast Railroad Museum (*see* Tour 8: South Dade, *above*).
Historical Museum of Southern Florida (*see* Tour 2: Downtown Miami, *above*).
Metromover rides (*see* Tour 2: Downtown Miami, *above*).
Metro Zoo (*see* Tour 8: South Dade, *above*).
Miami Museum of Science and Space Transit Planetarium (*see* Tour 5: Coconut Grove, *above*).
Miami Seaquarium (*see* Tour 6: Virginia Key and Key Biscayne, *above*).
Miami Youth Museum (*see* Tour 4: Coral Gables and South Miami, *above*).
Monkey Jungle (*see* Tour 8: South Dade, *above*).
Parrot Jungle (*see* Tour 4: Coral Gables and South Miami, *above*).
Venetian Pool (*see* Tour 4: Coral Gables and South Miami, *above*).
Vizcaya Museum and Gardens (*see* Tour 5: Coconut Grove, *above*).
Weeks Air Museum (*see* Tour 8: South Dade, *above*).

Shopping

Except in the heart of the Everglades, visitors to the Greater Miami area are never more than 15 minutes from a major shopping area. Downtown Miami long ago ceased to be the community's central shopping hub, as most residents moved to the suburbs. Today Dade County has more than a dozen major malls, an international free-trade zone, and hundreds of miles of commercial streets lined with storefronts and small neighborhood shopping centers. Many of these local shopping areas have an ethnic flavor, catering primarily to one of Greater Miami's immigrant cultures.

In the Latin neighborhoods, for example, children's stores sell *vestidos de fiesta* (party dresses) made of organza and lace. Men's stores sell the *guayabera*, a pleated, embroidered shirt that replaces the tie and jacket in much of the tropics. Traditional bridal shops display formal dresses that Latin families buy or rent for a daughter's *quince*, a lavish 15th-birthday celebration.

No standard store hours exist in Greater Miami. Call ahead. When you shop, expect to pay Florida's 6% sales tax unless you have the store ship your goods out of Florida.

Shopping Districts

Greater Miami is the fashion marketplace for the southeastern United States, the Caribbean, and Latin America. Many of the 500 garment manufacturers in Miami and Hialeah sell their clothing locally, in more than 30 factory outlets and discount fashion stores in the **Miami Fashion District**, east of I–95 along 5th Avenue from 25th Street to 29th Street. Most stores in the district are open Monday–Saturday 9–5 and accept credit cards.

The **Miami Free Zone** (MFZ) is an international wholesale trade center open to the public, a vast operation occupying more than 880,000 square feet on three floors. You can buy goods duty-free for export or pay duty on goods released for domestic use. More than 150 companies sell products from 65 countries, including aviation equipment, chemicals, clothing, computers, cosmetics, electronics, liquor, and perfumes. The 51-acre MFZ is five minutes west of Miami International Airport off the Dolphin Expressway (Route 836) and about 20 minutes from the Port of Miami. *Miami Free Zone, 2305 N.W. 107th Ave., Miami, tel. 305/591-4300. Open weekdays 9-5.*

The following retail shopping malls are located in neighborhoods visitors are likely to frequent:

Aventura Mall, anchored by Macy's, Lord & Taylor, J.C. Penney, and Sears, is in the northern suburb of Aventura. *19501 Biscayne Blvd., Aventura, tel. 305/935-4222. Open Mon.-Sat. 10-9:30, Sun. noon-5:30.*

Bal Harbour Shops is a swank collection of boutiques, featuring Martha, Gucci, Cartier, Nina Ricci, Fendi, Bruno Magli, Neiman Marcus, and Saks Fifth Avenue. *9700 Collins Ave., Bal Harbour, tel. 305/866-0311. Open Mon., Thurs., Fri. 10-9; Tues., Wed., Sat. 10-6; Sun. noon-5.*

Bayside Marketplace, the 16-acre mall on Biscayne Bay, has 150 specialty shops, entertainment, tour-boat docks, and a food court. *401 Biscayne Blvd., Miami, tel. 305/577-3344. Open Mon.-Sat. 10-10, Sun. noon-8.*

Cauley Square, a complex of clapboard, coral-rock, and stucco buildings, was erected 1907-20 for railroad workers who built and maintained the line to Key West. Crafts, antiques, and clothing shops are here now. Turn right off U.S. 1 at S.W. 224th Street. *22400 Old Dixie Hwy., Goulds, tel. 305/258-3543. Open year-round, Mon.-Sat. 10-4:30; Thanksgiving-Christmas Eve, also Sun. noon-5.*

Cocowalk offers three floors of specialty shops in the heart of Coconut Grove, where the shops stay open almost as late as the popular restaurants and clubs. *3015 Grand Ave., Coconut Grove, tel. 305/444-0777. Open Sun.-Thurs. 11-10, Fri.-Sat. 11 AM-midnight.*

Miracle Mile provides some 160 shops along a wide, tree-lined boulevard in Coral Gables. Shops range from posh boutiques to bargain-basement, from beauty salons to chain restaurants. As you go west, the quality increases. *Coral Way between 37th and 42nd Aves., Coral Gables, tel. 305/445-0591. Hrs vary from store to store.*

The Shops at 550, the shortest and most elegant shopping arcade in the metropolis, is in the marble halls of the Azteclike 550 Building on Biltmore Way, three blocks west of Miracle Mile in Coral Gables. Shops include the Stones of Venice jewelry store, Susan Sakolsky, Allure couture, Habib oriental rugs, and Muscles, a women's gym. *550 Biltmore Way, Coral Gables, tel. 305/447-9299. Open weekdays 10-5, some shops open later.*

Outdoor Markets

Coconut Grove Farmers Market is a laid-back, *Brigadoon*like happening that appears as if by magic in Coconut Grove each Saturday. Vendors set up outdoor stands to offer home-grown tropical fruits and vegetables (including organic produce), honey, seafood, macrobiotic foods, and ethnic fare from the Caribbean, the Middle East, and Southeast Asia. Nonfood items for sale include plants, handicrafts, candles, jewelry, and homemade clothing. *For new post-Hurricane Andrew location, opening in 1993, contact Coconut Grove Chamber of Com-*

*merce, 2820 McFarlane Rd., Coconut Grove, tel. 305/444–7270.
Open Sat. 8–3.*

Every weekend since 1984, more than 500 vendors sell a variety of goods at the **Flagler Dog Track.** *401 N.W. 38th Ct., Miami, tel. 305/649–3022. Admission: 50¢. Open weekends 9–5.*

Specialty Shops

Antiques **Alhambra Antiques Center** is a collection of seven antiques dealers selling high-quality decorative pieces from Europe. *3640 Coral Way, Coral Gables, tel. 305/446–1688.*

Books Greater Miami's best English-language bookstore, **Books & Books, Inc.,** specializes in books on the arts, architecture, Floridiana, and contemporary and classical literature. Collectors enjoy browsing through the rare-book room upstairs, which doubles as a photography gallery. There are frequent poetry readings and book signings. *296 Aragon Ave., Coral Gables, tel. 305/442–4408; Sterling Bldg., 933 Lincoln Rd., Miami Beach, tel. 305/532–3222.*

Children's Books and Toys The friendly staff at **A Likely Story** has been helping Miamians choose books and educational toys appropriate to children's interests and stages of development since 1978. *5740 Sunset Dr., South Miami, tel. 305/667–3730.*

Equally good is **A Kid's Book Shoppe,** which has been at this location since 1984. *1895 N.E. Miami Gardens Dr., North Miami Beach, tel. 305/937–2665.*

Clothing **Allure,** in the luxurious Shops at 550 mall in Coral Gables, sells fine women's wear. *550 Biltmore Way, Coral Gables, tel. 305/444–5252.*

Ninth Street Bizarre is a trendy Miami Beach minimart with vendors selling clothing and accessories from around the world. *900 Ocean Dr., Miami Beach, tel. 305/534–2254.*

Decorative and Gift Items **American Details** sells colorful, trendy crafts items. *3107 Grand Ave., Coconut Grove, tel. 305/448–6163.*

Art Deco Welcome Center has a gift shop worth checking out for deco-phernalia. *1244 Ocean Dr., Miami Beach, tel. 305/672–2014.*

The Indies Company, the Historical Museum of Southern Florida's gift shop, offers interesting artifacts reflecting Miami's history, including some inexpensive reproductions. *101 W. Flagler St., Miami, tel. 305/375–1492.*

Jewelry **The Stones of Venice,** operated by a two-time winner of the DeBeers Diamond Award for jewelry, sells ridiculously affordable creations. Customers have included actor Elliott Gould, Pope John Paul II, and film director Barbet Schroeder, among others. *550 Biltmore Way, Coral Gables, tel. 305/444–4474.*

Beaches

Miami Beach From Haulover Cut to Government Cut a broad sandy 300-foot-wide beach extends for 10 continuous miles—7.1 miles within Miami Beach proper, the other 2.9 miles in Surfside and Bal Harbour. Amazingly, it's all man-made. Seriously eroded during the mid-1970s, it was restored by the U.S. Army Corps of

Engineers in a $51.5 million project between 1977 and 1981. Between 21st and 46th streets Miami Beach built boardwalks and protective walkways atop a sand dune landscaped with sea oats, sea grape, and other native plants whose roots keep the sand from blowing away.

The new beach lures residents and visitors alike to swim and stroll—without question, Miami's favorite activity. Here's a guide to where kindred spirits gather:

From **1st to 14th streets** senior citizens predominate early in the day. Later a younger crowd appears, including family groups, which flock to the new children's play area in **Lummus Park,** between Ocean Drive and the beach at 5th and 14th streets. These beaches are opposite the Art Deco strip and attract many European tourists. In this area, in an effort to accommodate foreign visitors, city officials don't enforce the law against female bathers going topless, as long as everyone on the beach behaves with decorum. Gays like the beach between **11th and 13th streets.**

French-Canadians frequent the **72nd Street beach** and the area from **Surfside to 96th Street,** which is colonized by winter visitors from Québec.

During the winter, wealthy condominium owners cluster on the beach from **96th to 103rd streets** in Bal Harbour.

Older visitors especially complain about just how wide the beach is in the Deco District—feet burn easily on long marches across hot sand before reaching the water. If you want the water closer to the upland beach, try the beaches along **Haulover Beach Park** (*see* County Park Beaches, *below*) and through **Sunny Isles** to the far north of the Miami Beach area. The eroded sand was never replaced here, and the strand is mercifully narrow.

City of Miami Beach beaches are staffed by lifeguards and are open winter, daily 8–5, and summer, daily 9–sunset. Bal Harbour and Surfside have no lifeguards; beaches are open daily 24 hours. Beaches are free in all three communities, and there's metered parking nearby.

County-Park Beaches Metropolitan Dade County operates beaches at several of its major parks. Each county park operates on its own schedule, which varies from day to day and season to season. Call the park you plan to visit for current hours and information on special events.

Crandon Park has an Atlantic Ocean beach that's popular with young Hispanics and with family groups of all ethnic backgrounds. *4000 Crandon Park Blvd., Key Biscayne, tel. 305/ 361–5421. Admission: $3 per car. Open daily 8:30–5.*

Haulover Beach Park, also on the Atlantic Ocean, is a good place to avoid crowds—it's lightly used, compared to other public beaches. On weekends and in the peak tourist season, it attracts a diverse crowd. *10800 Collins Ave., Miami, tel. 305/ 947–3525. Admission: $3 per car. Open daily 8–sunset.*

Participant Sports

Miami's subtropical climate is ideal for active people. Here refugees from the frozen north can enjoy warm-weather outdoor sports, such as boating, swimming, and golf, all year long. During Miami's hot, humid summers, people avoid the sun's strongest rays by playing early or late in the day. We've listed some of the most popular individual and group sports.

Bicycling Dade County has about 100 miles of off-road bicycle trails. A color-coded map outlining Dade's 4,000 miles of roads suitable for bike travel is available for $3.50 from area bike shops and from the **Dade County Bicycle Coordinator** (Metropolitan Planning Organization, 111 N.W. 1st St., Suite 910, Miami 33128, tel. 305/375–4507). For information on dozens of monthly group rides contact the **Everglades Bicycle Club** (Box 430282, South Miami 33243–0282, tel. 305/598–3998). Among the best shops for renting bicycles are **Dade Cycle** (3216 Grand Ave., Coconut Grove, tel. 305/444–5997 or 305/443–6075) and **Gary's** (1260 Washington Ave., Miami Beach, tel. 305/534–3306).

Boating and Fishing Listed below are the major marinas in Greater Miami. The dock masters at these marinas can provide information on other marine services you may need. Also ask the dock masters for *Teall's Tides and Guides, Miami–Dade County*, and other local nautical publications.

The U.S. Customs Service requires boats of less than 5 tons that enter the country along Florida's Atlantic Coast south of Sebastian Inlet to report to designated marinas and call U.S. Customs on a direct phone line. The phones, located outside marina buildings, are accessible 24 hours a day. U.S. Customs phones in Greater Miami are at Haulover Marina and Watson Island Marina (both listed below).

Crandon Park Marina sells bait and tackle. *4000 Crandon Blvd., Key Biscayne, tel. 305/361–1161. Open weekdays 7–5, weekends 7–6.*

Dinner Key Marina has dockage with space for transients and a boat ramp. *3400 Pan American Dr., Coconut Grove, tel. 305/579–6980. Open daily 7 AM–11 PM.*

Haulover Marine Center offers a bait-and-tackle shop, marine gas station, and boat launch. *15000 Collins Ave., Miami Beach, tel. 305/945–3934. Open weekdays 8–5, weekends 8–6. Bait shop and gas station open 24 hrs.*

Miamarina's facilities include a bait-and-tackle shop and gas station. *Next to Bayside Marketplace, 401 Biscayne Blvd., Miami, tel. 305/579–6955. Open daily 7 AM–11 PM.*

Miami Beach Marina provides dockage, a boat ramp, a fueling station, a bait-and-tackle store, and bathrooms with showers. There is also a 24-hour guard with communications capability. This is one of five locations for renting Club Nautico power-boats (Pier E, tel. 305/673–2502). *300 Alton Rd., Miami Beach, tel. 305/673–6000. Open daily 8–6.*

Watson Island Marina's facilities include a bait-and-tackle shop, boat ramp, and a gas station. When the marina is busy it stays open until all boaters are served. *1050 MacArthur Causeway, Miami, tel. 305/579–6955. Open weekdays 7:30 AM–10 PM, weekends 6:30 AM–10 PM.*

Fishing Charters A few ocean fishing-charter operators sailing out of various parts of town are: **Abracadabra** (4000 Crandon Blvd., Key Biscayne, tel. 305/361–5625), **Bayside Fishing Charters** (Bayside Marketplace, 401 Biscayne Blvd., Miami, tel. 305/374–2092), **Blue Waters Fishing Charters** (16300 Collins Ave., Sunny Isles, tel. 305/944–4531), **Kelly Fishing Fleet** (Haulover Marina, 10800 Collins Ave., Miami Beach, tel. 305/945–3801 or 305/949–1173), and **Reward H** (1020 MacArthur Causeway, Miami Beach, tel. 305/372–9470).

Diving Summer diving conditions in greater Miami have been compared to those in the Caribbean. Winter diving can be adversely affected when cold fronts come through. Dive-boat schedules vary with the season and with local weather conditions.

Fowey, Triumph, Long, and Emerald Reefs are all shallow 10- to 15-foot dives good for snorkelers and beginning divers. These reefs are on the edge of the continental shelf, ¼ mile from depths greater than 100 feet. You can also paddle around the tangled prop roots of the mangrove trees that line Florida's coastline, peering at the fish, crabs, and other onshore creatures that hide there.

Dive Boats and Instruction Look for instructors affiliated with the Professional Association of Dive Instructors (PADI) or the National Association of Underwater Instructors (NAUI).

Bubbles Dive Center is an all-purpose dive shop located on Watson Island on the MacArthur Causeway. It has PADI affiliation. *2671 S.W. 27th Ave., Miami, tel. 305/856–0565. Open weekdays 10–7, Sat. 9–6.*

Divers Paradise Corp has a complete dive shop and diving-charter service, including equipment rental and scuba instruction. It has PADI affiliation. *4000 Crandon Blvd., Key Biscayne, tel. 305/361–3483. Open weekdays 10–6, weekends 7:30–6.*

Omega Diving International offers private instruction throughout Greater Miami, as well as equipment consultation and specialty courses, including instructor training and underwater photography. It has PADI affiliation. *13885 S.W. 70th Ave., Miami, tel. 305/238–3039 or 800/255–1966. Open daily 8–6.*

Golf From the famed "Blue Monster" at the Doral Resort & Country Club to the scenic Key Biscayne Golf Course overlooking Biscayne Bay, Greater Miami has more than 30 private and public courses. For information contact the appropriate parks-and-recreation department: City of Miami (tel. 305/575–5256), City of Miami Beach (tel. 305/673–7730), or Metro–Dade County (tel. 305/579–2968). Some 18-hole courses open to the public include: **Biltmore Golf Course** (1210 Anastasia Ave., Coral Gables, tel. 305/460–5364), **Don Shula's Golf Club** (N.W. 154th St., Miami Lakes, tel. 305/821–1150 or 800/247–4852), **Doral Hotel Golf Club** (4400 N.W. 87th Ave., Miami, tel. 305/592–2000 or 800/327–6334), **Key Biscayne Golf Club** (6700 Crandon Blvd., Key Biscayne, tel. 305/361–9129), **Normandy Shores Golf Course** (2401 Biarritz Dr., Miami Beach, tel. 305/868–6502), **Presidential Country Club** (19650 N.E. 18th Ave., North Miami Beach, tel. 305/933–5266), and **Turnberry Isle Country Club** (199th St. and Biscayne Blvd., North Miami Beach, tel. 305/932–6200 or 800/327–7028).

Jogging Try these recommended jogging routes: in Coconut Grove, along the pedestrian/bicycle path on South Bayshore Drive, cutting over the causeway to Key Biscayne for a longer run; from downtown, go south along the sidewalks of Brickell Avenue to Bayshore Drive, where you can run alongside the bay; in Miami Beach, along Bay Road (parallel to Alton Road); and in Coral Gables, around the Riviera Country Club golf course, just south of the Biltmore Country Club. Two good sources of running information are the **Miami Runners Club** (tel. 305/227–1500) and **Foot Works** running-shoe store (5724 Sunset Dr., South Miami, tel. 305/667–9322 or 305/666–7223).

Sailing Dinner Key and the Coconut Grove waterfront remain the center of sailing in Greater Miami, although sailboat moorings and rentals are located along other parts of the bay and up the Miami River. For instruction and rentals, **Easy Sailing** offers a fleet ranging from 19 to 127 feet for rent by the hour or the day. Services include sailboat lessons, scuba-diving lessons and certification, and on-board catering. *Dinner Key Marina, 3400 Pan American Dr., Coconut Grove, tel. 305/858–4001 or 800/780–4001. Reservation and advance deposit required. Open daily 9–sunset.*

Spa The **Doral Saturnia International Spa Resort,** on the grounds of the Doral Resort and Country Club, combines mud baths and other European pampering techniques with state-of-the-art American fitness-and-exercise programs. A one-day sampler is available. Formal Italian gardens contain the spa pool and a special waterfall under which guests can enjoy natural hydromassage from the gentle pounding of falling water. The spa's 100-foot-high atrium accommodates a 5,000-pound bronze staircase railing created in 1920 by French architect Alexandre-Gustave Eiffel and fabricated by artist Edgar Brandt for Paris's Bon Marché department store. *8755 N.W. 36th St., Miami 33178, tel. 305/593–6030. 48 suites. Facilities: 4 exercise studios (2 with spring-loaded floors), 2 outdoor heated pools, indoor heated pool, David fitness equipment, beauty salon, 2 restaurants.*

Tennis Greater Miami has more than 60 private and public tennis centers, of which 11 are open to the public. All public tennis courts charge nonresidents an hourly fee.

Coral Gables **Biltmore Tennis Center** has 10 well-maintained hard courts. *1150 Anastasia Ave., tel. 305/460–5360. Nonresident day rate $4.30, night rate $5 per person per hr. Open weekdays 8 AM–9 PM, weekends 8–8.*

Metropolitan Dade County The **International Tennis Center** provides 17 Laykold Cushion Plus hard courts, six of them lighted. Reservations are necessary for night play. This is the site of the annual Lipton International Players Championship, held in March. *7300 Crandon Blvd., Key Biscayne, tel. 305/361–8633. Open daily 8 AM–10 PM. Day rate $2, night rate $3 per person per hr. Racket rental: $5 per hr.*

Miami Beach **Flamingo Tennis Center** has 19 well-maintained clay courts. *1000 12th St., tel. 305/673–7761. Day rate $2.67, night rate $3.20 per person per hr. Open weekdays 8 AM–9 PM, weekends 8–7.*

Windsurfing The safest and most popular windsurfing area in city waters is south of town, by Hobie Island and Virginia Key. The best windsurfing on Miami Beach is at First Street, just north of the Government Cut jetty, and at 21st Street. You can also windsurf at Lummus Park at 10th Street and in the vicinity of 3rd, 14th, and 21st streets. Lifeguards discourage windsurfing from 79th to 87th streets.

Sailboards Miami, on Hobie Island, just past the tollbooth for the Rickenbacker Causeway to Key Biscayne, rents windsurfing equipment. *Key Biscayne, tel. 305/361-7245. Cost: $17 per hr, $95 for 10 hrs. 2-hr lesson: $39. Open daily 9:30–sunset.*

Spectator Sports

Greater Miami now has four major-league teams, in football, baseball, basketball, and ice hockey, plus more specialized events, such as boat racing and jai alai. For tickets to major events, call **Ticketmaster** (Dade County, tel. 305/358–5885; Broward County, tel. 305/523–3309; Palm Beach, tel. 407/839–3900), and charge to your credit card. Generally you can find daily listings of local sports events on the last page of the sports section in *The Miami Herald*. Friday's weekend section carries detailed schedules and coverage of spectator sports.

The activities of the annual **Orange Bowl** and **Junior Orange Festival** take place early November–late February. Best known for its King Orange Jamboree Parade and the Federal Express/Orange Bowl Football Classic, the festival also includes two tennis tournaments: the Rolex–Orange Bowl International Tennis Tournament, for top amateur tennis players 18 and under, and an international tournament for players 14 and under.

Auto Racing **Hialeah Speedway,** the Greater Miami area's only independent raceway, holds stock-car races on a ⅓-mile asphalt speedway in a 5,000-seat stadium. Five divisions of stock cars run weekly. The Marion Edwards, Jr., Memorial Race for late-model stock cars is held in November. The speedway is on U.S. 27, ¼ mile east of the Palmetto Expressway (Route 826). *3300 W. Okeechobee Rd., Hialeah, tel. 305/821-6644. Admission: $10 adults, under 12 free. Open late Jan.–early Dec., Sat. Gates open 5 PM, racing 7–11.*

The **Toyota Grand Prix of Miami** is typically held in February or April on a 1.9-mile, E-shape track in downtown Miami, south of MacArthur Causeway and east of Biscayne Boulevard. Drivers race for three hours; the driver completing the most laps wins. *Miami Motor Sports, Inc., 1110 Brickell Ave., Suite 206, Miami 33131; information, tel. 305/379-5660; tickets, tel. 305/ 379-7223, or call Ticketmaster (see above).*

Baseball The **Florida Marlins**—members of the Eastern Division of the National League—play home games at Joe Robbie Stadium, also home to the Miami Dolphins (*see* Football, *below*). It's 16 miles northwest of downtown Miami, accessible from I–95 and Florida's Turnpike. On game days the Metro-Dade Transit Authority runs buses to the stadium (bus information, tel. 305/ 638-6700). *Tickets: Florida Marlins, 100 N.E. 3rd Ave., Ft. Lauderdale 33301, tel. 305/779-7070, 305/930-7800 (toll-free in Miami), or call Ticketmaster (see above).*

Basketball The **Miami Heat,** Miami's National Basketball Association franchise, plays home games November–April at the Miami Arena (721 N.W. 1st Ave., 1 block east of Overtown Metrorail

Station). *Tickets: Miami Heat, Miami Arena, Miami 33136–4102, tel. 305/577–4328, or call Ticketmaster (see above).*

Dog Racing The Biscayne Kennel Club and the Flagler Dog Track in Greater Miami divide the annual racing calendar. Check with the individual tracks for dates.

At the **Biscayne Kennel Club,** greyhounds chase a mechanical rabbit around illuminated fountains in the track's infield. *320 N.W. 115th St., near I–95, Miami Shores, tel. 305/754–3484. Admission: table seats $1, grandstand $1, clubhouse $2, sports room $3. Parking: 50¢–$2.*

Flagler Dog Track, in the middle of Little Havana, is five minutes east of Miami International Airport off the Dolphin Expressway (Route 836) and Douglas Road (N.W. 37th Ave. and 7th St.). *401 N.W. 38th Ct., Miami, tel. 305/649–3000. Admission: $1, clubhouse $3. Parking: 50¢–$2.*

Football The **Miami Dolphins** play at state-of-the-art Joe Robbie Stadium—JRS, as the fans call it—which has 73,000 seats and a grass playing-field surface with built-in drainage under the sod to carry off rainwater. It's on a 160-acre site 16 miles northwest of downtown Miami, 1 mile south of the Dade-Broward county line, accessible from I–95 and Florida's Turnpike. On game days the Metro-Dade Transit Authority runs buses to the stadium (bus information, tel. 305/638–6700). *Tickets: Miami Dolphins, Joe Robbie Stadium, 2269 N.W. 199th St., Miami 33056, tel. 305/620–2578. Box office open weekdays 10–6, also Sat. during season; or call Ticketmaster (see above).*

Horse Racing **Calder Race Course,** opened in 1971, is Florida's largest glass-enclosed, air-conditioned sports facility. This means that Calder actually has two racing seasons, one in fall or winter, the other in spring or summer. Contact the track for this year's dates. Each year in either January or May, Calder holds the Tropical Park Derby for three-year-olds; if it's in May, this becomes the last major race in Florida before the Kentucky Derby. The track is on the Dade-Broward county line near I–95 and the Hallandale Beach Boulevard exit, ¾ mile from Joe Robbie Stadium. *21001 N.W. 27th Ave., Miami, tel. 305/625–1311. Admission $2, clubhouse $4, programs 75¢. Parking: $1–$3. Gates open 10:30 AM, post time 12:30, races end at about 5:30.*

A superb setting for thoroughbred racing, **Hialeah Park** has 228 acres of meticulously landscaped grounds surrounding paddocks and a clubhouse built in a classic French-Mediterranean style. Since it opened in 1925, Hialeah Park has survived hurricanes and now seems likely to survive even changing demographics as the racetrack crowd has steadily moved north and east. Racing dates are usually March–May or November–January. Alas, the park is no longer open for free tours, but call during racing season to see if there'll be an early gate opening on weekend mornings—if so, you can have breakfast at the track. You can watch the horses work out, explore Hialeah's gardens, munch an under-$10 buffet breakfast, and admire the park's breeding flock of 600 Cuban flamingos. Metrorail's Hialeah Station is on the grounds of Hialeah Park. *2200 E. 4th Ave., Hialeah, tel. 305/885–8000. Admission: $2 grandstand, $4 clubhouse. Parking $1–$3. Gates open during race season at 10:30, post time 12:30 or 1. Races end 5:30.*

Ice Hockey The **Florida Panthers** of the National Hockey League play at the Miami Arena (721 N.W. 1st Ave., 1 block east of Overton Metrorail station). *Tickets: Florida Panthers, Miami Arena, Miami 33136–4102, tel. 305/577–4328, or call Ticketmaster.*

Jai Alai Built in 1926, the **Miami Jai-Alai Fronton** is the oldest fronton in America. Each evening it presents 13 games—14 on Friday and Saturday—some singles, some doubles. This game, invented in the Basque region of northern Spain, is the world's fastest. Jai-alai balls, called *pelotas*, have been clocked at speeds exceeding 170 miles per hour. The game is played in a 176-foot-long court called a fronton. Players climb the walls to catch the ball in a *cesta*—a woven basket—with an attached glove. You can bet on a team to win or on the order in which teams will finish. *3500 N.W. 37th Ave., 1 mi e. of Miami International Airport, Miami, tel. 305/633–6400. Admission: $1, clubhouse $5. Dinner available. Open early Nov.–late Apr. and May–late Sept., 7:10–midnight; matinees Mon., Wed., and Sat. noon–5.*

Tennis The **Lipton International Players Championship (LIPC),** a 10-day spring tournament at the 64-acre International Tennis Center of Key Biscayne, is one of the largest in the world in terms of attendance, and, with $3 million in prize money in 1993, was fifth largest in purse. The two main professional tennis organizations—the Association of Tennis Professionals and the Women's International Tennis Association—helped create this tournament and own part of it. In 1994 the tournament will be played in the new 7,500-seat permanent stadium, with additional seating for the tournament for up to a whopping 14,000 fans. *7300 Crandon Blvd., Key Biscayne; tickets, tel. 305/361–5252, or call Ticketmaster (see above).*

Dining

By Rosalie Leposky and Herb Hiller

You can eat your way around the world in Greater Miami, enjoying just about any kind of cuisine imaginable, in every price category. The rich mix of nationalities encourages individual restaurateurs and chefs to retain their culinary roots. Thus Miami offers not just Latin fare but dishes native to Spain, Cuba, Nicaragua, and other Hispanic countries; not just Oriental fare but specialties of China, India, Thailand, Vietnam, and other Asian cultures. And don't neglect American fare. In recent years the city has gained eminence for the distinctive cuisine introduced by chefs who have migrated north from the tropics and here combine fresh, natural foods—especially seafoods—with classically inspired dedication. Dining is definitely one of the signs of Miami's coming of age.

Highly recommended restaurants are indicated by a star ★.

Category	Cost*
Very Expensive	over $50
Expensive	$35–$50
Moderate	$20–$35
Inexpensive	under $20

per person, excluding drinks, service, and 6% sales tax

American
Downtown Miami
★

The Pavillon Grill. The mahogany, jade marble, and leather appointments of the restaurant's salon and dining room exude the conservative bias of an English private club. A guitarist plays, and the attentive staff serves regional American fare, including items that are low in calories, cholesterol, and sodium for diners on restricted diets. Specialties include veal loin with wild mushrooms in a shallot-cream sauce; grilled medallions of venison with roasted figs and cassis sauce; and duck in two acts—duck breast with caramelized apples, and grilled leg on greens. For dessert the restaurant features a gratin of berries perfumed with Cointreau in an almond-cream sauce. The menu changes often, but there's always an extensive wine list. *100 Chopin Plaza, tel. 305/577–1000, ext. 4494 or 4462. Reservations advised. Jacket required. AE, DC, MC, V. No lunch. Sun. brunch only, noon–3. Very Expensive.*

Kendall
(S.W. Suburb)

Shorty's Bar-B-Q. Shorty Allen opened his barbecue restaurant in 1951 in a log cabin, and this place has since become a tradition; a second location opened in 1989 in Davie, in southeast Broward County. Parents bring their teenage children here to show them where Mom and Dad ate on their honeymoon. Huge fans circulate fresh air through the single, screened dining room, where meals are served family-style at long picnic tables. On the walls hang an assortment of cowboy hats, horns, saddles, an ox yoke, and heads of boar and caribou. Specialties include barbecued pork ribs, chicken, and pork steak slow-cooked over hickory logs and drenched in Shorty's own warm, spicy sauce, and side orders of tangy baked beans with big chunks of pork, corn on the cob, and coleslaw. *9200 S. Dixie Hwy., tel. 305/665–5732; 5989 S. University Dr., Davie, tel. 305/680–9900. No reservations. Dress: casual. MC, V at Davie location. Closed Thanksgiving, Christmas. Inexpensive.*

Miami Beach

A Mano. Acclaimed Florida chef Norman Van Aken (formerly with Key West's Louie's Backyard) opened this intimate Deco District restaurant in 1991 and instantly made it one of southern Florida's finest dining establishments. When speaking of the tropical cuisine prepared here, Van Aken says it's "Old World methods with New World ingredients." Terra-cotta floor tiles and black-trimmed aqua chairs accent a mottled orange wall with black panels. *A mano* means "by hand," reflecting the tradition and philosophy of food preparation at the restaurant. For an appetizer consider the triple-decker blue-corn tortilla with grilled duck and such accoutrements as smoky chipotle mayonnaise and tropical-fruit chutney. On any given evening the menu may include spiny lobster tail stir-fry with wasabi, soba noodles, and a ginger-lemongrass-tamari vinaigrette, among other inspired offerings. A separate dessert menu offers such delectables as berry trifle, pecan-caramel tart, and "fallen" chocolate-cognac cake with passion-fruit chantilly. Nightly A Mano features two fixed-price menus and a "signature dishes" tasting menu. There's an extensive wine list with some expensive choices. *1440 Ocean Dr., in Betsy Ross Hotel, tel. 305/531–6266. Reservations advised. Dress: casual but neat. AE, DC, MC, V. Closed Mon. Expensive (special menus, Very Expensive).*

The News Cafe. This is the hippest joint on Ocean Drive. Owners Mark Soyka, who trained on the cosmopolitan beach scene in Tel Aviv, and Jeffrey Dispenzieri, from New York, are right on the money here with quick, friendly waiters and waitresses who don't hurry guests who have come to schmooze or intel-

lects deep in a Tolstoi novel picked out of the book rack. A raw
bar has been added in back with 15 stools, but most visitors
prefer sitting outside to feel the salt breeze and look at the
beach. Offering a little of this and a little of that—bagels,
pâtés, chocolate fondue—the News Cafe attracts a big all-the-
time crowd, with people coming in for a snack, light meal, or
aperitif and, invariably, to indulge in the people parade. *800
Ocean Dr., tel. 305/538–6397. No reservations. Dress: casual.
AE, DC, MC, V. Open 24 hrs. Inexpensive.*

North Miami Beach **Chef Allen's.** In this art-deco world of glass block, neon trim,
★ and fresh flowers, your gaze remains riveted on the kitchen.
Chef Allen Susser designed it with a picture window 25 feet
wide, so you can watch him create new American masterpieces
almost too pretty to eat. For an appetizer, try the red-hot curried mussels with colorful peppers and cellophane noodles, or
rock-shrimp hash with crisp boniato, smoked corn, and mango
ketchup; for a salad, try fire-roasted peppers and asparagus
with eggplant-caviar crusts. Entrées include truffle-crusted
wahoo with rock shrimp, tarragon, leeks, and red wine; and
honey-chilled roasted duck with stir-fried wild rice and green-
apple chutney. Recent dessert choices have included white-
chocolate macadamia-nut mousse bombe; pecan-apple pie tim-
bales with toffee-crunch ice cream; and mango tarte Tatin with
mango sorbet. You can order fine wines by the glass from a
wine bar. *19088 N.E. 29th Ave., tel. 305/935–2900. Reservations accepted. Dress: casual. AE, MC, V. Expensive.*

★ **Mark's Place.** Behind the adobe facade lies a stylish, deco-de-
tailed dining room; in the kitchen, owner-chef Mark Militello
cooks regional Florida fare in a special oak-burning oven imported from Genoa. The menu changes nightly, based on the
availability of fresh ingredients (many of the vegetables are or-
ganically grown by staffers), but typical selections include appetizers of grilled garlic-studded Portobello mushrooms with
tomato salad and herb oil; curry-fried fresh Florida farmed
oysters with tamarind-banana salsa and orange sour cream;
and fresh cracked Bahamian conch with black bean–mango relish and vanilla-rum butter. Among entrées try Cuban spice–
marinated free-range chicken grilled under a brick with vegetable paella and cumin vinaigrette, or grilled Florida swordfish
in tomato sauce with Spanish sherry, caper berries, and pimiento. For dessert there's warm apple tart with homemade
cinnamon ice cream and caramel sauce, or warm chocolate decadence with chocolate sorbet and blackberry *coulis* (puree).
*2286 N.E. 123rd St., North Miami, tel. 305/893–6888. Reserva-
tions advised. Dress: casual but neat. AE, DC, MC, V. No
weekend lunch. Closed Thanksgiving, Christmas. Expensive.*

West Dade **Shula's.** Surrounded by memorabilia of coach Don Shula's perfect 1972 season with the Miami Dolphins, you can drink or dine
in this shrine for the NFL-obsessed. The certified Black Angus
beef is almost an afterthought to the icons, which include quar-
terback Earl Morall's rocking chair, assistant coach Howard
Schnellenberger's pipe, and a playbook autographed by President Richard Nixon. The ladies room mirrors the Orange Bowl
locker room from which the magic took place, with pictures of
the beefy perfect-season squad. Otherwise it's steaks, prime
rib, and fish (including dolphin) in a woody, fireplace-cheered,
cedar-shingled setting. *15400 N.W. 77th Ave., Miami Lakes,
tel. 305/822–2324. Reservations advised. Dress: casual but
neat. AE, DC, MC, V. Moderate–Expensive.*

Miami Area Dining

N

O C E A N

MIAMI BEACH

NORTH MIAMI BEACH

NORTH MIAMI

Miami Gdns. Dr.

Beach Blvd.

Biscayne Blvd.

Broad Causeway

JFK Causeway

Julia Tuttle Causeway

Collins Ave.

Biscayne Blvd.

Florida's Turnpike

Palmetto Expwy

Miami Gdns. Dr.

Red Rd.

Graigny Rd.

Robert Frost Expwy.

Miami River

Okeechobee Rd.

Miami International

Dairy Rd.

N.E. 6th Ave.
N.E. 135th St.
N.E. 103d St.
N.E. 95th St.
N.W. 2nd Ave.
N. Miami Ave.
N.W. 7th Ave.
N.W. 27th Ave.
N.W. 135th Ave.
N.W. 8th Ave.
W. 4th Ave.
N.W. 72nd Ave.
N.W. 58th Ave.
N.W. 87th Ave.
N.W. 39th St.
N.W. 20th St.
N.W. 36th St.
N.W. 54th St.
N.W. 62nd St.
N.W. 79th St.
N.W. 95th St.
N.W. 103rd St.
E. 25th St.
E. 49th St.
W. 49th St.
Hialeah Dr.

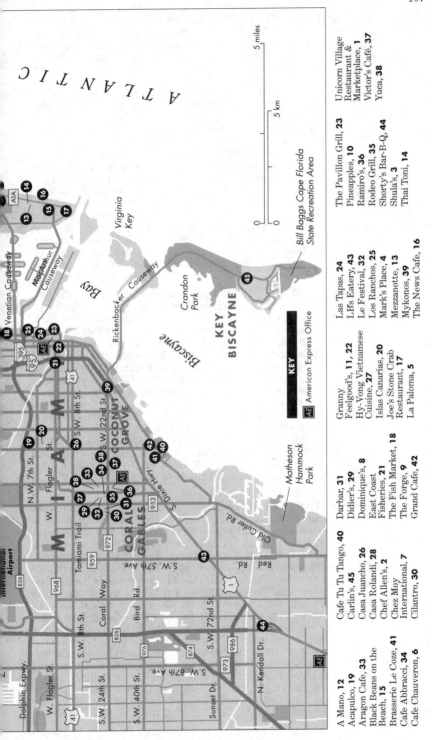

ATLANTIC

Venetian Causeway

MacArthur Causeway

Bay

Virginia Key

Rickenbacker Causeway

Crandon Park

Biscayne

KEY BISCAYNE

Matheson Hammock Park

Bill Baggs Cape Florida State Recreation Area

KEY

AE American Express Office

International Airport

Dolphin Expwy.

W. Flagler St.

S.W. 8th St.

S.W. 24th St.

S.W. 40th St.

Coral Way

Bird Rd.

Sunset Dr.

S.W. 87th Ave.

S.W. 72nd St.

N. Kendall Dr.

MIAMI

CORAL GABLES

COCONUT GROVE

Tamiami Trail

Red Rd.

Old Cutler Rd.

S. Dixie Hwy.

S.W. 57th Ave.

N.W. 7th St.

W. Flagler St.

S.W. 22nd St.

S.W. 8th St.

5 miles

5 km

A Mano, **12**
Acapulco, **19**
Aragon Cafe, **33**
Black Beans on the Beach, **15**
Brasserie Le Coze, **41**
Cafe Abbracci, **34**
Cafe Chauveron, **6**

Cafe Tu Tu Tango, **40**
Carlin's, **45**
Casa Juancho, **26**
Casa Rolandi, **28**
Chef Allen's, **2**
Chez Moy International, **7**
Cilantro, **30**

Darbar, **31**
Didier's, **29**
Dominique's, **8**
East Coast Fisheries, **21**
The Fish Market, **18**
The Forge, **9**
Grand Cafe, **42**

Granny Feelgood's, **11, 22**
Hy-Vong Vietnamese Cuisine, **27**
Islas Canarias, **20**
Joe's Stone Crab Restaurant, **17**
La Paloma, **5**

Las Tapas, **24**
LB's Eatery, **43**
Le Festival, **32**
Los Ranchos, **25**
Mark's Place, **4**
Mezzanotte, **13**
Mykonos, **39**
The News Cafe, **16**

The Pavillon Grill, **23**
Pineapples, **10**
Ramiro's, **36**
Rodeo Grill, **35**
Shorty's Bar-B-Q, **44**
Shula's, **3**
Thai Toni, **14**

Unicorn Village Restaurant & Marketplace, **1**
Victor's Café, **37**
Yuca, **38**

Brazilian   **Rodeo Grill.** Skewers aloft, waiters at the imaginative Rodeo
Coral Gables   Grill race about (just hope they don't trip), ready to carve off
hunks and slices of 10 kinds of meats. The philosophy at this
novel 180-seat restaurant in the heart of downtown Coral Gables seems to be "Eat 'til you drop." The idea comes from
rodizio, a Portuguese word referring to a continuous feed—
"rodeo" is an easy-to-pronounce corruption that makes you
think "meat"—and in southern Brazil, where they're big meat
eaters, that means beef ribs, chicken, lamb, London broil,
pork, sausage, and turkey, with sides of rice, potatoes, fried
yucca, and a big salad bar. If you have room for dessert you
might want to split an order of *quindim*, a cake-and-custard
combination made with coconuts and eggs. Restaurateur Tito
Valiente, a native of São Paulo and former owner of the largest
electronics store on Flagler Street, and his wife, Teresa, have
made the Rodeo Grill a great favorite among the 40,000 Brazilians who live in Dade County, as well as with other locals and
hordes of visiting Brazilians. The dining room is filled with
mostly whimsical Brazilian art, much of it for sale. *2121 Ponce
de Leon Blvd., tel. 305/447–6336. Weekend reservations advised. Dress: casual but neat. AE, D, DC, MC, V. Closed Sun.
Moderate.*

Continental   **Grand Cafe.** Understated elegance at all hours is the hall-
Coconut Grove   mark—a bilevel room with pink tablecloths and floral bou-
★   quets, sunbathed by day, dim and intimate after dark.
Japanese-born, French-trained executive chef Katsuo Sugiura
creates international cuisine (the menu theme changes every
six weeks: Look for special Brazilian, Caribbean, Cajun, and
Oriental specialties), combining ingredients from all over the
world in pleasing presentations that intrigue the palate. Specialties include black linguine (colored with squid ink); fresh
smoked salmon; a superbly rich she-crab soup with roe, sherry,
and cayenne pepper; "boned" Maine lobster meat presented in
the shape of a lobster, with artichokes and a cream sauce of vermouth and saffron. Dessert specialties include a white-choco-
late-and-pistachio mousse with blackberry sauce and
Beaujolais essence. *2669 S. Bayshore Dr., tel. 305/858–9600.
Reservations advised. Jacket advised. AE, DC, MC, V. Very
Expensive.*

Coral Gables   **Aragon Cafe.** If George Merrick, the founder of Coral Gables,
entered the bar of Aragon Cafe, he would see on display some of
his mother's hand-painted china and silver. In this restaurant
designed to look old and classy, subdued lighting emanates
from gaslight-style chandeliers and etched-glass wall sconces.
The menu now emphasizes lighter fare as well as fresh Florida
seafoods, although it still reflects Merrick's desire to re-create
the best of the Mediterranean in a Florida setting. Specialties
include salmon seared in soy sauce, with crab-and-arugula
spring roll, wood-ear mushrooms, and pickled ginger; grilled
Caribbean swordfish and scallops with caramelized plantains
and mango-curry sauce; and grilled veal chop with ricotta and
eggplant timbale and tomato-marsala sauce. Dessert offerings
include a baked apple tart with pecans, vanilla ice cream, and
caramel sauce; and a semisweet chocolate–almond terrine with
mocha sabayon. *180 Aragon Ave., in Colonnade Hotel, tel. 305/
448–9966. Reservations advised. Jacket required. Free valet
parking. AE, DC, MC, V. No Sat. lunch. Closed Sun. Expensive.*

★ **Ramiro's Restaurant.** This bright, gardenlike place doesn't depend on moody effects but rather on superb cuisine to satisfy guests. Maybe it's bright, too, because 30-year-old chef–part owner Benito del Cueto hails from sunny Puerto Rico. His presentations are delicate and brilliant, drawing imaginatively on fruits and vegetables. Appetizers, for example, may include a salad of organic lettuces with a raspberry vinaigrette, a grouper-and-shrimp seviche on pesto painting, or fresh green asparagus on a gratiné of natural tomato sauce. His dolphin entrée is prepared with a sauce of capers and tamarinds, the snapper with papaya, the beef tenderloin with a plum-Armagnac sauce, and the duck with a potato bird's nest on a sauce of port and raisins. For dessert, sherbets are served in a pastry cone with fruits of the day, mango is caramelized on puff pastry, and there's a five-milks flan with coconut. *2700 Ponce de Leon Blvd., tel. 305/443–7605 or 305/443–7607. Reservations advised. Dress: casual but neat. AE, DC, MC, V. No weekend lunch. Closed Thanksgiving, Christmas Eve. Expensive.*

Miami Beach **The Forge.** Miraculously reopened in late 1991 after a devastating fire, the Forge has in fact gained something: improved intimacy. The number of seats has been reduced to 175 through the loss of several rooms, which may reopen in time. This landmark (often compared to a museum) still stands behind a facade of 19th-century Parisian mansions, where an authentic forge once stood. Each of the intimate dining salons has its own historical artifacts, including a 250-year-old chandelier that hung in James Madison's White House. A fully stocked wine cellar contains an inventory of 380,000 bottles—including more than 500 dating from 1822 (and costing as much as $35,000) and recorked in 1989 by experts from Domaines Barons de Rothschild. Specialties include Norwegian salmon served over fresh garden vegetables with spinach vinaigrette; veal tenderloin roasted Tuscan-style over oak wood and marinated with fresh blackberries; and free-range Wisconsin duck roasted with black currants. Desserts are extravagant; try the famous blacksmith pie. *432 Arthur Godfrey Rd., tel. 305/538–8533. Reservations advised. Dress: casual but neat. AE, DC, MC, V. No lunch. Expensive.*

North Miami **La Paloma.** This fine Swiss Continental restaurant offers a total sensory experience: fine food, impeccable service, and the ambience of an art museum. In sideboards and cases throughout, owners Werner and Maria Staub display ornate European antiques they have spent decades collecting. The treasures include Baccarat crystal, Limoges china, Meissen porcelain, and Sèvres clocks. The staff speaks Spanish, French, German, Portuguese, and Arabic. Specialties include fresh local fish and seafood: Norwegian salmon Caroline (poached and served on a bed of spinach with hollandaise sauce); Wiener schnitzel; lamb chops à la *diable* (coated with bread crumbs, mustard, garlic, and herbs); veal chop with morel sauce; chateaubriand; and, for dessert, passion-fruit sorbet and kiwi soufflé with raspberry sauce. *10999 Biscayne Blvd., tel. 305/891–0505. Reservations advised. Jacket advised. AE, MC, V. No lunch. Closed Mon., July, part of Aug. Expensive.*

Cuban
Coral Gables
★
Yuca. This celebrity-favored Cuban eatery (Robert DeNiro, Carolina Herrera, Itzhak Perlman, Paloma Picasso, and Wolfgang Puck have eaten here) is chicly designed with track lighting, blond wood, tiles, and art prints. The cuisine, too, is

colorful, presented by chef Douglas Rodriguez, who takes advantage of the tropical foods available in Miami. Entrées include plantain-coated dolphin with tamarind tartar sauce, braised oxtail in a fiery La Mancha wine sauce, and barbecued baby ribs in a spicy guava sauce. Featured desserts include classic Cuban rice pudding in an almond basket. *177 Giralda Ave., tel. 305/444–4448. Reservations required. Dress: casual but neat. AE, DC, MC, V. No weekend lunch. Closed Thanksgiving, Christmas, New Year's Day. Expensive.*

Little Havana **Victor's Cafe.** This big, popular up-market restaurant draws its inspiration from the traditional Cuban *casona*, the great house of colonial Cuba. The mood is old Havana, with Cuban art and antiques, high ceilings, and a glassed-covered fountain courtyard. Owner Victor del Corral, who emigrated from Cuba in 1957, first made his mark in Manhattan before branching out to Miami. Now he works with his daughter Sonia Zaldivar and her son Luis. Come on Friday afternoon, when the *tapas* (hors d'oeuvres) bar is packed tightly as an airport on a holiday weekend, and lunch often lasts through dusk, in true Cuban fashion. The food is filling, well seasoned (although not peppery hot), and makes much use of traditional foods, including many root crops. Portions are immense, and all entrées are accompanied by rice and black beans. You could make a meal on the hot appetizers, such as a puff pastry filled with aromatically herbed lump crabmeat, or a savory cassava turnover filled with Florida lobster. An exceptional entrée is the red-snapper fillet "Miralda," marinated in bitter orange juice and garlic, sautéed in olive oil, and served over strips of fire-roasted pimientos, green peppers, and scallions; truly jumbo shrimp are served with yam quenelles in a creamy champagne sauce sprinkled with salmon roe. Very sentimental, romantic music is played nightly. *2430 SW 32nd Ave., tel. 305/445–1313. Reservations advised. Dress: casual but neat. AE, DC, MC, V. Moderate–Expensive.*

Islas Canarias. Since 1976 this has been a gathering place for Cuban poets, pop-music stars, and media personalities. Wall murals depict a Canary Islands street scene (the owners, the Garcia family, come from Tenerife). The menu includes such Canary Islands dishes as baked lamb, ham hocks with boiled potatoes, and tortilla *Española* (Spanish omelet with onions and chorizo), as well as Cuban standards including palomilla steak and fried kingfish. Don't miss the three superb varieties of homemade chips—potato, malanga, and plantain. Islas Canarias has another location in Westchester. *285 N.W. Unity Blvd. (N.W. 27th Ave.), tel. 305/649–0440; Coral Way and S.W. 137th Ave., Westchester, tel. 305/559–6666. No reservations. Dress: casual. No credit cards. Closes at 6 on Christmas and New Year's eves. Inexpensive.*

Family Style **LB's Eatery.** Town and gown meet at this sprout-laden haven a
Coral Gables half block from the University of Miami's baseball stadium. Kitschy food-related posters cover the walls of this relaxed restaurant with low prices. There are no waiters: You order at the counter, and pick up your food when called. Vegetarians thrive on LB's salads and daily meatless entrées, such as lasagna and moussaka. The place is famous for Saturday-night lobster—if you plan to come after 8, call ahead to reserve a lobster. Other specialties include barbecued baby-back ribs, lime chicken, croissant sandwiches, and carrot cake. *5813 Ponce de León*

Blvd., tel. 305/661–7091. No reservations. Dress: casual. D, MC, V. Closed Sun., major holidays. Inexpensive.

French Brasserie Le Coze. A tricolor flag flies out front, where tables
Coconut Grove line the sidewalk; art-nouveau and brass stylings within recre-
★ ate the essence of a stylish French brasserie on a quiet, leafy, two-block street just behind the Cocowalk hubbub. At this notable extension of the famed Le Bernardin restaurant run by Maguy LeCoze and her brother in Manhattan, you'll find topnotch bistro fare, the food the French think of as home cooking but Americans hope for only when dining out. Appetizers include sausages, ham, and pâté; and besides traditional endive-and-Roquefort salad you'll find imaginative new offerings like a shrimp–and–bean sprout salad with cashews in a ginger-soy vinaigrette. Main courses include melt-in-your-mouth roasted flakes of monkfish on savoy cabbage, and a stewy beef bourguignonne with buttery linguine. For dessert, choose among sorbets and ice creams, crepes, and a Rothschild-rich chocolate cake. *2901 Florida Ave., tel. 305/444–9697. Reservations accepted. Dress: casual but neat. AE, DC, MC, V. Closed Mon., Thanksgiving, and New Year's Day. Moderate–Expensive.*

Coral Gables Didier's. The atmosphere here is pure Provence: white walls,
★ beautiful paintings of the Côte d'Azur, terra-cotta tiles with painted inserts, big bouquets of fresh flowers, white-lace curtains, and straw-bottom chairs. Owner Didier Collongette, who hails from Burgundy via Cannes and Paris, opened this spot on his own after working for five years with New York nightclub owner Regine. All meals start with a mini baguette served warm and yeasty; the classic choices from then on include foie gras, bouillabaise, *coquilles St. Jacques* (scallops), *côtes de veau* (grilled veal chop) flamed with calvados, green peppercorn-grilled sirloin, and roasted rack of lamb. Fish preparations are tender and flaky—a tiptoe-delicate basil on the salmon, the tuna with an equally restrained mango sauce. Desserts? All the French favorites: *crème brulée* (caramel custard), tarte Tatin, and crepes suzette. The wine list is extensive, too. *325 Alcazar Ave., tel. 305/448–0312. Reservations advised. Dress: casual but neat. AE, DC, MC, V. Closed Sun., Thanksgiving, New Year's Day. Expensive.*

Le Festival. The modest canopied entrance to this classical French restaurant understates the elegance within. The decor includes etched-glass filigree mirrors and light pink walls. Appetizers of salmon mousse, baked oysters with garlic butter, and lobster in champagne sauce *en croute* (in pastry) lead the way for special entrées such as rack of lamb for two and medallions of veal with two sauces—a pungent, creamy lime sauce and a dark port-wine sauce with mushrooms. Dinners come with real french-fried potatoes. Don't pass up dessert here; the mousses and soufflés are positively decadent. The wine list includes 100 selections, about a third of them priced less than $30. *2120 Salzedo St., tel. 305/442–8545. Reservations required for dinner and for lunch parties of 5 or more. Dress: casual but neat. AE, DC, MC, V. No weekend lunch. Closed Sun. and Sept.–Oct. Expensive.*

Miami Beach Dominique's. Woodwork and mirrors from a Vanderbilt home
★ and other demolished New York mansions create an intimate setting for a unique nouvelle-cuisine experience in either of two enclosed patios, both glass-sided for views of the ocean. Spe-

cialties include exotic appetizers such as buffalo sausage, sautéed alligator tail, and rattlesnake-meat salad; entrées such as rack of lamb (which accounts for 35% of the restaurant's total sales) and fresh seafood; and an extensive wine list. The restaurant also serves brunch on Sunday. *Alexander Hotel, 5225 Collins Ave., tel. 305/865-6500 or 800/327-6121. Reservations advised. Jacket advised. AE, DC, MC, V. Very Expensive.*

★ **Cafe Chauveron.** After a lapse of service, this café again reigns as doyen of traditional French cuisine in Miami. The international clientele is personally tended by an attentive, multilingual staff. Stellar chef Jean-Claude Plihon offers Escoffier cookery with a nouvelle presentation in a setting that overlooks Indian Creek. Consider as an appetizer the crab cake with chives, cayenne, saffron, and a touch of garlic in lobster sauce. A *feuilleté* of lobster is elegant in its pastry shell. The broiled pheasant with truffle and goose-liver pâté is flambéed with cognac and served with fried potato slivers filled with inoke and chanterelle mushrooms. The bouillabaisse is suffused with saffron in an herbed fish stock and includes mussels, scallops, lobster, clams, and shrimp. For dessert, indulge in a Grand Marnier soufflé served with raspberry, chocolate, and custard sauce. *9561 E. Bay Harbor Dr., tel. 305/866-8779. Reservations advised. Jacket required. AE, DC, MC, V. Closed June–Sept. Expensive.*

Greek
Southwest Miami

Mykonos. This family restaurant has served typical Greek fare since 1974. There's a lovely mural of the Aegean outside; inside, the 74-seat dining room is painted a smart blue and white and adorned with Greek travel posters. Specialties include gyro, moussaka, marinated lamb and chicken, calamari and octopus sautéed in wine and onions, and sumptuous Greek salads thick with feta cheese and briny olives. *1201 Coral Way, tel. 305/856-3140. Dinner reservations accepted. Dress: casual. AE, MC, V. No Sun. lunch. Closed July 4, Thanksgiving, Christmas Eve, New Year's Eve, New Year's Day. Inexpensive.*

Haitian
Little Haiti

Chez Moy International. Seating is outside on a shaded patio or in a pleasant room with oak tables and high-back chairs. Specialties include *grillot* (pork boiled then fried with spices), fried or boiled fish, stewed goat, and conch with garlic and hot pepper. Try a tropical fruit drink such as sweet sop (also called *anon* or *cachiman*) or sour sop (also called *guanabana* or *corrosol*) blended with milk and sugar, and sweet-potato pie for dessert. *1 N.W. 54th St., tel. 305/757-5056. Reservations accepted. Dress: casual. No smoking. No credit cards. Inexpensive.*

Indian
Coral Gables
★

Darbar. Owner Bobby Puri's impeccably arranged Darbar is the glory of Miami's Indian restaurants. Although it's small, Darbar (Punjabi for "Royal Court") reigns with authenticity, down to the portraits of turbaned Puri ancestors, including kings and princes. Flavors rise as if in a dance from the *bangan bharta*, a dish of eggplant skinned and mashed with onions, tomatoes, herbs, and spices and baked in a tandoor. The limited menu's focus is on northern Indian or frontier cuisine, although there are also curries from different regions and *biryani* specialties prepared with basmati rice and garnished with boiled egg, tomato, nuts, and raisins. Among the northern Indian and Khyber Pass specialties you'll find various kebabs, tandoori platters, and *tikkas*—pieces of chicken or lamb marinated in yogurt and spices and cooked tandoori style. Everything, including the unusual Indian breads, is cooked to order. In the early evening you'll hear *santoor* (a stringed instrument) music. *276 Alhambra Circle, tel. 305/448–9691; 11099 Biscayne Blvd., Miami, tel. 305/895–8345. Reservations advised. Dress: casual but neat. AE, DC, MC, V. Closed Sun., major holidays. Moderate.*

Italian **Cafe Abbracci.** Owner Nino Pernetti now has two standout res-
Coral Gables taurants in the Gables, this and **Caffe Baci** (which serves more traditional Italian food). Although the kitchen closes at about 11 or midnight, the last wave of customers—usually Brazilians—is still partying to the flamenco or salsa music on weekends at 2 in the morning. The setting is graciously deco, with huge bursts of flowers, frosted glass, gallery lighting, and fresh roses on white linens; lights above each table are on individual dimmers. After the cold and hot antipasti—various carpaccios, porcini mushrooms, calamari, grilled goat cheese, shrimps, mussels—come festive entrées. Most of the pasta is made fresh on the premises, so consider ordering sample portions of two or three, maybe with pesto sauce, Gorgonzola, and fresh tomatoes. The *agnolotti al burro e salvia* are pasta pockets filled with ricotta cheese and spinach; the *tortelloni rossi verdi* are green and red pastas filled with veal and asparagus and veiled in a lavish Gorgonzola-and-basil sauce. The tuna carpaccio surrounded with cracked peppers comes seared in olive oil; the grilled swordfish is marinated in balsamic vinegar, rosemary, lemon zest, and olive oil. A pounded veal chop—*costoletta tricolore*—is to die for, grilled and crowned with marinated tomatoes, radicchio, and arugula. Room for dessert? The little Napoleons are made here daily, as is the tiramisu, and there's always a choice of fresh fruit tarts. *318 Aragon Ave., tel. 305/441–0700. Reservations required. Dress: casual but neat. AE, DC, MC, V. No weekend lunch. Moderate–Expensive.*

Key Biscayne **Carlin's.** You wouldn't expect in a shopping center anything so evocative as this wonderful dining room, made more wonderful late in 1992 when chef Fabio Rolandi came to perform his kitchen magic. Carlin is Carlos Semsch, longtime operator of La Rosa Nautica in the Miraflores section of Lima, Peru. Here he has reproduced an Old World memory with terra-cotta floors, rosy chintz drapes, brass chandeliers, lots of dried flowers, hunting prints, and stained glass, all under open beams that rise nearly as high as a lighthouse. The menu features Swiss and northern Italian favorites: half a dozen pastas, including *papardelle al funghi porcini* (sauteed porcini with rosemary and white wine and a scent of truffles), risottos, grills that include *paillard de vitello Key Biscayne* (thin slices of veal with tomato, arugula, radicchio, romaine, and Boston lettuces, served with olive oil, raspberry vinegar, salt, pepper, and lime), and fish courses such as dolphin with blueberries, green onions, wine, and herbs. Very popular here is the $7.95 all-you-can-eat weekday buffet lunch, which includes dessert. There is a disco upstairs Thursday–Saturday nights. *320 Crandon Blvd., tel. 305/361–8877. Reservations accepted. Dress: casual but neat. AE, DC, MC, V. No Sat. lunch. Moderate.*

Miami Beach **Mezzanotte.** Chic but not intimate, this restaurant is noted for fine food at moderate prices. Among the entrées is *zuppe nettuno* (fish, octopus, squid, and crab served with angel-hair pasta). The *spiedano Romano* includes sautéed porcini mushrooms under melted fontina cheese in a white-wine sauce and capers with mustard and garlic served over bread. Mezzanotte is known for its pastas, especially the capellini *prima vera* (with vegetables) and for its veal dishes, including *piccata* (prepared with lemon-butter sauce and roasted peppers), *lombata* (lightly breaded with radicchio, endive, tomatoes, and onions), and six scaloppines. *1200 Washington Ave., tel. 305/673–4343. Reservations accepted for 5 or more. Dress: casual but neat. AE, DC, MC, V. No lunch. Moderate.*

Latin
Coconut Grove
Cafe Tu Tu Tango. Brilliant local artists such as William DeLaVega set up their easels in the rococo-modern arcades of this eclectic, imaginative café-lounge on the second story of the highly popular Cocowalk. Throngs of people frequent this place to savor the frittatas, cosas frías, and empanadas. Hot recorded jazz sets the mood, and you can sit indoors or out; the latter offers some of the best people-watching in the South. Beneath ceiling fans in the oak-floored dining room, guests at the more than 250 seats graze on chips, dips, breads, and spreads. House specials include crusted tempura-like "fritangas" of ham and crabmeat, and *boniato relleno* (white sweet tubers stuffed with picadillo). A few wines are available, none of which costs too much. Don't miss this place. *3015 Grand Ave. (Cocowalk), tel. 305/529–2222. No reservations. Dress: casual but neat. AE, DC, MC, V. Closed Christmas. Moderate.*

Mexican
Little Havana
Acapulco. Authentic Mexican cuisine is served here by Cuban-born Haydee Ruiz, who was raised in New York City and is married to a Mexican. The intimate 70-seat dining room has adobe walls, wood beams, tabletops of Mexican tiles, and sombreros on the walls. As soon as you sit down a waiter descends on you with a free, ample supply of *totopos*, homemade corn chips served hot and crunchy, salt free, with a fiery *pico de gallo* sauce. Specialties include rich, chunky guacamole; *carnitas asadas* (marinated pork chunks in lemon-butter sauce); *mole poblano* (chicken in chocolate sauce); shrimp and rice in cherry-wine sauce; and fajitas and shrimps Cancun with whipping cream, garlic, and cilantro. *727 N.W. Unity Blvd. (N.W. 27th Ave.), tel. 305/642–6961. Weekend reservations advised. Dress: casual. AE, DC, MC, V. Moderate.*

Natural
Downtown Miami
Granny Feelgood's. "Granny" is a shrewd gentleman named Irving Field, who caters to health-conscious lawyers, office workers, and cruise-ship crews in two downtown locations. Since 1989 Jack Osman has owned the original Granny's and, with Field, he plans to franchise locations outside Miami. Specialties include chicken salad with raisins, apples, and cinnamon; spinach fettuccine with pine nuts; grilled tofu; apple crumb cake; and carrot cake. *190 S.E. 1st Ave., tel. 305/358–6233; 111 N.W. 1st St., tel. 305/579–2104; 647 Lincoln Road Mall, Miami Beach, tel. 305/672–3606. No reservations. Dress: casual. No smoking. AE, MC, V. Closed Sun. Inexpensive.*

Miami Beach
Pineapples. Art-deco pink pervades this health-food store and restaurant. Specialties include Chinese egg rolls; lasagna filled with tofu and mushrooms; spinach fettuccine with feta cheese, fresh garlic, walnuts, and cream sauce; and salads with full-flavored Italian-style dressing. *530 Arthur Godfrey Rd., tel. 305/532–9731. No reservations. Dress: casual. No smoking. AE, MC, V. Closed Rosh Hashanah, Yom Kippur. Moderate.*

North Miami Beach ★ **Unicorn Village Restaurant & Marketplace.** Far and away the top choice in its field in the north end of the city, this 300-seat restaurant, now in its 14th year, caters to vegetarian and nonvegetarian diners. In an outdoor setting of free-form ponds and fountains by a bayfront dock, or in the plant-filled interior under three-story-high wood-beam ceilings, guests enjoy spinach lasagna; a Tuscan vegetable sauté with Italian seasonings; grilled honey-mustard chicken; wok-barbecued shrimp; spicy seafood cakes; fresh fish, poultry, and Coleman natural beef; and the Unicorn's spring roll of uncooked veggies wrapped in thin rice paper with cellophane noodles. The adjacent 16,000-square-foot food market is the largest natural-foods source in Florida and features desserts baked on premises. *3565 N.E. 207th St., tel. 305/933–8829. No reservations. Dress: casual. No smoking. MC, V. Moderate.*

Nicaraguan
Downtown Miami **Los Ranchos.** Carlos Somoza, owner of this beautiful bayside establishment, is a nephew of Nicaragua's late president Anastasio Somoza. Carlos, who came to south Florida in 1979, sustains a tradition begun 30 years ago in Managua, when the original Los Ranchos instilled in Nicaraguan palates a love of Argentine-style beef—lean, grass-fed tenderloin with *chimichurri*, a green sauce of chopped parsley, garlic, oil, vinegar, and other spices. Nicaragua's own sauces are a tomato-base marinara and the fiery *cebollitas encurtidas*, with slices of jalapeño pepper and onion pickled in vinegar. Specialties include chorizo, *cuajada con maduro* (skim cheese with fried bananas), and shrimp sautéed in butter and topped with creamy jalapeño sauce. There is live entertainment at lunch and dinner. *Bayside Marketplace, 401 Biscayne Blvd., tel. 305/375–8188 or 305/375–0666; 125 S.W. 107th Ave., Little Managua, tel. 305/221–9367; Kendall Town & Country, 8505 Mills Drive, Miami, tel. 305/596–5353; The Falls Shopping Center, 8888 S.W. 136th St., Suite 303, Miami. Reservations advised. Dress: casual. AE, DC, MC, V. Closed Good Friday, Christmas Eve, New Year's Day. Moderate.*

Seafood
Downtown Miami **The Fish Market.** Tucked away in a corner of the Omni International Hotel's lobby, this fine restaurant has a kitchen staff fluent in seafood's complexities. The menu changes with the availability of fresh fish, fruits, and vegetables, but typical items include sautéed Florida grouper on marinated eggplant, sesame-roasted red snapper with buckwheat pasta and soy broth, and seared medallion of salmon on fresh spinach with ginger-spiced cream. The chocolate-pecan tart and pistachio-chocolate terrine with orange-cream sauce are two of the featured desserts. *Biscayne Blvd. at 16th St., tel. 305/374–0000. Reservations advised. Jacket advised. Free valet parking. AE, DC, MC, V. No Sat. lunch. Closed Sun. Moderate–Expensive.*
East Coast Fisheries. This family-owned restaurant and retail fish market on the Miami River features fresh Florida seafood from its own 38-boat fleet in the Keys. From tables along the second-floor balcony, watch the cooks prepare your dinner in the open kitchen below. Specialties include a complimentary fish-pâté appetizer, blackened pompano with owner David Swartz's personal herb-and-spice recipe, lightly breaded fried grouper, and a homemade Key lime pie so rich it tastes like ice cream. *360 W. Flagler St., tel. 305/373–5515. Reservations accepted for parties of 6 or more. Dress: casual. Beer and wine only. AE, MC, V. Moderate.*

Miami Beach   **Joe's Stone Crab Restaurant.** A south Florida tradition since 1913, Joe's is a family restaurant in its fourth generation. You go to wait, people-watch, and finally settle down to an ample à la carte menu. About a ton of stone-crab claws is served daily, with drawn butter, lemon wedges, and piquant mustard sauce (recipe available). Popular side orders include vinegary cole-slaw; salad with a brisk vinaigrette house dressing; creamed garlic spinach; french-fried onion rings, sweet potatoes, and eggplant; cheddar grilled tomatoes; and hash-brown potatoes. Save room for dessert—a slice of Key lime pie with graham-cracker crust and real whipped cream or apple pie with a crumb-pecan topping. To minimize the wait, come for lunch at 11:30, for dinner at 5 or after 9. *227 Biscayne St., tel. 305/673–0365; take-out orders and overnight shipping, tel. 800/780–2722. No reservations. Dress: casual; no T-shirts or tank tops. AE, D, DC, MC, V. Closed May 15–Oct. 15. Moderate.*

Southwestern   **Cilantro.** Owner-chef Cindy Rothman at one time was chef at
Coral Gables   Las Puertas, a kindred Mexican restaurant across the street. Here she hosts guests in a blue-and-white café setting of open galvanized pipe leavened by fanciful Western art. All guests are treated to blue corn chips with a pico de gallo sauce, and all meals are accompanied by seasoned rice (poblano peppers, corn, cheese, seasoned sour cream, diced onions, and cilantro) and beans cooked in Tecate beer. Top entrées include twin grilled medallions of filet mignon stuffed with roasted poblano chiles, onions, and cheese; blue-corn seafood enchiladas, with shrimp, scallops, and leeks in a mildly spiced tomato sauce; and duck-breast fajitas with flour tortillas, tomato relish, and gua-camole. For dessert, try tangy mango-and-lime cheesecake, co-conut flan, or crème brulée in a flour tortilla cup. Beers include Anchor Steam and the hard-to-find Rattlesnake Lager from New Orleans. *139 Giralda, tel. 305/444–6858. Reservations accepted. Dress: casual but neat. AE, DC, MC, V. No weekend lunch. Closed Mon., major holidays. Moderate.*

Spanish   **Las Tapas.** Overhung with dried meats and enormous show
Downtown Miami   breads, this popular spot offers a lot of imaginative creations. Tapas ("little dishes") give you a variety of tastes during a single meal. Specialties include *la tostada* (smoked salmon on melba toast, topped with a dollop of sour cream, baby eels, black caviar, capers, and chopped onion) and *pincho de pollo a la plancha* (grilled chicken brochette marinated in brandy and onions). Also available are soups, salads, sandwiches, and standard-size dinners. *Bayside Marketplace, 401 Biscayne Blvd., tel. 305/372–2737. Reservations required for large parties. Dress: casual. AE, DC, MC, V. Moderate.*

Little Havana   **Casa Juancho.** A meeting place for the movers and shakers of
★   Miami's Cuban community, Casa Juancho serves a cross section of Spanish regional cuisines. The interior recalls old Castile: brown brick, rough-hewn dark timbers, and walls adorned with colorful Talavera platters. Strolling balladeers (universi-ty students from Spain) will serenade you. Specialties include *cochinillo Segoviano* (roast suckling pig) and *parrillada de mariscos* (fish, shrimps, squid, and scallops grilled in a light garlic sauce) from the Pontevedra region of northwest Spain. For dessert, the *crema Catalana* has a delectable crust of burnt caramel atop a rich pastry custard. The wine list includes fine labels from Spain's Rioja region. *2436 S.W. 8th St., tel. 305/642–2452. Reservations advised; not accepted after 8 Fri. and*

Sat. *Dress: casual but neat. AE, DC, MC, V. Closed Christmas Eve. Expensive.*

Miami Beach **Black Beans on the Beach.** This wonderful 72-seat restaurant has brought Latin swank to the Deco District food scene, and chef Marcelino has staked his claim in this somewhat seedy neighborhood. A big oil painting pays homage to Tenerife, where he cooked for years. The look is tropical deco—gorgeous sea greens with black trim and a touch of gold leaf, with tropical murals and sumptuous greenery. Some favorite dishes are cream of black bean soup; grilled palomilla steak; fried pork chunks; grilled beef with onions and garlic; and big stewy rice dishes for two, including paella Valenciana, *arroz con mariscos*—both with seafood—and oven-baked *arroz con pollo* (chicken with rice). For dessert, there's flan, guava shells with cream cheese, lemon pie, and anisette pastry cream topped with burned sugar. Dine inside or on the covered terrace. *635 Collins Ave., tel. 305/531-7111. Reservations accepted. Dress: casual but neat. AE, DC, MC, V. Moderate.*

Swiss/ **Casa Rolandi.** Italian art and two working brick ovens add a
Northern Italian warm feeling here. Among the tasty entrées you'll find
Coral Gables *agnolotti Fiorentina* (spinach pasta stuffed with ricotta cheese
★ and topped with tomato sauce and sage); *fusilli al pesto*, with pine nuts, parsley, basil, olive oil, Parmesan cheese, and a touch of cream; and *tortelloni de fonduta al sugo d'arrosto di vitello e tartufi* (homemade cheese tortelloni served with veal-juice demiglaze and pared white truffles). The snapper *livornesa*—a special, baked in the brick oven—comes with compote of green and yellow squash, radicchio, and parsley potatoes arranged on a plate shaped like a scallop shell. All meals come with a pita-style house bread baked with virgin olive oil. For dessert, the tiramisù is a winner. *1930 Ponce de León Blvd., tel. 305/444-2187. Reservations required. Dress: casual but neat. AE, DC, MC, V. No weekend lunch. Closed Thanksgiving, Christmas, New Year's Day. Expensive.*

Thai **Thai Toni.** Thai silks, bronze Buddhas, ceiling drapes, and two
Miami Beach raised platforms for guests who want to dine seated on cushions highlight this fine eatery. The mellow Thai Singha beer sets you up for the spicy grilled-squid appetizer or the vegetarian or pork *pad Thai* (rice noodles tossed with shrimp, egg, bean sprouts, and peanuts). Traditional entrées include hot-and-spicy deep-fried whole snapper garnished with basil leaves and mixed vegetables. Try the homemade lemonade. *890 Washington Ave., tel. 305/538-8424. Dress: casual but neat. AE, MC, V. No lunch. Moderate.*

Vietnamese **Hy-Vong Vietnamese Cuisine.** Beer-loving Kathy Manning has
Little Havana introduced a half-dozen top brews since taking over in 1989
★ (Double Grimbergen, Moretti, and Spaten, among them), and magic continues to pour forth from the tiny kitchen of this 36-seat restaurant. Come before 7 to avoid a wait. Specialties include spring rolls, a Vietnamese version of an egg roll, with ground pork, cellophane noodles, and black mushrooms wrapped in homemade rice paper; whole fish panfried with *nuoc man* (a garlic-lime fish sauce); and thinly sliced pork, barbecued with sesame seeds and fish sauce, served with bean sprouts, rice noodles, and slivers of carrots, almonds, and peanuts. *3458 S.W. 8th St., tel. 305/446-3674. Reservations accepted for 5 or more. Dress: casual. No smoking. No credit*

cards. *No lunch. Closed Mon., American and Vietnamese/ Chinese New Years, and 2 weeks in Aug. Inexpensive.*

Lodging

Few urban areas can match Greater Miami's diversity of hotel accommodations. The area has hundreds of hotels and motels with lodgings in all price categories, from $8 for a night in a dormitory-style hostel to $2,000 for a night in the luxurious presidential suite atop a posh downtown hotel. As recently as the 1960s many hotels in Greater Miami opened only in winter to accommodate Yankee snowbirds. Now all hotels stay open all year. In summer they cater to European and Latin American vacationers, who find Miami congenial despite the heat, humidity, and intense afternoon thunderstorms.

Although some hotels (especially on the mainland) have adopted year-round rates, many still adjust their rates to reflect the ebb and flow of seasonal demand. The peak occurs in winter, with only a slight dip in summer, when families with school-age children take vacation. You'll find the best values between Easter and Memorial Day (a delightful time in Miami but a difficult time for many people to travel) and in September and October (the height of hurricane season).

The list that follows is representative of the best hotels and motels, organized geographically. The rate categories in the list are based on the all-year or peak-season price; off-peak rates may be a category or two lower.

Highly recommended lodgings are indicated by a star ★.

Category	Cost*
Very Expensive	over $150
Expensive	$90–$150
Moderate	$60–$90
Inexpensive	under $60

All prices are for a standard double room, excluding 6% state sales tax and nominal tourist tax.

Coconut Grove
★ **Grand Bay Hotel.** This modern high rise overlooking Biscayne Bay features rooms with traditional furnishings and original art. The building's stepped facade, like a Maya pyramid, gives each room facing the bay a private terrace, but the best views come from rooms at the northeast corner, which look out on downtown Miami. Only slightly more special than most rooms is 814, Luciano Pavarotti's two-level suite with a baby-grand piano, circular staircase, and canopied king-size bed. You can rent it when he's not there. Most remarkable, however, is the meticulous attention the staff pays to guests' desires. *2669 S. Bayshore Dr., 33133, tel. 305/858–9600, fax 305/859–2026. 132 rooms with bath, including 20 nonsmoker rooms; 49 suites. Facilities: restaurant, lounge, poolside bar, afternoon tea, outdoor pool, hot tub, health club, saunas, masseur. AE, DC, MC, V. Very Expensive.*
Grove Isle. This luxurious mid-rise urban resort sits on a 26-acre island and adjoins equally posh condominium-apartment towers and a private club. Developer Martin Margulies dis-

plays selections from his extensive private art collection on the premises. The oversize rooms have patios, bay views, ceiling fans, and tropical decor with area rugs and Spanish tiles; the rooms with the most light and best view are 201–205. *4 Grove Isle Dr., 33133, tel. 305/858–8300. 40 rooms with bath, 9 suites. Facilities: restaurant, outdoor freshwater pool and whirlpool, 12 tennis courts, 85-slip marina, running track, in-room refreshment bar and coffee maker, free cable TV. AE, DC, MC, V. Very Expensive.*

Mayfair House. This European-style luxury hotel sits within an exclusive open-air shopping mall, Mayfair (*see* Tour 5: Coconut Grove in Exploring Miami, *above*). Public areas have Tiffany windows, polished mahogany, marble walls and floors, and imported ceramics and crystal. Also impressive is the glassed-in elevator that whisks you to the corridor on your floor; a balcony overlooks the mall's central fountains and walkways. All rooms are suites, with outdoor terraces facing the street, screened from view by vegetation and wood latticework. Each has a Japanese hot tub on the balcony or a Roman tub in the suite; otherwise, each room is individually furnished. The Sunset (Room 505) is one of 48 suites with antique pianos. Other luxury touches: All bathrooms have double sinks, makeup lights, and scales, and all closets are lighted. Some suites used to have nightclub noise, but the club has been closed—it got too much competition from Cocowalk across the street. *3000 Florida Ave., 33133, tel. 305/441–0000 or 800/433–4555, fax 305/447–9173. 181 suites, including 22 nonsmoker suites. Facilities: snack bar, rooftop recreation area with sauna, small outdoor freshwater swimming pool. AE, DC, MC, V. Very Expensive.*

Coral Gables

★ **The Biltmore Hotel.** This is Miami's grand boom-time hotel, one of a handful in Florida that recaptures an era of uncompromised elegance. Now part of the Westin chain, the Biltmore was built in 1926 as the centerpiece of George Merrick's "city beautiful," and it rises like a sienna-color wedding cake in the heart of the Coral Gables residential district. A golf course, tennis courts, and waterway surround the hotel. The lobby is spectacularly vaulted with hand-painted rafters on a background sky of twinkling blue; travertine marble, Oriental rugs, and palms in blue porcelain pots set the tone that continues through the fountain patio and opulent ballrooms. Guest rooms are spacious, completely modernized in a restrained Moorish style during the 1986 overhaul, when the hotel reopened after decades of neglect. *1200 Anastasia Ave., 33134, tel. 305/445–1926 or 800/445–2586, fax 305/442–9496. 240 rooms with bath, 35 suites. Facilities: restaurant, coffee shop, lounge, 18-hole championship golf course, 10 lighted tennis courts, health spa with sauna, pool. AE, DC, MC, V. Very Expensive.*

★ **The Colonnade Hotel.** The twin 13-story towers of this $65 million hotel, office, and shopping complex dominate the heart of Coral Gables. Architectural details echo the adjoining two-story Corinthian-style rotunda on Miracle Mile, from which 1920s developer George Merrick sold lots in his fledgling city. Merrick's family provided old photos, paintings, and other heirlooms that are on display throughout the hotel. The oversize rooms come in 26 floor plans, each with a sitting area, built-in armoires, and traditional furnishings of mahogany. The hospitality bars feature marble counters and gold-plated faucets with 1920s-style ceramic handles. The pool on a 10th-floor ter-

Miami Area Lodging

121

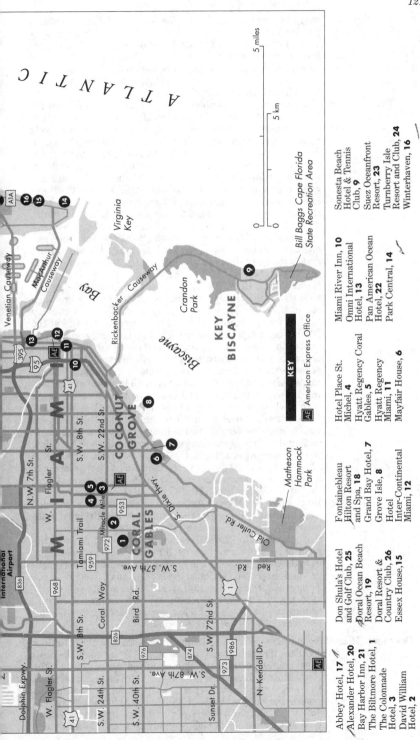

ATLANTIC

Bill Baggs Cape Florida
State Recreation Area

KEY

AE American Express Office

Abbey Hotel, **17**
Alexander Hotel, **20**
Bay Harbor Inn, **21**
The Biltmore Hotel, **1**
The Colonnade
Hotel, **3**
David William
Hotel, **2**

Don Shula's Hotel
and Golf Club, **25**
Doral Ocean Beach
Resort, **19**
Doral Resort &
Country Club, **26**
Essex House, **15**

Fontainebleau
Hilton Resort
and Spa, **18**
Grand Bay Hotel, **7**
Grove Isle, **8**
Hotel
Inter-Continental
Miami, **12**

Hotel Place St.
Michel, **4**
Hyatt Regency Coral
Gables, **5**
Hyatt Regency
Miami, **11**
Mayfair House, **6**

Miami River Inn, **10**
Omni International
Hotel, **13**
Pan American Ocean
Hotel, **22**
Park Central, **14**

Sonesta Beach
Hotel & Tennis
Club, **9**
Suez Oceanfront
Resort, **23**
Turnberry Isle
Resort and Club, **24**
Winterhaven, **16**

race looks south toward Biscayne Bay. Ask for a room with a private balcony. *180 Aragon Ave., 33134, tel. 305/441–2600 or 800/533–1337, fax 305/445–3929. 157 rooms, including 18 non-smoker rooms and 4 rooms for disabled guests; 17 bilevel suites. Facilities: 2 restaurants, outdoor heated pool and Jacuzzi with 2 saunas, Nautilus equipment, 24-hr room service. AE, DC, MC, V. Very Expensive.*

★ **Hyatt Regency Coral Gables.** Opened in 1987, this high-rise hotel patronized by business travelers is part of a megastructure that includes two office towers. The entire complex reflects Spanish Mediterranean architecture, with tile roofs, white-frame casement windows, and a pink-stucco exterior. The hotel's interior decor of pastels and antique-style furnishings gives a comfortable, residential feel to the public areas and guest rooms, in which all fabrics were replaced in 1993. Rooms have king-size beds and sofas. Rooms facing the pool are best; the worst face north toward the airport. *50 Alhambra Plaza, 33134, tel. 305/441–1234, fax 305/443–7702. 192 rooms with bath, including 60 nonsmoker rooms; 50 suites. Facilities: restaurant; lounge; 2 ballrooms; pool; outdoor whirlpool; health club with Nautilus equipment, LifeCycles, sauna, steam rooms. AE, DC, MC, V. Very Expensive.*

David William Hotel. Easily the most affordable of the top Gables hotels, the DW (as aficionados call it) was the first high rise of Miami's modern era, standing 13 stories tall with a distinctive waffled facade. That dates it from the 1960s, but the DW has been kept in top shape. The hotel is solidly built, like a fort, so the rooms are very private and very quiet. Guest rooms are large, with marble baths; all those facing south (the sunnier exposure) have balconies. Many rooms have kitchens. The decor features new furniture trimmed with braids of varicolored wood, upholstered in tan and blue. The lobby is a bit tacky, with newly installed tables outside the elegant Chez Vendôme, a popular traditional French restaurant. The excellent desk staff is more concerned with helping guests than with maintaining airs. Rooftop cabana guest rooms are the best bargains. *700 Biltmore Way, 33134, tel. 305/445–7821; outside FL, 800/327–8770; fax 305/445–5585. 150 rooms with bath, some with kitchens, some nonsmoker rooms. Facilities: restaurant, bar, rooftop freshwater pool. AE, DC, MC, V. Expensive.*

★ **Hotel Place St. Michel.** Art-nouveau chandeliers suspended from vaulted ceilings grace the public areas of this intimate jewel in the heart of downtown Coral Gables. The historic low-rise hotel, built in 1926 and restored 1981–86, is filled with the scent of fresh flowers, circulated by the paddle fans hanging from the ceilings. Each room has its own dimensions, personality, and imported antiques from England, Scotland, and France. *162 Alcazar Ave., 33134, tel. 305/444–1666 or 800/247–8526, fax 305/529-0074. 24 rooms with bath, 3 suites. Facilities: restaurant, lounge, snack shop, complimentary Continental breakfast. AE, DC, MC, V. Expensive.*

Downtown Miami
★ **Hotel Inter-Continental Miami.** Stand outside on the fifth-floor pool deck for the best view of downtown. You see only the clean upper stories of the city, nothing of the ragtag street—the view Miami likes best of itself, with its Disneyesque Metromover, the booming port, the beautiful bay. The marble grain in the lobby of this 34-story landmark matches that in *The Spindle*, a massive centerpiece sculpture by Henry Moore. With all that marble, the lobby could easily look like a mausole-

um—and did before the addition of palm trees, colorful umbrellas, and oversize wicker chairs and tables. Atop a five-story atrium, a skylight lets in the afternoon sun. *100 Chopin Plaza, 33131, tel. 305/577–1000 or 800/327–3005, fax 305/577–0384. 644 rooms with bath, including 48 nonsmoker rooms; 34 suites; corner rooms have extra-wide doors for the disabled. Facilities: 2 restaurants, lounge, outdoor heated pool, ¼-mile jogging track, in-room minibar. AE, DC, MC, V. Very Expensive.*

Hyatt Regency Miami. This centrally located, 24-story convention hotel adjoins the James L. Knight International Center (*see* Tour 2: Downtown Miami in Exploring Miami, *above*). Nestled beside the Brickell Avenue Bridge on the north bank of the Miami River, the Hyatt offers views of tugboats, freighters, and pleasure craft from its lower lobby. The best rooms are on the upper floors, facing east toward Biscayne Bay. *400 S.E. 2nd Ave., 33131, tel. 305/358–1234 or 800/233–1234, fax 305/358–0529. 615 rooms with bath, including 43 nonsmoker rooms and 17 rooms for the disabled; 25 suites. Facilities: 2 restaurants, lounge, outdoor freshwater pool, $10 admission to nearby Downtown Athletic Club, in-room safe, in-house pay-TV movies. AE, DC, MC, V. Very Expensive.*

Omni International Hotel. This 20-story hotel, built in 1977 but constantly updated, stands atop the 10½-acre multilevel Omni International Mall, which includes a J.C. Penney store, many specialty shops, a food court, Children's Workshop child-care center, and a hand-made Italian wood carousel. The lowest hotel floor is five stories up; rooms on upper floors have spectacular views of downtown Miami and Biscayne Bay. Many rooms feature a blue-and-tan color scheme and mahogany furniture. Direct covered access to the Metromover downtown-transportation system is expected to open in spring 1994. *1601 Biscayne Blvd., 33132, tel. 305/374–0000 or 800/843–6664, fax 305/374–0020. 535 rooms, including 25 nonsmoker rooms and 2 rooms for the disabled; 50 suites. Facilities: restaurant, bar, café, outdoor heated pool, access to nearby health club and spa. AE, DC, MC, V. Very Expensive.*

★ **Miami River Inn.** Preservationist Sallye Jude has restored this landmark property (the oldest continuously operating inn south of St. Augustine) as an oasis of country hospitality at the edge of downtown. It is a 10-minute walk across the 1st Street Bridge to the heart of the city and a few hundred feet from José Martí Park (one of the city's prettiest, although lately a haven for the homeless). The inn—dating to 1904—consists of five clapboard buildings that are the only concentration of houses remaining from that period. The inn offers 40 antiques-filled rooms, a room with breakfast area, small meeting space, outdoor pool and patio, and an oval lawn. As part of the same property—officially designated the Riverside Historic District—four modified-deco midcentury masonry buildings house long-term renters. The best rooms are second- and third-story river views with stunning vistas of the city. Avoid the tiny rooms in Building D that overlook the stark condo to the west. *118 S.W. S. River Dr., 33130, tel. 305/325–0045, fax 305/325–9227. 40 rooms, 39 with bath, some with tub only. Facilities: complimentary Continental breakfast, freshwater outdoor pool and heated Jacuzzi, use of refrigerator. Moderate.*

Key Biscayne **Sonesta Beach Hotel & Tennis Club.** Among the features of this ★ eight-story beachfront resort are displays of museum-quality modern art by prominent painters and sculptors. Don't miss

Andy Warhol's three drawings of rock star Mick Jagger in the hotel's disco bar, Desires. The best rooms, on the eighth floor, face the ocean. All guest rooms were completely refurbished in 1991 and 1992; this hotel was hard hit by Hurricane Andrew and was not expected to reopen before winter 1993. *350 Ocean Dr., 33149, tel. 305/361–2021 or 800/766–3782. 267 rooms with bath, 12 suites, 11 villas (3-, 4-, and 5-bedroom homes with full kitchen and screened pool). Facilities: 4 restaurants, snack bar, deli, lounge with live entertainment; 750-ft ocean beach; outdoor freshwater heated Olympic-size pool and whirlpool; water sports, including sailboarding; 10 tennis courts (3 lighted); health center with Jacuzzi, steam rooms, aerobic-dance floor, weight room, massage room, tanning room. AE, DC, MC, V. Very Expensive.*

Miami Beach
★ **Alexander Hotel.** Located amid the high rises of the mid-Beach district, this 16-story hotel represents the elegance for which the Beach was once famous, with immense suites furnished with antiques and reproductions, each with ocean or bay views. Everything is understated, from the landscaped lobby to the oceanfront dining rooms. *5225 Collins Ave., 33140, tel. 305/865–6500 or 800/327–6121, fax 305/864–8525. 212 1- and 2-bedroom suites with 2 baths and kitchen. Facilities: restaurant, coffee shop, ocean beach, 2 outdoor heated freshwater pools, 4 poolside Jacuzzis, spa, cabanas, Sunfishes and catamarans for rent, in-room minibars. AE, DC, MC, V. Very Expensive.*

★ **Doral Ocean Beach Resort.** Of the great Miami Beach hotels, this 18-story glass tower is the youngest—it opened in 1962. It's still a standout, with the only rooftop restaurant in town (Alfredo, the Original of Rome), the only rooftop ballroom (with 8,000 twinkling ceiling lights), two presidential suites designed in consultation with the Secret Service, an F.A.A.-licensed helipad, and the kind of service that's kept the Beach going through the years—waitresses call guests in the coffee shop "Honey" and declare anybody who comes in twice "my favorite customer." Some of the staff have worked here for 20 or 30 years, and the hotel remembers hospitality as it was before voice mail, when you could still get a bellhop. It's got all the amenities, from aqua sports when you want the sun, to lobby-level shops for when you want to be out of it. It's got meeting space, workout space, and disco space. The guest rooms are large, with tons of closet space and swagged drapes over soft curtains—tropical, but in calm foam-greens, blues, and peach; the regal bathrooms have blue-green tiles. Relish one of the best. *4833 Collins Ave., Miami Beach 33140, tel. 305/532–3600 or 800/223–6725, fax 305/534–7409. 293 rooms with bath, including 66 nonsmoker rooms and 4 rooms for the disabled; 127 suites. Facilities: 3 restaurants, 4 lounges, ocean beach with cabanas, water sports, Olympic-size swimming pool, 2 all-weather lighted tennis courts, Saturnia fitness center, free transportation to Doral Resort and Country Club, (see West Dade, below) and Doral Saturnia International Spa Resort (see Spa in Participant Sports, above). AE, DC, MC, V. Very Expensive.*

Fontainebleau Hilton Resort and Spa. The Miami area's foremost convention hotel has an opulent lobby with massive chandeliers, a sweeping staircase, and new meeting rooms in art-deco hues. There are always some rooms in the hotel that are under renovation; most recently completed in mid-1992, as part of a $10 million program, are 375 rooms in the north-tower building, which have been redone in Lifesavers colors and have new bathrooms. In 1993 all 60 suites were remodeled, including a wraparound ocean-view suite only slightly smaller than the state of Rhode Island. Decor in the different wings varies: you can request a '50s look or one that's contemporary. Even the smallest rooms are large. Upper-floor rooms in the Chateau Building have the best views. *4441 Collins Ave., 33140, tel. 305/ 538–2000, fax 305/673–5351. 1,206 rooms with bath, including 120 nonsmoker rooms and 2 rooms for the disabled; 60 suites. Facilities: 12 restaurants and 4 lounges, nightclub, ocean beach with 30 cabanas, 1 fresh- and 1 saltwater outdoor pool, marina, windsurfing, parasailing, Hobie Cats, volleyball, 3 whirlpool baths, 7 lighted tennis courts, health club with exercise classes, saunas, free children's activities. AE, DC, MC, V. Very Expensive.*

Pan American Ocean Hotel, A Radisson Resort. This beach hotel built in 1954 sits back from Collins Avenue behind a refreshing garden of coconut palms and seasonal flowers. It is easily the pick of the litter along the Sunny Isles strip. The most recent renovation of all guest rooms was completed in 1993. The best view is from Rooms 330, 332, and 333 on the third floor of the north wing, which overlooks the ocean. North- and south-facing rooms have only a sliver view of ocean or bay. *17875 Collins Ave., 33160, tel. 305/932–1100 or 800/327–5678, fax 305/ 935–2769. 138 rooms, including 10 for the disabled, 4 suites. Facilities: restaurant, coffee shop, bar, lounge, 400-ft ocean beach, outdoor heated pool, 4 hard-surface tennis courts, tennis pro and pro shop, 2 shuffleboard courts, 9-hole putting green, exercise room, volleyball, beauty salon, ping-pong room, video-game room, card room, free shuttle service to Bal Harbour and Aventura shopping malls, in-room minibars. AE, D, DC, MC, V. Very Expensive.*

Park Central. Across the street from the glorious beach, this seven-story Deco hotel—painted blue, with wraparound corner windows—makes all the right moves to stay in the forefront of the Art Deco revival. Most of the fashion models visiting town come to this property, which dates to 1937. Black-and-white photos of old beach scenes, hurricanes, and familiar faces attest to the hotel's longevity. Stylishly, rooms are decorated with Philippine mahogany furnishings—originals that have been restored. An Italian theme prevails, with the Barocco Beach restaurant and espresso served in the lobby. *640 Ocean Dr., 33139, tel. 305/538–1611, fax 305/534–7520. 85 rooms with bath. Facilities: restaurant, bar, espresso bar. AE, DC, MC, V. Expensive–Very Expensive.*

Essex House. This was one of the premier lodgings of the Art Deco era, now painted in cool pastel gray with sulphur-yellow trim. They got it right from the start: designed by architect Henry Hohauser, Everglades mural by Earl LaPan. Here are the ziggurat arches, the hieroglyph-style ironwork, etched-glass panels of flamingos under the palms, 5-foot rose-medallion Chinese urns. Hallways have recessed showcases with original Deco sculptures. The original 66 rooms from 1938 are now 41, plus two petite suites and six grand suites. Amenities include designer linens and towels, feather-and-down pillows and sofa rolls, and individually controlled air-conditioning and central heat plus ceiling fans. The rooms are soundproofed from within (otherwise unheard of in beach properties of the '30s), and rooms to the east have extra-thick windows to reduce the band noise from a nearby hotel. The smallest rooms are yellow-themed and face north. Best are the two-room ocean-view suites: 205, 208, 305, and 308. Continental breakfast is free. *1001 Collins Ave., 33139, tel. 305/534–2700 or 800/553–7739, fax 305/532–3827. 51 rooms with bath, 9 suites. Facilities: breakfast room. AE, MC, V. Expensive.*

Bay Harbor Inn. Here you'll find down-home hospitality in the most affluent zip code in the county. Retired Washington lawyer Sandy Lankler and his wife, Celeste, operate this 38-room lodging in two sections, two moods. Townside is the oldest building in Bay Harbor Islands, vaguely Georgian in style but dating from 1940. Behind triple sets of French doors under fan windows, the lobby is full of oak desks, hand mills, grandfather clocks, historical maps, and potted plants. Rooms are antiques-filled, and no two are alike. Along Indian Creek the inn incorporates the former Albert Pick Hotella, a shipshape tropical-style set of rooms on two floors, off loggias surrounded by palms, with all rooms facing the water. The decor here is midcentury modern, with chintz. The popular Miami Palm restaurant is located townside and B. C. Chong's Seafood Garden creekside, with the London Bar serving the best ½-pound hamburger in the city. *9660 E. Bay Harbor Dr., Bay Harbor Islands 33154, tel. and fax 305/868–4141. 25 rooms with bath, 12 suites, penthouse. Facilities: 2 restaurants, lounge, complimentary Continental breakfast, outdoor freshwater pool, 2 restaurants, lounge. AE, DC, MC, V. Moderate–Expensive.*

The Winterhaven. This 64-room, mid-1930s Art Deco property right on Ocean Drive is a top buy. You're across from the beach and within walking distance of everything in the Deco District, including the Lincoln Road Mall. The six-story hotel has been painted pale blue, green, and cream, with sculptured "eyebrows" over the windows and center masonry folds that do a number with sunlight and shadow all day. The two-story yellow-green lobby features sensuous curves and fluting. Rooms are typically Deco-era—small, decorated in blues and white, with shell-pattern quilted bed covers and original black Deco furniture. The bathrooms and closets are small, too. Central air-conditioning was installed in 1992–93. *1400 Ocean Drive, 33139, tel, 305/531–5571 or 800/395–23224, fax 305/538–3337. 64 rooms with bath. Facilities: restaurant, complimentary Continental breakfast, in-room safes. AE, DC, MC, V. Moderate–Expensive.*

Abbey Hotel. Just north of the Deco District and Lincoln Road, a few blocks from the beach, lies a quiet neighborhood of less pretentious hotels with modest rates. Best in comfort, service, and price is the 50-room Abbey, a Deco-style hotel dating from the late '30s. It's across the street from the Bass Museum and its gardens, and many of the Abbey's rooms look onto the gardens. Rooms are large for a Deco-era hotel, and all are newly refurbished. The lobby is stylish gray and tan with rattan furniture and wall niches for art and ceramics. A boon: 24-hour free parking on adjacent Liberty Avenue—although you have to capture one of the spaces. Co-managers Terri Bankin and John Calu have been here since 1990 and are devoted to their guests. *300 21st St., 33139, tel. 305/531–0031. 50 rooms with bath. Facilities: in-room microwave and fridge, if not complete kitchen; complimentary Continental breakfast. AE, DC, MC, V. Moderate.*

Suez Oceanfront Resort. They call this Miami Beach, and it is on the beach, although it's several miles north of the municipality of Miami Beach, in the section called Sunny Isles—more popularly referred to as Motel Row. This is affordable Miami Beach, chockablock with fancy motels but few of distinction. The carousel-stripe Suez, however, is a standout, a side-by-side pair of two-story buildings from the 1960s. Get past the tacky sphinx icons, go upstairs in the main building, and you're in a quiet, gardenlike rattan-and-palm lounge. Heading toward the beach you enter a landscaped palm courtyard. It feels like a resort, generous with space—out by the beach is a popular bar and restaurant, two pools (freshwater and salt), a tennis court, and kids' playground. Rooms are newly redone, with matched chinois furniture, and they dazzle with color to counteract the generally small spaces. The worst rooms are in the north wing, where both sides face the parking lot, and on the north side of the main building, which also faces parking. Modified American Plan dining and special kids rates make this an especially good value. Free laundry service is a bonus. *18215 Collins Ave., 33160, tel. 305/932–0661 or 800/327–5278; in FL, 800/432–3661, fax 305/937–0058. 196 rooms. Facilities: restaurant, bar, tennis court, playground, shuffleboard and volleyball courts, beachfront, fresh and saltwater pools. AE, D, DC, MC, V. Moderate.*

North Dade **Turnberry Isle Resort and Club.** Finest of the Miami-area grand
★ resorts, Turnberry sits on 300 superbly landscaped acres by the bay. The newest addition is an $80 million three-wing Mediterranean-style annex, with new restaurants and the *Ms. Turnberry* (a custom-built yacht). Guests can also choose from the European-style Marina Hotel, the Yacht Club, or the Mizner-style Country Club Hotel, beside one of the two Robert Trent Jones–designed golf courses. Interiors of the oversize rooms feature light woods and earth tones (a nautical-blue motif at the hotel), large curving terraces, Jacuzzis, honor bar, and in-room safes. *19999 W. Country Club Dr., Aventura 33180, tel. 305/932–6200 or 800/327–7028, fax 305/933–6560. 300 rooms with bath, 40 suites. Facilities: 5 restaurants; lounge; nightly entertainment; Ocean Club with 250-ft private beach; diving gear; Windsurfers and Hobie Cats for rent; complimentary shuttle service to hotel; 4 outdoor freshwater pools; 24 tennis courts (18 lighted); 2 18-hole golf courses; helipad; marina with moorings for 117 boats up to 150 ft; spa with saunas, steam rooms, whirlpools, facials, herbal wraps, Nautilus equipment, indoor racquetball courts, outdoor jogging course. AE, DC, MC, V. Very Expensive.*

West Dade **Don Shula's Hotel and Golf Club.** This low-rise suburban resort is part of a planned town developed by Florida senator Bob Graham's family about 14 miles northwest of downtown Miami. The golf resort opened in 1962 and added two wings in 1978. Its decor is English-traditional throughout, rich in leather and wood. All rooms have balconies. The hotel opened in 1983 with a typically Florida-tropics look—light pastels and furniture of wicker and light wood. In both locations the best rooms are near the lobby for convenient access; the worst are near the elevators. *Main St., Miami Lakes 33014, tel. 305/821–1150. 269 rooms with bath, 32 suites. Facilities: 2 restaurants, 1 lounge, 2 outdoor freshwater heated pools, 9 lighted tennis courts, 18-hole par-72 championship golf course, lighted 18-hole par-54 executive course, golf school, saunas, steam rooms, whirlpools, 8 indoor racquetball courts, athletic club with Nautilus fitness center, full-size gym for volleyball and basketball, aerobics classes. AE, DC, MC, V. Very Expensive.*

★ **Doral Resort & Country Club.** Millions of airline passengers annually peer down upon this 2,400-acre jewel of an inland golf-
   and-tennis resort while fastening their seat belts. It's 4 miles
   west of Miami International Airport and consists of eight separate three- and four-story lodges nestled beside the golf links.
   The resort follows a tropical theme, with light pastels, wicker,
   and teak furniture. All guest rooms have minibars; most have
   private balconies or terraces with views of the golf courses or
   tennis courts. This is the site of the Doral Ryder Open Tournament, played on the Doral "Blue Monster" golf course. *4400
   N.W. 87th Ave., Miami 33178, tel. 305/592–2000, fax 305/591–
   6447. 592 rooms with bath, 58 suites. Facilities: 4 restaurants,
   3 lounges, 5 18-hole golf courses, 9-hole par-3 executive course,
   pro shop, 15 tennis courts (4 lighted), Olympic-size heated outdoor freshwater pool, 3-mi jogging and bike path, bicycle rentals, lake fishing, transportation to beach. AE, DC, MC, V.
   Very Expensive.*

The Arts

Performing-arts aficionados in Greater Miami will tell you they
survive quite nicely, despite the area's historic inability to support a professional symphony orchestra. In recent years this
community has begun to write a new chapter in its performing-
arts history.

The New World Symphony, a unique advanced-training orchestra, begins its seventh season in 1994. The Miami City Ballet
has risen rapidly to international prominence in its eight-year
existence. The opera company ranks with the nation's best, and
a venerable chamber-music series brings renowned ensembles
here to perform. Several churches and synagogues run classical-music series with international performers. In theater Miami offers English-speaking audiences an assortment of
professional, collegiate, and amateur productions of musicals,
comedy, and drama. Spanish theater also is active. In the cinema world, the Miami Film Festival attracts more than 45,000
people annually to screenings of new films from all over the
world—including some made here.

Information Greater Miami's English-language daily newspaper, *The Miami Herald*, publishes reliable reviews and comprehensive listings in its Weekend section on Friday and in the Lively Arts
section on Sunday. Call ahead to confirm details.

If you read Spanish, check *El Nuevo Herald* (a Spanish version
of *The Miami Herald*) or *Diario Las Américas* (the area's largest independent Spanish-language paper) for information on
the Spanish theater and a smattering of general performing-
arts news.

Another good source of information on the performing arts is
the calendar in *Miami Today*, a free weekly newspaper available each Thursday in downtown Miami, Coconut Grove, and
Coral Gables. The best, most complete source is the *New
Times*, a free weekly distributed throughout Dade County
each Wednesday. Various tabloids reporting on Deco District
entertainment and society come and go on Miami Beach.

The free *Greater Miami Calendar of Events* is published twice
a year by the Dade County Cultural Affairs Council (111 N.W.
1st St., Suite 625, Miami 33128, tel. 305/375–4634).

Guide to the Arts/South Florida is a pocket-size publication produced 10 times a year ($2 per issue, $15 per year) that covers all the cultural arts in Dade, Broward, and Palm Beach counties and is available from Kage Publications (3800 S. Ocean Dr., Hollywood 33019, tel. 305/456–9599).

Real Talk/WTMI (93.1 FM) provides concert information on its Cultural Arts Line (tel. 305/358–8000, ext. 9398).

To order tickets for performing-arts events by telephone, call **Ticketmaster** (Dade County, tel. 305/358–5885; Broward County, tel. 305/523–3309; Palm Beach, tel. 407/839–3900) and charge tickets to a major credit card.

Ballet The **Miami City Ballet** (905 Lincoln Rd., Miami Beach 33139, tel. 305/532–7713) is Florida's first major, fully professional, resident ballet company. Edward Villella, the artistic director, was a principal dancer of the New York City Ballet under George Balanchine. Now the Miami City Ballet re-creates the Balanchine repertoire and introduces new works of its own during its September–March season. Performances are held at the Dade County Auditorium; the Broward Center for the Performing Arts; Bailey Concert Hall, also in Broward County; the Raymond F. Kravis Center for the Performing Arts; and at the Naples Philharmonic Center for the Arts. Demonstrations of works in progress are given at the 800-seat Lincoln Theater in Miami Beach. Villella narrates the children's and works-in-progress programs.

Cinema The **Alliance Film/Video Project** (927 Lincoln Rd. Mall, Suite 119, Sterling Building, Miami Beach 33139, tel. 305/531–8504) presents cutting-edge cinema from around the world, with special midnight shows.
The **Miami Film Festival** (444 Brickell Ave., Suite 229, Miami 33131, tel. 305/377–3456) screens new films from all over the world for 10 days every February, in the Gusman Center for the Performing Arts.

Concerts **Concert Association of Florida** (555 Hank Meyer Blvd., Miami Beach 33139, tel. 305/532–3491), a not-for-profit organization directed by Judith Drucker, is the South's largest presenter of classical artists.
Friends of Chamber Music (44 W. Flagler St., Miami 33130, tel. 305/372–2975) presents an annual series of chamber concerts by internationally known guest ensembles, such as the Beaux Arts Trio, the Tokyo Quartet, and the Juilliard String Quartet.

Drama **Acapai** (6161 N.W. 22nd Ave., Miami 33142, tel. 305/758–3534), whose name stands for African Caribbean American Performing Artists, Inc., mounts productions year-round at various area stages.
Acme Acting Company (955 Alton Rd., Miami Beach 33139, tel. 305/531–2393) presents thought-provoking, on-the-edge theater by new playwrights in its winter and summer seasons.
Actor's Playhouse (8851 S.W. 107th Ave., Miami 33176, tel. 305/595–0010) is a seven-year-old professional equity company based in Kendall that performs adults' and children's productions year-round.
Area Stage (645 Lincoln Rd., Miami Beach 33139, tel. 305/673–8002) performs provocative off-Broadway-style productions throughout the year.
Coconut Grove Playhouse (3500 Main Hwy., Coconut Grove

33133, tel. 305/442–4000) stages Broadway-bound plays and musical reviews and experimental productions.

Gold Coast Mime Company (905 Lincoln Rd., Miami Beach 33139, tel. 305/538–5500) is a new company performing at the Lincoln Theater, where it shares studios with the Miami City Ballet.

Miami Skyline (174 E. Flagler St., Miami 33131, tel. 305/358–7529), a much-heralded nonprofit regional repertory theater, was scheduled to debut by November 1993, with a schedule of four productions by its resident acting company at the downtown Gusman Center for the Performing Arts.

Minorca Playhouse (2121 Ponce de Leon Blvd., Suite 550, Coral Gables 33134, tel. 305/446–1116), the long-established home of several theater companies, including the Florida Shakespeare Theatre and the Hispanic Theatre Festival, now performs at a new 125-seat theater in the Colonnade Hotel.

New Theatre (65 Almeria St., Coral Gables 33134, tel. 305/443–5909) showcases contemporary and classical plays.

Ring Theater (1380 Miller Dr., Coral Gables 33146, tel. 305/284–3355), is the 311-seat hall of the University of Miami's Department of Theatre Arts, where eight plays a year are performed.

Opera The **Greater Miami Opera** (1200 Coral Way, Miami 33145, tel. 305/854–7890, box office open weekdays 9–4) is Miami's resident opera company, presenting four operas each year in the Dade County Auditorium. The International Series brings such luminaries as Placido Domingo and Luciano Pavarotti; the National Series features rising young singers in the principal roles, with the same sets and chorus but with more modest ticket prices. All operas are sung in the original language, with titles in English projected onto a screen above the stage.

Symphony **New World Symphony** (541 Lincoln Rd., Miami Beach 33139; box office, tel. 305/673–3331; main office, tel. 305/673–3330), conducted by Michael Tilson Thomas, performs October–April. Greater Miami has no resident symphony orchestra, and this group helps fill the void. Musicians ages 22–30 who have finished their academic studies perform here before moving on to other orchestras.

Theaters **Dade County Auditorium** (2901 W. Flagler St., Miami 33135, tel. 305/545–3395) satisfies patrons with 2,498 comfortable seats, good sight lines, and acceptable acoustics. Opera, concerts, and touring musicals are usually on the schedule.

Gusman Center for the Performing Arts (174 E. Flagler St., Miami 33131, tel. 305/372–0925), in downtown Miami, has 1,739 seats seemingly made for sardines—and the best acoustics in town. Concerts, ballet, and touring stage productions are seen here. An ornate former movie palace, the hall resembles a Moorish courtyard. Lights twinkle, starlike, from the ceiling.

Gusman Concert Hall (1314 Miller Dr., Coral Gables 33146, tel. 305/284–2438), a 600-seat concert hall on the University of Miami's Coral Gables campus, has good acoustics and plenty of room. Parking is a problem when school is in session.

Jackie Gleason Theater of the Performing Arts (TOPA, 1700 Washington Ave., Miami Beach 33139, tel. 305/673–7300) has finally brought its acoustics and visibility up to par for all 2,750 seats. The Broadway Series each year presents five or six major productions (or other performances); contact the box office (505 17th St., Miami Beach 33139, tel. 305/673–8300).

Jan McArt's International Room (Marco Polo Hotel, 19201 Collins Ave., Miami Beach 33161, tel. 305/932–7880) is the new Miami-area venue for musicals, which are performed September–June in the 270-seat hotel theater.

Spanish Theater Spanish theater prospers, although many companies have short lives. About 20 Spanish companies perform light comedy, puppetry, vaudeville, and political satire. To locate them, read the Spanish newspapers. When you call, be prepared for a conversation in Spanish—few box-office personnel speak English.

Prometeo (Miami-Dade Community College, New World Center Campus, 300 N.E. 2nd Ave., Miami 33132, tel. 305/237–3263) has produced three or four Spanish-English plays each year for 20 years. Admission is free.

Teatro Avante (Box 453005, Miami 33134, tel. 305/858–4155) stages three to six productions annually at El Carrusel (235 Alcazar Ave., tel. 305/445–8877). A Hispanic theater festival is held each June.

Teatro de Bellas Artes (2173 S.W. 8th St., Miami 33135, tel. 305/325–0515), a 255-seat theater on Calle Ocho, Little Havana's main commercial street, presents eight Spanish plays and musicals per year.

Nightlife

Greater Miami has no concentration of night spots like Bourbon Street in New Orleans or Rush Street in Chicago, but nightlife is found throughout the area in scattered locations, notably in the Deco District of Miami Beach, Little Haiti, Little Havana, Coconut Grove, the fringes of downtown Miami, and south-suburban Kendall.

Individual clubs offer jazz, reggae, salsa, various forms of rock, and top-40 sounds on different nights of the week. Some clubs refuse entrance to anyone under 21; others set the age limit at 25. On Miami Beach, where the sounds of jazz and reggae spill into the streets, fashion models and photographers frequent the lobby bars of small Art Deco hotels. Throughout the Greater Miami area, bars and cocktail lounges in larger hotels operate discos nightly, with live entertainment on weekends. Many hotels extend their bars into open-air courtyards, where patrons dine and dance under the stars throughout the year.

For current information, see the Weekend section in the Friday edition of *The Miami Herald;* the calendar in *Miami Today,* a free weekly newspaper available each Thursday in downtown Miami, Coconut Grove, and Coral Gables; *The New Times,* a free weekly distributed throughout Dade County each Wednesday; and in the proliferating Deco District tabloids.

WLVE radio (93.9 FM) sponsors an entertainment line (tel. 305/654–9436) with information on touring groups of all kinds, except classical. **Blues Hot Line** (tel. 305/666–6656) lists local blues clubs and bars. **Jazz Hot Line** (tel. 305/382–3938) lists local jazz programs.

Bars **Hungry Sailor** (3064½ Grand Ave., tel. 305/444–9359) has ex-
Coconut Grove panded to two bars, serving Jamaican-English food, British beer, and live reggae nightly.

Taurus Steak House (3540 Main Hwy., tel. 305/448–0633) is an unchanging oasis in the trendy Grove. The bar, built in 1922 of native cypress, draws an over-30 singles crowd nightly that drifts outside to a patio. A band plays on weekends.

Coral Gables **Stuart's Bar-Lounge** (162 Alcazar Ave., tel. 305/444–1666) was named one of the best new bars of 1987 by *Esquire*; seven years later, locals still favor it. Built in 1926, it is decorated with beveled mirrors, mahogany paneling, French posters, pictures of old Coral Gables, and art-nouveau lighting. It's closed Sunday.

Key Biscayne **Sundays on the Bay** (5420 Crandon Blvd., tel. 305/361–6777) is a classic Miami over-the-water scene on Key Biscayne with an upscale menu. The clientele include lots of Latins who love Miami the way it was. There's a disco nightly and live entertainment Friday–Sunday ($5–$10 cover).

Miami **Churchill's Hideaway** (5501 N.E. 2nd Ave., tel. 305/757–1807) is an Anglo enclave in Little Haiti, redolent of English pubbery despite its new outside barbecue. Its satellite dish picks up BBC news, and a video system plays tapes of international soccer and rugby games. There's live music Tuesday and Thursday–Saturday.

Tobacco Road (626 S. Miami Ave., tel. 305/374–1198), opened in 1912, holds Miami's oldest liquor license. Upstairs, in space occupied by a speakeasy during Prohibition, local and national blues bands perform Friday and Saturday and in scheduled weeknight concerts. There's excellent bar food.

Miami Beach **Cactus Cantina** (630 6th St., tel. 305/532–5095) is an unpretentious hangout, now with live music nightly. The food is Tex-Mex, and the bar serves 45 brands of tequila and Mexican beer.

Lasso Lounge (754 Washington Ave., tel. 305/532–0228) serves no food, but its atmosphere is steer-skull Western, with country-and-western karaoke and a pool table.

Mac's Club Deuce (222 14th St., tel. 305/673–9537) is a South Beach gem where top international models pop in to have a drink and shoot some pool. All you get late at night are minipizzas, but the pizzazz lasts.

Re Bar (1121 Washington Ave., tel. 305/672–4788) is a new "in" spot where people dance on the floor, on pool tables, even on the bar. There's a fire-blowing bartender, a sheeps' trough full of beer, and a lively crowd of gays and straights.

Shabeen Cookshack and Bar (1200 Collins Ave., in Marlin Hotel, tel. 305/673–8770) is Jamaican all the way—brilliant island decor, food, and upbeat Caribbean music.

The Spot (218 Espanola Way, tel. 305/532–1682) features American heroes from Mickey Mouse to Marilyn Monroe to Jim Morrison. Very hip, full of black light and neon, it almost feels like it's underwater.

Comedy Clubs Three comedy clubs make the scene in this popular part of *Coconut Grove* town: **Coconuts Comedy Club**, at the Peacock Cafe (2977 McFarlane Rd., tel. 305/446–2582); **Improv** (3015 Grand Ave., tel. 305/441–8200), in the Cocowalk mall; and the long-standing and outrageous **Mental Floss** (3138 Commodore Plaza, tel. 305/448–1011).

Miami **Uncle Funny's Comedy Club** (Mark Twain's Riverboat Playhouse, 13700 N. Kendall Dr., tel. 305/388–1992) presents a 1990s version of vaudeville comedy—humor that's adult but not obscene. There are two acts per show, new performers each week, a cover charge, and a two-drink minimum. Shows are weekends 9:30 and 11:30.

Disco, Jazz, and Rock Clubs
Coconut Grove

Baja Beach Club (3015 Grand Ave., Cocowalk, tel. 305/445–0278), the Number 1 party place in the Grove, has waiters and waitresses dressed in beach attire.

Key Biscayne

Stefano's of Key Biscayne (24 Crandon Blvd., tel. 305/361–7007) is a northern Italian restaurant cum disco; the music's live Tuesday–Sunday.

Miami Beach

Facade (3509 N.E. 163rd St., N. Miami Beach, tel. 305/948–6868) is an upscale, twentysomething scene with a top northern Italian kitchen. It's very purple.

Paragon (1235 Washington Ave., tel. 305/535–1235) is a beautifully styled, entertaining spot with brilliant Deco-District gay-scene ambiguity. Skating waiters wear skimpy underwear below tux shirts. There's a cover charge after 11.

Nightclubs
Miami

Les Violins Supper Club (1751 Biscayne Blvd., tel. 305/371–8668) is a reliable standby owned for 26 years by the Cachaidora-Currais family, who ran a club and restaurant in Havana. There's a live dance band and a wood dance floor. Reservations are advised; the cover charge is $15.

Miami Beach

Club Tropigala at La Ronde (4441 Collins Ave., in Fontainebleau Hilton Hotel, tel. 305/672–7469) is a seven-level round room decorated with orchids, banana leaves, and philodendrons to resemble a tropical jungle. Two bands play Latin music for dancing on the wood floor. Reservations are advised.

Stephen Talkhouse (616 Collins Ave., tel. 305/531–7557) is a top venue for national blues, rock, rhythm-and-blues, and zydeco acts, plus the best of the locals. It's an intimate spot, although it has 250 seats, and seafood and barbecue are served. The cover charge varies.

Van Dome (1532 Washington Ave., tel. 305/534–4288), housed in an old Masonic temple, is an upscale club featuring fashion shows, models, and champagne. There's a $10 cover Friday and Saturday nights.

The Whiskey (1250 Ocean Dr., tel. 305/531–0713) is a rock lounge in a hotel lobby with red love seats on a terrazzo floor. A celebrity scene, it's a spin-off of Manhattan's pop hotel, The Paramount.

5 The Everglades

*By George and
Rosalie Leposky*

*Updated by Herb
Hiller*

Greater Miami is the only metropolitan area in the United States with two national parks virtually in its backyard: Everglades National Park and Biscayne National Park. In late 1992, Hurricane Andrew turned everything ass-over-teakettle through the towns nearest the two parks, and as if this wasn't bad enough, 1992–1993 was the wettest winter on record, which severely upset the mating cycle of Everglades wildlife. Even before Hurricane Andrew, the long-term survival of both parks was besieged by environmental problems. It's still a beautiful, fascinating area to visit, but it's also an environmental case study, an example of a fragile ecosystem threatened by both man and the ravages of nature.

Everglades National Park, created in 1947, was meant to preserve the slow-flowing "river of grass"—a freshwater river 50 miles wide but only six inches deep, flowing through marshy grassland—which was under stress from channelizing and from weirs installed for flood control. But the water has been increasingly polluted by pesticide runoff from local farms, and the disrupted flow has caused subtle but steady changes in the Everglades wildlife habitat. Visitors to the park over the years note diminished numbers of birds; the black bear has been eliminated and the Florida panther reduced to near extinction. In 1992 the nonprofit group American Rivers declared the Everglades the fourth most endangered river in North America.

Biscayne National Park, established as a national monument in 1968, and 12 years later expanded and upgraded to park status, lies mostly underwater. The park includes the northernmost sections of Florida's tropical reef, which is under assault from the massive outflow of the polluted canals that drain the Everglades. The coral is also directly damaged by boat anchors and by commercial ships that run off course and onto the reefs.

Besides hurting the wildlife habitat, the 1992 hurricane ruined visitor facilities at both parks, and it will take a while to replace them. The main center at Everglades National Park was so badly damaged it had to be destroyed (a temporary center will serve visitors through 1994). Manmade facilities were quickly restored—boardwalks, outlooks, launch ramps—but the long-term effects of the hurricane are hard to gauge. One concern: a lot of fast-growing non-native seeds were blown into the swamp, complicating efforts to root out such unwanted trees as the melaleuca and fast-growing peppers, which could, over time, overcome the indigenous habitat. The heavy rains of winter 1993 only aggravated the situation.

The visitor center at Biscayne National Park, already only a temporary facility, continues to operate, since construction plans for an elaborate new center were put on hold after the hurricane. Worst hit were visitor centers on the park's remote islands, which already attracted fewer visitors than they deserved. The park's offshore coral reefs bore only slight damage from Andrew, but the mangrove trees—the backbone of coastal ecology—were ravaged by the winds: an estimated 80 percent damaged if not destroyed. Long-term effects threaten fish and bird life as well as water quality, in turn threatening the reefs.

We urge you to experience the real Everglades by getting your feet wet—but most people who visit the park won't do that. Boat tours at Everglades City and Flamingo, a tram ride at

Shark Valley, and boardwalks at several locations along the main park road allow you to see the Everglades with dry feet. You must take a boat ride to visit most of Biscayne National Park, which is 96% under water, and you really have to snorkel or scuba dive to appreciate it fully.

Many visitors to the two parks stay in the big-city portion of Greater Miami and spend a day visiting one or both of the parks. Serious outdoors people, however, will want to stay closer to the parks to devote more time to nature study and recreation.

Homestead and Florida City sprang up early in this century as agricultural communities attached to the Florida East Coast Railroad. Over the years, they developed a triple personality— part farming towns, part Miami suburbs, and part gateway to the parks. Both towns were devastated by Hurricane Andrew, however, which leveled entire neighborhoods, historic buildings, walls, and royal palm groves. Those losses can't quickly be reversed, although local food crops came back quickly and most of the motels, restaurants, and shopping centers that serve park visitors have reopened.

The other entrance to the Everglades is Everglades City, 35 miles east of Naples along U.S. 41. This is an older community—it's been around since the Seminole Wars, in the 19th century—and there are plenty of motels, restaurants, and guided Everglades tours based here.

Essential Information

Important Addresses and Numbers

Tourist Information
South Dade Visitors Information Center (160 U.S. 1, Florida City 33034, tel. 305/245–9180 or 800/388–9669).
Greater Homestead–Florida City Chamber of Commerce (550 Homestead Blvd., Homestead 33030, tel. 305/247–2332).
Everglades City Chamber of Commerce (corner of State Road 29 and U.S. 41, Everglades City 33929, tel. 813/695–3941).
Everglades National Park Gulf Coast Ranger Station (Rte. 29, Everglades City, tel. 813/695–3311).
Everglades National Park, Main Visitor Center (11 mi west of Homestead on Rte. 9336; Box 279, Homestead 33030; tel. 305/242–7700).
Biscayne National Park, Convoy Point Information Station (east end of North Canal Dr. [S.W. 328th St.], Homestead 33033, tel. 305/247–PARK).

Emergencies
Dial 911 for **police** and **ambulance** in an emergency.

In the national parks, rangers answer police, fire, and medical emergencies. Phone the park switchboards: **Biscayne** (tel. 305/247–2044) or **Everglades** (tel. 305/247–6211).

Hospitals
South Miami Hospital of Homestead (160 N.W. 13th St., Homestead, tel. 305/248–3232; physician referral, tel. 305/633–2255).

Marine Phone Numbers
Florida Marine Patrol (tel. 305/325–3346), a division of the Florida Department of Natural Resources, maintains a 24-hour telephone service for reporting boating emergencies and natural resource violations.

National Weather Service supplies local forecasts through the National Hurricane Center office in Coral Gables. *Tel. 305/665–0429; 24-hr recording, tel. 305/661–5065. Open weekdays 8–4:30.*

U.S. Coast Guard **Miami Beach Coast Guard Base** (tel. 305/535–4314 or 305/535–4315, VHF-FM Channel 16) responds to local marine emergencies and reports of navigation hazards.

Arriving and Departing

By Plane **Miami International Airport** (MIA) is the closest commercial airport to Everglades National Park and Biscayne National Park. It's 34 miles from Homestead and 83 miles from the Flamingo resort in Everglades National Park.

Between the Airport and Towns **Super Shuttle** (tel. 305/871–2000) operates 11-passenger air-conditioned vans between MIA and Homestead. Service from *By Van* MIA is available around the clock, on demand; go to the Super Shuttle booth outside most luggage areas on the lower level. 24-hour advance reservation is requested when returning to MIA. The cost is $28–$40 per person, $12 for each additional person traveling from the same residence.

The Airporter (tel. 305/247–8874) runs shuttle bus services four times a day between the Homestead–Florida City area and the airport. Pick-up points in Homestead are the Holiday Inn in Homestead and the Holiday Inn in Cutler Ridge (pending post-Hurricane repairs). Service from Florida City is 6:10 AM–5:20 PM; from the airport, 7:30 AM–6 PM. Trips take approximately 1 hour. Airport pick-ups are arranged at all baggage claim areas. The cost is $20 one way; reservations are required.

By Bus **Metrobus** Route 1A runs from Homestead to MIA only during peak weekday hours: 6:30–9 AM and 4–6:30 PM.

Greyhound/Trailways operates three trips daily north from Homestead to the Greyhound/Trailways depot in Miami (4111 N.W. 27th St. tel. 305/871–1810), which is about a $5 cab ride from MIA. Coming from the airport, you can connect with one of Greyhound's three daily buses south to Homestead; take an ARTS (Airport Region Taxi Service) car for about $5 from MIA to the Greyhound/Trailways depot (5 N.E. 3rd Rd., Homestead, tel. 305/247–2040).

By Car From Miami to Biscayne National Park, take the turnpike extension to the Tallahassee Road (S.W. 137th Ave.) exit, turn left, and go south. Turn left at North Canal Drive (S.W. 328th St.), go east, and follow signs to park headquarters at Convoy Point. The park is about 30 miles from downtown Miami.

From Miami, the main highways to Homestead–Florida City are U.S. 1, the Homestead Extension of the Florida Turnpike, and Krome Avenue (Rte. 997/old U.S. 27).

To reach Biscayne National Park from Homestead, take U.S. 1 or Krome Avenue to Lucy Street (S.E. 8th St.) and turn east. Lucy Street becomes North Canal Drive (S.W. 328th St.). Follow signs for about 8 miles to the park headquarters.

To reach Everglades National Park's Main Visitor Center and Flamingo from Florida City, turn right (west) onto Route 9336 and follow signs to the park entrance. The Main Visitor Center is 11 miles from Homestead; Flamingo is 49 miles from Homestead.

To reach the south end of Everglades National Park in the Florida Keys, take U.S. 1 south from Homestead. It's 27 miles to the Key Largo Ranger Station (between miles 98 and 99 on the Overseas Hwy.).

To reach the western gateway to Everglades National Park, take U.S. 41 (the Tamiami Trail) 35 miles east from Naples to Everglades City's Gulf Coast Ranger Station. Continue along U.S. 41 to reach the Shark Valley Information Center, about two hours from Naples. From Miami, west on U.S. 41, it's 40 miles to Shark Valley and 83 miles to Everglades City.

By Taxi   The only cab company here is **Kendall Taxi** (tel. 305/388–8888), which has two cabs stationed in the Homestead–Florida City area, so it's best to reserve cab needs well in advance.

Rental Cars   **American Eagle Rent-A-Car** (28400 S. Dixie Hwy., Homestead 33033, tel. 305/245–0300 or 305/247–0873), **Enterprise Rent-a-Car** (30428 S. Federal Hwy., Homestead 33030, tel. 305/246–2056).

By Boat   If you're entering the U.S. by boat, you must stop and phone U.S. Customs at either **Watson Island Marina** (1050 MacArthur Causeway, Miami, tel. 305/371–2378), about 25 nautical miles from Biscayne National Park headquarters and 50 nautical miles from Flamingo, or **Tavernier Creek Marina** (mile 90.5, U.S. 1, Tavernier, tel. 305/252–0194 from Miami, tel. 305/852–5854 from the Keys), about 48 nautical miles from Biscayne National Park headquarters, 25 nautical miles from Flamingo.

Guided Tours

Tours of Everglades National Park and Biscayne National Park typically focus on native wildlife, plants, and park history. Concessionaires operate Everglades tram tours and the boat cruises in both parks. In addition, the National Park Service organizes a variety of free programs at Everglades National Park. Ask a ranger for the daily schedule.

From Miami   **All Florida Adventure Tours** (8263-B S.W. 107th Ave., Miami 33173–3729, tel. 305/270–0219) operates from one-day to two-week custom tours that emphasize nature, history, and ecology.

From Homestead–
Florida City   **Air Tours of South Florida** (Homestead General Aviation Airport, 28720 S.W. 217th Ave., Homestead 33030, tel. 305/248–
Air Tours   1100) may be back in service by 1994, offering 50-minute narrated tours ($59 per person) of the Everglades.

Airboat Tours   **Everglades Alligator Farm** (40351 S.W. 192nd Ave., tel. 305/AIRBOAT) runs a 4-mile, 30-minute tour of the River of Grass, leaving every half hour. The tour includes free hourly alligator feedings and reptile shows. The cost is $11 adults; $6 children 4–12, under 4 free; $10 senior citizens.

Boat Tours   **Biscayne National Park Tour Boats** (east end of North Canal Dr. [S.W. 328th St.], Homestead, tel. 305/247–2400) explore the park's living coral reefs 10 miles offshore on a 53-foot glass-bottom boat. The cost is $16.50 adults, $8.50 children, $24.50 snorkelers.

From Flamingo
Boat Tours

Back Country Tour (Flamingo Marina, Flamingo, tel. 305/253–2241 or 813/695–3101, fax 813/695–3921) is a two-hour cruise aboard a 40-passenger catamaran. The cost is $11.50 adults, $5.50 children 6–12, under 6 free.

Flamingo Lodge Marina & Outpost Resort (TW Services Inc., Everglades National Park, Box 428, Flamingo 33030, tel. 305/253–2241 or 813/695–3101) helps you arrange in advance for charter fishing-boat captains to give individual tours out of Flamingo. Cost is $265 a day (for up to 3 persons), $165 a half day, additional persons $20 each.

Florida Bay Cruise (Flamingo Marina, Flamingo, tel. 305/253–2241 or 813/695–3101) is a 90-minute tour of Florida Bay aboard *Bald Eagle*, a 90-passenger catamaran. It costs $8 adults, $4 children 6–12.

Tram Tours

Wilderness Tram Tour (Flamingo Lodge, tel. 305/253–2241 or 813/695–3101) visits Snake Bight, an indentation in the Florida Bay shoreline, aboard a 48-passenger screened tram. This two-hour tour passes through a mangrove forest and a coastal prairie to a 100-yard boardwalk over the mud flats at the edge of the bight. The cost is $7.25 adults, $3.65 children 6–12.

From Shark Valley
Airboat Rides

Buffalo Tiger's Florida Everglades Airboat Ride (12 mi west of Krome Ave., 20 mi west of Miami city limits [Rte. 997], tel. 305/559–5250) is led by the former chairman of the Miccosukee tribe, who will take you on a 40- to 45-minute airboat ride through the Everglades, with a stop at an old Indian camp. It costs $10 adults, $6 children under 10.

Coopertown Airboat Ride (Tamiami Trail, 5 mi west of Krome Ave., tel. 305/226–6048) is a 30-minute airboat ride through the Everglades saw grass, visiting two hammocks (subtropical hardwood forests) and alligator holes. The cost is $8 per person; minimum $20 for the boat.

Tram Tours

Shark Valley Tram Tours (Shark Valley entrance to Everglades National Park, off Tamiami Trail, tel. 305/221–8455) follow a 15-mile elevated loop road into the interior, stopping at the observation tower. Cost is $7 adults, $3.50 children 12 and under, $6.25 senior citizens. Reservations are recommended December–March.

From Everglades City
Airboat Tour

Florida Boat Tours (200 Rte. 29, tel. 813/695–4400 or in FL 800/282–9194) are 30- to 40-minute back-country tours aboard custom-designed Jet-Airboats. Cost is $10.95 adults, $5.50 children 4–12.

Wooten's Everglades (Wooten's Alligator Farm, U.S. 31, tel. 813/695–2781) runs a variety of airboat and swamp-buggy tours through the Everglades.

Boat Tours

Everglades National Park Boat Tours (Gulf Coast Ranger Station, Rte. 29, tel. 813/695–2591 or in FL 800/445–7724) carry from 40 to 140 passengers (the two largest boats have food and drink concessions) on three separate 14-mile tours through the Ten Thousand Islands region along the Gulf of Mexico on the western margin of the park. The cost is $10 adults, $5 children 6–12, under 6 free.

Majestic Tours (Box 241, Everglades City 33929, tel. 813/695–2777 or 800/638–5051, ext. 574) are led by exceptionally well-informed guides, Frank and Georgia Garrett. The 3½- to 4-hour tours depart from Smallwood's Store on Chokoloskee Island on a 24-foot pontoon boat into the Ten Thousand Islands, ending up at The Watson Place. Tours are limited to six passengers and includes brunch or afternoon snacks. It costs $60 per person, $40 for children under 12.

Swampland Airboat Tours (Box 619, Everglades City 33929, tel. 800/344–2740 or 813/695–2740) offer personalized tours of the Everglades or the Big Cypress National Preserve. The cost for one to three persons is $60 per hour, plus $20 for each additional person; the limit is six passengers. Reservations are required.

Exploring the Everglades

Highlights for First-Time Visitors

Biscayne National Park Tour Boat
Everglades park drive from Homestead to Flamingo
The Loop Road, Big Cypress National Preserve
Miccosukee Indian Village, Shark Valley
Rod and Gun Club, Everglades City
Shark Valley Tram Tour, Shark Valley
Smallwood's Store, Chokoloskee Island

Biscayne National Park

Numbers in the margin correspond to points of interest on the Everglades and Biscayne National Parks map.

Biscayne National Park, the nation's largest marine park, is the only national park in the continental United States with living coral reefs. The park encompasses almost 274 square miles, of which 96% are under water. The park boundary encompasses the continental shelf to a depth of 60 feet. East of that boundary, the shelf falls rapidly away to a depth of 400 feet at the edge of the Gulf Stream.

Biscayne includes 18 miles of inhospitable mangrove shoreline on the mainland and 45 mangrove-fringed barrier islands 7 miles to the east across Biscayne Bay. The bay is a lobster sanctuary and a nursery for fish, sponges, and crabs. Manatees and sea turtles also frequent its warm, shallow waters.

The islands (called keys) are fossilized coral reefs that emerged from the sea when glaciers trapped much of the world's water supply during the Ice Age. Today a tropical hardwood forest grows in the crevices of these rocky keys. From December through April, when the mosquito population is relatively quiescent, you can comfortably explore several of the islands, if you have your own boat.

East of the keys another 3 miles lies the park's main attraction: living coral reefs, some the size of a student's desk, others as broad as a large parking lot. The reefs attract divers and snorkelers (*see* Participant Sports and Outdoor Activities, *below*), and you can visit them by boat, either your own or one operated by the park concession. A diverse population of colorful fish flits through the reefs: angelfish, gobies, grunts, parrot fish, pork fish, wrasses, and many more. Fortunately, Hurricane Andrew did only minor damage to the reefs.

❶ The main gateway to the park is the **Convoy Point Information Station.** A new park headquarters was to have opened in 1993, but it was put on hold following Hurricane Andrew and is not expected to open before 1995. Instead a small temporary building provides an outdoor kiosk with bulletin boards; nearby are a launching ramp for canoes and sailboards, a boardwalk over shallow water to a jetty, a path along the jetty, and a picnic area. At the dock here, you can board tour boats to the reefs and Elliott Key. *At east end of North Canal Dr. (S.W. 328th St.), Homestead, tel. 305/247–PARK. Admission free. Station open daily 8:30–6 winter, 9–5 summer. Park open 8–sunset year-round.*

❷ On an offshore island, you can visit the **Elliott Key Reception Center** which should be open by late 1993. The previous facility was badly damaged by Hurricane Andrew; this new replacement has more limited materials for visitors. *Tel. 305/247–PARK. Open most weekends and holidays 10–4.*

❸ Just north is **Boca Chita Key,** once owned by Mark C. Honeywell, former president of Minneapolis's Honeywell Company. Of the facilities built here, all except one stone structure were blown away or so badly damaged by Hurricane Andrew that they had to be torn down. Island use should resume in late 1994 or 1995.

❹ **Adams Key Information Station** is expected to reopen in late 1993 with limited facilities, after sustaining major hurricane damage. A boat dock, picnic area, rest rooms, and short nature trail were here.

The Everglades

Winter is the best time to visit Everglades National Park. Temperatures and mosquito activity are moderate. Low water levels concentrate the resident wildlife around sloughs that retain water all year. Migratory birds swell the avian population. Winter is also the busiest time in the park. Make reservations and expect crowds at the most popular visitor service areas— Flamingo, the main visitor center, and Royal Palm.

In spring the weather turns increasingly hot and dry, and tours and facilities are less crowded. Migratory birds depart, and you must look harder to see wildlife. Be especially careful with campfires and matches; this is when the wildfire-prone sawgrass prairies and pinelands are most vulnerable.

Summer brings intense sun and billowing clouds that unleash torrents of rain on the Everglades. Thunderstorms roll in almost every afternoon; water levels rise and wildlife disperses. Mosquitoes hatch, swarm, and descend on you in voracious clouds. It's a good time to stay away, although some brave souls do come to explore. Europeans constitute 80% of the summer visitors.

In mid-October, the first cold front sweeps through. The rains cease, water levels start to fall, and the ground begins to dry out. Wildlife moves toward the sloughs. Flocks of migratory birds and tourists swoop in, as the cycle of seasons builds once more to the winter peak activity.

Florida City to Flamingo Before you reach Everglades National Park, you mght want to stop off in **Florida City** to visit the **Florida Pioneer Museum,**

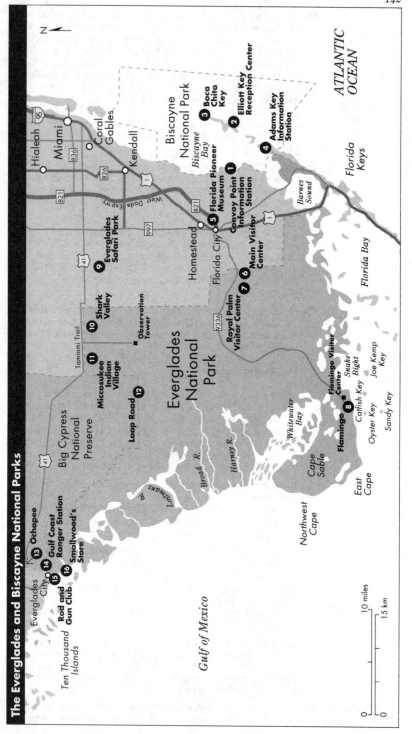

The Everglades and Biscayne National Parks

⑤ where in a former station agent's house you can pore over a collection of articles from daily life that evoke the homestead period here, on the last frontier of mainland America. They recall the time when Henry Flagler's railroad vaulted the Florida Keys on its epic extension to Key West, and Homestead and Florida City were briefly the take-charge supply outposts. Another part of the museum, the old East Coast Railway Station, was demolished by Hurricane Andrew, but its caboose, which was tumbled on its side, has since been righted. *826 N. Krome Ave., Florida City 33034, tel. 305/246–9531. Call for latest admission information and hours.*

⑥ Enter the park at the **Main Visitor Center,** where some limited interpretive materials are available in a temporary facility, replacing the park headquarters that was ruined by Hurricane Andrew. *11 mi west of Homestead on Rte. 9336, tel. 305/242–7700. Park Admission: $5 per car, $3 per person on foot, bicycle, or motorcycle, U.S. citizens over 62 free. Visitor center open daily 8–5.*

⑦ A short distance away, at the **Royal Palm Visitor Center,** you can stroll along the Anhinga Trail boardwalk or follow the Gumbo Limbo Trail through a hardwood hammock (a tree island). The visitor center has an interpretive display, a bookstore, and vending machines. *Open 8–noon, 1–4:30.*

The main Everglades park road travels 38 miles from the Main Visitor Center to Flamingo, across a cross section of the park's eight distinct ecosystems: hardwood hammock, freshwater prairie, pineland, freshwater slough, cypress, coastal prairie, mangrove, and marine/estuarine. Highlights of the trip include a dwarf cypress forest, the ecotone (transition zone) between saw grass and mangrove forest, and a wealth of wading birds at Mrazek and Coot Bay ponds. Boardwalks and trails along the main road and several short spurs allow you to see the Everglades without getting your feet wet.

⑧ At the far end, **Flamingo** offers access to Florida Bay; tour boats and fishing guides leave from here. The temporary visitor center here offers an interpretive display; there's also a lodge, restaurant, lounge, gift shop, marina, and campground. *Tel. 305/242–7700 (Park Service), tel. 305/253–2241 (Everglades Lodge). Visitor center open daily 8–5.*

Along the Tamiami Trail Another way to visit the Everglades is to follow the Tamiami Trail (U.S. 41) for the scenic 83 miles between Miami and Naples. The following tour assumes drivers will begin at the Main Visitor Center near Homestead and drive west to the Gulf Coast Ranger Station in Everglades City; the tour can just as easily be made in the opposite direction. (Keep in mind that the sun will be in your eyes after noon while driving the tour east to west.)

From Homestead, go north on Krome Avenue (Rte. 997) to U.S. Highway 41, then head 9 miles west. Turn left to **⑨** **Everglades Safari Park.** This commercial attraction includes an airboat ride, jungle trail, observation platform, alligator wrestling, wildlife museum, gift shop, and restaurant. *Tamiami Trail (U.S. 41), tel. 305/226–6923 or 305/223–3804. Admission: $10 adults, $5 children under 12. No credit cards. Open daily 8:30–5.*

⑩ Continue on U.S. 41 to the **Shark Valley** visitor center, which has rotating exhibits and a bookstore. From here you can walk along a ¼-mile boardwalk, follow hiking trails, or take a tram tour (*see* Guided Tours, *above*) that visits a 50-foot observation tower built on the site of an oil well drilled in the 1940s. From atop the tower you can view the Everglades' vast "river of grass" sweeping south toward the Gulf of Mexico. *Box 42, Ochopee 33943, tel. 305/221–8776. Park admission: $4 per car, $2 per person on foot, bicycle, or motorcycle U.S. citizens over 62 free. Visitor center open daily 8:30–5.*

⑪ Near the Shark Valley entrance to Everglades National Park, the Miccosukee tribe operates the **Miccosukee Indian Village** as a tourist attraction. You can watch Indian families cooking and making clothes, dolls, beadwork, and baskets. You'll also see an alligator-wrestling demonstration. The village has a boardwalk and a museum. Airboat rides (*see* Guided Tours, *above*) depart from here. *Mailing address: Box 440021, Miami 33144, tel. 305/223–8380. Admission: $5 adults, $3.50 children. Open 9–5.*

⑫ Continuing west on the Tamiami Trail, you'll drive through the **Big Cypress National Preserve,** with its variegated pattern of wet prairies, ponds, marshes, sloughs, and strands. Just west of the Miccosukee Indian Reservation turn onto SR 94, the 29-mile **Loop Road.** It starts out paved, turns to dirt, and traverses deep, clear cypress swamps of rare beauty. Be sure to keep car windows rolled up when you stop, especially in summer, because mosquitoes can be a severe problem—lather on repellent if you leave the car to explore along the road beside ponds. Walk silently and you may see 'gators, deer, rabbits, and other wildlife, as well as orchids and bromeliads. The road returns to the Tamiami Trail at **Monroe Station,** midway between the Miccosukee Indian Reservation and Everglades City.

⑬ Just before Route 29 turns off south to Everglades City, on the Tamiami Trail you'll pass through **Ochopee,** site of the smallest post office in North America. Buy a picture postcard of the little one-room shack and mail it to a friend, thereby helping keep this picturesque post office in business.

⑭ The western entrance to Everglades National Park is at the **Gulf Coast Ranger Station.** Turn south from the Tamiami Trail onto Route 29, drive 3 miles to Everglades City, and continue to the visitor center, which offers exhibits and a gift shop. Back-country campers can pick up the required camping permits (free) here. This station offers access to the Ten Thousand Islands region along the Gulf of Mexico (*see* Guided Tours, *above*), but there are no roads from here to other sections of the park. *Tel. 813/695–3311. Admission free. Open daily in winter 7–4:30, reduced hours in summer.*

⑮ Stop in **Everglades City** at the **Rod and Gun Club** (200 Riverside Dr., tel. 813/695–2101), and take a time-warp trip back to the '20s, when wealthy hunters, fishermen, and yachting parties from all over the world came here for the winter season. Founded in 1889, the club is built on the foundations of the first house on the south bank of the Barron River. Breakfast, lunch, and dinner are still served in its original dining room or on the wide veranda; there are 17 cottages available at reasonable rates for overnight stays. As in days of yore, if you catch a "keeper" fish, the chef will prepare it for your dinner.

16 Three miles from Everglades City across a toll-free causeway is **Smallwood's Store,** a perfectly restored old trading post that dates from 1906. Ted Smallwood pioneered this last American frontier deep in the Everglades, a 3,000-square-foot pine store raised on pilings in Chokoloskee Bay. Smallwood's grand-daughter Lynn McMillin reopened it in 1989 after it had been closed several years, and she installed a small museum and gift shop. *360 Mamie St., Chokoloskee Island, tel. 813/965–2989. Admission: $2.50 per person, children under 12 free when accompanied by a parent. Open daily 10–5, closed major holidays.*

Shopping

Florida City **Robert Is Here** is a remarkable fruit stand that sells vegetables and some 40 kinds of tropical fruits, including carambola, egg fruit, lychees, monstera, sapodilla, soursop, sugar apple, tamarind, as well as fresh juices. *19200 Palm Dr. (S.W. 344th St.), tel. 305/246–1592. Open daily 8–7.*

For the sheer fun as well as the bargain, you can't beat a stint in any of the local fields that welcome visitors to pick their own produce. The season runs from November to April, and you can expect to find strawberries for maybe $2 a pound, corn at $1.25 a dozen ears, and tomatoes for 50¢ a pound. Drive and look for signs—in season they're everywhere among the fields—or call the **South Dade Visitors Information Center** (*see* Important Addresses and Numbers, *above*). You can also buy fresh-picked produce at stands that border fields if you don't want to save quite as much.

Homestead Homestead's main shopping streets are **Homestead Boulevard** (U.S. 1), **Campbell Drive** (S.W. 312th St. and N.E. 8th St.), and **Krome Avenue** (Rte. 997), where the heart of old Homestead, with brick sidewalks and lots of antiques stores, is located.

Shark Valley The most unusual crafts found in south Florida are the bead-work, dolls, baskets, and patchwork dresses and jackets sold at the **Miccosukee Indian Village** (*see* Tamiami Trail, *above*).

Participant Sports and Outdoor Activities

Most of the sports and recreational opportunities in Everglades National Park and Biscayne National Park are related in some way to water or nature study, or both. Even on land, be prepared to get your feet wet on the region's marshy hiking trails. In summer, save your outdoor activities for early or late in the day to avoid the sun's strongest rays, and use a sunscreen. Carry mosquito repellent at any time of year.

Bicycling and In **Biscayne National Park,** rangers used to lead informal na-
Hiking ture walks on Elliott Key; check whether the walks have resumed. On your own you can walk the length of the 7-mile key along a rough path locally referred to as the "spite highway," which developers bulldozed before the park was created.

In **Everglades National Park,** you can rent bikes at the Shark Valley visitor center. Ride or hike along the Shark Valley Loop Road, 15 miles round-trip. *Shark Valley Tram Tours, Box 1729, Tamiami Station, Miami 33144, tel. 305/221–8455. Cost: $2 per hr. Open daily 8:30–3.*

Ask the rangers for *Foot and Canoe Trails of the Flamingo Area,* a leaflet that also lists bike trails. Inquire about water levels and insect conditions before you go. Get a free back-country permit if you plan to camp overnight.

Boating Bring aboard the proper *NOAA Nautical Charts* before you cast off to explore the waters of the parks. The charts cost $15.95 each and are sold at many marine stores in south Florida, at the Convoy Point Visitor Center in Biscayne National Park, and in Flamingo Marina.

Waterway Guide (southern regional edition) is an annual publication that many boaters use as a guide to these waters. Bookstores all over south Florida sell it, or you can order it directly from the publisher. *Communications Channels, Book Department, 6151 Powers Ferry Rd., Atlanta, GA 30339, tel. 800/233–3359. Cost: $31.95 plus $3 shipping and handling.*

Marinas Listed below are the major marinas serving the two parks. The dock masters at these marinas can provide information on other marine services you may need.

Black Point Park is a 155-acre Metro-Dade County Park with a hurricane-safe harbor basin. Although badly mauled by Hurricane Andrew, it reopened in early 1993. **Black Point Marina's** facilities include storage racks for 300 boats, 178 wet slips, 10 ramps, fuel, a bait-and-tackle shop, canoe-launching ramp, power-boat rentals from **Marine Management** (tel. 305/258–3500), and an outside grill serving lunch and dinner. From Florida's Turnpike, exit at S.W. 112th Avenue, go two blocks north, turn east on Coconut Palm Drive (S.W. 248th St.) and drive to the end. *24775 S.W. 87th Ave., Naranja, tel. 305/258–4092. Office open daily 8:30–5; park open 6 AM–sundown.*

Pirate's Spa Marina, just west of the Black Point Park entrance, offers boat hoist, wet and dry storage, fuel, bait and tackle, and boat rental. *8701 Coconut Palm Dr. (S.W. 248th St.), Naranja, tel. 305/257–5100.*

Homestead Bayfront Park, just 5 miles south of Black Point Park, has a marina with a dock and wet slips, fuel, bait and tackle, ice, boat hoist, and ramp; the park also has a tidal swimming area and concessions. *North Canal Dr., Homestead, tel. 305/245–2273. Admission: $3 per car, $5 for boat ramp, hoist available for $10.*

Flamingo Lodge Marina & Outpost Resort has a 50-slip marina that rents 40 canoes, 10 power skiffs, and five houseboats; several private boats are also available for charter. There are two ramps, one for Florida Bay, the other for Whitewater Bay and the back country. The hoist across the plug dam separating Florida Bay from the Buttonwood Canal can take boats up to 26 feet long. A small marina store sells food, camping supplies, bait and tackle, and automobile and boat fuel. *Tel. 305/253–2241 from Miami, 813/695–3101 from the Gulf Coast.*

Canoeing The subtropical wilderness of southern Florida is a mecca for flat-water paddlers. In winter, you'll find the best canoeing that the two parks can offer. Temperatures are moderate, rainfall is minimal, and the mosquitoes are tolerable.

Before you paddle into the back country and camp overnight, get a required free permit from the rangers in the park where you plan to canoe (at Convoy Point, Elliott Key, and Adams Key for Biscayne; at Everglades City or Flamingo for Everglades).

You don't need a permit for day trips, but tell someone where you're going and when you expect to return. Getting lost out here is easy, and spending the night without proper gear can be unpleasant, if not dangerous.

At Biscayne, you can explore five creeks through the mangrove wilderness within 1½ miles of park headquarters at Convoy Point.

Everglades has six well-marked canoe trails in the Flamingo area, including the southern end of the 100-mile Wilderness Waterway from Flamingo to Everglades City. **North American Canoe Tours** in Everglades City (*see below*) runs a three-hour shuttle service to haul people, cars, and canoes between Everglades City and Flamingo (cost $100 for 2 canoes).

The vendors listed below all rent aluminum canoes. Most have 17-foot Grummans. Bring your own cushions.

Biscayne National Park Tour Boats (Convoy Point in Biscayne National Park, tel. 305/247–2400) rents canoes for $5 per hour, $17.50 for four hours, $22.50 per day. Open daily 8:30–6.

Everglades National Park Boat Tours (Gulf Coast Ranger Station in Everglades City, tel. 813/695–2591, in FL 800/445–7724) rents canoes for $15 per half day, $20 per full day. Open daily 8:30–5.

North America Canoe Tours at Glades Haven (The Ivey House, 800 S.E. Copeland Ave., Box 5038, Everglades City 33929, tel. 813/695–4666) is an established source for canoes, sea kayaks, guided Everglades trips approved by the National Park Service (Nov.–Apr.), and single-speed bikes for local touring. Canoes cost $20 the first day, $18 for every day after. Reservations required; open daily 7 AM–9 PM.

Diving
Dive Boats and Instruction
Biscayne National Park Tour Boats is the official concessionaire for Biscayne National Park. The center provides equipment for dive trips and sells equipment. Snorkeling and scuba trips include about two hours on the reefs. *Reef Rover IV and V*, glass-bottom dive boats, each carry up to 48 passengers. The resort course and private instruction lead to full certification. *Office and dive boat at Convoy Point. Mailing address: Box 1270, Homestead 33030, tel. 305/247–2400. Cost: $24.50 snorkeling, $34.50 scuba. Reservations required. Open daily 7:30–6. Snorkeling and scuba trips daily 1:30–5 PM; group charters any day.*

Fishing
The rangers in the two parks enforce all state fishing laws and a few of their own. Ask at each park's visitor centers for that park's specific regulations.

Swimming
Homestead Bayfront Park has a saltwater atoll pool, adjacent to Biscayne Bay, which is flushed by tidal action. It's popular with local family groups and teenagers. Highlights include a newly installed "tot-lot" playground, ramps for disabled people (including a ramp that leads into the swimming area), and four new barbecues in the picnic pavilion. *N. Canal Dr., Home-*

stead, tel. 305/247–1543. Admission: $3 per car. Open daily 7 AM–sundown.

Elliott Key has a 30-foot-wide sandy beach (the only beach in Biscayne National Park), where boaters like to anchor off for a swim. It's about a mile north of the harbor on the west (bay) side of the key.

Dining and Lodging

Dining Although the two parks are wilderness areas, there are restaurants within a short drive of all park entrances: between Miami and Shark Valley along the Tamiami Trail (U.S. 41), in the Homestead–Florida City area, in Everglades City, and in the Keys along the Overseas Highway (U.S. 1). The only food service in either park is at Flamingo in the Everglades.

The list below is a selection of independent restaurants in Flamingo, the Homestead–Florida City area, along the Tamiami Trail, and in Everglades City. Many of these establishments will pack picnic fare that you can take to the parks. (You can also find fast-food establishments with carryout service on the Tamiami Trail and in Homestead–Florida City.)

Highly recommended restaurants are indicated by a star ★.

Category	Cost*
Very Expensive	over $50
Expensive	$35–$50
Moderate	$20–$35
Inexpensive	under $20

per person, excluding drinks, service, and 6% sales tax

Lodging Southwest of Miami, Homestead has become a bedroom community for both parks. You'll find well-kept older properties and shiny new ones, chain motels, and independents. Prices tend to be somewhat lower than in the Miami area. At Shark Valley, due west of Miami, there are no lodgings—only the Miccosukee Indians live there. Hotel and motel accommodations are available on the Gulf Coast at Everglades City and Naples.

The rate categories in the list are based on the all-year or peak-season price; off-peak rates may be a category or two lower.

Highly recommended lodgings are indicated by a star ★.

Category	Cost*
Very Expensive	over $150
Expensive	$90–$150
Moderate	$60–$90
Inexpensive	under $60

All prices are per room, double occupancy, excluding 6% state sales tax and modest resort tax.

Everglades City
Dining
★

The Oyster House. An established local favorite, this rustic sea-food house was built in 1984, with the Florida fishing-village look accented by mounted swampcats, gator heads, deer, crabs, nets, shells, and anchor chains. Lanterns from the A-frame ceiling burnish plank walls. You sit at booths and tables set without cloths. They'd serve on the porch, too, but the insects can get too pesty—though winters, when the bugs relent, guests with a drink from the bar sit out here waiting for tables. Fresh oysters are shucked daily; main course favorites include the broiled or grilled pompano, black-tip shark, frog's legs, gator tail, and custom-cut steaks. Desserts include a home-made key lime pie, carrot cake, and Black Forest cake. *Hwy. 29 (Chokoloskee Causeway), tel. 813/695–2073. Reservations accepted. Dress: casual. Closed Thanksgiving and Christmas. MC, V. Moderate*

Susie's Station. There's a real Susie at Susie's Station—Susie Olson from the Catskills, who fell in love with Everglades City and in 1992, after years running a pizza and sub shop, expanded by building her 85-seat restaurant next door. You'd swear the place dates from Everglades City's heyday, with its white-balustered screened porch, the gas station memorabilia, the 1898 horse-drawn oil tanker, the old Ford pick-up truck, and the Chevvy coupe. Replica '20s lamps are strung over booths set with beige cloths. There are three dining areas, one with original area art by Camille Baumgartner, another fixed up like an old general store, and the third on the screened porch. Susie features stone crabs in season, a cold seafood plate with lobster salad, seafood, steaks, and pizzas. Best buy is the nightly dinner special—maybe lasagna, baked chicken, or salisbury steak. The home-made Key lime pie sells out daily (whole pies to go cost $12). *103 S.W. Copeland Ave., tel. 813/695–2002. Reservations accepted. Dress: casual. Closed Thanksgiving and Christmas. Beer and wine only. No credit cards. Inexpensive.*

Dining and Lodging
★

The Rod & Gun Club. Hurricane Donna in 1960 did more damage than Andrew in 1992, but the pool and veranda were quickly restored at this landmark inn on the banks of the Collier River. With dark cypress and a nautical theme, the Rod & Gun is a vestige of backwoods glory days when imperial developer Barron Collier greeted U.S. presidents, Barrymores, and Gypsy Rose Lee here for days of leisurely fishing. Most of them flew in to the private landing strip; in the evenings they were fed by one of Collier's big catches, a chef who once worked for Kaiser Wilhelm. The old guest rooms, upstairs from the restaurant and bar, aren't open anymore, but you can stay in comfortable cottages (basic, with the standard amenities except room phone), and the food's more than passable. *200 Riverside Dr., Everglades City 33929, tel. 813/695–2101. 25 rooms with bath. Facilities: screened freshwater pool, tennis courts, restaurant, lounge. No credit cards. Moderate.*

Lodging

Ivey House. It's clean, homey, friendly, and a bargain, run by the folks who operate North American Canoe Tours—there are always adventure travelers around in the big living room, and lots of chatter over breakfast. The house is trailerlike, set upon blocks, and was a popular boarding house in the days when workers stayed here while building the Tamiami Trail. Earl Ivey's wife ran it back in the '20s; there was nothing at all fancy about it then, or now. Men's and women's baths are down the hall, but the rooms are private. *107 Camellia St., Ever-*

glades City 33929, tel. 813/695–3299. 10 rooms with shared baths. Open Nov.–Apr., but may stay open year-round beginning summer 1994. MC, V. Inexpensive.

Flamingo
Dining

Flamingo Restaurant. The view from this three-tier dining room on the second floor of the Flamingo Visitor Center will knock your socks off. Picture windows overlook Florida Bay, giving you a bird's-eye view (almost) of soaring eagles, gulls, pelicans, terns, and vultures. Try to dine at low tide when flocks of birds gather on a sandbar just offshore. Specialties include a flavorful, mildly spiced conch chowder; teriyaki chicken breast; and pork loin roasted Cuban-style with garlic and lime. The tastiest choices, however, are the seafood. If marlin is on the dinner menu, order it fried so that the moisture and flavor of the dark, chewy meat are retained. Picnic baskets available. They will cook the fish you catch if you clean it at the marina. There's buffet service only in summer; the snack bar at the marina store stays open all year to serve pizza, sandwiches, and salads. *Flamingo Visitor Center, Everglades National Park, Flamingo, tel. 305/253–2241 from Miami, 813/695–3101 from the Gulf Coast. Reservations advised at dinner. Dress: casual. AE, D, DC, MC, V. Moderate.*

Lodging

Flamingo Lodge Marina & Outpost Resort. This rustic low-rise wilderness resort, the only lodging inside Everglades National Park, is a strip of tentative civilization 300 yards wide and 1½ miles long. Accommodations are basic but attractive and well kept. An amiable staff with a sense of humor helps you become accustomed to alligators bellowing in the sewage-treatment pond down the road, raccoons roaming the pool enclosure at night, and the flock of ibis grazing on the lawn. The rooms have wood-paneled walls, contemporary furniture, floral bedspreads, and art prints of flamingos and egrets on the walls. All motel rooms face Florida Bay but don't necessarily overlook it. The cottages are in a wooded area on the margin of a coastal prairie. Ask about reserving tours, skiffs, and canoes when you make reservations. *Box 428, Flamingo 33090, tel. 305/253–2241 from Miami, 813/695–3101 from Gulf Coast. 125 units with bath, including 101 motel rooms, one 2-bath suite for up to 8 people, 24 kitchenette cottages (2 for handicapped guests). Facilities: outdoor pool, restaurant, lounge, marina, marina store with snack bar, gift shop, coin laundry. AE, D, DC, MC, V. Moderate.*

Florida City
Dining
★

Richard Accursio's Capri Restaurant and **King Richard's Room.** One of the oldest family-run restaurants in Dade County—since 1958—this is where locals dine out: business groups at lunch, the Rotary Club each Wednesday at noon, and families at night. Specialties include pizza with light, crunchy crusts and ample toppings; mild, meaty conch chowder; mussels in garlic-cream or marinara sauce; Caesar salad with lots of cheese and anchovies; antipasto with a homemade, vinegary Italian dressing; pasta shells stuffed with rigatoni cheese in tomato sauce; yellowtail snapper Française; and Key lime pie with plenty of real Key lime juice. *935 N. Krome Ave., Florida City, tel. 305/ 247–1544. Reservations advised. Dress: casual. AE, D, MC, V. Closed Sun. except Mother's Day. Closed Christmas. Moderate–Inexpensive.*

Lodging

Hampton Inn. This two-story, 102-unit motel just off the highway has good clean rooms and some public-friendly policies. There's a free Continental breakfast daily, free local calls, and the TV gets the Disney Channel at no extra charge. All rooms have at least two upholstered chairs, twin reading lamps, and a desk and chair. Units are color-coordinated and carpeted. Baths have tub-showers. *124 E. Palm Dr., Florida City 33034, tel. 800/426–7866 or 305/247–8833, fax 305/247–8833. Facilities: outdoor pool. AE, D, DC, MC, V. Moderate.*

Homestead
Dining

Mutineer Restaurant. Former Sheraton Hotels builder Allan Bennett built this stylish roadside restaurant with its indoor-outdoor fish and duck pond at a time (1980) when Homestead was barely on the map. Bilevel dining rooms (doubled in size in 1990) are upscale, with sea-scene dividers in etched glass, striped velvet chairs, stained glass, and a few portholes, but there's no excess. The Wharf Lounge behind its solid oak doors is equally imaginative, with magnified aquarium and nautical antiques such as a crow's nest with a real stuffed crow, gold parrot, and treasure chest. The big menu features 18 seafood entrées plus another half dozen daily seafood specials, as well as game, ribs, and steaks. Favorites include quail & tail (quail stuffed with blended wild rice and a broiled Florida lobster tail), and snapper Oscar (topped with crabmeat and asparagus). Enjoy live music Thursday–Saturday evenings. *11 S.E. 1st Ave., tel. 305/245–3377. Reservations accepted. Dress: casual but neat. AE, D, DC, MC, V. Moderate.*

★ **El Toro Taco.** The Hernandez family came to the United States from San Luis Potosí, Mexico, to pick crops. They opened this Homestead-area institution in 1971, where they make their own salt-free tortillas and nacho chips with corn from Texas that they grind themselves. The cilantro-dominated salsa is mild, for American tastes; if you like more fire on your tongue, ask for a side dish of minced jalapeño peppers to mix in. Specialties include *chile rellenos* (green peppers stuffed with meaty chunks of ground beef and topped with three kinds of cheese), and chicken *fajitas* (chunks of chicken marinated in Worcestershire sauce and spices, grilled in butter with onions and peppers, and served with tortillas and salsa). *1 S. Krome Ave., tel. 305/245–5576. No reservations. Dress: casual. BYOB. No credit cards. Inexpensive.*

Potlikker's. This southern country-style restaurant takes its name from the broth—pot liquor—left over from the boiling of greens. Live plants dangle from the sides of open rafters in the lofty pinelined dining room. Specialties include a lemon-pepper chicken breast with lemon sauce, fresh-carved roast turkey with homemade dressing, and at least 11 different vegetables to serve with lunch and dinner entrées. For dessert, try Key lime pie—four inches tall and frozen; it tastes great if you dawdle over dessert while it thaws. *591 Washington Ave., tel. 305/248–0835. No reservations. Dress: casual. AE, MC, V. Closed Christmas Day. Inexpensive.*

Tiffany's. This country-French cottage with shops and restaurant under a big banyan tree looks like a converted pioneer house with its high-pitched roof and lattice. That's because fourth-generation Miamian Rebecca DeLuria, who built it in 1984 with her husband, Robert, wanted a place that reminded her of the Miami she remembered. Teaberry-colored tables, satin-like floral placemats, marble-effect floor tiles, fresh flowers on each table, and lots of country items lend to the tea-room style found here. Featured entrées include hot crabmeat au gratin, asparagus supreme (rolled in ham with hollandaise sauce), and quiche of the day. Homemade desserts are to die for: old-fashioned (very tall) carrot cake, strawberry whipped-cream cake, and a harvest pie with double crust that layers apples, cranberries, walnuts, raisins, and a caramel topping. *22 N.E. 15th St., tel. 305/246–0022. Reservations accepted. Dress: casual but neat. AE, MC, V. No dinner. Closed Memorial Day, Labor Day, Christmas, New Year's Day. Inexpensive.*

Lodging   **Holiday Inn.** This low-rise motel is situated on a commercial strip. The best rooms look out on the landscaped pool and adjoining Banana Bar. Rooms have contemporary walnut furnishings and firm, bouncy mattresses. A guest laundry and fitness room were added in 1992. *990 N. Homestead Blvd., Homestead 33030, tel. 305/247–7020 or 800/HOLIDAY. 150 rooms with bath. Facilities: outdoor pool, restaurant, lounge, poolside bar. AE, D, DC, MC, V. Moderate.*

Nearby Miami   **Coopertown Restaurant.** This rustic 30-seat restaurant is full of
Dining   Floridiana, including alligator skulls, stuffed alligator heads, and alligator accessories (belts, key chains, and the like). Specialties include alligator and frogs' legs, breaded and deep-fried in vegetable oil, available for breakfast, lunch, or dinner. *22700 S.W. 8th St., Miami, tel. 305/226–6048. Reservations accepted. Dress: casual. No credit cards. Inexpensive.*

The Pit Bar-B-Q. This place will overwork your salivary glands with its intense aroma of barbecue and blackjack oak smoke. You order at the counter, then come when called to pick up your food. Specialties include barbecued chicken and ribs with a tangy sauce, french fries, coleslaw, and a fried biscuit, and catfish, frogs' legs, and shrimp breaded and deep-fried in vegetable oil. *16400 S.W. 8th St., Miami, tel. 305/226–2272. Dress: casual. No reservations. Closed Christmas Day. MC, V. Inexpensive.*

Shark Valley   **Miccosukee Restaurant.** Murals with Indian themes depict
Dining   women cooking and men engaged in a powwow. Specialties include catfish and frogs' legs breaded and deep-fried in peanut oil, Indian fry bread (a flour-and-water dough deep-fried in peanut oil), pumpkin bread, Indian burger (ground beef browned, rolled in fry bread dough, and deep-fried), and Indian tacos (fry bread with chili, lettuce, tomato, and shredded cheddar cheese on top). *Tamiami Trail, near Shark Valley entrance to Everglades park, tel. 305/223–8380, ext. 332. No reservations. Dress: casual. AE, DC, MC, V. Inexpensive.*

Camping

Biscayne National Park. You can camp on designated keys 7 miles offshore at primitive sites or in the backcountry. Carry all your food, water, and supplies onto the keys, and carry all trash off when you leave. Bring plenty of insect repellent. *Free. No reservations. No ferry or marina services. For backcountry camping, obtain a required free permit from rangers at Adams Key, Convoy Point, or Elliott Key.*
Everglades National Park. The park includes three developed campsites with drinking water, sewage dump station, restrooms, cold showers, and hand-laundry. **Long Pine Key** offers 108 campsites. **Flamingo** offers 235 drive-in sites and 60 walk-in sites. **Chekika** offers 20–25 sites plus a group site for up to 20, and additionally offers both hot and cold showers. Primitive campgrounds are located throughout the park but offer no water or electricity. Come early to get a good site, especially in

winter. Bring plenty of insect repellent. *Admission: $8 per site in winter, free in summer except for walk-in sites at Flamingo, which are $4. Stay limited to 14 days Nov. 1–Apr. 30. Check-out time 10 AM. Register at campground. Open all year.*

Everglades National Park Backcountry Sites. Deep in the park are 48 designated sites (two accessible by land, others only by canoe), 14 with chickees (raised wood platforms with thatch roofs). All have chemical toilets, including the 29 ground sites. Four chickee sites and nine of the ground sites are within an easy day's canoeing of Flamingo; five of the ground sites are within an easy day's canoeing of Everglades City. Call ahead for information on handicap accessibility and updates. Carry all your food, water, and supplies in; carry out all trash. Get free permit from rangers at Everglades City or Flamingo. Permits issued for a specific site. Capacity and length of stay limited. Call for daily updates, but sites available first come, first served. *Flamingo Ranger Station, Backcountry Reservations Office, Box 279, Homestead 33034, tel. 305/242–7700 or 813/695–3101, ext. 182.*

6 Fort Lauderdale

**Updated by
Herb Hiller**

If you think of Fort Lauderdale only as a spring-break mecca for collegians seeking sun, suds, and surf, your knowledge is both fragmentary and out-of-date. It's true that after the 1960 film *Where the Boys Are* attracted hordes of young people to the city's beaches, Fort Lauderdale became so popular with students on spring break that upscale visitors began to shun the city year-round. But city officials intentionally discouraged college revelers after a record number of 350,000 appeared in 1985; by 1992 that number dropped to fewer than 15,000 (most have relocated to Daytona Beach and Panama City).

Today, visitors who choose Fort Lauderdale and its nearby beachfront communities generally do so because they prefer a quieter, less pretentious, and slightly less expensive style of vacationing. They like the fact that the beach here is more open and accessible than Miami Beach and less eroded than Palm Beach. A variety of affordable, well-maintained, mom-and-pop lodgings, located only minutes from the beach, line this stretch of coast. Beautiful new development downtown along the riverfront has kept Fort Lauderdale appealing, but the emphasis is on culture, history, and education, not on trendy publicity-grabbing attractions. It's primarily intended to improve the quality of life for people who *live* here, although it ends up making for high-quality vacations as well.

Broward County is also blessed with near-ideal weather, with about 3,000 hours of sunshine a year. The average temperature is about 77 degrees—66 degrees in winter, 84 degrees in summer.

Sandwiched between Miami to the south and Palm Beach to the north along southeast Florida's Gold Coast, Fort Lauderdale is the county seat of huge Broward County, which has 23 miles of Atlantic Ocean beach frontage. Broward County is named for Napoleon Bonaparte Broward, Florida's governor from 1905 to 1909, whose drainage schemes around the turn of the century opened much of the marshy Everglades region for farming, ranching, and settlement. Fort Lauderdale's first known white settler, Charles Lewis, established a plantation along the New River in 1793. Major William Lauderdale built a fort at the river's mouth in 1838 during the Seminole Indian wars—hence the name Fort Lauderdale.

Incorporated in 1911, with just 175 residents, Fort Lauderdale grew rapidly during the Florida boom of the 1920s. Today the city has a population of 150,000, while its suburban areas keep growing and growing. New homes, offices, and shopping centers have filled in the gaps between older communities along the coastal ridge; now they're marching west along I–75, I–595, and the Sawgrass Expressway as well. Once a home for retirees, Broward County now attracts younger, working-age families, too. All in all, it's a sane and pleasant place to spend a vacation.

Essential Information

Important Addresses and Numbers

Tourist Information Dania Chamber of Commerce (Box 838, Dania 33004, tel. 305/927–3377).

Deerfield Beach Chamber of Commerce (1601 E. Hillsboro Blvd., Deerfield Beach 33441, tel. 305/427–1050).
Greater Fort Lauderdale Chamber of Commerce (512 N.E. 3rd Ave., tel. 305/462–6000).
Greater Fort Lauderdale Convention & Visitors Bureau (200 E. Las Olas Boulevard, Suite 1500, tel. 305/765–4466; tel. 800/22-SUNNY for brochures) is open weekdays 8:30–5.
Hollywood Chamber of Commerce (4000 Hollywood Blvd., Suite 265 S, Hollywood 33021, tel. 305/985–4000).
Lauderdale-by-the-Sea Chamber of Commerce (4201 Ocean Dr., Lauderdale-by-the-Sea 33308, tel. 305/776–1000).
Pompano Beach Chamber of Commerce (2200 E. Atlantic Blvd., Pompano Beach 33062, tel. 305/941–2940).

Emergencies Dial 911 for **police** and **ambulance** in an emergency.

Poison Control (tel. 800/282–3171).

Hospitals The following hospitals have a 24-hour emergency room: **Holy Cross Hospital** (4725 N. Federal Hwy., Fort Lauderdale, tel. 305/771–8000; physician referral, tel. 305/776–3223), **Imperial Point Hospital** (6401 N. Federal Hwy., Fort Lauderdale, tel. 305/776–8610; physician referral, tel. 305/355–4888), and **Broward General Medical Center** (1600 S. Andrews Ave., Fort Lauderdale, tel. 305/355–5700; physician referral, tel. 305/355–4888).

24-Hour Pharmacies **Eckerd Drug** (1385 S.E. 17th St., Fort Lauderdale, tel. 305/525–8173; Commercial Blvd. at N.E. 18th Ave., Fort Lauderdale, tel. 305/771–0660; and 154 University Dr., Pembroke Pines, tel. 305/432–5510). **Walgreens** (2855 Stirling Rd., Fort Lauderdale, tel. 305/981–1104; 5001 N. Dixie Hwy., Oakland Park, tel. 305/772–4206; and 289 S. Federal Hwy., Deerfield Beach, tel. 305/481–2993).

Arriving and Departing

By Plane **Fort Lauderdale–Hollywood International Airport (FLHIA)** (tel. 305/357–6100), just off U.S. 1, 4 miles south of downtown Fort Lauderdale, is Broward County's major airline terminal. Scheduled airlines include American (tel. 800/433–7300), Braniff (tel. 800/BRANIFF), Chalk's International (tel. 800/432–8807), Comair (tel. 800/354–9822), Continental (tel. 800/525–0281), Delta (tel. 800/221–1212), Midwest Express (tel. 800/452–2022), Northwest (tel. 800/225–2525), Paradise Island (tel. 800/432–8807), TWA (tel. 800/221–2000), United (tel. 800/241–6522), USAir (tel. 800/842–5374), and Airways International (tel. 305/887–2794).

Between the Airport and Center City **Broward Transit**'s bus route No. 1 operates between the airport and its main terminal at N.W. 1st Street and 1st Avenue in the center of Fort Lauderdale. Service from the airport begins daily at 5:40 AM; the last bus from the downtown terminal to the airport leaves at 9:30 PM. The fare is 85¢. Limousine service is available from **Airport Express** (tel. 305/527–8690) to all parts of Broward County. Fares to most Fort Lauderdale beach hotels are in the $6–$8 range. **Economy Shuttle** (tel. 305/722–7433) operates van service, if booked 24 hours in advance. Fares run from $6 (to Las Olas Boulevard or to Hollywood Beach) to $14 (all the way north to Deerfield Beach).

By Car The access highways to Broward County from the north or south are Florida's Turnpike I–95, U.S. 1, and U.S. 441. I–75

(Alligator Alley) connects Broward County with the west coast of Florida, paralleled by Route 84.

By Train **Amtrak** (tel. 800/872–7245) provides daily service to Broward County, with stops at Hollywood, Fort Lauderdale, and Deerfield Beach. The Fort Lauderdale station (tel. 305/463–8251) is at 200 S.W. 21st Terr.

Tri-Rail (tel. 305/728–8445; locally, 800/874–7245) operates train service daily, 5 AM–11 PM (more limited on weekends), around Broward, Dade, and Palm Beach counties. There are six stations in Broward County, all of them west of I–95.

By Bus **Greyhound/Trailways** buses stop at the Fort Lauderdale bus station (513 N.E. 3rd St., tel. 305/764–6551).

Getting Around

By Car Except during rush hour, Broward County is a fairly easy place in which to travel. East–west I–595 runs from westernmost Broward County to link I–75 and U.S. 1, providing handy access to Fort Lauderdale–Hollywood International Airport. The scenic but slow Route A1A generally parallels the beach area.

A 2-mile stretch of I–95, between Route 84 and Sunrise Boulevard, is being widened, with crews working through mid-1994; expect major bottlenecks.

By Bus **Broward County Mass Transit** serves the entire county. The fare is 85¢ (40¢ senior citizens, the disabled, and students), plus 10¢ for a transfer. Some bus routes start as early as 5 AM; some continue until 9 PM. Call for route information (tel. 305/357–8400). Special seven-day tourist passes, which cost $8, are good for unlimited use on all county buses. These are available at some hotels, at Broward County libraries, and at the main bus terminal at Broward Boulevard at S.W. 1st Avenue.

By Taxi It's difficult to hail a taxi on the street; sometimes you can pick one up at a major hotel. Otherwise, phone ahead. Fares are not cheap; meters run at a rate of $2.20 for the first mile and $1.50 for each additional mile; waiting time is 25¢ per minute. The major company serving the area is **Yellow Cab** (tel. 305/565–5400).

By Water Taxi **Water Taxi** (tel. 305/565–5507) provides service along the Intracoastal Waterway between Port Everglades and Commercial Boulevard 10 AM–1 AM and between Atlantic Boulevard and Hillsboro Boulevard in Pompano Beach noon–midnight. The boats stop at more than 30 restaurants, hotels, shops, and nightclubs; the fare is $5 one-way, $13 for an all-day pass, $45 weekly.

Guided Tours

Carrie B. (Riverwalk at S.E. 5th Ave. tel. 305/768–9920) operates a 300-passenger day-cruiser up the New River and Intracoastal Waterway.

Jungle Queen (Bahia Mar Yacht Center tel. 305/462–5596) operates 155-passenger and 578-passenger tour boats on day and night cruises up the New River, through the heart of Fort Lauderdale.

Las Olas Horse and Carriage (610 E. Las Olas Blvd., tel. 305/763–7393) operates in-town tours and transportation to and from the Performing Arts Center.

River/Walking Tours (219 S.W. 2nd Ave., tel. 305/463–4431), co-sponsored by the Fort Lauderdale Historical Society, trace the New River by foot and by boat.

South Florida Trolley Tours (tel. 305/522–7701); offers fully narrated, 90-minute tours on *Lolly the Trolley* daily from 9 to 5, starting from the Welcome Station on Route A1A, with pick-ups along Las Olas Blvd.

Exploring Fort Lauderdale

Highlights for First-Time Visitors

Beachfront promenade (North on Scenic A1A)
Bonnet House (North on Scenic A1A)
International Swimming Hall of Fame (North on Scenic A1A)
Las Olas Boulevard shopping (Downtown Fort Lauderdale)
Museum of Art (Downtown Fort Lauderdale)
Riverwalk (Downtown Fort Lauderdale)

Downtown Fort Lauderdale

Numbers in the margin correspond to points of interest on the Fort Lauderdale Area map.

❶ This tour begins, appropriately enough, at **Stranahan House,** home of pioneer businessman Frank Stranahan and the oldest standing structure in Fort Lauderdale. Stranahan arrived in 1892 and began trading with the Seminole Indians; in 1901 he built a store, and later made it his home. Now it's a museum with many of his furnishings on display. *1 Stranahan Pl. (335 S.E. 6th Ave.), tel. 305/524–4736. Admission: $3 adults, $2 children under 12. Open Wed., Fri., Sat. 10–3:30.*

❷ Go north on S.E. 6th Avenue to **Las Olas Boulevard.** From S.E. 6th Avenue to S.E. 11th Street, Las Olas is an upscale shopping street with Spanish-Colonial buildings housing high-fashion boutiques, jewelry shops, and art galleries. If you drive east on
❸ Las Olas, you'll cross into **The Isles,** Fort Lauderdale's most expensive and prestigious neighborhood, where the homes line a series of canals with large yachts beside the seawalls.

Return on Las Olas to Andrews Avenue, turn right, and park in one of the municipal garages while you walk around downtown
❹ Fort Lauderdale. First stop is the **Museum of Art,** which features a major collection of works from the CoBrA (Copenhagen, Brussels, and Amsterdam) movement, plus Native American, pre-Columbian, West African, and Oceanic ethnographic art. Edward Larabee Barnes designed the museum building, which opened in 1986. The museum has a notable collection of works by celebrated Ashcan School artist William Glackens and other early 20th-century American painters. *1 E. Las Olas Blvd., tel. 305/525–5500. Admission: $3.25 adults, $2.75 senior citizens, $1.25 students, under 12 free; free 1-hour tours. Open Tues. 11–9, Wed.–Sat. 10–5, Sun. noon–5.*

Fort Lauderdale Area

Art and Cultural
Center of Hollywood, **16**
Bonnet House, **11**
Broadwalk, **17**
Brooks Memorial
Causeway, **8**
Broward County
Main Library, **5**
Deerfield Island
Park, **15**

Hillsboro Light, **14**
Hollywood North
Beach Park, **18**
Hugh Taylor Birch
State Recreation
Area, **10**
International Swimming
Hall of Fame Museum
and Pool, **9**

The Isles, **3**
John U. Lloyd Beach
State Recreation
Area, **19**
Las Olas Boulevard, **2**
Lauderdale-by-the-
Sea, **12**
Museum of Art, **4**

Ocean World, **7**
Pompano Beach, **13**
Riverwalk, **6**
Stranahan House, **1**

5 Walk one block north to the **Broward County Main Library,** in a distinctive building designed by Marcel Breuer. On display here are many works from Broward's Art in Public Places program, including a painting by Yaacov Agam; a wood construction by Marc Beauregard; an outdoor, aluminum-and-steel sculpture by Dale Eldred; and ceramic tile by Ivan Chermayeff. Productions from theater to poetry readings are presented in a 300-seat auditorium. *100 S. Andrews Ave., tel. 305/357–7444; 305/357–7457 for self-guided Art in Public Places walking tour brochure. Admission free. Open. Mon.–Thurs. 10–9, Fri.–Sat. 9–5, Sun. 12:30–5:30. Closed holidays.*

6 Go north to Broward Boulevard, turn left, and head toward palm-lined **Riverwalk,** a lovely, paved promenade on the north bank of the New River. By the mid-1990s, Riverwalk will extend 2 miles on both sides of the beautiful urban stream, connecting a magnificent cluster of new facilities collectively known as the **Arts and Science District.** Outdoor **Esplanade Park** features several science exhibits, but the star science attraction is the **Museum of Discovery and Science**, opened in 1992. It has the Blockbuster IMAX Theater and interactive exhibits on ecology, health, outer space, and other topics. *401 S.W. 2nd St., tel. 305/467–6637 (museum), tel. 305/463–4629 (IMAX). Admission: $6 adults, $5 senior citizens and children; children under 3 free. Open weekdays 10–5, Sat. 10–8:30, Sun. noon–5.*

The adjacent **Broward Center for the Performing Arts,** a massive glass-and-concrete structure by the river, opened in 1991. *201 S.W. 5th Ave., tel. 305/462–0222.*

East of the Esplanade along the Riverwalk is the **Fort Lauderdale Historical Society Museum,** which surveys the city's history from the Seminole Indian era to World War II. A model in the lobby depicts old Fort Lauderdale. The building also houses a research library and a bookstore. *219 S.W. 2nd Ave., tel. 305/463–4431. Admission: $2 adults, $1 children 6–12, children under 6 free. Open Tues.–Sat. 10–4, Sun. 1–4.*

North on Scenic A1A

7 About a mile east of the intersection of U.S. 1 and S.E. 17th Street, you'll find the entrance to **Ocean World,** an intimate marine park. Six shows daily feature trained dolphins and sea lions. Display tanks hold sharks, sea turtles, alligators, and river otters. You can feed and pet a dolphin here. *1701 S.E. 17th St., tel. 305/525–6611. Admission: $10.95 adults, $8.95 children 4–12, under 4 free. Boat tour admission: $6 adults, $5 children 4–12, under 4 free. Tours at 12:30, 2:50, and 5:05 last about an hour. Open 10–6, last show starts 4:15.*

Across 17th Street is the new **Greater Fort Lauderdale/Broward County Convention Center,** home of boat shows, antique shows, and mammoth meetings.

Time Out **Joe's Bel-Air's** (1717 Eisenhower Blvd., tel. 305/527–5637), a longtime favorite diner, has been somewhat subdued now in order to attract conventioneers—wisecracking signs and waitresses were its hallmark back when only port types found their way here. Still, the same affordable down-home cooking is served up around the clock—including breakfast whenever you want.

⑧ Go east on S.E. 17th Street across the **Brooks Memorial Causeway** over the Intracoastal Waterway, and bear left onto Seabreeze Boulevard (Route A1A). You'll pass through a neighborhood of older homes set in lush vegetation before emerging at the south end of Fort Lauderdale's beachfront strip. On your left at **Bahia Mar Resort & Yachting Center,** novelist John McDonald's fictional hero, Travis McGee, is honored with a plaque at marina slip F-18, where he docked his houseboat. *801 Seabreeze Blvd., tel. 305/764–2233 or 800/327–8154.*

⑨ Three blocks north, visit the **International Swimming Hall of Fame Museum and Pool,** with its 10-lane, 50-meter pool. An expanded exhibition building features photos, medals, and other souvenirs from major swimming events around the world. *1 Hall of Fame Dr., museum tel. 305/462–6536, pool tel. 305/468–1580. Museum admission: $3 adults; $1 children 6–21, senior citizens, and military personnel; $7 family. Pool admission: $3 adults; $2 students; $1 resident students, senior citizens, military personnel. Museum and pro shop open daily 9–7 (subject to change).*

North of Las Olas Boulevard, Route A1A is lined with hotels, restaurants, and shops on your left, the ocean on your right. For 2½ miles, this stretch of beach road (Rte. A1A) and beachfront have been improved with planters, palms, and a beachfront wall of ornamental entrances, whorled and scrolled. Throughout the beach area, you'll see distinctive signs, street furniture, and a repeated wave motif. More than ever, the boulevard is worth promenading.

⑩ Turn left off Route A1A at Sunrise Boulevard, then right into **Hugh Taylor Birch State Recreation Area.** Amid the 180-acre park's tropical greenery, you can stroll along a nature trail, visit the Birch House Museum, picnic, play volleyball, pitch horseshoes, and paddle a canoe. *3109 E. Sunrise Blvd., tel. 305/564–4521. Admission: $3.25 per car. Open 8–sundown. Ranger-guided nature walks Fri. 10:30.*

⑪ Cross Sunrise Boulevard south and go to visit the **Bonnet House** (closed in winter, unfortunately). This lovely house built by artist Frederic Clay Bartlett stands on land he was given by his first father-in-law, Hugh Taylor Birch. The house and its subtropical 35-acre estate contain original works of art, whimsically carved animals, a swan pond, and, most of all, tranquility. *900 N. Birch Rd., tel. 305/563–5393. Admission (by reserved tour only): $8 adults; $6 senior citizens, students, and military personnel; children under 6 free. Open May–Nov., Tues.–Thurs. 10 and 1:30, Sun. 1:30.*

North of Birch Park, Route A1A edges back from the beach through a section known as the **Galt Ocean Mile,** marked by beach-blocking high rises. The pattern changes again in **⑫** **Lauderdale-by-the-Sea,** a low-rise family resort town. One block east of Route A1A, you can drive along lawn-divided El Mar Drive, lined by garden-style motels.

Time Out   Where Commercial Boulevard meets the ocean, you can walk out onto **Anglin's Pier,** stretching 875 feet into the Atlantic. Stop in at the coffee shop or at any of the popular restaurants clustered around the seafront plaza. **Aruba Beach Cafe** (tel. 305/776–0001) is your best bet: a big beachside barn, always crowded, always happy, serving large portions of Caribbean conch chowder, Cuban black bean soup, fresh tropical salads, burgers, sandwiches, and seafood.

⑬ North of Lauderdale-by-the-Sea, Route A1A enters **Pompano Beach,** where the high-rise procession begins again. At Atlantic Boulevard turn east to drive along the shore; here A1A is called Pompano Beach Boulevard. Behind a low coral rock wall, a park extends north and south of **Fisherman's Wharf** along the road and beach. The road swings back from the beach, and then returns to it crossing **Hillsboro Inlet.** To your left across the in-⑭ let you can see **Hillsboro Light,** the brightest light in the Southeast. The light is on private property and is inaccessible to the public.

Route A1A now enters onto the so-called **Hillsboro Mile** (actually more than 2 miles), which only a few years ago was one of the outstanding residential corridors of Florida. Changes in zoning laws, however, have altered the area—except for sections in the south and north, the island seems destined to sink under the weight of its massive condominiums. The road runs along a narrow strip of land between the Intracoastal Waterway and the ocean, with bougainvillea and oleanders edging the way and yachts docked along both banks. In winter, the traffic often creeps at a snail's pace along here, as vacationers and retirees gawk at the views. Turn left on Hillsboro Boulevard (Route 810). Make a sharp right just over the bridge to Riverview Road, and park at the Riverview Restaurant to take ⑮ a free boat ride to **Deerfield Island Park** (1 Deerfield Island, Deerfield Beach, tel. 305/428–5474, open Wednesdays and Saturdays). This 8 ½-acre island, officially designated an urban wilderness area, resulted from the dredging of the Intracoastal Waterway and from construction of the Royal Palm Canal. Its mangrove swamp provides a critical habitat for gopher tortoises, gray foxes, raccoons, and armadillos.

At this point you're right across the county line from Palm Beach County (*see* Chapter 7). You can return to Fort Lauderdale along Route A1A, or turn west and head south along U.S. 1 or I–95.

Hollywood

Begin exploring at the junction of U.S. 1 and Hollywood Boulevard, called **Young Circle** after Joseph W. Young, a California real estate developer who in 1921 began developing the community of Hollywood from the flatwoods. Just east of here, you can ⑯ visit an art gallery in the **Art and Cultural Center of Hollywood,** set in a 1924 Mediterranean-style residence, typical of its era. *1650 Harrison St., Hollywood, tel. 305/921–3274. Admission: $2 Wed.–Sat., $3 Sun., donations accepted Tues. Open Tues.–Sat. 10–4, Sun. 1–4.*

Drive east along wide Hollywood Boulevard, a remaining glory of Young's era. You will cross the Intracoastal Waterway in front of the **Hollywood Beach Resort Hotel** (101 N. Ocean Dr., tel. 305/921–0990), opened by Young in 1922 and now a timeshare. To the rear of the hotel is the retail and entertainment mall **Oceanwalk**—a good idea that has never been consistently successful.

Take the ramp north onto Route A1A. The Intracoastal Waterway parallels Route A1A to the west; the beach and ocean lie
17 just beyond the 2.2-mile **Broadwalk,** a paved promenade since 1924, popular with pedestrians and cyclists. Especially during the winter, expect to hear French spoken: Hollywood Beach has been a favorite winter getaway for Québecois ever since Joseph Young hired French-Canadians to work here in the 1920s.

Time Out One-half mile north on the left is **Le Tub** (1100 N. Ocean Dr., Hollywood Beach, tel. 305/921–9425), formerly a Sunoco gas station and now a quirky waterside saloon with an affection for clawfoot bathtubs—hand-painted tubs are everywhere, under ficus, seagrape, and palm trees. Le Tub is highly favored by locals for affordable food, mostly shrimp and barbecue.

18 The Broadwalk ends at **Hollywood North Beach Park** (Rte. A1A and Sheridan St., tel. 305/921–1553). No high-rises overpower the scene, nothing hip or chic, just a laid-back old-fashioned place for enjoying sun, sand, and sea.

Continue north along Route A1A. The wilderness area west across the waterway is part of the large, 1,400-acre **West Lake Park** (1200 Sheridan St., tel. 305/925–8377).

At Dania Beach Boulevard, Route A1A turns west and crosses the waterway onto the mainland for a couple of miles. You may,
19 however, want to continue north into **John U. Lloyd Beach State Recreation Area** (6503 North Ocean Dr., tel. 305/923–2833), with its pleasant pine-shaded beach and a jetty pier where you can fish. There are good views from here, north to Palm Beach County and south to Miami Beach. From the road, look west across the waterway to Port Everglades, with its deepwater freighters and cruise ships.

What to See and Do with Children

Butterfly World is a screened-in aviary in a tropical rain forest on 2.8 acres of land, where thousands of caterpillars pupate and emerge as butterflies, up to 150 species. *3600 W. Sample Rd., Coconut Creek, tel. 305/977–4400. Admission: $7.95 adults, $5 children 3–12, $6.95 senior citizens. Open Mon.–Sat. 9–5, Sun. 1–5.*

Everglades Holiday Park and Campground offers a 60-minute, narrated airboat tour and an alligator-wrestling show featuring Seminole Indians. The park has a 100-space campground that accommodates recreational vehicles and tents. *21940 Griffin Rd., Ft. Lauderdale 33332, tel. 305/434–8111 (Broward County), 305/621–2009 (Miami). Tour: $12 adults, $6 children, under 3 free. Open daily 9–5.*

Flamingo Gardens offers gators, crocodiles, river otters, birds of prey, a 23,000-square-foot walk-through aviary, a plant house, and an Everglades Museum in the pioneer Wray Home. Admission includes a 1½-hour guided tram ride through a citrus grove and wetlands area. *3750 Flamingo Rd., tel. 305/473–2955. Admission: $6 adults, $2.50 children 4–12; $4.80 senior citizens. Open daily 9–5.*

Museum of Discovery & Science and IMAX Theater (*see* Downtown Fort Lauderdale, *above*).

Ocean World (*see* North on Scenic A1A, *above*).

Seminole Native Village is a reservation where Seminole Indians sell native arts and crafts and run a high-stakes bingo parlor (4150 N. Rte. 7, tel. 305/961–5140 for recorded information or 305/961–3220 for general information). At the adjacent **Anhinga Indian Museum and Art Gallery,** Joe Dan and Virginia Osceola display a collection of artifacts from the Seminoles and other American Indian tribes. They also sell contemporary Indian art and craft objects. *5791 S. Rte. 7, tel. 305/581–8411. Open daily 9–5.*

Spykes Grove & Tropical Gardens takes visitors aboard a tractor-pulled tram for a 15-minute tour of working citrus groves, in operation since 1944. A bear born in captivity, gators, prairie dogs, roosters, and peacocks are also on exhibit. *7250 Griffin Rd., tel. 305/583–0426. Admission free. Tours hourly 11–4. Open Oct.–June, daily 9–5:30.*

Shopping

Shopping Districts
Major Malls

Broward Mall, the county's largest upscale shopping center, features such stores as Burdines, J.C. Penney, and Sears. *8000 W. Broward Blvd., Plantation, tel. 305/473–8100. Open Mon.–Sat. 10–9, Sun. noon–5:30.*

Fashion Mall features Macy's and Lord & Taylor among 150 shops, boutiques, and restaurants in a three-level, 669,000-square-foot, landscaped, glass-enclosed facility. *University Blvd., Plantation, tel. 305/370–1884. Open Mon.–Sat. 10–9, Sun. noon–6.*

Galleria Mall on Sunrise Boulevard, just west of the Intracoastal Waterway, occupies more than one million square feet and includes Neiman-Marcus, Lord & Taylor, Saks Fifth Avenue, and Brooks Brothers. *Tel. 305/564–1015. Open Mon.–Sat. 9–10, Sun. noon–5:30.*

Pompano Square in Pompano Beach has 110 shops with three department stores and food stalls. *2255 N. Federal Hwy., tel. 305/943–4683. Open Mon.–Sat. 10–9, Sun. noon–5:30.*

Sawgrass Mills Mall is an immense, candy-colored, Disney-style discount mall with more than two million square feet of stores, restaurants, and entertainment activities. Among the major stores: Macy's Outlet, Saks Outlet, Ann Taylor, and Spiegel's Outlet. *Intersection of Flamingo Rd. and Sunrise Blvd., tel. 305/846–2350. Open Mon.–Sat. 10–9:30, Sun. 11–6.*

Antiques

More than 75 dealers line U.S. 1 (Federal Hwy.) in **Dania,** ½ mile south of the Fort Lauderdale International Airport and ½ mile north of Hollywood. *Exit Griffin Rd E. off I–95.*

Flea Market

Some 600 vendors set up daily at the **Festival Marketplace,** the largest market of its type in the county. *2900 W. Sample Rd., Pompano Beach, tel. 305/979-4555. Open daily 9:30–5.*

Upscale Boutiques

If only for a stroll and some window shopping, don't miss **The Shops of Las Olas,** the city's best one-of-a-kind boutiques plus top restaurants (many affordable) along a beautiful landscaped street. It's located a block off the New River just west of Federal Highway (U.S. 1).

Participant Sports

Biking Cycling is popular in Broward County, though statistically this is one of the most dangerous places to ride in Florida. So it's good news that the new 330-meter **velodrome** opened at Brian Piccolo Park (Sheridan St. and N.W. 101st Ave.) in Cooper City. This outdoor track has public hours throughout the week. For a schedule of public hours and spectator events, call the **County Bicycle Coordinator** (115 S. Andrews Ave., Fort Lauderdale 33301, tel. 305/357–6661). Otherwise, the most popular routes are along Route A1A, especially early in the morning before traffic builds. Many shops along the beach rent bikes. A new map for cycling Broward's streets is available from many shops or from the county bicycle coordinator.

Diving Good diving can be enjoyed within 20 minutes of the shore along Broward County's coast. Among the most popular of the county's 80 dive sites is the 2-mile-wide, 23-mile-long **Fort Lauderdale Reef,** the product of Florida's most successful artificial reef-building program. The project began in 1984 with the sinking of a 435-foot freighter donated by an Oklahoma marine electronics manufacturer. Since then more than a dozen houseboats, ships, and oil platforms have been sunk to provide a habitat for fish and other marine life, as well as to help stabilize beaches. The most famous sunken ship is the 200-foot German freighter *Mercedes*, which was blown ashore in a violent Thanksgiving storm onto Palm Beach socialite Mollie Wilmot's pool terrace in 1984: the ship has now been sunk a mile off Fort Lauderdale beach. For more information, contact the Greater Fort Lauderdale Convention & Visitors Bureau (*see* Important Addresses and Numbers, *above*).

Dive Boats and All **Force E** stores rent scuba and snorkeling equipment. In-
Instruction struction is available at all skill levels. Dive boat charters are available. *2700 E. Atlantic Blvd., Pompano Beach, tel. 305/ 943–3483 open in winter, Mon.–Sat. 8–7, Sun. 8–5; in summer, weekdays 8–8:30, Sat. 8–7, Sun. 8–5. 2104 W. Oakland Park Blvd., Oakland Park, tel. 305/735–6227; open in winter, weekdays 9–8, Sat. 8–7, Sun. 8–4; in summer, weekdays 8–9, Sat. 8–7, Sun. 8–4.*

Lauderdale Diver arranges dive charters throughout the county. Dive trips typically last four hours. Nonpackage reef trips are also open to divers for $35, to snorkelers for $25 (including snorkel equipment); scuba gear is extra. PADI affiliated. *1334 S.E. 17th St. Causeway, Fort Lauderdale, tel. 305/467–2822 or 800/654–2073. Open weekdays 9–6, Sat. 8–6, Sun. 8–1.*

Pro Dive, the area's oldest diving operation, offers packages with Bahia Mar Resort & Yachting Center, from where its 60-foot boat departs. Nonpackage snorkelers can go out for $25 on the four-hour dive trip, or for $20 on the two-hour snorkeling trip, which includes snorkel equipment but not scuba gear. *Bahia Mar Resort & Yachting Center, Rte. A1A, Fort Lauderdale, tel. 305/761–3413 or 800/772–DIVE outside FL.*

Fishing Two primary centers for saltwater charter boats are Fort
Charters Lauderdale's **Bahia Mar Yachting Center** and the **Fish City Marina** on Route A1A and Hillsboro Inlet in Pompano Beach. Half-

day charters usually run from $200 to $250 for up to six people; full-day charters are between $400 and $475. Skipper and crew, plus bait and tackle, are included. Split-parties can be arranged at a cost of about $50 per person.

Among marinas catering to freshwater fishing are **Sawgrass Recreation** (U.S. 27 north of I–595, tel. 305/426–2474) and **Everglades Holiday Park** (21940 Griffin Rd., tel. 305/434–8111 or 305/621–2009), where you can rent a 14-foot, flat-bottomed John boat carrying up to four people for about $30–$32.50 for five hours. Tackle rents for $5–$8; bait is extra.

Fishing Piers   Fishing piers draw anglers for pompano, amberjack, bluefish, snapper, blue runners, snook, mackerel, and Florida lobsters. Pompano Beach's **Fisherman's Wharf** extends 1,080 feet into the Atlantic. The cost is $1.95 for adults, 95¢ for children under 10; rod-and-reel rental is $4.75. **Anglin's Fishing Pier** in Lauderdale-by-the-Sea reaches 875 feet and is open for fishing 24 hours a day. Fishing is $2.50 for adults and $1.75 for children up to 12, tackle rental $5.

Golf   More than 50 courses, public and private, green the landscape in metro Fort Lauderdale, including some famous championship links. Members of the general public usually can arrange to play at: **Bonaventure Country Club** (250 Racquet Club Rd., tel. 305/389–3300 or 800/327–8090, 36 holes); **Colony West Country Club** (6800 N.W. 88th Ave., Tamarac, tel. 305/726–8430, 36 holes); **Inverrary Country Club** (3840 Inverrary Blvd., Coral Springs, tel. 305/733–7550, 54 holes); **The Oaks Golf & Racquet Club** (3701 Clubhouse Dr., Pompano Beach, tel. 305/978–1737 or 800/336–2108, 36 holes); **Palm-Aire resort** (2601 Palm-Aire Dr. N., Pompano Beach, tel. 305/972–3300 or 800/272–5624, 40 holes); **Rolling Hills** (3501 Rolling Hills Circle, Davie, tel. 305/475–3010, 27 holes); **Tournament Players Club at Eagle Trace** (1111 Eagle Trace Blvd., Coral Springs, tel. 305/753–7600, 18 holes); and the site of the PGA Honda Classic, **Weston Hills** (2600 Country Club Way, Fort Lauderdale, tel. 305/384–4653, 18 holes).

Skiing   A unique water-skiing cableway, which pulls water-skiers across the water is at **Quiet Waters Park** (Power Line Rd., Pompano Beach, tel. 305/360–1315; open weekends; admission $1 driver, 75¢ per passenger), just north of the Pompano Harness Track. At the park, **Ski Rixen** (tel. 305/429–0215) offers waterskiing lessons for beginners, plus skis and life vests.

Spas   If you watch "Lifestyles of the Rich and Famous" on TV, you'll recognize the names of Greater Fort Lauderdale's two world-famous spas, the Bonaventure Resort & Spa and Palm-Aire Spa Resort. At each resort, women comprise 75%–80% of the spa clientele. Both resorts offer single-day spa privileges to nonguests, including body massage, exercise classes, facials, herbal wraps, spa-cuisine lunches, and other spa facilities and services. Price and availability of services vary with seasonal demand; resort guests have priority. Bring your own sneakers and socks—the spa provides everything else you'll need. Each spa will help you design a personal exercise-and-diet program tied to your lifestyle at home. If you already have an exercise program, bring it with you. If you have a medical problem, bring a letter from your doctor.

Bonaventure Resort and Spa (250 Racquet Club Rd., Fort Lauderdale, tel. 305/389–3300 or 800/327–8090) offers complimentary caffeine-free herbal teas in the morning, and fresh fruit in the afternoon. The staff nutritionist follows American Heart Association and American Cancer Society guidelines, and can accommodate macrobiotic and vegetarian diets. The full-service beauty salon is open to the public.

Palm-Aire Spa Resort (2601 Palm-Aire Dr. N, Pompano Beach, tel. 305/972–3300 or 800/272–5624) is a 192-room, 750-acre health, fitness, and stress-reduction spa offering exercise activities, personal treatments, and calorie-controlled meals. It's 15 minutes from downtown Fort Lauderdale.

Less elaborate facilities are available at Spa LXVI of **Pier Sixty Six Resort & Marina** (2301 S.E. 17th St., Fort Lauderdale, tel. 305/525–6666 or 800/327–3796; in FL, 800/432–1956), a 22-acre site on the Intracoastal Waterway, minutes from the beach.

Tennis   Some 20 sites offer public courts throughout the county. Best known to Broward Countians (and largest) is **Holiday Park** (701 N.E. 12th Ave., Fort Lauderdale, tel. 305/761–5378), with 18 clay and three hard surface courts lighted for night play in the downtown area, 10 minutes from the beach. This is where former pro Jimmy Evert taught his daughter Chris the game that made her a world champion.

Spectator Sports

For tickets to sporting events, call **Ticketmaster** (tel. 305/523–3309).

Baseball   The New York Yankees hold spring training in 7,000-seat Fort Lauderdale Stadium (5301 N.W. 12th Ave., Fort Lauderdale, tel. 305/776–1921).

The **Fort Lauderdale Yankees** compete between April and August in the Florida State League, as do the **Pompano Beach Miracles**, both at Pompano Municipal Stadium (1799 N.E. 8th St., tel. 305/783–2111).

Greyhound Racing   Hollywood Greyhound Track (831 N. Federal Highway, Hallandale, tel. 305/454–9400) has plenty of dog-racing action during its season, from December 26 until late April. Post time is 7:45 Mon.–Sat., 7 on Sundays.

Harness Racing   **Pompano Harness Track** (1800 S.W. 3rd St., Pompano Beach, tel. 305/972–2000) is Florida's only harness track. Since 1992, the 327-acre facility has been for sale. So far, however, it's still business as usual, though you'll need to call to find out when the racing dates are. The Top 'O The Park restaurant overlooks the finish line. Post time: 7:30.

Jai Alai   **Dania Jai-Alai Palace** (301 E. Dania Beach Blvd., Dania, tel. 305/428–7766) offers one of the fastest games on the planet year-round.

Rodeo   **Davie Arena for Rodeo** (6591 S.W. 45th St. [Orange Dr.], Davie 33314, tel. 305/797–1145) holds rodeos throughout the year. Admission for jackpot events is $4 adults, $2 children; for five-star rodeo, $8 adults, $5 children.

Rugby   The **Fort Lauderdale Knights** play September–April on the green at Holiday Park (off U.S. 1, 2 blocks south of Sunrise Blvd., Fort Lauderdale, tel. 305/561–5263 for a recorded message). Games are Saturday at 2 PM; admission is free.

Thoroughbred **Gulfstream Park Race Track** (901 S. Federal Hwy., tel. 305/
Racing 454–7000) is home of the Florida Derby, one of the southeast's
foremost horse racing events, and the Breeders Cup. Race
dates are always during winter.

Beaches

Fort Lauderdale's beachfront extends for miles without inter-
ruption, although the character of the communities behind the
beach changes. For example, in Hallandale at far south
Broward County, the beach is backed by towering condominiums; in Hollywood, by motels and the hoi-polloi Broadwalk;
and just north of there—blessedly—there's nothing at all.

The most crowded portion of beach is along **Ocean Boulevard,**
between Las Olas Boulevard and Sunrise Boulevard in Fort
Lauderdale. This is the one-time "strip" famed from *Where the
Boys Are* and the era of spring break madness, now but a memory. Parking is readily available, often at parking meters.

Dania, Lauderdale-by-the-Sea, Pompano Beach, and **Deerfield
Beach** each have piers where you can fish in addition to their
beaches.

John U. Lloyd Beach State Recreation Area is the locals' favorite beach area. It offers a beach for swimmers and sunners, but
also 251 acres of mangroves, picnic facilities, fishing, and canoeing. *6503 N. Ocean Dr., Dania, tel. 305/923–2833. Admission: $3.25 per car. Open 8 AM–sunset.*

Dining

The list below is a representative selection of restaurants in
Fort Lauderdale and Broward County, organized by type of
cuisine. Unless otherwise noted, they serve lunch and dinner.

Highly recommended restaurants are indicated by a star ★.

Category	Cost*
Very Expensive	over $50
Expensive	$35–$50
Moderate	$20–$35
Inexpensive	under $20

per person, excluding drinks, service, and 6% sales tax

American **Burt & Jack's.** This restaurant, situated at the far end and most
scenic lookout of Port Everglades, has been around in some
capacity since the late 1970s. Finally, after three restaurants failed here, in 1984 Burt Reynolds and Jack Jackson
hit it right. Though signs leading the way are far and few between, diners find their way through the port-management
maze. Behind the heavy mission doors and bougainvillea,
guests are rewarded with Maine lobster, steaks, and chops.
The two-story gallery of hacienda-like dining rooms surrounded by glass have stunning views of the Intracoastal
Waterway and John U. Lloyd State Park. Come to this very
romantic spot Saturday or Sunday in early evening for cocktails
(served from 4:30, dinner from 5) and watch the cruise ships

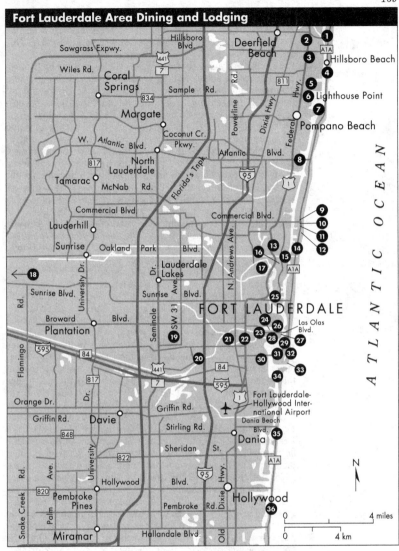

Fort Lauderdale Area Dining and Lodging

Lodging

Bahia Cabana Beach Resort, **29**
Banyan Marina Apartments, **24**
Blue Seas, **11**
Carriage House Resort Motel, **4**
Driftwood On the Ocean, **36**
Lago Mar Resort Hotel & Club, **33**

A Little Inn by-the-Sea, **10**
Marriott's Harbor Beach Resort, **32**
Nina Lee Motel, **27**
Pier 66 Resort and Marina, **31**
Pier Pointe Resort, **12**
Riverside Hotel, **28**
Royal Flamingo Villas, **1**
Tropic Seas Resort Inn, **9**

Dining

Bimini Boatyard, **30**
Brooks, **2**
Burt & Jack's, **34**
Cafe Arugula, **6**
Cafe Grazia, **5**
Cafe Maxx, **8**
Cap's Place, **7**
Casa Vecchia, **26**
Don Arturo, **19**
Down Under, **15**
Ernie's Bar-B-Q & Lounge, **22**
Grainary Cafe, **3**

Il Tartufo, **16**
Martha's, **35**
Old Florida Seafood House, **17**
Renaissance Resturant, **18**
Rustic Inn Crabhouse, **20**
Sage, **13**
Santa Lucia, **23**
Sea Watch, **14**
Shirttail Charlie's, **21**
Studio One French Bistro, **25**

steam out. The entire dining area is now nonsmoking. *Berth 23, Port Everglades, Fort Lauderdale, tel. 305/522–2878 or 305/ 525–5225. Reservations advised. Jacket required. AE, DC, MC, V. No lunch. Closed Christmas. Expensive.*

★ **Cafe Maxx.** As you enter Cafe Maxx, you're greeted by the aroma of fragrant spices issuing from the open theater kitchen. The decor includes art deco–style black wood chairs and cut flowers. Booth seating is best; the tables are quite close together. Owner-chef Oliver Saucy's specialties include such appetizers as banana lime grilled shrimp on brochette with banana and dijon dipping sauce, and pistachio fried oysters with mango-pineapple salsa and creole remoulade; and among main courses, sweet onion-crusted yellowtail snapper with madeira sauce and crispy gaufrette potatoes, and pompano with macadamia nut crust, plantain chips, and grilled pineapple salsa. Daily dessert specials include a vanilla-bean crème brulée with pineapple rum sauce and seasonal berries, and a cappuccino mousse torte with hazelnut crust and chocolate shavings. *2601 E. Atlantic Blvd., Pompano Beach, tel. 305/782–0606. Reservations advised. Dress: casual but neat. AE, D, DC, MC, V. No lunch. Closed Super Bowl Sun. Expensive.*

Bimini Boatyard. With a sky-high sloped roof, loads of windows, and paddle fans, this is a rarity among architecturally distinctive restaurants: affordable menu, ambience, and a quality bar. Try a Bass Ale with a loaf of Bimini bread or buffalo chicken wings. Heartier fare? Go for the *fettuccine al salmone affumicato* (smoked salmon, capers, whole-grain mustard, white wine, cream, and leeks). The extensive menu includes salads, burgers, and dishes from the cookbooks of the Bahamas, Jamaica, and Indonesia (grilled chicken breast with peanut sauce). The restaurant is on the 15th Street canal, where outdoor seating lets you look at the year-round boat show. On weekends Bimini hosts progressive jazz bands. *1555 S.E. 17th St., tel. 305/525–7400. Reservations accepted for groups. Dress: casual. AE, MC, V. Closed Christmas. Moderate.*

Ernie's Bar-B-Q & Lounge. Soup you can chew, thick barbecue between slabs of Bahama bread, and a wacky wall collection of memorabilia from a previous owner make Ernie's a must. Since 1976, Jeff Kirtman (from Brooklyn) has run this two-story eatery, which has an open-deck patio upstairs overlooking six-lane Federal Highway. The downstairs murals tout zany slogans and are adorned with former owner Ernie Siebert's dodo birds. Current owner Kirtman has supplied plenty of new reasons for visiting, including his conch-rich thick chowder, the hot barbecued pork-and-beef sandwiches, and the ribs-and-chicken combo dinner with corn on the cob and baked beans. *1843 S. Federal Hwy., Fort Lauderdale, tel. 305/523–8636. No reservations. Dress: casual. MC, V. Inexpensive.*

Continental **Cafe Arugula.** Former adman Dick Cingolani describes his cooking as "cuisines of the sun"—it draws upon culinary traditions from several warm climates, from Italy to the American Southwest. The decor, too, blends Southwestern with Mediterranean looks—mauve velvet booths beneath steamboat-wheel window surrounds; an entire wall of chili peppers, corn, cactus, and garlic cloves surrounds the display kitchen. The best of the abundant seafood appetizers are sautéed calamari cutlet with tomato vinaigrette on a bed of arugula, jumbo lump crabcakes with creole mustard sauce, and oak-grilled jumbo shrimp with Cajun spicy andoille sausage, served with sweet-and-sour figs and black bean salsa. Entrées include pan-sauteed, pecan-crusted Keys yellowtail snapper; citrus- and pepper-painted grouper; and oak-grilled Cuban marinated pork loin. A winning dessert is the white chocolate mousse cannoli. *3110 N. Federal Hwy., Lighthouse Point, tel. 305/785–7732. Reservations advised. Dress: casual but neat. AE, DC, MC, V. No lunch. Closed Easter, Thanksgiving, Christmas, New Year's Day. Expensive.*

Down Under. When Al Kocab and Leonce Picot opened Down Under in 1968, the Australian government sent them a boomerang as a gift. The name actually describes the restaurant's location, below a bridge approach at the edge of the Intracoastal Waterway. The restaurant has antique brick deliberately laid off-plumb, and an open-air upstairs. Dishes include a classic cobb salad, Florida seafoods (snapper, crab, lobster), duck, and beef Wellington, all in traditional presentations. Other specialties include fresh baked oysters, Florida blue crab cakes, Brutus salad (Down Under's version of Caesar salad), sautéed fresh Idaho trout topped with blue crab and hollandaise sauce, and a pan-seared Jamaican jerk- and molasses-seasoned roast pork tenderloin. Desserts include a variety of soufflées. *3000 E. Oakland Park Blvd., tel. 305/563–4123. Reservations advised. Dress: casual but neat. AE, D, DC, MC, V. Expensive.*

Martha's. Situated on the Intracoastal across from a 417-acre mangrove preserve, just below the Dania Boulevard Bridge, the restaurant is dressy downstairs—tables adorned with orchid buds, fanned napery, etched glass dividers, brass, rosewood, and an outdoor patio surrounded by a wildly floral mural. Here piano music accompanies happy hour, and at night, a band and dancing set a supper-club mood. The upstairs dining area (reached by elevator) is casual, with a tropical setting of painted orchids, stained glass, and wave-shape outdoor furniture. The same menu downstairs and up features outstanding seafood preparations: flaky dolphin in a court-bouillon; shrimp dipped in a piña colada batter, rolled in coconut, pan fried with orange mustard sauce; and snapper prepared 17 ways. An assortment of rolls and banana bread come with entrées. For dessert, try fresh sorbet and vanilla and chocolate ice cream topped with meringue and hot fudge brandy sauce. *6024 N. Ocean Dr., Hollywood, tel. 305/923–5444. Reservations advised. Dress: casual but neat downstairs, casual upstairs. AE, D, DC, MC, V. Expensive.*

★ **Brooks.** A French perfectionist (born in Poitiers), Bernard Perron serves a very affordable menu in a series of brilliantly set rooms, filled with replicas of Old Masters, cut glass, antiques, and tapestry-like floral wallpapers, though the shed-like dining room still feels very Florida. For Bernard the secret is fresh ingredients, which translate into a distinctly Floridian cuisine. You will find such appetizers as tempura shrimp fritters and pan-fried soft-shell crab; main courses include red snapper in papillotte, broiled filet of pompano with seasoned root vegetables, a sweet lemon-grass linguini with bok choy and julienne of crisp vegetables, and a chicken breast marinated in orange tamarind sauce with macadamia nuts and coconut rice. Desserts include southern pecan pie with banana ice cream, a filo purse filled with chocolate ganache and strawberries, and rum-basted bananas with coconut ice cream and toasted macadamia nuts. *500 S. Federal Hwy., Deerfield Beach, tel. 305/427–*

9302. Reservations accepted. Dress: casual but neat. AE, MC, V. Closed Christmas, Super Bowl Sun. Moderate.

Cuban **Don Arturo.** Waiters in tuxedos belie the friendly style of this family-run, romantically lit restaurant popular with the courthouse crowd. Avoid the party room that's near a noisy service area. If you're new to Cuban food, try the tri-steak sampler (chicken filet, palomilla steak, and pork fillet), or one of the dinners for two, such as the *zarzuela de mariscos* (assorted seafood and fish smothered in tangy Spanish red sauce). Wash it down with the homemade sangria. English is spoken in this restaurant located four stoplights west of I–95, just north of Davie Boulevard. *1198 S.W. 27th Ave., tel. 305/584–7966; 6522 W. Atlantic Blvd., Margate, tel. 305/968–1608. Reservations accepted. Dress: casual but neat. AE, D, DC, MC, V. No Sun. lunch. Closed July 4, Thanksgiving, Christmas, New Year's Day. Moderate.*

French **Sage.** One of the best values in Fort Lauderdale is this joyous, country-French café in a country-American setting: exposed brick walls, captain's chairs, lace curtains, herbal art, and baskets of dried grains and flowers. The menu is a happy mix of very affordable quiches and pâtés, savory and dessert crêpes, salads, and main course specialties. Entrées include coq au vin, boeuf bourguignon, *cassoulet à l'Armagnac* (layers of duck and garlic sausage with white beans), and a platter of fresh vegetables that's a veritable garden of legumes. There's a superb collection of beers (Anchor Steam, Sam Adams, Harp) and wines by the glass. *2378 N. Federal Hwy., Fort Lauderdale, tel. 305/565–2299. No reservations. Dress: casual but neat. D, MC, V. Inexpensive.*

★ **Studio One French Bistro.** As if one great bargain French restaurant weren't enough, Fort Lauderdale offers a second. Studio One is more like a gallery of art—intimate, black-and-white, mirrored—and, if anything, it serves even more bountiful portions of food than Sage does. The extraordinary profusion of food is thoughtfully presented, from high-gluten breads through a dozen or so appetizers, dinner-size salads, and entrées that include a grilled fillet of Norwegian salmon with mustard dill sauce, veal-stuffed tortellini with a vodka Alfredo sauce, and a grilled chicken breast with corn chili sauce. For dessert try the mildly sweet custard apple tart. The fetching creole logo, by the way, dates from Grenoble-born chef Laurent Tasic's years in Martinique. Wife Carol greets guests by name—the locals who return time and again, typically bringing out-of-town guests. *2447 E. Sunrise Blvd., Fort Lauderdale, tel. 305/565–2052. Reservations accepted. Dress: casual but neat. AE, MC, V. No lunch. Closed Mon. and New Year's Day. Inexpensive.*

Italian **Casa Vecchia.** This old house *(casa vecchia)* stands beside the ★ Intracoastal Waterway, surrounded by a formal garden from which you can watch boats cruise past. The garden also grows herbs that flavor the restaurant's fare. Casa Vecchia was built in the late 1930s, and diners are encouraged to roam through the building to admire antique furnishings and original statuary and paintings. Spanish tiles decorate Casa Vecchia's walls and many tabletops. The menu changes every three months, but it is generally light fare—few sauces, lots of grills and seared meats. Appetizers include linguine pesto and soft polenta with grilled portobello mushrooms; salads include a Belgian endive with pine nuts and goat cheese crostini. Among the entrées you'll find capellini with sea scallops and jade sauce, and roasted Florida lobster with herb linguine and a niçoise olive vinaigrette. Desserts include full-flavored sorbets of fresh seasonal fruit prepared on the premises. *209 N. Birch Rd., tel. 305/463-7575. Reservations advised. Jacket advised. AE, MC, V. No lunch. Expensive.*

Il Tartufo. In this hint of a Ligurian garden with a cherub fountain, new added space has simply meant that the 16 tables are set farther apart and a wood-burning Tuscan oven has been installed. Specials include fresh truffles in November and December, but exquisite preparations can be found year-round in this family-run restaurant. Try an antipasto of portobello mushrooms with white wine, garlic, olive oil, herbs, and lemon; or a jumbo shrimp on radicchio flavored with balsamic vinegar, garlic, olive oil, and cilantro. Exceptional pastas include: cannelloni stuffed with parmesan and ricotta cheeses and spinach in a béchamel-tomato sauce; a home-made *pappardelle* pasta (wide noodles) with pesto sauce; and ravioli stuffed with veal in a white Genovese sauce. *2980 N. Federal Hwy., Fort Lauderdale, tel. 305/564-0607. Reservations advised. Dress: casual but neat. AE, MC, V. No lunch. Closed Mon., Thanksgiving, and Christmas. Moderate.*

Santa Lucia. "You gotta taste the ocean," says owner/chef Angelo Ciampa, a veteran of 44 years in the restaurant biz, who now draws packed houses to his little 13-table storefront restaurant next to the fashionable Riverside Hotel on Las Olas Boulevard. The place smells like it ought to at home: pungent with a lot of subtle wafts. Try the whole grilled yellowtail snapper or the *rigatoni à la Russa* (tomato, garlic, hot pepper, parmesan, and basil with a splash of vodka). The *zuccotto* (a homemade sponge cake) is made with whipped cream, liqueurs, roasted pine nuts, almonds, and walnuts. Ask for the Moretti beer, a full-bodied Italian gift to the world. Or choose from three dozen Italian wines. *602 E. Las Olas Blvd., tel. 305/525-9530. Reservations advised. Dress: casual but neat. AE, MC, V. No lunch Tues.-Fri. Closed Aug. and Sun. and Mon. in summer. Moderate.*

★ **Cafe Grazia.** This happy green-red-and-white recollection of an Italian garden is so close to the highway that its bar glasses jiggle to the passing of 18-wheelers. Not to worry—exuberance is what really shakes the scene. Chef Ace Gonzalez and his wife Estelita have created a happy case of the best for less: dinners on the low side of what we call "moderate," and downright inexpensive if you come between 5 and 6:30 for the early-bird specials, a choice of three-course dinners priced at $6.95 in summer, $8.95 in winter. Pocketbook-pleasing, too, are the regular menu's 15 pasta selections, including *penne arrabiata e vodka* (round pasta with hot chilies, vodka, tomatoes, and cream), and *roselline de pasta* (fresh pasta rosettes with fontina cheese, smoked ham, and spinach in a cream-parmesan sauce). Other entrées include fowl, veal, and grills. A big rave. *3850 N. Federal Hwy., Lighthouse Point, tel. 305/942-7207. Reservations accepted. Dress: casual but neat. AE, MC, V. No weekend lunch. Closed Christmas. Inexpensive–Moderate.*

Natural
★ **Grainary Cafe.** Tucked away in the little Palm Plaza on the west side of Federal Highway, this is the premier natural food restaurant in the county, offering gourmet vegetarian food priced for family pocketbooks. Lunch specials include various brown

rice combination plates and Middle Eastern specialties (tabouli, hummus, falafel), and items such as an eggless tofu yung, seitan stir fry, and mock-chicken tamale pie. In the evening entrées come with brown rice, unlimited bread basket (including macrobiotic brown rice bread, pita, and outstanding sourdough rolls) with miso-tahini spread and soy margarine, and soup or salad. House-filleted fresh fish is served in a lemon-ginger sauce, broiled, Cajun-blackened, or in a West Indian sauté that's served hot and spicy or mild and plain. You can get vegetable dumplings, a vegetarian primavera marinara, blackened tofu, veggie lasagna (non-dairy), and a raja's delight—vegetable stir-fry with tofu, nuts, and curry. Desserts include fresh-baked cookies and tofu-based, rice syrup–sweetened pies. *847 S. Federal Hwy., Deerfield Beach, tel. 305/360–0824. Reservations accepted. Dress: casual. AE, D, MC, V. BYOB. No Sun. lunch. Closed Christmas. Inexpensive.*

Seafood **Renaissance Restaurant.** This gourmet restaurant in the Bonaventure Resort and Spa, five-star-rated by the Confrérie de la Chaine des Rôtisseurs, features mesquite-grilled seafood and California cuisine with Florida adaptations. You dine in a rain forest setting, with views of a waterfall surrounded by palm and ficus trees, ferns and blooming flowers, and a pond with variegated, foot-long carp. Specialties include chilled cream of avocado and cucumber soup; hot cream of poblano pepper soup with chunks of brie; a spinach-and-bean sprout salad with pickled eggs and rosemary vinaigrette dressing; whole wheat fettuccine sautéed with chunks of Maine lobster, scallops, and chives in a lobster sauce; and mako shark in a lime-parsley-butter sauce. *250 Racquet Club Rd., tel. 305/389–3300 or 800/327–8090. Reservations required. Jacket advised. AE, DC, MC, V. No lunch. Expensive.*

★ **Cap's Place.** This restaurant, located on an island previously inhabited by a rum runner, boasts having served such celebrities as Winston Churchill, Franklin D. Roosevelt, and John F. Kennedy. "Cap" was Captain Theodore Knight, born in 1871, who floated a derelict barge with partner-in-crime Al Hasis to the area in the 1920s. Today, the rustic restaurant, built atop the site, is run by descendants of Hasis who make freshness and excellence a priority. Baked wahoo steaks are lightly glazed and meaty; the long-cut french fries arouse gluttony; hot and flaky rolls are baked fresh several times a night, and tangy lime pie is the finishing touch. *Cap's Dock, 2765 N.E. 28th Ct., Lighthouse Point (follow double-line road leading east on N.E. 24th St. off Federal Hwy. 2 blocks north to Pompano Fashion), tel. 305/941–0418. No reservations. Dress: casual. AE, MC, V. No lunch. Closed Sun. June–Nov. Moderate–Expensive.*

Old Florida Seafood House. Owner Bob Wickline has run this traditional seafood restaurant since 1978 with a West Virginian's eye toward giving value for money: it's plain on atmosphere and friendly on price, with nothing frozen and nothing portion-controlled. He'll bring out a whole swordfish to show that it's fresh. Try the veal Gustav (sautéed veal topped with a lobster tail), and a snapper New Orleans (sautéed with mushrooms and artichokes, laced with a light brown sauce). There's usually a 30-minute wait weekends. *1414 N.E. 26th St., Wilton Manors, tel. 305/566–1044; 4535 Pine Island Rd., Sunrise, tel. 305/572–0444. Dress: casual but neat. AE, MC, V. No weekend lunch. Closed Thanksgiving. Moderate.*

Rustic Inn Crabhouse. Wayne McDonald started with a cozy one-room roadhouse saloon in 1955 when this was a remote service road just west of the little airport. Now, the plain, rustic place seats 700. Steamed crabs seasoned with garlic and herbs, spices, and oil are served with mallets on tables covered with newspapers; peel-and-eat shrimp are served either Key West–style with garlic and butter, or spiced and steamed with Old Bay seasoning. The big menu includes other seafood items as well. Pies and cheesecakes are offered for dessert. *4331 Ravenswood Rd., Fort Lauderdale, tel. 305/584–1637; 100 S. State Rd. 7, Margate, tel. 305/968–9791. No reservations. Dress: casual. AE, D, DC, MC, V. Closed Thanksgiving, Christmas. Moderate.*

Shirttail Charlie's. Overlooking the New River, you can watch the world go by from the outdoor deck or upstairs dining room of Shirttail Charlie's, named for a yesteryear Seminole Indian who wore his shirts in the traditional way with the tails out. Diners may take a free 30- to 40-minute after-dinner cruise on the *Shirttail Charlie's Express*, which chugs upriver past an alleged Al Capone speakeasy or across the river to and from the Broward Center for the Performing Arts. Charlie's itself is built to look old, with a 1920s tile floor that leans toward the water. Florida-style seafood offerings include an alligator-tail appetizer served with *tortuga* sauce (a béarnaise with turtle broth and sherry); conch served four ways; crab balls; swordfish bites; blackened tuna with Dijon mustard sauce; crunchy coconut shrimp with a not-too-sweet piña colada sauce; and a superbly tart Key lime pie with graham-cracker crust. *400 S.W. 3rd Ave., tel. 305/463–3474. Reservations advised upstairs. Dress: casual but neat. AE, D, MC, V. Moderate.*

Sea Watch. It's back from the road and easy to miss—but not missed by many. Waiting for a table, you're likely to hear announced, "Party of 47, your tables are ready!" After 20 years, this nautical-theme restaurant by the sea stays packed lunch and dinner. Waits can be as long as 30 minutes, but the time passes quickly in the sumptuous upstairs lounge with its comfy sofas and high-back rattan chairs. The menu has all the right appetizers: oysters Rockefeller, Florida Gulf shrimp, clams casino, and Bahamian conch fritters. Typical daily specials might be sauteed yellowtail snapper, oat-crusted with roasted red bell pepper sauce and basil, or a charbroiled dolphin fillet marinated with soy sauce, garlic, black pepper, and lemon juice. Desserts include a Granny Smith apple crisp cheesecake, cappuccino brownie, and strawberries romanoff. Good early-bird specials. *6001 N. Ocean Blvd., Fort Lauderdale, tel. 305/781–2200. No reservations. Dress: casual but neat. AE, MC, V. Closed Christmas. Inexpensive–Moderate.*

Lodging

In Fort Lauderdale, Pompano Beach, and the Hollywood–Hallandale area, dozens of hotels line the Atlantic Ocean beaches, ranging from economy motels to opulent luxury resorts. Inland, the major chain hotels along I–95 north and south of the airport cater primarily to business travelers and overnight visitors en route to somewhere else.

An innovative Superior Small Lodging program, set up by the Greater Fort Lauderdale Convention and Visitors Bureau and administered by the hospitality department of Broward County's Nova University, has led to substantial upgrading of many smaller properties, many of which charge modest rates.

Wherever you plan to stay in Broward County, reservations are a good idea throughout the year. Tourists from the northern United States and Canada fill up the hotels from Thanksgiving through Easter. In summer, southerners and Europeans create a second season that's almost as busy. The rate categories below are based on the all-year or peak-season price; off-peak rates may be a category or two lower.

Highly recommended hotels are indicated by a star ★.

Category	Cost*
Very Expensive	over $150
Expensive	$90–$150
Moderate	$60–$90
Inexpensive	under $60

All prices are for a standard double room, excluding 6% state sales tax and nominal tourist tax.

Deerfield Beach **Royal Flamingo Villas.** This small community of houselike villas, built in the 1970s, reaches from the Intracoastal Waterway to the sea in quiet Deerfield Beach. The 40 villas are all condominium owned, so they're fully furnished the way owners want them. (Many are no-smoking.) Choose from either one or two bedrooms. All are so quiet that you hear only the soft click of ceiling fans and kitchen clocks. Living rooms have tile floors; there's carpet in the bedrooms. The development is wisely set back a bit from the beach, which is eroded anyway, though enjoyable at low tide. The lawns here are so lushly landscaped you might trip. The villas are roomy and comfortable, so if you don't need lavish public facilities, this is your value choice. *1225 Hillsboro Mile (Rte. A1A), Hillsboro Beach 33062, tel. 305/427-0669, 305/427-0670, or 800/241-2477. 40 1- and 2-bedroom villas. Facilities: heated pool, beach, dock, boat rentals, shuffleboard, putting green, coin laundry. D, MC, V. Expensive–Very Expensive.*

★ **Carriage House Resort Motel.** Very clean and tidy, this good 30-unit beachfront motel sits one block from the ocean. Run by a French-American couple (who speak German and some Spanish as well), the two-story, black-shuttered white Colonial-style motel is actually two buildings connected by a second-story sun deck. Steady improvements have been made to the facility, including the addition of Bahama beds that feel and look like sofas. Kitchenettes are equipped with quality utensils. Rooms are self-contained and quiet. *250. S. Ocean Blvd., 33441, tel. 305/427-7670, fax 305/428-4790. 30 rooms with bath, 14 efficiencies, 10 apartments. Facilities: heated pool, shuffleboard. AE, MC, V. Moderate.*

Fort Lauderdale **Lago Mar Resort Hotel & Club.** No one steadily upgrades re-
Beach sort property like Walter Banks, who in early 1993 opened a new signature wing at this sprawling resort owned by the Banks family since the early 1950s. The new lobby is Babylonian-scale, with fanlight surrounds, a coquina rock fireplace, and an eye-popping saltwater aquarium behind the registration desk. Allamanda trellises edge the new swimming lagoon, and

guests have the use of the broadest beach in the city. Lago Mar is less a big resort, more a small town—still personally run after all these years. *1700 S. Ocean La., 33316, tel. 305/523–6511 or 800/255–5246, fax 305/523–6511. 44 rooms with bath, 135 suites. Facilities: 4 restaurants, 2 outdoor heated pools, 4 tennis courts, 2 volleyball courts, 4 shuffleboard courts, miniature golf. AE, DC, MC, V. Very Expensive.*

Marriott's Harbor Beach Resort. This sprawling resort, built in 1984, is the resort of the Surplus Age. No other hotel gives you so much to take advantage of. Located south of the big public beach, it's a property of imperial dimensions—16 acres on the sea. Seen at night from upper stories (14 in all), the grounds, with their waterfall-pool beset by tall pines, shimmer like a jewel. Sheffield's, one of the resort's five restaurants, is one of the city's top spots. The spacious guest rooms, furnished in rattan and cane, lack design distinction, but each has a balcony facing either the ocean or the Intracoastal Waterway. *3030 Holiday Dr., 33316, tel. 305/525–4000 or 800/228–9290, fax 305/766–6152. 588 rooms with bath, 36 suites. Facilities: 5 restaurants, 3 lounges, beach, cabanas, windsurfing, Hobie cats, 65' catamaran, parasailing, outdoor heated freshwater pool and whirlpool, 5 tennis courts, fitness center, men's and women's saunas, masseuse, in-room minibars, complimentary 1-hr. weekly adult bike tours, 108 nonsmoker rooms, 7 rooms for disabled. AE, DC, MC, V. Very Expensive.*

Bahia Cabana Beach Resort. *Boating Magazine* ranks this resort's waterfront bar and restaurant among the 10 best in the world. Rooms are spread out in five contiguous buildings furnished in tropical-casual style, redone with new carpets, paint, tiles, and new landscaping and patio furniture in 1992/1993. Added at the same time was a new video bar with a great view of the marina. Rooms in the 500 Building are more motel-like and overlook the parking lot, but rates here are lowest. The bar-restaurant is far enough from guest rooms so that the nightly entertainment does not disturb anyone. *3001 Harbor Dr., Fort Lauderdale 33316, tel. 305/524–1555 or 800/232–2437 in FL, 800/922–3008, fax 305/764–5951. 52 rooms with bath, 37 efficiencies, 10 suites. Facilities: restaurant, café, pool bar, patio bar, 3 heated freshwater pools, Jacuzzi, saunas, marina, shuffleboard court. AE, D, DC, MC, V. Expensive.*

Nina Lee Motel. This 14-unit motel is typical of the modest, affordable 1950s-style lodgings that can be found within a block or two of the ocean along the Fort Lauderdale shore. Be prepared for plain rooms—homey and clean, but not tiny, with at least a toaster, coffee pot, and fridge; the efficiencies have gas kitchens, large closets, and tub-showers. The pool is set in a garden, and the entire property is just removed enough from the beach causeway so that it's quiet. *3048 Harbor Dr., Fort Lauderdale 33316, tel. 305/524–1568. 14 units with bath. Facilities: heated pool; in-room toasters, coffee makers, and refrigerators. MC, V. Moderate.*

Fort Lauderdale Downtown and Beach Causeways ★

Pier 66 Resort and Marina. Phillips Petroleum built Fort Lauderdale's landmark high-rise resort, best known for its revolving rooftop Pier Top Lounge. Its tower and lanai lodgings are "tops" from the ground up. The 17-story tower dominates a 22-acre spread that includes a 142-slip marina. A complete spa was added in 1989. *2301 S.E. 17th St., 33316, tel. 305/525–6666 or 800/327–3796; in FL, 800/432–1956, fax 305/728–3541. 380 rooms with bath, 8 suites. Facilities: 7 restaurants and* *lounges, water taxi to beach, outdoor freshwater pool, heated Jacuzzi, full-service marina with 142 wet slips, scuba diving, snorkeling, parasailing, small boat rentals, waterskiing, fishing and sailing yacht charters, 2 clay tennis courts, LXVI Spa. AE, DC, MC, V. Very Expensive.*

★ **Riverside Hotel.** This six-story hotel, on Fort Lauderdale's most fashionable shopping thoroughfare, was built in 1936, and has been steadily upgraded since 1987. In-room coffee makers are a new feature. The tropical murals are the work of Bob Jenny, who painted a New Orleans–style mural across 725 square feet of the hotel's Las Olas facade. An attentive staff includes many who have been with the hotel for two decades or more. Each room is unique, with antique oak furnishings, framed French prints on the walls, in-room refrigerators, and European-style baths. The best rooms face south, overlooking the New River; the worst rooms, where you can hear the elevator, are the 36 series. *620 E. Las Olas Blvd., 33301, tel. 305/ 467–0671 or 800/325–3280, fax 305/462–2148. 111 rooms with bath, 5 suites. Facilities: 2 restaurants, poolside bar, heated freshwater pool beside New River, 540' of dock (mooring space available by advance reservation), volleyball court, 15 non-smoker rooms. AE, DC, MC, V. Expensive.*

★ **Banyan Marina Apartments.** Outstanding waterfront apartments on a residential island just off Las Olas Boulevard feature imaginative landscaping that includes a walkway through the upper branches of a banyan tree, dock space for eight yachts, and exemplary housekeeping. Luxurious units with leather sofas, springy carpets, real potted plants, sheer curtains and full drapes, and jalousies for sweeping the breeze in make these apartments as comfortable as any first-class hotel—but for half the price. Also included is a full kitchen, dining area, water view, and beautiful gardens. This is Florida the way you want it to be. *111 Isle of Venice, tel. 305/524–4430, fax 305/764–4870. 10 hotel rooms with bath, 1 efficiency, 4 1-bedroom apts., 2 2-bedroom apts. Facilities: swimming pool, waterfront deck. MC, V. Moderate–Expensive.*

Hollywood **Driftwood on the Ocean.** This attractive motel in three buildings, built in 1959, was completely refurbished in 1992/1993 following Hurricane Andrew. Its lawn faces the beach at the secluded south end of Surf Road in Hollywood. Most units have a kitchen; all one-bedroom apartments have a daybed, and all standard rooms a queen-size Murphy bed. All units are tropical in feel and have balconies. *2101 S. Surf Rd., 33019, tel. 305/923–9528, fax 305/922–1062. 10 rooms with bath, 39 efficiencies. Facilities: beach, heated pool, shuffleboard, bicycles, laundry, barbecue. AE, MC, V. Moderate.*

Lauderdale- **Pier Pointe Resort.** Built in the 1950s, this oceanfront resort in
by-the-Sea Lauderdale-by-the-Sea, located a block off the main street (Route A1A) and a block from the fishing pier, reminds one of the Gold Coast 40 years ago. The aqua-color canopied entry opens onto two- and three-story buildings (most units with kitchens) set among brick pathways on cabbage palm lawns. The attractive wood pool deck is set off by sea grapes and rope-strung bollards. Rooms are plain, comfortable, and have balconies. *4324 El Mar Dr., 33308, tel. 305/776–5121 or 800/ 331–6384, fax 305/491–9084. 98 suites, 30 efficiencies, and 24 apartments. Facilities: beach, 3 heated freshwater pools, gardens, barbecues. AE, DC, MC, V. Expensive.*

Tropic Seas Resort Inn. It's only a block off A1A, but it might as well be a mile. It's a million-dollar location—directly on the beach, two blocks from municipal tennis courts. Built in the 1950s, units are plain but clean and comfortable, with tropical rattan furniture and ceiling fans. Managers Sandy and Larry Lynch maintain the largely repeat family-oriented clientele. Added features include a weekly wiener roast and rum swizzle party—both are good opportunities to mingle with other guests. *4616 El Mar Dr., 33308, tel. 305/772–2555, fax 305/771–5711. 16 rooms with bath, 6 efficiencies, 7 apartments. Facilities: beach, heated freshwater pool, shuffleboard, barbecue. AE, D, DC, MC, V. Expensive.*

A Little Inn by-the-Sea. Chuck Murawski, who was a Palm Springs councilman after an Emmy Award–winning career in TV, could have settled anywhere. He chose Lauderdale-by-the-Sea because of the accessible cultural life—all construction over three stories is banned, vacationers forget to use their cars, and dozens of good restaurants and shops are nearby. In this felicitous setting, Chuck and partner Larry Krick took over two old motels, completely renovated them, and in 1992 opened their 29-room inn, the first bed-and-breakfast around. The guest rooms show what Chuck and Larry think Florida is all about, themed with shells or boats or birds or fish. They've installed tile floors, and all rooms have at least a fridge (if not complete kitchens). Many rooms have balconies. Plantings surround the pool, and the furniture can be taken onto the beach. The entire fountain lobby, where breakfast is served, is given over to guest use. *4546 El Mar Dr., 33308, tel. 305/772–2450, fax 305/938–9354. 29 rooms with bath, 13 efficiencies, 6 apts. Facilities: beach, heated pool, hot tub, bikes, daily newspaper in season, poolside barbecues. AE, MC, V. Moderate.*

Blue Seas. Bubbly innkeeper Cristie Furth runs this 13-unit, one- and two-story motel in Lauderdale-by-the-Sea with her husband, Marc. The setting is attractive, with its brick patio and garden-set pool, and the guest quarters feature terracotta tiles, bright Haitian and Peruvian art, and generally Tex-Mex and Danish furnishings, which work well together in their woody textures. A good buy in a quiet resort area. *Blue Seas, 4525 El Mar Dr., 33308, tel. 305/772–3336. 13 units with bath. Facilities: heated pool, shuffleboard, kitchenettes, coin laundry. Inexpensive–Moderate.*

The Arts and Nightlife

For the most complete weekly listing of events, read the "Showtime!" entertainment insert and events calendar in the Friday *Fort Lauderdale News/Sun Sentinel*.

Tickets are sold at individual box offices and through **Ticketmaster** (tel. 305/523–3309 in Broward County).

The Arts

Concerts **Bailey Concert Hall** (Central Campus of Broward Community College, 3501 S.W. Davie Rd., tel. 305/475–6884 for reservations) is a popular place for classical music concerts, dance, drama, and other performing arts activities, especially October–April.

The Florida Philharmonic Orchestra (1430 N. Federal Hwy., 33304, tel. 305/561–2997), south Florida's only fully professional orchestra, is Broward-based but performs in six locations in Broward, Dade, and Palm Beach counties.

Opera **The Fort Lauderdale Opera Guild** (333 S.W. 2nd St., 33312, tel. 305/728–9700) presents the current production of the Greater Miami Opera and of the Palm Beach Opera, as well as productions of the Guild itself, in the Broward Center for the Performing Arts. For tickets, contact the Guild office.

Theater **Broward Center for the Performing Arts** (201 S.W. 5th Ave., Fort Lauderdale, tel. 305/522–5334) is the waterfront centerpiece of Fort Lauderdale's new outdoor complex. More than 500 events a year are scheduled at the performing arts center, including Broadway musicals, plays, dance, symphony and opera, rock, film, lectures, comedy, and children's theater.
Parker Playhouse (808 N.E. 8th St., Holiday Park, Fort Lauderdale, tel. 305/764–0700) features Broadway plays, musicals, drama, and local productions.
Sunrise Musical Theatre (5555 N.W. 95th Ave., Sunrise, tel. 305/741–7300) stages Broadway musicals, a few dramatic plays with name stars, and concerts by well-known singers throughout the year. The theater is 14 miles west of Fort Lauderdale Beach via Commercial Boulevard.
Vinnette Carroll Theatre (503 S.E. 6th St., Fort Lauderdale, tel. 305/462–2424), a multiethnic theater company, housed in a renovated church, has mounted productions of such Broadway hits as *Your Arms Too Short to Box with God* and *Don't Bother Me I Can't Cope.*

Nightlife

Bars and **Baja Beach Club** (Coral Ridge Mall, 3200 N. Federal Hwy.,
Nightclubs Fort Lauderdale, tel. 305/561–2432) offers trendy entertainment: Karaoke, lip sync, virtual reality, performing bartenders, temporary tatoos—plus a 40-foot free buffet.
Cheers (941 E. Cypress Creek Rd., tel. 305/771–6337) is a woody night spot with two bars and dance floor. Monday is New Orleans jazz, and every night has a special something.
Confetti (2660 E. Commercial Blvd., tel. 305/776–4081) is a high-energy "in" spot for 35 to 50-year-olds.
Crocco's (3339 N. Federal Hwy., Oakland Park, tel. 305/566–2406) is the action place for singles. Free drinks for women Wednesday night from 8 to 11.
Musicians Exchange (729 W. Sunrise Blvd., tel. 305/764–1912) is a long-running venue for the best of blues, jazz, rock-and-roll, and reggae performers. Every Thursday there's a tribute to the Grateful Dead.
The Parrot Lounge (911 Sunrise La., Fort Lauderdale., tel. 305/563–1493) is a loony feast for the eyes, with a very casual, friendly, local crowd. Ten TVs and frequent singalongs add to the fun.
Squeeze (2 S. New River Dr., tel. 305/522–2068) welcomes a wide-ranging clientele—hard-core new-wavers to yuppie types.
Sushi Blues (1836 Young Circle, Hollywood, tel. 305/929–9560), a small restaurant with great Japanese food, where good music plays in the evenings.
Yesterday's (East Oakland Park Blvd. at the Intracoastal, tel. 305/561–4400) is an upscale disco that attracts middle-agers, but it's no sleeper—more like *Saturday Night Fever.*

Comedy Clubs **The Comic Strip** (1432 N. Federal Hwy., tel. 305/565–8887) headlines stand-up comedians from New York, performing among framed old newspaper funnies.

Country and **Desperado** (2520 S. Miami Rd., Fort Lauderdale, tel. 305/463–
Western 2855) features a mechanical bull and free line-dance lessons.
Do-Da's Country Music Emporium (700 S. U.S. 441, Plantation, tel. 305/792–6200) has buckboard tables and a 2,100-square-foot sunken dance floor, popular for square dancing.

7 Palm Beach and the Treasure Coast

Updated by Herb Hiller

In recent years Palm Beach County—sometimes called the Gold Coast—has really begun to define itself as South Florida's hub of the arts. The heart of the action is downtown West Palm Beach, the county seat and commercial center of Palm Beach County. Here you'll find the Palm Beach Opera, Ballet Florida, the expanding Norton Gallery of Art, the upcoming Palm Beach County School of the Arts, and the new Kravis Center for the Performing Arts. This downtown area, newly landscaped and beautified, saw some major public buildings open in 1992 and 1993, accompanied by a host of new restaurants, stores, and galleries.

In Palm Beach, the elegant barrier island where high society has made headlines for a hundred years, the arts flourish with two equity theaters, the Society of the Four Arts, galleries galore, and a singular commitment to historic preservation. Boca Raton, an upscale community developed in the 1920s by society architect Addison Mizner, today is home to the Boca Raton Museum of Art, the Caldwell Theater, and Jan McArt's Royal Palm Dinner Theater, and retains much of its Spanish Revival architecture and ambience through strict zoning.

Delray Beach, which began as an artists' retreat and a small settlement of Japanese farmers, today has the Morikami Museum, America's leading center for Japanese and American cultural exchange. Downtown Delray has its Old School Square Cultural Arts Center. North in the county past the golfing center of Palm Beach Gardens, the town of Jupiter, with its dune-fringed beach, boasts such institutions as the Burt Reynolds Institute for Theater Training, the Jupiter Dinner Theatre, the Lighthouse Gallery, and the Loxahatchee Historical Museum. To the west, the Dolly Hand Cultural Arts Center in Belle Garde offers a window on the performing arts where Palm Beach County fronts on huge Lake Okeechobee.

Surprising as this arts profusion may strike visitors, no one would be more surprised than Henry Morrison Flagler, who created Palm Beach in 1894 as a resort for his wealthy friends. He never expected West Palm Beach to amount to more than a place for his workers to live, and the rest of the county he saw simply as agricultural land to benefit his railroad. Flagler, who had helped John D. Rockefeller establish the Standard Oil Company, put his retirement money into Florida railroads and real estate. He bought a small railroad between Jacksonville and St. Augustine and extended it southward, to eventually become the Florida East Coast Railroad. Along the rail line he built grand hotels, like the Royal Poinciana and The Breakers, to generate traffic.

Flagler created an international high-society resort at Palm Beach, attracting the affluent for the Season: New Year's Day to Washington's Birthday. The affluent then departed for Europe, extolling Palm Beach's virtues and collecting great art to ship back to the mansions they were building on the island.

Socialites and celebrities still flock to Palm Beach. They attend charity galas at The Breakers. They browse in the stores along Worth Avenue, regarded as one of the world's classiest shopping districts. They swim on secluded beaches that are nominally public but lack convenient parking and access points. They pedal the world's most beautiful bicycle path beside Lake Worth. And what they do, *you* can do—if you can afford it.

But despite its prominence and affluence, the Town of Palm Beach occupies far less than 1% of the land area of Palm Beach County, which is a remarkably diverse political jurisdiction.

The coast north of Palm Beach County, called the Treasure Coast, encompasses Martin, St. Lucie, and Indian River counties. Remote and sparsely populated as recently as the late 1970s, the Treasure Coast lost its relative seclusion in 1987, when I–95's missing link from Palm Beach Gardens to Fort Pierce was completed. Now hotels, restaurants, and shopping malls crowd most corridors between I–95 and the beaches from Palm Beach north to Vero Beach.

The interior here is largely devoted to citrus production, with cattle ranching in rangelands of pine-and-palmetto scrub. Along the coast, the broad expanse of the Indian River (actually a tidal lagoon) separates the barrier islands from the mainland. It's a sheltered route for boaters on the Intracoastal Waterway, a nursery for many saltwater game fish, and a natural radiator keeping frost away from the tender orange and grapefruit trees that grow near its banks. Sea turtles come ashore at night from April to August to lay their eggs on the beaches, and you may join organized turtle-watches run by local conservation groups, chambers of commerce, and resorts.

Essential Information

Important Addresses and Numbers

Tourist Information
Palm Beach County Convention & Visitors Bureau (1555 Palm Beach Lakes Blvd., Suite 204, West Palm Beach 33401, tel. 407/471–3995) is open weekdays 8:30–5.
Chamber of Commerce of the Palm Beaches (401 N. Flagler Dr., West Palm Beach 33401, tel. 407/833–3711) is open weekdays 8:30–5.
Palm Beach Chamber of Commerce (45 Cocoanut Row, Palm Beach 33480, tel. 407/655–3282) is open weekdays 9–5.
Stuart/Martin County Chamber of Commerce (1650 S. Kanner Hwy., Stuart 34994, tel. 407/287–1088) is open weekdays 9–5.
St. Lucie County Tourist Development Council (2300 Virginia Ave., Ft. Pierce 34954, tel. 800/344–TGIF or 407/468–1535) is open weekdays 9–5.
Indian River County Tourist Council (1216 21st St., Box 2947, Vero Beach 32961, tel. 407/567–3491) is open weekdays 9–5.

Emergencies
Dial 911 for **police** and **ambulance** in an emergency.

Hospitals
Three hospitals in West Palm Beach with 24-hour emergency rooms are **Good Samaritan Hospital** (Flagler Dr. and Palm Beach Lakes Blvd., tel. 407/655–5511; doctor referral, tel. 407/650–6240); **Palm Beach Regional Hospital** (2829 10th Ave. N, tel. 407/967–7800; doctor referral, tel. 800/237–6644); and **St. Mary's Hospital** (901 45th St., tel. 407/844–6300; doctor referral, tel. 407/881–2929).

24-Hour Pharmacies
Eckerd Drugs (3343 S. Congress Ave., Palm Springs, tel. 407/965–3367; 7016 Beracasa Way, Boca Raton, tel. 407/391–8770).
Walgreen Drugs (1688 Congress Ave., Palm Springs, tel. 407/968–8211; 7561 N. Federal Hwy., Boca Raton, tel. 407/241–9802; 1208 Royal Palm Beach Blvd., Royal Palm Beach, tel. 407/

798–9048; 6370 Indiantown Rd., Jupiter, tel. 407/744–6822; 20 E. 30th St., Riviera Beach, tel. 407/848–6464).

Arriving and Departing

By Plane **Palm Beach International Airport (PBIA)** (Congress Ave. and Belvedere Rd., West Palm Beach, tel. 407/471–7400) is served by American/American Eagle (tel. 800/433–7300); Bahamasair (tel. 800/222–4262); Continental (tel. 407/832–5200); Delta (tel. 407/655–5300); Northwest (tel. 800/225–2525); Paradise Island (tel. 800/432–8807); TWA (tel. 407/655–3776); United (tel. 800/241–6522); and USAir (tel. 800/428–4322).

Between the Airport and City Center Route 10 of **Tri-Rail Commuter Bus Service** runs from the airport to Tri-Rail's Palm Beach Airport station during weekday rush hours only. For schedule, call 800/TRI–RAIL. For connections with CoTran (Palm Beach County Transportation Authority) routes, call 407/233–1111 in Palm Beach, 407/272–6350 in Boca Raton–Delray Beach. Route 4–S operates from the airport to downtown West Palm Beach every two hours on the half hour from 7:30 AM until 5:30 PM. Fare is 90¢.

Palm Beach Transportation (tel. 407/689–4222) provides taxi and limousine service from PBIA. Reserve at least a day in advance for a limousine. Lowest fares are $1.50 per mile, with the meter starting at $1.25. Depending on your destination, a flat rate (from PBIA only) may save money.

By Car I–95 runs north–south, linking West Palm Beach with Miami and Fort Lauderdale to the south, and with Daytona, Jacksonville, and the rest of the Atlantic Coast to the north. To get to central Palm Beach, exit at Belvedere Road or Okeechobee Boulevard. Florida's Turnpike runs up from Miami through West Palm Beach before angling northwest to reach Orlando.

By Train **Amtrak** (201 S. Tamarind Ave., West Palm Beach, tel. 800/872–7245 or 407/832–6169) connects West Palm Beach with cities along Florida's east coast and the northeast daily.

By Bus **Greyhound/Trailways** buses arrive at the station in West Palm Beach (100 1st St., tel. 407/833–0825).

Getting Around

A new downtown facility to open in 1994 at Clearwater Drive and Banyan, the western entrance to downtown, will link together all sorts of transport including Amtrak, Greyhound/Trailways, TriRail (the commuter line that links Dade, Broward, and Palm Beach counties), CoTran (the county bus system), and taxis.

By Car U. S. 1 threads north–south along the coast, connecting most coastal communities, while the more scenic Route A1A ventures out onto the barrier islands. The interstate, I–95, runs parallel to U.S. 1 a bit farther inland. Southern Boulevard (U.S. 98) runs east–west from West Palm Beach out to Lake Okeechobee.

By Train Tri-Rail, the commuter rail system, has six stations in Palm Beach County. For details, call 800/TRI–RAIL or 305/728–8445.

By Bus **CoTran** (Palm Beach County Transportation Authority) buses require exact change (90¢, 45¢ for senior citizens and handicapped persons, plus 20¢ for a transfer). Service is provided from 5 AM to 8:30 PM, with individual route variations. For details, call 407/233–1111 (Palm Beach) or 407/272–6350 (Boca Raton–Delray Beach).

A new shuttle system introduced in 1993, **Palmtran** (tel. 407/833–8873) provides free transportation around downtown West Palm Beach from 7 to 7 weekdays.

By Taxi Call **Palm Beach Transportation** (tel. 407/689–4222) for a cab. Meters start at $1.25, and the charge is $1.25 per mile within West Palm Beach city limits; if the trip at any point leaves the city limits, the fare is $1.50 per mile. Some cabs may charge more. Waiting time is 25¢ per 75 seconds.

Guided Tours

Boat Tours **Loxahatchee Everglades Tours** (tel. 407/482–6107) operates air boat tours from west of Boca Raton through the marshes between the built-up coast and Lake Okeechobee.

Star of Palm Beach (tel. 407/842–0882) offers sightseeing as well as dinner-dance tours that cruise the Intracoastal Waterway from Phil Foster Park.

Manatee Queen (tel. 407/744–2191) offers day and evening cruises on the Intracoastal Waterway and into the cypress swamps of Jonathan Dickinson State Park between November and May.

The Spirit of St. Joseph (tel. 407/467–2628) offers lunch, dinner, and family sightseeing cruises along the Indian River from alongside the St. Lucie County Historical Museum, November through April.

Land Tours **Old Northwood Historic District Tours** (tel. 407/863–5633) offers year-round group walking tours through the 1920s-era historic district of West Palm Beach, including historic home interiors.

Boca Raton Historical Society (71 N. Federal Hwy., Boca Raton 33429, tel. 407/395–6766) offers afternoon tours of the Boca Raton Resort & Club, November to April, as well as group tours to other south Florida sites.

Tropical Florida Tours (1422 Tropical Dr., Lake Worth, tel. 407/582–5947) offers year-round guided day tours of South Florida and the Everglades.

Indian River County Historical Society (2336 14th Ave., Vero Beach, tel. 407/778–3435) expects to begin offering tours of the historic 7-mile Jungle Trail along the Indian River beginning in the winter of 1993–94.

Exploring Palm Beach and the Treasure Coast

Highlights for First-Time Visitors

The Breakers, Palm Beach
Highway A1A along the shore, South Palm Beach County
Historic Downtown Stuart, Treasure Coast

Island of Palm Beach, Palm Beach
The Jungle Trail, Treasure Coast
Morikami Museum, South Palm Beach County
Norton Gallery of Art, West Palm Beach
Whitehall, Palm Beach
Worth Avenue, Palm Beach

Palm Beach

Numbers in the margin correspond to points of interest on the Palm Beach and Palm Beach County map.

Palm Beach is an island community 12 miles long and no more than ¼ mile across at its widest point. Three bridges connect Palm Beach to West Palm Beach and the rest of the world.

Begin at Royal Palm Way and County Road in the center of Palm Beach. Go north on County Road past the Episcopal church, **Bethesda-by-the-Sea,** built in 1927 by the first Protestant congregation in southeast Florida. Inspiring stained-glass windows and a lofty, vaulted sanctuary grace its Spanish-Gothic design. A stone bridge with an ornamental tile border spans the pond; bubbling fountains feed it. *141 South County Rd., Palm Beach, tel. 407/655-4554. Gardens open 8-5. Services Sun. 8, 9, and 11 AM in winter, 8 and 10 June–Aug.; phone for weekday schedule.*

Continue north on County Road past **The Breakers** (1 S. County Rd., Palm Beach), an ornate Italian renaissance hotel (*see* Lodging, *below*) built in 1926 by Henry M. Flagler's widow to replace an earlier hotel, which had burned, twice. Explore the elegant public spaces—especially on a Sunday morning, when you can enjoy the largest champagne brunch in Florida at The Beach Club.

Continue north on County Road to Royal Poinciana Way. Go inside the **Palm Beach Post Office** to see the murals depicting Seminole Indians in the Everglades and royal and coconut palms. *95 N. County Rd., Palm Beach, tel. 407/832-0633 or 407/832-1867. Open weekdays 8:30-5.*

Continue 3.9 miles north on County Road to the north end of the island, past the very-private **Palm Beach Country Club** and a neighborhood of expansive (and expensive) estates. From the coastal road you can catch glimpses of Singer Island, with its Oz-like scenery.

You must turn around at **E. Inlet Drive,** the northern tip of the island, where a dock offers a view of Lake Worth Inlet, the U.S. Coast Guard Reservation on Peanut Island, and the Port of Palm Beach across Lake Worth on the mainland. Observe the no-parking signs; Palm Beach police will issue tickets.

Turn south and make the first right onto Indian Road, then the first left onto Lake Way. You'll return to the center of town through an area of newer mansions, past the posh, private Sailfish Club. Lake Way parallels the **Palm Beach Bicycle Trail** along the shoreline of Lake Worth, a palm-fringed path through the backyards of some of the world's priciest homes. Watch on your right for metal posts topped with a swatch of white paint, marking narrow public-access walkways between houses from the street to the bike path.

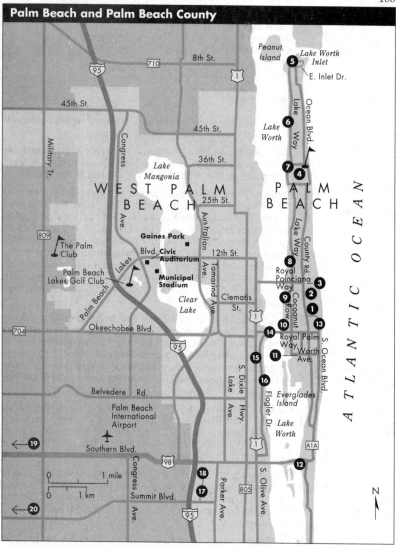

Palm Beach and Palm Beach County

Ann Norton Sculpture Gardens, **16**

Bethesda-by-the-Sea, **1**

The Breakers, **2**

Canyon of Palm Beach, **7**

Dreher Park Zoo, **17**

E. Inlet Drive, **5**

Lion Country Safari, **19**

Mar-A-Lago, **12**

Norton Gallery of Art, **15**

Palm Beach Bicycle Trail, **6**

Palm Beach Biltmore Hotel, **8**

Palm Beach Country Club, **4**

Palm Beach Post Office, **3**

Pine Jog Environmental Education Center, **20**

Public Beach, **13**

Royal Palm Bridge, **14**

Society of the Four Arts, **10**

South Florida Science Museum, **18**

Whitehall, **9**

Worth Ave., **11**

Lake Way runs into Country Club Road, which takes you
❼ through the **Canyon of Palm Beach,** a road cut about 25 feet
deep through a ridge of sandstone and oolite limestone.

As you emerge from the canyon, turn right onto Lake Way and
continue south. Lake Way becomes Bradley Place. You'll pass
❽ the **Palm Beach Biltmore Hotel,** now a condominium. Another
flamboyant landmark of the Florida boom, it cost $7 million to
build and opened in 1927 with 543 rooms.

As you cross Royal Poinciana Way, Bradley Place becomes Co-
❾ coanut Row. Stop at **Whitehall,** the palatial 73-room mansion
that Henry M. Flagler built in 1901 for his third wife, Mary Lily
Kenan. After the death of Flagler, and later of his widow, the
mansion was turned into a hotel. In 1960, Flagler's grand-
daughter, Jean Flagler Matthews, bought the building. She
turned it into a museum, with many of the original furnishings
on display. The art collection includes a Gainsborough portrait
of a girl with a pink sash, displayed in the music room near a
1,200-pipe organ. Exhibits also depict the history of the Florida East Coast Railroad. Flagler's personal railroad car, "The
Rambler," is parked behind the building. A tour by well-
informed guides takes about an hour; afterwards, you may
browse on your own. *Cocoanut Row at Whitehall Way, Palm
Beach, tel. 407/655–2833. Admission: $5 adults, $2 children 6–
12. Open Tues.–Sat. 10–5, Sun. noon–5. Closed Mon.*

Continue south on Cocoanut Row to Royal Palm Way. Turn
❿ right and then right again onto the grounds of the **Society of the
Four Arts.** This 58-year-old cultural and educational institution
is privately endowed and incorporates an exhibition hall for
art, concerts, films, and lectures; a library open without
charge; 13 distinct gardens; and the Philip Hulitar Sculpture
Garden. *Four Arts Plaza, tel. 407/655–7226. Admission: suggested donation $3. Concert and lecture tickets for nonmem-
bers may be purchased one week in advance. Tickets for Fri.
films available at time of showing. Exhibitions and programs,
Dec.–mid-Apr., Mon.–Sat. 10–5, Sun. 2–5. Library open
Nov.–Apr., Mon.–Sat. 10–5; May–Oct., weekdays 10–5. Gardens open Nov.–Apr., Mon.–Sat. 10–5; Jan.–Apr. 15, Sun.
2:30–5; May–Oct., weekdays 10–5.*

Return to Royal Palm Way and County Road, where we began
⓫ this tour. Now go south on County Road, until you reach **Worth
Avenue,** regarded by many as the world's classiest shopping
street (*see* Shopping, *below*). Immediately on your left is the
Colony Hotel in its lovely lemony yellow (*see* Lodging, *below*).

County Road runs south along a mansion row fronted by thick
stands of palm trees and high hedges, some hedgerows higher
than 20 feet. You will see de rigeur barrel tile roofs on the
houses. After a mile, County Road joins Ocean Boulevard to become the shore road (now officially designated A1A). A low
wall separates the road from the sea and hides the badly eroded
beach. Here and there where the seaside strand deepens a bit,
homes have been built directly on the beach.

⓬ Grandest of homes along this road is **Mar-A-Lago** (1100 S.
Ocean Blvd.), its Italianate towers silhouetted against the sky.
Mar-A-Lago, the former estate of breakfast-food heiress Marjorie Meriweather Post, has lately been owned by real estate
magnate Donald Trump, who is trying to subdivide it. The
property curves for ⅓ mile along the road.

Rather than cross the bridge to the mainland, turn around and return to Ocean Boulevard, heading north along one of Florida's most scenic drives. The road follows the dune top, with the beach eroding to surf on your right and some of Palm Beach's most opulent mansions on your left. As you approach Worth **⑬** Avenue, the **public beach** begins. Parking meters along Ocean Boulevard between Worth Avenue and Royal Palm Way signify the only stretch of beach in Palm Beach with convenient public access.

West Palm Beach

⑭ Royal Palm Way runs across the **Royal Palm Bridge** from Palm Beach into West Palm Beach. Newly widened and relandscaped, Okeechobee Boulevard leads west from here to downtown, past the **Kravis Center for the Performing Arts** (*see* the Arts, *below*). Besides the Kravis Center, which opened in 1992, new buildings on the skyline include the mammoth Palm Beach County Judicial Center and Courthouse and the State Administrative Building, both opened in 1993.

Rather than drive into downtown, however, once you have reached the mainland side of the bridge turn left onto Flagler Drive. Running along the west shore of Lake Worth, the body of water that separates Palm Beach from the mainland, Flagler Drive has been spruced up with a new $4.2 million waterfront restoration project.

One-half mile south of the bridge, turn right onto Actaeon Street, which is the north edge of a sloping mall leading up to **⑮** the **Norton Gallery of Art.** Founded in 1941 by steel magnate Ralph H. Norton, the Norton Gallery boasts an extensive permanent collection of 19th- and 20th-century American and European paintings with emphasis on 19th-century French Impressionists, Chinese bronze and jade sculptures, a sublime outdoor patio with sculptures on display in a tropical garden, and a library housing more than 3,000 art books and periodicals. *1451 S. Olive Ave., West Palm Beach, tel. 407/832–5194. Admission free; $5 donation requested. Open Tues.–Sat. 10–5, Sun. 1–5.*

Return to Flagler Drive, go ½ mile south to Barcelona Road, **⑯** and turn right again. You're at the entrance to the **Ann Norton Sculpture Gardens,** a monument to the late American sculptor Ann Weaver Norton, second wife of Norton Gallery founder Ralph H. Norton. In three distinct areas of the 3-acre grounds, the art park displays seven granite figures and six brick megaliths. Plantings were designed by Norton, an environmentalist, to attract native birdlife. Native plants include 150 different kinds of palms. Other sculptures in bronze, marble, and wood are on display in Norton's studio. *253 Barcelona Rd., West Palm Beach, tel. 407/832–5328. Admission: $2 adults, children under 12 free. Open Tues.–Sat. 10–4 or by appointment.*

Return again to Flagler Drive and continue south to Southern Boulevard (U.S. 98). Turn right and go west almost a mile, turn left onto Parker Avenue, and go south about a mile. Turn right onto Summit Boulevard, and at the next stoplight you'll find **⑰** the **Dreher Park Zoo.** The 29-acre zoo has more than 400 animals representing more than 100 different species, including an endangered Florida panther. Of special interest are the reptile collection, the petting zoo, and a new elevated boardwalk running through natural Florida hammock land. *1301 Summit Blvd., West Palm Beach, tel. 407/547–WILD (recording) or 407/533–0887. Admission: $5 adults, $4.50 senior citizens over 60, $3.50 children 3–12. Open daily 9–5.*

⓲ About ¼ mile from the zoo is the **South Florida Science Museum.** Here you'll find hands-on exhibits, aquarium displays with touch-tank demonstrations, planetarium shows, and a chance to observe the heavens Friday nights through the most powerful telescope in south Florida (weather permitting). *4801 Dreher Trail N, West Palm Beach, tel. 407/832–1988. Admission: $5 adults, $4.50 senior citizens over 62, $3 students 13–21, $2 children 4–12; laser show $2 extra. Planetarium admission: $1.75 extra. Open daily 10–5, Fri. 10–10.*

⓳ Leaving the science museum, return to Southern Boulevard (Rte. 98) and go about 16 miles west to **Lion Country Safari,** where you drive (with car windows closed) on 8 miles of paved roads through a 500-acre cageless zoo where 1,000 wild animals roam free. Lions, elephants, white rhinoceroses, giraffes, zebras, antelopes, chimpanzees, and ostriches are among the species in residence. Try to go early in the day, before the park gets crowded. *Box 16066, West Palm Beach 33416, tel. 407/793–1084. Admission: $11.95 adults, $8.55 senior citizens over 65, $9.95 children 3–16, under 3 free; car rental $5 per hour. Open daily 9:30–5:30.*

⓴ Returning to town on Southern Boulevard, turn right onto Jog Road, left onto Summit Boulevard to the **Pine Jog Environmental Education Center.** The 150-acre site is mostly undisturbed Florida pine flatwoods. There's a self-guided ½-mile trail, and formal landscaping around the five one-story buildings features an array of native plants. Dioramas and displays show native ecosystems, and environmental education programs are offered. *6301 Summit Blvd., West Palm Beach, tel. 407/686–6600. Admission free. Open weekdays 9–5, weekends 1–4. Closed major holidays.*

South to Boca Raton

Numbers in the margin correspond to points of interest on the Gold Coast and Treasure Coast map.

This driving tour carries you along the coast of south Palm Beach County, nearly 40 miles along Highway A1A through an almost uninterrupted realm of the rich and famous that has earned the sobriquet "the Gold Coast." Little commuter traffic occurs, but the route all the way is two-lane and slow moving in winter. Watch for cyclists and joggers.

Starting from the center of Palm Beach, on Royal Palm Way, head south on County Road. It soon joins Ocean Boulevard and proceeds south, as Highway A1A, along the barrier island. On
❶ the left is **Phipps Ocean Park** with a Palm Beach County landmark: the **Little Red Schoolhouse,** which dates from 1886, the first schoolhouse in what was then Dade County. (Dade County today is metropolitan Miami, but at one time extended all the way to Lake Okeechobee.) The schoolhouse displays its pine floor, pine desks, little chairs on iron bases riveted to the floor, and a row of sandbuckets for use in case of fire. *Phipps Ocean*

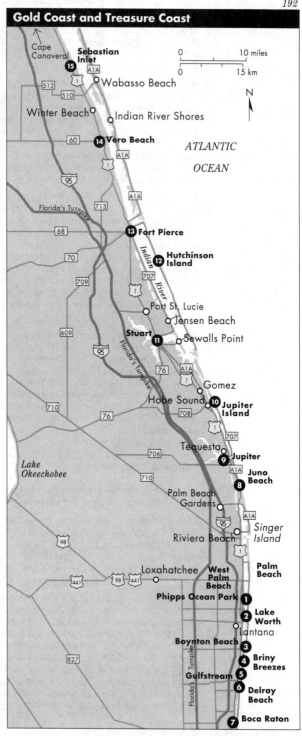

Gold Coast and Treasure Coast

Cape Canaveral

Sebastian Inlet
15 A1A

Wabasso Beach

512
510

Winter Beach

Indian River Shores

60 **14 Vero Beach**
A1A

ATLANTIC

OCEAN

95

713

68

70

709

13 Fort Pierce

12 Hutchinson Island

707

Indian River

Port St. Lucie

Jensen Beach

Stuart Sewalls Point
11

76

A1A
1

609

Florida's Turnpike

Gomez

Hobe Sound **10 Jupiter Island**

708

710

76

1

707

Tequesta **Jupiter**
706 **9** A1A

Lake Okeechobee

710

Juno Beach
8

Palm Beach Gardens

95
A1A

98

Singer Island

Riviera Beach

1

Loxahatchee **West Palm Beach**

Palm Beach

441 98 441

Phipps Ocean Park **1**

2 Lake Worth

Lantana

Boynton Beach **3**

4 Briny Breezes

Gulfstream **5**

827

6 Delray Beach

Florida's Turnpike

7 Boca Raton

0   10 miles
0   15 km

N

Park. Open 8 AM–6 PM, parking 25¢ for 20 minutes, 75¢ per hr.,
quarters only.

Just below Phipps Ocean Park, **Palm Beach Golf Club** extends
its course to either side of the road. You are now leaving Palm
❷ Beach and entering the town called **Lake Worth.** Turn right at
the causeway into Casino Park (also known as Lake Worth Municipal Park).

Time Out About the only time the line lets up at **John G's** (Lake Worth
Casino, tel. 407/585–9860) is when the restaurant closes. The
menu is as big as the crowd: eggs every which way, including a
UN of ethnic omelets; big fruit platters; sandwich board superstars; grilled burgers and seafood. The Greek shrimp (seven at
recent count) come on fresh linguini topped by feta cheese.

Across Boynton Inlet you enter the towns of Manalapan and
Ocean Ridge. **The Ritz-Carlton Hotel** (100 S. Ocean Blvd.,
Manalapan, tel. 407/533–6000) is on the left, then the **Ocean
Club Golf Course** to the west, its villas and beach club to the
❸ east. The little **Boynton Beach** city park provides a good swimming beach, but only at a prohibitive parking fee for non-resi-
dents: $10 in winter, half that other times of year.

Just below the crossing of SR 804 (East Ocean Avenue), a niche
road (Old Ocean Boulevard) cuts off directly along the beach to
❹ enter **Briny Breezes,** a wonderful old blue-collar town, 42 acres
directly on the sea. It's an incongruous neighbor in these pre-
cincts of the high and mighty, but here it has been, incorporated since 1963. Beyond this you'll pass another anomaly in
this ritzy area—a row of mildly ramshackle houses, with overgrown yards full of rusting gear—then come to the beautiful
❺ little community of **Gulfstream.** The road passes beneath a canopy of palms and pines that thickly tint the air gray-green.
You'll pass the very private St. Andrews County Club and the
bougainvillea-topped walls of the Gulfstream Club, part of the
Addison Mizner legacy, where a private policeman may come
onto the road to halt traffic for the moment it takes a golfer to
cross in his or her cart.

❻ At the edge of **Delray Beach,** across Northeast 8th Street
(George Bush Boulevard) begins a lovely pedestrian way along
the big broad swimming beach that extends north and south of
Atlantic Avenue. Reach the water via dune walks through the
dense beach shrubbery. Atlantic Avenue is Delray's main
street, running for about 12 store-lined blocks west from the
ocean; along here you'll see the Mediterranean-revival **Colony
Hotel** (525 E. Atlantic Ave., tel. 407/276–4123), still open only
for the winter season as it has been for more than 60 years. Just
off Atlantic Avenue, the **Old School Square Cultural Arts Center** (51 N. Swinton Ave., tel. 407/243–7922) houses museums
and a performing arts center in restored school buildings dating from 1913 and 1926. The main tourist attraction in Delray
Beach is the **Morikami Museum and Japanese Gardens,** a 200-
acre cultural and recreational facility. Some programs and exhibits are in the new lakeside museum building and theater; an
earlier building, modeled after a Japanese imperial villa,
houses a permanent exhibition detailing the history of the
Yamato Colony, Japanese farmers who came in 1905 to farm the
vicinity under the encouragement of Henry Flagler's Florida
East Coast Railroad. The grounds include a 1-mile nature trail,

four picnic pavilions, a library and audiovisual center on Japanese culture, museum shop, snack bar/café, and various gardens, including the only collection known to exist of bonsai Florida plants. *4000 Morikami Park Rd., Delray Beach 33446, tel. 407/495–0233. Admission: $4 adults, $3.50 senior citizens, $2 children 6–18. Park open daily sunrise–sunset; museum open Tues.–Sun. 10–5.*

South of Linton Boulevard the beachfront character changes, becoming more high-rise. You enter the town of **Highland Beach,** which has been completely developed in the last 25 years. In the 1960s there was only dune here (and some of the best surfing along the Gold Coast); today the shoreside is packed with condominiums, and across the Intracoastal Waterway, mansions. An older section commences, then development again. The road here is called South Ocean Boulevard.

➐ Where the road rises along the dune, you enter into **Boca Raton.** This visionary city, developed by architect Addison Mizner in the 1920s, had barely made it off the drawing board when the Depression hit. Mizner's development company went bust and a man named Clarence Geist bought up its assets in 1929. For half a century after this, Boca Raton grew along the beach and along U.S. 1, without ever really becoming a town in its own right. Off to the right ahead you will see the peachy-plum-color Boca Tower of the **Boca Raton Resort & Club**; alongside it, lower to the ground, is the nucleus of the hotel, the original Cloister Inn built by Addison Mizner. To the left is the Boca Beach Club, a newer part of the same property.

Cross the drawbridge over Boca Inlet and drive on to Camino Real, a six-lane boulevard with a double row of Malaysian dwarf palms down the center. Cross Federal Highway (U.S. 1), and just before Dixie Highway, turn left at 2 E. Camino Real into the parking lot of **Addison's Flavor of Italy** restaurant (tel. 407/391–9800), with its enormous twin banyan trees in front. Built in 1925 by the Mizner Development Corporation to house the city administration, this building shows Mizner's characteristic Spanish Revival architectural style: pecky cypress, wrought-iron grills, a barrel tile roof, and hand-made tiles around the courtyard.

Turn right onto South Dixie Highway. Immediately on your left is the restored **Raton Florida East Coast Railroad Station,** once a stop on the Florida East Coast Railroad. It's now the **Count De Hoernle Pavilion,** named for a benefactor of the project, and is used for small community meetings. The two stainless steel coaches on the south side and the locomotive and freight car on the north side are from the Seaboard Coast Line, which ran through another station to the west, no longer in use.

As you continue north on Dixie Highway, on your right notice the distinctive Boca look: buildings in pink and burnt sienna, all with barrel tile roofs, many with canopies and iron balconies. One block past Palmetto Park Road, turn right onto Boca Raton Road; on your right is the **Old Town Hall,** built in 1927 to a Mizner design. Of special interest are the pecky cypress ceiling and fanlight windows, the original tile and hardwood floors, the cypress millwork throughout, and the historical Mizner artifacts in display cabinets of the library. A gift shop is located in the original Mayor's office. *Open weekdays 10–4.*

Turn left on North Federal Highway, and at Northeast 3rd Street you'll find **Mizner Park,** the new heart of downtown Boca Raton, with its shopping promenade, apartments, and offices (*see* Shopping, *below*). This successful development has quickly become Boca's downtown heart, giving the community a focal point it sorely needed.

Exit Mizner Park across Northeast 2nd Street and continue west across the railroad tracks. The new **Boca Raton City Hall** is on your left, designed in the style of the original, set among enormous banyan trees. The grounds also house the **Boca Raton Community Center.**

Return to Palmetto Park Road to visit the **Boca Raton Museum of Art,** with its whimsical metal sculptures outdoors on the lawn. The museum's permanent collection includes works by Picasso, Degas, Matisse, Klee, Modigliani, and notable pre-Columbian art. *801 W. Palmetto Park Rd., tel. 407/392–2500. Admission: free. Open Mon.–Fri. 10–4, Sat.–Sun. noon–4.*

The residential area behind the museum is **Old Floresta,** developed by Addison Mizner starting in 1925 and landscaped with many varieties of palms and cycads. The houses are mainly Mediterranean-style, many with upper balconies supported in the Mizner style by exposed wood columns.

The Treasure Coast

This tour takes you north from Palm Beach along the coast as far as Sebastian Inlet, but you can break away at any intermediate point and return to Palm Beach on I–95. From downtown West Palm Beach, take U.S. 1 about 5 miles north to Blue Heron Boulevard (Route A1A) in Riviera Beach, turn right, and cross the **Jerry Thomas Bridge** onto Singer Island. Continue on Route A1A as it turns north onto Ocean Boulevard, past hotels and high-rise condominiums to **John D. MacArthur State Park** (10900 Rte. A1A, North Palm Beach, tel. 407/624–6952), which offers almost 2 miles of beach and interpretive walks to a mangrove estuary in the upper reaches of Lake Worth.

8 North of MacArthur State Park, Route A1A rejoins U.S. 1, then veers east again 1½ miles north at **Juno Beach.** Take Route A1A north to the **Loggerhead Park Marine Life Center of Juno Beach,** established by Eleanor N. Fletcher, "the turtle lady of Juno Beach." Museum displays interpret the sea turtles' natural history; hatchlings are raised in saltwater tanks, tagged, and released into the surf. Also on view are displays of coastal natural history, sharks, whales, and shells. *1111 Ocean Dr., but enter at 1200 U.S. 1, on the west side of the park, Juno Beach, tel. 407/627–8280. Admission free. Open Tues.–Sat. 10–3, Sun. noon–3.*

9 From Juno Beach north to **Jupiter,** Route A1A runs for almost 4 miles atop the beachfront dunes. At the northwest corner of Indiantown Road and Route A1A is the **Jupiter Dinner Theatre** (formerly the Burt Reynolds Jupiter Theater). Actor Burt Reynolds grew up in Jupiter; his father was a Palm Beach County sheriff. More than 150 Broadway and Hollywood stars have performed here since the theater opened in 1979. *1001 E. Indiantown Rd., Jupiter, tel. 407/747–5566.*

Leave the theater grounds on Route A1A, and continue a little more than ½ mile to Jupiter Beach Road. Turn right and immediately left onto Dubois Road. At the end of the road, in **Dubois Park,** is the **Dubois Home,** a modest pioneer home that dates from 1898. The house, with design features that include Cape Cod as well as "cracker," sits atop an ancient Jeaga Indian mound 20 feet high, looking onto Jupiter Inlet. Even if you visit when the house is closed, the park is worth the visit for its lovely beaches around swimming lagoons. *Dubois Rd., Jupiter, tel. 407/747–6639. Admission by voluntary donation. Open Sat.–Sun. 1–4.*

Return to A1A, turn right to U.S. 1, then turn left (south) for ⅓ mile. On the east side of the highway, in Burt Reynolds Park, is the **Loxahatchee Historical Society Museum.** Permanent exhibits emphasize Seminole Indians, the steamboat era, pioneer life on the Loxahatchee River, shipwrecks, railroads, and modern-day development. *805 N. U.S. 1, Jupiter, tel. 407/747–6639. Admission: $3 adults, $2 senior citizens, $1 children 6–18. Open Tues.–Fri. 10–4, weekends 1–4. Closed Mon.*

Return north on U.S. 1 across the Loxahatchee River and just across the Jupiter Inlet Bridge, pick up Route 707 (Beach Road). On your right is the **Jupiter Inlet Light Station,** a redbrick Coast Guard navigational beacon that has operated here since 1866. A giant banyan tree sits in front of the 105-foot light; a museum is located in its base (open Sun. only, 1–4).

⑩ Continue north on Route 707 from the lighthouse onto **Jupiter Island** and stop at the Nature Conservancy's 73-acre **Blowing Rocks Preserve.** Within the preserve you'll find plant communities native to beachfront dune, strand (the landward side of the dunes), marsh, and hammock (tropical hardwood forest). Sea grape, cabbage palms, saw palmetto, and sea oats help to anchor the dunes. Also on the grounds are live pelicans, seagulls, ospreys, redbellied and pileated woodpeckers, and a profusion of warblers in spring and fall. The best time to go is early morning, before the crowds. The parking lot holds just 18 cars, with room for three cars to wait; Jupiter Island police will ticket cars parked along the road shoulder. *Box 3795, Tequesta 33469, tel. 407/575–2297 (office), 407/747–3113 (preserve). Donation requested. Open daily 6–5.*

Continue north through the town of Jupiter Island, a posh community with estates screened from the road by dense vegetation. At the north end of Jupiter Island, **Hobe Sound National Wildlife Refuge** has a 3½-mile beach where turtles nest and shells wash ashore. High tides and strong winds in 1991 and 1992 severely eroded the beach; only at low tide is there any beach to walk on (admission: $3 per vehicle).

Return to the mainland, to the town of Hobe Sound along U.S. 1, to visit the refuge headquarters, the **Elizabeth W. Kirby Interpretive Center.** An adjacent ½-mile trail winds through a forest of sand pine and scrub oak—one of Florida's most unusual and endangered plant communities. *13640 S.E. Federal Hwy., Hobe Sound, tel. 407/546–2067, refuge tel. 407/546–6141. Trail open sunrise to sunset. Nature center open weekdays 9–11 and 1–3, call for Sat. hours; group tours by appointment.*

Return to U.S. 1 and proceed north. Quality-of-life values are

⑪ most apparent in **Stuart**—the county seat—a one-time fishing village that has become a magnet for people who want to live and work in a small-town atmosphere. Strict architectural and zoning standards guide civic renewal projects in the older section of Stuart. Recent achievements include most of a 2-mile riverwalk, due for completion early in 1994; start of a new pleasure boat marina; beautification of **Confusion Corner,** a complex traffic exchange adored by townsfolk; and a 200-seat amphitheater at the foot of St. Lucie Street. The old courthouse has been opened for cultural exhibits, and a newly built gazebo features free music performances. The Lyric Theater has been revived for performing and community events.

Time Out   In an old bank building, the **Jolly Sailor Pub** (1 S.W. Osceola St., tel. 407/221–1111) is owned by a retired 27-year British Merchant Navy veteran, which may account for the endless ship paraphernalia—a veritable Cunard museum, with its model of the *Brittania*, prints of 19th-century sidewheelers, and a big bar painting of the *QE2*. There's a wonderful brass-railed wood bar, a dart board, and such pub grub as fish and chips, cottage pie, and bangers (sausage) and mash, with Guinness and Harp ales on tap.

⑫ Continue north on Route A1A to **Hutchinson Island.** At Indian River Plantation, turn right onto MacArthur Boulevard 1½ miles to the **House of Refuge Museum,** built in 1875 as one of 10 such structures erected by the U.S. Life Saving Service (an ancestor of the Coast Guard) to aid stranded sailors. Exhibits include antique lifesaving equipment, maps, artifacts from nearby wrecks, and boatmaking tools. The 35-foot watch-tower in the front yard was used during World War II by submarine spotters (but is off-limits for climbing). *301 S.E. MacArthur Blvd., Stuart, tel. 407/225–1875. Admission: $1 adults, 50¢ children 6–13, under 6 free. Open Tues.–Sun. 1–4, winter Tues.–Sun. 11–4. Closed Mon. and holidays.*

Return to Route A1A and go ³⁄₁₀ mile north to the pastel-pink **Elliott Museum,** built in 1961 in honor of Sterling Elliott, inventor of an early automated addressing machine and a four-wheel bicycle. In addition, the museum features antique automobiles, dolls and toys, and fixtures from an early general store, blacksmith shop, and apothecary shop. *825 N.E. Ocean Blvd., Stuart, tel. 407/225–1961. Admission: $2.50 adults, 50¢ children 6–13, under 6 free. Open daily 11–5 (no admittance after 4).*

Across the road is the **Coastal Science Center** (890 N.E. Ocean Blvd., Stuart 34996, tel. 407/225–0505) of the Florida Oceanographic Society. Its nearly 44-acre site combines a coastal hardwood hammock and mangrove forest. Resources include temporary displays about coastal ecology, a library program, and an interpretive nature trail. Construction is expected to begin before 1994 on a visitor center, auditorium, permanent library, research laboratories, and aquariums.

Continue up Route A1A as far as the Jensen Beach Bridge. Cut back to the mainland and turn right on Indian River Drive, Route 707. This scenic road full of curves and dips follows the
⑬ course of early-20th-century pineapple plantations. In **Fort Pierce,** turn right over the South Beach Causeway Bridge. On the east side, take the first road left onto the grounds of the **St. Lucie County Historical Museum.** Among its exhibits are historic photos, early-20th-century memorabilia, vintage farm tools, a restored 1919 American La France fire engine, replicas of a general store and the old Fort Pierce railroad station, and the restored 1905 Gardner House. *414 Seaway Dr., Fort Pierce,*

tel. 407/468–1795. Admission: $2 adults, $1 children 6–11, under 6 free. Open Tues.–Sat. 10–4, Sun. noon–4.

From here, backtrack to the mainland, head north (right), and then turn east across North Beach Causeway. Follow Route A1A north to Pepper Park and the **UDT-Seal Museum,** beside the beach where more than 3,000 Navy frogmen trained during World War II. Exhibits tell the story of Navy divers from the 1944 Normandy invasion through Korea, Vietnam, and astronaut landings at sea. *3300 N. AIA, Ft. Pierce, tel. 407/595–1570. Admission: $2 adults, $1 children 6–11, under 6 free. Open Tues.–Sat., 10–4, Sun. noon–4.*

About 1 mile north of Pepper Beach, turn left to the parking lot for the 958-acre **Jack Island Wildlife Refuge,** accessible only by footbridge. The 1½-mile Marsh Rabbit Trail across the island traverses a mangrove swamp to a 30-foot observation tower overlooking the Indian River. You'll see ospreys, brown pelicans, great blue herons, ibis, and other water birds. Trails cover 4⅓ miles altogether.

⓮ Return to Route A1A and go north to **Vero Beach,** an affluent city of about 30,000; retirees comprise half the winter population. In the exclusive Riomar Bay section, north of the 17th Street Bridge, "canopy roads" shaded by massive live oaks cross the barrier island between Route A1A and Ocean Drive. **Painted Bunting Lane,** a typical canopy road, is lined with elegant homes—many dating from the 1920s.

Continue north on Route A1A past the John's Island development. Turn left onto Old Winter Beach Road: The pavement turns to hard-packed dirt as the road curves north, indicating the old **Jungle Trail.** Portions of the trail along the Indian River are still undeveloped, with palms and moss-covered oaks abounding, and provide a glimpse of yesteryear Florida.

Return to Route A1A to visit the **McLarty Museum,** a National Historical Landmark site, its displays dedicated to the 1715 hurricane that sank a fleet of Spanish treasure ships. *13180 N. Hwy. A1A, Sebastian, tel. 407/589–2147. Admission: $1, children under 6 free. Open daily 10–5.*

⓯ Turn left and proceed 7 miles to **Sebastian Inlet.** The high bridge over the Intracoastal Waterway offers spectacular views. Immediately after crossing the bridge, turn left and follow the signs to the **Environmental Learning Center** (255 Live Oak Dr., Vero Beach 32963, tel. 407/589–5050), an outstanding 51-acre facility with exhibits, a 600-foot section of boardwalk through mangrove shore, and a 1-mile canoe trail.

Return east across U.S. 1 on Route 510, which curves twice and becomes Route 512 before reaching I–95, where you can head south to return to Palm Beach.

What to See and Do with Children

At the **Burt Reynolds Ranch and Mini Petting Farm,** a 160-acre working horse ranch owned by the famous actor, visitors can take a 1½-hour tour by air-conditioned bus, with stops that include movie sets, a chapel, tree house, and wherever else filming may be in progress. Farm and exotic animals can be petted. *16133 Jupiter Farms Rd., Jupiter (2 mi west of I–95 off exit 59-B), tel. 407/747–5390. Admission free to petting farm; tour* *admission $10 adults, $5 children. Open daily 10–4:30. Closed major holidays.*

Children's Museum of Boca Raton at Singing Pines is a learning center featuring hands-on exhibits, workshops, and special programs. *498 Crawford Blvd., Boca Raton, tel. 407/368–6875. Admission: $1. Open Tues.–Sat. noon–4.*

Children's Science Explorium features 40 hands-on exhibits as well as ongoing special events. On Saturday there's a Wizard's Workshop that features crafts for young children. *Royal Palm Plaza, Suite 15, 131 Mizner Blvd., Boca Raton, tel. 407/395–8401. Admission: $3.50 adults, $3 senior citizens and children over 3. Open Tues.–Sat. 10–5, Sun. noon–5.*

Gumbo Limbo Nature Center lets children view four 20-foot-diameter saltwater sea tanks, stroll a 1,628-foot boardwalk through a dense tropical forest, and climb a 50-foot tower to overlook the tree canopy. The forest is a coastal hammock, with tropical species growing north of the tropics. One tree species you're sure to see—the gumbo-limbo, with its red peeling bark—is often called "the tourist tree." The center's staff leads guided turtle walks to the beach to see nesting mothers come ashore and lay their eggs. *1801 N. Ocean Blvd., Boca Raton, tel. 407/338–1473. Admission: $3. Open Mon.–Sat. 9–4. Nighttime turtle tour: admission free, though tickets must be obtained in advance; tours late-May–mid-July Mon.–Thurs. 9 PM–midnight.*

Off the Beaten Track

Arthur R. Marshall Loxahatchee National Wildlife Refuge Loxahatchee Refuge is 221 square miles of sawgrass marshes, wet prairies, sloughs, and tree islands. From the visitor center, there are two walking trails—-a boardwalk through a dense cypress swamp and a marsh trail to a 20-foot-high observation tower overlooking a pond—as well as a 5½-mile canoe trail. You can see alligators and birds (including the rare snail kite), fish for bass and panfish, or paddle your own canoe through this watery wilderness. *Headquarters off U.S. 441 between Boynton Blvd. (Rte. 804) and Atlantic Ave. (Rte. 806), west of Boynton Beach; mailing address: Rte. 1, Box 278, Boynton Beach 33437–9741, tel. 407/734–8303. Open 6 AM–sunset. Refuge admission: $3 per car, $1 per pedestrian.*

Lake Okeechobee Fifty miles in from the coast lies 448,000-acre Lake Okeechobee, the fourth-largest natural lake in the United States. The lake's bass and perch attract fisherfolk; catfish devotees prize the hearty flavor of succulent Okeechobee "sharpies." Drive on U.S. 98/441 west from West Palm Beach; when the two roads split, stay on Route 441 to reach the marina at **Belle Glade,** or stay on U.S. 98 and then follow the lake shore 2 miles south to reach the marina at **Pahokee.**

Shopping

Boca Raton **Mizner Park** (Federal Hwy. between Palmetto Park Rd. and Glades Rd., tel. 407/362-0606), a 30-acre shopping village within the city of Boca Raton, debuted in 1991, and its gardenlike spaces make for distinctive shopping. Visitors have some three dozen retail stores to choose among, including the excellent Liberties Fine Books & Music, a new Jacobson's specialty department store, six restaurants with sidewalk cafés, and eight movie screens.

Gallery Center is a hub of eight art galleries (608 Banyan Trail, Boca Raton, open Nov.–Mar., Mon.–Sat. 10:30–5; Apr.–Oct., Tues.–Sat. 11–5) specializing in modern, contemporary, and Latin American art.

Delray Beach Unlike many cities along this resort coast, Delray Beach has a thriving old-fashioned downtown with hundreds of shops and restaurants, centered on a mile of east–west Atlantic Avenue, which ends at the oceanfront. Stores worth visiting include **Sundy House Antiques** (108 S. Swinton Ave., tel. 407/278–2163), a Queen Anne original dating from 1902 where lunch and tea are served daily; and **Cason Cottage** (5 N.E. 1st St., tel. 407/243–0223), a home that dates from about 1915, now the gift shop and offices of the Delray Beach Historical Society.

Fort Pierce One of Florida's best discount malls, the **Manufacturer's Outlet Center** contains 41 stores offering such brand names as American Tourister, Jonathan Logan, Aileen, Polly Flinders, Van Heusen, London Fog, Levi Strauss, and Geoffrey Beene. It's on Route 70, at exit 65 off I–95; stores are open Monday–Saturday 9–8, Sunday 11–5.

Palm Beach One of the world's showcases for quality shopping, **Worth Avenue** runs ¼ mile east–west across Palm Beach, from the beach to Lake Worth. The street has more than 250 shops: The 300 block, with a series of Italianate villas designed by Addison Mizner, retains a quaint charm; the 100 and 200 blocks are more overtly commercial. Most merchants open at 9:30 or 10 AM, and close at 5:30 or 6 PM.

Many "name" stores associated with fine shopping have a presence on Worth Avenue, including Brooks Brothers, Cartier, F.A.O. Schwarz, Gucci, Hermès, Pierre Deux, Saks Fifth Avenue, Tiffany, and Van Cleef & Arpels. These upscale firms tend to send their best merchandise to Worth Avenue to appeal to the discerning tastes of their Palm Beach clientele.

Also appealing to shoppers are the six blocks of **South County Road,** north of Worth Avenue.

West Palm Beach Numerous malls include **The Gardens,** with Bloomingdale's, Burdines, Macy's, Saks Fifth Avenue, and Sears (PGA Blvd. in Palm Beach Gardens, tel. 407/622–2115), and **Palm Beach Mall,** with Burdines, J.C. Penney, Lord & Taylor, and Sears (Palm Beach Lakes Blvd. at I–95, tel. 407/683–9186).

Vero Beach Along Ocean Drive near Beachland Boulevard, a specialty shopping area includes art galleries, antiques shops, and upscale clothing stores.

Beaches

The widest beaches in Palm Beach County are in the Jupiter area, on Singer Island, and in Boca Raton; many of the beaches in Palm Beach County have begun to erode.

Boca Raton Three of the most popular beaches in Boca Raton are **South Beach Park** (400 N. Hwy. A1A), which has no picnic facilities, and **Red Reef Park** (1400 N. Hwy. A1A) and **Spanish River Park** (3001 N. Hwy. A1A), both with picnic tables, barbeque grills, and playgrounds. All are open 8 AM to sunset.

Boynton Beach **Oceanfront Park** (Ocean Ridge at Hwy. A1A) offers a board-walk, concessions, grills, a jogging trail, and playground, but parking is expensive for non-Boynton residents ($10 in winter, $5 for the rest of the year).

Delray Beach **Municipal Beach** (Atlantic Ave. at Hwy. A1A) has a boat ramp and volleyball court, and is open from 8 AM to sunset.

Hutchinson Island **Bathtub Beach** is ideal for children because the waters are shal-low for about 300 feet offshore and usually calm. At low tide bathers can walk to the reef. Facilities include rest rooms and showers.

Jupiter **Carlin Park** (400 Rte. A1A, tel. 407/964–4420), provides beachfront picnic pavilions, hiking trails, a baseball diamond, playground, six tennis courts, and fishing sites. The Park Gal-ley, serving snacks and burgers, is usually open daily 9–5.

Lake Worth **Lake Worth Municipal Beach** has an olympic-size swimming pool (admission: $2 adults, $1 senior citizens and children) with a free fishing pier, picnic areas, shuffleboard, restaurants, and shops on the upland side of the street. Metered parking costs 25¢ an hour.

Palm Beach **Phipps Ocean Park** (Hwy. A1A) offers picnic tables. Meters are 25¢ for 20 minutes.

Vero Beach All through town there are beach-access parks (open daily 7 AM–10 PM, admission free) with boardwalks and steps bridging the foredune. **Humiston Park** has a large children's play area and picnic tables, and is across the street from shops.

Participant Sports

Biking By 1994, bike lanes will be marked by stripes on Palm Beach streets. Two good rides for less experienced cyclists include a 10-mile path bordering **Lake Worth** in Palm Beach, from the Flagler Bridge to the Lake Worth Inlet, and a 5-mile ride along **Flagler Drive** on the Intracoastal Waterway, in West Palm Beach. Both rides are almost completely free of cross streets. For on-the-road rides, group rides, and schedules of longer rides and general cycling savvy, contact the **West Palm Beach Bicycle Club** (Tracy Chambers, Public Affairs Director, tel. 407/659–7644 day, 407/832–9945 evening). Other contacts: **Palm Beach County Bicycle Coordinator** (Wendell Phillips, tel. 407/684–4170); **Juno Beach Bicycle Coordinator** (Susan Guffey, tel. 407/626–1122); **Boca Raton Bicycle Coordinator** (Chad Danos, tel. 407/393–7700). Rentals, including mopeds and rollerblades, are available at **Palm Beach Bicycle Trail Shop** (223 Sunrise Ave., Palm Beach, tel. 407/659–4583).

Canoeing **Bill Rogers Outdoor Adventures** (408 Ponoka St., Sebastian, tel. 407/388–2331) outfits canoe trips down the Sebastian River, along Indian River Lagoon, through Pelican Island Wildlife Refuge, and more distant locations.

Canoe Outfitters of Florida (4100 W. Indiantown Rd., Stuart, tel. 407/746–7053) outfits canoe trips along the Loxahatchee River, Florida's only designated wild and scenic river.

Jonathan Dickinson State Park (tel. 407/546–2771) and **Arthur G. Marshall Loxahatchee National Wildlife Refuge** (tel. 407/734–8303) are good spots for canoeing, call the parks for up-dates.

Diving   You can drift dive or anchor dive along Palm Beach County's 47-mile Atlantic Coast. Drift divers take advantage of the Gulf Stream's strong currents and proximity to shore—sometimes less than a mile. A group of divers joined by nylon line may drift across coral reefs with the current; one member of the group carries a large, orange float that the charter-boat captain can follow. Drift diving works best from Boynton Beach north. South of Boynton Beach, where the Gulf Stream is farther from shore, diving from an anchored boat is more popular. Among the more intriguing artificial reefs in the area is a 1967 Rolls-Royce Silver Shadow in 80 feet of water off Palm Beach.

Ocean Reef Park (3860 N. Ocean Dr., Riviera Beach, tel. 407/966–6655) is attractive for snorkeling because the reefs are close to shore in shallow water. You may see angelfish, sergeant majors, rays, robin fish, and occasionally a Florida lobster (actually a species of saltwater crayfish). Wear canvas sneakers and cloth gloves.

In **Vero Beach,** snorkelers and divers can swim out to explore reefs 100–300 feet off the beach. Summer offers the best diving conditions. At low tide you can see the boiler and other remains of an iron-screw steamer, *Breconshire*, which foundered in 1894 on a reef just south of Beachland Boulevard.

Dive Boats and   The following **Force E** stores rent scuba and snorkeling equip-
Instruction   ment: **West Palm Beach,** 1399 N. Military Trail, tel. 407/471–2676; **Riviera Beach,** 155 E. Blue Heron Blvd., tel. 407/845–2333; **North Palm Beach,** 11911 U.S. 1, Suite 101–G, tel. 407/624–7136; **Boca Raton,** 877 E. Palmetto Park Rd., tel. 407/368–0555 or 7166 Beracasa Way, tel. 407/395–4407. All stores have PADI affiliation and instruction available at all skill levels; dive-boat charters are also available.

Fishing   Palm Beach County and the Treasure Coast are fisherfolks' heaven, from deep-sea strikes of fighting sailfish and wahoo to the bass, speckled perch, and bluegill of Lake Okeechobee. In between there are numerous fishing piers, bridges, and waterways where pompano, sheepshead, snapper, and grouper are likely catches. The best inlet fishing is at **Sebastian Inlet State Recreation Area,** where the catch includes bluefish, flounder, jack, redfish, sea trout, snapper, snook, or Spanish mackerel. Representative of the fleets and marinas are:

Deep-Sea Fishing   **B-Love Fleet** (314 E. Ocean Ave., Lantana, tel. 407/588–7612). $19 per person includes rod, reel, and bait.

Lake Fishing   **Slim's Fish Camp** (Drawer 250, Belle Glade 33430, tel. 407/996–3844). Guided tour for one or two people costs $185 per day, boat rental $35 per day.

J-Mark Fish Camp (Box 2225, Belle Glade 33430, tel. 407/996–5357). Guided tour for one or two people costs $200 per day, boat rental $50 per day.

Golf   There are 145 public, private, and semiprivate golf courses in the Palm Beach County area. A **Golf-A-Round** program lets guests at any of 92 hotels play at one of 10 courses each day, without greens fees, between April and December. For details, contact the Palm Beach County Convention & Visitors Bureau (*see* Important Addresses and Numbers, *above*).

Top-flight courses that you can arrange to play on include:

Boca Raton **Boca Raton Resort & Club** (501 E. Camino Real, Boca Raton 33432, tel. 407/395–3000 or 800/327–0101; 36 holes).

Boynton Beach **Boynton Beach Municipal Golf Course** (8020 Jog Rd., Boynton Beach 33437, tel. 407/969–2200; 27 holes).

Hutchinson Island **Indian River Plantation** (555 N.E. Plantation Rd., Hutchinson Island 33494, tel. 407/225–3700 or 800/444–1432; 18 holes).

Palm Beach Area **Breakers Hotel Golf Club** (1 S. County Rd., Palm Beach 33480, tel. 407/655–6611 or 800/833–3141; 36 holes); **Emerald Dunes Golf Club** (2100 Emerald Dunes Dr., West Palm Beach 33411, tel. 407/684–4653; 18 holes); **Palm Beach Polo & Country Club** (13198 Forest Hill Blvd., West Palm Beach 33414, tel. 407/798–7000 or 800/327–4204; 45 holes); **PGA National Golf Club** (1000 Ave. of Champions, Palm Beach Gardens 33418, tel. 407/627–1800; 90 holes); **Royal Palm Beach Country Club** (900 Royal Palm Beach Blvd., Royal Palm Beach 33411, tel. 407/798–6430; 18 holes).

Spas **Hippocrates Health Institute** was founded in Boston in 1963 by Ann Wigmore and moved to its present 10-acre site in 1987. Guests receive complete examinations by traditional and alternative health-care professionals. Personalized programs include juice fasts and the eating of raw foods. *1443 Palmdale Ct., West Palm Beach 33411, tel. 407/471–8876.*

The Spa at PGA National Resort, in a 17,800-square-foot building styled after a Mediterranean fishing village, has six outdoor therapy pools, men's and women's Jacuzzis and saunas, and 22 rooms for private treatments, including Swedish and shiatsu massage, hydrotherapy, and mud treatments. A 26,000-square-foot Health & Racquet Center offers five racquetball courts, complete Nautilus center, aerobics and dance studios, men's and women's locker rooms, and a fitness-oriented Health Bar. *400 Ave. of the Champions, Palm Beach Gardens 33418–3698, tel. 407/627–2000 or 800/633–9150.*

Spectator Sports

The *Palm Beach Post's* weekly "TGIF" section on Friday carries information on sports activities. For tickets to Sporting events call **Ticketmaster** (tel. 407/839–3900).

Auto Racing Drag racing, stock-car racing, and other two-axle racing takes place mid-January–November at the **Moroso Motorsports Park** (17047 Beeline Hwy., Palm Beach Gardens; for information write to Box 31907, Palm Beach Gardens 33420; tel. 407/622–1400).

Baseball The **Atlanta Braves** and the **Montreal Expos** both conduct spring training in West Palm Beach's Municipal Stadium, which is also home to the **Palm Beach Expos,** a Class-A team in the Florida State League. *1610 Palm Beach Lakes Blvd., Box 3087, West Palm Beach 33402, tel. 407/683–6012. Expos tickets: Box 3566, West Palm Beach 33402, tel. 407/689–9121. Braves tickets: Box 2619, West Palm Beach 33402, tel. 407/683–6100.*

The **Los Angeles Dodgers** train each March in the 6,500-seat Holman Stadium at Dodgertown (4101 26th St., Vero Beach; for information write to Box 2887, Vero Beach 32961; tel. 407/569–4900).

The **New York Mets** hold spring training in the 7,300-seat St. Lucie County Sport Complex (525 N.W. Peacock Blvd., Port St. Lucie 34986, tel. 407/871–2115), home stadium for the Florida League's **St. Lucie Mets.** Take Exit 63C off I–95 and follow St. Lucie West Boulevard east to Peacock Boulevard.

Equestrian Sports and Polo Palm Beach County and the Treasure Coast are home to four major polo organizations. Although only the affluent can support a four-member polo team, you don't have to be rich to watch—admission is free for some games and priced reasonably for others.

Polo teams play under a handicap system in which the U.S. Polo Association ranks each player's skills; a team's total handicap reflects its members' individual handicaps. The best players have a 10-goal handicap. The average polo game lasts about 90 minutes. Each game consists of six periods or chukkers of 7½ minutes each.

Gulf Stream Polo Club, the oldest club in Palm Beach, began in the 1920s and plays medium-goal polo (for teams with handicaps of 8–16 goals). It has six polo fields. *4550 Polo Rd., Lake Worth 33467, tel. 407/965–2057. Season runs Dec.–Apr., games Fri. 3 PM and Sun. 1 PM. Admission free.*

Palm Beach Polo and Country Club, founded in 1979, is the site each spring of the $100,000 World Cup competition. *13420 South Shore Blvd., West Palm Beach, 33414, tel. 407/793–1440. General admission $6, reserved $10, lower level $14, upper level $17. Games Sun. 3 PM Dec.–Apr.*

Royal Palm Polo, founded in 1959 by Oklahoma oilman John T. Oxley, has seven polo fields with two stadia. The complex is home to the $100,000 International Gold Cup Tournament. *6300 Old Clint Moore Rd., Boca Raton 33496, tel. 407/994–1876. General admission $6, box seats $15, $3 children and students. Games at 1 and 3 PM Jan.–Apr.; at 5 PM June–Oct.*

Windsor opened in February 1989 with a special charity game in which England's Prince Charles played. Charity events here benefit the international Friends of Conservation, of which Prince Charles is a patron. *3125 Windsor Blvd., Vero Beach 32963, tel. 407/388–5050 or 800/233–POLO. Season runs mid-Jan.–early Apr.*

Greyhound Racing **Palm Beach Kennel Club** opened in 1932 and has 3,000 seats. Call for schedule. *1111 N. Congress Ave., Palm Beach 33409, tel. 407/683–2222. Admission: 50¢ general admission, $2 dining rooms, matinees free; free parking. Races Wed., Thurs., Sat. 12:30 and 7:30; Tues. and Fri. 7:30; Sun. 1.*

Jai Alai **Fort Pierce Jai Alai** is a source for jai alai action. *1750 Kings Hwy., Ft. Pierce, off Okeechobee Rd., tel. 800/JAI–ALAI or 407/464–7500. Admission: $1. Gates open 6:30 PM. Open winter only, inquire for dates.*

Palm Beach Jai Alai is the site of two world records: for the largest payoff ever, $988,325, and for the fastest ball ever thrown, 188 mph. *1415 45th St., West Palm Beach, ¼ mi east of I–95 off exit 54, tel. 407/844–2444. Admission: 50¢–$3.50, senior citizens free Wed., Fri., Sat. matinees. Women admitted free Tues. night. Game time is 7 PM. Schedule changes seasonally.*

Dining and Lodging

Dining   The wealth and sophistication of Palm Beach County's seasonal residents ensures a good supply of top-end restaurants here; quick, casual, cheap restaurants are a bit harder to find. Along the Treasure Coast, restaurants woo business with dollar-saving early-bird menus. Unless otherwise noted, restaurants serve lunch and dinner.

Highly recommended restaurants are indicated by a star ★.

Category	Cost*
Very Expensive	over $50
Expensive	$35–$50
Moderate	$20–$35
Inexpensive	under $20

per person, excluding drinks, service, and 6% sales tax

Lodging   Palm Beach County deserves its nickname "the Gold Coast"— hotel prices hover at the high end of the scale, and it's tough to find a bargain. Delray Beach and Lake Worth are two communities where accommodations are a bit more affordable. One way to save money is to visit the area off-season, when rates may be significantly lower. The following price categories are based on peak-season rates.

If you plan to stay overnight along the Treasure Coast, reservations are a must. There's less to choose from because tourism came later to the Treasure Coast than to the Gold Coast, but prices are generally lower. Even beachfront lodgings can be affordable.

Highly recommended lodgings are indicated by a star ★.

Category	Cost*
Very Expensive	over $150
Expensive	$90–$150
Moderate	$60–$90
Inexpensive	under $60

All prices are for a standard double room, excluding 6% state sales tax and nominal tourist tax.

Boca Raton
Dining

Gazebo Cafe. The locals who patronize this popular restaurant know where it is, even though there is no sign and it's difficult to find: Look for the Barnett Bank Pantry Pride Plaza, a block north of Spanish River Boulevard. Once you find the place, await your table in the open kitchen where chef Paul Sellas (co-owner with his mother Kathleen) and his staff perform a gastronomic ballet. The high noise level of the main dining room has been reduced with an acoustical ceiling but you may still be happier in the smaller back dining room. Specialties include lump crabmeat with an excellent glaze of Mornay sauce on a marinated artichoke bottom; spinach salad with heart of palm, egg white, bacon, croutons, mushrooms, fruit garnish, and a dressing of olive oil and Dijon mustard; Paul Sellas's "classic" bouillabaisse with Maine lobster, shrimp, scallops, clams, and mussels topped with julienne vegetables in a robust broth flavored with garlic, saffron, and tomatoes; and raspberries with a Grand Marnier-Sabayon sauce. *4199 N. Federal Hwy., Boca Raton, tel. 407/395–6033. Reservations advised. Jacket preferred. AE, D, DC, MC, V. Closed Sun. mid-May–Dec. Expensive.*

★ **La Vieille Maison.** This elegant French restaurant occupies a two-story dwelling that dates from the 1920s (hence the name, meaning "old house"). The structure, believed to be an Addison Mizner creation, has been renovated repeatedly, but still retains details which typify the architect's style. Closets and cubbyholes have been transformed into intimate private dining rooms. You may order from a fixed-price or an à la carte menu throughout the year; in summer, a separate fixed-price menu available Sunday through Thursday offers a sampling of the other two at a more modest price. Specialties include *pompano aux pecans* (pompano fillets sautéed in butter strewn with pecans under a creamy chardonnay sauce) and *le saumon fumé aux endives* (smoked salmon, onions, and Belgian endive with light vinaigrette). Dessert specialties include *crêpe soufflé au citron* and a chocolate tart. *770 E. Palmetto Park Rd., tel. 407/391–6701 in Boca Raton, 407/737–5677 in Delray Beach and Palm Beach. Reservations suggested. Jacket preferred. AE, D, DC, MC, V. Expensive.*

Tom's Place. "This place is a blessing from God," says the sign over the fireplace, to which, when you're finally in and seated (this place draws long lines) you'll add, "Amen!" That's in between mouthfuls of Tom Wright's soul food—sauce-slathered ribs, pork chop sandwiches, chicken cooked in a peppery mustard sauce over hickory and oak, sweet potato pie. You'll want to leave with a bottle or two of Tom's BBQ sauce: $2.25/pint. You'll return, though, just as Mr. T, Sugar Ray Leonard, Joe Frazier, and a rush of NFL pro players do. You can bet the place is family run. *7251 N. Federal Hwy., tel. 407/997–0920. No reservations. Dress: casual but neat. No lunch Mon. Closed Sun., holidays, and for a month around Sept. MC, V. Inexpensive.*

Lodging **Boca Raton Resort & Club.** Architect and socialite Addison
★ Mizner designed and built the original Cloister Inn in 1926; the 27-story tower was added in 1961 and the ultramodern Boca Beach Club in 1981. In 1991 an eight-year, $55 million renovation was completed, upgrading the tower accommodations, adding a new fitness center, redesigning the Cloister lobby and adjacent golf course, and creating a new restaurant, Nick's Fishmarket, at the Beach Club. In 1992 the 27-story-high Top of the Tower Italian Restaurant opened. Room rates during the winter season are European Plan (no meals included). The rooms in the older buildings tend to be smaller and cozily traditional; those in the newer buildings are light, airy, and contemporary in color schemes and furnishings. An international concierge staff speaks at least 12 languages. *501 E. Camino Real, 33431–0825, tel. 407/395–3000 or 800/327–0101. 963 rooms: 100 in Cloister Inn, 333 in the 1931 addition, 242 in Tower Building, 214 in Boca Beach Club, plus Golf Villas. Facilities: 1½ mi of beach, 5 outdoor pools, two 18-hole golf courses, 37 tennis courts (9 lighted), 3 fitness centers, 23-slip marina, fishing and sailing charters, 7 restaurants, 3 lounges,*

in-room safes. *AE, DC, MC, V. Daily MAP supplement (breakfast and dinner) $50 per person. Very Expensive.*

Delray Beach
Lodging

The Seagate Hotel & Beach Club. The best garden hotel in Palm Beach County: it offers value, comfort, style, and personal attention. You can dress up and dine in a smart little mahogany-and-lattice-trimmed beachfront salon or have the same Continental fare in casual attire in the equally stylish bar. Lodgings are on the west side of the two-lane road, and it still feels like the country here. The deluxe one-bedroom suite looks sharp in chintz and rattan, with plenty of upholstered pieces. Kitchens in the least expensive studio suites are compact but complete behind foldaway doors. The standard one-bedroom suite has its own touches: make-up lights, double doors between bedroom and living room, and access to the bathroom from both. The beachfront facility is actually a private club to which overnight guests can gain membership. Winter rates are high, but after May 1st until mid-November they drop substantially. *400 S. Ocean Blvd., 33483, tel. 407/276-2421 or 800/233-3581 (U.S. and Canada). 70 1- and 2-bedroom suites, including 2 penthouses. Facilities: beach, pool, heated saltwater pool, Jacuzzi, beach cabanas ($10/day), restaurant, lounge. AE, DC, MC, V. Very Expensive.*

The Blue Surf. Considering its top location—across the street from the Gulf Stream Bath & Tennis Club, across from the beach, in very resorty but quiet Delray—the Blue Surf is an exceptional buy. The look is garden-apartment white with aqua trim; the one- and two-story buildings are set around beautiful lawns. Each of the 23 studios and one- or two-bedroom apartments has a full kitchen. Furnishings include lots of floral prints, brocaded pieces, and French provincial reproductions, which create a beachy yet homey look. Though dating from the 1950s, it's beautifully maintained and super clean. *820 N. Ocean Blvd., 33483, tel. 407/276-7496. 23 studios, 1-, and 2-bedroom apartments with bath. Facilities: full kitchen, heated pool, shuffleboard, gas barbecue, coin laundry. MC, V. Moderate–Expensive.*

Riviera Palms Motel. This small 1950s-era motel has two chief virtues: it's clean and it's well located, across Highway A1A from mid-rise apartment houses on the water, with beach access between them. Hans and Herter Grannemann have owned this two-story property, three wings surrounding a grassy front yard and heated pool, since 1978, and they have lots of repeat guests—you'll have to book early in winter. The decor uses Danish modern furniture and colors of blue, brown, and tan. Rooms have at least a fridge but no phone. *3960 N. Ocean Blvd., 33483, tel. 407/276-3032. 17 rooms, efficiencies, and suites with bath. Facilities: heated pool. No credit cards. Inexpensive–Moderate.*

Fort Pierce
Dining

Mangrove Mattie's. Since its opening six years ago, this upscale rustic spot on Fort Pierce Inlet has provided dazzling views and imaginative decor with seafood to match. Try the coconut fried shrimp or the chicken and scampi; on Thursday evenings, build your own roast beef sandwich for $1; and Friday evenings you can get ¼-pound shrimp for $1, and 25¢ oysters and clams. The dinner-at-dusk early bird specials offer a half dozen entrées under $10 with a glass of wine (5 to 6:30 seven days a week). *1640 Seaway Dr., tel. 407/466-1044. Reservations advised. Dress: casual but neat. AE, MC, V. Closed Christmas. Moderate.*

Theo Thudpucker's Raw Bar. Businesspeople dressed for work mingle here with people who come in off the beach wearing shorts. On squally days everyone piles in off the jetty. Specialties include oyster stew, smoked fish spread, conch salad and fritters, fresh catfish, and alligator tail. *2025 Seaway Dr. (South Jetty), tel. 407/465–1078. No reservations. Dress: casual. No credit cards. Closed Christmas, Thanksgiving. Inexpensive.*

Jensen Beach **Conchy Joe's.** This classic Florida stilt-house full of antique fish
Dining mounts, gator hides, and snakeskins dates from the late 1920s, though Conchy Joe's, like a hermit crab sidling into a new shell, only sidled up in '83 from West Palm Beach for the relaxed atmosphere of Jensen Beach. Under a huge Seminole-built *chickee* with a palm through the roof, you get the freshest Florida seafoods from a menu that changes daily—though some things never change: grouper marsala, the house specialty; broiled sea scallops; fried cracked conch. Try the rum drinks with names like Goombay Smash, Bahama Mama, and Jamaica Wind, while you listen to steel band calypsos Thursday through Sunday nights. Happy Hour 3–6 daily. *3945 N. Indian River Dr., tel. 407/334–1131. No reservations. Dress: casual. AE, D, MC, V. Closed Thanksgiving, Christmas, Superbowl Sunday; Christmas Eve lunch only. Moderate.*

★ **11 Maple Street.** This 16-table cracker-quaint restaurant run by Margee and Mike Perrin offers Continental gourmet specialties on a nightly changing menu. Appetizers might include walnut bread with melted fontina cheese; pan-fried conch with balsamic vinegar; or pear, gorgonzola, and pine nut salad with balsamic vinegar and grilled polenta. Among the entrées might be rosemary spiced salmon with leeks; lobster and blue crab cake; or dried porcini mushroom risotto. Desserts might include a cherry *clafouti* (like a bread pudding), a white chocolate custard with blackberry sauce, or an old-fashioned chocolate cream pie with poached pear. *3224 Maple Ave., tel. 407/334–7714. Reservations required. Dress: casual but neat. MC, V. Closed Mon. and Tues. No lunch. Moderate.*

Lodging **Hutchinson Inn.** Sandwiched among the high rises, this modest and affordable two-story motel from the mid-1970s has the feel of a bed-and-breakfast, thanks to its pretty canopies, bracketing, and the fresh produce stand across the street. You do in fact get an expanded Continental breakfast in the well detailed, homey lobby—where you can also borrow a book or a stack of magazines to take to your room, where milk and cookies are served in the evenings. Rooms range from small but comfy, with chintz bedcovers, wicker chair, and contract dresser, to fully equipped efficiencies and seafront suites with private balconies. *9750 S. Ocean Dr., 34957, tel. 407/229–2000. 21 units. Facilities: tennis court, heated pool, beach, complimentary Continental breakfast and Sat. noon barbeque. AE, MC, V. Moderate–Expensive.*

Jupiter **Log Cabin Restaurant.** "Too much!" exclaim first-timers, re-
Dining sponding to the decor and whopping portions of American food. Everybody takes home a doggie bag, unless you've ordered the nightly all-you-can-eat special, for which the policy is suspended. This rustic roadhouse (very easy to miss driving past) has old bikes, sleds, clocks, and quilts hanging from the rafters. Dine indoors or on the porch. The big early bird breakfast (7–8:30) is $1.95. *631 N. Hwy. A1A, tel. 407/746–6877. No res-*

ervations. Dress: casual. AE, D, DC, MC, V. Closed Christmas. Inexpensive–Moderate.

Charlie's Crab (*see* Palm Beach, *below*).

Lighthouse Restaurant. Dutch brothers John and Bill Verehoeven bought this long-established place late in 1991, but they've left intact the people-pleasing formula of more than 60 years: low prices, 'round-the-clock service (except for 10 PM Sunday–6 AM Monday), and daily menu changes that take advantage of the best market buys. Typical daily specials include veal parmigiana with spaghetti, hearty beef stew, or grilled center cut pork chops with apple sauce. Also served nightly are affordable "lite dinners." You can get breakfast 24 hours a day, and Sunday dinner at noon. *1510 U.S. 1, tel. 407/746–4811. No reservations. Dress: casual. D, MC, V. Closed Christmas Eve. Inexpensive.*

Lake Worth
Lodging

Gulfstream Hotel. The Gulfstream reopened in 1990, after an edgy three-year hiatus, and the new owners have tapped into Lake Worth's Finnish heritage with attentive, unfussy hospitality. Built in 1925, this arcaded, six-story, pink stucco landmark sits across the street from Bryant Park and the Intracoastal Waterway. Restored and repainted, it's perfect for guests who are undemanding about luxury—it offers all the basics and none of the extra pricing. Would you believe $100 suites in winter? Public rooms include a two-story-high old-fashioned lobby and dining room and a mood-right chandeliered lounge. Granted, much of the room furniture is metallic, but the colors are warm mauves and aquas. Most bathrooms have tub-showers. *1 Lake Ave., 33460, tel. 407/586–9250, fax 407/586–9256. 121 rooms, 2 suites, 13 apartments, all with bath. Facilities: heated pool, restaurant, lounge. AE, MC, V. Moderate–Expensive.*

Sea Wulf Inn. Ah, Lake Worth—the budget traveler's destination. This 13-unit, one-story motel that dates from the 1950s comes up against busy (though not noisy) two-lane Federal Highway south of downtown. With the air conditioning on, and especially in rooms at the rear, sleep will not be disturbed. Heinz Wulf, who has run the motel since 1975, keeps the place looking country comfy. The three wings surround a big yard full of fruit-bearing trees and nautical bric-a-brac, with chaises for sunning, and old-fashioned mosaic tile-top stone tables. Rooms are clean, the look wood-panel cozy; browns and tans dominate. The furniture is mixed contemporary, but nothing crummy. Rooms range in size from efficiencies to two-bedroom apartments. All baths have tub showers; there are no in-room phones. *1016 S. Federal Hwy., 33460, tel. 407/586–5550. 13 units. Facilities: shuffleboard, morning coffee in season. Inexpensive.*

Lantana
Dining

Old House. Partners Wayne Cordero and Captain Bob Hoddinott have turned the old Lyman House, dating from 1889, into an informal, old-Florida seafood house. Located on the water, the house has been expanded many times into a patchwork of shed-like spaces. Baltimore steamed crab is a specialty, though most of the seafood's from Florida. All dinners come with unlimited salad, fresh baked bread, fries, and parsley potatoes or rice. *300 E. Ocean Ave., tel. 407/533–5220. No reservations. Dress: casual. AE, MC, V. Moderate.*

Palm Beach
Dining
★

Cafe L'Europe. Sumptuous oak paneling, shirred curtains over fanlight windows, extravagant dried-flower bouquets, and vintage Sinatra in the background set the mood here. Even the barflys are elegantly coiffed, surrounded by details of brass, etched and leaded glass, and tapestry fabrics. Choose from spa cuisine (grilled loin of swordfish with black bean ragout and balsamic beurre blanc); Mandarin way cuisine (minced squab with Virginia ham, mushrooms and water chestnuts in a lettuce cup); or the café cuisine (rack of lamb ratatouille with fine herb sauce and minted couscous). Desserts include numerous fruit tarts and chocolate cakes prepared daily in the café bakery. *150 Worth Ave. in the Esplanade, tel. 407/655–4020. Reservations required in winter. Jacket and tie required in main dining room. AE, DC, MC, V. No lunch Sun. Expensive–Very Expensive.*

Bice Ristorante. "Bice" is short for Beatrice, mother of Roberto Ruggeri, who founded the Milanese original in 1926. Branches are in Palm Beach and other smart places—Paris, New York, Chicago, Washington, Atlanta, Dallas, Beverly Hills. Brilliant flower arrangements and Italian stylings—brass, greens, and a dark beige-and-yellow color scheme—are matched by exquisite aromas of *antipasti* and *piatti del giorno* laced with basil, chive, and oregano. Divine home-baked *focaccia*—a Tuscan-style bread—accompanies such house favorites as *robespierre alla moda della bice* (sliced steak topped with arugula salad); *costoletta di vitello impanata alla milanese* (breaded veal cutlet with a tomato salad); and *trancio di spada alla mediterranea* (grilled swordfish with black olives, capers, and plum tomatoes). Leave room for the *gelati* and other desserts. *313½ Worth Ave., tel. 407/835–1600. Reservations advised. Jackets preferred. AE, DC, MC, V. Closed Christmas, New Year's Day. Expensive.*

The Breakers. The main hotel dining area at The Breakers consists of the elegant Florentine Dining Room, decorated with fine 15th-century Flemish tapestries; the adjoining Celebrity Aisle where the maître d' seats his most honored guests; and the Circle Dining Room, with a huge circular skylight framing a bronze-and-crystal Venetian chandelier. Continental specialties include rack of lamb Dijonnaise; salmon *en croûte* with spinach, herbs, and sauce Véronique (a grape sauce); *vacherin glacé* (praline-flavored ice cream encased in fresh whipped cream and frozen in a baked meringue base); and Key lime pie. *1 S. County Rd., tel. 407/655–6611 or 800/833–3141. Reservations required. Jacket and tie requested in winter. AE, DC, MC, V. Expensive.*

★ **Jo's.** This is an intimate, candlelit bistro with flowers on pink cloths, greenery against lattice backdrops, and, after nine years, a well-rehearsed French menu. The three-soup sampler is tried and true: buttery lobster bisque, potage St. Germain (green pea soup), and beef consommé. Osso buco, always on the chalkboard, is served with rice and vegetables. Chef Richard Kline, Jo's son, faithfully prepares a moist (but never rare) half roast duckling (boned) with orange demiglaze. For dessert try the fresh apple *tarte tatin* or fresh raspberries Josephine. Jo's is tucked off County Road behind the Church Mouse Thrift Shop. *200 Chilian Ave., tel. 407/659–6776. Reservations advised. Jacket preferred. Dinner only. MC, V. Closed Aug. and Christmas. Expensive.*

Charley's Crab. Audubon bird prints, fresh flowers, and French posters accent the walls of this Palm Beach seafood favorite perched across the street from the beach. During the season, the dinner line forms early. A wine and cheese bar has lately replaced the raw bar. Dressier than most seafood houses, Charley's offers its fanciest dining rooms toward the back. Menus change daily. Specialties include 8–10 daily fresh fish specials. *456 S. Ocean Blvd., tel. 407/659–1500; also at 1000 N. U.S. 1, Jupiter, tel. 407/744–4710. Reservations advised. Dress: casual. AE, D, DC, MC, V. Moderate–Expensive.*

Chuck & Harold's. Boxer Larry Holmes and thespians Brooke Shields and Burt Reynolds are among the celebrities who frequent this combination power-lunch bar, celebrity sidewalk café, and nocturnal big band/jazz garden restaurant. Locals who want to be part of the scenery frequent the front-porch area, next to pots of red and white begonias mounted along the sidewalk rail. Specialties include a mildly spiced conch chowder with a rich flavor and a liberal supply of conch; an onion-crunchy gazpacho with croutons, a cucumber spear, and a dollop of sour cream; a *frittata* (an omelet of bacon, spinach, pepperoncini, potatoes, smoked mozzarella, and fresh tomato salsa); and a tangy Key lime pie with a graham cracker crust and a squeezeable lime slice for even more tartness. A big blackboard lists daily specials and celebrity birthdays. *207 Royal Poinciana Way, tel. 407/659–1440. Reservations advised. Dress: casual but neat. AE, DC, MC, V. Moderate.*

Dempsey's. A New York–style Irish pub under the palms: green baize, plaid café curtains, brass rods, burgundy banquettes, paddlefans, horse prints, and antique coach lanterns. George Dempsey was a Florida horse rancher until he entered the restaurant business 16 years ago. This place is packed, noisy, and as electric as Black Friday at the stock exchange when major sports events are on the big TV. Along with much socializing, people put away fresh Maine lobster, fresh Florida seafood, plates of chicken hash Dempsey (with a dash of Scotch), shad roe, prime rib, and hot apple pie. *50 Cocoanut Row, tel. 407/835–0400. Reservations advised for 6 or more. Dress: casual but neat. AE, MC, V. Closed Thanksgiving, Christmas. Moderate.*

Ta-boo. Real estate investor Franklyn P. deMarco, Jr. has teamed up with Maryland restaurateur Nancy Sharigan to successfully re-create the legendary Worth Avenue bistro that debuted in 1941. Decorated in gorgeous pinks, greens, and florals, the space is divided into discrete salons: one resembles a courtyard; another, an elegant living room with a fireplace; a third, a gazebo under a skylight. The Tiki Tiki bar is frequented by regulars. The round-the-clock menu includes chicken and arugula from the grill, prime ribs and steaks, gourmet pizzas, and main course salads (a tangy warm steak salad, for instance, comes with grilled strips of marinated filet mignon tossed with greens, mushrooms, tomato, and red onion). *221 Worth Ave., tel. 407/835–3500. Reservations advised. Jacket preferred. AE, MC, V. Closed Christmas. Moderate.*

TooJay's. New York deli food served in a California-style setting—what could be more Florida? Menu includes matzoh ball soup, corned beef on homemade rye, killer cake with five chocolates, and homemade whipped cream. A sandwich of Hebrew National kosher salami layered with onions, muenster cheese, cole slaw, and Russian dressing on rye is a house favorite. There's also dill chicken; seafood with crabmeat, shrimp, and sour cream; and for the vegetarians, hummus, tabouleh, and a wheatberry salad. On the High Holidays look for carrot *tzimmes* (a sweet compote), beef brisket with gravy, potato pancakes, and roast chicken. Wise-cracking waitresses set the fast pace of this bright restaurant with a high, open packing-crate board ceiling, and windows overlooking the gardens. In addition to this location, Palm Beach County has seven other TooJay's restaurants. *313 Royal Poinciana Plaza, tel. 407/659–7232. No reservations. Dress: casual. AE, D, DC, MC, V. Beer and wine only. Closed Thanksgiving, Christmas. Inexpensive.*

Lodging

★ **Brazilian Court.** The color palette at the Brazilian Court captures the magic of the bright Florida sun indoors and out. With its 134 courtyard rooms and suites, the BC remains the pick of Palm Beach without snoot. Spread out over half a block, the yellow-stucco facade with gardens and a red tile roof helps you imagine what the place must have been like 68 years ago, at its birth. Rooms are brilliantly floral—yellows, blues, greens—with theatrical bed canopies, big white-lattice patterns on carpets, and sunshiny pane windows. Shelf space is small in the bathrooms, but closets will remind you that people once came with trunks enough for the entire season. French doors, bay windows, rattan loggias, cherub fountains, chintz garden umbrellas beneath royal palms are just some of the elements that compose the lyrical style. *301 Australian Ave., 33480, tel. 407/655–7740 or 800/552–0335, 800/228–6852 in Canada. 128 guest rooms and 6 suites. Facilities: pool, 2 restaurants, bar. AE, D, DC, MC, V. Very Expensive.*

★ **The Breakers.** Only The Breakers can complete a five-year, $50 million renovation of guest rooms, public spaces, and back-of-the-house, and immediately follow it up with a $40-million-dollar commitment to do more. This palatial seven-story ocean-front resort hotel, built in Italian Renaissance style in 1926 and enlarged in 1969, sprawls over 140 acres of splendor in the heart of some of the most expensive real estate in the world. Cupids wrestle alligators in the Florentine fountain in front of the main entrance. Inside the lofty lobby, your eyes lift to majestic ceiling vaults and frescoes. The hotel still blends formality with tropical resort ambiance, even if, conceding to the times, men and boys are no longer *required* (only requested) to wear jackets and ties after 7 PM. Room decor follows two color schemes: cool greens and soft pinks in an orchid-pattern English cotton chintz fabric; and shades of blue, with a floral and ribbon chintz. Both designs include white plantation shutters and wall coverings, Chinese porcelain table lamps, and original 1920s furniture restored to its period appearance. The original building has 15 different room sizes and shapes. If you prefer more space, ask to be placed in the newer addition. *1 S. County Rd., 33480, tel. 407/655–6611 or 800/833–3141. 528 rooms with bath, including 40 suites. Facilities: ½ mi of beachfront, heated pool, 20 tennis courts, 2 golf courses, health club, saunas, lawn bowling, croquet, shuffleboard, shopping arcade, 4 restaurants, lounge. AE, DC, MC, V. Very Expensive.*

★ **The Chesterfield Hotel Deluxe.** You'll be met at the airport in the house limousine, whereupon you'll be conveyed to the finest European hotel in Florida. A little pretense, a lot of style, and a superabundance of service marks this 57-room property located a block from Worth Avenue. The Chesterfield may be a Mizner copy, but its luxury aura is all its own. Dating from 1926 when it opened as the Royal Palm, it's currently decorated with rich chintz, mahogany, leather, and brass. The lobby boasts chintz and plaid with flowered dust ruffles and frou-frou drapes; the Game Room has baize tables so red they could only be a dare; the Library has an aura of brandy in the air after the hunt, with the important newspapers racked and waiting;

the Key West–style pool patio has pink keystone. The dining room is luxuriously adorned in pink and green. No two of the English-country-style bedrooms are alike, but expect lots of wood and brass, with beds recessed into stagey nooks. Details on the upholstery, quilts, ruffles, and drapes keep rooms unique. Baths are travertine with full amenities. *363 Cocoanut Row, 33480, tel. 407/659–5800. 58 rooms and suites with bath. Facilities: heated pool, restaurant, lounge. AE, D, DC, MC, V. Very Expensive.*

★ **The Colony.** The legend remains the legend. This is where the glitterati show after the charity balls, where Roxanne Pulitzer retreated after her infamous seven-week marriage of 1992. Only steps from Worth Avenue, The Colony has been a Palm Beach legend since its completion in 1947. The new director of operations is Frederick Danielski, the hotel's retired former manager, whose World War II espionage inspired the role of Rick played by Humphrey Bogart in *Casablanca*. A 1990 redecoration transformed the lobby into a Park Avenue salon of plush white silks, chandeliers, and a baby grand piano, and outfitted guest rooms in cool neutral colors; in 1992, acceding to guests' preference, the manager reintroduced touches of color. Low-rise maisonettes built in the mid-1950s, and apartments from the 1960s, are across the street, as well as seven neighborhood villas. *155 Hammon Ave., Palm Beach 33480, tel. 407/655–5430, fax 407/832–7318. 106 rooms, including 36 suites and apartments and 7 villas. Facilities: heated pool, restaurant, spa. AE, D, DC, MC, V. Very Expensive.*

★ **The Ocean Grand.** This six-acre property at the south end of Palm Beach is cooly elegant, but warm in detail and generous in amenities. Marble, art, fanlight windows, swagged drapes, chintz, and palms create an ambience of Grecian serenity. In the Restaurant and the Ocean Bistro you'll be serenaded with piano, harp, and guitar music that accompanies the skilled cuisine. In the Living Room cocktails are served daily, and there is jazz on weekend evenings and classical recitals on Sunday afternoon. Although the hotel's name suggests grandeur, it's more like a small jewel, with only four stories and a long beach. All rooms are spacious—equivalent to suites in other hotels. All have private balconies and are furnished in finery typical of Palm Beach. Muted natural tones prevail in guest rooms, with teal, mauve, and salmon accents. Each room has a loveseat, upholstered chairs, desk, TV, armoire, and large closet. A thoughtful touch: all lamps have three-way bulbs. *2800 S. Ocean Blvd., 33480, tel. 407/582–2800, fax 407/547–1557. 210 rooms, including suites. Facilities: 2 restaurants, lounge, beachfront, heated pool, 3 tennis courts, health club, saunas. AE, MC, V. Very Expensive.*

Plaza Inn. This small hotel operates bed-and-breakfast style, including a full cooked breakfast with room rate. The hotel is deco-designed from the 1930s, with pool and gardens where a $9.99 Friday-night Indian buffet is served, and a paella for the same price on Thursday. Inn owner Ajit Azrani is a retired Indian Army officer who raises show horses and polo ponies. Room lighting is so-so (bedlamps may be inadequate for reading) and housekeeping inconsistent (dirt may accumulate behind headboards), yet the courteous staff, the location in the heart of Palm Beach, and the rate make the inn worth recommending. *215 Brazilian Ave., 33480, tel. 800/BED AND B, 407/832–8666, fax 407/835–8776. 50 rooms. AE, MC, V. Expensive.*

Sea Lord Hotel. If you don't need glamor or brand names, and you're not the bed-and-breakfast type, this garden-style hideaway is for you. Choose from a room that overlooks Lake Worth, the pool, or the ocean. The reasonably priced 20-seat café, which attracts repeat clientele, adds to the at-home, comfy feeling you'll get from this place. Rooms are plain but not cheap, and come with carpet, at least one comfortable chair, small or large fridge, and tropical print fabrics. Most were refurbished in 1991. *2315 S. Ocean Blvd., 33480, tel. 407/582–1461. 40 units, including 15 efficiencies and suites all with bath. Facilities: beach, pool, restaurant. No credit cards. Moderate–Expensive.*

Palm Beach Gardens
Dining
★

The Explorers. You sit in red leather hobnail chairs at tables lit with small brass and glass lanterns. Above you hovers a ceiling mural of stars and the Milky Way; about the room are memorabilia of famous explorers: Daniel Boone, John Glenn, Sir Edmund Hillary, Tenzing Norkay. The à la carte menu includes a variety of international and American regional preparations, including such specialties as a fresh sushi appetizer with soy, wasabi, and pickled ginger; a 9-ounce snapper fillet prepared with saffron ginger in sesame-seed broth and bok choy; veal chop with sundried tomatoes, pine nuts, calamata olives, and mascarpone cheese; and almond snow eggs, an egg-shape meringue poached in almond cream, plated between three-fruit coulis (boysenberry, mango, and tamarillo) and garnished with a nest of butter caramel. A complete spa menu is also offered. The Explorers Wine Club meets fortnightly for wine and food tastings and is open to the public without charge. Contact the club for a schedule of events. *400 Ave. of the Champions, tel. 407/627–2000. Reservations advised. Jacket required. Dinner only. AE, MC, V. Closed Sun.–Mon. May–Sept. Expensive.*

Lodging

PGA National Resort & Spa. The $10 million spa that opened in 1992 is to rave about, as are the limitless sports facilities and The Explorers restaurant (*see* Dining, *above*). This sprawling resort is the focus of the 2,340-acre PGA National community of 39 neighborhoods and 4,250 residences and is home to the Professional Golfers Association of America and the United States Croquet Association. Its championship golf courses and croquet courts are adorned with 25,000 flowering plants and situated amidst a 240-acre nature preserve. *400 Ave. of the Champions, 33418, tel. 407/627–2000 or 800/633–9150. 275 rooms and 60 suites, with bath. Nonsmoker rooms, rooms for handicapped guests. 85 2-bedroom, 2-bath cottages with fully equipped kitchens. Facilities: 5 golf courses; 19 tennis courts (12 lighted); 5 croquet courts; 3 indoor racquetball courts; pool; sand beach on 26-acre lake; sailboats, canoes, and kayaks for rent; spa; sauna; whirlpool; aerobic dance studio; 7 restaurants; 2 lounges. AE, DC, MC, V. Very Expensive.*

Rio
Dining

The Country Place. This cozy little English country-style restaurant, rich in lace, burgundy, and paisley, makes a pleasant stop on the winding road between Stuart and Jensen Beach. Family culinary tradition stems from Bournemouth brothers Barry (chef) and John (maître d'), whose father was a chef on the original *Queen Elizabeth.* Nightly specials may include jumbo scallops in black bean sauce; raspberry duck; or a seafood Wellington of salmon, scallops, shrimp, and crabmeat beautifully layered in a puff pastry on a bed of spinach, with plenty of fresh basil from Lucky, the Thai waitress and gardener. Save room for the homemade whisky pie, the crème brûlée, or strawberries Grand Marnier. *1205 N.E. Dixie Hwy. (S.R. 707), tel. 407/334–4563. Reservations advised. Dress: casual but neat. Beer and wine only. Dinner only. AE, MC, V. Closed Sun. and Mon. June–Dec., New Year's Day, Super Bowl Sunday, Christmas. Moderate.*

Sebastian
Dining

Hurricane Harbor. A year-round crowd of retirees and locals frequent this down-home, open-beam, old-Florida–style waterfront restaurant (though note, it's all indoors), built in 1927 as a garage and during Prohibition used as a smugglers' den. Guests love the window seats on stormy nights when sizeable waves break outside in the Indian River Lagoon. The menu features seafood, steaks, and grills, along with sandwiches, soups, and salads. Friday and Saturday nights they open the Antique Dining Room, with its linen, stained glass, and a huge antique breakfront. There's live music nightly—jazz, pop, Dixieland, German, country-and-western, or oldies. *1540 Indian River Dr., tel. 407/589–1773. Reservations accepted. Dress: casual. Closed Christmas, Mon. AE, D, MC, V. Inexpensive–Moderate.*

Lodging

The Davis House Inn. Vero native Steve Wild modeled his two-story, 12-room inn after the clubhouse at Augusta National. Wide overhung roofs shade wraparound porches. In a companion house that Steve calls the Gathering Room, he serves an expanded Continental breakfast. Though the inn is new—opened late in 1992—it looks old, and it fits right in with the fishing-town look of Sebastian, on the Indian River Lagoon. Rooms are huge—virtual suites, with a large sofa sitting area—though somewhat underfurnished. Each room has a hand-painted, pine, king-size bed and microwave kitchenette. Terrific value. *607 Davis St., 32958, tel. 407/589–4114. 12 efficiencies with bath. Facilities: free cruiser bikes, Jacuzzi, complimentary Continental breakfast. MC, V. Inexpensive–Moderate.*

Stuart
Dining

The Ashley. Opened in 1990, this art- and plant-filled restaurant is on the site of an early Stuart bank that was robbed three times by the Ashley gang. The bank impression has been revived with an old cashier's cage, original tile floor, open-beam ceiling, and brick columns. The big outdoor mural in the French Impressionist style (owner-chef Bernard Nigondis comes from near Lyon) was paid for by good sports helping revive downtown, all duly inscribed now on wall plaques inside. The Continental menu appeals with the freshest foods, and features lots of salads, fresh fish, and pastas. *61 S.W. Osceola St., tel. 407/221–9476. Dress: casual but neat. AE, MC, V. Breakfast Sat. and Sun. Closed Sun. evening, Mon., and major holidays. Moderate.*

The Emporium. Indian River Plantation's coffee shop is an old-fashioned soda fountain and grill that also serves hearty breakfasts. Specialties include eggs Benedict, omelets, deli sandwiches, and salads. *555 N.E. Ocean Blvd., Hutchinson Island, tel. 407/225–3700. No reservations. Dress: casual. AE, DC, MC, V. Inexpensive.*

★ **Mahony's Oyster Bar.** Mike Mahony ensures the personal touch by limiting what he buys to what he can carry on his bike. Well, the beer's trucked in—real brew like Anchor Steam and Negra Modelo, and Molson on draft. Choose from 12 tables and booths, or sit at the 14-stool bar, where Mike's got 13 hot sauces lined up to go with the oysters, clams, and shrimp stew. A chalkboard lists such items as sardines and greens on toast, with green onions, red pepper ring, and parsley and a basic pub salad. Decor consists of wind socks, oars, fish traps, nets, and charts, as well as a couple of worshipful paintings of Mike and his bar, and another of Chief Osceola. *201 St. Lucie Ave., tel. 407/286–9757. No reservations. Dress: casual. Beer and wine only. No credit cards. Closed Sun. and dinner Mon.–Wed., major holidays, and Aug.–Sept. Inexpensive.*

Lodging **Indian River Plantation.** Situated on a 192-acre tract of land on Hutchinson Island, this resort includes a three-story luxury hotel that is an architectural gem in the Victorian Beach Revival style, with tin roofs, shaded verandas, pink stucco, and much latticework. Seventy new oceanfront rooms and suites with microwave and range-top kitchens opened in 1992. Its gourmet restaurant, Scalawags, is excellent. *555 N.E. Ocean Blvd., Hutchinson Island, 34996, tel. 407/225–3700 or 800/444–3389. 200 hotel rooms with bath, including 10 rooms for handicapped guests; 54 1- and 2-bedroom oceanfront apartments with full kitchens. Facilities: 3 pools, outdoor spa, 13 tennis courts (7 lighted), golf course, 77-slip marina, power boat and jet-ski rentals, beach club with tiki bar and grill, 5 restaurants. AE, DC, MC, V. Very Expensive.*

The Homeplace. The house was built in 1913 by pioneer Sam Matthews, who contracted much of the early town construction for railroad developer Henry Flagler; to preserve the structure, present-day developer Jim Smith moved it from Frazier Creek to Creekside Common. Smith's wife Jean Bell has restored the house to its early look, from hardwood floors to fluffy pillows. Fern-filled dining and sun rooms, full of chintz-covered cushioned wicker, overlook a pool and patio. Three guest rooms are Captain's Quarters, Opal's Room, and Prissy's Place. *501 Akron Ave., 34994, tel. 407/220–9148. 3 rooms with bath. Facilities: pool, hot tub. MC, V. Moderate–Expensive.*

HarborFront. On a piece of land sloping to the St. Lucie River in an historic enclave west of the highway, this bed-and-breakfast offers a mix of rooms and cottages as cozy as they are eclectic. Choose from a spacious chintz-covered suite or apartment, or maybe the 33-foot moored sailboat (small rowing dinghy provided). Rooms include wicker and antiques, some airy and bright with private deck, others more tweedy and dark. From hammocks in the yard you can watch pelicans and herons. *310 Atlanta Ave., tel. 407/288–7289. 8 apartments, cottages, suites, rooms, boat with bath. No credit cards. Inexpensive–Expensive.*

Vero Beach **The Black Pearl.** This intimate restaurant (19 tables) with pink *Dining* and green art-deco furnishings offers entrées that combine fresh local ingredients with the best of the Continental tradition. Specialties include chilled leek-and-watercress soup, local fish in parchment paper, feta cheese and spinach fritters, mesquite-grilled swordfish, and pan-fried veal with local shrimp and vermouth. *1409 Rte. A1A, tel. 407/234–4426. Reservations advised. AE, MC, V. Dinner only. Closed major holidays and Super Bowl Sun. Moderate.*

Ocean Grill. Opened by Waldo Sexton as a hamburger shack in 1938, the Ocean Grill has since been refurbished and outfitted with antiques—Tiffany lamps, wrought-iron chandeliers, and Beanie Backus paintings of pirates and Seminole Indians. The menu has also changed with the times and now includes black bean soup, crisp onion rings, jumbo lump crabmeat salad, at least three kinds of fish every day, prime rib, and a tart Key lime pie. *1050 Sexton Plaza (Beachland Blvd. east of Ocean Dr.), tel. 407/231–5409. Reservations accepted for parties of 5 or more. AE, D, DC, MC, V. Closed weekend lunch, Thanksgiving, Super Bowl Sunday, 2 weeks following Labor Day. Moderate.*

Lodging **Guest Quarters Suite Hotel.** Built in 1986, this five-story rose-color stucco hotel on Ocean Drive provides easy access to Vero Beach's specialty shops and boutiques. First-floor rooms have patios opening onto the pool. All suites have balconies and ocean views. *3500 Ocean Dr., 32963, tel. 407/231–5666 or 800/ 742–5388. 55 1- and 2-bedroom suites with bath. Facilities: pool, pool bar, movie rentals, coffeemakers, VCRs. AE, D, DC, MC, V. Very Expensive.*

Capt. Hiram's Islander Resort. The aqua- and white-trim Islander was completely redone Key West–style at the end of 1992, so its snoozy mood fits stylishly well with the smart shops across the beach along Ocean Drive. Jigsaw-cut brackets and balusters and beach umbrellas dress up the pool. All rooms feature white wicker, pickled paneled walls, Caribbean art, colorful carpets, floral bedcovers, and paddle fans hung from vaulted ceilings. Just right for beachside Vero. *3101 Ocean Dr., 32963, tel. 800/952–5886, 407/231–4431. 16 rooms and efficiencies with bath. Facilities: pool, barbeque grill. AE, D, DC, MC, V. Moderate-Expensive.*

West Palm Beach
Dining
Comeau Bar & Grill. Everybody still calls it Roxy's, its name from 1934 until it moved into this art deco downtown high-rise in 1989. Outside there are tables under the canopy; inside is a clubby pecky cypress-paneled room. It's no-surprise, all-American food: steaks, shrimp, chicken, duck, with some pastas and Caesar and Greek salads. Try the Roxy Burger: a combination of veal and beef herbed and spiced. *319–323 Clematis St., tel. 407/833–2402 or 407/833–1003. Reservations accepted. Dress: casual but neat. AE, MC, V. Inexpensive–Moderate.*

Narcissus. Get acquainted with the vitality of downtown West Palm Beach at this lively two-level jazz café across the park from the public library. The grazing menu features salads, pastas, crab cake, tuna pizza melt, burgers, and specialty sandwiches like falafel. During the daily happy hour, 4:30–7, drinks and hors d'oeuvres are half price. There's a live jazz brunch Sunday noon–4 and jazz jamming 5–10. *200 Clematis St., tel. 407/659–1888. Reservations accepted. Dress: casual but neat. AE, MC, V. Inexpensive–Moderate.*

Lodging **Palm Beach Polo and Country Club.** Individual villas and condominiums are available in this exclusive 2,200-acre resort where Britain's Prince Charles has come to play polo. The Major Dawnay Polo Clinic is conducted during the sport's season (February–April), and there's a seven-week equestrian festival. Arrange to rent a dwelling closest to the sports activity that interests you: polo, tennis, or golf. Each residence is designed and furnished by its owner according to standards of quality set by the resort. *13198 Forest Hill Blvd., 33414, tel. 407/798–7000 or 800/327–4204. 100 privately owned studios, 1- and 2-bedroom villas, and condominiums available for daily, weekly, or monthly rental. Facilities: 10 pools; 24 grass, clay, and hard-surface tennis courts (20 lighted); two 18-hole and one 9-hole golf courses; men's and women's saunas; 10 polo fields, 9 polo barns, equestrian club, riding trails, 7 stable barns; 2 lighted croquet lawns; squash and racquetball courts;*

sculling equipment and instruction; 5 dining rooms. AE, DC, MC, V. Very Expensive.

Hibiscus House. This Cape Cod–style bed-and-breakfast offers eight rooms and many public rooms, full of antiques, and a beautifully landscaped, tropical pool area. Owners Raleigh Hill and Colin Rayner have been prime movers in revitalizing the historic Old Northwood neighborhood. *501 30th St., 33407, tel. 407/863–5633. 8 rooms with bath. Facilities: pool. No credit cards. Moderate.*

West Palm Beach Bed & Breakfast. Also in Old Northwood, but more informal and Key West–like, this cottage-style B&B has a clump of rare paroutis palms out front. Its three guest rooms include a splashy-colored poolside carriage house, which is where you want to be. (The aqua room is AQUA, the pink room PINK.) The parlor has a delightful montage of work by Florida's favorite painter of hotel art, Eileen Seitz. Owners are Dennis Keimel and Ron Seitz (unrelated to the artist Seitz). *419 32nd St., 33407, tel. 407/848–4064 or 800/736–4064, fax 407/842–1688. 3 rooms with bath. Facilities: pool. No credit cards. Moderate.*

The Arts and Nightlife

The *Palm Beach Post*, in its "TGIF" entertainment insert on Friday, lists all events for the weekend, including concerts. Admission to some cultural events is free or by donation. Call **Ticketmaster** (tel. 407/839–3900) for tickets for performing arts events.

Performing Arts Center The **Raymond F. Kravis Center for the Performing Arts** (701 Okeechobee Blvd., West Palm Beach, tel. 407/832–7469) a new $55 million, 2,200-seat glass-copper-and-marble showcase, opened in late 1992 on the highest ground in West Palm Beach. Some 300 performances are scheduled a year, featuring everything from gospel and blue grass to jazz and classics.

Nightclub **Wildflower Waterway Cafe** (551 E. Palmetto Park Rd., Boca Raton, tel. 407/391–0000) has nightly DJs spinning the top of the pops for a mostly young crowd.

Theater **Caldwell Theatre Company** (7873 N. Federal Hwy., Boca Raton 33487, tel. 407/241–7432 [Boca Raton], 407/832–2989 [Palm Beach], 305/462–5433 [Broward County]), a professional Equity regional theater, hosts the annual multimedia Mizner Festival each April–May and presents four shows each winter.

Jan McArt's Royal Palm Dinner Theatre (303 S.E. Mizner Blvd., Royal Palm Plaza, Boca Raton 33432, tel. 407/426–2211 or 800/841–6765), an Equity theater in its 16th year, presents five musicals on a year-round schedule.

Royal Poinciana Playhouse (70 Royal Poinciana Plaza, Palm Beach 33480, tel. 407/659–3310) performs six productions each year between December and April.

Riverside Theatre (3250 Riverside Park Dr., Vero Beach 32963, tel. 407/231–6990) performs six shows a season and hosts road shows and visiting performers in its 633-seat performance hall.

8 The Florida Keys

By George and
Rosalie Leposky

Updated by Herb
Hiller

The Florida Keys are a wilderness of flowering jungles and shimmering seas, a jade pendant of mangrove-fringed islands dangling toward the tropics. The Florida Keys are also a 110-mile traffic jam lined with garish billboards, hamburger stands, shopping centers, motels, and trailer courts. Unfortunately, you can't have one without the other. A river of tourist traffic gushes southward along the only highway—U.S. 1—to Key West. Many residents of Monroe County live by diverting some of that river's green dollar flow to their own pockets, sometimes blighting the Keys' fragile beauty—at least on the 34 islands linked to the mainland by the 42 bridges of the Overseas Highway. In effect, the Keys' natural resources have paid the price.

The environmental impact of such development is still mounting, but new legislation promises to help restore the natural beauty of the Keys. Since 1992, county legislation has severely restricted new building, with an eye to protecting the environment as well as to improving hurricane evacuation procedures. In 1994 the National Oceanic and Atmospheric Administration is expected to implement a management plan for the 200-mile-long Florida Keys National Marine Sanctuary (largest in the nation), intended to help protect the coral reefs of the Keys and restore badly depleted fish reserves. This will include a new maritime zoning concept that restricts commercial and recreational activities in designated areas. Dive shops and places where visitors stay will alert people to these zones.

For now, however, take pleasure as you drive down U.S. 1 through the islands. The silvery blue and green Atlantic, with its great living reef, is on your left; Florida Bay, the Gulf of Mexico, and the back country are on your right. At points the ocean and the gulf are 10 miles apart; on the narrowest landfill islands, they are separated only by the road.

The Overseas Highway varies from a frustrating traffic-clogged trap to a mystical pathway skimming across the sea. There are more islands than you will be able to remember. Follow the green mile markers by the side of U.S. 1, and even if you lose track of the names of the islands, you won't get lost.

There are many things to do along the way, but first you have to remind yourself to get off the highway. Once you leave this road, you can rent a boat and find a secluded anchorage at which to fish, swim, and marvel at the sun, sea, and sky. To the south in the Atlantic, you can dive to spectacular coral reefs or pursue dolphin, blue marlin, and other deep-water game fish. Along the Florida Bay coastline you can seek out the bonefish, snapper, snook, and tarpon that lurk in the grass flats and in the shallow, winding channels of the back country.

Along the reefs and among the islands are more than 600 kinds of fish. Diminutive deer and pale raccoons, related to but distinct from their mainland cousins, inhabit the Lower Keys. And throughout the islands you'll find such exotic West Indian plants as Jamaica dogwood, pigeon plum, poisonwood, satinwood, and silver and thatch palms, as well as tropical birds, including the great white heron, mangrove cuckoo, roseate spoonbill, and white-crowned pigeon.

Another Keys attraction is the weather: in the winter it's typically 10 degrees warmer in the Keys than on the mainland; in the summer it's usually 10 degrees cooler. The Keys also get substantially less rain, around 30 inches annually compared to 55–60 inches in Miami and the Everglades. Most of the rain falls in brief, vigorous thunderstorms on summer afternoons. In winter, continental cold fronts occasionally stall over the Keys, dragging temperatures down to the 40s.

The Keys were only sparsely populated until the early 20th century. In 1905, however, railroad magnate Henry Flagler began building the extension of his Florida railroad south from Homestead to Key West. His goal was to establish a rail link to the steamships that sailed between Key West and Havana, just 90 miles away across the Straits of Florida. The railroad arrived at Key West in 1912 and remained a lifeline of commerce until the Labor Day hurricane of 1935 washed out much of its roadbed. For three years thereafter, the only way in and out of Key West was by boat. The Overseas Highway, built over the railroad's old roadbeds and bridges, was completed in 1938.

Although on the surface the Keys seem homogenous to most mainlanders, they are actually quite different from each other. Key Largo, the largest of the keys and the one closest to the mainland, is becoming a bedroom community for Homestead, South Dade, and even the southern reaches of Miami. Most of the residents of the Upper Keys moved to Florida from the Northeast and Midwest; many are retirees. In the Middle Keys, fishing dominates the economy, and most residents are descendants of people who moved here from other southern states. The Lower Keys have a diverse population: native "Conchs" (white Key Westers, many of whom trace their ancestry to the Bahamas), freshwater Conchs (longtime residents who migrated from somewhere else years ago), gays (who now make up at least 20% of Key West's citizenry), Bahamians, Hispanics (primarily Cubans), recent refugees from the urban sprawl of Miami and Fort Lauderdale, transient Navy and Air Force personnel, students waiting tables, and a miscellaneous assortment of vagabonds, drifters, and dropouts in search of refuge at the end of the road.

Essential Information

Important Addresses and Numbers

Tourist Information
Florida Keys & Key West Visitors Bureau (Box 1147, Key West 33041, tel. 800/352–5397).
Key Largo Chamber of Commerce (MM 106, BS, 105950 Overseas Hwy., Key Largo 33037, tel. 305/451–1414 or 800/822–1088).
Islamorada Chamber of Commerce (MM 82.5, BS, Box 915, Islamorada 33036, tel. 305/664–4503 or 800/322–5397).
Greater Marathon Chamber of Commerce (MM 48.7, BS, 3330 Overseas Hwy., Marathon 33050, tel. 305/743–5417 or 800/842–9580).
Lower Keys Chamber of Commerce (MM 31, OS, Box 511, Big Pine Key 33043, tel. 305/872–2411 or 800/872–3722).
Greater Key West Chamber of Commerce (402 Wall St., Key West 33040, tel. 305/294–2587 or 800/527–8539).

Emergencies
Dial 911 for **ambulance** and **police**.

Hospitals
The following hospitals have 24-hour emergency rooms: **Mariners Hospital** (MM 88.5, BS, 50 High Point Rd., Tavernier,

Plantation Key 33070; physician-referral service, tel. 305/852–9222), **Fishermen's Hospital** (MM 48.7, OS, 3301 Overseas Hwy., Marathon, tel. 305/743–5533), and **Lower Florida Keys Health System** (MM5, BS, 5900 Junior College Rd., Stock Island, tel. 305/294–5531).

Late-Night The Keys have no 24-hour pharmacies. Hospital pharmacists
Pharmacies will help with emergencies after regular retail business hours.

Arriving and Departing

By Plane Recent improvements in service now link airports in Miami, Fort Lauderdale/Hollywood, Orlando, and Tampa directly with **Key West International Airport** (S. Roosevelt Blvd., tel. 305/296–5439). Service is provided by American (tel. 800/433–7300), American Eagle (tel. 800/225–9920), Comair (tel. 800/354–9822), Delta (tel. 800/221–1212), and USAir/USAir Express (tel. 800/842–5374).

Chalk's International (1000 MacArthur Cswy., tel. 305/371–8628 or 800/432-8807), the venerable seaplane service operating out of Miami, flies 17-passenger Grumman Mallard seaplanes daily into Key West Harbor, with free water taxi transfer to Mallory Square. Depending on how far in advance you buy your ticket, round-trip fare ranges between $169 and $189.

Carriers that provide direct service between Miami and **Marathon Airport** (MM 52, BS, 9000 Overseas Hwy., tel. 305/743–2155) include Airways International (tel. 305/743–0500) and American Eagle (tel. 800/433–7300); direct service between Marathon and Fort Lauderdale is provided by Air Sunshine (tel. 305/434–8900; in FL, 800/432–1744).

Car Rentals Only two rental-car firms have booths at Key West International Airport: **Avis** (tel. 305/296–8744 or 800/831–2847) and **Dollar** (tel. 305/296–9921 or 800/800–4000). **Avis** (tel. 305/743–5428) also serves Marathon Airport. Companies in other Key West locations include **Hertz** (3840 N. Roosevelt Blvd., tel. 305/294–1039 or 800/654–3131); **Thrifty** (2516 N. Roosevelt Blvd., tel. 305/296–6514), **Tropical Rent A-Car** (1300 Duval St., tel. 305/294–8136), and **Value** (3820 N. Roosevelt Blvd., tel. 305/296–7733 or 800/468–2583). **Enterprise Rent-A-Car** (tel. 305/876–9749, 305/451–3998, or 305/292–0220; in Miami, 800/325–8007) has several Keys locations, including at participating hotels. Don't fly into Key West and drive out; the rental firms have substantial drop-off charges for leaving a Key West car in Miami.

Between Miami **The Airporter** (88890 Overseas Hwy., MM 88.8, Tavernier
International 33070, tel. 305/852–3413 or 305/247–8874) operates scheduled
Airport and the van and bus service from MIA's baggage areas to major hotels
Keys in Key Largo and Islamorada. Drivers post Airporter signs with the names of clients they are to meet ($30 per person to Key Largo, $33 per person to Islamorada; children under 12 ride for half fare). Reservations are required.

Island Taxi (tel. 305/664–8181, 305/743–0077, or 305/872–0128) meets arriving flights at MIA. Reservations are required 24 hours in advance for arrivals, one hour for departures. Accompanied children under 12 ride free. Fares for one or two persons: $80 to Key Largo, $100 to Islamorada, $175 to Marathon, $200 to Key West; each additional person $5, except to Key West $10.

By Car If you want to avoid Miami traffic on the mainland en route to the Keys, take the Homestead Extension of Florida's Turnpike; although it's a toll road that carries a lot of commuter traffic, it's still the fastest way to go. If you prefer traffic to tolls, take U.S. 1.

Just south of Florida City, the turnpike joins U.S. 1 and the Overseas Highway begins. Eighteen miles farther on, you cross the Jewfish Creek bridge at the north end of Key Largo, and you're officially in the Keys.

By 1994 work could begin on widening at least a portion of this road to four lanes; Jewfish Creek bridge, too, is scheduled for replacement. If this happens, to avoid even worse traffic than usual, from Florida City take Card Sound Road (Route 905A) 13 miles southeast to the Card Sound Bridge (toll: $1), which will take you across to north Key Largo. Continue ahead until you reach the only stop sign, then turn right onto Route 905, which cuts through some of the Keys' last remaining jungle. You'll rejoin U.S. 1 in north Key Largo, 31 miles from Florida City.

By Bus **Greyhound/Trailways** (tel. 305/374–7222) makes scheduled stops between Miami and Key West: downtown Miami (700 Biscayne Blvd., tel. 305/379–7403), Miami Airport (4111 N.W. 27th St., tel. 305/871–1810), Marathon (6363 Overseas Hwy., tel. 305/743–3488), Big Pine Key (U.S. 1 tel. 305/872–4022), and Key West (615½ Duval St., tel. 305/296–9072). You can also flag down a bus anywhere along the route.

By Boat Boaters can travel to Key West either along the Intracoastal Waterway through Florida Bay, or along the Atlantic Coast. The Keys are full of marinas that welcome transient visitors, but they don't have enough slips for everyone who wants to visit the area. Make reservations in advance, and ask about channel and dockage depth—many Key marinas are quite shallow.

Florida Marine Patrol (MM 49, OS, 2835 Overseas Hwy., Marathon, tel. 305/289–2320).

Coast Guard Group Key West provides 24-hour monitoring of VHF-FM Channel 16. Safety and weather information is broadcast at 7 AM and 5 PM Eastern Standard time on VHF-FM Channel 16 and 22A. *Key West 33040, tel. 305/292–8727. 3 stations in Keys: Islamorada, tel. 305/664–4404; Marathon, 305/743–6778; Key West, 305/292–8856.*

Getting Around

The only address many people have is a mile marker (MM) number. The markers themselves are small green rectangular signs along the side of the Overseas Highway (U.S. 1). They begin with MM 126 a mile south of Florida City and end with MM 0 on the corner of Fleming and Whitehead streets in Key West. Keys residents also use the abbreviation BS for the Bay Side of U.S. 1, and OS for the Atlantic Ocean Side of the highway.

The best road map for the Florida Keys is published by the Homestead/Florida City Chamber of Commerce. You can obtain a copy for $2 from the **Tropical Everglades Visitor Center** (160 U.S. Hwy. 1, Florida City 33034, tel. 305/245–9180).

Throughout the Keys, the local chambers of commerce, marinas, and dive shops will offer you the local **Teall's Guide**—a land

and nautical map—free or for $1, which goes to build mooring buoys to protect living coral reefs from boat anchors. The whole set includes the entire Keys, John Pennekamp Coral Reef State Park, Everglades National Park, and Miami to Key Largo; you can buy the set for $6.95, postage included, from **Teall's Florida Guides** (111 Saguaro Ln., Marathon 33050, tel. 305/743–3942).

By Car The Overseas Highway is only two lanes wide from Florida City to Key Largo, with heavy traffic (especially on weekends). The highway is four lanes wide in Key Largo, Marathon, and Stock Island (just north of Key West), but narrow and crowded elsewhere. Expect delays behind large tractor-trailer trucks, cars towing boats, and rubbernecking tourists. Allow at least five hours from Florida City to Key West on a good day. After midnight, you can make the trip in three hours—but then you miss the scenery.

In Key West's Old Town, parking is scarce and costly ($1.50 per hour at Mallory Square). Use a taxicab, bicycle, moped, or your feet to get around. Elsewhere in the Keys, however, having a car is crucial. Gas prices are higher in the Keys than on the mainland, so it's wise to fill your tank in Miami and top it off in Florida City.

By Bus The **City of Key West Port and Transit Authority** (tel. 305/292–8165) operates two bus routes: Mallory Square (counterclockwise around the island) and Old Town (clockwise around the island). The fare is 75¢ (exact change); 35¢ senior citizens, students, children under 5, and disabled riders.

By Taxi **Island Taxi** (tel. in Upper Keys, 305/664–8181; in Middle Keys, 305/743–0077; in Lower Keys, 305/745–2200) offers 24-hour service anywhere from Key Largo to Boca Chica Key. Accompanied children ride free. There is service to downtown Key West but no pick-up there. Fares are calculated at $4 for first 2 miles, then $1.50 per mile.

Maxi-Taxi Sun Cab System (tel. 305/294–2222 or 305/296–7777) provides 24-hour service in Key West.

By Limousine **Carriage Trade Limousine Service** (tel. 305/296–0000) provides local metered service: $1.40 for the first ⅕ mile, 35¢ each additional ⅕ mile. Inquire for group and zone rates.

Guided Tours

Orientation Tours **The Conch Tour Train** (tel. 305/294–5161) is a 90-minute, narrated tour of Key West, traveling 14 miles through Old Town and around the island, daily 9–4:30. Board at Mallory Square Depot every half hour, or at Roosevelt Boulevard Depot (just north of the Quality Inn) every hour on the half hour.

Old Town Trolley (1910 N. Roosevelt Blvd., Key West 33040, tel. 305/296–6688) operates 12 trackless trolley-style buses, departing every 30 minutes daily 9–4:30, for 90-minute, narrated tours of Key West. The trolleys are smaller than the Conch Tour Train and go places the train won't fit. You may disembark at any of 14 stops and reboard a later trolley.

Special-Interest Tours
Air Tours **Island Aeroplane Tours** (3469 S. Roosevelt Blvd., at Key West airport, tel. 305/294–8687) fly up to two passengers in an open cockpit biplane, for tours ranging from a quick overview of Key West ($50 for two), to a 50-minute look at the offshore reefs ($200 for two, other tours priced in between).

Key West Seaplane Service (5603 Junior College Rd., Key West 33040, tel. 305/294–6978) operates half-day or full-day trips to the Dry Tortugas in single-engine seaplanes, departing from Stock Island (last island before Key West). Camping trips are also available. Capacity is five passengers per plane.

Boat Tours **Vicki Impallomeni** (23 Key Haven Terr., Key West 33040, tel. 305/294–9731), an authority on the ecology of Florida Bay, features half-day and full-day charters in her 22-foot Aquasport open fisherman, *The Imp II.* Families especially like exploring with Captain Vicki because of her ability to teach youngsters. Tours depart from Paradise Marina on Stock Island. Reservations are necessary, at least a month ahead in winter.

Canoe Tours **Canoeing Nature Tours** (MM 28, BS, Box 62, Big Pine Key 33043, tel. 305/872–2620), led by Stan Becker, are full-day, 5-mile canoe and hiking trips in the Key Deer National Wildlife Refuge. Reservations required.

Kayak Tours **Mosquito Coast Island Outfitters & Kayak Guides** (1107 Duval St., Key West, tel. 305/294–7178) run full-day, guided, sea kayak tours around the lush backcountry marsh just east of Key West. Reservations are required.

Sunset and Harbor Boat Tours Throughout the Keys, many motor yacht and sailboat captains take paying passengers on sunset cruises. Contact local chambers of commerce and hotels for information.

M/V *Miss Key West* (0 Duval St., in front of Ocean Key House, tel. 305/296–8865) offers a one-hour, narrated cruise that explores Key West's harbor up to ½ mile from shore. The sundown cruise includes live music.

Walking Tours **Pelican Path** is a free walking guide to Key West published by the **Old Island Restoration Foundation.** The tour discusses the history and architecture of 43 structures along 25 blocks of 12 Old town streets. Pick up a copy at the Key West Chamber of Commerce.

Solares Hill's Walking and Biking Guide to Old Key West, by local historian Sharon Wells, contains at least six walking tours of the city and a short tour of the Key West cemetery. Free copies are available from Key West Chamber of Commerce and many hotels and stores.

Exploring the Florida Keys

We have divided our exploration of the Keys into three sections: the Upper Keys, from Key Largo to Long Key Channel; the Middle Keys, from Long Key Channel through Marathon to Seven Mile Bridge; and the Lower Keys, from Seven Mile Bridge down to Key West. The fourth tour is a walking tour around Key West.

Highlights for First-Time Visitors

Bahia Honda State Recreation Area, Lower Keys
City Cemetery, Key West
Crane Point Hammock, Middle Keys
East Martello Tower, Key West
Hemingway House, Key West
John Pennekamp Coral Reef State Park, Upper Keys
Mallory Square, Key West

San Carlos Institute, Key West

The Upper Keys

Numbers in the margin correspond to points of interest on the Florida Keys map.

This tour begins on Key Largo, the northeasternmost of the Florida Keys accessible by road. The tour assumes that you have come south from Florida City on **Card Sound Road** (Rte. 905A). If you take the Overseas Highway (U.S. 1) south from Florida City, you can begin the tour with Key Largo Underseas Park. Attractions are listed by island or by mile marker (MM) number.

Cross the **Card Sound Bridge** onto **North Key Largo,** where Card Sound Road forms the eastern boundary of **Crocodile Lakes National Wildlife Refuge.** In the refuge dwell some 300 to 500 crocodiles, the largest single concentration of these shy, elusive reptiles in North America. There's no visitor center here—just 6,800 acres of mangrove swamp and adjoining upland jungle. For your best chance to see a crocodile, park on the shoulder of Card Sound Road and scan the ponds along the road with binoculars. In winter, crocodiles often haul themselves out to sun on the banks farthest from the road. Don't leave the road shoulder; you could disturb tern nests on the nearby spoil banks or aggravate the rattlesnakes.

Take Card Sound Road to Route 905, turn right, and drive for 10 miles through **Key Largo Hammock,** the largest remaining stand of the vast West Indian tropical hardwood forest that once covered most of the upland areas in the Florida Keys. The state and federal governments are busy acquiring as much of the hammock as they can to protect it from further development, and they hope to establish visitor centers and nature trails. For now, it's best to admire this wilderness from the road. According to law-enforcement officials, this may be the most dangerous place in the United States, a haven for modern-day pirates and witches. The "pirates" are drug smugglers who land their cargo along the ocean shore or drop it into the forest from low-flying planes. The "witches" are practitioners of voodoo, *santeria*, and other occult rituals. What's more, this jungle is full of poisonous plants. The most dangerous, the manchineel or "devil tree," has a toxin so potent that rainwater falling on its leaves and then onto a person's skin can cause sores that resist healing. Florida's first tourist, explorer Juan Ponce de León, died in 1521 from a superficial wound inflicted by an Indian arrowhead dipped in manchineel sap.

Just after you come onto the four-lane highway, on your right is the new **St. Justin Martyr Catholic Church** (MM 105.5, tel. 305/451–1316), notable for its architecture, which evokes the colors and materials of the Keys. Among its art are a beautiful fresco of the Last Supper and an altar table formed of a 5,000-pound mass of Carrara marble quarried in Tuscany.

❶ Continue on U.S. 1 to Transylvania Avenue (MM 103.2) and turn left to visit the **Key Largo Undersea Park.** The family attractions include an underwater museum that you have to snorkel or dive to reach, underwater music, and an air-conditioned grotto theater with a 13-minute multimedia slide show devoted to the history of man and sea. *Key Largo Undersea Park, 51*

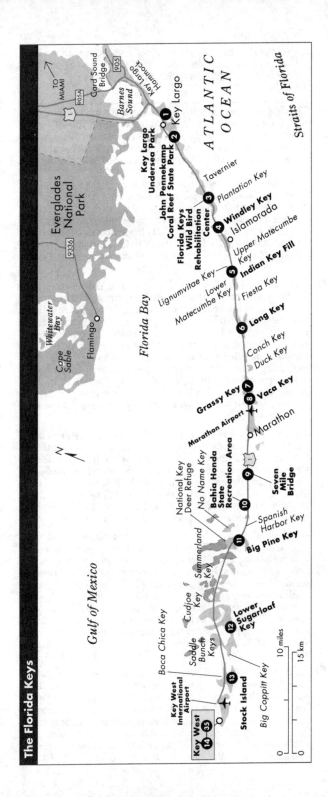

The Florida Keys

Shoreland Dr., Key Largo, tel. 305/451–2353. Aquarium thea-ter admission free; scuba fee, including tanks and gear: $20–$30; snorkel fee, including gear: $10, $35 for family of 4. Open daily 9–3.

Time Out The first real hangout you come to in the Keys is the **Caribbean Club** (MM 103, BS, Key Largo, tel. 305/451–9970), a local bar where scenes from the classic 1948 Bogart-Bacall flick *Key Largo* were shot. The place is plastered with memorabilia of Bogart films. Stop here for fabulous sunset views.

Less than 1 mile south on the Overseas Highway is the new **Maritime Museum of the Florida Keys.** This small but earnest museum offers exhibits depicting the history of shipwrecks and salvage efforts along the Keys: retrieved treasures, recon-structed wreck sites, and artifacts in various stages of preser-vation. *MM 102, Key Largo, tel. 305/451–6444. Admission: $5 adults, $3 children, under 6 free. Open daily except Thurs., 10–5.*

② One-half mile farther on U.S. 1 is the entrance to **John Pennekamp Coral Reef State Park.** The primary attraction here is diving on the offshore coral reefs (*see* Participant Sports, *be-low*), but even a landlubber can appreciate the superb interpre-tive aquarium in the park's visitor center. A concessionaire rents canoes and sailboats and offers boat trips to the reef. The park also includes a nature trail through a mangrove forest, a swimming beach, picnic shelters, a snack bar, a gift shop, and a campground. *MM 102.5, OS, Key Largo, tel. 305/451–1202. Admission: $3.25 per vehicle for up to 8 persons plus $1 each additional, and 50¢ per person county surcharge. Open daily 8 AM–sunset.*

Return to U.S. 1 and turn left. At MM 100, turn left again into the parking lot of the Holiday Inn Key Largo Resort. In the ad-joining Key Largo Harbor Marina you'll find the **African Queen,** the steam-powered work boat on which Katharine Hepburn and Humphrey Bogart rode in their movie of the same name. Also displayed at the resort is the *Thayer IV,* a 22-foot mahogany Chris Craft built in 1951 and used by Ms. Hepburn and Henry Fonda in Fonda's last film, *On Golden Pond.*

Continuing south on U.S. 1 you'll cross **Plantation Key** (MM 93–87), named for the plantings of limes, pineapples, and tomatoes cultivated here at the turn of the century. In 1991, woodcarver **③** and teacher Laura Quinn moved her **Florida Keys Wild Bird Re-habilitation Center** here. Nowhere else in the Keys can you see birdlife so close up. Many are kept for life because of injuries that can't be healed. Others are brought for rehabilitation and then set free. At any time there's likely to be lots of pelicans, cormorants, terns, and herons of various types. *93600 Overseas Hwy., MM 93.6, BS, Tavernier 33070, tel. 305/852–4486. Ad-mission free, donations accepted. Open daily sunrise–sunset.*

④ Next comes **Windley Key,** notable for **Theater of the Sea,** where nine dolphins, two sea lions, and an extensive collection of trop-ical fish swim in the pits of a 1907 railroad quarry. Allow at least two hours to attend the dolphin and sea lion shows and vis-it all the exhibits, which include an injured birds of prey exhib-it, a "bottomless" boat ride, touch tank, shark-feeding pool, and a 300-gallon "living reef" aquarium with invertebrates and small reef fishes. *MM 84.5, OS, Box 407, Islamorada, tel. 305/*

664–2431. Admission: $11.75 adults, $6.25 children 3–12. Swim with dolphins (30-min orientation and 30 min in the water): $65, reservations required with 50% deposit; video or still photos $65 (inquire at concession). AE, MC, V. Open daily 9:30 AM–4 PM.

Watch for the **Hurricane Memorial** (MM 82) beside the highway. It marks the mass grave of 423 victims of the 1935 Labor Day hurricane. Many of those who perished were veterans who had been working on the Overseas Highway; they died when a tidal surge overturned a train sent to evacuate them. The art deco–style monument depicts wind-driven waves and palms bowing before the storm's fury.

Near here are three unusual state parks accessible only by water. To reach the **San Pedro Underwater Archaeological Preserve,** you can get on the *Coral Sea* glass-bottom boat from the dive shop at Bud 'n' Mary's Fishing Marina (MM 79.5, OS, Islamorada tel. 305/664–2461): this park features an underwater, wrecked, 18th-century Spanish treasure fleet. From the dock on **Indian Key Fill** (MM 78, BS), boat tours aboard the M/V *Monroe* will take you to the other two parks on Indian Key and Lignumuitae Key. (Tour service was temporarily discontinued in late 1992 for lack of state funds; inquire whether service has resumed.) **Indian Key State Historic Site** (OS) was a county seat town and base for shipwreckers until an Indian attack wiped out the settlement in 1840. Dr. Henry Perrine, a noted botanist, was killed in the raid. Today you'll see his plants overgrowing the town's ruins. *For information and boat reservations, contact Long Key State Recreation Area, Box 776, Long Key, tel. 305/664–4815. Indian Key open daily 8 AM–sunset. Tour boat admission: $7 adults, $3 children under 12. 3-hr tours Thurs.–Mon. at 8:30 AM.*

A virgin hardwood forest still cloaks **Lignumvitae Key State Botanical Site** (BS), punctuated only by the home and gardens that chemical magnate William Matheson built here as a private retreat in 1919. *For information and boat reservations, contact Long Key State Recreation Area, Box 776, Long Key, tel. 305/664–4815. Lignumvitae Key admission for private boats: $1 adults, children under 6 free; admission with tour boat: $7 adults, $3 children under 12. 1-hr guided tour Thurs.–Mon. at 10:30 AM, 1 PM, and 2:30 PM for visitors from private boats; 3-hr tours for tour boat visitors Thurs.–Mon. 1:30 PM.*

❻ Continue on the Overseas Highway down to **Long Key** (MM 69), where you'll pass a tract of undisturbed forest on the right (BS) just below MM 67. Watch for a historical marker partially obscured by foliage. Pull off the road here and explore **Layton Trail,** named after Del Layton, who incorporated the city of Layton in 1963 and served as its mayor until his death in 1987. The marker relates the history of the Long Key Viaduct, the first major bridge on the rail line, and the Long Key Fishing Club that Henry Flagler established nearby in 1906. Zane Grey, the noted western novelist, was president of the club. It consisted of a lodge, guest cottages, and storehouses—all obliterated by the 1935 hurricane. The clearly marked trail, which should take 20–30 minutes to walk, leads through the tropical hardwood forest to a rocky Florida Bay shoreline overlooking shallow grass flats offshore.

Less than 1 mile below Layton Trail, turn left into **Long Key State Recreation Area,** then left again to the parking area for the **Golden Orb Trail.** This trail leads onto a boardwalk through a mangrove swamp alongside a lagoon where many herons and other water birds congregate in winter. The park also has a campground, a picnic area, a canoe trail through a tidal lagoon, and a not-very-sandy beach fronting on a broad expanse of shallow grass flats. Bring a mask and snorkel to observe the marine life in this rich nursery area. *Box 776, Long Key, MM 67.5, OS, tel. 305/664–4815. Admission: $3.25 per car for up to 8 persons, $1 per additional person, plus 50¢ per person county surcharge. Bike or canoe rental $10 deposit and $2.14 per hour (includes tax). Open daily 8 AM–sunset.*

The Middle Keys

Below Long Key, the Overseas Highway crosses Long Key Channel on a new highway bridge beside the railroad's **Long Key Viaduct.** The second-longest bridge on the former rail line, this 2-mile-long structure has 222 reinforced-concrete arches. It ends at **Conch Key** (MM 63), a tiny fishing and retirement community. Below Conch Key, the causeway on your left at MM 61 leads to **Duck Key,** an upscale residential community and the **Hawk's Cay Resort** (*see* Lodging, *below*).

❼ Next comes **Grassy Key** (MM 59). Watch on the right for the **Dolphin Research Center** and the 35-foot-long concrete sculpture of the dolphin Theresa and her offspring Nat outside the former home of Milton Santini, creator of the original *Flipper* movie. The 14 dolphins here today are free to leave and return to the fenced area that protects them from boaters and predators. *MM 59, BS, Box Dolphin, Marathon Shores, tel. 305/289–0002. Admission: $7.50 adults, $5 donation children 4–12. Walking tours at 10 AM, 12:30, 2, and 3:30 PM. Swim with dolphins (20 min., part of 2½-hr instruction/education program): $80 per person. Children 5–12 must swim with an accompanying, paying adult. Reserve for dolphin swim on the first day of any month for the next month after. Visitor center open Wed.–Sun. 9 AM–4 PM, closed Christmas, New Year's Day, Thanksgiving. MC, V.*

❽ Continuing down U.S. 1, you'll pass the road to **Key Colony Beach** (MM 54, OS), an incorporated city developed in the 1950s as a retirement community. It has a golf course and boating facilities. Soon after, you'll cross a bridge onto **Vaca Key** and enter **Marathon** (MM 53–47), the commercial hub of the Middle Keys.

On your right (BS) at 55th Street is **Crane Point Hammock,** a 63-acre tract that includes the last known undisturbed thatch-palm hammock, owned by the Florida Keys Land Trust, a private, non-profit conservation group. Behind a stunning bronze-and-copper door crafted by Roy Butler of Plantation, Florida, the Trust operates **The Museum of Natural History of the Florida Keys** with dioramas and displays on the Keys' geology, wildlife, and cultural history. Check to see if the exotic plant arboretum, several archaeological sites, and the remnants of a Bahamian village, with the oldest surviving example of Conch-style architecture outside Key West, are open to the public. From November to Easter, weekly Hammock tours may be included in your admission; bring good walking shoes and bug repellent. *MM 50, BS, 5550 Overseas Hwy., Box 536, Marathon 33050, tel. 305/743–9100. Admission: $5 adults, $2.50 senior citizens, $1 children 13–17 and students. Open Mon.–Sat. 9–5, Sun. noon–5.*

❾ As you approach the new **Seven Mile Bridge,** turn right at MM 47 to the entrance to the **Old Seven Mile Bridge.** An engineering marvel in its day, the bridge rested on 546 concrete piers spanning the broad expanse of water that separates the Middle and Lower Keys. Monroe County maintains a 2-mile stretch of the old bridge to provide access to **Pigeon Key** (MM 45), where the county's public schools and community college-run marine-science classes in a railroad work camp built around 1908. In 1990, Pigeon Key was placed on the National Register of Historic Places, a status the Old Seven Mile Bridge already enjoyed. *For information, contact James Lewis, Chairman, Pigeon Key Advisory Authority, 2945 Overseas Hwy., Marathon 33050, tel. 305/743–6040.*

Return to U.S. 1 and proceed across the new **Seven Mile Bridge** (actually only 6.79 miles long). Built between 1980 and 1982 at a cost of $45 million, the new Seven Mile Bridge is the world's longest segmental bridge, with 39 expansion joints separating its cement sections. Each April runners gather in Marathon for the annual Seven Mile Bridge Run.

The Lower Keys

❿ At **Bahia Honda State Recreation Area** (MM 36.5) on Bahia Honda Key, you'll find a sandy beach most of the time. Lateral drift builds up the beach in summer; winter storms whisk away much of the sand. The park's Silver Palm Trail leads you through a dense tropical forest where you can see rare West Indian plants, including the Geiger tree, sea lavender, Key spider lily, bay cedar, thatch and silver palms, and several species found nowhere else in the Florida Keys: the West Indies yellow satinwood, Catesbaea, Jamaica morning glory, and wild dilly. The park also includes a campground, cabins, gift shop, snack bar, marina, and dive shop offering snorkel trips to offshore reefs. *MM 36.5, OS, Rte. 1, Box 782, Big Pine Key, tel. 305/872–2353. Admission: $3.25 per vehicle for up to 8 passengers plus $1 per additional person and 50¢ per person county surcharge. Open daily 8 AM–sunset.*

⓫ Cross the Bahia Honda Bridge and continue past Spanish Harbor Key and Spanish Harbor Channel onto **Big Pine Key** (MM 32–30), where prominent signs warn drivers to be on the lookout for Key deer. Every year cars kill 50 to 60 of the delicate creatures. A subspecies of the Virginia white-tailed deer, Key deer once ranged throughout the Lower and Middle Keys, but hunting and habitat destruction reduced the population to fewer than 50 in 1947. In 1954, the **National Key Deer Refuge** was established to protect them. To visit the refuge, turn right at the stoplight, bear left at the fork onto Key Deer Boulevard (Route 940) and follow the signs. Under protection, the deer herd grew to about 750 by the early 1970s. But the government owns only about a third of Big Pine Key, and as the human population on the remaining land grew during the 1980s, the deer herd declined again until today only 250 to 300 remain. Plans for a new road that may have threatened the remaining deer were canceled in 1991.

The best place in the refuge to see Key deer is on **No Name Key,** a sparsely populated island just east of Big Pine Key. To get there from the Refuge Headquarters, return east on Watson Boulevard to Wilder Road, and turn left. You'll go 2 miles from Key Deer Boulevard to the middle of the Bogie Channel Bridge, which links Big Pine and No Name Keys, and 1½ miles from there across No Name Key. If you get out of your car at the end of the road to walk around, close all doors and windows to keep raccoons from wandering in. Deer may turn up along this road at any time of day—especially in early morning and late afternoon. Admire their beauty, but don't try to feed them—it's against the law.

Return to U.S. 1 and continue on down the Keys across **Big Torch, Middle Torch,** and **Little Torch Keys** (named for the torchwood tree, which settlers used for kindling because it burns easily even when green). Next comes **Ramrod Key** (MM 27.5), a base for divers in **Looe Key National Marine Sanctuary,** 5 miles offshore (*see* Participant Sports, *below*).

Time Out Find top dining at **Mangrove Mama's** (MM 20, BS, tel. 305/745–3030), a lattice-front conch house, remnant from a time when trains outnumbered cars in the Keys, around 1919. Fresh fish, seafood, some decent beers, and rave-worthy Key lime pie are served. Concrete floors, Keys art on the walls, a Tennessee oak bar, and lights twinkling at night in the banana trees all contribute to the romantic ambience here.

⑫ On **Lower Sugarloaf Key,** you'll find the Sugar Loaf Lodge (MM 17, BS), an attractive motel known for its performing dolphin named Sugar, who lives in a lagoon behind the restaurant (*see* Lodging, *below*). Follow the paved road northwest from the motel for ½ mile past an airstrip, and keep going on an unpaved spur. There, in bleak, gravel-strewn surroundings, you'll find a reconstruction of R. C. Perky's **bat tower.** Perky, an early real estate promoter, built the tower in 1929 to attract mosquito-eating bats, but no bats ever roosted in it.

Continue on through the Saddlebunch Keys and Big Coppitt Key to **Boca Chica Key** (MM 10), site of the Key West Naval Air Station. You may hear the roar of jet fighter planes in this vicin-
⑬ ity. At last you reach **Stock Island** (MM 5), the gateway to Key West. Pass the 18-hole **Key West Resort Golf Course,** then turn right onto Junior College Road and pause at the **Key West Botanical Garden,** where the Key West Garden Club has labeled an extensive assortment of native and exotic tropical trees.

Key West

Numbers in the margin correspond to points of interest on the Key West map.

In April 1982, the U.S. Border Patrol threw a roadblock across the Overseas Highway just south of Florida City to catch drug runners and illegal aliens. Traffic backed up for miles as Border Patrol agents searched vehicles and demanded that the occupants prove U.S. citizenship. City officials in Key West, outraged at being treated like foreigners by the federal government, staged a mock secession and formed their own "nation," the so-called Conch Republic. They hoisted a flag and distributed mock border passes, visas, and Conch currency.

The embarrassed Border Patrol dismantled its roadblock, and now an annual festival recalls the secessionists' victory.

The episode exemplifies Key West's odd station in life. Situated 150 miles from Miami and just 90 miles from Havana, this tropical island city has always maintained its strong sense of detachment, even after it was connected to the rest of the United States—by the railroad in 1912 and by the Overseas Highway in 1938.

14 The U.S. government acquired **Key West** from Spain in 1819 along with the rest of Florida. The Spanish had named the island Cayo Hueso (Bone Key) in honor of Indian skeletons they found on its shores. In 1822, Uncle Sam sent Commodore David S. Porter to the Keys to chase pirates away.

For three decades, the primary industry in Key West was "wrecking"—rescuing people and salvaging cargo from ships that foundered on the nearby reefs. According to some reports, when business was slow, the wreckers hung out lights to lure ships aground. Their business declined after 1852, when the federal government began building lighthouses along the reefs.

In 1845 the Army started to construct Fort Taylor, which held Key West for the Union during the Civil War. After the war, an influx of Cuban dissidents unhappy with Spain's rule brought the cigar industry to Key West. Fishing, shrimping, and sponge-gathering became important industries, and a pineapple-canning factory opened. Major military installations were established during the Spanish-American War and World War I. Through much of the 19th century and into the second decade of the 20th, Key West was Florida's wealthiest city in per-capita terms.

In the 1920s the local economy began to unravel. Modern ships no longer needed to stop in Key West for provisions, the cigar industry moved to Tampa, Hawaii dominated the pineapple industry, and the sponges succumbed to a blight. Then the Depression hit, and even the military moved out. By 1934 half the population was on relief. The city defaulted on its bond payments, and the Federal Emergency Relief Administration took over the city and county governments.

Federal officials began promoting Key West as a tourist destination. They attracted 40,000 visitors during the 1934–35 winter season. Then the 1935 Labor Day hurricane struck the Middle Keys, sparing Key West but wiping out the railroad and the tourist trade. For three years, until the Overseas Highway opened, the only way in and out of town was by boat.

Ever since, Key West's fortunes have waxed and waned with the vagaries of world affairs. An important naval center during World War II and the Korean conflict, the island remains a strategic listening post on the doorstep of Fidel Castro's Cuba.

As a tourist destination, Key West has a lot to sell—superb frost-free weather with an average temperature of 79°F, quaint 19th-century architecture, and a laid-back lifestyle. Promoters have fostered fine restaurants, galleries and shops, and new museums to interpret the city's intriguing past. There's also a growing calendar of artistic and cultural events and a lengthening list of annual festivals—including the Conch Republic celebration in April, Hemingway Days in July, and a Halloween Fantasy Fest rivaling the New Orleans Mardi Gras.

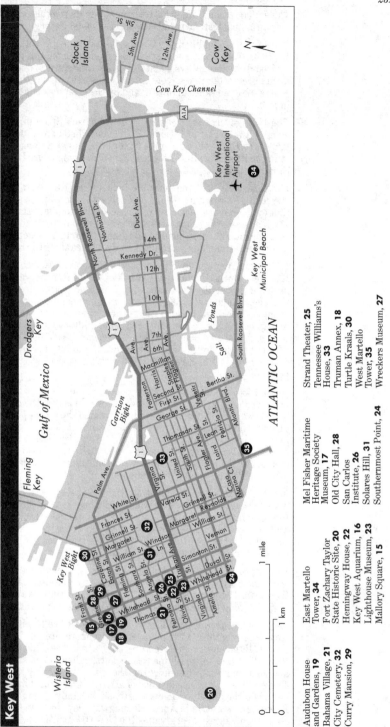

Key West

234

Audubon House
and Gardens, **19**
Bahama Village, **21**
City Cemetery, **32**
Curry Mansion, **29**

East Martello
Tower, **34**
Fort Zachary Taylor
State Historic Site, **20**
Hemingway House, **22**
Key West Aquarium, **16**
Lighthouse Museum, **23**
Mallory Square, **15**

Mel Fisher Maritime
Heritage Society
Museum, **17**
Old City Hall, **28**
San Carlos
Institute, **26**
Solares Hill, **31**
Southernmost Point, **24**

Strand Theater, **25**
Tennessee Williams's
House, **33**
Truman Annex, **18**
Turtle Kraals, **30**
West Martello
Tower, **35**
Wreckers Museum, **27**

⑮ Start your tour at **Mallory Square,** named for Stephen Mallory, secretary of the Confederate Navy, who later owned the Mallory Steamship Line. On the nearby **Mallory Dock,** a nightly sunset celebration draws street performers, food vendors, and thousands of onlookers.

⑯ Facing Mallory Square is the **Key West Aquarium,** which features hundreds of brightly colored tropical fish and other fascinating sea creatures from the waters around Key West. A touch tank enables visitors to handle starfish, sea cucumbers, horseshoe and hermit crabs, even horse and queen conchs—living totems of the Conch Republic. Built in 1934 by the Works Progress Administration as the world's first open-air aquarium, the building has been enclosed for all-weather viewing. *1 Whitehead St., tel. 305/296–2051. Guided tours 11 AM, 1, 3, 4:30; shark feeding on every tour. Admission: $6 adults, $5 senior citizens, $3 children 8–15. Open daily, 10–6.*

Go east on Front Street and turn right to **Clinton Place,** where a Civil War memorial to Union soldiers stands in a triangle formed by the intersection of Front, Greene, and Whitehead streets. On your right is the **U.S. Post Office and Customs House,** a Romanesque Revival structure designed by prominent local architect William Kerr and completed in 1891. Tour guides claim that federal bureaucrats required the roof to have a steep pitch so it wouldn't collect snow.

⑰ On your left is the **Mel Fisher Maritime Heritage Society Museum,** which displays gold and silver bars, coins, jewelry, and other artifacts recovered in 1985 from the Spanish treasure ships *Nuestra Señora de Atocha* and *Santa Margarita.* The two galleons foundered in a hurricane in 1622 near the Marquesas Keys, 40 miles west of Key West. In the museum you can lift a gold bar weighing 6.3 Troy pounds and see a 77.76-carat natural emerald crystal worth almost $250,000. *200 Greene St., tel. 305/294–2633. Museum admission: $5 adults; $1.50 children 6–12. Open daily 9:30–5; last video showing 4:30.*

Mel Fisher's museum occupies a former navy storehouse that he bought from Pritam Singh, a Key West hippie-turned-**⑱** millionaire. Singh is the developer behind **Truman Annex,** a 103-acre former military parade grounds and barracks. During World War II, Truman Annex housed some 18,000 military and civilian employees. Singh is successfully transforming it into a suburban community of pastel, picket, and lattice charm, a mix of affordable condominiums and grassy-yard family homes surrounded by colorful bougainvillea and allamanda vines. The whole community is set behind high black wrought iron gates and architecturally designed in the Victorian style that knits Old Town together. Pedestrians and cyclists are welcome on the grounds daily between 8 AM and sunset. Also on the grounds is the **Harry S. Truman Little White House Museum,** the president's former vacation home, with Truman family memorabilia on display. *111 Front St., tel. 305/294–9911. Admission: $6 adults, $3 children 12 and under. Open daily 9–5.*

From Mel Fisher's museum, cross Whitehead Street to visit **⑲** the **Audubon House and Gardens.** A museum in this three-story dwelling built in the mid-1840s commemorates ornithologist John James Audubon's 1832 visit to Key West. On display are several rooms of period antiques, a children's room, and a large collection of Audubon engravings. There is a self-guided walking tour of the tropical gardens, keyed to an eight-page brochure. *205 Whitehead St., tel. 305/294–2116. Admission: $5 adults, $1 children 6–12. Open daily 9:30–5.*

Continue up Whitehead Street to **301 Whitehead Street**, which was once the first headquarters of Pan American World Airways, the first U.S. airline to operate scheduled international air service. The inaugural flight took off from Key West International Airport on October 28, 1927: Passengers paid $9.95 for the 90-mile, 80-minute flight from Key West to Havana aboard *The General Machado*, a Fokker F–7 trimotor.

Turn right onto Southard Street and follow the signs to the ㉔ **Fort Zachary Taylor State Historic Site.** Built between 1845 and 1866, the fort served as a base for the Union blockade of Confederate shipping during the Civil War. More than 1,500 Confederate vessels captured while trying to run the blockade were brought to Key West's harbor and detained under the fort's guns. What you will see at Fort Taylor today is a fort within a fort, with a new moat dug to suggest how the fort originally looked when it was surrounded by water. Snorkeling is excellent here because of an artificial reef, except when the wind blows south-southwest and muddies the water. *Box 289, tel. 305/292–6713. Free 90-min tour daily at 2 PM. Admission: $3.25 per car for up to 8 passengers, $1 per additional passenger, $1 per pedestrian or bicyclist, plus 50¢ county surcharge per person. Park open daily 8–sunset, fort open 8–5.*

Time Out Pause for a libation at the open-air **Green Parrot Bar** (601 Whitehead St., corner of Southard St., tel. 305/294–6133). Built in 1890, the bar is said to be Key West's oldest, a sometimes-rowdy saloon where locals outnumber the tourists, especially on weekends when bands play.

Return to Thomas Street, turn right two blocks to the corner of ㉑ Petronia Street, and you're in the heart of **Bahama Village**, where Bahamians settled Key West a century-and-a-half ago. **Blue Heaven** (729 Thomas St., tel. 305/296–8666) is a popular little conch- and Caribbean-food restaurant in an old blue-on-blue clapboard, peach-and-yellow-trim Greek Revival Bahamian house. Not too long ago it was a bordello where Ernest Hemingway refereed boxing matches and customers watched cockfights. There's still a rooster graveyard out back, as well as a water tower hauled here from Little Torch Key in the 1920s.

Return to Whitehead Street east on Petronia Street and turn ㉒ right one block to the **Hemingway House**, now a museum dedicated to the novelist's life and work. Built in 1851, this two-story Spanish colonial dwelling was the first house in Key West to have running water and a fireplace. Hemingway bought the house in 1931 and wrote about 70% of his life's work here, including *For Whom the Bell Tolls* and *The Old Man and the Sea*. Three months after Hemingway died in 1961, local jeweler Bernice Dickson bought the house and its contents from Hemingway's estate and two years later opened it as a museum. Of special interest are the huge bed with a headboard made from a 17th-century Spanish monastery gate, a ceramic cat by Pablo Picasso (a gift to Hemingway from the artist), the hand-blown Venetian glass chandelier in the dining room, and the swimming pool. The museum staff gives guided tours rich with anecdotes about Hemingway and his family and feeds the 42 fe-line habitants (for the 42 bridges in the Keys), descendants of Hemingway's own 50 cats. Kitten adoptions are possible (for a fee), but there's a five-year waiting list. Tours begin every 10 minutes and take 25–30 minutes; then you're free to explore on your own. *907 Whitehead St., tel. 305/294–1575. Admission: $6 adults, $1.50 children 6–12. Open daily 9–5.*

23 Down the block and across the street from Hemingway House (behind a spic-and-span white picket fence) is the **Lighthouse Museum,** a 92-foot lighthouse built in 1847 and an adjacent 1887 clapboard house where the keeper lived. You can climb 98 steps to the top of the lighthouse for a spectacular view of the island town, as well as of the first order (biggest) Fresnel lens, installed at a cost of $1 million in the 1860s. On display in the keeper's quarters are vintage photographs, ship models, nautical charts, and lighthouse artifacts from all along the Key reefs. *938 Whitehead St., tel. 305/294–0012. Admission: $3 adults, $1 children 6–12. Open daily 9:30–5.*

24 Continue to the foot of Whitehead Street, where a huge concrete marker proclaims this spot to be the **Southernmost Point** in the United States. Most tourists snapping pictures of each other in front of the marker are oblivious to Key West's real southernmost point, on a nearby navy base off limits to civilians but visible through the fence to your right. Bahamian vendors of shells and straw hats line the sidewalk and blow a conch horn at passing Conch Tour Trains and Old Town Trolleys.

Turn left on South Street. To your right are two dwellings that both claim to be the **Southernmost House**—the Spanish-style home built in the 1940s at 400 South Street by Thelma Strabel, author of *Reap the Wild Wind,* a novel about the wreckers who salvaged ships aground on the reef in Key West's early days, and the adjoining cream-brick Queen Anne mansion at 1400 Duval Street. Neither is open to the public. Take the next right onto Duval Street, which ends at the Atlantic Ocean and the **Southernmost Beach.** *Admission free. Open daily 7 AM–11 PM.*

Now go north on Duval Street toward downtown Key West. Pause at the **Cuban Club** (1108 Duval St.). The original building—a social club for the Cuban community—burned in 1983 and has been replaced by shops and luxury condominiums; some of the original facade was retained. Continuing on Duval Street, you'll pass several art galleries from the 1100 block through the 800 block.

25 Pause to admire the colorful marquee and ornamental facade of the **Strand Theater** (527 Duval St.) built in 1918 by Cuban craftsmen. After a period as a movie theater and as a live music hall, the Strand is now the **Odditorium,** one of a chain of **Ripley's Believe It or Not** museums, displaying weird and eccentric artifacts. *527 Duval St., tel. 305/293–9694. Admission: $9.75 adults, $6.75 children 4–11. Open daily 10–10.*

26 Continue on to the **San Carlos Institute,** a Cuban-American heritage center, which houses a museum and research library focusing on the history of Key West and of 19th- and 20th-century Cuban exiles. The San Carlos Institute was founded in 1871 by Cuban immigrants who wanted to preserve their language, customs, and heritage while organizing the struggle for Cuba's independence from Spain. Cuban patriot Jose Martí delivered many famous speeches in Key West from the balcony of the auditorium. Opera star Enrico Caruso sang in the 400-seat hall of the Opera House, which reportedly has the best acoustics of any concert hall in the South. The current building was completed in 1924, replacing the original built in 1871 that burned in the Key West fire of 1886, in which two-thirds of the city was destroyed. A second building succumbed to the hurricane of 1919. After Cuba and the United States broke off diplomatic relations in 1961, the building deteriorated. It was saved from demolition when Miami attorney Rafael A. Peñalver, Jr. secured a $3 million state grant for its restoration. The building reopened January 3, 1992, exactly 100 years after Martí founded the Cuban Revolutionary Party here. A self-guided tour of the premises takes 30–40 minutes; on weekends you can top it off by watching the 30-minute documentary film *Nostalgia Cubano*, about Cuba in the 1930s through the 1950s. *516 Duval St., tel. 305/294-3887. Open Tues.–Fri. 11–5, Sat. 11–9, Sun. 11–6. Admission: $3 adults, $1 children.*

27 Continue north on Duval Street to the **Wreckers Museum,** which is alleged to be the oldest house in Key West. It was built in 1829 as the home of Francis Watlington, a sea captain and wrecker. He was also a Florida state senator, but resigned to serve in the Confederate Navy during the Civil War. Six of the home's eight rooms are now a museum furnished with 18th- and 19th-century antiques. In an upstairs bedroom is an eight-room miniature dollhouse of Conch architectural design, outfitted with tiny Victorian furniture. *322 Duval St., tel. 305/294-9502. Open daily 10–4; closed Christmas. Admission: $2 adults, 50¢ children 3–12.*

28 Take Duval Street to Front Street, turn right, go two blocks to Simonton Street, turn right again and go one block to Greene Street to see the restored **Old City Hall** (510 Greene St.), where the City Commission has its meetings. Designed by William Kerr, the architect also responsible for the Customs House, the Old City Hall opened in 1891. It has a rectangular tower with four clock faces and a fire bell. The ground floor was used as a city market for many years. Inside Old City Hall is a permanent exhibition of old Key West photographs, including an 1845 Daguerreotype, the oldest known photographic image of Key West.

Time Out Stop next door to the **Cuban Coffee Queen Cafe** (512 Greene St., tel. 305/296-2711), run by a mother/daughter team from Central Chaparra, in Cuba's Oriente Province. Locals love the hot bollos, conch fritters, pigs feet, ham and eggs, sangría, and Cuban coffee.

29 Return to Simonton Street, go one block south to Caroline Street, and turn right to the **Curry Mansion.** Built in 1899 for Milton Curry, the son of Florida's first millionaire, this 22-room Victorian mansion is an adaptation of a Parisian town house. It has the only widow's walk open to the public in Key West. Owners Edith and Al Amsterdam have restored and redecorated most of the house and turned it into a winning bed-and-breakfast (*see* Lodging, *below*). Take an unhurried self-guided tour with a comprehensive brochure, which includes floor plans, full of detailed information about the history and contents of the house. *511 Caroline St., tel. 305/294-5349. Admission: $5 adults, $1 children under 12. Open daily 10–5.*

30 Go east on Caroline Street to Margaret Street and turn left to reach the harbor docks. At the **Turtle Kraals,** the Florida Marine Conservancy runs a hospital for sea creatures. Biologist Linda Bohl maintains a touch tank with horseshoe crabs, sea anemones, sea urchins, and other benign beasts you can fondle—but keep your fingers away from Hawkeye and Gonzo, a churlish pair of 150-pound, 32-year-old hawksbill turtles. A fish pond on the premises gives you a good look at live denizens of local waters, including barracuda, bluefish, lemon and nurse sharks, and yellowtail snapper. *231 Margaret St., tel. 305/294–2640. Admission free; donation accepted. Open 11 AM–1 AM Mon.–Sat., Sun. noon–1 AM.*

Time Out Return along the waterfront to William Street and **Schooner Wharf Waterfront Bar** (202 William St., tel. 305/292–9520), a laid-back tiki hut where the town's waiters and waitresses hang out. You can hear live music weekends (and sometimes at other times) in the warehouse space next door.

Go south on Margaret Street to the corner of Angela Street.

31 Just west of you, on Angela Street, rises **Solares Hill,** the steepest natural grade in Key West. Its summit, the island's loftiest elevation, is 18 feet above sea level.

32 Go down Windsor Lane to Passover Lane, turn left, and go to Margaret Street to the entrance of the **City Cemetery.** Clustered near a flagpole resembling a ship's mast are the graves of 22 sailors killed in the sinking of the battleship U.S.S. *Maine. Tel. Susan Olsen at 305/296–3913 for tour. Admission free. Tour donation: $5. Open sunrise–sunset. Guided tours weekends by appointment.*

33 Walk east to White Street, turn right and go south to Duncan Street, then go three blocks east to walk past **Tennessee Williams's House** (1431 Duncan St., at the corner of Duncan and Leon Sts.), a modest Bahamian-style cottage where the playwright lived from 1949 until his death in 1983. After years of neglect, the house was purchased in 1992 and fixed up by a couple named Paradise; it's not open to the public.

34 The last few Key West sights are better visited on wheels, either car or bicycle. Take Truman Avenue (U.S. 1) east from downtown, past **Garrison Bight Yacht Basin,** where many charter-fishing boats dock. Continue east, as U.S. 1 becomes North Roosevelt Boulevard. Past the turnoff to Stock Island at the east end of Key West, North Roosevelt Boulevard (now Route A1A) swings south and then, at the bottom of the island, turns west, becoming South Roosevelt Boulevard. On your left is a small community of houseboats. On your right, just past the entrance to Key West International Airport, stands **East Martello Tower,** one of two Civil War forts of similar design overlooking the Atlantic Ocean. Housed in a portion of this tower (restored in 1993) are military uniforms and relics of the battleship U.S.S. *Maine,* which was blown up in Havana Harbor in 1898. Also, the **Key West Art and Historical Society** operates a museum in East Martello's vaulted casemates. The collection includes Stanley Papio's "junk art" sculptures, Cuban primitive artist Mario Sanchez's chiseled and painted wood carvings of historic Key West street scenes, memorabilia from movies shot on location in the Keys, and a display of books by many of the 55 famous writers (including seven Pulitzer Prize winners) who lived in Key West. Historical exhibits have been developed to present a chronological history of the Florida Keys. A circular 48-step staircase in the central tower leads to a platform overlooking the airport and surrounding waters. *3501 S. Roosevelt Blvd., tel. 305/296–6206 or 305/296–3913. Admission: $3 adults, $1 children. Open daily 9:30–5.*

Continue west on South Roosevelt Boulevard past Smathers Beach on your left. To your right are the **salt ponds,** where early residents evaporated seawater to collect salt. This area, a vestige of the old Key West and for years a wildlife sanctuary, in 1991 was saved from condo development and turned into **Little Hamaca Park,** with a boardwalk leading into the natural area. Where South Roosevelt Boulevard ends at Bertha Street, turn right, then make the first left onto Atlantic Avenue. Near White Street are **Higgs Memorial Beach** (a Monroe County park) and **West Martello Tower,** a fort built in 1861 and used as a lookout post during the Spanish-American War. Within its walls the Key West Garden Club maintains an art gallery and tropical garden. *Corner of Atlantic and White Sts., tel. 305/294–3210. Donations accepted. Open Wed.–Sun. 9:30–3:30. Closed major holidays.*

Shopping

In season, supermarkets and roadside stands sell tropical fruits. Look for Key limes (April to January), guavas (August to October), lychee nuts (June), and sapodillas (February to March).

Islamorada   **The Rain Barrel** (MM 86.7, BS, 86700 Overseas Hwy., tel. 305/852–3084), a 3-acre crafts village attended by free-running cats, represents 450 local and national artists and has eight resident artists. During the third weekend of March each year the largest arts show of the Keys takes place here, when some 20,000 visitors view the work of 100 artists.

Key West   **Fast Buck Freddie's** (500 Duval St., tel. 305/294–2007) sells imaginative items you'd never dream of, including battery-operated alligators that eat Muenster cheese, banana leaf–shape furniture, fish-shape flatwear, and every flamingo item anyone's ever come up with.

Fausto's Food Palace (522 Fleming St., tel. 305/294–5221) may be under a roof, but it's a market in the traditional town-square style, where everyone meets to catch up on the week's gossip. Here since 1926, Fausto's is also where you chill out in summer, because it's got the heaviest air-conditioning in town.

Gingerbread Square Gallery (1207 Duval St., tel. 305/296–8900), the oldest gallery in Key West, owned by former two-time Key West Mayor Richard Heyman, mainly represents Keys artists who have attained national prominence.

Greenpeace (719 Duval St., tel. 305/296–4442) is operated by Greenpeace, an international conservation organization known for its efforts to prevent the killing of whales and seals. Conservation-oriented educational materials, gift items, and T-shirts are sold here.

Haitian Art Co. (600 Frances St., tel. 305/296–8932) sells the works of 200 or more Haitian artists.

H. T. Chittum & Co. (725 Duval St., tel. 305/292–9002) sells the kind of informal clothing beloved by Key Westers (and Key West visitors)—aviator hats and fish-cleaning knives as well as smart ready-to-wear. There's also a branch in Islamorada (Overseas Hwy., MM 82.7, OS, tel. 305/664–4421).

Key West Aloe (524 Front St., tel. 305/294–5592 or 800/445–2563) was founded in a garage in 1971; today it produces some 300 perfume, sunscreen, and skin-care products for men and women. You can also visit the factory store (corner of Greene and Simonton Sts.), where you watch the staff measure and blend ingredients, then fill and seal the containers.

Key West Hand Print Fabrics (201 Simonton St., tel. 305/294–9535) was made famous in the 1960s by Lilly Pulitzer's designs. Shoppers can watch workers making handprinted fabric on five 50-yard-long tables in the Curry Warehouse, a brick building erected in 1878 to store tobacco.

Key West Island Bookstore (513 Fleming St., tel. 305/294–2904) is the literary bookstore of the large Key West writers' community.

Old Town Fish Market (513 Green St., tel. 305/294–8046) is one place to go for good daily catches.

Pelican Poop (314 Simonton St., tel. 305/292–9955) sells Haitian and Ecuadorean art. It's worth buying something just to gain admittance to the lush, tropical courtyard garden—the kind of place you could imagine Tennessee Williams coming for inspiration. (Hemingway actually once lived here, in the apartments out back called Casa Antigua.)

P. S. Lane Gallery (1000 Duval St., tel. 305/294–0067) is an art gallery specializing in Key West artists.

Tikal Trading Co. (129 Duval St., tel. 305/296–4463) sells its own well-known line of double-stitched women's clothing of hand-woven Guatemalan cotton.

Waterfront Market (201 William St., tel. 305/294–8418 or 305/296–0778) sells health and gourmet foods, deli items, fresh produce, salads, cold beer, and wine. If you're there, be sure to check out the best bulletin board in Key West. In the same building are **Waterfront Fish Market, Inc.** (tel. 305/294–0778) for fresh seafood and **Waterfront Baits & Tackle** (tel. 305/292–1961) for bait and fishing gear.

Marathon **Food For Thought** (MM 51, BS, 5800 Overseas Hwy., in the Gulfside Village, tel. 305/743–3297) is a bookstore and a natural-foods store with a good selection of Florida titles—including *The Monroe County Environmental Story*, "must" reading for anyone who wants the big picture on the Keys ($35—not cheap but worth it).

Participant Sports

Biking A bike path parallels the Overseas Highway from Key Largo through **Tavernier** and onto **Plantation Key**, from MM 106 (at the Route 905 junction) to MM 86 (near the Monroe County Sheriff's Substation). **Key Largo Bikes** (MM 99.4, 99275 Overseas Hwy., tel. 305/451–1910) stocks adult, children's, and tandem bikes, all single-speed with coaster brakes, and multispeed mountain bikes.

The **Marathon** area is popular with bikers. Some of the best areas include the paths along Aviation Boulevard on the bay side of Marathon Airport; the new four-lane section of the Overseas Highway through Marathon; Sadowski Causeway to Key Colony Beach; Sombrero Beach Road from the Overseas Highway to the Marathon public beach; the roads on Boot Key (across a bridge from Vaca Key on 20th Street, OS); and a 2-mile section of the old Seven Mile Bridge that remains open to Pigeon Key, where locals like to ride to watch the sunset. **KCB Bike Shop** (MM 53, 11518 Overseas Hwy., tel. 305/289–1670) rents single-speed adult and children's bikes.

Key West is a cycling town, but many tourists aren't accustomed to driving with so many bikes around, so ride carefully. Some hotels rent bikes to their guests; others will refer you to a nearby bike shop and reserve a bike for you. **Keys Moped & Scooter** (523 Truman Ave., tel. 305/294–0399) rents beach cruisers with large baskets as well as mopeds and scooters. **Moped Hospital** (601 Truman Ave., tel. 305/296–3344) supplies balloon-tire bikes with yellow safety baskets, as well as mopeds.

Camping   The State of Florida operates recreational-vehicle and tent campgrounds in **John Pennekamp Coral Reef State Park** (MM 102.5, Box 1560, Key Largo 33037, tel. 305/451–1202); **Long Key State Recreation Area** (MM 67.5, Box 776, Long Key 33001, tel. 305/664–4815); and **Bahia Honda State Recreation Area** (MM 36.5, Rte. 1, Box 782, Big Pine Key 33043, tel. 305/872–2353). Bahia Honda also has rental cabins. Best bet to reserve one is to call at 8 AM 60 calendar days before your planned visit.

Diving   Although there are reefs and wrecks all along the east coast of Florida, the state's most extensive diving grounds are in the Keys. Divers come for the quantity and quality of living coral reefs within 6 or 7 miles of shore, the kaleidoscopic beauty of 650 species of tropical fish, and the adventure of probing wrecked ships that foundered in these seemingly tranquil seas during almost four centuries of exploration and commerce.

Underwater Parks   **John Pennekamp Coral Reef State Park** encompasses 78 square
and Sanctuaries   miles of coral reefs, sea grass beds, and mangrove swamps on the Atlantic Ocean side of Key Largo. The park is 21 miles long and extends to the seaward limit of state jurisdiction 3 miles offshore. Its reefs contain 40 of the 52 species of coral in the Atlantic Reef System. *MM 102.5, OS, tel. 305/451–1202. Park admission: $3.25 per car for up to 8 persons, plus $1 per additional person, and 50¢ per person county surcharge. Park open daily 8 AM–sunset. Coral Reef Park Co., a concessionaire, offers glass-bottom boat, scuba, sailing, and snorkeling tours: Box 1560, Key Largo 33037, tel. 305/451–1621.*

The **Key Largo National Marine Sanctuary** (Box 1083, Key Largo 33037, tel. 305/451–1644) protects 103 square miles of coral reefs from the eastern boundary of John Pennekamp Coral Reef State Park, 3 miles off Key Largo, to a depth of 300 feet some 8 miles offshore. Managed by the National Oceanic and Atmospheric Administration (NOAA), the sanctuary includes Elbow, French, and Molasses reefs; the 1852 Carysfort Lighthouse and its surrounding reefs; Christ of the Deep; Grecian Rocks; Key Largo Rocks; and the torpedoed WW II freighter *Benwood*. A popular dive destination, the 9-foot **Christ of the Deep** statue was a gift to the Underwater Society of America from an Italian dive equipment manufacturer. The statue is about 6 miles east–northeast of Key Largo's South Cut in about 25 feet of water. It's a smaller copy of the 50-foot Christ of the Abysses off Genoa, Italy.

San Pedro Underwater Archaeological Preserve is an underwater park in 18 feet of water about 1 mile off the western tip of Indian Key. The *San Pedro* was part of a Spanish treasure fleet wrecked by a hurricane in 1733. You can get there on the *Coral Sea*, a 40-passenger glass-bottom dive and snorkel boat, from the dive shop at Bud 'n' Mary's Fishing Marina (MM 79.5, OS, Box 1126, Islamorada 33036, tel. 305/664–2211 for reservations). Cost: $15 adults, $20 if snorkeling, $35 with scuba gear, $7.50 children under 12.

Marathon Marine Sanctuary, off the Middle Keys in Hawk Channel opposite MM 50, OS, runs from Washerwoman Shoal on the west to navigation marker 48 on the east. The 2-square-mile underwater park contains a dozen patch reefs ranging from the size of a house to about an acre. Write to: Greater Marathon Chamber of Commerce, MM 49, BS, 3330 Overseas Hwy., Marathon, tel. 305/743–5417 or 800/842–9580.

National Key Deer Refuge (Box 430510, Big Pine Key 33043, tel. 305/872–2239) and **Great White Heron National Wildlife Refuge** contain reefs where the Keys' northern margin drops off into the Gulf of Mexico. These parks attract fewer divers than the better-known Atlantic Ocean reefs. A favorite Gulf spot for local divers is the **Content Keys,** 5 miles off Big Pine Key (MM 30).

Looe Key National Marine Sanctuary (Rte. 1, Box 782, Big Pine Key 33043, tel. 305/872–4039) contains a reef 5 miles off Ramrod Key (MM 27.5), perhaps the most beautiful and diverse coral community in the entire region. It has large stands of elkhorn coral on its eastern margin, large purple sea fans, and ample populations of sponges and sea urchins. On its seaward side, it has an almost-vertical dropoff to a depth of 50–90 feet. The reef is named for H.M.S. *Looe,* a British warship wrecked there in 1744.

Snorkeling Sites From shore or from a boat, snorkelers can easily explore grass flats, mangrove roots, and rocks in shallow water almost anywhere in the Keys. You may see occasional small clusters of coral and fish, mollusks, and other sea creatures. Ask dive shops for snorkeling information and directions. Diving and snorkeling are prohibited around bridges and near certain keys.

Dive Shops Dive shops all over the state organize Keys dives and offer diving instruction. South Florida residents fill dive boats on weekends, so plan to dive Monday through Thursday, when the boats and reefs are less crowded.

All of the dive shops listed below organize dives, fill air tanks, and sell or rent all necessary diving equipment. All have NAUI and/or PADI affiliation. Listings are arranged geographically, from the Upper Keys to Key West.

Quiescence Diving Service, Inc. (MM 103.5, BS, 103680 Overseas Hwy., Key Largo, tel. 305/451–2440) takes groups of up to six people per boat.
Coral Reef Park Co. (John Pennekamp Coral Reef State Park, MM 102.5, OS, Key Largo, tel. 305/451–1621) provides scuba trips, sailing and snorkeling trips on a 38-foot catamaran, and glass-bottom boat tours, as well as rental boats and equipment for sailing, canoeing, and windsurfing.

Capt. Corky's Diver's World of Key Largo (MM 100.2, OS, Box 1663, Key Largo 33037, tel. 305/451–3200; outside FL, 800/445–8231) offers reef and wreck-diving packages, exploring the *Benwood*, Coast Guard cutters *Bibb* and *Duane*, and French and Molasses reefs.

Florida Keys Dive Center (MM 90.5, OS, 90500 Overseas Hwy., Box 391, Tavernier 33070, tel. 305/852–4599 or 800/433–8946) organizes dives from John Pennekamp Coral Reef State Park to Alligator Light. This center has two Coast Guard–approved dive boats and offers training from introductory scuba through instructor course.

Treasure Divers, Inc. (MM 85.5, BS, 85500 Overseas Hwy., Islamorada, tel. 305/664–5111 or 800/356–9887), tucked just across Snake Creek Bridge on Windley Key, is a full-service dive shop with instructors, that arranges dives to reefs, Spanish galleons, and other wrecks.

Hall's Dive Center and Career Institute (MM 48.5, BS, 1994 Overseas Hwy., Marathon, tel. 305/743–5929 or 800/331–4255) offers trips to Looe Key, Sombrero Reef, Delta Shoal, Content Key, and Coffins Patch.

Looe Key Dive Center (MM 27.5, OS, Box 509, Ramrod Key, tel. 305/872–2215 or 800/942–5397), the dive shop closest to Looe Key National Marine Sanctuary, offers overnight dive packages.

Captain's Corner (513 Greene St., Key West, tel. 305/296–8918) provides dive classes in English, French, German, Italian, and Japanese. All captains are licensed dive masters. Reservations are accepted for regular reef and wreck diving, spear and lobster fishing, and archaeological and treasure hunting. The shop also runs fishing charters and a 60-foot dive boat—*Sea Eagle*—which departs daily.

Diver's Hotel   **Jules Undersea Lodge** (MM 103.2, OS, Box 3330, Key Largo 33037, tel. 305/451–2353), the world's first underwater hotel, takes reservations 30 days in advance from divers who want to stay in its two-room lodge in 30 feet of water. A resort course for new divers is offered. PADI and NAUI affiliations.

Fishing and Boating   Fishing is popular throughout the Keys. You have a choice of deep-sea fishing on the ocean or the gulf or flat-water fishing in the mangrove-fringed shallows of the backcountry. Each of the areas protected by the state or federal government has its own set of rigorously enforced regulations. Check with your hotel or a local chamber of commerce office to find out what the rules are in the area where you're staying. The same sources can refer you to a reliable charter-boat or party-boat captain who will take you where the right kind of fish are biting.

Glass-bottom boats, which depart daily (weather permitting) from docks throughout the Keys, are popular with visitors who want to admire the reefs without getting wet. If you're prone to seasickness, don't try to look through the glass bottom in rough seas.

Motor yachts, sailboats, Hobie Cats, Windsurfers, canoes, and other water-sports equipment are all available for rent by the day or on a long-term basis. Some hotels have their own rental services; others will refer you to a separate vendor.

The following well-established suppliers are listed geographically, from the Upper Keys to Key West:

Gibbsail (MM 102.5, OS, Key Largo, tel. 305/451–1621) rents Windsurfers, Hobie Cats, and canoes.

Coral Reef Park Co. (John Pennekamp Coral Reef State Park, MM 102.5, OS, Key Largo, tel. 305/451–1621) provides glass-bottom boat tours and rents boats and equipment for sailing, canoeing, and windsurfing.

Key Largo Princess (MM 100, OS, Key Largo, tel. 305/451–4655) offers glass-bottom boat trips and sunset cruises on a luxury 70-foot motor yacht with a 280-square-foot glass viewing area, departing from the Holiday Inn Docks.

Sailors Choice (MM 100, OS, Key Largo, tel. 305/451–1802 or 305/451–0041) operates daily charters, including a nighttime trip, on a 50-foot, 49-passenger boat, departing from the Holiday Inn Docks.

Florida Bay Outfitters (MM 99.4, OS, at Key Largo Bikes, Key Largo, tel. 305/451–3018) arranges camping, canoeing, kayaking, and sailing adventures in the upper Keys and beyond, from 1 to 14 days.

Treasure Harbor Marine (MM 86.5, OS, 200 Treasure Harbor Dr., Islamorada, tel. 305/852–2458 or 800/352–26287, fax 305/852–5743) rents bareboat and crewed sailboats, from a 19-foot Cape Dory to a 41-foot custom-built ketch; and powerboats that include a 34-foot Mainship and 36-foot Grand Banks. Treasure Harbor also offers American Sailing Association courses. Reservations and advance deposit required; $100 per day captain fee.

Caloosa (MM 83.5, OS, Whale Harbor Marina, tel. 305/852–3200) is a 65-foot party fishing boat captained by Ray Jensen and his son David.

Gulf Lady (MM 79.8, OS, Islamorada, tel. 305/664–2628 or 305/664-2451) is a 65-foot deluxe party boat operating full day and night fishing trips from Bud 'n' Mary's Marina.

Captain Jack (MM 68.5, BS, Long Key, tel. 305/664–0750) operates snorkel and sunset cruises on six-passenger catamarans from Lime Tree Bay Resort.

Marathon Lady and *Marathon Lady III* (MM 53, OS, Marathon, tel. 305/743–5580) are a pair of 65-footers that offer half-day and full-day fishing charters from the Vaca Cut Bridge just north of Marathon.

Captain Pip's (¼ mile east of Seven Mile Bridge, MM 47.5, BS, Marathon, tel. 305/743–4403) lets you rent your own 20-foot or larger motor-equipped boat.

Strike Zone Charters (MM 28.5, OS, at Dolphin Marina, Little Torch Key, tel. 305/872–9863 or 800/654-9560) is run by Lower Keys native Capt. Larry Threlkeld, who operates fishing and diving trips into the backcountry, to Looe Key, and offshore, including three- and five-day trips into the Dry Tortugas.

Scandia-Tomi (MM 25, BS, at the Summerland Chevron Station, Summerland Key, tel. 305/745–8633 or 800/257–0978), under Capt. Bill Hjorth, takes up to six passengers on reef fishing trips; he also takes divers and snorkelers to Looe Key.

M/V *Discovery* (Land's End Marina, 251 Margaret St., tel. 305/293–0099), and the 65-foot **M/V *Fireball*** (Ocean Key House, 0 Duval St., tel. 305/296–6293 or 305/294–8704) are two glass-bottom boats operating out of Key West.

Wolf (Schooner Wharf, Key West Seaport [end of Greene St.], tel. 305/296–9653) is Key West's tall ship, a 44-passenger topsail schooner operating day cruises as well as sunset and starlight cruises with live music.

Linda D III (Dock 19, Amberjack Pier, City Marina, Garrison

Bight, Key West, tel. 305/296–9798), captained by third-generation Key Wester Bill Wickers, Jr., offers sportfishing by the half day or full day or night.

Golf Two of the five golf courses in the Keys are open to the public.

Key Colony Beach Par 3 (MM 53.5, 8th St., Key Colony Beach, tel. 305/289–1533), a nine-hole course near Marathon, charges $5.50 greens fees.

Key West Resort Golf Course (6450 E. Junior College Rd., Key West, tel. 305/294–5232) is an 18-hole course on the bay side of Stock Island. Fees are $28 for 18 holes ($10 for cart), $23 for nine holes ($6 for cart).

Beaches

Keys shorelines are either mangrove-fringed marshes or rock outcrops that fall away to mucky grass flats. Most pleasure beaches in the Keys are man-made, with sand imported from the U.S. mainland or the Bahamas. There are public beaches in **John Pennekamp Coral Reef State Park** (MM 102.5), **Long Key State Recreation Area** (MM 67.5), **Sombrero Beach** in Marathon (MM 50), **Bahia Honda State Recreation Area** (MM 36.5), and at many roadside turnouts along the Overseas Highway. Many hotels and motels also have their own small, shallow-water beach areas.

When you swim in the Keys, wear an old pair of tennis shoes to protect your feet from rocks, sea-urchin spines, and other potential hazards.

Key West **Atlantic Shores Motel** (510 South St.) has a beach where female guests can go topless.

Dog Beach at Vernon and Waddell streets is the only beach in Key West where dogs are allowed.

Fort Zachary Taylor State Historic Site has several hundred yards of beach near the western end of Key West, with an adjoining picnic area with barbecue grills in a stand of Australian pines. Snorkeling is good except when winds blow from the south–southwest. This beach is relatively uncrowded and attracts more locals than tourists; nude bathing is not allowed.

Higgs Memorial Beach, near the end of White Street, is a popular sunbathing spot. A nearby grove of Australian pines provides shade and the **West Martello Tower** provides shelter should a storm suddenly sweep in.

Pier House hotel (1 Duval St.) has a beach for its guests; locals may join the beach club here, and patrons of certain nearby guest houses are also welcome. Female guests can go topless.

Simonton Street Beach, at the north end of Simonton Street, facing the Gulf of Mexico, is a great place to watch boat traffic in the harbor, but parking here is difficult.

Smathers Beach features almost 2 miles of sand beside South Roosevelt Boulevard. Trucks along the road will rent you rafts, Windsurfers, and other beach "toys."

Southernmost Beach, on the Atlantic Ocean at the foot of Duval Street, is popular with tourists at nearby motels. It has limited parking and a nearby buffet-type restaurant.

Dining and Lodging

Dining Denizens of the Florida Keys may be relaxed and wear tropical-casual clothes, but these folks take food seriously. A number of young, talented chefs have settled here in the last few years to enjoy the climate and contribute to the Keys' growing image as a fine-dining center. Best-known among them is Doug Shook, who made his reputation at Louie's Backyard, along with lately departed (for Miami Beach's Art Deco District) Norman Van Aken, whose book, *Feast of the Sunlight* (Random House, 1988) describes the delights of Key West's "fusion cuisine," a blend of Florida citrus, seafood, and tropical fruits with Southwestern chilis, herbs, and spices.

The restaurant menus, the rum-based fruit beverages, and even the music reflect the Keys' tropical climate and their proximity to Cuba and other Caribbean islands. The better American and Cuban restaurants serve imaginative and tantalizing dishes that incorporate tropical fruits and vegetables, including avocado, carambola (star fruit), mango, and papaya.

Freshly caught local fish have been on every Keys menu in the past, but that is starting to change. Because many venerable commercial fish houses have abandoned the business in the past decade, there's a good chance the fish you order in a Keys restaurant may have been caught somewhere else. Since 1985, the U.S. government has protected the queen conch as an endangered species, so any conch you order in the Keys has come fresh-frozen from the Bahamas, Belize, or the Caribbean. Florida lobster and stone crab should be local and fresh from August through March.

Purists will find few examples of authentic Key lime pie: a yellow lime custard in a Graham-cracker crust with a meringue top. Many restaurants now serve a version made with white-pastry crust and whipped cream, which is easy to prepare and hold for sale. For the real thing, try **Papa Joe's** (MM 79.7, BS, Islamorada on Upper Matecumbe Key) or **Mangrove Mama's** (MM 20, BS, Sugarloaf Key).

Note that small restaurants down here don't hold too strictly to their stated hours of business; sometimes they close for a day or a week, or cancel lunch for a month or two, just by posting a note on the door.

Highly recommended restaurants are indicated by a star ★.

Category	Cost*
Very Expensive	over $50
Expensive	$35–$50
Moderate	$20–$35
Inexpensive	under $20

per person, excluding drinks, service, 6% state sales tax, and local tourist tax

Lodging Some hotels in the Keys are historic structures with a charming patina of age; others are just plain old. Salty winds and soil play havoc with anything man-made in the Keys. Constant maintenance is a must, and some hotels and motels don't get it.

Inspect your accommodations before checking in. The best rooms in the Keys have a clear bay or ocean view and a deep setback from the Overseas Highway. The city of Key West offers the greatest variety of lodgings, from large resorts to bed-and-breakfast rooms in private homes.

Accommodations in the Keys are more expensive than elsewhere in south Florida. In part this is due to the Keys' popularity and ability to command top dollar, but primarily it's because everything used to build and operate a hotel costs more in the Keys.

Highly recommended hotels are indicated by a star ★.

Category	Cost*
Very Expensive	over $150
Expensive	$90–$150
Moderate	$60–$90
Inexpensive	under $60

All prices are for standard double room, excluding 7% state sales tax and local tourist tax.

Florida City
Dining

Alabama Jack's. In 1953 Alabama Jack Stratham opened his restaurant on two barges at the end of Card Sound Road, 13 miles southeast of Homestead in an old fishing community between Card and Barnes sounds. The spot, something of a no-man's-land, belongs to the Keys in spirit thanks to the Card Sound toll bridge, which joined the mainland to upper Key Largo in 1969. Regular customers include Keys fixtures such as balladeer Jimmy Buffett, Sunday cyclists, local retirees, boaters who tie up at the restaurant's dock, and anyone else fond of dancing to country-western music and clapping for cloggers. You can also admire the tropical birds cavorting in the nearby mangroves and the occasional crocodile swimming up the canal. Though Jack has been gone since the early 1980s, owner Phyllis Sague has kept the favorites, including peppery homemade crab cakes, crispy-chewy conch fritters, crunchy breaded shrimp, homemade tartar sauce, and a tangy cocktail sauce with horseradish. Ask about availability of dive boats. *58000 Card Sound Rd., tel. 305/248–8741. No reservations. Dress: casual. No credit cards. Closes at 7 weekdays, 7:30 weekends. Live band on weekends. Inexpensive.*

Islamorada
Dining

Green Turtle Inn. Photographs of locals and famous visitors dating from 1947 line the walls and stuffed turtle dolls dangle from the ceiling over the bar. Henry Rosenthal, the restaurant's third owner, retains many of the original dishes. Specialties include a turtle chowder; conch fritters, nicely browned outside, light and fluffy inside; conch salad with vinegar, lime juice, pimiento, and pepper; alligator steak (tail meat) sautéed in an egg batter; and Key lime pie. Whole pies are available for carryout. For $9.95, nightly specials include such entrées as seafood marinara and pork chops Milanese with soup, salad, vegetable, potato, and beverage. *MM 81.5, OS, tel. 305/664–9031. No reservations. Dress: casual. AE, D, DC, MC, V. Closed Mon. and Thanksgiving. Moderate.*

★ **Marker 88.** The best seats in chef/owner Andre Mueller's main dining room catch the last glimmers of sunset. Hostesses recite a lengthy list of daily specials and offer you a wine list with more than 200 entries. You can get a good steak or veal chop here, but 75% of the food served is seafood. Specialties include a robust conch chowder; banana blueberry bisque; salad Trevisana, made with radicchio, leaf lettuce, Belgium endive, watercress, and sweet-and-sour dill dressing (President Bush's favorite); sautéed conch or alligator steak meunière; grouper Rangoon, served with chunks of papaya, banana, and pineapple in a cinnamon and currant jelly sauce; and Key lime pie. *MM 88 Overseas Hwy., BS, Plantation Key, tel. 305/852-9315. Reservations advised. Dress: casual. AE, D, DC, MC, V. No lunch. Closed Mon. Moderate.*

Papa Joe's Landmark Restaurant. Never mind the heavily chlorinated water and the pasty white bread when you can savor succulent dolphin and fresh green beans and carrots al dente. Here, they will still clean and cook your own catch: $8.95 up to one pound per person fried, broiled, sautéed; $10.95 any other style, which includes meunière, blackened, coconut-dipped, Cajun, amandine, or Oscar (sautéed, topped with béarnaise sauce, crabmeat, and asparagus). Joe's—which dates from 1937—includes an upper-level, over-the-water tiki bar with 25 seats. "Early American dump," is how owner Frank Curtis describes the look: captain's chairs, mounted fish, hanging baskets, fish buoys, and driftwood strung year-round with Christmas lights. The decor never gets ahead of the food, which is first rate. An early-bird menu from 4 to 6 PM is priced $7.95–$8.95. For dessert dive into the Grand Marnier cheesecake, the mud pie, or the rum chocolate cake. *MM 79.7 Overseas Hwy., BS, tel. 305/664-8756. No reservations. Dress: casual. AE, MC, V. Closed Thanksgiving, Christmas. Moderate.*

Whale Harbor Inn. This coral rock building has oyster shells cemented onto the walls, an old Florida Keys bottle collection, and a water mark at the seven-foot mark as a reminder of Hurricane Donna's fury in 1960. Several restaurant employees rode out the storm in the building's lighthouse tower. The main attraction is the 50-foot-long, all-you-can-eat buffet, which includes a stir-fry area for wok cookery and a plentiful supply of shrimp, mussels, crayfish, and snow crab legs. The adjoining Dockside Restaurant and Lounge are open for breakfast, while upstairs the wood-trimmed raw bar and grill overlooking the marina are open to midnight. *MM 83.5, OS, Upper Matecumbe Key, tel. 305/664-4959. No reservations. Dress: casual. AE, DC, MC, V. Moderate.*

Lodging ★ **Cheeca Lodge.** Winner of numerous awards for its environmental responsibility, and host of an annual fund-raising dinner that benefits The Cousteau Society, this 27-acre, low-rise resort on Upper Matecumbe Key places its emphasis on an environmental ethic. Camp Cheeca employs marine science counselors to make learning about the fragile Keys environment fun for children age 6–12. Biodegradable products are used, almost everything is recycled, and the resort has banned motorized watersports, both to ensure a quiet setting and to reduce oily discharges into the water. The beachfront pioneer burial ground of the Matecumbe United Methodist Church is preserved on the grounds, and tranquil fish-filled lagoons and gardens surround. Guest rooms and suites feature periwinkle blue/strawberry and green/hot orange color schemes; all have British colonial–style furniture of tightly woven wicker, cane, and bamboo. Touches include intriguing hand-painted mirror frames, faintly surreal art prints and romantic waterscapes, and natural shell soap dishes. Suites have full kitchens and private screened balconies; fourth-floor rooms in the main lodge open onto terraces with either ocean or bay views. The dining room's stunning carpet imitates the rippled pattern of the sea floor. *MM 82, Upper Matecumbe Key, Box 527, 33036, tel. 305/ 664–4651 or 800/327–2888. 139 rooms with bath, 64 suites. Facilities: 2 restaurants, lounge, in-room minibars, 9-hole par-3 golf course, 6 lighted tennis courts, 2 heated pools and 1 saltwater tidal pool, 525' fishing pier, water-sports equipment rentals (Hobie Cats, rafts, snorkeling and fishing gear, parasailing gear, and nonmotorized boats), 60 nonsmoker rooms, 5 rooms for the disabled. AE, D, DC, MC, V. Very Expensive.*

Ragged Edge Resort. One-quarter mile off the Overseas Highway you'll find this spread-out, grassy little resort, with 10 units at the ocean end of a road. The 2-story buildings are covered with rustic planks outside; inside, the rooms are decorated with pine paneling, tile, carpet, chintz-covered furniture, and matching drapes. Each unit has a large tiled bath suite; motel rooms have a fridge, other units have full kitchens with island counters, chopping blocks, lots of cabinets, and irons and ironing boards. Upper units are best because they have more windows and are lighter. Ragged Edge feels expensive, though it's surprisingly affordable because there's no staff to speak of and there aren't a lot of resort extras. You will find, however, a few amenities—a two-story thatch-roof observation tower, picnic areas with barbecue pits, and free coaster brake bikes. You can swim off the large dock, though there's no beach to speak of; the dock's a virtual rookery when boating activity isn't disturbing the birds—pelicans, herons, anhingas, and terns all crowd around. Look north and south, and only mangroves cluster the near distance. *MM 86.5, OS, 243 Treasure Harbor Rd., 33036, tel. 305/852–5389. 10 motel rooms with bath, 9 of which have kitchens; 3 of them are 2-bedroom apartments. Facilities: freshwater pool, barbecue grills, shuffleboard, free bikes. No in-room phones. MC, V. Moderate–Expensive.*

Key Largo
Dining
Crack'd Conch. Behind the white clapboard lattice exterior and the green and violet trim, foreign money and patrons' business cards festoon the main dining room, where vertical bamboo stakes support the bar. There's also a screened outdoor porch and outdoor garden. This was originally a fish camp from the 1930s. Specialties include conch (cracked and in chowder, fritters, and salad), an award-winning lobster taco, fried alligator, smoked chicken, and 90 kinds of beer. Big portions; they use lots of take-out containers. *MM 105, OS, Rte. 1, 105045 Overseas Hwy., tel. 305/451–0732. No reservations. Dress: casual. AE, D, MC, V. Closed Wed., also Tues. Easter–Memorial Day and Sept.–Christmas. Moderate.*

Harriette's Retreat. Typical of one of those roadside places where the Coca-Cola sign appears larger than the restaurant's, this place hangs thick with down-home personality. Owner Harriette Mattson makes it her business to know many of her guests by name, and even takes the trouble to remember what they eat. Wise-cracking waitresses, perfectly styled for this joint, will tell you that the three-egg omelet is usually a six-egg omelet because Harriette has a heavy hand. Harriette's is famous for its breakfasts: steak and eggs with hash browns or

grits and toast and jelly for $5.95; or old-fashioned hot cakes
with whipped butter and syrup and sausage or bacon for $3.25.
Count on a strictly homey, tacky atmosphere with crafts and
photos on consignment. *MM 95.7, 95710 Overseas Hwy., BS,
tel. 305/852-8689. No reservations. Dress: casual. No credit
cards. No dinner. Closed Thanksgiving, Christmas. Inexpensive.*

★ **Mrs. Mac's Kitchen.** Hundreds of beer cans, beer bottles, and
expired auto license plates from all over the world decorate the
walls of this wood-paneled, open-air restaurant. At lunchtime,
the counter and booths fill up early with locals. Regular nightly
specials are worth the stop: meatloaf on Monday, chef's choice
on Tuesday, Italian on Wednesday, and seafood Thursday
through Saturday. The chili is always good, and the imported
beer of the month is $1.50 a bottle or can. *MM 99.4, Rte. 1, tel.
305/451-3722. No reservations. Dress: casual. No credit cards.
Closed Sun., major holidays. Inexpensive.*

Lodging **Holiday Inn Key Largo Resort & Marina.** New owners in 1993
refurbished all guest rooms at this top of the Keys resort. Former owner James W. Hendricks still docks the *African Queen*
at the adjacent Key Largo Harbor Marina. This is the closest
resort to Pennekamp Reef. Many of the rooms, which have contemporary decor, have large windows overlooking the harbor.
*MM 100, OS, 99701 Overseas Hwy., 33037, tel. 305/451-2121,
800/465-4329, or 800/843-5397. 132 rooms with bath. Facilities: restaurants, 2 pools (1 with waterfall), Jacuzzi, marina
with 35 transient spaces, dive and glass-bottom tour boats, boat
rentals, 29 nonsmoker rooms, 1 room for disabled. AE, D, DC,
MC, V. Expensive.*

Marina Del Mar Resort and Marina. This resort beside the Key
Largo Harbor Canal caters to sailors and divers. All rooms contain original watercolors by Keys artist Mary Boggs and the
best rooms are suites 502, 503, and 504, each of which has a full
kitchen and plenty of room for large families or dive groups.
The fourth-floor observation deck offers spectacular sunrise
and sunset views. Advance reservations are suggested for boat
slips. *MM 100, OS, Box 1050, 33037, tel. 305/451-4107, 305/
451-4107, or 800/451-3483. 52 rooms with bath, 8 suites, 16 studios with kitchen. Facilities: restaurant and bar with live
nightly entertainment, in-room refrigerators, 40-slip full-
service marina, pool, 2 lighted tennis courts, weight room, free
Continental breakfast in lobby, dive packages, diving and
snorkeling charters, fishing charters, 8 nonsmoker suites, 16
nonsmoker rooms, 3 rooms for the disabled. AE, D, DC, MC,
V. Expensive.*

Sheraton Key Largo Resort. This is first of the large, amenity-
filled, enclave resorts on the way south. Service can be imper-
sonal, as happens at chain resorts, but day by day, one staff
person or another wins you over (typically the chambermaids).
The look of this four-story hotel, with hanging gardens, fits
well in its surroundings. The three-story atrium with its win-
dowpane and coral-rock walls, Mexican tile floor, and rattan
furniture strikes the mood. Least desirable rooms are the 230,
330, and 430 series that overlook the parking lot, but all are
spacious and comfortable. Mulched nature trails and boardwalks lead through hammocks to mangrove overlooks by the
shore. (Bring bug spray for your walk.) Both Cafe Key Largo,
for three meals a day, and Christina's, the gourmet dinner-only
room, guarantee grand views three stories above the bay. *MM*

97, BS, 97000 Overseas Hwy., 33037, tel. 305/852–5553 or 800/
325–3535; in eastern Canada, 800/268–9393, in western Canada, 800/268–9330. 190 rooms with bath, 10 suites. Facilities: 2
restaurants, 3 lounges, 2 heated pools, 2 lighted tennis courts,
nature trail, sailboat and Windsurfer rental, fishing and dive
charters, 21-slip dock for hotel guests, minibars. AE, DC, MC,
V. Expensive.

Bay Harbor Lodge. Owner Laszlo Simoga speaks German,
Hungarian, and Russian and caters to an international clientele. Situated on two heavily landscaped acres, this resort
offers a rustic wood lodge, tiki huts, and concrete block cottages; every room has either a small fridge or full kitchen. Unit
14, a large efficiency apartment with a deck, has a wood ceiling,
original oil paintings, and a dining table made from the hatch
cover of a World War II Liberty Ship. Laszlo and his wife
Sandra are the kind of caring hosts who make mom-and-pop
lodges such as this worth your patronage. The rates and the
waterfront setting make this place specially good. MM 97.5,
BS, 97702 Overseas Hwy., 33037, tel. 305/852–5695. 16 rooms
with bath. Facilities: Jacuzzi, saltwater shower, Olympic
weight equipment, barbecue grills, paddle boats, rowboats,
canoes, 2 docks, cable TV, boat-trailer parking. D, MC, V.
Inexpensive–Moderate.

★ **Largo Lodge.** No two rooms are the same in this vintage 1950s
resort, but all are cozy with rattan furniture and screened
porches with Cuban tile floors. The prettiest palm alley you've
ever seen sets the mood. Tropical gardens with more palms, sea
grapes, and orchids surround the guest cottages. Late in the
day, wild ducks, pelicans, herons, and other birds come looking
for a handout from long-time owner Harriet "Hat" Stokes. If
you're looking for an affordable tropical hideaway without going far into the Keys, this is it. MM 101.5, BS, 101740 Overseas
Hwy., 33037, tel. 305/451–0424 or 800/468–43786. 6 apartments with kitchen, 1 efficiency. Facilities: 200' of bay frontage, boat ramp, 3 slips. AE, MC, V. Inexpensive–Moderate.

Sunset Cove Motel. Statues of lions, tigers, and dinosaurs seem
to be attracting waterbirds that fly in each morning and afternoon, while an orphaned manatee swims by for a daily visit.
The 10 guest units all have kitchens and original hand-painted
murals. Special discounts are offered to senior citizens and
members of conservation groups. MM 99.5, BS, Box 99, 33037,
tel. 305/451–0705. 10 units with bath, dormitory house with
kitchen for up to 15 people. Facilities: free water-sports equipment (canoes, glass-bottom and regular paddle boat, sailboats,
trimaran, Windsurfers), 115' fishing pier, boat ramp. MC, V.
Inexpensive–Moderate.

Key West **Louie's Backyard.** Abstract art and old Key West paintings
Dining adorn the interior of this oceanfront Key West institution,
★ while outside you dine under the mahoe tree and feel the cool
breeze coming off the sea. The ambience, however, takes second place to executive chef Doug Shook's culinary expertise.
The loosely Spanish-Caribbean menu changes twice yearly,
but might include such house specials as loin of venison with
port, wild mushrooms, and goat cheese strudel, or pan-cooked
grouper with Thai peanut sauce, and stir-fried Asian vegetables. Top off the meal with Louie's lime tart or an irresistible
chocolate brownie brulée. 700 Waddell Ave., tel. 305/294–1061.
Reservations advised. Dress: casual but neat. AE, DC, MC, V.
Expensive.

★ **Pier House Restaurant.** Steamships from Havana once docked at this pier jutting out into the Gulf of Mexico. Now it's an elegant place to dine, indoors or out, and to watch boats gliding by in the harbor. At night the restaurant shines lights into the water, attracting schools of brightly colored parrot fish. The menu highlights American and Caribbean cuisine, featuring such dishes as grilled tuna with cracked peppercorns; a New York strip steak with a gouda sauce accompanied by spinach, tomato, and pearl onions; grilled sea scallops with black bean cake; and lobster ravioli in a creamy pesto sauce and salmon caviar. Ordered specially, a poached yellowtail is served with broccoli florets and red peppers triangulated on alternate rounds of yellow and green squash. Even simple food becomes art. *1 Duval St., tel. 305/296–4600, ext. 555. Reservations advised. Dress: casual but neat. AE, DC, MC, V. Expensive.*

Cafe des Artistes. This intimate, 75-seat restaurant occupies part of a hotel building constructed in 1935 by C. E. Alfeld, Al Capone's bookkeeper. Haitian paintings and Keys scenes by local artists decorate the walls. Dining is in two indoor rooms or on a roof-top open deck beneath a big sapodilla tree. Executive chef Andrew Berman presents a French interpretation of tropical cuisine, using fresh local seafood and produce and light, flour-free sauces. Specialties include the restaurant's award-winning "lobster tango mango" (lobster with Cognac, served with shrimp in a mango-saffron beurre blanc), the half roast duckling with raspberry sauce, and the yellowtail "Atocha" sauteed with shrimps and scallops in lemon butter with basil. *1007 Simonton St., tel. 305/294–7100. Reservations advised. Dress: casual but neat. AE, MC, V. No lunch. Moderate–Expensive.*

Antonia's. Since 1979, co-chefs Antonia Berto and Phillip Smith have turned out fluent northern Italian renditions of Keys' seafood with homemade pastas. The setting is an 1861 building, formerly the site of the Blue Boar Bar and the hippie coffeehouse Crazy Ophelia's, with a stained-glass transom and bay windows. Order such dishes as homemade mozzarella appetizers, braised veal shank, and the generous dolphin fillet with subtle caper sauce. All pastas and breads are home baked. Many Italian wines are offered by the glass. Room for dessert? Try the tiramisù, cannoli, or Amaretto pie in coconut cream sauce. The ice creams and sorbets are made in house. *615 Duval St., tel. 305/294–6565. Reservations advised. Dress: casual but neat. MC, V. No lunch. Closed 1 month in summer. Moderate.*

★ **The Buttery.** The Buttery's waiters have come to be known as "buttercups," a nickname they share with the house's special drink, a blended frozen concoction of vodka, Kahlúa, Amaretto, coconut milk, and cream. Each of this seafood restaurant's six rooms has its own character. The back room with the bar has wood paneling, skylights, and lots of greenery; a small private dining room in front has a crystal chandelier, and floral wallpaper; another is eclectically tropical with bamboo chairs, dark louvered shutters, and ceiling fans. In its 14th year, The Buttery experiments with specials that find their way onto the seasonally changing menu. Lately rave-worthy were the scallops *Tova* (wrapped in salmon atop a spinach hollandaise sauce); steak "Ricardo" (fillets of tenderloin sautéed with mushrooms in Madeira wine sauce); and chilled Senegalese cream of celery soup made with curry, heavy cream, and mango chutney. *1208 Simonton St., tel. 305/294–0717. Reservations advised. Dress: casual but neat. AE, D, DC, MC, V. No lunch. Moderate.*

Cafe Marquesa. The secret of this small café's success is its openness in all respects: It is open to innovative cuisine; it has an open-hearted, friendly staff; and you can view the open kitchen through a *trompe l'oeil* pantry mural. Meals include arugula salad with sun-dried tomatoes, fresh mushrooms, corn kernels, and bacon; a delicate blue corn pasta layered with spinach, mushrooms, red bell peppers, ricotta, and parmesan cheeses, with a vegetarian béchamel on a bed of zucchini coulis; grilled shrimp with *piripiri* sauce (a salsa of tomatoes, chilis, garlic, cilantro, and shallots). Limitless helpings of the excellent sesame flatbread with black pepper accompany all meals. For dessert try the fruit tart with kiwi, strawberries, and crème fraîche. *600 Fleming St., tel. 305/292–1244. Reservations accepted. Dress: casual but neat. AE, MC, V. No lunch. Closed Tues. in summer. Moderate.*

Market Bistro. The Pier House's deli and fine-dining snack shop, which recently added an espresso bar, sells the hotel's classic Key lime pie by the slice, as well as a chocolate decadence: a triple chocolate flourless torte with raspberry sauce and rose petals. A cooler holds tropical fruit juices, beer, and mineral water. Other specialties include sandwiches, salads, gourmet cheeses, pâtés, and homemade pastries. *1 Duval St., in Pier House, tel. 305/296–4600. No reservations. Dress: casual. AE, DC, MC, V. Moderate.*

Pepe's Cafe and Steak House. Judges, police officers, carpenters, and fisherpeople rub elbows every morning in their habitual breakfast seats, at tables or high-back, dark pine booths under a huge paddle fan. Outdoors under a huge rubber tree are more tables and an open-air bar under a canvas tarp. Pepe's was established downtown in 1909 (which makes it the oldest eating house in the Keys) and moved to the current site in 1962. The specials change nightly: barbecued chicken, pork tenderloin, ribs, potato salad, red or black beans, and corn bread on Sunday; meatloaf on Monday; seafood Tuesday and Wednesday; a full traditional Thanksgiving dinner every Thursday; filet mignon on Friday; and prime rib on Saturday. *806 Caroline St., tel. 305/294–7192. No reservations. Dress: casual. D, MC, V. Moderate.*

Half Shell Raw Bar. "Eat It Raw" is the motto, and even off-season the oyster bar keeps shucking. You eat at shellacked picnic tables and benches in a shed, with ship models, life buoys, mounted dolphin, and old license plates hanging overhead. Classic signs offer homage to Keys' passions. Reads one: "Fishing is not a matter of life and death. It's more important than that." Once a fish market, the Half Shell looks out onto the deep-sea fishing fleet. Specials, chalked on the blackboard, may include broiled dolphin sandwich or linguine seafood marinara. *Land's End Marina, tel. 305/294–7496. No reservations. Dress: casual. No credit cards. Inexpensive–Moderate.*

★ **Mangia Mangia.** Fresh homemade pasta is served alfredo, marinara, meaty, or pesto style, either in the twinkly garden or in the classic old-house dining room with the splashy Save the Rainforests mural. One of the best restaurants in Key West, Mangia Mangia is run by Elliot and Naomi Baron, ex-Chicago restaurateurs who couldn't resist the warmth and laid-back style of Key West. Everything that comes out of the open kitchen is heaven, the pasta divine, all made with 100% semolina and fresh eggs. Made-on-the-premises Key lime pie or Mississippi mud pie are winners for dessert. In a quirky neglect, the restaurant serves no decaf and no espresso, so enjoy another glass of wine, or try to talk Elliot into a sample of his flower-light homebrewed lager. *900 Southard St., tel. 305/294-2469. No reservations. Dress: casual but neat. MC, V. No lunch. Closed Thanksgiving, Christmas Eve, Christmas Day. Inexpensive-Moderate.*

El Siboney. This family-style restaurant serves traditional Cuban food. Specials include chicken and rice every Friday, oxtail stew with rice and beans on Saturday. Always available are roast pork with *morros* (black beans and white rice) and cassava, paella, and *palomilla* steak. *900 Catherine St., tel. 305/296-4184. No reservations. Dress: casual. No credit cards. Closed 2 wks in June, Thanksgiving, Christmas, New Year's Day. Inexpensive.*

Sunset Pier Bar. When the crowds get too thick on the Mallory Dock at sunset, you can come up here, have a piña colada and a snack, and watch the action from afar. This establishment, on a 200-foot dock behind Ocean Key House, has a limited but flavorful menu: freshly smoked fish, crunchy conch salad, crispy conch fritters, steamed lobster (in season), potato salad, and shrimp. Live island music is featured nightly. *Ocean Key House, 0 Duval St., tel. 305/296-7701. No reservations. Dress: casual. AE, D, DC, MC, V. Inexpensive.*

Guest Houses **Artist House.** Dressed in French Empire and Victorian style, with lavender shutters on white clapboard, latticework, wrought-iron spear fencing, and a grand tin-shingled turret, this guest home is a real show stopper. All rooms are antique filled and have Dade County pine floors. Among the rooms you'll find a mix-and-match of brocade sofas, Japanese screens, pull-latch doors, clawfoot tubs, four-poster beds, and elaborate moldings. The little garden out back has a Jacuzzi with a stone lion's head, surrounded by a brick deck, and there's a pond. Rates include full breakfast in winter, Continental breakfast in summer. *534 Eaton St., 30040, tel. 305/296-3977 or 800/582-7882, fax 305/296-3210. 6 rooms with bath, 2 suites. Facilities: Jacuzzi, garden. AE, D, DC, MC, V. Expensive-Very Expensive.*

★ **The Curry Mansion Inn.** Careful dedication to detail by Key West architect Thomas Pope and owners Al and Edith Amsterdam have produced a near-perfect match between the Victorian Curry Mansion (1899) and its modern bed-and-breakfast addition. Each room has a different color scheme using tropical pastels; all rooms have carpeted floors, wicker headboards and furnishings, and quilts from the Cotton Gin Store at MM 94.5 in Tavernier. Rooms 1 and 8, honeymoon suites, feature canopy beds and balconies. Guests are welcome to a complimentary Continental breakfast and happy hour with an open bar and live piano music. *511 Caroline St., 33040, tel. 305/294-5349. 15 rooms with bath. Facilities: pool, refrigerator, wet bars, wheelchair lift, guest privileges at Pier House Beach Club, 2 rooms for disabled. AE, DC, MC, V. Expensive-Very Expensive.*

Island City House. This guest house is actually three separate buildings: the vintage-1880s Island City House, Arch House (a former carriage house), and a 1970s reconstruction of an old cigar factory that once stood on the site. Arch House features a dramatic high carriage entry from the street to the lush courtyard beneath its second story, but its rooms, while most old Key West in character, are least desirable because they are too near busy Eaton Street. Rooms in Cigar House are largest; those in the original Island City House best decorated. The chintz and Victorian patterns fit well in the house's somewhat darker (read Romantic) spaces. Floors throughout are pine, and each of the 24 suites is furnished with antiques. Guests share a private tropical garden and are given free Continental breakfasts. *411 William St., 33040, tel. 305/294-5702 or 800/634-8230. 24 parlor suites with bath and kitchen. Facilities: pool, Jacuzzi, bike rental. MC, V. Expensive-Very Expensive.*

★ **The Watson House.** Small in number of rooms but big in amenities, this guest house provides utmost privacy with Duval Street convenience: It's a block from the bustle but light years from the hassle. Ed Czaplicki with partner Joe Beres has restored the house to its 1860s Bahamian look that guests find caressingly soothing. The three units are the deco Cabana Suite by the two-tier pool gardens, the William Suite on the second floor of the house with its new wainscoting and wallpapers, and the connecting or private Susan Room, also with new wallpapers. French doors and gingerbread trim dress up the pristine yellow-and-white exterior. *525 Simonton St., 30040, tel. 305/294-6712 or 800/621-9405. 1 room with bath, 2 suites with full kitchen. Facilities: heated pool, whirlpool, off-street parking. AE, MC, V. Expensive-Very Expensive.*

The Mermaid & The Alligator. The owners of this smartly styled B&B are former New York and Chicago TV news producers Ursula and Michael Keating, who sailed their way south. They know what it takes to be happy in Key West, and give guests good advice on enjoying the local scene. The house dates from 1904, built of Dade County pine; it was completely renovated by the Keatings. One room has Japanese styling, another a canopied four-poster bed; the big third-story suite has an entire floor all to itself. Rooms facing busy Truman Avenue, which used to be noisy, are now double-glazed and, especially with the AC on, quiet for sleep. *729 Truman Ave., 33040, tel. 305/294-1894. 5 rooms with bath. Facilities: heated Jacuzzi, complimentary breakfast. AE, MC, V. Moderate-Expensive.*

Hotels **The Banyan Resort.** A time-share resort across the street from the Truman Annex, the Banyan Resort includes five Victorian houses, a former cigar factory listed on the National Registry of Historic Places, and three modern buildings in the Victorian style. The award-winning gardens are a tropical cornucopia of avocado, Barbados cherry, eggfruit, papaya, Persian lime, and sapodilla. The rooms have a gray, maroon, and mauve color scheme and rattan and wicker furniture. *323 Whitehead St., 33040, tel. 305/296-7786 or 800/225-0639. 38 suites. Facilities: 2 pools (1 heated), Jacuzzi, bar. AE, D, MC, V. Very Expensive.*

Hyatt Key West. A first for Hyatt, this "baby grand" resort consists of three four-story buildings surrounding a tropical piazza. The lobby features a Mexican terra-cotta tile floor and cherry wood fixtures; the room decor employs mint, lilac, peach, and teal blue hues with light-wood dressers and wicker chairs. *601 Front St., 33040, tel. 305/296-9900, 800/233-1234, or 800/233-1234; in HI and AK, 800/228-9005. 116 rooms with bath, 4 suites. Facilities: pool, Jacuzzi, hot tub, fitness room, massage studio, beach, bicycle and motor-scooter rental, 6-slip marina, 60' rental ketch, wave runners, reef trips, 16 nonsmoker rooms, 6 rooms for disabled. AE, DC, MC, V. Very Expensive.*

★ **The Marquesa Hotel.** Key West architect Thomas Pope supervised the coolly elegant restoration of this four-story 1884 home and added onto it in a compatible style. The lobby resembles a Victorian parlor, with antique furniture, Audubon prints, fresh flowers, and wonderful photos of early Key West, including one of Harry Truman driving by in an open convertible. Rooms have Queen Anne and eclectic antique and reproduction furnishings and dotted Swiss curtains. Botanical print fabrics match bedcovers with drapes. There are marble vanities in some baths, marble floors in others. Everything's beautifully thought out and crisply clean as a trousseau. Continental breakfast is served poolside ($6 extra). *600 Fleming St., 33040, tel. 305/292–1919 or 800/869–4631. 15 rooms with bath. Facilities: restaurant, heated pool, in-room safe, free off-street parking. AE, MC, V. Very Expensive.*

Marriott's Casa Marina Resort. Henry Morrison Flagler's heirs built La Casa Marina in 1921 at the end of the Florida East Coast Railroad line. The entire 13-acre resort revolves around an outdoor patio and lawn facing the ocean. The lobby has a beam ceiling, polished Dade County pine floor, and wicker furniture; guest rooms are decorated in mauve and green pastels and Key West scenes. Among the best rooms are the two-bedroom loft suites with balconies facing the ocean, and the lanai rooms on the ground floor of the main building with French doors opening directly onto the lawn. Flagler's, the showplace dining room, serves a light cuisine that emphasizes pasta and seafood. *1500 Reynolds St., 33040, tel. 305/296–3535 or 800/ 228-9290; in FL, 800/235–4837. 249 rooms with bath, 63 suites. Facilities: restaurant, poolside bar, heated pool, whirlpool, 600' fishing pier, health club, massage studio and sauna, 3 tennis courts, children's activity center, exercise room, watersports rentals (deep-sea, light-tackle, and party-boat fishing; Hobie Cats, Sunfish, jet skis; scuba and snorkel trips), bicycle and moped rentals, 60 nonsmoker rooms, 6 rooms for disabled. AE, DC, MC, V. Very Expensive.*

★ **Pier House.** This is the catbird seat for touring Key West—just off the intersection of Duval and Front streets and within an easy walk of Mallory Square and downtown. Yet inside the hotel grounds you feel the tranquility of a remote tropical island. New since 1990 is the Caribbean Spa: 22 rooms and suites with hardwood floors and two-poster plantation beds. Eleven of the baths convert to steam rooms; the others have whirlpool tubs. In the new rooms (615 and 619 are one-bedroom suites) you'll be spoiled by the VCRs and a library of movies and CD players with compact discs. You can also avail yourself of a loofa rub, massages, aromatherapy, or facial in the new fitness center. Weathered-gray buildings flank a courtyard filled with tall coconut palms and hibiscus blossoms. Locals gather around the thatch-roof tiki bar at the Beach Club. The complex's eclectic architecture includes an original Conch house. *1 Duval St., 33040, tel. 305/296–4600 or 800/327–8340. 129 rooms with bath, 13 suites in 5 separate low-rise buildings. Facilities: 5 restaurants, 5 bars, heated pool. AE, MC, V. Very Expensive.*

La Concha Holiday Inn. This seven-story Art Deco hotel in the heart of downtown Key West is the city's tallest building and dates to 1926. The lobby's polished floor of pink, mauve, and green marble and a conversation pit with comfortable chairs are among the details beloved by la Concha's guests. Large rooms are furnished with 1920s-era antiques, lace curtains, and big closets. The restorers kept the old building's original louvered room doors, light globes, and floral trim on the archways. You can enjoy the sunset from "The Top," a restaurant and lounge that overlooks the entire island. *430 Duval St., 33040, tel. 305/296–2991, 800/745–2191, or 800/465–4329. 158 rooms with bath, 2 suites. Facilities: restaurant, 3 bars, pool, sun deck, whirlpool, bicycle and motor-scooter rentals, 18 non-smoker rooms, 8 rooms for disabled. AE, D, DC, MC, V. Expensive–Very Expensive.*

Best Western Key Ambassador Inn. If you want to stay in a hotel near the airport, this is the place to visit. Even though the 100 rooms are typical motel style—functional and non-luxurious—and the Ambassador was built in 1952, the surroundings are well cared for and the property offers lots of resort features. Each room has a balcony and most offer ocean and pool views. The mood at the pool bar is upbeat and often swings to a reggae sound. A mangrove-lined stream runs through some of the seven acres and connects the salt ponds in the back with the ocean in front across the road. *375 S. Roosevelt Blvd., 33040, tel. 305/296–3500 or 800/432–4315, fax 305/296–9961. 100 rooms with bath. Facilities: snack bar, bar, outdoor heated pool, outdoor fitness course, shuffleboard, complimentary Continental breakfast. AE, D, DC, MC, V. Expensive.*

House and Condominium Rentals

Key West Reservation Service makes hotel reservations and helps visitors locate rental properties (hotels, motels, bed-and-breakfasts, oceanfront condominiums, luxury vacation homes). *628 Fleming St., Drawer 1689, 33040, tel. 305/294–8850 or 800/327–4831; in FL, 800/356–3567; fax 305/296–6291. AE, MC, V.*

Property Management of Key West, Inc., offers lease and rental service for condominiums, town houses, and private homes, including renovated Conch homes. *1213 Truman Ave., 33040, tel. 305/296–7744. AE, MC, V.*

Motels

Harborside Motel & Marina. The 13 units here, all efficiencies, are tucked away between a quiet street and Garrison Bight, the charter boat harbor, between Old Town and New Town. Rooms are boxy with little patios. Clean, basic, carpeted, the rooms have phone and basic color cable TV. *903 Eisenhower Dr., 33040, tel. 305/294–2780. 13 efficiencies. Facilities: freshwater pool, tiki hut, coin laundry. MC, V. Moderate.*

Lord's Motel. A tropical patio adds charm to this otherwise plain motel, painted peach-color with white shutters and lattice accents. The terrazzo floors were recently carpeted over, unfortunately, but the new kidney-shape pool is a pleasant addition. Close to Old Town in the motel district, it's a couple of blocks from the beach. *625 South St., 33040, tel. 305/296–2829. 5 rooms with bath, 10 efficiencies. AE, D, MC, V. Moderate.*

Southwinds. This is a pastel, 1940s-style motel with mature tropical plantings and a pool in a raised deck, all nicely set back from the street a block from the beach. Rooms have basic furnishings; it's as good as you'll find at the price. *1321 Simonton St., 33040, tel. 305/296–2215. 17 rooms with bath, 5 efficiencies. Facilities: freshwater pool. AE, D, MC, V. Moderate.*

Little Torch Key Lodging
★

Little Palm Island. The lobby is located off the Overseas Highway on Little Torch Key, but the resort itself is a 3-mile boat ride away on a palm-fringed island at the western end of the Newfound Harbor Keys. There you'll find 14 thatch-roof villas, each with two suites. An additional suite is located in the Great House, a cypress fishing lodge built in 1928. Each suite has a

Mexican-tile bath and dressing area, Jacuzzi, beds draped with mosquito netting, and Mexican and Guatemalan wicker and rattan furniture. Built on stilts 9 feet above mean high tide, all villas are 20 feet from the water. A 56-foot motor yacht contains another suite called **The Wooker.** The island is in the middle of Coupon Bight State Aquatic Preserve and is the closest point of land to the Looe Key National Marine Sanctuary. *MM 28.5, Overseas Highway, Rte. 4, Box 1036, 33042, tel. 305/872–2524 or 800/343–8567. 30 suites. Facilities: restaurant, tiki bar, air conditioners, wet bars, stocked refrigerators, room safes, heated lagoon-style pool, sauna, exercise room, 12-slip marina, airport pickup ($80 per couple), free launch service, guided tours and excursions, 1 suite for disabled. AE, DC, MC, V. Very Expensive.*

Long Key
Lodging

Lime Tree Bay Resort Motel. Some more imagination and bucks invested here could make this little 2½-acre resort a winner. It's a long, motel-like row with an attractive bayfront setting, but most of the rooms lack detail or charm. The best are the spacious, comfortably furnished rooms in the cottage rows out back (no bay views, unfortunately), and the four deluxe rooms upstairs, which have high cathedral ceilings with skylights, ceiling fans, and linoleum floors with area rugs. Best bet for two couples traveling together is the upstairs Tree House—it has a palm tree growing through its private deck and a divine canvas sling chair with its separately strung footrest. You can swim and snorkel in the shallow grass flats just offshore. *MM 68.5, BS, Box 839, Layton, 33001, tel. 305/664–4740. 29 rooms with bath. Facilities: restaurant, outdoor pool, Jacuzzi, tennis court, barbecue, picnic tables, shuffleboard, horseshoe pit, power and sailboat rentals, dive boats, charter boats. AE, D, MC, V. Moderate.*

Lower Sugarloaf Key
Lodging

Sugar Loaf Lodge. This well-landscaped older motel overlooking mangrove islands and Upper Sugarloaf Sound has one building with soft beds and an eclectic assortment of furniture and another with high ceilings, wall murals, and balconies on the second floor. A friendly dolphin named Sugar inhabits a lagoon just outside the restaurant; diners can watch her perform through a picture window. *MM 17, BS, Box 148, 33044, tel. 305/745–3211. 55 rooms with bath. Facilities: restaurant, lounge, pool, tennis court, 18-hole miniature-golf course. AE, D, DC, MC, V. Moderate.*

Marathon
Dining

Kelsey's. The walls in this restaurant at the Faro Blanco Marine Resort are hung with boat paddles inscribed by the regulars and such celebrities as Joe Namath and Ted Turner. All entrées here are served with fresh-made yeast rolls brushed with drawn butter and Florida orange honey. You can bring your own cleaned and filleted catch for the chef to prepare. Dessert offerings change nightly and may include Mrs. Kelsey's original macadamia pie (even though she's sold out and gone to the old Riverview Hotel in New Smyrna Beach) and Key lime cheesecake. *MM 48, BS, 1996 Overseas Hwy., tel. 305/743–9018. Reservations required. Dress: casual. AE, MC, V. No lunch. Closed Mon. Moderate.*

Ship's Pub and Galley. At this restaurant at the Hawk's Cay Resort, you can dine indoors or under the dockside canopy. A collection of historic photos on the restaurant walls depicts the railroad era in the Keys, the development of Duck Key (which later became Hawk's Cay), and many of the notables who have visited here. Dinners include soup and a 40-item salad bar with all the steamed shrimp you can eat. Specialties include home-made garlic bread, Swiss onion soup, certified New York Angus beef, Florida stone crab claws (in season), and mile-high shoofly mud pie, a 6-inch-high coffee ice-cream pie with a whipped-cream topping. *MM 61, OS, tel. 305/743–7000, ext. 3627. Reservations accepted. Dress: casual. AE, DC, MC, V. No lunch. Moderate.*

Grassy Key Dairy Bar. Look for the Dairy Queen–style concrete ice cream cones near the road. Locals and construction workers stop here for quick lunches. Owners/chefs George and Johnny Eigner are proud of their fresh-daily homemade bread, soups and chowders, fresh seafood, and fresh-cut beef. *MM 50.5 OS, 6350 Overseas Hwy., tel. 305/743–6373. No reservations. Dress: casual. No credit cards. No Sat. lunch. Closed Sun., Mon. Inexpensive.*

Herbie's Bar. A local favorite for lunch and dinner since the 1940s, Herbie's has three small rooms with two bars. Indoor diners sit at wood picnic tables or the bar; those in the screened outdoor room use concrete tables. Specialties include spicy conch chowder with chunks of tomato and crisp conch fritters with homemade horseradish sauce. *MM 50.5, BS, 6350 Overseas Hwy., tel. 305/743–6373. No reservations. Dress: casual. No credit cards. Closed Sun. and 1 month in spring or fall. Inexpensive.*

★ **Mile 7 Grill.** This open-air diner built in 1954 at the Marathon end of Seven Mile Bridge has walls festooned with beer cans, mounted fish, sponges, and signs describing individual menu items. Specialties include conch chowder, the fresh fish sandwich of the day, and a foot-long chili dog on a toasted sesame roll. Even if you're not a dessert eater, don't pass up the peanut-butter pie, served near frozen, in a chocolate-flavor shell. Made with cream cheese, it's a cross between pudding and ice cream. *MM 47.5, BS, 1240 Overseas Hwy., tel. 305/743–4481. Dress: casual. No credit cards. Closed Wed., Thurs., Christmas Eve–1st Fri. after New Year's, and at owner's discretion Aug.–Sept. Inexpensive.*

Lodging **Hawk's Cay Resort.** Morris Lapidus, architect of the Fontaine-
★ bleau Hilton hotel in Miami Beach, designed this rambling West Indies–style resort, which opened in 1959 as the Indies Inn and Marina. Over the years it has entertained a steady stream of politicians (including Harry Truman, Dwight Eisenhower, and Lyndon Johnson) and film stars who come to relax and be pampered by a friendly, low-key staff. Decor features wickerwork rattan, a sea-green-and-salmon color scheme, and original contemporary artwork in guest rooms and public areas. Most rooms face the water. Twenty-two two-bedroom marina villas are available to hotel guests. *MM 61, OS, 33050, tel. 305/743–7000 or 800/432–2242. 160 rooms with bath, 16 suites. Facilities: 4 restaurants, 2 lounges, complimentary breakfast buffet, heated pool, 2 whirlpool spas, 1-mi fitness trail, 8 tennis courts, Killington Tennis School, use of Sombrero Golf Course in Marathon, 60-slip full-service marina, PADI-certified and disabled-diving–certified dive boats, Club Nautico boat rentals, fishing and sailing charters, video-game room, summer children's program, 10 rooms for disabled. AE, D, DC, MC, V. Very Expensive.*

Rainbow Bend Fishing Resort. First you notice the shocking-pink exterior, then the well-kept appearance of this 2.7-acre resort built in the late 1950s as a lumberyard and CIA base. Each guest room is uniquely decorated. A restaurant offering complimentary breakfast overlooks an ample manmade beach and barbecue area, good bonefish flats just a few yards offshore, and a dock with boats available free to guests, except for minimum $5 fuel charge. *MM 58, OS, Grassy Key, Rte. 1, Box 159, 33050, tel. 305/289-1505, fax 305/743-0257. 4 rooms with bath, 19 suites, 21 efficiencies. Facilities: restaurant, heated pool, Jacuzzi, small fishing pier, bait-and-tackle shop, free use of sailboats and canoe. AE, MC, V. Expensive.*

Conch Key Cottages. Conch Key Cottages is on its own little island bridged by a pebbly causeway, all slightly larger than a tot's sandbox. The look is castaway, hidden; the mood live-and-let-live. Allamanda, bougainvillea, and hibiscus jiggle colorfully, and the beach curves around a little mangrove-edged cove. Ten lattice-trimmed cottages rise up on pilings, old-fashioned in Dade County pine; try to get one of the three that directly face the beach. Owners Wayne Byrnes and Ron Wilson have lately replaced pine floors with cool tile, and pine doors with glass, mucking up the authentic look somewhat. Furnishings are reed, rattan, and wicker, with hammocks out front—people are meant to live comfortably here, without a lot of fuss, without a lot of clothes. *MM 62.3 OS, RR 1, Box 424, 33050, tel. 305/289-1377 or 800/330-1577. 10 cottages with equipped kitchen. Facilities: beach. D, MC, V. Moderate–Expensive.*

Valhalla Beach Resort Motel. Guests come back year after year to this unpretentious motel with the waterfront location of a posh resort. It has no less than three little beaches, while many Keys resorts have none. Rhonda and Bruce Schofield are second-generation proprietors of this 1950s-era plain-Jane place. Clean, straightforward, with rattan and laminate furniture, it's excellent for families because of the safe, shallow beaches. It's also far off the highway, so don't miss the highway sign. *MM 56.5, OS, Crawl Key, Rte. 1, Box 115, 33050, tel. 305/289-0616. 4 rooms with bath, 8 efficiencies. Facilities: boat ramp, dock, beaches, refrigerators in rooms. No credit cards. Inexpensive–Moderate.*

Sea Cove Motel. Cheap—and, believe it or not, charming, if you really want to be *on* the water. Next to its land-built motel rooms and efficiencies, this property offers three houseboats at a plain but private dockside. One has multiple rooms on upper and lower decks, the other two are self-contained units. Houseboat units have no bath. The motel has zero amenities, but bathrooms are cleaned at least twice a day. There is nothing cheaper in the Keys. *MM 54, OS, 12685 Overseas Hwy., 33050, tel. 305/289-0800. 28 rooms, efficiencies, most with shared bathroom. Facilities: fishing pier, barbecue. AE, D, MC, V. Inexpensive.*

Ramrod Key
Lodging

Looe Key Reef Resort and Dive Center. This two-story motel attracts divers because of its scuba facilities. In the tiny lobby, the front desk doubles as a package liquor store. Rooms are spartan but comfortable, with firm mattresses and ocean-blue bedspreads and carpets. The least desirable rooms are the three singles without a canal view. Guests can make an appointment for free pickup from the private airstrip on Summerland Key. *MM 27.5, US 1, OS, Box 509, 33042, tel. 305/872-2215 or 800/942-5397. 23 rooms with bath. Facilities: restaurant, poolside tiki bar and raw bar, air conditioners, cable TV, outdoor pool, PADI-rated 5-star dive shop, 400' of boat* *dock, 3 Coast Guard–certified dive boats, dive and snorkel packages, 1 room for disabled. D, MC, V. Inexpensive.*

The Arts and Nightlife

The Arts

The Keys are more than warm weather and luminous scenery—a vigorous and sophisticated artistic community flourishes here. Key West alone currently claims among its residents 55 full-time writers and 500 painters and craftsmen. Arts organizations in the Keys sponsor many special events, some lasting only a weekend, others spanning an entire season.

The monthly *Island Navigator,* Monroe County's only countywide, general-interest newspaper, is free at banks, campgrounds, and stores. Its monthly community calendar lists cultural and sports events.

Three free publications covering Key West arts, music, and literature are available at hotels and other high-traffic areas. The weekly *Island Life,* the most current and complete, is published by JBM Publications (517 Duval St., Suite 200, Key West 33040, tel. 305/294–1616). *Solares Hill,* a monthly community newspaper, is published by Key West Publications, Inc. (1217 White St., Key West 33040, tel. 305/294–3602). In the Upper and Middle Keys, the weekly *Free Press* (Box 469, Islamorada 33036, tel. 305/664–2266) is available at hotels, motels, and retail outlets.

Theater   **Red Barn Theater** (319 Duval St. [rear], Key West, tel. 305/296–9911), a professional, 94-seat theater in its 13th year, performs dramas, comedies, and musicals, including plays by new playwrights.

Tennessee Williams Fine Arts Center (Florida Keys Community College, 5901 W. Junior College Rd., Key West, tel. 305/296–9081, ext. 326) presents chamber music, dance, jazz concerts, and plays (dramatic and musical) with national and international stars, and other performing-arts events, November–April.

Waterfront Playhouse (Mallory Sq., Key West, tel. 305/294–5015) is a mid-1850s wrecker's warehouse that was converted into a 185-seat, non-Equity community theater presenting comedy and drama November–May.

Nightlife

Key Largo   **Coconuts Restaurant and Bar** (MM 100, OS, in the Marina Del Mar Resort and Marina, tel. 305/451–4107) starts out the evening with soft island music, changing to top 40 after 10 PM.

Key West   **Capt. Tony's Saloon** (428 Greene St., tel. 305/294–1838) is a landmark bar owned until 1988 by a legend in his own right, Captain Tony Tarracino—a former bootlegger, smuggler, mercenary, gunrunner, gambler, and raconteur. The building dates from 1851 when it was first used as a morgue and ice house; later it was Key West's first telegraph station. The bar here was the original Sloppy Joe's from 1933 to 1937. Hemingway was a regular here, and Jimmy Buffet got his start at Capt. Tony's. Live country and rhythm-and-blues make the scene nowadays, and the house drink, the Pirates' Punch, contains a secret rum-based formula.

American Express offers Travelers Cheques built for two.

American Express® Cheques *for Two*. The first Travelers Cheques that allow either of you to use them because both of you have signed them. And only one of you needs to be present to purchase them.

Cheques *for Two* are accepted anywhere regular American Express Travelers Cheques are, which is just about everywhere. So stop by your bank, AAA* or any American Express Travel Service Office and ask for Cheques *for Two*.

Travelers Cheques

Havana Docks Lounge (1 Duval St., tel. 305/296–4600) is a high-energy disco club popular with young locals and visitors. The Havana Docks deck is a good place to watch the sun set when Mallory Square gets too crowded.

Margaritaville Cafe (500 Duval St., tel. 305/292–1435) is owned by Key West resident and recording star Jimmy Buffett, who has been known to perform here, but not very often. The house special drink is, of course, a margarita. Live music nightly.

Sloppy Joe's (201 Duval St., Key West, tel. 305/294–5717) is the successor to a famous speakeasy named for its founder, Captain Joe Russell. Ernest Hemingway liked to gamble in a partitioned club room in back. Decorated with Hemingway memorabilia and marine flags, the bar is popular with tourists and is full and noisy all the time. Live entertainment nightly.

The Top Lounge (430 Duval St., tel. 305/296–2991) is located on the seventh floor of the La Concha Holiday Inn, Key West's tallest building, and it's one of the best places from which to view the sunset. The Top features Coconuts Comedy Club Wednesday through Sunday. Also at La Concha, on the ground floor, is Crazy Daizy's, serving deli food and presenting weekend entertainment.

9 Walt Disney World® and the Orlando Area

By Catherine
Fredman

Long before the strains of "It's A Small World" echoed through the palmetto scrub, other theme parks tempted visitors away from the beaches into the scruffy interior of Central Florida. I–4 hadn't even been built when Dick and Julie Pope created Cypress Gardens, which now holds the record as Central Florida's oldest continuously running attraction. Busch Gardens was founded a quarter-century later, in 1959, as an exotic animal sideshow attached to a brewery and beer garden.

But when the Magic Kingdom opened on October 1, 1971, and was immediately successful, the Central Florida theme park scene became big business. Sea World filled its tanks two years afterward. Epcot Center debuted in 1982. Disney–MGM Studios Theme Park threw down the movie gauntlet in 1989; Universal Studios answered the challenge one year later.

The problem for visitors with tight schedules or slim wallets is that each of the parks is worth a visit. But if you're staying in the Orlando area, a decision can be made on the basis of distance. Cypress Gardens is a 60-minute drive through the dusty citrus groves, which sometimes seems to take forever. The Magic Kingdom, Epcot Center, and Sea World are not to be missed. Of the two movie parks, Universal Studios and Disney–MGM Studios, the former is probably the more spectacular.

All this grew up around a clean, sleepy farming town founded as a military outpost, Fort Gatlin, in 1838. Though not on any major waterway, Orlando was surrrounded by small, clear, spring-fed lakes, and transplanted northerners planted spawling oak trees, which vary the original landscape of palmetto scrub and citrus groves. Though this graceful, quiet city often seems to visitors to be lost in the shadow of the theme parks, most of the tourist development is in southern Orlando, along the I–4 corridor south of Florida's Turnpike. Orlando itself has become a growing center of national and international business activity, and north of downtown are several handsome, prosperous suburbs, most notably Winter Park, where the pace of life is still leisurely and refined.

The Orlando area is an obvious destination for vacationing families. All the theme parks get high marks from young travelers. And parents appreciate the good hotel facilities for children, which range from okay to fabulous. The only problem is that the times that you can go, because your youngsters are out of school, are the times when every other child in the universe is out of school and every other parent is packing up the car to drive to Orlando. These crowds may not be a problem, or they may—preschoolers can find them overwhelming. For that reason, if your children are of varying ages and those in school are good students, consider taking them out school so that you can visit in the less congested off-season. If your children cannot afford to miss school, try to take your vacation in late May or early June (as soon as the school year ends).

Essential Information

Important Addresses and Numbers

Visitor
Information For general information about Walt Disney World, contact **Walt Disney World** (Guest Letters, Box 10040, Lake Buena Vista, FL 32830, tel. 407/824–4321, TDD 407/827–5141). Request the

Walt Disney World Vacation Guide (free). For reservations or accommodations and entertainment, phone the Central Reservations Office (CRO, tel. 407/W–DISNEY; TDD, 407/345–5984). To be a member of the audience at a show being taped at Disney–MGM Studios, call Production Information (tel. 407/560–3434).

Other area visitors bureaus include:

Kissimmee/St. Cloud Convention and Visitors' Bureau (1925 E. Irlo Bronson Hwy., Kissimmee, FL 34744, tel. 407/847–5000, 407/363–5800, or 800/327–9159).

Orlando/Orange County Convention and Visitors Bureau (8445 International Dr., Orlando, FL 32819, tel. 407/363–5800).

Winter Park Chamber of Commerce (Box 280, Winter Park, FL 32790, tel. 407/644–8281).

Emergencies **Police** or **ambulance** (tel. 911). All the area's major theme parks have first-aid centers.

Hospitals Hospital emergency rooms are open 24 hours a day. The most accessible hospital is the **Orlando Regional Medical Center/Sand Lake Hospital,** located in the International Drive area (9400 Turkey Lake Rd., tel. 407/351–8500).

24-Hour **Eckerd Drugs** (908 Lee Rd., Orlando, tel. 407/644–6908) is just
Pharmacies off I–4 at the Lee Road exit, and **Walgreen's** (6201 International Drive, tel. 407/345–8311) is opposite Wet 'n' Wild.

Dentists **Emergency dental referral** (tel. 407/847–7474).

Arriving and Departing

By Plane More than 21 scheduled airlines and more than 30 charter firms operate in and out of Orlando International Airport, providing direct service to more than 100 cities in the United States and overseas. At last count, **Delta Airlines,** the official airline of Walt Disney World, had more than 90 flights daily to and from Orlando International. The airport is also a major hub for **United Airlines.** Other airlines serving the airport include **America West, American, Bahamasair, British Airways, Continental, Icelandair, KLM, Mexicana, Northwest, TransBrasil, TWA,** and **USAir.**

Between the Find out in advance whether your hotel offers free airport
Airport and shuttles; if not, ask for a recommendation.
the Hotels
Public buses operate between the airport and the main terminal of the **Tri-County Transit Authority** (1200 W. South St., Orlando, tel. 407/841–8240). Though the cost is 75¢, other options are preferable since downtown is far from most of the hotels used by theme park vacationers.

Mears Transportation Group (tel. 407/423–5566) has meet-and-greet service—they'll meet you at the gate, help you with your luggage, and whisk you away, either in an 11-passenger van, a town car, or a limo. Vans run to Walt Disney World and along U.S. 192 every 30 minutes; prices range from $12.50 one-way for adults ($8.50 for children 4–11) to $22 round-trip adults ($16 children 4–11). Limo rates run around $50–$60 for a town car that will accommodate three or four and $90 for a stretch limo that will seat six. **Town & Country Limo** (tel. 407/828–3035) charges $30 to $40 one-way for up to seven, depending on the hotel, while **First Class Transportation** (tel. 407/578-0022) charges $45 one-way for up to four people.

Taxis take only a half hour to get from the airport to most hotels used by WDW visitors, and charge about $25 plus tip to the International Drive area, about $10 more to the U.S. 192 area.

By Train **Amtrak** (tel. 800/USA-RAIL) operates the Silver Star and the Silver Meteor to Florida. Both stop in Winter Park (150 Morse Blvd.), in Orlando (1400 Sligh Blvd.), and then, 20 minutes later, in Kissimmee (416 Pleasant St.).

If you want to have your car in Florida without driving it there, board the **Auto-Train** in Lorton, VA, near Washington, DC. Its southern terminus is Sanford, FL, some 23 miles from Orlando.

By Bus **Greyhound** (consult directory for number in your locality) buses stop in Orlando at 555 N. Magruder Avenue, tel. 407/843-7720.

Getting Around

Though public transportation in Orlando is practically nonexistent and taxis are expensive because of the distances involved, it is by no means absolutely necessary to rent a car when you are in Orlando. If you are staying at a Disney hotel, or if you purchase a four- or five-day passport instead of buying daily admission tickets to the Disney parks, your transportation within Walt Disney World is free. (*See* Exploring Walt Disney World, *below*.) Outside Walt Disney World, just about every hotel, and even many motels, are linked to one of several private transportation systems that shuttle travelers back and forth to most of the area attractions for only a few dollars. However, should you want to visit the major theme parks outside Walt Disney World, venture off the beaten track, or eat where most tourists don't, then a rental car is essential. Fortunately, Orlando offers some of the lowest rental car rates in the entire United States.

By Car The most important artery in the Orlando area is **I–4**. This interstate highway, which links the Atlantic Coast to Florida's Gulf of Mexico, ties everything together, and you'll invariably receive directions in reference to it. The problem is that I–4, though considered an east–west expressway in our national road system (where even numbers signify an east–west orientation and odd numbers a north–south orientation), I–4 actually runs north and south in the Orlando area. So when the signs say east, you are usually going north, and when the signs say west, you are usually going south. Think north–EAST and south–WEST.

Another main drag is **International Drive**, a.k.a. I-Drive, which has many major hotels, restaurants, and shopping centers. You can get onto International Drive from I–4 Exits 28, 29, and 30B.

The other main road, **U.S. 192,** cuts across I–4 at Exits 25A and 25B. This highway goes through the Kissimmee area and crosses Walt Disney World property, taking you to the Magic Kingdom's main entrance. U.S. 192 is sometimes called by its former names, Spacecoast Parkway and Irlo Bronson Memorial Highway.

By Bus If you are staying along International Drive, in Kissimmee, or in Orlando proper, you can ride public buses to get around the immediate area. To find out which bus to take, ask your hotel clerk or call the **Tri-County Transit Authority Information Office** (tel. 407/841–8240) during business hours. Fares are 75¢, 10¢ extra for transfers.

By Taxi Taxi fares start at $2.45 and cost $1.40 for each mile thereafter. Call **Yellow Cab Co.** (tel. 407/699–9999) or **Town and Country Cab** (tel. 407/828–3035). Sample fares are: to WDW's Magic Kingdom, about $20 from International Drive, $11–$15 from U.S. 192; to Universal Studios, $6–$11 from International Drive, $25–$30 from U.S. 192; to downtown Orlando's Church Street Station, $20–$25 from International Drive, $30–$40 from U.S. 192.

From the Hotels to the Attractions Scheduled service and charters linking just about every hotel and major attraction in the area are available from **Mears Transportation Group** (tel. 407/839–1570), **Gray Line of Orlando** (tel. 407/422–0744), **Rabbit Bus Lines** (tel. 407/291–2424), and **Phoenix Tours** (tel. 407/859–4211). In addition, many hotels run their own shuttles especially for guests; to arrange a ride, ask your hotel's concierge, inquire at the front desk, or phone the operator directly.

One-way fares are usually $6–$7 per adult, a couple of dollars less for children 4–11, between major hotel areas and the Disney parks. Excursion fares to Cypress Gardens are $27 per person, including admission as well as round-trip fare.

Guided Tours

Theme Park Orientation Tours Walt Disney World's **Magic Kingdom** operates 3½- to 4-hour guided orientation tours ($5 per adult, $3.50 per child, plus park admission). Tours include visits to some of the rides, but don't expect to go to the head of the line—you still have to wait your turn. For schedules, ask at City Hall.

Reserve up to three weeks in advance for the two four-hour behind-the-scenes tours of **Epcot Center,** open to guests 16 and up ($20 plus park admission; tel. 407/345–5860): Hidden Treasures of the World Showcase (Sun., Wed., and Fri. 9:30–1:30) and Gardens of the World (Mon.–Wed., 9–1).

Among many other educational programs, **Sea World**'s guided, 90-minute **Behind-the-Scenes Tour** ($5.95 adults, $4.95 children 3–9) provides a close-up look at the park's breeding, research, and training facilities, and is as interesting to children as to adults, as is the 45-minute **Let's Talk Training** presentation ($5.95 adults, $4.95 children 3–9), which introduces guests to Sea World's animal behavior and training techniques.

Balloon Rides **Balloons by Terry** (93529 Edgewater Dr., Orlando, tel. 407/422–3529) will give you an early wake-up call, meet you at Church Street Station for juice and coffee, then transport you to the balloon launch site, take you floating above the city for an hour, and return you to Church Street for a champagne breakfast. The fare is $150 per adult, $100 for children.

Aerial Adventures (124 W. Pine St., Orlando, tel. 407/841–UPUP) offers blimp rides as well as hot-air balloon trips. The 30- and 60-minute blimp trips cost $75 and $150 per passenger, the balloon rides the same as those from Balloons by Terry (but no reductions for children).

Rise & Float Balloon Tours (5767 Major Blvd., opposite Universal Studios at the Mystery Fun House, Orlando, tel. 407/352–8191) takes you up in a 10-passenger hot-air balloon decorated with two hot-pink flamingoes and a giant palm tree. There's a regular Champagne Balloon Excursion ($150 per adult, $280 per couple, $85 for children under 11), and a romantic For Lovers Only trip goes aloft with one couple at a time, with a picnic basket laden with champagne, fruits, cheeses, crackers, and pastries ($350 per couple).

Boat Tour **Scenic Boat Tour** (312 E. Morse Blvd., Winter Park, tel. 407/644–4056) is a relaxing, hour-long cruise past 12 miles of fine old homes and through the grounds of Rollins College, on one of Winter Park's three main lakes, which are connected by 100-year-old canals.

Helicopter Rides Six different area tours are available from the **Falcon Helicopter Service** (8990 International Dr., next to Caruso's Palace, Orlando, tel. 407/352–1753; at the Hyatt Hotel at I–4 and U.S. 192, (no phone); at the Howard Johnson's (5071 W. Irlo Bronson Memorial Hwy., Kissimmee, tel. 407/397–0228); and at Universal Studios (no phone). Trips range from a four-minute overflight of Sea World, a five-minute foray above Universal Studios and Wet & Wild, an eight-minute trip above all three, and a 15-minute aerial tour of Walt Disney World, to a special half-hour Grand Tour flight that shows off all the major theme parks plus downtown Orlando. Fares range from $15–$130 for adults, $15–$100 for children ages 3–11.

Exploring
Walt Disney World

Numbers in the margin correspond to points of interest on the Orlando Area map.

➊ **Walt Disney World** (WDW) has its own complete transportation system that can get you wherever you want to go. It's fairly simple to understand once you get the hang of it.

The elevated **monorail** serves many important destinations. It has two loops: one linking the Magic Kingdom, an area known as the Transportation and Ticket Center (TTC), and a handful of resorts, including the Contemporary and Polynesian Village; and the other looping from the TTC direct to Epcot Center.

Motor **launches** connect WDW destinations located on waterways. Specifically, they operate between the Epcot Center resorts (except the Caribbean Beach) and Disney–MGM Studios and between Discovery Island, in Bay Lake, and the Magic Kingdom, Fort Wilderness, and the Polynesian, Contemporary, and Grand Floridian resorts (Discovery Island admission ticket, WDW resort ID, or multiday admission ticket required).

In addition, **buses** provide direct service from every on-site resort to both major and minor theme parks, and express buses go direct between the major theme parks. To Typhoon Lagoon, you can go direct from (or make connections at) the Disney Vil-

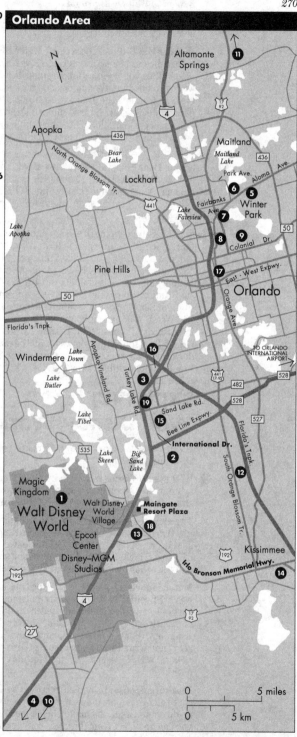

Orlando Area

lage Marketplace, Epcot Center, and the Epcot Center resorts (the Beach and Yacht Clubs, the Caribbean Beach Resort, the Swan, and the Dolphin).

From the Epcot Center resort area, **trams** operate to the International Gateway of the park's World Showcase section.

Monorail, launches, buses, and trams all operate during the hours that you'll want them—usually from early in the morning until at least midnight. (Hours are shorter during early closing periods.) Check on the operating hours of the service you need if you plan to be out later than that.

All of this transportation is free if you are staying at an on-site resort, or if you hold a three-park ticket. If not, you can buy yourself unlimited transportation within Walt Disney World for $2.50 a day.

Every theme park has a parking lot—and all are huge. Always write down exactly where you park your car and take the number with you. Trams make frequent trips between the parking area and the parks' turnstile areas. For each lot, the cost is $4 (free to Walt Disney World resort guests with ID), except for Typhoon Lagoon and River Country, where parking is free.

To make the most of your time at the parks, here are a few tips:

- See the three-star attractions either first thing in the morning, during a parade, or at the very end of the day.

- Whenever possible when you're visiting the theme parks, eat in a restaurant that takes reservations, or have meals before or after mealtime rush hours (from 11 AM to 2 PM and again from 6 to 8 PM). Or leave the theme parks altogether for a meal in one of the hotels.

- Spend afternoons in high-capacity sit-down shows or catching live entertainment—or leave the park entirely for a swim in your hotel pool.

- If you plan to take in Typhoon Lagoon, go early in your visit (but not on a weekend). You may like it so much that you'll want to go again.

- If a meal with the characters is in your plans, save it for the end of your trip, when your youngsters will have become accustomed to these large, looming figures.

- Familiarize yourself with all age and height restrictions—and don't let your younger children get excited about rides they're too short or too young to experience.

Admission Fees Visiting Walt Disney World is not cheap, especially if you have a child or two along. Everyone 10 and older pays adult prices; reductions are available for children 3–9. Children under age 3 get in free. No discounted family tickets are available.

Tickets In Disneyspeak, "ticket" refers to a single day's admission to the Magic Kingdom, Epcot Center, or the Disney–MGM Studios. A ticket is good in the park for which you buy it only on the day you buy it; if you buy a one-day ticket and later decide to extend your visit, you can apply the cost of it toward the purchase of any passport (but only before you leave the park). Exchanges can be made at City Hall in the Magic Kingdom, at Earth Station in Epcot Center, or at Guest Relations at Disney–MGM.

Passports Both the **4-day Super Pass** and the **5-day Super Duper Pass** admit you to all three major theme parks and include unlimited use of Disney's transportation system. A Super Duper Pass also admits you to WDW's minor parks—Discovery Island, Pleasure Island, River Country, and Typhoon Lagoon—for up to seven days from the day you first use it. Each time you use a passport the entry date is stamped on it; remaining days may be used years in the future. A variety of annual passes are also available, at a cost only slightly more than a five-day Super Duper Pass; if you plan to visit twice in a year, these are a good deal.

Prices At press time (July 1993), WDW admission prices were as follows, not including 6.5% tax.

One-day ticket	$35 adults, $28 children
Four-day Super Pass	$125 adults, $98 children
Five-day Super Duper Pass	$170 adults, $135 children
River Country	$13.25 adults, $10.50 children
Combined River Country/ Discovery Island	$16.75 adults, $12.25 children
Discovery Island	$8.50 adults, $4.75 children
Typhoon Lagoon	$20.50 adults, $16.50 children
Pleasure Island	$13.95 adults, $13.95 children

Italicized prices are for visitors staying in Disney-owned on-site resorts and for most resorts on Hotel Plaza Boulevard near Disney Village Marketplace.

Tickets and passports to Walt Disney World, Epcot Center, and Disney–MGM Studios Theme Park can be purchased at admission booths at the TTC, in all on-site resorts (if you're a registered guest), and at the Walt Disney World kiosk at Orlando International Airport (2nd floor, main terminal). American Express, Visa, and MasterCard are accepted, as are cash, personal checks (with ID), and traveler's checks.

Opening and Closing Hours Operating hours for the Magic Kingdom, Epcot Center, and Disney–MGM Studios Theme Park vary widely throughout the year and change for school and legal holidays. In general, the longest days are during the prime summer months and over the year-end holidays, when the Magic Kingdom is open to midnight (later on New Year's Eve); Epcot Center is open to 11 PM; and Disney–MGM is open to 9 PM.

At other times, Epcot Center and Disney–MGM are open until 8 and the Magic Kingdom until 6 (Main Street until 7)—but there are variations, so call ahead.

Note that though the Magic Kingdom, Epcot Center, and Disney–MGM officially open at 9 AM, visitors may enter at 8:30, and sometimes at 8. The parking lots open at least an hour before the parks. Arriving at the Magic Kingdom turnstiles before "rope drop," the official opening time, you can breakfast in a restaurant on Main Street, which opens before the rest of the park, and be ready to dash to one of the popular attractions in other lands at rope drop. Arriving in Epcot Center or Disney–MGM studios, you can make dinner reservations before the crowds arrive and take in some of the attractions and pavilions well before the major crowds descend, which is usually at about 10.

Ratings Every visitor leaves the Magic Kingdom, Epcot Center, and Disney–MGM Studios with a different opinion about what was "the best." Some attractions get raves from all visitors, while others are enjoyed most by young children or older travelers. To take this into account, our descriptions rate each attraction with ★, ★ ★, or ★ ★ ★, depending on the strength of its appeal to the visitor group noted by the italics.

Magic Kingdom

For most people, the Magic Kingdom *is* Walt Disney World. Certainly it is both the heart and soul of the Disney empire. The Magic Kingdom is comparable to California's Disneyland; it was the first Disney outpost in Florida when it opened in 1972, and it is the park that traveled, with modifications, to France and Japan. In fact, for many years it was the only Disney outpost, Epcot Center not having opened until 10 years later and Disney–MGM seven years after that.

For a park that wields such worldwide influence, the Magic Kingdom is surprisingly small: At barely 98 acres, it is the tiniest of Walt Disney World's Big Three. However, packed into six different "lands" are some 46 major crowd-pleasers, and that's not counting all the ancillary attractions: shops, eateries, live entertainment, cartoon characters, fireworks, and parades.

The park is laid out on a north-south axis, with Cinderella Castle at the epicenter and the various lands surrounding it in a broad circle. Upon passing through the entrance gates, you immediately discover yourself in **Town Square,** a central area containing **City Hall,** the principal information center. Here you can pick up the *Magic Kingdom Guide Book* and a schedule of daily events; search for misplaced belongings or companions; and ask questions of the omnisicient staffers behind the desk.

Town Square directly segues into **Main Street,** a boulevard filled with Victorian-style stores and dining spots. Main Street runs due north and ends at **The Hub,** a large tree-lined circle in front of Cinderella Castle. Moving clockwise from The Hub, the Magic Kingdom's different lands are **Adventureland, Frontierland, Liberty Square, Fantasyland** (located directly behind Cinderella Castle), and **Tomorrowland.**

Step right up to the elevated platform above the Magic Kingdom's entrance for a ride on the **Walt Disney World Railroad.** The 1½-mile track runs along the perimeter of the Magic Kingdom, through the woods and past Tom Sawyer Island and other attractions; stops are in Frontierland and Mickey's Starland. It's a great introduction to the layout of the park and a much welcome relief for tired feet. The four trains run at five- to seven-minute intervals; a complete circuit takes 21 minutes. *Audience: All ages. Rating:* ★

Main Street Although attractions with a capital "A" are minimal on Main Street, there are plenty of inducements to spend more than the 40 minutes most visitors usually take. The stores that most of the structures house range from the **House of Magic,** complete with trick-showing proprietors, to the **Harmony Barber Shop,** where you can have yourself shorn and shaved, to a milliner's

Walt Disney World

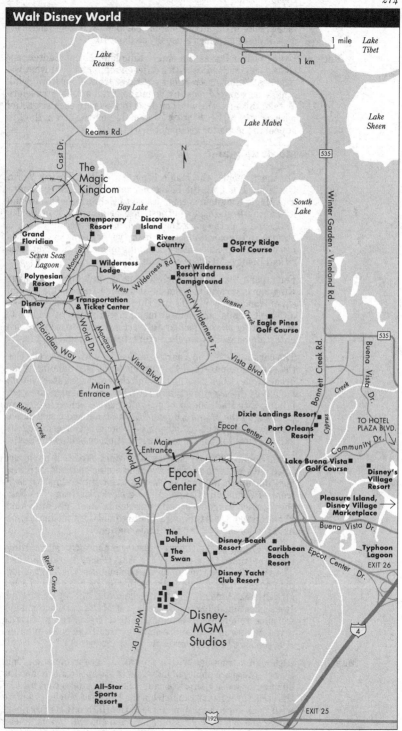

Lake Tibet

Lake Reams

Lake Mabel

Lake Sheen

Reams Rd.

Cast Dr.

535

Winter Garden - Vineland Rd.

The Magic Kingdom

South Lake

Bay Lake

Contemporary Resort

Discovery Island

Osprey Ridge Golf Course

Grand Floridian

River Country

Seven Seas Lagoon

Wilderness Lodge

Fort Wilderness Resort and Campground

Bonnet Creek

Polynesian Resort

West Wilderness Rd.

Eagle Pines Golf Course

Disney Inn

Transportation & Ticket Center

Monorail

Fort Wilderness Tr.

535

Floridian Way

World Dr.

Monorail

Vista Blvd

Vista Blvd.

Bonnett Creek Rd.

Buena Vista Dr.

Reedy Creek

Main Entrance

Cypress Creek

Dixie Landings Resort

TO HOTEL PLAZA BLVD.

Main Entrance

Port Orleans Resort

Community Dr.

Epcot Center Dr.

Epcot Center

Lake Buena Vista Golf Course

Disney's Village Resort

World Dr.

Pleasure Island, Disney Village Marketplace

Buena Vista Dr.

The Dolphin

Disney Beach Resort

Reedy Creek

The Swan

Caribbean Beach Resort

Epcot Center Dr.

Typhoon Lagoon

EXIT 26

Disney Yacht Club Resort

Disney-MGM Studios

I-4

World Dr.

All-Star Sports Resort

192

EXIT 25

0   1 mile
0   1 km

N

emporium stocking Cat-in-the-Hat fantasies, to all sorts of snacks and souvenirs. The **Penny Arcade** lets you try vintage coin-operated games and kinescopes. The best time to shop is mid-afternoon, when the lines at the rides are long and slow.

Six screens run continuous vintage Disney cartoons in the cool, air-conditioned quiet of the **Main Street Cinema,** halfway up Main Street on the right. It's a great opportunity to see the genius of Walt Disney and to see *Steamboat Willie,* Mickey Mouse's debut cartoon. *Audience: All ages. Rating:* ★ ★

Adventureland From the scrubbed brick, manicured lawns, and meticulously pruned trees of the Central Plaza, an artfully dilapidated wooden bridge leads to Adventureland, Disney's version of jungle fever. The landscape artists went wild here: South African Cape honeysuckle droops, Brazilian bougainvillea drapes, Mexican flame vines cling, spider plants clone, and three different varieties of palm trees sway, all creating a seemingly spontaneous mess. **Swiss Family Treehouse** is the first attraction on your left (the camouflaged entrance is *way* over to the left). Based on the classic novel by Johann Wyss about the adventures of a family shipwrecked on the way to America, the treehouse shows what you can do with a big banyan and a lot of imagination: The kitchen sink is made of a giant clamshell, the boys' room, strewn with clothing, has two hammocks instead of beds, and an ingenious system of rain barrels and bamboo pipes provides running water in every room (German visitors seem especially fascinated by this). *Audience: All ages; toddlers unsteady on their feet may have trouble with the stairs. Rating:* ★ ★

During the **Jungle Cruise,** you glide through three continents along four rivers: the Congo, the Nile, the Mekong, and the Amazon. The canopied launches pack in visitors tighter than sardines, the safari-suited guide makes a point of checking his pistol, and the *Irrawady Irma* or *Mongala Millie* is off for another "perilous" journey. The guide's spiel is surprisingly funny, with just the right blend of cornball humor and the gently snide. *Audience: All ages. Rating:* ★ ★

Time Out Among the fast munchies in the Magic Kingdom, some of the best are the fresh pineapple spears at Adventureland's **Aloha Isle.**

"Avast, ye scurvy scum!" is the sort of greeting your kids will proclaim for the next week—which gives you an idea of the impact of the stellar **Pirates of the Caribbean.** This 10-minute boat ride is Disney at its best: memorable vignettes, incredible detail, a gripping story and catchy music. Emerging from a pitch-black tunnel of time, you're literally in the middle of a furious battle as a pirate ship, cannons blazing, attacks a stone fortress. Audio-Animatronic pirates hoist the Jolly Roger while brave soldiers scurry to defend the fort. The wild antics of the pirates result in a conflagration, the town goes up in flames, and everyone goes to their just reward. *Audience: All ages. Rating:* ★ ★

Inside the blessedly air-conditioned Polynesian longhouse that houses the **Enchanted Tiki Birds,** the "Tropical Serenade" is sung and whistled by hundreds of Audio-Animatronic figures: exotic birds, swaying flowers, and Tiki god statues with blinking red eyes. This was Disney's first Audio-Animatronics attraction; the animatronics still hold up fine but the audio could use an update. *Audience: All ages. Rating:* ★

Frontierland Located in the northwest quadrant of the Magic Kingdom, Frontierland invokes the spirit of the American frontier, with Disney staffers dressed in checked shirts, leather vests, cowboy hats, and brightly colored neckerchiefs. Banjo and fiddle music twang from tree to tree.

At rope drop, the hordes hoof it to **Splash Mountain.** Based on the animated sequences in Disney's 1946 film, *Song of the South,* it features AudioAnimatronic creations of Brer Rabbit, Brer Bear, Brer Fox, and a menagerie of brer beasts. An eight-person hollowed-out log carries you through a lily pond and up the mountain. You get one heart-stopping pause at the top—just long enough to grab the safety bar—and then the boat plummets down the world's longest and sharpest flume drop right into a gigantic briar patch. *Audience: All ages. No pregnant women or guests wearing back, neck, or leg braces; minimum height 42 inches. Rating:* ★ ★ ★

Scoot across the footbridge to another classic Disney ride, **Big Thunder Mountain Railroad.** As any true rollercoaster lover can tell you, this three-minute ride is a tame one, but the thrills are there, thanks to the intricate details and stunning scenery. Set in Gold Rush days, the runaway railroad train rushes and rattles past 20 Audio-Animatronic figures—including donkeys, chickens, a goat and a grizzled old miner surprised in his bathtub—a derelict mining town, hot springs, and a flash flood. *Audience: All except young children. No pregnant women or guests in back, neck, or leg braces; minimum height 40 inches. Rating:* ★ ★ ★

Head back across the footbridge past Splash Mountain and continue to your left along Frontierland's main drag to the landing stage for the rafts to **Tom Sawyer Island**—actually, two islands connected by an old-fashioned swing bridge. Most of the attractions are located on the main island: the mystery cave, a pitch-black (almost) labyrinth where the wind wails in a truly spooky fashion; Injun Joe's cave, all pointy stalactites and stalagmites; Harper's Mill, an old-fashioned grist mill (nothing scary here); and, in a clearing at the top of the hill, a rustic playground for younger kids. On the other island is Fort Sam Clemens, a log fortress from which you can fire air guns (with great booms and cracks) at the soporific passengers on the Liberty Square Riverboat. *Audience: All ages. Rating:* ★ ★

Back on the main street, a row of barns, false-fronted buildings, and other structures straight out of Dodge City house shops, eateries, and two theaters. The first one on your right houses the **Country Bear Jamboree,** a stage show in which wisecracking, corn-pone Audio-Animatronics bears joke, sing, and play country music and 1950s rock 'n' roll. *Audience: All ages. Rating:* ★ ★ ★

The riproaring, raucous, corny, high-kicking **Diamond Horseshoe Jamboree** features a sextet of dance hall girls and high-spirited cowboys, a lovelorn saloon keeper, and Lily, a shimmying, feather-boa-toting, reincarnation of Mae West. Seating begins half an hour before curtain time and snacks and light refreshments may be purchased at your table. *Showtimes: 10:45, 12:15, 1:45, 3:30, and 4:45; reservations essential. Book in early morning at the Main Street booth in front of the Disneyana*

Collectibles (12:15 show fills up first) or show up 30 minutes before showtime to wait for cancellations. Audience: All except young children. Rating: ★ ★

Liberty Square The weathered siding gives way to neat clapboard and solid brick, the mesquite and cactus are replaced by stately oaks and masses of azalea, and the rough-and-tumble western frontier gently slides into colonial America. The shops in this area tend to sell more arts than kitsch, and the **Liberty Tree Tavern,** a gracious, table-service restaurant that could have been airlifted from Colonial Williamsburg, is one of the best at the Magic Kingdom; reservations are essential.

The **Hall of Presidents,** a 30-minute multimedia tribute to the Constitution, is another marvel of Audio-Animatronics. The two-part show starts with a film discussing the importance of the Constitution; the second half is a roll call of all 42 American presidents, including William Jefferson Clinton. The detail is lifelike right down to the brace on Franklin Delano Roosevelt's leg, and the robots can't resist nodding, fidgeting, and even whispering to each other while waiting for their name to come up. *Audience: Older children and adults. Rating:* ★ ★

The **Liberty Square Riverboat** is a real old-fashioned steamboat, the *Richard F. Irvine* (named for a key Disney designer), authentic from the big rear paddlewheel to the gingerbread trim on its three decks and its calliope whistle. The 15-minute trip is slow and certainly not thrilling, but it's a relaxing break for all concerned. *Audience: All but young children. Rating:* ★

The **Mike Fink Keel Boats** ply the same waters as the Liberty Square Riverboat, but these craft are short and dumpy and you have to listen to a heavyhanded, noisy spiel about those roistering, roustabout days along the Missouri. *Strategy: Skip this on your first visit. Audience: All ages. Rating:* ★

Part walk-through, part ride on a "doom buggie," the eight-minute **Haunted Mansion** ride is scary but not terrifying, and the special effects are phenomenal. Catch the glowing bat's eyes on the wallpaper; the strategically placed gusts of damp, cold air; the wacky inscriptions on the tombstones; and the spectral xylophone player. *Audience: All except young children. Rating:* ★ ★ ★

Fantasyland You can enter Fantasyland from Frontierland or by skyway from Tomorrowland, but the classic introduction is a stroll through the glistening white towers of the **Cinderella Castle.** Although often confused with Disneyland's Sleeping Beauty Castle, at 180 feet this castle is more than 100 feet taller and, with its elongated towers and lacy fretwork, immeasurably more graceful.

The whirling, musical heart of Fantasyland—and maybe even of the entire Magic Kingdom—the antique **Cinderella's Golden Carrousel** has 90 prancing horses, each one completely different. The rich notes of the band organ—no calliope here—play favorite tunes from Disney movies. *Audience: All but young children. Rating:* ★ ★ ★

The first attraction on the left as you enter Fantasyland, the 3-D **Magic Journeys,** is a plotless 18-minute film about the mind-travels of five children. Once you've donned the goofy, purple 3-D glasses, you can't help reaching out to touch the apple blossoms blooming in front of you, or trying to catch the kite above your head, or leaping back from the lightning bolts. *Audience: All ages. Rating:* ★ ★

Moving clockwise through Fantasyland brings you to **Peter Pan's Flight,** a truly fantastic indoor ride. You board two-person (or one-adult, two-children) magic sailing ships, whose brightly striped sails catch the wind and soar into the skies above London en route to Never-Never-Land. Adults will especially enjoy the dreamy views of London by moonlight. *Audience: All ages. Rating:* ★ ★

Visiting Walt Disney World and *not* stopping for **It's a Small World**—why, the idea is practically un-American. Disney raided the remains of the 1964–65 New York World's Fair for this exhibit. Moving somewhat slower than a snail, barges inch through several barnlike rooms, each crammed with musical moppets dressed in various national costumes and madly singing the theme song, "It's A Small World After All." But somehow by the time you reach the end of the 11-minute ride, you're grinning and humming too. *Audience: All ages. Rating:* ★ ★

Dumbo, the Flying Elephant is one of Fantasyland's most popular rides. Jolly Dumbos fly around a central column, each pachyderm packing a couple of kids and a parent. A joystick controls each Dumbo's vertical motion, so that it appears to swoop and soar. Alas, the ears do not flap. *Audience: Young children. Rating:* ★

Baed on the Jules Verne novel and Disney's 1954 film adaptation, **20,000 Leagues under the Sea** takes passengers on 61-foot, bug-eyed, otherworldly submarines through an 11½-million-gallon pool, a world of kelp and sea grass, fantastic fish and clams, coral and icebergs, and a grasping, tentacled squid. *Audience: All ages. Rating:* ★

In the **Mad Tea Party,** based on the 1951 Disney film of *Alice in Wonderland,* you hop into oversized, pastel-color teacups and whirl for two minutes around a giant platter. If the centrifugal force hasn't shaken you up too much, check out the soused mouse that pops out of the teapot centerpiece. *Rating:* ★

Mr. Toad's Wild Ride, based on the 1949 Disney release *The Adventures of Ichabod and Mr. Toad* (itself derived from Kenneth Grahame's classic children's novel, *The Wind in the Willows*), puts you in the jump seat of the speed-loving amphibian's fliv-ver for a jolting, jarring three-minute jaunt through the English countryside. Marginally less scary than Snow White's Adventure, this ride may still startle young children. *Audience: All ages. Rating:* ★ ★

There's a surprising dearth of friendly heigh-ho-ing dwarves on **Snow White's Adventures.** In fact, from the wicked witch with the wart on her nose and the evil cackle to a forest of malevolent shrubbery, the content of this three-minute indoor spookhouse ride is unremittingly scary. *Audience: All ages; toddlers may be scared. Rating:* ★ ★

The **Skyway to Tomorrowland** takes off on its one-way aerial trip to Tomorrowland from an enchanted attic perched above the trees in the far left corner of Fantasyland. *Audience: All ages. Rating:* ★

Mickey's Starland, built in 1988 to celebrate Mickey Mouse's 60th birthday, is a rarely crowded 3-acre niche set off to the side of Fantasyland. The attractions are located in the imaginary town of Duckburg (yes, Donald and Huey, Dewey, and Louie are all here, along with a cast of other Disney characters), whose pastel-color houses are positively Lilliputian, with miniature driveways and toy-size picket fences and signs scribbled with finger paint. **Mickey's Starland Show and Hollywood Theater,** held under a yellow-and-white stripe big top, presents the television stars of "The Disney Afternoon" in a cheerful sing-along musical comedy that kids adore. Afterward, all the kids dash around backstage to **Mickey's Dressing Room,** where the star graciously signs autographs and poses for pictures with his adoring public. There's also a petting zoo with live animals at **Grandma Duck's Farm. Mickey's Treehouse** and **Minnie's Doll House** offer opportunities for climbing and exploring, and the **Mousekamaze** offers a place to get lost. *Audience: Young children, mainly. Rating:* ★ ★

Tomorrowland Frankly, this 1960s view of the future is distressingly charm-free: lots of bare white concrete and almond-color plastic, metal spires resembling elongated lightning rods, and unisex *Star Trek*–type uniforms whose silver coating and brown lining has caused them to be nicknamed "baked potatoes." The Disney Imagineers already have plans for a complete overhaul—"Discoveryland," which will portray a view of the future as imagined by past sci-fi writers. Rehabilitation is planned sometime in the mid- to late-'90s.

CircleVision 360 "American Journeys" is the first attraction on the far right as you cross the bridge into Tomorrowland. The air-conditioned circular theater holds up to 3,100 people; note that we don't say "seats"—the theater is standing-room only, so you can pirouette to catch as many as possible of the spectacular shots projected onto the 360° screen. As the name implies, the 21-minute film shown here captures the breadth and beauty of this country from sea to shining sea. *Audience: All ages. Rating:* ★ ★ ★

There's almost never a wait at **Delta Dreamflight,** which should put your suspicions on red alert. Sponsored by Delta Airlines, this ride takes a look at the adventure and romance of flying. The idea is cute but the execution—surprising given Disney's experience with special effects tricks—falls far short of thrilling. *Audience: All ages. Rating:* ★

Tune up your imagination for the two-part, standing-and-sitting **Mission to Mars,** a 20-minute simulated trip to the Red Planet, with seats that jolt in a so-called hyperspace jump, tilt and shake during hyperspace penetration, and whir and chug like one of the cars on the Grand Prix Raceway. *Audience: All ages. Rating:* ★

Who can resist **Starjets,** an old-fashioned thrill ride with small two-passenger planes swooping around a central column shaped like a Saturn rocket? Judging from the lines, neither adults nor children. The two-minute trip in the open-cockpit airplanes can be tame or exciting, depending on how you raise and lower your airplane and adjust its pitch and yaw. Ferris wheel–like view over the park all around. *Audience: All ages. Rating:* ★ ★

Just to the right of the Starjets, the open-air, five-car trains of the **WEDway PeopleMover** provide an appealing tour of Tomorrowland. Tooling along at 10 miles per hour around about

1 mile of track, Disney's vision of future mass transit is smooth and noiseless, thanks to an electromagnetic linear induction motor that has no moving parts, uses little power and emits no pollutants. *Audience: All ages. Rating:* ★

Walt Disney World picked up the **Carousel of Progress** from New York's 1964–65 World's Fair. The 22-minute show takes place in a revolving theater, where an Audio-Animatronics family hymn the improvements in American life that have resulted from the use of electricity. *Audience: All ages. Rating:* ★

Set off to the extreme left corner of Tomorrowland opposite the land's main block of shops and restaurants, **Grand Prix Raceway** incites instant addiction among kids: brightly colored Mark VII model gasoline-powered cars swerve around the four 2,260-foot tracks with much vroom-vroom-vrooming. But there's way too much waiting. *Must be 52 inches to drive. Audience: Older children. Rating:* ★

The needlelike spires and gleaming white concrete cone of **Space Mountain** are a Magic Kingdom landmark. Inside this 180-foot-high structure is arguably the world's most imaginative roller coaster. The ride only lasts two minutes and 38 seconds, and attains a top speed of 28 miles per hour, but the devious twists and invisible drops, and the fact that you can't see where you're going, make it seem twice as long and four times as thrilling. *Audience: All but young children. Rating:* ★ ★ ★

The brightly colored cable cars of the one-way **Skyway to Fantasyland** can be picked up at the station right outside of Space Mountain for the commute to the far western end of Fantasyland. *Audience: All ages. Rating:* ★

Entertainment A 30-minute-long **daily parade** proceeds down Main Street through Frontierland beginning at 3; it boasts floats, balloons, cartoon characters, dancers, singers (usually lip-synching to music played over the PA system), and much waving and cheering. **SpectroMagic** is an incredible 30-minute nighttime extravaganza of battery-lighted floats, sequined costumes, sparkling decorations and twinkling trees. **Fantasy in the Sky** is the Magic Kingdom fireworks display. Heralded by a dimming of all the lights along Main Street, a single spotlight illuminates the top turret of the Cinderella Castle and—poof!—Tinkerbell emerges in a shower of pixie dust to fly over the treetops and the crowds. Her disappearance signals the start of the fireworks.

Epcot Center

Walt Disney World was created because of Walt Disney's dream of EPCOT, an "Experimental Prototype Community of Tomorrow." He envisioned a future in which nations co-existed in peace and harmony, reaping the miraculous harvest of technological achievement. He suggested the idea as early as October 1966. But with Disneyland hemmed in by development, Disney had to search for new land. He found it in central Florida. The permanent community that he envisioned has not yet come to be, but instead we have Epcot Center, which opened in 1982, years after Disney's death, a showcase, ostensibly, for the concepts that would be incorporated into the EPCOTs of the future. Then, as now, it was composed of two parts: **Future World,** whose 10 pavilions are sponsored by major American corporations and **World Showcase,** whose 11 exhibition areas each represent a different country.

Epcot is that rare paradox—an educational theme park—and a very successful one, too. Although rides have been added over the years to try to amuse the young 'uns, the thrills are mostly in the mind. Consequently, Epcot is best suited for older children and adults. A dedicated visitor really needs two days to explore it all; to cram it into one day, get to the park early, don't waste time at sit-down meals, see the shows when the park is empty, and slow down and enjoy the shops and the live entertainment when the crowds thicken.

Epcot Center is divided into two distinct areas separated by the 40-acre World Showcase Lagoon. The monorail drops you off at the official entrance, in Future World; trams from the Walt Disney World Dolphin and Swan hotels and Disney's Yacht Club and Beach Club resorts drop you off at International Gateway, the entrance to World Showcase.

Future World Future World's inner core is composed of the **Spaceship Earth** geosphere and, just beyond it, two crescent-shape wings— **CommuniCore East** to the left and **CommuniCore West** to the right. Seven pavilions comprise the outer ring of the circle, containing both rides and interactive displays.

Balanced like a giant golf ball waiting for some celestial being to tee off, the multifaceted silver geosphere of **Spaceship Earth** is to Epcot Center what the Cinderella Castle is to the Magic Kingdom. It weighs 1 million pounds, measures 164 feet in diameter and 180 feet in height, and encompasses more than 2 million cubic feet of space. The anodized aluminum sheath is composed of 954 triangular panels, not all of equal size or shape. Since it is not a geodesic dome (which is only a half sphere), the name "geosphere" was invented for it.

Earth Station, underneath Spaceship Earth, is the principal Epcot Center information center, the place to pick up schedules of live entertainment, park brochures, and the like. The computerized WorldKey Information System kiosks, most located in Earth Station, let you obtain detailed information about every pavilion, leave messages for companions, and most important of all, make reservations for Epcot restaurants.

Besides the Earth Station information center, Spaceship Earth contains the **Spaceship Earth ride** (★ ★ ★) hands down the most popular ride at Epcot Center. Scripted by science-fiction writer Ray Bradbury and narrated by Walter Cronkite, the 15-minute journey begins in the darkest tunnels of time, proceeds through history as we know it, and ends poised on the edge of the future. Audio-Animatronic figures present history in astonishing detail.

CommuniCore East and West contain an electronic funhouse of interactive digital panels, computers, and video screens. There are so many different exhibits that you could easily spend a morning here.

Universe of Energy, the first of the pavilions on the left, or east, side of Future World, occupies a large, lopsided pyramid, sheathed in thousands of mirrors, which serve as solar collectors to power the ride and films within. One of the most technologically complex shows at Epcot Center, the Exxon-sponsored exhibit combines one half-hour ride, two films, the largest Audio-Animatronic animals ever built, 250 prehistoric trees, and enough cold, damp fog to make you think you've been transported to the inside of a defrosting icebox. (★ ★ ★)

A towering statue of a DNA double helix stands outside the gold-crowned dome of Metropolitan Life's popular **Wonders of Life** pavilion, which takes an amusing but serious and educational look at health, fitness, and modern lifestyles. One improvisational theater revue, two films, and dozens of interactive gadgets that whiz, bleep, and blink make up the Fitness Fairground. Walt Disney World's first flight simulator, **Body Wars** (★ ★ ★), takes visitors on a five-minute bumpy platelet-to-platelet ride through the human circulatory system. And the 20-minute multimedia presentation, **Cranium Command** (★ ★ ★), reveals the workings of the mind of a typical 12-year-old boy during the course of an ordinary day.

Time Out   Met Life practices its preaching at **Pure & Simple,** a food stall offering healthy snacks and full meals, and proves that nutritious can also be delicious. The prices won't give you a heart attack either.

At **Horizons** (★ ★), General Electric sponsors a relentlessly optimistic look at the once and future future. After being enjoined to "live your dreams," you ride a tram for 15 minutes past visions of the future, where great minds imagine what the world might have been like in a hundred years or so. The tram then moves past a series of tableaux of life in a future space colony. The Omega Centuri tableau, portraying a free-floating space colony, prefigures virtual reality with its games of zero-gravity basketball and simulated outdoor sports.

Shaped like a wheel, General Motors' **World of Motion** features the **TransCenter,** a 33,000-square-foot exhibit and auto showroom displaying new and experimental car models, and the 15-minute **World of Motion ride** (★ ★) essentially a dippy, feel-good frolic through scenarios depicting the history of human attempts to get somewhere else faster.

United Technologies' **Living Seas** is a favorite among children (★ ★ ★). An imaginative fountain flings surf in a never-ending wave against a rock garden beneath the stylized marquee. Inside is a 5.7-million-gallon central aquarium. The three-minute **Caribbean Coral Reef Ride** encircles the acrylic tank. Sometimes you'll catch sight of a diver, testing out the latest scuba equipment, surrounded by a cloud of parrot fish as he scatters food for the tank's denizens. After the ride, you may want to circumnavigate the tank at your own speed on an upper level, pointing out barracudas, stingrays, parrot fish, sea turtles, and even sharks, before exploring the two levels of **Sea Base Alpha,** a prototype undersea research facility. There are six interactive modules, each dedicated to a specific subject, such as the history of robotics, ocean exploration, ocean ecosystems, dolphins, porpoises, and sea lions.

Shaped like an intergalactic greenhouse, the enormous skylighted **The Land** pavilion sponsored by Nestlé dedicates 6 acres and a host of different attractions to everyone's favorite topic: food. You can easily spend two hours exploring here. The main event is a 14-minute ride called **Listen to the Land**

(★ ★ ★) where you putter through three biomes (rain forest, desert, and prairie ecological communities) and into an experimental greenhouse that demonstrates how food sources may be grown in the future, not only on Earth but also in outer space. The **Kitchen Kabaret Revue** (★) is a 12-minute Audio-Animatronics show featuring dancing fruits, vegetables, and dairy products. The **Harvest Theater** is home to a *National Geographic*–like film called *Symbiosis* (20 minutes long: ★ ★), an intelligent look at how we can profit from the earth's natural resources while ensuring that the earth benefits, too.

The last of the big three pavilions on the west side, **Journey into Imagination,** presented by Eastman Kodak, sets your mind spinning. The **Journey into Imagination Ride** (★ ★ ★) is a dreamy exploration of how creativity works. Laser beams zing back and forth, lightning crackles, letters leap out of a giant typewriter, an iridescent painting unfolds across a wall. The **Image Works** (★ ★ ★) is an electronic funhouse crammed with interactive games and wizardry. Starring Michael Jackson and Angelica Huston, the 3-D film **Captain EO** draws long lines (★). The music can be deafening, and the plot is banal, but the special effects are fascinating and hey, this is a chance to see Michael Jackson while his nose still looked normal.

World Showcase The 40-acre World Showcase Lagoon is 1⅓ miles around, but in that space, you circumnavigate the globe.

A striking rocky chasm and tumbling waterfall make just one of the high points of **Canada.** Like the Rocky Mountains and the Great Canadian North, the scale of the structures seems immense; unlike the real thing, it's managed with a trick called forced perspective, which exaggerates the smallness of the distant parts to make the entire thing look humongous. The top attraction is the 17-minute CircleVision film, **O Canada!** (★ ★ ★).

A pastiche of there-will-always-be-an-England architecture, the **United Kingdom** rambles between the elegant mansions lining a London square to the bustling, half-timbered shops of a village High Street to the thatched-roof cottages from the countryside (their thatch made of plastic broom bristles). The pavilion has no single major attraction. Instead, you can wander through shops selling tea and tea accessories, Welsh handicrafts, Royal Doulton figurines, and woolens and tartans from Pringle of Scotland, while outside, the strolling Old Globe Players coax audience members into participating in their definitely low-brow versions of Shakespeare.

You don't need the scaled-down model of the Eiffel Tower to tell you that you've arrived in **France,** specifically Paris. There's the poignant accordion music wafting out of concealed speakers, solid Mansard-roof mansions crowned with iron filigree, and delicious aromas surrounding the *Boulangerie Pâtisserie* bakeshop. The intimate Palais du Cinema, inspired by the royal theater at Fontainebleau, screens the 18-minute film **Impressions de France,** a five-screen homage to the glories of the country. (★ ★ ★)

Walk through the pointed arches of the Bab Boujouloud gate, ornamented with beautiful wood carvings and encrusted with intricate mosaics, into **Morocco.** You can take a guided tour of the pavilion (inquire of any cast member), check out the ever-changing exhibit in the **Gallery of Arts and History,** and entertain yourself examining the wares at such shops as Casablanca Carpets, Jewels of the Sahara, the Brass Bazaar, and Berber Oasis. The belly-dancing in **Restaurant Marrakesh** is tame, but youngsters like it (reservations required).

A brilliant vermillion *torii* gate epitomizes the striking yet serene mood that pervades **Japan.** Disney horticulturists deserve a hand here for their achievement in constructing a very Japanese landscape, complete with rocks, pebbled streams, pools, and hills out of all-American plants and boulders. The heart of the pavilion is a brilliant blue winged pagoda, based on the 8th-century Horyuji Temple in Nara. Entertainment is provided by Japanese musicians and demonstrations of traditional Japanese crafts.

Time Out Westerners with a yen for Asian tastes will be satisfied here at the **Yakitori House,** which serves broiled chicken and beef (a sort of Japanese shish-kebab) and batter-fried seafood and vegetables, respectively, as well as such Japanese specialties as clear soup and pickled ginger.

The **American Adventure,** housed in a scrupulous reproduction of Philadelphia's Liberty Hall presents a 100-yard dash through history called the **American Adventure show,** which uses evocative sets, the world's largest rear-projection screen (72 feet in width), enormous movable stages, and 35 Audio-Animatronics players (★ ★ ★). Beginning with the arrival of the Pilgrims at Plymouth Rock, Ben Franklin and a wry, pipe-smoking Mark Twain narrate 30 minutes of episodes—both praiseworthy and shameful—that have shaped the American spirit. Outside, a convoy of pushcarts offers heritage handicrafts, and directly opposite the pavilion on the edge of the Lagoon, the open-air **American Gardens Theatre** presents lively, high-stepping song-and-dance shows about four times a day.

Saunter around the corner into the replica of Venice's Piazza San Marco and you've moved to **Italy.** The star is the architecture: a reproduction of Venice's Doge's Palace that's true right down to the gold leaf on the angel perched 100 feet atop the Campanile, gondolas tethered to a seawall stained with age, and Romanesque columns, Byzantine mosaics, Gothic arches, and stone walls carefully "antiqued" to look historic. Inside, shops sell Venetian beads and glasswork, leather purses and belts, and Perugina chocolate "kisses."

Germany is a jovial make-believe village that distills the best folk architecture from all over that country. You'll hear hourly chimes from the specially designed glockenspiel on the clock-tower, musical toots and tweets from multitudinous cuckoo clocks, folk tunes from the spinning dolls and lambs sold at Der Teddybär, and the satisfied grunts of hungry visitors chowing down on hearty German cooking. Other than the four-times-a-day oompah band show in the Biergarten restaurant (reservations required), Germany's pavilion doesn't offer any specific entertainment, but it does boast the most shops of any pavilion.

Time Out The **Sommerfest** pretzel-and-bratwurst cart is one of the rare snacking options in this part of the World.

At **China,** a shimmering red-and-gold, three-tier replica of Beijing's Temple of Heaven towers over a serene Chinese garden, an art gallery displaying treasures from the People's Republic, a spacious emporium devoted to Chinese goods, and two restaurants. The garden, planted with rose bushes native to China, a 100-year-old mulberry tree, and water oaks (whose twisted branches look Asian but are actually Florida homegrown), is one of the most peaceful spots in Epcot Center. The 19-minute film **Wonders of China** (★ ★ ★) is dramatically portrayed on a 360° CircleVision screen.

In **Norway,** there are rough-hewn timbers and sharply pitched roofs (so the snow will slip right off), bloom-stuffed window boxes, figured shutters, and lots of smiling, blond and blue-eyed young Norwegians. The pavilion complex contains a 14th-century stone fortress that mimics Oslo's Akershus, cobbled streets, rocky waterfalls, and a wood stave church with wood dragons glaring from the eaves. The church houses an exhibit called "To The Ends of the Earth," which tells the story of two early 20th-century polar expeditions with vintage artifacts. Norway also has a dandy boat ride: **Maelstrom** in which dragon-headed longboats take a 10-minute voyage through time (★ ★).

Housed in a spectacular Mayan pyramid surrounded with a tangle of tropical vegetation, **Mexico** contains an exhibit of pre-Colombian art, a restaurant, a shopping plaza, and the **El Rio del Tiempo** ride. This nine-minute journey from the jungles of the Yucatán to modern-day Mexico City is enlivened by video images of feathered Toltec dancers, by Spanish-colonial Audio-Animatronic dancing puppets, and by film clips of the cliff divers in Acapulco, the speed boats in Manzanillo, and snorkeling around Isla Mujeres (★).

Entertainment Walt Disney World uses the lagoon for the spectacular **Illumi-Nations** sound-and-light show every night a half hour before closing. Best viewing spots are on the bridge between France and the United Kingdom, the promenade in front of Canada and Norway, and the bridge between China and Germany.

Disney–MGM Studios Theme Park

When Walt Disney Company Chairman Michael Eisner opened Disney–MGM Studios in May 1989, he welcomed visitors to "the Hollywood that never was and always will be." Modeled after Southern California's highly successful Universal Studios tour (an even more successful version of which is just down I-4), Disney–MGM combined Disney detail with MGM's motion-picture expertise in an amalgamation that blends theme park with fully functioning movie and television production center, breathtaking rides with instructional tours, nostalgia with high-tech wonders.

Although there are attractions that will interest young children, Disney–MGM is really best for teenagers old enough to watch old movies on television and catch the cinematic references.

When the lines are minimal, the park can be easily covered in a day with time for repeat rides. The **Crossroads of the World kiosk** in the Entrance Plaza dispenses park maps, entertainment schedules, brochures, and the like. The **Production Information Window** (tel. 407/560–3434), also in the Entrance Plaza, is the place to find out what's being taped when and how to sit in the audience for any of these shows.

Hollywood Boulevard With its palm trees, pastel buildings and flashy neon, Hollywood Boulevard paints a rosy picture of Tinseltown in the 1930s and 1940s. The sense of having walked right onto a movie set is enhanced by vintage automobiles that putt-putt back and forth, strolling brass bands, and roving actors dressed in costume and playing everything from would-be starlets to nefarious agents. Hollywood Boulevard is crammed with souvenir shops and memorabilia collections, such as **Oscar's Classic Car Souvenirs & Super Service Station,** easily identified by the grape-color 1947 Buick parked in front; **Sid Cahuenga's One-of-a-Kind** antiques and curios, where you might find (and acquire) Brenda Vaccaro's shawl, Liberace's table napkins, or autographed stars' photos; and **Cover Story,** where you can have your picture put on the front cover of a major magazine. Also on the boulevard is the **Theater of the Stars,** which presents musical revues.

At the head of Hollywood Boulevard is the fire-engine red, pagoda'd replica of Grauman's Chinese Theatre, which houses the **Great Movie Ride.** Disney–MGM pulls out all the stops on this 22-minute tour of great moments in film. Movie memorabilia fills the lobby; the pre-show area screens film clips; then you ride open trams for a tour—past AudioAnimatronics characters, and past scrim, smoke, and Disney magic—of cinematic climaxes. *Audience: All but young children (for whom it may be too intense). Rating:* ★ ★ ★

Studio Courtyard As you exit the Chinese Theater, veer left through the high arched gateway to the Studio Courtyard. You're now at one end of Mickey Avenue. A boxy building on the left invites you to join Ariel, Sebastian, and the underwater gang in the **Voyage of the Little Mermaid** stage show, which condenses the movie into a 15-minute presentation of the greatest hits. *Audience: All ages. Rating:* ★ ★

The **Magic of Disney Animation,** a 30-minute self-guided tour through the Disney animation process, is one of the funniest and most engaging attractions at the park. You'll watch a hilarious eight-minute film in which Walter Cronkite and Robin Williams explain the basics of animation. You then follow walkways with windows overlooking the working animation studios where you see actual salaried Disney artists at their drafting tables doing everything you just learned about. This is better than magic—this is real. *Audience: All but toddlers. Rating:* ★ ★ ★

The **Backstage Studio Tour,** a combination tram ride and walking tour, takes you on a 25-minute tour of the backlot building blocks of movies: set design, costumes, props, lighting, and special effects. You literally ride through working offices, peering through windows as Foley artists mix sound, as lighting crews sort cables, as costumiers stitch seams, and so on. At Catastrophe Canyon, the tram bounces up and down in a simulated earthquake, an oil tanker explodes in gobs of smoke and flame, and a water tower crashes to the ground, touching off a flash flood. *Audience: All but young children. Rating:* ★ ★ ★

The **Inside the Magic Special Effects and Production Tour,** a one-hour walking tour, explains how clever cameramen make illusion seem like reality through camera angles, miniaturization, matte backgrounds, and a host of other magic tricks. You visit the soundstages used for filming the *Mickey Mouse Club, Ed McMahon's Star Search,* and assorted movies. In the Post-Production area, Star Wars director George Lucas, aided by the robots R2D2 and C3PO, explains how film editors use computers for editing, and Mel Gibson and PeeWee Herman switch voices in a lecture on soundtracks. *Audience: Older children and adults. Rating:* ★ ★ ★

The Backlot In this rather amorphous area, you can tour the New York Street sets on foot as long as crews aren't filming—and it's worth it, for the wealth of detail to be seen in the store windows. Take a left at the corner of Mickey Avenue and New York Street and let the kids run free in the **Honey, I Shrunk the Kids Movie Set Adventure,** a state-of-the-art playground based on the movie about lilliputian children in a larger-than-life world. *Audience: Children. Rating:* ★ ★ ★

Jim Henson's Muppet*Vision 3-D is a combination of 3-D movie and musical revue. The theater was constructed especially for this spectacular 30-minute show, with special effects literally built into the walls. All the Muppet characters make an appearance. *Audience: All ages. Rating:* ★ ★ ★

Backlot Annex This niche contains two of the park's most high-powered attractions. The **Indiana Jones Epic Stunt Spectacular** features the stunt choreography of veteran coordinator Glenn Randall (*Raiders of the Lost Ark, Indiana Jones and the Temple of Doom, E.T.,* and *Jewel of the Nile* are among his credits). Presented in a 2,200-seat amphitheater, this 30-minute show teaches the audience how breathtaking movie stunts are pulled off, with the help of 10 audience participants. *Audience: All but young children. Rating:* ★ ★ ★

The annex's other attraction, **Star Tours,** is a real showstopper: a flight simulator inspired by the *Star Wars* films. Piloted by Star Wars characters R2D2 and C3PO, you board a 40-passenger StarSpeeder for a 7-minute flight that soon goes awry: You shoot into deep space, dodge giant ice crystals and comet debris, innocently bumble into an intergalactic battle, and whiz through the canyons of some planetary city before coming to a heart-stopping halt. The lines are incredibly long, but don't go first thing in the morning—it'll spoil you for the rest of the park. *Audience: Older children and adults. Rating:* ★ ★ ★

Lakeside Circle Set off to the left, or west side, of Hollywood Boulevard, Lakeside Circle is an idealized California with two major attractions.

At **SuperStar Television,** 28 volunteers are chosen from the 1,000-person audience to "play" the starring roles on everything from "I Love Lucy" to "Gilligan's Island." While the volunteers are led off to makeup and costume, the audience files into a 1,000-seat theater reminiscent of the days of live television broadcasting. On 6-foot-wide monitors, you see both what appears on the set and on the screen—where electronic dubbing merges the action on the stage with historic clips from classic shows. *Audience: All but young children. Rating:* ★ ★

Despite its name, the **Monster Sound Show** is anything but scary. Rather, it's a delightful, multifaceted demonstration of the use of movie sound effects. Volunteer sound-effects specialists dash around trying to coordinate their sound effects with the short movie being shown simultaneously, where a hilariously klutzy Chevy Chase plays an insurance man on a visit to a haunted house. *Rating:* ★ ★ ★

Discovery Island

Originally conceived as a re-creation of the setting of Robert Louis Stevenson's *Treasure Island,* complete with wrecked ship and Jolly Roger, Discovery Island evolved gradually into its contemporary status as an animal preserve where visitors can see and learn about some 100 different species of exotic birds and animals amid 11½ lushly landscaped acres. Although it's possible to "do" Discovery Island in less than an hour, anything more than a stop-and-start saunter would do it injustice. You can wander along the boardwalks at your own pace, stopping to inspect the bougainvillea or visit with a rhinocerous hornbill. You can picnic on the beach or on one of the benches in the shade and watch trumpeter swans glide by. The only thing you may not do is go swimming—the Water Sprites and motor launches come just too close for safety.

Just past the first right-hand bend in the boardwalk is the **Discovery Island Bird Show,** presented in an open amphitheater equipped with benches and numerous perches. There's usually a show every hour; most last about 15 minutes.

Typhoon Lagoon

Four times the size of River Country, Typhoon Lagoon offers a full day's worth of activities: bobbing in 4-foot waves in a surf lagoon the size of two football fields; speeding down arrow-straight water slides and around twisty storm slides; bumping through whitewater rapids; and snorkeling in **Shark Reef,** a 360,000-gallon snorkeling tank (closed November–April) containing an artificial coral reef and 4,000 real tropical fish. More mellow folks can float in inner-tubes along the 2,100-foot **Castaway Creek,** which circles around the entire park (it takes about 30 minutes to do the whole circuit; you can stop as you please along the way). A children's area, **Ketchakiddie Creek,** replicates adult rides on a smaller scale (all children *must* be accompanied by an adult). It's Disney's version of a day at the beach—complete with lifeguards in spiffy red-and-white striped, fisherman's T-shirts.

Typhoon Lagoon is popular—in the summer and on weekends, the park often reaches capacity (7,200 people) by mid-morning. If you must go during the summer, go for a few hours during the dreamy late afternoons or when the weather clears up after a thundershower. (Typically, rainstorms drive away the crowds, and lots of people simply don't come back.) If you plan to make a whole day of it, avoid weekends—Typhoon Lagoon is big among locals as well as tourists.

River Country

Imagine a mountain in Utah's red-rock country. Put a lake at the bottom, and add a verdant fuzz of maples and pines here and there up the sides. Then plant some water slides among the greenery, call it a "good ole fashion swimmin' hole." That's River Country, adjoining the Fort Wilderness Campground Resort.

It was the first of Walt Disney World's water parks. Where larger, glitzier Typhoon Lagoon is balmy and tropical, this is rustic and rugged. Walking from the dressing rooms brings you to the 330,000-gallon swimming pool, bright blue and concrete-paved, like something out of a more modern Midwest; there are a couple of short, steep water slides here. Beyond that is **Bay Cove,** the roped-off corner of Bay Lake that's the main section of River Country. Rope swings hang from a rustic boom and there are various other woody contraptions from which kids dive and cannonball. Two big waterslides, 100 and 260 feet long, respectively, descend the side of the mountain, while **White Water Rapids,** a series of short chutes and swirling pools that you descend in jumbo inner tubes, provides a more leisurely trip. In summer, come first thing in the morning or in late afternoon to avoid crowds.

Exploring Sea World, Universal Studios, and Beyond

Sea World

2 Aptly named, 135-acre **Sea World** is the world's largest zoological park and is devoted entirely to the mammals, birds, fish, and reptiles that live in the ocean and its tributaries. Every attraction is designed to teach visitors about the beauty of the marine world and how it is threatened by human thoughtlessness. Yet the presentations are rarely dogmatic, never pedantic, and almost always memorable as well as enjoyable. The park rivals Disney properties for sparkly cleanliness, smiley staff, and attention to detail.

Sea World is organized around the nucleus of a 17-acre central lake. As you enter, the lake is to your right. You can orient yourself by the Sky Tower, whose revolving viewing platform is generally visible even above the trees; it's directly opposite Shamu Stadium.

Walk straight through the park to the **Sea World Theatre** to see "Window to the Sea" (20 minutes long), both to orient yourself and to get a sense of the larger vision of the park. Then whip into **Penguin Encounter** early, to visit one of the most spectacular attractions at its least crowded time. This refrigerated re-creation of Antarctica is home to 17 species of penguins; a Plexiglass wall on the viewers' side of the tank lets you see that the penguins are as graceful in the water as they are awkward on land. Proceed to **Terrors of the Deep,** where videos and walk-through plexiglass tunnels let you get acquainted with the world's largest and most unique collection of such dangerous sea creatures as eels, barracuda, venomous and poisonous fish, and sharks. Then stop in to visit the hulking Clydesdale horses, the Ansheuser-Busch trademark, at **Clydesdale Hamlet.**

Follow the crowds across the bridge to **Shamu Stadium**; while they're watching Sea World's orca mascot perform, you can sneak into **Mission: Bermuda Triangle,** a flight simulator ride that replicates a deep-sea dive afflicted by forces beyond its control. Stop by the nearby concession for shopping or food, or get a lakeside table at Mango Joe's to catch the **Atlantis Water Ski Show.**

While on this side of the lagoon, visit the **Pinniped Habitat,** a new 2½-acre home for fun-loving California sea lions and harbor and fur seals; **Manatees: The Last Generation?,** where you can view a film, then watch manatees splash about in their 300,000-gallon tank (there's also a 30,000-gallon nursing lagoon for manatee moms and their babies); and the **Shamu Breeding Pool and Nursery.** That should put you right in place for the afternoon Shamu show. Go as much as 45 minutes early to get a seat—even the wait is fun, as you watch the whales swim around their tank.

Wander back across the bridge and treat yourself to some interactive exhibits: the **Dolphin Community Pool, Harbor Seal Community, Stingray Lagoon,** and **Tide Pool** (do these during the day because the herring concessions close at dusk). This is one of the most rewarding experiences in the park for all ages, and the snack-happy animals are obligingly hungry all day. Keep an eye on the time: You'll want to intersperse these with the delightful shows at the **Whale & Dolphin Stadium** (20 minutes long) and the **Sea Lion & Otter Stadium** (40 minutes long).

By now, you'll be feeling a little frayed. If you've got kids, this may be the time to let them unwind at **Shamu's Happy Harbor,** a 3-acre outdoor play area. Otherwise, head for the soothing **Tropical Reef,** an indoor attraction built around a cylindrical mega-aquarium where more than 1,000 tropical fish swim around a 160,000-gallon manmade coral reef. The **"Water Fantasy,"** back in the Sea World Theater, is another good option: after 5, the theater is turned into a giant wading pool with 36 revolving nozzles spraying water into fountains, waving plumes, and helices, all set to music and colored lights. Restored and in good humor for one last show, trek across the lake for **"Shamu Night Magic."**

7007 Sea World Dr. (just off intersection of I–4 and Bee Line Expwy.), Orlando, FL 32821, tel. 407/351–3600; in FL, 800/ 432–1178; outside FL, 800/327–2424. Admission: $31.95 adults, $27.95 children 3–9. Parking: $4 per car, $6 per RV or camper. Open daily 9–7, except 9–9 July–Aug. and during Thanksgiving and Christmas holidays.

Universal Studios Florida

Far from being a "me-too" version of Disney–MGM Studios, ❸ **Universal Studios Florida,** which opened in June 1990, is a theme park with plenty of personality of its own. It's saucy, sassy, and hip—and doesn't hesitate to invite comparisons to the competition. When a stuntman in the Wild, Wild, Wild West Stunt Show falls into a well, he emerges spitting water and shouting, "Look, Ma, I'm Shamu!" Disney–MGM's strolling actors are pablum compared to the Blues Brothers peeling rubber in the Bluesmobile. And let's face it, even the Muppets are matched by the E.T., Tickli Moot Moot, and other inventions of Steven Spielberg, Universal's genius on call.

The lofty adult ticket price raises expectations very high indeed. They are met most of the time but can easily be dashed by long lines and the park's unabashed attempt to soak you extra at every step at ubiquitous concession stands and overpriced snackeries. With Disney–MGM just down the road, is Universal worth the visit? The answer is an unqualified yes. Actually, Universal Studios and Disney–MGM dovetail rather than replicate each other. Its attractions are more geared to older children than the stroller set.

The 444 acres of Universal Studios are a bewildering conglomeration of stage sets, shops, reproductions of New York and San Francisco, and anonymous sound stages housing theme attractions as well as genuine movie-making paraphernalia. On the map, these sets are neatly divided into six neighborhoods, surrounding a huge blue lagoon, the setting for the **Dynamite Nights Stunt Spectacular,** a shoot-em-up stunt show (performed on water skis, no less!) presented nightly at 7. As you walk around the park, however, expect to get lost, and if you do, just ask directions of the nearest staffer.

The Front Lot is essentially a scene-setter, and the place to find many services. The main drag, the Plaza of the Stars, stretches from the marble-arched entrance gateway straight down to the other end of the lot.

Angling off to the right of Plaza of the Stars, Rodeo Drive forms the backbone of **Hollywood.** Among its attractions, **Lucy: A Tribute** is a basically just a walk-through collection of Lucille Ball's costumes, accessories, and other memorabilia, best for real fans of the ditzy redhead. The **Gory, Gruesome & Grotesque Horror Make-Up Show** is especially appreciated by kids and teens (young children may be frightened), showing as it does what goes into and oozes out of the most mangled monsters in movie history.

Production Central contains six huge warehouses containing working sound stages, as well as several attractions. Follow Nickelodeon Way left from the Plaza of the Stars to the embarkation point for the **Production Tram Tour,** a 20-minute nonstop narrated ride around the park that neither orients you nor takes you inside any of the soundstages. It lets you off right back where you started, where the Green Slime Geyser entices visitors into **Nickelodeon Studios,** a 40-minute tour showing how a television show is produced. With its yellow stairwells and bright orange zigzags, black squiggles, and blue blobs, this is a post-modern funhouse, appropriate for the home of the world's only television network designed for kids. About 90% of the Nickelodeon shows are made on Nick's pair of sound stages, so visitors can always expect to see some action. Lines are often long, so you may want to skip it if no shows are taping. The **Funtastic World of Hanna-Barbera,** a combination ride-video-interactive display at the corner of Nickelodeon Way and Plaza of the Stars, is one of the most popular attractions at Universal Studios and always crowded. Using Hanna-Barbera animated characters (Yogi Bear, the Jetsons, the Flintstones) you're shown how cartoons are made, and given eight minutes of thrills in the process. (It may be too much for toddlers.) **Alfred Hitchcock's 3-D Theatre,** across the Plaza of the Stars from Hanna-Barbera, is a dandy 40-minute multimedia tribute to the master of suspense (young children may be frightened). **"Murder, She Wrote" Mystery Theatre,** based on the popular TV series starring Angela Lansbury as senior citizen sleuth Jessica Fletcher, is presented in a large sit-down theater, where the audience is placed in the role of executive producer, racing the clock to put together an episode of the show. **"The Adventures of Rocky & Bullwinkle"** is a musical revue starring Bullwinkle the Moose, his faithful friend Rocky Squirrel, and those two Russian no-goodniks, Boris Badenov and his slinky sidekick, Natasha, staged hourly on an animated set at the edge of Universal's New York backlot.

The **New York** backlot has been rendered with surprising verisimilitude, right down to the cracked concrete and slightly stained cobblestones. The **Blues Brothers Bluesmobile** regularly cruises the neighborhood and musicians hop out to give impromptu performances at 70 Delancey. New York is also home to **Ghostbusters,** a 15-minute show that's part special-effects demonstration, part high-tech haunted house. **Kongfrontation** is a very popular five-minute ride just down the street from Ghostbusters.

San Francisco/Amity combines two sets: one the wharves and warehouses of San Francisco's Embarcadero and Fisherman's Wharf district, with cable-car tracks and the distinctive redbrick Ghiradelli chocolate factory; the other the New England fishing village terrorized by the shark in *Jaws.* Attractions here include **Beetlejuice's Graveyard Revue,** a live 16-minute sound-and-light spectacle starring the ghoul of the same name, from the 1991 movie starring Michael Keaton. Rock 'n' roll and monsters is the theme; it's carried off with lots of noise, smoke, and wit. Just next door, **Earthquake—The Big One** starts off with a pre-show that reproduces choice scenes from the movie "Earthquake," then takes you on San Francisco Bay Area Rapid Transit subway cars to ride out an 8.3 Richter scale tremor and its consequences: fire, flood, blackouts. Unlike Disney–MGM's Disaster Canyon, there are no "safe" seats on this ride; it's not for younger children. It lasts 20 minutes and the lines are always long. Stagger out of San Francisco into Amity to stand in line for the revamped **Jaws** ride, a terror-filled boat ride with concommitant explosions, noise, and shaking, and gnashing of sharp sharkteeth. The **Wild, Wild, Wild West Stunt Show,** presented in a covered amphitheater at the very end of Amity Avenue, involves trapdoors, fistfights, bullwhips, water gags, explosions, shoot-outs, horseback riding, and jokes that skewer every other theme park in Central Florida.

Expo Center, which takes up the southeastern corner of the park, contains another treasure trove of attractions. **Back to the Future . . . The Ride** is the flight simulator to beat all others, even (probably) those yet to be built. A seven-story, one-of-a-kind Omnimax screen surrounds your Delorean-shape simulator so that you lose all sense of perspective as you rush backwards and forwards in the space-time continuum—and there are no seatbelts. You may have to wait up to two hours for this five-minute ride unless you make a beeline here first thing in the morning. The same is true of the somewhat gentler **E.T. Adventure,** where you board bicycles mounted on a movable platform and pedal through fantastic forests, and across the moon in an attempt to help the endearing extraterrestrial find his way back to his home planet. For younger children, **Fievel's Playland,** just around the corner, is a true gift. Based on the adventures of Steven Spielberg's mighty-if-miniature mouse, this gigantic playground incorporates a four-story net climb, tunnel slides, water play areas, ball crawls, a 200-foot water slide, and a harmonica slide that plays music when you slide along the openings.

1000 Universal Studios Plaza (entrance is ½ mile north of I–4 Exit 30B), Orlando, FL 32819-7610, tel. 407/363–8000, TDD 407/363–8265). Tickets also available by mail through Ticketmaster (tel. 800/745–5000); discounted tickets available at Orlando/Orange County Convention and Visitors Bureau ticket office (8445 International Dr.). One-day admission: $34 adults, $27 children 3–9. Two-day admission: $53 adults, $42 children 3–9. Parking: $4. Open daily 9–7, with hours as late as 10 during summer and holiday periods.

Cypress Gardens

A botanical gardens, amusement park, and water-skiing circus rolled into one, **Cypress Gardens** is a uniquely Floridian combination of natural beauty and utter kitsch. A 45-minute drive from Walt Disney World, the park now encompasses 233 acres, and contains more than 8,000 varieties of plants gathered from 75 countries. More than half of the grounds are devoted to flora, ranging from natural landscaping to cutesy-poo topiary to chrysanthemum cascades. Even at a sedate pace, you can see just about everything in six hours.

The souvenir-shop-ridden main entrance funnels visitors straight to the **Water Ski Stadiums** for a stunt-filled half-hour water-skiing revue presented every 2 hours. To the right are the Botanical Gardens, where you can board a boat for the **Botanical Gardens Cruise,** which floats through the cypress-hung canals of the Botanical Gardens, passing hoop-skirted Southern belles, flowering shrubs, 27 different species of palm, and the occasional baby alligator.

The path leading from the ski stadiums to the amusement park area meanders through the **Exhibition Gardens,** where the landscaping philosophy is heroic in intent and hilariously vulgar in execution.

The **Crossroads Arena,** at the far southern end of the park, is presently home to a whizbang half-hour performance of aerial stunts, trampoline acts, and high-wire acrobatics. Many of the park's attractions are clustered around Southern Crossroads; they include the bird show at the Cypress Theatre; a huge walk-through butterfly conservatory; a museum of antique radios; Cypress Junction, the nation's most elaborate model railroad exhibit; and Cypress Roots, a clapboard shack chockful of fascinating memorabilia about the Gardens' founders, Dick and Julie Pope. The American Waterskiing Museum, which takes up permanent residence at Cypress Gardens in 1994, tells the history of the sport that Cypress Gardens made famous. Kodak's Island in the Sky, a 153-foot-high revolving platform, provides aerial views of the park, and Carousel Cove is the kids' playground, with lots of ball rooms and bouncing pads plus a lovely old carousel.

Box 1, Cypress Gardens, FL 33884 (take I–4 Exit U.S. 27S and follow signs), tel. 813/324–2111, 800/282–2123 in FL, 800/237–4826 outside FL. Admission: $22.95 adults, $16.45 children 3–9. Open daily 9–6, with extended hours in summer.

Winter Park

Once the winter refuge of some wealthy Northerners, the community of Winter Park, though part of Orlando's metro area, maintains a proud, independent, and tony identity. **Park Avenue** in downtown Winter Park is lined with trendy boutiques and restaurants; long and narrow Central Park stretches through the heart of the shopping district, and benches under the ancient trees offer a respite from the hustle and bustle. His-
❺ toric **Rollins College,** a private liberal arts school, is at the south end of Park Avenue. Take time to look at the Spanish-style architecture, especially Knowles Memorial Chapel, home to the Bach Festival Society. Also on campus is the **Cornell Fine Arts Museum,** which has the largest collection of American and European art in Central Florida. *1000 Holt Ave., Winter Park, tel. 407/646–2526. Admission free. Open Tues.–Fri. 10–5, weekends 1–5; closed major holidays.*

❻ The elegant **Charles Hosmer Morse Museum of American Art** features an outstanding collection of stained-glass windows, blown glass, and lamps by Louis Tiffany (son of Charles Tiffany of New York jewelry fame). There's also a collection of paintings by 19th- and 20th-century American artists, as well as jewelry and pottery. *133 E. Welbourne Ave., Winter Park, tel. 407/645–5311. Admission: $2.50 adults, $1 students and children. Open Tues.–Sat. 9:30–4, Sun. 1–4; closed major holidays.*

Heading west out of town on Fairbanks Avenue, take a left fork onto Orange Avenue and, after ½ mile, turn left onto Denning
❼ Avenue for a visit to 55-acre **Mead Gardens,** which has been intentionally left to grow as a natural preserve. Plans are under way to build a boardwalk to provide a better view of the delicate wetlands. *S. Denning Ave., Winter Park, tel. 407/623–3334. Admission free. Open daily 8–sundown.*

With entrances on both Rollins and Princeton streets (1 mile
❽ east off I–4's Exit 43), **Loch Haven Park** is a grassy field with three of the city's museums. The **Orlando Science Center** is full of hands-on and interactive exhibits, including a special preschoolers' water play area and a planetarium. *810 E. Rollins St., Orlando, tel. 407/896–7151. Admission: $6.50 adults, $5.50 children 3–11. Open Mon.–Thurs. and Sat. 9–5, Fri. 9–9, Sun. noon–5. Cosmic Concerts: admission: $5; Fri. and Sat. 9 PM, 10:30 PM, and midnight.*

The **Orange County Historical Museum** is a storehouse of Orlando memorabilia, photographs, and antiques. Permanent exhibits explore Native American and cracker (native Floridian) culture, and show off a country store, a Victorian parlor, a print shop, and an actual 1926 brick firehouse. *812 E. Rollins St., Orlando, tel. 407/897–6350. Admission: $2 adults, $1.50 senior citizens, $1 children 6–11. Open Mon.–Sat. 9–5, Sun. noon–5.*

The **Orlando Museum of Art** displays 19th- and 20th-century American art and a permanent exhibit of pre-Columbian artifacts from a Mayan excavation. Young children will enjoy the first-class Art Encounter, created with the help of Walt Disney World. *2416 N. Mills Ave., Orlando, tel. 407/896–4231. Admission (suggested donation): $4 adults, $2 children 4–11. Open Tues.–Sat. 9–5, Sun. noon–5; tours Sept.–May, Wed. and*

Sun. 2 PM; Art Encounter Tues.–Fri. and Sun. noon–5, Sat. 10–5; café Tues.–Sun. 11–2.

⑨ A short distance from Loch Haven Park is **Leu Botanical Gardens,** Orlando's 56-acre horticultural extravaganza. Formerly the estate of the late industrialist and citrus industry entrepreneur Harry P. Leu, it has a collection of historical blooms, many varieties having been established before 1900. You'll see ancient oaks, a 50-foot floral clock, an orchid conservatory, and one of the largest camellia collections in eastern North America (in bloom October through March). Mary Jane's Rose Garden is the largest rose conservatory south of Atlanta. The simple 19th-century Leu House Museum, once the Leu family home, preserves the furnishings and appointments of a well-to-do, turn-of-the-century Florida family. *1730 N. Forest Ave., Orlando, tel. 407/246–2620. Admission: $3 adults, $1 children 6–16. Open daily 9–5; museum Tues.–Sat. 10–3:30, Sun.–Mon. 1–3:30; closed Christmas.*

Other Sites of Interest

⑩ A one-hour drive south of Orlando, **Bok Tower Gardens** is a sanctuary of plants, flowers, trees, and wildlife native to subtropical Florida. Shady paths meander through pine forests in this peaceful world of silvery moats, mockingbirds and swans, blooming thickets, and hidden sundials. There is a quirky appeal to the majestic 200-foot Bok Tower, constructed of coquina (from seashells) and pink, white, and gray marble. The tower is carved with wildlife designs, each very symbolic, and bronze doors are decorated with reliefs that tell the complete story of Genesis. The tower houses a carillon with 57 bronze bells that ring every half-hour after 10 AM. Also on the grounds is the 230-room, Mediterranean Revival–style Pinewood House, built in 1930. Take I–4 to U.S. 27 south. About 5 miles past the Cypress Gardens turnoff, turn right on Route 17A to Alternate U.S. 27. Past the orange groves, turn left on Burns Avenue and follow about 1½ miles to gardens. *Burns Ave. and Tower Blvd., Lake Wales, tel. 813/676–1408. Admission: $3 adults. Open daily 8–5. Pinewood House tours: admission (suggested donation): $5 adults, $4 children under 12; Sept. 15–May 15, Tues. and Thurs. 12:30 and 2, Sun. at 4.*

⑪ A visit to **Central Florida Zoological Park** will disappoint you if you're expecting a grand metro zoo. However, this is a respectable display of 230 animals on 110 acres, tucked under pine trees in a natural setting, and, like the city of Orlando, it continues to grow. A new boardwalk extends through a wetland tour. The elephant exhibit is popular, as are the playful otters. The zoo is becoming specialized in small- and medium-size exotic cats, including servals, caracals, and jaguarundis. There is a petting area and weekend elephant and pony rides. *3755 N. U.S. 17–92, Sanford, tel. 407/323–4450. Admission: $5 adults, $3 senior citizens ($1.50 on Tues.), $2 children 3–12. Open daily 9–5; closed Thanksgiving and Christmas.*

⑫ Long before Walt Disney World, there was **Gatorland,** a kitschy attraction south of Orlando on U.S. 441 that has endured since 1949. Through the monstrous aqua gator-jaw doorway lie thrills and chills in the form of more than 5,000 alligators and crocodiles, swimming and basking in the Florida sun. In addition to the gators and crocs, a zoo houses many other reptiles, animals, and birds. A free train ride provides an overview of the park, and a three-story observation tower overlooks the gator breeding marsh. Don't miss the Gator Jumparoo show, the Gator Wrestling show, and the educational Snakes Alive show, with 30–40 rattlesnakes in the pit around the speaker. *14501 S. Orange Blossom Trail, between Orlando and Kissimmee, tel. 407/855–5496 or 800/393–JAWS. Admission: $9.95 adults, $6.95 children 3–11. Open daily 8–dusk.*

⑬ More than 100 personal items and three of the King's cars are on display at the **Elvis Presley Museum,** tucked in Kissimmee's Old Town shopping area. The owner, a former singer who claims to have been Elvis's personal friend for more than 24 years, periodically changes the exhibits of clothing, costumes, jewelry, and furniture. *Old Town, 5770 Irlo Bronson Memorial Hwy., Kissimmee, tel. 407/396–8594. Admission: $4 adults, $3 children 7–12. Open daily 10–10.*

⑭ The **Flying Tigers Warbird Air Museum** is a working aircraft restoration facility and a museum displaying about 25 vintage planes in its hangar, with a few big ones out on the tarmac. Tour guides are full of facts and personality and have an infectious passion for the planes. *231 Hoagland Blvd., Kissimmee, tel. 407/933–1942. Admission: $6 adults, $5 senior citizens and children under 5. Open Mon.–Sat. 9–5:30, Sun. 9–5 (extended hrs in peak seasons).*

⑮ The new **Ripley's Believe It or Not!** museum in the heart of tourist territory is part of a national chain displaying all sort of weird and amazing artifacts. Children love it, but the displays are strictly for looking—no touching. *8201 International Dr., Orlando, tel. 407/363–4418. Admission: $8.95 adults, $5.95 children 3–11. Open daily 10 AM–11 PM (extended hrs in peak seasons).*

⑯ **Mystery Fun House** is an 18-chamber Mystery Maze, which comes with the warning that it is "90% dark" and full of gory and distorted images. Outside there's an 18-hole Mystery Mini-Golf, a video arcade, and the high-tech Starbase Omega laser game, in which you are suited up, given a reflector gun and badge, and transported to an arena for a group game of laser tag. *5767 Major Blvd., Orlando, tel. 407/351–3355. Admission: maze $7.95, minigolf $2.95, laser game $5.95, all 3 for $11.85. Open daily 10–10 (to midnight in peak seasons).*

⑰ Visit a haunted house all year round at **Terror on Church Street.** There's also a gift shop with all kinds of creepy things. *Church St. and Orange Ave., Orlando, tel. 407/649–3327. Admission: $10 adults, $8 children under 18. Open Tues.–Sat. 7 PM–1 AM.*

⑱ **Water Mania** has all the requisite rides and slides without the aesthetics you'll find at Walt Disney World. However, it's the only water park around to have Wipe Out, a surfing simulator, where you grab a body board and ride a continuous wave form. The giant Pirate Ship in the Rain Forest, one of two children's play areas, is equipped with water slides and water cannons. The Abyss, similar to Wet 'n' Wild's Black Hole *(see below),* is an enclosed tube slide through which you twist and turn on a one- or two-person raft for 300 feet of deep-blue darkness. The park also offers miniature golf, a sandy beach, snack bars, gift shops, and periodic concerts. *6073 W. Irlo Bronson Memorial Hwy., Kissimmee, tel. 407/239–8448 in Orlando, 407/396–2626 in Kissimmee, or 800/527–3092. Admission: $17.95 adults,*

$15.95 children 3–12. Open daily 10–5 (till about 8 in summer).

⑲ Wet 'n' Wild is best known for its outrageous water slides, especially the Black Hole—a 30-second, 500-foot, twisting, turning ride on a two-person raft through total darkness propelled by a 1,000 gallon-a-minute blast of water. There's also an elaborate Kid's Park, for those 4 feet tall and under, full of miniature versions of the bigger rides. The latest addition is the Bubba Tub, a six-story, triple-dip slide with a tube big enough for the entire family to ride in together. The park has snack stands, but visitors are allowed to bring their own food and picnic around the pool or on the lakeside beach. *6200 International Dr., Orlando, tel, 407/351–3200. Admission: $19.95 adults, $16.95 children 3–9. Open 10–5 (till about 9 in summer) daily except for Orlando's few really cold days.*

Shopping

Altamonte Mall (451 Altamonte Ave., ½ mi east of I–4 on Rte. 436, Altamonte Springs, tel. 407/830–4400) is an airy, spacious two-level mall containing Sears, Gayfers, Burdines, and J.C. Penney department stores and 165 specialty shops.

Church Street Exchange (Church St. Station, 129 W. Church St., Orlando, tel. 407/422–2434) is a decorative, brassy, Victorian-theme "festival marketplace" filled with more than 50 specialty shops. Perhaps the best demonstration is at the Fudgery, where free samples are distributed during a light-hearted look at the process of making fudge. Across the street from the complex is Bumby Emporium, a Church Street souvenir shop, and across the railroad tracks is yet another collection of unusual shops and pushcarts, known as the **Historic Railroad Depot.**

The Crossroads of Lake Buena Vista (Rte. 535 and I–4, tel. 407/827–7300), across the street from the entrance to the hotels at Lake Buena Vista, contains nine restaurants and 18 shops that are convenient for tourists—the necessities, such as a 24-hour grocery and pharmacy, post office, bank, and cleaners, are all there, and while you shop, your offspring can entertain themselves at Pirate's Cove Adventure Golf.

Disney Village Marketplace, nestled along the shores of Buena Vista Lagoon, is a complex of 17 shops packed with art, fashions, crafts, and more. If you are looking for one-stop shopping for Disney collectibles and souvenirs, this is the place. *Lake Buena Vista, tel. 407/824–4321. Open daily 9:30 AM–10 PM.*

Florida Mall (8001 S. Orange Blossom Trail, 4½ mi east of I–4 and International Dr., tel. 407/851–6255), the largest in Central Florida, includes Sears, J.C. Penney, Belk Lindsey, Gayfers, Dillard's, 200 specialty shops, seven theaters, and one of the better food courts around.

The Spanish-style **Mercado Mediterranean Village** (8445 International Dr., Orlando, tel. 407/345–9337), houses more than 60 specialty shops. A walkway circles the courtyard, where live entertainment can be enjoyed throughout the day. The clean, quick, and large food court offers a selection of food from around the world.

Old Town (5770 Irlo Bronson Memorial Hwy., Kissimmee, tel. 800/843–4202) is a shopping-entertainment complex featuring a 1928 ferris wheel, a 1909 carousel, and more than 70 specialty shops in a re-creation of a turn-of-the-century Florida village.

The recently redesigned **Orlando Fashion Square** (3201 E. Colonial Dr., 3 mi east of I–4 Exit 41, tel. 407/896–1131) has 130 shops including J.C. Penney, Sears, Camelot Music, the Gap, Lerner, and Lechters.

Outlet Stores The International Drive area is filled with factory outlet stores, including **Belz Factory Outlet Mall and Annexes** (5401 W. Oakridge Rd., tel. 407/352–9611), with nearly 170 stores; and **Quality Outlet Center** and **Quality Center East** (5409 and 5529 International Dr., tel. 407/423–5885), two interconnected strip shopping centers containing 20 brand-name factory outlet stores. On U.S. 192, **Kissimmee Manufacturers' Outlet Mall** (1 mi east of Rte. 535, Kissimmee, tel. 407/396–8900) contains approximately 20 stores.

Flea Market **Flea World** (U.S. 17–92, 3 mi east of I–4 Exit 50 on Lake Mary Blvd., then 1 mi South on U.S. 17–92), between Orlando and Sanford, tel. 407/321–1792) claims to be America's largest flea market under one roof, with more than 1,600 booths selling only new merchandise—everything from car tires, ginsu knives, and pet tarantulas to gourmet coffee, leather lingerie, and beaded evening gowns. Kids love Fun World next door, which offers miniature golf, arcade games, go-carts, bumper cars, bumper boats, kiddie rides, and batting cages.

Sports and the Outdoors

Participant Sports

Golf **Golfpac** (Box 940490, Maitland 32794, tel. 407/660–8559) packages golf vacations and prearranges tee times at more than 40 courses around Orlando. Rates vary based on hotel and course, and 60–90 days advance notice is required to set up a vacation.

Be sure to reserve tee times well in advance. Greens fees usually vary by season—we list the highest and lowest figures, all including mandatory cart rental.

At WDW Walt Disney World's five championship courses—all on the PGA Tour route—are among the busiest and most expensive in the region. Greens fees run $75–$85, or $35–$45 if you tee off after 3 PM. For tee times on any of the five, phone 407/824–2270. The five courses, which are all 18 holes, are: **Eagle Pines** (Bonnet Creek Golf Club, 6,722 yds); **Lake Buena Vista** (Lake Buena Vista, 6,829 yds); **Magnolia** (Disney Inn, 6,642 yds); **Osprey Ridge** (Bonnet Creek Golf Club, 7,101 yds); and **The Palm** (Disney Inn, 6,957 yds).

Elsewhere **Cypress Creek Country Club** (5353 Vineland Rd., Orlando, tel. 407/351–2187, 6,955 yds) is a demanding 18-hole course with 16 water holes and lots of trees; greens fees run $20–$35.

Grand Cypress Golf Club (1 N. Jacaranda, Orlando 32836, tel. 407/239–4700) has 45 holes designed by Jack Nicklaus, including the New Course, a re-creation of the famed Old Course in St. Andrews, Scotland. Greens fees are high, in the over-$75 range.

Grenelefe Golf and Tennis Resort (3200 Rte. 546, Haines City, tel. 813/422–7511 or 800/237–9549), about 45 minutes from Orlando, has three excellent 18-hole courses, of which the toughest is the 7,325-yard West Course. Greens fees run $39–$94.

Horseback Riding **Fort Wilderness Campground** (tel. 407/824–2803) offers tame trail rides through backwoods. Children must be over nine, and adults must be under 250 pounds. Trail rides cost $16 for 45 minutes. Rides daily at 9, 10:30, noon, 2.

Jogging Walt Disney World has several scenic jogging trails. Pick up jogging maps at any Disney resort. **Fort Wilderness Campground** (tel. 407/824–2900) has a 2.3-mile jogging course with plenty of fresh air and woods as well as numerous exercise stations along the way.

Water Sports Marinas at the Caribbean Beach Resort, Contemporary Resort, Disney Village Market Place, Fort Wilderness Campground, Grand Floridian, Polynesian Village, and Yacht and Beach Club rent Sunfish, catamarans, motor-powered pontoon boats, pedal boats, and tiny two-passenger Water Sprites—a hit with kids—for use on their nearby waters: Bay Lake, Seven Seas Lagoon, Lake Buena Vista, Club Lake, or Buena Vista Lagoon. The Polynesian Village marina also rents outrigger canoes, and Fort Wilderness rents canoes for paddling along the placid canals in the area. For waterskiing reservations ($65 an hour), call 407/824–1000.

Spectator Sports

In addition to teams in various sports and leagues who play their regular seasons in and around Orlando, there are also major league baseball clubs that make their spring-training home in the area.

Basketball The NBA **Orlando Magic** (Box 76, 600 W. Amelia St., 2 blocks west of I–4 Amelia St. Exit, Orlando, tel. 407/839–3900) plays in the new 15,077-seat Orlando Arena.

Dog Racing **Sanford Orlando Kennel Club** (301 Dog Track Rd., Longwood, tel. 407/831–1600) has dog racing as well as South Florida horse-racing simulcasts, November–May.

Seminole Greyhound Park (2000 Seminola Blvd., Casselberry, tel. 407/699–4510), open May–October, is a newer track.

Jai Alai **Orlando–Seminole Jai–Alai** (6405 S. U.S. 17–92, Fern Park, tel. 407/331–9191), about 20 minutes north of Orlando off I–4, offers South Florida horse-racing simulcasts and betting in addition to jai alai at the fronton (closed May).

Dining

Many of Orlando's fine restaurants are in the stylish hotels in areas close to Walt Disney World. These dining establishments like to flaunt their sophisticated menus and wine lists, but many of them are overrated. If you're watching your pennies or like your restaurants with a certain regional flavor, it will be worth your while to drive a ways to eat in a local spot, where you'll find a taste of Orlando and considerable savings. Many restaurants are in rather mundane-looking shopping centers, and getting to places is almost always complicated, so always call for directions.

Walt Disney World is full of places to snack and eat. The theme parks are chockablock with fast-food spots; all have full-service, sit-down restaurants, too. The best of these in the Magic Kingdom are **Liberty Tavern** and **King Stefan's Banquet Hall,** which is inside Cinderella Castle. At Disney–MGM Studios, the lines can be enormous and reservations are routinely late. Moreover, reservations must be made in person at the restaurant—for popular seating times, first thing in the morning. Top picks there are **Brown Derby,** the **50's Prime Time Cafe,** and the **Sci-Fi Dine-In Theater,** a re-creation of an actual drive-in. Epcot Center's World Showcase offers some of the finest dining to be found in the entire Orlando area, with many of the restaurants operated by the same people who own internationally famous restaurants in their home countries. However, you have to pay Epcot Center admission to get in, and reservations can be hard to come by. Make reservations first thing in the morning at the **Earth Station;** if you're staying in an on-site property, you can make reservations in advance by phoning 407/560–7277. All restaurants, unless otherwise noted, are open for lunch and dinner daily. Lunch reservations may be easier to get, and the meal will be cheaper.

Unless otherwise noted in our reviews, casual dress prevails—that means comfortably presentable, in shorts, sneakers, or T-shirts.

Category	Cost*
Very Expensive	over $40
Expensive	$30–$40
Moderate	$20–$30
Inexpensive	under $20

per person, excluding drinks, service, and 6% sales tax

Highly recommended restaurants are indicated by a star ★.

Beer, Wine, and Spirits The Magic Kingdom's no-liquor policy does not extend to the rest of Walt Disney World, and in fact, most restaurants and watering holes, particularly those in the on-site hotels, mix elaborate fantasy drinks based on fruit juices or flavored with liqueurs.

In and Around Walt Disney World

American
Expensive
★
Dux. Expert service and innovative American cuisine focusing on fresh regional specialties make this intimate Peabody Hotel dining room, decorated in warm earth tones, one of the finest restaurants in this or any other city. Chef Scott Maurer, a graduate of the Culinary Institute of America, changes the menu three times a year; in winter good choices include warm "Turtle Creek" goat cheese salad with fried green tomatoes or mixed baby greens in a basil-flavored balsamic vinaigrette, followed by mesquite-grilled veal chops served with cranberry compote, baby fall vegetables, and wild rice cakes with five-peppercorn sauce. The wine cellar boasts more than 470 vintages from around the world. *Peabody Hotel, 9801 International Dr., Orlando, tel. 407/352–4000. Reservations advised. AE, DC, MC, V. Closed Sat. lunch and Sun.*

Moderate **Empress Lilly restaurants.** Moored at the far end of Disney village Marketplace, this 220-foot replica of a 19th-century Mississippi-style riverboat is complete with brass lamps, velvet loveseats, and acres of gleamy mahogany paneling and moldings. Inside are four restaurants, all a little different. The **Steerman's Quarters** serves beef, and the **Fisherman's Deck,** replete with gingerbread woodwork painted in sunset pastels, offers seafood. In the **Baton Rouge Lounge,** John Charles performs musical comedy while you eat all you want from a Southern-style buffet, heavy on the carbohydrates. Overall, meals can be fun and congenial, despite the undistinguished food. Only 10% of the tables are open for reservations (up to a month in advance); visitors without reservations are advised to arrive early, add their names to the list, and wait for as long as an hour. The **Empress Room,** the only expensive restaurant of the lot, is extremely formal, serves Continental cuisine, and requires reservations; you'll also need to dress up. *Disney Village Marketplace, tel. 407/828–3900. AE, MC, V.*

Pebbles. This restaurant serves California cuisine with a Florida twist, using native produce and fish. A favorite of Orlando residents, the original restaurant in the suburbs was such a big hit that three more have opened. Choose the hamburger or try a selection of appetizers and a salad or soup for either lunch or dinner. Desserts are good, and the wine list is interesting and well priced. *At Lake Buena Vista entrance to Walt Disney World, Orlando, tel. 407/827–1111; 17 W. Church St., tel. 407/839–0892; 2516 Aloma Ave., Winter Park, tel. 407/678–7001; 2100 Rte. 434, Longwood, tel. 407/774–7111. No reservations. AE, D, DC, MC, V.*

Chinese **Ming Court.** Although the dishes' names may sound familiar,
Moderate this kitchen's creative flair makes each one stand out from the standard rendition. Try the jumbo shrimp in lobster sauce flavored with crushed black beans, or the Hunan kung pao chicken with peanuts, cashews, and walnuts. Glass walls allow you to look out onto a pond and floating gardens. *9188 International Dr., Orlando, tel. 407/351–9988. Reservations advised. AE, DC, MC, V.*

Sum Chows. The hokey name belies the food and ambience in this gourmet Chinese restaurant in the Walt Disney World Dolphin Hotel. Specialties include stir-fried swordfish and Cantonese lamb steak with lemon sauce. Everyone raves about the crispy fried spinach. *Walt Disney World Dolphin, Lake Buena Vista, tel. 407/934–4000. AE, D, DC, MC, V. No lunch Wed.–Sun.*

Continental **Arthur's 27.** This fancy restaurant on the top floor of the Buena
Very Expensive Vista Palace Hotel serves up gorgeous views of the Magic Kingdom and Epcot Center and elegant, well-prepared meals, featuring such specialties as venison with papaya and dates, and sautéed breast of duck with honey-ginger sauce. There's a four-course prix fixe dinner for $45, a six-course prix fixe for $60; à la carte tabs run even higher. Arthur's is very popular on weekends and there is only one seating per night, so reserve your table when you reserve your room. *Buena Vista Palace Hotel, Walt Disney World Village, Lake Buena Vista, tel. 407/827–3450. Reservations necessary. Jacket required. AE, D, DC, MC, V.*

French **La Coquina.** The menu ranges from Normandy to Flanders,
Expensive from the Basque country to the Côte d'Azur. But the best bet is

Sunday brunch, which is all-American and served in the restaurant's kitchen. Try to sit by the windows so you can enjoy the tropical view as you listen to the harpist. Start with salads or smoked fishes, go back for omelets or waffles, and then try one of the chef's selections of the day. *Hyatt Regency Grand Cypress Blvd., Orlando; tel. 407/239–1234. Reservations advised. Jacket and tie required for dinner. AE, DC, MC, V. Closed Sun. night and Mon., June–Sept.*

Italian
Moderate

Portobello Yacht Club. The Levys, longtime Chicago restaurateurs, have brought their highly touted home-town restaurant to Pleasure Island. The food and service fall far short of the original, but the atmosphere is appealing, the catch of the day is fresh, and the selection of Italian and domestic wines is good. Moreover, the kitchen keeps late hours—worth knowing about when you're partying the night away. You don't have to pay the Pleasure Island cover charge to eat here. *Pleasure Island, Walt Disney World, tel. 407/934–8888. Reservations accepted. AE, DC, MC, V.*

Inexpensive–
Moderate

Rosario's. This cheerful little place, in a New England–style clapboard house that looks refreshingly out of place in Kissimmee, serves Italian food that's way above average. The *spaghetti aglio olio* is sauced with fresh garlic, basil, and diced tomatoes sautéed in olive oil. The hearty *pasta e fagioli* soup is filled with cannelini beans, prosciutto, escarole, pasta, and flavored with brandy and a touch of marinara sauce. *4838 W. Irlo Bronson Hwy., Kissimmee. 407/239–0118. Children's menu. AE, D, DC, MC, V. Beer and wine only. Closed for lunch.*

Japanese
Moderate

Ran-Getsu. For Orlando, the Japanese food served here is pretty good, fresh and carefully prepared. Sit at the curved, dragon's-tail-shape sushi bar and order the matsu platter—an assortment of *nigiri-* and *maki*-style sushis. Or if you're with a group, have your meal Japanese-style at the low tables overlooking a carp-filled pond and decorative gardens. Specialties include sukiyaki and shabu-shabu, the latter thinly sliced beef prepared tableside in a boiling seasoned broth and served with vegetables. *8400 International Dr., Orlando, tel. 407/345–0044. Reservations advised. AE, DC, MC, V.*

Seafood
Expensive

Ariel's. Fish is the speciality at this favorite of Disney executives in Disney's Beach Club Resort, whose centerpiece is a 2,500-gallon saltwater tank. The seafood is most often simply grilled over a hardwood fire. Want something more exotic? Start with the Tuckernut shellfish gumbo with *andouille* sausage and then have Ariel's strudel—chicken and ricotta cheese wrapped in a flaky basil-perfumed pastry. *Disney's Beach Club Resort, Lake Buena Vista, tel. 407/834–8000. Reservations accepted. No smoking. AE, MC, V.*

Moderate–Expensive
★

Hemingway's. Located by the pool at the Hyatt Regency Grand Cypress, this restaurant serves up all sorts of sea creatures from conch, scallops, and squid to grouper, pompano, and monkfish. Be sure to order Florida stone crabs during the season (October through March), and don't miss the beer-battered coconut shrimp. *Hyatt Regency Grand Cypress Resort, 1 Grand Cypress Blvd., Orlando, tel. 407/239–1234. Reservations advised. AE, DC, MC, V.*

Epcot Center

British
Moderate
Rose and Crown. At day's end, visitors mingle with Disney employees at this friendly British pub on the shore of World Showcase Lagoon while knocking off pints of crisp Bass Ale and blood-thickening Guinness Stout with Stilton cheese. "Wenches" serve up simple pub fare, such as steak-and-kidney pie, lamb, and fish and chips. Dark wood floors, rustic pub chairs, and brass lamps create a warm, homey atmosphere. At 4, a traditional tea is served.

French
Expensive
Les Chefs de France. To create this sparkling French café– restaurant, three of France's most famous culinary artists came together: Paul Bocuse, who operates one restaurant north of Lyon and two in Tokyo; Gaston Lenôtre, noted for his pastries and ice creams; and Roger Vergé, proprietor of France's celebrated Mougins near Cannes. The three developed the menu, trained the chefs, and look in frequently to make sure the food and service stay up to snuff. And they do. Start with a hot chicken-and-duck pâté in a light pastry crust, follow up with a classic *coq au vin* (chicken in red wine) or broiled salmon with sorrel sauce, and end up with chocolate-doused ice cream-filled pastry shells.

Moderate–Expensive
★
Bistro de Paris. This quiet, elegant restaurant on the second floor of the France pavilion, above Chefs de France, specializes in simple country-French fare. Bouillabaisse and sautéed veal tenderloin with apple and Calvados sauce are always good. Come late, ask for a window seat, and plan to linger to watch IllumiNations. The French wines are moderately priced and available by the glass. Open for lunch during busy seasons only.

German
Moderate
Biergarten. The cheerful—some would say raucous—atmosphere is what you would expect in a place with an oompah band. Waitresses in typical Bavarian garb serve hot pretzels, sauerbraten, bratwurst, and stout pitchers of beer and wine, while patrons pound on their long communal tables.

Italian
Expensive
L'Originale Alfredo di Roma Ristorante. If you love fettuccine Alfredo, you owe it to yourself to try it in this restaurant, a cousin of the one founded in 1914 by Alfredo de Lelio, who invented the now-classic dish—pasta sauced with cream, butter, and loads of freshly grated Parmesan cheese. Stick with pasta when dining here for the other menu items are pretty much undistinguished.

Japanese
Moderate–Expensive
★
Mitsukoshi. This complex of dining areas overlooking tranquil gardens is actually three restaurants: The **Yakitori,** a fast-food stand in a small pavilion modeled after a teahouse in Kyoto's Katsura Summer Palace, offers broiled skewers of chicken basted with teriyaki sauce; *gyudon,* paper-thin beef simmered in a spicy sauce and served with noodles; and Japanese desserts. At the **Tempura Kiku,** diners sit around a central counter and watch the chefs prepare sushi, sashimi, and tempura (batter-dipped deep-fried shrimp, scallops, and vegetables). In the **Teppanyaki Rooms,** chefs skillfully chop vegetables, meat, and fish at lightning speed and then stir-fry them at grills set into communal dining tables.

Mexican
Moderate
★
San Angel Inn. The lush, tropical surroundings—cool, dark, and almost surreal—make this restaurant in the courtyard inside the Mexican pavilion perhaps the most exotic in Walt Dis-

ney World. The best seats are along the restaurant's outer edge, directly alongside the pavilion's "river," where boatloads of sightseers stream by; above looms an Aztec pyramid. On the roster of authentic Mexican dishes, one specialty is *mole poblano*—chicken simmered in a rich sauce of chiles, green tomatoes, ground tortillas, coriander seed, and 11 other spices mixed with cocoa. Fresh tortillas are made every day.

Moroccan
Moderate–Expensive

Marrakesh. Belly dancers and a three-piece Moroccan band set a North African mood. The food is mildly spicy and relatively inexpensive. Try the couscous, the national dish of Morocco, served with vegetables; or *bastila*, an appetizer made of alternating layers of sweet-and-spicy pork and a thin pastry, redolent of almonds, saffron, and cinnamon.

Norwegian
Inexpensive

Restaurant Akershus. Norway's tradition of seafood and cold-meat dishes is highlighted at the *koldtboard*, or Norwegian buffet, in this restaurant, four dining rooms occupying a copy of Oslo's Akershus Castle. It is traditional to make several trips: first for appetizers (usually herring, which comes several ways here), then such cold seafood as gravlax (salmon cured with salt, sugar, and dill), followed by cold salads and meats, then hot lamb, veal, or venison. The selection of desserts, offered à la carte, includes cloudberries, delicate seasonal fruits that grow on the tundra.

Elsewhere in Orlando

American
Moderate–Expensive
★

Chatham's Place. The Chatham brothers, Culinary Institute of America graduates, prepare everything to order here. It's housed in an office building next to the Marketplace shopping mall, but the meticulously prepared food rises above the setting. Try the black grouper with pecan butter, spaghetti à la Grecque, or the duck breast, grilled to crispy perfection. *7575 Dr. Phillips Blvd., Orlando, tel. 407/345–2992. Reservations advised. MC, V. Dinner only.*

Jordan's Grove. One of Orlando's most popular restaurants, Jordan's Grove occupies an old house built in 1912. The rather avant-garde menu changes daily; depending on the day, the season, and the mood of the chef, the food ranges from just plain ordinary to quite extraordinary. *1300 S. Orlando Ave. (U.S. 17–92), Maitland, tel. 407/628–0020. Reservations advised. AE, DC, MC, V. Closed Mon. and lunch Sat.*

Moderate

Sam Snead's Tavern. A tribute to the venerable golf champion, Sam Snead, this restaurant's wood-panel walls are chockablock with pictures and memorabilia of his illustrious career. The kitchen does well with an eclectic variety of foods ranging from hamburgers and grilled chicken to veal chops and fish. *2461 S. Hiawassee Rd., Orlando, tel. 407/295–9999. Reservations accepted. AE, DC, MC, V.*

Inexpensive

Hard Rock Café Orlando. You can enter this guitar-shape building from the Universal Studios theme park or from the street. Besides the rock music and rock memorabilia, Orlando's Hard Rock features a Hollywood room. Food includes hamburgers, barbecue, and sandwiches. *Universal Studios Florida, 5800 Kirkman Rd., Orlando, tel. 407/351–7625. No reservations accepted. AE, MC, V.*

Dexter's. Winter Park locals, from Rollins College students to the owners of the area's lakefront estates, hang out at this combination wine shop and wine bar. Sample the interesting vintages for sale by the glass, or have a meal at the counter or at bar-height wood tables. The made-from scratch soups are a hearty choice as is the ratatouille, served in a hollowed out roll. *200 W. Fairbanks Ave., Winter Park, tel. 407/629–1150. AE, MC, V. Closed Sun.*

Chinese
Inexpensive–
Moderate
★
The Forbidden City. The Hunan style food at this restaurant in a reconstructed gas station is terrific. Start with the diced chicken with pine seeds in a package, icy lettuce cups wrapped around spicy chicken, which offer a delightful mix of cold and hot sensations. The sesame chicken, large chunks of sesame-coated poultry sautéed in a sweet sauce, goes perfectly with bright-green broccoli in a subtle garlic sauce. The traditional 10-ingredient lo mein is full of fresh shrimp, chicken, beef, and pork. *948 N. Mills Ave., Orlando, tel. 407/894–5005. MC, V. Closed Sat. lunch and Sun.*

Cuban
Inexpensive
★
Rolando's Cuban Restaurant. Cuban cuisine has become a Florida staple, and Rolando's is one of the best places in Orlando to try it. Black bean soup, dirty rice, and chicken with yellow rice are just a few of the specialties. *870 Semoran Blvd., Casselberry, tel. 407/767–9677. No reservations. MC, V.*

Deli
Inexpensive
Ronnie's. Others have tried but failed to compete with Ronnie's, the only place in town to get a decent corned-beef sandwich and Dr. Brown's soda. At lunchtime, city bigwigs fill up the back tables, and late at night, Ronnie's is still serving coffee and Danish. The tuna-fish salad is terrific. *Colonial Plaza, 2702 E. Colonial Dr. (bet. Bumby and Primrose Aves.), Orlando, tel 407/894–4951. No credit cards.*

French
Expensive
Le Cordon Bleu. Over the last two decades Georges and Monique Vogelbacher have won a loyal clientele with their traditional French cuisine. The room is comfortable, and so is the menu, which offers a well-prepared version of Caesar salad, lamb with vegetables, and poached Norwegian salmon. *537 West Fairbanks Ave., Winter Park, tel. 407/647–7575. Reservations advised. AE, D, DC, MC, V. Closed Sat. lunch and Sun.*

Moderate
★
Le Coq au Vin. The atmosphere here is country French, heavy on the country. Charming owners Louis Perrotte and his wife, Magdalena, make the place feel warm and homey, and it is almost always filled with a friendly group of Orlando residents. The traditional French fare is first-class: homemade chicken liver pâté, fresh rainbow trout with Champagne, and roast Long Island duck with green peppercorn sauce. For dessert, try the crème brûlée. *4800 S. Orange Ave., Orlando, tel. 407/851–6980. Reservations advised. AE, DC, MC, V.*

Italian
Expensive
Christini's. Locals and tourists alike gladly pay the price at Christini's, one of Orlando's best for traditional northern Italian cuisine. As a result, the place always feels as if there's a party going on, particularly in the center of the room. Try the pasta with lobster, shrimp, and clams; or the huge veal chops, perfumed with fresh sage. *7600 Dr. Phillips Blvd., in the Marketplace, Orlando, tel. 407/345–8770. Reservations advised. AE, DC, MC, V.*

★
Enzo's on the Lake. Enzo's is Orlando's most popular restaurant. The Roman charmer who owns the place, Enzo Perlini, has turned a rather ordinary lake-front house in suburban Longwood, about 30 minutes' drive from I-Drive, into a delightful Italian villa. It's worth the trip to sample the antipasto, the array of fresh grilled vegetables, the homemade frittatas

and pâtés, and the marinated seafood salad. The *bucatini à la Enzo*, a combination of sautéed bacon, mushrooms, and peas served over long hollow noodles, is satisfying. Even people with reservations don't mind waiting at the bar (as is often necessary); they just get into the party. *1130 S. U.S. 17–92, Longwood, tel. 407/834–9872. Reservations necessary. AE, DC, MC, V. Closed Sun.–Mon.*

Inexpensive– **Gargi's Italian Restaurant.** If you crave old-fashioned spaghetti
Moderate and meatballs, lasagna, or manicotti made with sauces that you know have been simmering all day, this store-front hole-in-the-wall a little north of downtown Orlando is the place. Well-heeled Orlandoans eat here before Orlando Magic basketball games. Located well off the beaten tourist track, it's a welcome change from I-Drive. *1421 N. Orange Ave., Orlando, tel. 407/894–7907. Reservations accepted. Beer and wine only. MC, V. Closed Sun.–Mon.*

Positano. One side of this restaurant is a bustling family-style pizza parlor; the other is a more formal dining room. Although you can't order pizza in the dining room, you can get anything on the entire menu in the pizzeria, which serves the closest thing to New York–style pies in Central Florida. Try the unusual and piquant *ziti aum, aum,* ziti with mozzarella, Parmesan cheese, eggplant, and fresh basil in a tomato sauce. *8995 West Colonial Dr. (1 mi. W. of Hiawassee), in Good Homes Plaza, Orlando, tel. 407/291–0602. Reservations in dining room only. AE, D, DC, MC, V.*

Mexican **Border Cantina.** With its pink walls and neon lights, this third-
Inexpensive floor restaurant at the southern end of Winter Park's Park Avenue is trendy Tex-Mex. But you won't have any complaints about the food. The kitchen does fajitas better than most, and the salsa is a fresh, chunky mix that will suit all tastes. *329 S. Park Ave., Winter Park, tel. 407/740–7227. Reservations advised for parties of 8 or more. AE, MC, V.*

Middle Eastern **Phoenician.** This is the latest addition to the rich culinary
Inexpensive clique at the Marketplace. *Hummus* (chick pea purée flavored with tahini), *babaganoush* (roasted eggplant purée), and lebneh top the menu. The best bet is to order a tableful of *mezes* (appetizers) and sample as many as possible. *7600 Dr. Phillips Blvd., in The Marketplace, Orlando, tel. 407/345–1001. No reservations. AE, MC, V.*

Seafood **Straubs Fine Seafood.** Seafood restaurants in Orlando are sur-
Moderate prisingly ordinary. The two Straubs establishments, which look like upscale coffee shops, are good bets, serving adequate seafood at fair prices. If you want fish, ask your server which is the freshest; you can order it blackened, grilled, or sautéed, with salad or coleslaw, and red potatoes or rice pilaf. *5101 E. Colonial Dr., Orlando, tel. 407/273–9330, and 512 E. Altamonte Dr., Altamonte Springs, tel. 407/831–2250. Reservations accepted. AE, D, DC, MC, V.*

Steak **Linda's La Cantina.** Twenty years ago, when this steakhouse
Moderate was in a little frame house, customers lined up on its doorstep
★ to eat the juicy, oversize New York strip and porterhouse steaks and drink bottles of the house wine. A few years ago the owners ripped down the original place and replaced it with a big, unattractive, barnlike structure. But loyal customers still wait eagerly (though now in a bar around a fireside pit). Without exception this is Orlando's best and most popular steak-

house. Other than spaghetti with meat sauce, which is tasty, the Italian food seems offered only to fill up the menu. *4721 E. Colonial Dr., Orlando. tel. 407/894–4491. Reservations advised. AE, DC, MC, V. Lunch only; closed Sun.–Mon.*

Thai
Moderate

Siam Orchid. The authentic Thai cuisine includes Siam wings appetizer—a chicken wing stuffed to look like a drumstick—and *pla lad prig*, a whole, deep-fried fish covered with a sauce flavored with red chili, bell peppers, and garlic. If you like your food spicy, specify "Thai hot." *7575 Republic Dr., Orlando, tel. 407/351–0821. Reservations advised. AE, DC, MC, V.*

Vietnamese
Inexpensive

Little Saigon. The friendly folks at Little Saigon love to introduce novices to their healthy, delicious national cuisine. Try the spring or summer rolls, then move on to a traditional soup (filled with vegetables, rice, noodles, and chicken or seafood), or the grilled pork and egg on rice and noodles. *1106 E. Colonial Dr., Orlando, tel. 407/423–8539. Beer and wine only. MC, V.*

Lodging

Your basic options come down to properties that are (1) owned and operated by Disney on WDW grounds, (2) not owned or operated by Disney but located on Disney property, and (3) not located on WDW property. There are advantages to each. If you are coming to Orlando for only a few days and are interested solely in the Magic Kingdom, Epcot Center, and the other Disney attractions, the resorts on Disney property—whether or not they're owned by Disney—are the most convenient. But if you plan to spend time sightseeing in and around Orlando, it makes sense to look into the alternatives. On-site hotels are generally more expensive, though there are now some moderately priced establishments on Disney property. But Orlando is not huge, and even apparently distant properties are only a half hour's drive from Disney toll plazas.

On-site hotels were built with families in mind. Rooms are usually large enough to accommodate up to five; all accommodations offer baby-sitting and cable TV with the Disney Channel. As an on-site guest, you can call in advance to make reservations at any of the restaurants in Epcot Center and Disney–MGM Studios. For Disney dinner show reservations, on-site guests can book as far in advance as they want (outsiders can only reserve seats 30 to 45 days in advance, depending on the show). In addition, on-site guests can gain admission to the Magic Kingdom one hour before regular park opening. Even when the theme parks or water parks have reached capacity (as River Country, Typhoon Lagoon, and Disney–MGM Studios sometimes do), on-site guests are guaranteed entry. In addition, on-site hotels offer many of their own special events. Best of all, Walt Disney World buses and monorails are free to guests at on-site resorts (as well as to those who have purchased multiday passports), making it easy to shuttle from one Disney park to another.

Although not owned or operated by the Disney organization, the other on-site hotels are "official" Walt Disney World hotels and offer their guests many of the same courtesies available to guests at Disney-owned properties—for instance, guests can make telephone reservations for restaurants and dinner shows in Walt Disney World in advance of the general public.

Near to Walt Disney World, hotels are clustered in several principal areas: along International Drive, a few minutes south of downtown Orlando; within the boundaries of Kissimmee, the town that is actually closest to Walt Disney World (where hotels tend to be small and cheap); and in the Disney Maingate area around WDW's northernmost entrance, just off I–4. Nearly all hotels in all these areas provide frequent transportation to and from Walt Disney World.

For real bargains and basic accommodations, head for the U.S. 192 strip—a.k.a the Irlo Bronson Memorial Highway—crammed with mom-and-pop motels and bargain basement hotels, cheap restaurants, fast-food spots, nickel-and-dime attractions, gas stations, and minimarts. Room rates start at $20 a night—lower at the right time of year, if you can cut the right deal. As a rule, the greater the distance from Walt Disney World, the lower the room rates.

In all but the smallest motels there is little or no charge for children under 18 who share a room with an adult.

Reservations All on-site accommodations, Disney-owned or not, may be booked through the **Walt Disney World Central Reservations Office** (Box 10100, Suite 300, Lake Buena Vista, FL 32830, tel. 407/934–7639). You must give a deposit for your first night's stay within three weeks of making your reservation. Reservations should be made several months in advance—as much as a year in advance for the best rooms during high season (historically, Christmas vacation, summer, and from mid-February through the week after Easter). Many hotels and attractions offer discounts up to 40% from September to mid-December.

Land packages, including admission tickets, car rentals, and hotels both on and off Disney property, can be made through your travel agent or **Walt Disney Travel Co.** (1675 Buena Vista Dr., Lake Buena Vista, FL 32830, tel. 407/828–3255). Land/air packages, with accommodations both on and off Disney property, can be booked through **Disney Reservation Service** (tel. 800/828–0228).

Ratings Highly recommended properties are indicated by a star ★. Unless otherwise noted, these are high-season rates for two adults traveling with up to two children under 18.

Category	Cost*
Very Expensive	over $150
Expensive	$120–$150
Moderate	$65–$120
Inexpensive	under $65

All prices are for a double room, excluding 9% tax.

Inside Walt Disney World

For locations of these hotels and resorts, *see* the Walt Disney World map, except for the resorts on Hotel Plaza Boulevard, which are shown on the Orlando Lodging map.

Disney-Owned Properties **Contemporary Resort.** This modern 15-story A-frame in the Magic Kingdom resort area has a slick, space-age impersonali-

Orlando Area Lodging

Best Western–Grosvenor Resort, **17**
Best Western Kissimmee, **28**
Buena Vista Palace, **19**
Casa Rosa Inn, **27**
Chalet Suzanne, **33**
Days Inn Orlando/Lakeside, **2**
Doubletree Club Hotel, **11**
Embassy Suites, **5**
Embassy Suites Resort Orlando, **13**
The Enclave Suites at Orlando, **3**
Grand Cypress Resort, **12**
Guest Quarters, **14**
Hilton at WDW Village, **20**
Holiday Inn Lake Buena Vista, **21**
Howard Johnson, Lake Buena Vista, **18**
Marriott's Orlando World Center, **22**
Orlando Heritage Inn, **7**
Parc Corniche, **9**
Park Inn International, **31**
Park Plaza Hotel, **1**
Peabody Orlando, **6**
Quality Suites Maingate East, **32**
Ramada Resort Maingate at the Parkway, **23**
Record Motel, **25**
The Residence Inn by Marriott on Lake Cecile, **30**
Royal Plaza, **16**
Sevilla Inn, **26**
Sheraton Lakeside Inn, **34**
Sol Orlando Village, **29**
Sonesta Villa Resort Orlando, **10**
Summerfield Suites Hotel, **4**
Travelodge Hotel, **15**
Vistana Resort, **24**
Wynfield Inn-Westwood, **8**

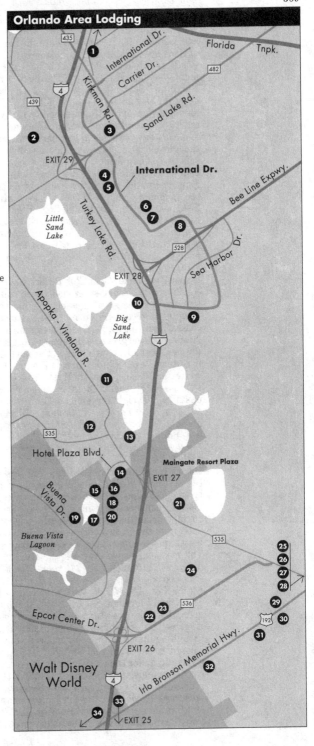

ty. It seems to be crowded with children and conventioneers, yet it is also the center of action, with entertainment, shops, and restaurants. Tower rooms are the most expensive because of their spectacular views, looking out toward the Cinderella Castle or onto Bay Lake, though they can be somewhat noisy at night—sounds rise through the busy atrium. Rooms in the North and South Gardens overlook the hotel's pool and gardens; the best are on the shore of Bay Lake. (Units described as having a view of the Magic Kingdom really look onto the parking lot.) Regardless of location, all rooms have a small terrace and most have two queen-size beds and a small additional bed, though you can request a room with a king-size bed and double sofa bed. The recently renovated rooms have oak furniture, paddle fans, and large bathrooms with black granite sinks. Many recreational facilities are right on the property; one of the swimming pools is WDW's largest. Kids will be happy to disappear into the Fiesta Fun Center, one of the biggest games rooms ever. *Tel. 407/824–1000. 1,053 rooms. Facilities: 3 restaurants, 2 snack bars, 2 lounges, 2 outdoor pools, lakeside beach, health club, 6 lighted tennis courts, children's program, volleyball, shuffleboard, boat rentals, water skiing. AE, MC, V. Very Expensive.*

Disney Beach and Yacht Club Resort. Set on a 25-acre lake, accessible from Epcot Center via a boardwalk, these two properties are New England inns on a grand scale. The five-story Yacht Club recalls the turn-of-the-century New England seacoast with its hardwood floors, gleaming brass, gray clapboard facade, and evergreen landscaping; there's even a lighthouse on its pier. Equally impressive is the blue-and-white, three- to five-story Beach Club, where a croquet lawn, cabana-dotted white-sand beach, and staffers' 19th-century "jams" and T-shirts set the scene. Both establishments are refreshingly unstuffy, just right for families. *Tel. 407/934–8000 (Beach) and 407/934–7000 (Yacht). 1,214 rooms. Facilities: 6 restaurants, 4 lounges, 2½-acre pool with water slides, 2 pools, marina with boat rentals, health club, golf, 2 lighted tennis courts, croquet court, volleyball court, child care for children 3–12 (4:30–midnight). AE, MC, V. Very Expensive.*

Disney Inn. Formerly called the Golf Resort, since it sits between two world-class 18-hole golf courses, this smaller property is a great spot for anyone who wants to get away from the more frenzied activity found at the other resorts. Rooms are slightly larger than in most other Disney resorts and accommodate up to five in two queen-size beds and a sleeper sofa. The least expensive units have views of the gardens or the fairways. The most expensive overlook the pool, though these can be noisy. *Tel. 407/824–2200. 284 rooms. Facilities: restaurant, 2 snack bars, lounge, 2 18-hole golf courses, 9-hole short course, health club. AE, MC, V. Very Expensive.*

★ **The Grand Floridian.** Set on the shores of the Seven Seas Lagoon, this looks like a turn-of-the-century summer resort, with its gabled red roof, brick chimneys, and rambling verandas. Although equipped with every modern convenience, the softly colored rooms have real vintage charm, especially the attic nooks, up under the eaves. Even the resort's monorail station carries the elegant Victorian theme. *Tel. 407/824–3000. 901 rooms and suites. Facilities: 6 restaurants, 3 lounges, outdoor pool, beach, whirlpool, health club, marina, boat rentals, children's program, playground. AE, MC, V. Very Expensive.*

Polynesian Resort. This resort is the most popular of all owned by Disney. An atrium full of orchids, coconut palms, and volcanic rock fountains is the centerpiece; guest rooms are in 11 two- and three-story "longhouses" stretching from this main building. All offer two queen-size beds and a smaller sleeper sofa to accommodate up to five, and except for some second-floor rooms, all have a balcony or patio. Lagoon-view rooms—the priciest—include a host of upgraded amenities and services. The least expensive rooms overlook the other buildings, the monorail, and the parking lot across the street. One of the two pools is an extravagantly landscaped free-form affair with rocks and caverns. The Neverland Club, the hotel's child-care center, even offers its guests a dinner show. *Tel. 407/824–2000. 855 rooms. Facilities: 3 restaurants, 2 snack bars, 2 lounges, 2 outdoor pools, lakeside beach, health club, playground, children's program. AE, MC, V. Very Expensive.*

Wilderness Lodge. Guests at this rustic lodge modeled after the turn-of-the-century structures in America's national parks won't exactly rough it. This pricey six-story establishment is scheduled to open in late summer 1994 on the southwest shore of Bay Lake, in the Magic Kingdom resort area. Its massive lobby features a huge, three-sided stone fireplace, enormous iron chandeliers with Indian and buffalo motifs, and two giant totem poles. All over the property there are porches, reading areas, and other intimate spaces. The large swimming pool area begins as a hot spring in the main lobby, flows under a window wall to an upper courtyard, and widens into a rushing waterfall. *WDW Central Reservations, Box 10100, Lake Buena Vista 32830, tel. 407/934–7639. 725 rooms. Facilities: 3 restaurants, lounge, outdoor pool, children's pool, golf, children's program. AE, MC, V. Very Expensive.*

Disney's Village Resort. Here you can choose among five clusters of villas, each with its own character and ambience. Though they are not quite as plush as rooms in the resort hotels, they are more spacious. Since the villas are not on the monorail, transportation to the parks can be slow. Free shuttle buses operate every 20 minutes to take you anywhere on the property. The upscale **Grand Vista Suites** (5 units) offer all the comforts of a luxury hotel, including nightly turndown service and stocked refrigerator. **One-bedroom villas** (139 units) have kitchens, a king-size bed in one room, and a queen-size sofa bed in the living room; **two-bedroom villas** (87 units), which also have kitchens, sleep six, with a sofa bed in the living room and either a king-size bed or two twins in each bedroom. Located right on the fairways of the Lake Buena Vista Golf Course, the **two-bedroom deluxe villas** (64 units) are built of cedar and are more tastefully decorated than some of the other villas. Very spacious, they have two bedrooms and a full loft and sleep up to six. Forest retreats built on stilts, the **two-bedroom resort villas with study** (60 units) are isolated within a peaceful wooded area ribboned with canals. All units have a kitchen, breakfast bar, and washer/dryer, and sleep six—two queen-bedded bedrooms, a double-bedded study, and two bathrooms. **One-bedroom suites** (324 units) are built of cedar and have one bedroom, a sofa bed in an adjacent sitting area, and a wet bar—but no kitchen; a few deluxe units have whirlpools. *Tel. 407/827–1100. Facilities: 4 outdoor pools, playground, 4 lighted tennis courts, boat rentals. AE, MC, V. Expensive–Very Expensive.*

All-Star Sports Resort. In this moderately priced resort, there are three-story stairwells in the shape of soda cups, lifeguard shacks, and tennis cans, plus larger-than-life football helmets, surfboards, and baseball bats; the entrance features a baseball scoreboard, a huge whistle, and a tennis umpire's chair. Rooms are designed to accommodate four people. *WDW Central Reservations, Box 10100, Lake Buena Vista 32830, tel. 407/W–DISNEY. 1,920 rooms. Facilities: food court, restaurant, outdoor pool, children's pool, children's program. AE, MC, V. Moderate.*

★ **Caribbean Beach Resort.** This immensely popular 200-acre property surrounding a 42-acre lake, just east of Epcot Center and Disney–MGM Studios theme parks, is comprised of five palm-studded island "villages," awash with the bright colors of the Caribbean, each with its own pool and white-sand beach. Bridges over the lake connect the mainland with 1-acre Parrot Cay, where there's a play area for children. Attractive, pastel-hue guest rooms are equipped with minibars and coffee makers. The only drawbacks compared to other on-site properties are somewhat smaller rooms, limited dining options, and no supervised children's program. *WDW Central Reservations, 10100 Lake Buena Vista, 32830, tel. 407/W–DISNEY. 2,112 rooms. Facilities: food court, lounge, whirlpool, 6 outdoor pools, children's pool, beach, playground, bike rentals, marina with boat rentals, jogging track. AE, MC, V. Moderate.*

Dixie Landings Resort. Disney's Imagineers drew inspiration from the architecture of the Old South for this sprawling resort complex. Rooms, which accommodate four, are in three-story plantation-style mansions and two-story rustic bayou dwellings. The well-designed food court, Colonel's Cotton Mill and Market, offers burgers, sandwiches, breakfast items, and pizza (which can be delivered to your room upon request). The pool, a 3½-acre old-fashioned swimming hole complex called Ol' Man Island, looks like something out of a Mark Twain novel; it has slides, rope swings, and an adjacent play area. *WDW Central Reservations, Box 10100, Lake Buena Vista 32830, tel. 407/W–DISNEY. 2,048 rooms. Facilities: food court, restaurant, whirlpool, heated outdoor pool, children's pool, marina, boat rentals, play area, golf. AE, MC, V. Moderate.*

Port Orleans Resort. Disney's version of New Orleans's French Quarter consists of ornate row-house buildings, with wrought iron balconies and hanging plants, clustered around squares with stone fountains and lush plantings. Lamplit sidewalks edge the streets, which are named after authentic French Quarter thoroughfares. New Orleans specialties, such as jambalaya, cajun chicken, and beignets, are served (along with the usual burgers, deli sandwiches, and pizza) at the hotel's food court; the restaurant offers Creole and other Louisiana-style fare. The large, freeform pool ("Doubloon Lagoon") is one of the most exotic of all Disney hotel pools. Note that most rooms here have two double beds and accommodate four; for quarters with one king-size bed, book early. *Tel. 407/934–5502. 1,008 rooms. Facilities: food court, restaurant, whirlpool, outdoor pool, children's pool, bike rentals, marina with boat rentals. AE, MC, V. Moderate.*

Other Walt Disney World Hotels

★ **Hilton at Walt Disney World Village.** The Hilton has an unimpressive facade, but the interiors are richly decorated in peach, mauve, and green; tastefully carpeted; and full of gleaming brass and glass. The lobby is rich with tile and latticework, and the pool area has an attractive deck and gazebo. Each guest room has a king-size bed or two double beds. The most expensive have views of Disney Village Market place and Lake Buena

Vista, but pool-view rooms are also good. Parents are particularly enthusiastic about the Hilton's Youth Hotel, a supervised playroom with large-screen television and six-bed dormitory that operates every evening; meals are served on schedule, and the cost is $6 an hour. *1751 Hotel Plaza Blvd., Lake Buena Vista 32830, tel. 407/827–4000 or 800/782–4414 for reservations. 813 rooms. Facilities: 4 restaurants, 2 lounges, Continental breakfast, 3 outdoor heated pools, outdoor whirlpool, 2 lighted tennis courts, health club, business center, valet parking. AE, DC, MC, V. Very Expensive.*

★ **Walt Disney World Dolphin.** This unforgettable Disney landmark features two mythical 56-foot sea creatures—labeled dolphins by the hotel's noted architect, Michael Graves—perched atop each end of the building; between them soars a 27-story pyramid, one of the highest structures in Walt Disney World. A waterfall cascades down the facade; the coral-and-turquoise facade displays a mural of giant banana leaves. Inside, chandeliers are shaped like monkeys and brightly painted wooden benches sprout wooden palm trees. Rooms are equally colorfully furnished; the best overlook Epcot Center and have a stunning view of its nightly fireworks-and-laser show. The 12th–20th Tower floors are concierge levels. With its emphasis on the convention trade, this hotel is more urban and adult than many other on-site properties. *1500 Epcot Resort Blvd., Lake Buena Vista 32830, tel. 407/934–4000 or 800/227–1500. 1,510 rooms (140 suites and 185 Tower rooms). Facilities: 7 restaurants, 4 lounges, 3 outdoor heated pools, beach, 8 lighted tennis courts, children's program. AE, DC, MC, V. Very Expensive.*

Walt Disney World Swan. Two 45-foot swans grace the rooftop of this coral-and-aquamarine hotel, which is connected by a covered causeway to the Dolphin. Inside, architect Michael Graves has canopied the ceiling with tall, gathered papyrus reeds and lined up a regiment of columns with palm-frond capitals. Rooms are decorated in coral, peach, teal, and yellow floral and geometric patterns; each has an in-room safe and stocked refrigerator. As at the Dolphin, the atmosphere is less family-oriented than many other on-site properties. *1200 Epcot Resorts Blvd., Lake Buena Vista 32830, tel. 407/934–3000, 800/248–7926, or 800/228–3000. 758 rooms (45 concierge rooms on 11th and 12th floors). Facilities: 3 restaurants, 2 lounges, outdoor pool, beach, health club, 8 lighted tennis courts, children's program, baby-sitting. AE, DC, MC, V. Very Expensive.*

Best Western–Grosvenor Resort. Offering a wealth of facilities and comfortable rooms for a fair price, this attractive hotel is probably the best deal in the neighborhood. Rooms are average in size, but colorfully decorated, and have their own safes, refrigerators, minibars, and coffee maker, plus cable TV, and a VCR (the lobby rents movies as well as videocameras). Public areas are spacious, with columns, high ceilings, cheerful colors, and plenty of natural light. *1850 Hotel Plaza Blvd., Lake Buena Vista 32830, tel. 407/828–4444 or 800/624–4109. 630 rooms. Facilities: 3 restaurants, lounge, 2 outdoor pools, children's pool, whirlpool, 2 lighted tennis courts, playground, shuffleboard, basketball court, volleyball court. AE, DC, MC, V. Expensive–Very Expensive.*

Buena Vista Palace and Palace Suite Resort at Walt Disney World Village. This bold, modern hotel, the largest at Lake Buena Vista, seems small and quiet when you enter its lobby. Don't be fooled. Upper-floor rooms are more expensive; the best ones look out toward Epcot Center. Ask for a room in the 27-story main tower, to avoid the late-night noise that reverberates through the atrium from the Kookaburra nightclub. All bedrooms have a small balcony and come with one king- or two queen-size beds. At the top of the hotel, the Top of the Palace Lounge offers a ringside seat on the local sunsets and Epcot Center's nightly laser-and-fireworks show. Suites in the adjacent Palace Suite Resort accommodate up to eight people; these have private balconies, living rooms with sleeper sofas, and dining areas (sink, coffee-maker, microwave, and refrigerator). *1900 Lake Buena Vista Dr., Lake Buena Vista 32830, tel. 407/827-2727 or 800/327-2990. 1,028 rooms. Facilities: 3 restaurants, 2 lounges, snack bar, 1 indoor-outdoor pool, 1 outdoor lap pool, health club, whirlpool, playground, 3 lighted tennis courts, business center, VCR in rooms, children's program. AE, DC, MC, V. Expensive–Very Expensive.*

Travelodge Hotel. Although unexceptionally furnished, the amenities make this a good choice for families. All guest rooms have recently been refurbished with pastel colors, attractive furniture, and touches of brass. There's nightly entertainment in the 18th-floor Topper's Nightclub, which overlooks Epcot Center. *2000 Hotel Plaza Blvd., Lake Buena Vista 32830, tel. 407/828-2424, 800/423-1022 in FL, or 800/348-3765 outside FL. 325 rooms. Facilities: restaurant, lounge, 2 snack bars, pool, playground. AE, DC, MC, V. Expensive.*

Guest Quarters. This all-suite hotel attracts a quiet family crowd and few of the noisy conventioneers often found at larger, splashier properties. Each unit has a bedroom with two double beds or a king, plus a separate living area equipped with a sofa bed; each can accommodate up to six (if not particularly comfortably). There's a television in each room (including a small one in the bathroom), refrigerator, wet bar, and coffeemaker; microwave ovens are available on request. *2305 Hotel Plaza Blvd., Lake Buena Vista 32830, tel. 407/934-1000 or 800/424-2900. 229 units. Facilities: restaurant, lounge, ice cream parlor, pool bar, pool, children's pool, 2 lighted tennis courts, whirlpool, exercise room, jogging trail. AE, DC, MC, V. Moderate–Very Expensive.*

Howard Johnson, Lake Buena Vista. Though somewhat charmless, with its lobbyful of white Formica and nondescript 14-story atrium, this is undeniably one of the most reasonably priced places to stay on Walt Disney World property, and it's popular with young couples and senior citizens. The Howard Johnson's restaurant, open until midnight, is better than average. *1805 Hotel Plaza Blvd., Lake Buena Vista 32830, tel. 407/828-8888 or 800/223-9930. 323 rooms. Facilities: restaurant, lounge, 2 heated pools, children's pool, whirlpool, games room, coffee maker in rooms, baby-sitting, guest laundry. AE, DC, MC, V. Moderate–Very Expensive.*

Royal Plaza. Though dated in comparison to the slick hotels in the neighborhood, this casual, lively establishment is quite popular among families with young kids and teenagers. Each of the generously proportioned rooms has a terrace or balcony, and the best ones overlook the pool. Lower-floor rooms can be noisy—the Giraffe, the hotel's Top-40 nightclub, hops until the wee, wee hours. *1905 Hotel Plaza Blvd., Lake Buena Vista 32830, tel. 407/828-2828 or 800/248-7890. 396 rooms. Facilities: 2 restaurants, 2 lounges, outdoor pool, whirlpool, sauna, tanning salon, 4 lighted tennis courts, putting green. AE, DC, MC, V. Moderate–Very Expensive.*

Around Walt Disney World

International Drive   **Peabody Orlando.** From afar, this 27-story structure looks like a high-rise office building, but don't be put off. Inside, the place is very impressive and handsomely designed, from the lobby's rich marble floors and fountains to the sweeping views and the modern art throughout the hotel. Like its parent property in Memphis, Tennessee, the Orlando Peabody has a resident flock of ducks splashing in the lobby fountain. The most panoramic rooms have views of Walt Disney World; those in the Peabody Club on the top three floors enjoy special concierge service. The restaurants are noteworthy. Located across the street from the Orlando Convention and Civic Center, the hotel attracts rock stars and other performers as well as convention-eers. *9801 International Dr., Orlando 32819, tel. 407/352-4000 or 800/732-2639. 891 rooms. Facilities: 3 restaurants, 2 lounges, Olympic-size pool, children's pool, 4 lighted tennis courts, whirlpool, health club and spa, children's program, golf privileges. AE, DC, MC, V. Very Expensive.*

Sonesta Villa Resort Orlando. In this complex of lakefront town houses, each unit is a homey, comfortable apartment, small but fully equipped with a kitchenette, dining area, living room, small patio, bedroom, and private ground-floor entrance; some units are bilevel. The conveniently located outdoor facilities are equally attractive. If you want to cook at "home" but are too busy to shop, the hotel will pick up groceries for you and deliver them while you're out. *10000 Turkey Lake Rd., Orlando 32819, tel. 407/352-8051 or 800/766-3782. 369 units. Facilities: 2 restaurants, lounge, pool bar and grill, ice cream parlor, outdoor pool, children's pool, 11 whirlpools, water sports (water ski, jet ski, and paddleboat rental), 2 lighted tennis courts, children's program, volleyball, shuffleboard, jogging path. AE, DC, MC, V. Moderate–Very Expensive.*

Embassy Suites. This all-suites hotel serves a free buffet breakfast with cooked-to-order items, yet room rates are less than a single room in the topnotch hotels. Each unit has both a bedroom and a full living room equipped with wet bar, refrigerator, pull-out sofa, two TVs. With its marble floors, pillars, hanging lamps, and ceiling fans, the lobby has an expansive, old-fashioned feel. Tropical gardens with mossy rock fountains give a distinctive Southern humidity to the atrium. *8978 International Dr., Orlando 32819, tel. 407/352-1400 or 800/432-7272. 245 suites. Facilities: restaurant, lounge, complimentary breakfast and cocktails, indoor pool, whirlpool, steam room, sauna, children's program. AE, DC, MC, V. Moderate–Expensive.*

The Enclave Suites at Orlando. With three 10-story buildings surrounding an office, restaurant, and recreation area, this all-suite hotel is less a hotel than a condominium complex. You get a complete apartment, with significantly more space than in other all-suite hotels. Accommodating up to six, the units have full kitchens, living rooms, two bedrooms, and small terraces. *6165 Carrier Dr., Orlando 32819, tel. 407/351-1155 or 800/457-0077. 321 suites. Facilities: restaurant, lounge, in-suite kitchens, 2 heated outdoor pools, indoor pool, whirlpool, sauna, exercise room, lighted tennis court, playground. AE, DC, MC, V. Moderate–Expensive.*

Parc Corniche Resort. Framed by an 18-hole Joe Lee–designed golf course called the International Golf Club, this all-suite resort is ideal for golf enthusiasts. Each of the one- and twobedoom suites is decked out in pastels and tropical patterns and has a patio or balcony with a golf course view as well as a kitchen. The largest accommodations, a two-bedroom, two-bath unit, can sleep up to six. The resort serves a complimentary Continental breakfast daily, and Sea World is only a few blocks away. *6300 Parc Corniche Dr., Orlando 32821, tel. 407/239-7100 or 800/446-2721. 210 suites. Facilities: restaurant, lounge, pool, children's pool, whirlpool, golf, playground. AE, D, MC, V. Moderate–Expensive.*

Summerfield Suites Hotel. A great option for big families, the all-suites Summerfield is small enough that guests get plenty of personal attention, but accommodations are quite roomy. Two-bedroom units, the most popular, have fully equipped kitchens (complete with stove, coffee maker, microwave, jumbo refrigerator, dishes, and pots and pans), plus a living room with TV and VCR. All the bedrooms have full baths and TVs. The courtyard shelters a small but pretty pool. If you don't want to hassle with whipping up eggs in the morning, you can sample the hotel's free Continental buffet. *8480 International Dr., Orlando 32819, tel. 407/352-2400 or 800/833-4353. 146 suites (42 with 1 bedroom, 104 with 2). Facilities: lounge, outdoor pool, children's pool, convenience store, exercise room, rental movies. AE, DC, MC, V. Moderate–Expensive.*

Orlando Heritage Inn. If you want a small, simple hotel with reasonable rates but plenty of charm, look into this establishment next door to the towering Peabody. Recalling Victorian-era Florida, it's full of reproduction turn-of-the-century furnishings, French windows, and brass lamps, interspersed with 19th-century antiques. In the guest rooms, folk art hangs on the walls, lace curtains the double French doors, and quilted spreads cover the beds. The staff is strong on southern hospitality. Dinner shows are presented in the rotunda several nights weekly. *9861 International Dr., Orlando 32819, tel. 407/352-0008 or 800/447-1890. 150 rooms. Facilities: restaurant, lounge, dinner theater, outdoor pool. AE, DC, MC, V. Moderate.*

Days Inn Orlando/Lakeside. Among the budget motels in the International Drive area, this Days Inn is tops. That's not only because of its location on the shores of Spring Lake, across I-4 from International Drive, but also because of its good facilities. Rooms are basic but just fine, and suites with coffee maker, microwave, and refrigerator are also available. *7335 Sand Lake Rd., Orlando 32819, tel. 407/351-1900 or 800/777-3297. 695 rooms. Facilities: restaurant, cafeteria, snack bar, 3 outdoor pools, beach, 2 playgrounds. AE, DC, MC, V. Inexpensive–Moderate.*

Wynfield Inn–Westwood. This two-story motel is a find. Its cheerful, contemporary rooms are smartly appointed with colorful, floral print bedspreads and understated wall hangings. In the recently renovated lobby, complimentary fruit, coffee, and tea is served daily. The staff is friendly and helpful. Children 17 and under stay free in their parents' room (with a maximum of four guests per room). *6263 Westwood Blvd., Orlando 32821, tel. 407/345-8000 or 800/346-1551. 300 rooms. Facilities: 2 outside pools, pool bar, in-room movies. AE, D, MC, V. Inexpensive–Moderate.*

Maingate **Grand Cypress Resort.** Perhaps the Orlando area's most spectacular resort, the 1,500-acre Grand Cypress offers virtually every resort facility and then some. Golf facilities are world-class, with 45 Jack Nicklaus-designed holes, making up four nine-hole courses, and a high-tech golf school. The huge, three-level swimming pool is fed by 12 cascading waterfalls, and there's a 45-acre Audubon nature reserve. Accommodations are divided between the 750-room Hyatt Regency Grand Cypress hotel and the 146-unit Villas of Grand Cypress. Rooms are unmemorable but spacious; those with the best views overlook the pool and Lake Windsong. The service is attentive and the restaurants excellent. This huge resort has just one drawback: the king-size conventions that it commonly attracts. *1 Grand Cypress Blvd., Orlando 32836, tel. 407/239–1234 or 800/233–1234. 750 rooms. Facilities: 7 restaurants, 5 lounges, ice cream parlor, 2 outdoor pools, children's pool, 3 whirlpools, health club, 45-hole golf complex, 12 tennis courts (5 lighted), 2 jogging trails, fitness course, bicycle rental, equestrian center, croquet court, water sports (paddleboat, sail boat, and canoe rentals), health club, children's program. AE, DC, MC, V. Very Expensive.*

Marriott's Orlando World Center. At this massive Marriott, the line-up of amenities seems endless; one of the four swimming pools is the largest in the state. The lobby is a huge, opulent atrium, and the rooms are clean and comfortable. Luxurious villas, the Royal Palms and Sabal Palms, are available for daily and weekly rentals. If you like your hostelries cozy, you'll consider the size of this place a definite negative; otherwise, its single unappealing aspect is the crowd of conventioneers it attracts. *8701 World Center Dr., Orlando 32821, tel. 407/239–4200 or 800/228–9290. 1,504 rooms. Facilities: 7 restaurants, 3 lounges, 3 outdoor pools, indoor pool, children's pool, 4 whirlpools, health club, 18-hole golf course, 12 lighted tennis courts, children's program. AE, DC, MC, V. Very Expensive.*

Vistana Resort. Consider this peaceful resort if you're interested in tennis: Its clay and all-weather courts can be used without charge; private or semiprivate lessons are available for a fee. It's also a good bet for families or a group of friends. The spacious, tastefully decorated villas and town houses are spread over 95 landscaped acres and have two bedrooms each, plus a living room, full kitchen, washer/dryer, and so on. The price may seem high, but considering that each unit can sleep six or eight, it's a bargain. *8800 Vistana Centre Dr., Orlando 32821, tel. 407/239–3100 or 800/877–8787. 722 units. Facilities: 2 restaurants, 2 lounges, 5 outdoor pools, 5 children's pools, 7 whirlpools, health club, 3 basketball courts, shuffleboard, miniature golf course, convenience store, children's program. AE, DC, MC, V. Very Expensive.*

Embassy Suites Resort Orlando. Some local folks have been shocked by this all-suite hotel's wild turquoise, pink, and yellow facade, clearly visible from I–4. But it's an attractive option—just 1 mile from Walt Disney World, 5 miles from Sea World, and 7 miles from Universal Studios Florida. The central atrium lobby, loaded with tropical vegetation and soothed by a rushing fountain, is a great place to enjoy the complimentary breakfast. *8100 Lake Ave., Lake Buena Vista 32830, tel. 407/239–1144 or 800/362–2779. 280 suites. Facilities: restaurant, lounge, snack bar, indoor–outdoor pool, children's pool, whirlpool, fitness room, lighted tennis court, shuffleboard, basketball, volleyball, fitness course, children's program, playground. AE, DC, MC, V. Expensive–Very Expensive.*

★ **Ramada Resort Maingate at the Parkway.** With its attractive setting, good facilities, and competitive prices, this bright, spacious Ramada may offer the best deal in the neighborhood. Its delicatessen comes in handy when you want to assemble a picnic. Generously proportioned rooms are decked out in tropical patterns and pastel colors; those with the best view and light face the pool. *2900 Parkway Blvd., Kissimmee 34746, tel. 407/396-7000, 800/634-4774, or 800/225-3939 in FL. 716 rooms. Facilities: restaurant, lounge, deli, snack bar, outdoor pool, children's pool, 2 whirlpools, sauna, 2 lighted tennis courts, volleyball. AE, DC, MC, V. Moderate–Very Expensive.*

Holiday Inn Lake Buena Vista. From its sweeping, covered entrance to its striking, terra-cotta-color facade, this big Holiday Inn is most impressive. It's also an excellent value. Furnished with two queen-size beds or one king and a sleeper, all rooms have a TV and VCR plus a kitchenette equipped with refrigerator, microwave, and coffee maker. In the hotel courtyard is a wonderfully huge, free-form pool, plus a whirlpool and a vast wading pool. But what really earns the kudos here is the Camp Holiday children's program, free to guests—the hotel even rents beepers to parents who want to stay in close touch with their children. *13351 Rte. 535, Lake Buena Vista 32821, tel. 407/239-4500, 800/366-6299, or 800/465-4329. 507 rooms. Facilities: restaurant, lounge, outdoor pool, children's pool, whirlpool, children's program. AE, DC, MC, V. Moderate–Expensive.*

Doubletree Club Hotel. This six-story hotel features the Doubletree Club, a 5,000-square-foot living room full of big couches, where guests can read a book or watch the big-screen TV. You don't expect such homey touches when you see the building, which looks as if it belongs in a sterile office park, but the service and amenities more than make up for the less-than-inspiring facade. *8688 Palm Pkwy., Lake Buena Vista 32830, tel. 407/239-8500 or 800/228-2846. 167 rooms. Facilities: restaurant, lounge, outdoor pool, whirlpool, health club. AE, DC, MC, V. Moderate.*

U.S. 192 Area   **Quality Suites Maingate East.** Ideal for large families, the spacious rooms are designed to sleep 6 or 10, and come equipped with a microwave, refrigerator, and dishwasher. Suites have two bedrooms with two double beds each and a living room with a double pullout couch. Children will enjoy the motel's restaurant: A toy train chugs along overhead. No-smoking suites are available. *5876 W. Irlo Bronson Memorial Hwy., Kissimmee 34746, tel. 407/396-8040, 800/221-2222, or 800/848-4148 in FL. 225 units. Facilities: restaurant, lounge, poolside bar, outdoor pool, whirlpool, playground, convenience store. AE, D, DC, MC, V. Moderate–Very Expensive.*

The Residence Inn by Marriott on Lake Cecile. Of the all-suite hotels on U.S. 192, this complex of town houses is probably the best. One side of the complex faces the highway, the other overlooks an attractive lake, where you can sail, water-ski, Jet-ski, and fish. Penthouse units accommodate four, with complete kitchens, small living rooms, loft bedrooms, and fireplaces. All others accommodate two and are like studio apartments, but still have full kitchens and fireplaces. Each suite has a private entrance. While the price may seem high considering the location, there is no charge for additional guests, so you can squeeze in the whole family, and both Continental breakfast and a grocery shopping service are complimentary. *4786 W. Irlo Bronson Memorial Hwy., Kissimmee 34746, tel. 407/396–*

2056, 800/648–7408 in FL, or 800/468–3027 outside FL. 160 units. Facilities: outdoor pool, whirlpool, tennis court, basketball court, playground. AE, DC, MC, V. Moderate–Expensive.

Sol Orlando Village Resort Hotel. Owned by a major Spanish hotel company, this hotel has the look of a resort on the Costa del Sol, with its red tile roof and stucco villa buildings on neatly landscaped grounds. Each of the one-, two-, and three-bedroom units has a living and dining area, a kitchen, and two TVs; the three-bedroom villa sleeps up to eight comfortably. Wooden bridges span the small waterway that meanders through the palm-studded property. *4787 W. Irlo Bronson Memorial Hwy., Kissimmee 34746, tel. 407/397–0555. 150 villas. Facilities: restaurant, lounge, outdoor pool, children's pool, whirlpool, health club, tennis court, squash and racquetball court, convenience store. AE, MC, V. Moderate–Expensive.*

Best Western Kissimmee. Overlooking a nine-hole, par-three executive golf course, this independently owned and operated three-story hotel is a hit with golf-loving seniors as well as families. The two swimming pools in the well-landscaped garden courtyard are amply shaded. The spacious, newly decorated rooms are done in soft pastels, with light wood furniture and attractive wall hangings. Units with king-size beds and kitchenettes are available. *2261 E. Irlo Bronson Memorial Hwy., Kissimmee 34744, tel. 407/846–2221. 281 rooms. Facilities: restaurant, lounge, 2 outdoor pools, playground, picnic area. AE, D, MC, V. Moderate.*

Sheraton Lakeside Inn. This comfortable if undistinguished resort, a complex of 15 two-story buildings spread over 27 acres, offers quite a few recreational facilities for the money. The nondescript beige rooms have either two double- or one king-size bed; each has a refrigerator and safe. *7769 W. Irlo Bronson Memorial Hwy., Kissimmee 34746, tel. 407/239–7919, 800/325–3535, or 800/422–8250 in FL. 651 rooms. Facilities: 2 restaurants, lounge, deli, 3 outdoor pools, children's pool, 4 tennis courts, children's program, miniature golf, paddleboat and fishing equipment rental. AE, DC, MC, V. Moderate.*

★ **Casa Rosa Inn.** For simple motel living—no screaming kids or loud music, please—this pink, Spanish-motif spot run by a Chinese immigrant family is the place you want. It's simple and doesn't have much in the way of facilities aside from its pool and free in-room movies. But it's a good, serviceable option, and the price is right. *4600 W. Irlo Bronson Memorial Hwy., Kissimmee 34746, tel. 407/396–2020 or 800/432–0665. 54 rooms. Facilities: outdoor pool, guest laundry. AE, DC, MC, V. Inexpensive.*

Park Inn International. The Mediterranean-style architecture is not likely to charm you off your feet, but the staff is friendly and the property has all the facilities you're likely to want—and it's on a lake. Ask for a room as close to the water as possible. There is a restaurant, but for an extra $10 you can get a room with a kitchenette. *4960 W. Irlo Bronson Memorial Hwy., Kissimmee 34741, tel. 407/396–1376 or 800/327–0072. 197 rooms. Facilities: restaurant, outdoor pool, whirlpool. AE, DC, MC, V. Inexpensive.*

Record Motel. This simple property is the kind of few-frills, rock-bottom-rates mom-and-pop operation that made U.S. 192 famous. Clean rooms with free HBO and a solar-heated pool are the major amenities. What the place lacks in luxuries and ambience it more than makes up for with its friendy staff. *4651 W.*

Irlo Bronson Memorial Hwy., Kissimmee 34746, tel. 407/396–8400. 57 rooms. Facilities: outdoor pool. AE, MC, V. Inexpensive.

Sevilla Inn. This classy, family-operated motel is one of the best buys in the Orlando area. Stucco and wood on the outside, the three-story building has up-to-date rooms inside, with colorful bedspreads, tasteful wall hangings, a fresh paint job, and cable TV. The pool area, encircled by palm trees and tropical flowers, feels like something you'd find in a much fancier resort. *4640 W. Irlo Bronson Memorial Hwy., Kissimmee 34746, tel. 407/396–4135 or 800/367–1363. 46 rooms. Facilities: outdoor pool. AE, D, MC, V. Inexpensive.*

Orlando Suburbs

Winter Park
★

Park Plaza Hotel. Small and intimate, this 1922-vintage establishment feels almost like a private home, but there are nice touches: A newspaper is slid under your door each morning, for example. Rooms—mostly on the small side—have either a double-, queen-, or king-size bed; all open onto one long balcony abloom with ferns and flowers and punctuated by wicker chairs and tables, with views of Park Avenue or Central Park. This old-fashioned spot is definitely not for you if you want recreational facilities or have young children. But if you are hoping for real Southern charm and hospitality, it's the only choice. *307 Park Ave. S, Winter Park 32789, tel. 407/647–1072 or 800/228–7220. 27 rooms. Facilities: restaurant, lounge. AE, DC, MC, V. Moderate–Expensive.*

Lake Wales
★

Chalet Suzanne. You'll find this friendly, homespun mom-and-pop operation in the orange grove territory some 60 miles southwest of Orlando and about a half-hour drive from Walt Disney World. A homemade billboard directs you down a country road that turns into a palm-lined drive, then cobblestone paths lead to a balconied chalet-style house and cabins with thatch roofs. Fields and gardens extend to one side, a lake on the other. The happily quirky grounds are decorated with colorful tilework from Portugal, ironwork from Spain, pottery from Italy, and porcelain from England and Germany. In the rooms and public spaces, furnishings vary wildly from the rare and valuable to the garage-sale one-of-a-kind. Each room has its own personality; all have eccentrically tiled bathrooms with old-fashioned tubs and washbasins. The most charming rooms face the lake. There is a gourmet dining room. *Box AC, Lake Wales 33859, tel. 813/676–6011. 30 rooms. Facilities: restaurant. AE, DC, MC, V. Moderate–Expensive.*

The Arts and Nightlife

Until a few years ago, you could have compared Orlando's nightlife to that of Oskaloosa, Iowa. But, slowly, an after-dark scene has developed. Disney and other Orlando entrepreneurs have now caught on that there is a fortune to be had satisfying the fun-hungry night owls who flock to this city. New night spots are opening constantly—everything from flashy discos to ballroom dancing palaces, country-and-western saloons, Broadway dinner theaters, and even medieval jousting tournaments.

The Arts

Check out the local fine arts scene in *The Weekly*, a local entertainment magazine, or "Calendar," which is printed every Friday in the *Orlando Sentinel*. They are available at most newsstands. The average price of a ticket to performing arts events in the Orlando area rarely exceeds $12, and is often half that price.

The **Carr Performing Arts Centre** (401 Livingston St., Orlando, tel. 407/849–2020) presents a different play each month, with evening performances Wednesday through Saturday and Sunday matinees. The Broadway series features new productions on the way to Broadway and current road shows.

During the school year, Winter Park's **Rollins College** (tel. 407/646–2233) has a choral concert series that is open to the public and usually free. The first week of March there is a Bach Music Festival (tel. 407/646–2182) that has been a Winter Park tradition for more than 55 years. Also at the college, the Annie Russell Theater (tel. 407/646–2145) has a regular series of productions.

The **Orange County Convention and Civic Center** (tel. 407/345–9800), on the south end of International Drive, and the **Orlando Arena,** downtown (tel. 407/849–2020), play host to many big-name performing artists.

Civic Theatre of Central Florida (1001 E. Princeton St., tel. 407/896–7365) in Loch Haven Park stages productions throughout the year. The MainStage Series offers traditional Broadway musicals and dramas; the SecondStage Series has off-Broadway–style, cutting-edge works; and family classics are performed in the Theatre for Young People.

Nightlife

There's been a recent surge in the number of Orlando nightclubs, but there still isn't a full-fledged nightlife scene in Orlando. Early in the week, many of the clubs are mostly deserted much of the night. Nightclubs in Orlando proper have significantly more character than those in the areas around Walt Disney World, but clubs on Disney property are allowed to stay open later—you can get a drink there as late as 2:45 AM.

Walt Disney World Inside Walt Disney World, every hotel has its quota of bars and lounges. Jazz trios and bluegrass bands, DJs and rockers tune up and turn on their amps after dinner's done. In addition, there's a trio of long-run dinner shows that give you and your family an evening of song, dance, and a meal for a single price—a fairly steep price, somewhere in the range of $30–$45 for adults, $15–$25 for children. **Broadway at the Top,** the show at the Top of the World Nightclub atop the Contemporary Resort (tel. 407/934–7639), is a spirited revue with a cast of high-energy dancers and singers performing some of Broadway's greatest hits; it runs for about an hour after each of the two nightly seatings for dinner. The **Hoop-Dee-Doo Revue,** staged at Fort Wilderness Resort's rustic Pioneer Hall (tel. 407/934–7639 in advance, 407/824–2748 on the day of the show), may be corny, but it is also the liveliest show in Walt Disney World. A troupe of jokers called the Pioneer Hall Players stomp their feet, wisecrack, and otherwise make merry while the audience chows down on barbecued ribs, fried chicken, corn on the cob, strawberry shortcake, and all the fixin's. There are three shows nightly; the prime times sell out months in advance in busy seasons. The **Polynesian Revue** (tel. 407/934–7639), better known as the Luau, is an outdoor barbecue with the Polynesian-theme entertainment appropriate to its colorful, South Pacific setting at the Polynesian Resort. There are two shows nightly, plus an earlier wingding for children called **Mickey's Tropical Revue,** wherein Disney characters do a few numbers decked out in South Seas garb.

Pleasure Island (tel. 407/934–7781) is a 6-acre after-dark entertainment complex, an island with a cluster of vintage buildings, connected to Disney Village Marketplace and the mainland by three footbridges. It's a short stroll from the Empress Lilly, a riverboat full of restaurants. In addition to seven clubs, there's also a 10-screen AMC movie theater (tel. 407/827–1309) that starts showing at 1:30 PM. A pay-one-price admission ($12.95) gets you in to all the clubs and shows except the movie house. The **Adventurers Club** whimsically re-creates a private club of the 1930s; the **Comedy Warehouse** has an improvisational setup, with five shows nightly; **Mannequins Dance Palace** is a high-tech Top–40 dance club with a revolving dance floor and special effects; live country-and-western music is the focus of the **Neon Armadillo Music Saloon;** the **Rock & Roll Beach Club** throbs with live rock music of the 1950s and 1960s.

Church Street Station **Church Street Station** (129 W. Church St., Orlando, tel. 407/422–2434) is a complete entertainment complex, with old-fashioned saloons, dance halls, dining rooms, and shopping arcades that are almost Disneyesque in their attention to detail. Unlike much of what you see in Walt Disney World, this place doesn't just look authentic—it is. The train on the tracks is an actual 19th-century steam engine; the whistling calliope was especially rebuilt to blow its original tunes. Just about everything down to the cobblestones that clatter under the horse-drawn carriages are the real McCoy. For a single $15.95 admission price ($9.95 for children 4–12), you can wander freely and stay as long as you wish. Food and drink cost extra and are not cheap. Parts of the complex are open during the day, but the place is usually quiet then; the pace picks up at night, especially on weekends, with crowds thickest from 10 to 11.

Rosie O'Grady's Good Time Emporium, the original bar on Church Street, is a turn-of-the-century saloon with dark wood, brass trim, a full Dixieland band, can-can and tap dancers, and vaudeville singers. Quiet **Apple Annie's Courtyard** offers easy-listening music from Jimmy Buffett to James Taylor. **Lili Marlene's Aviator's Pub and Restaurant** has the relaxed wood-paneled atmosphere of an English pub and the finest dining on Church Street—hearty, upscale, very American food, mostly steaks, ribs, and seafood. **Phineas Phogg's Balloon Works,** a disco that plays contemporary dance tunes on a sound system that will blow your socks off, draws a good-looking yuppie tourist crowd and a few local young singles; the place is jammed by midnight. In the **Orchid Garden Ballroom,** iron latticework, arched ceilings, and stained-glass windows create a striking Victorian setting where visitors sit, drink, and listen to a first-rate band pounding out popular tunes from the 1950s to present. **Cracker's Oyster Bar,** behind the Orchid Garden, is a good place to get a quick gumbo or chowder fix; it's also got one of the largest wine cellars in Florida. The immensely popular **Cheyenne Saloon and Opera House** occupies a trilevel former opera house, now full of moose racks, steer horns, buffalo heads, and Remington rifles; the seven-piece country-and-western band that plays there darn near brings the house down. The upstairs restaurant serves chicken-and-ribs fare.

Clubs and Bars **Laughing Kookaburra Good Time Bar** (Buena Vista Palace Hotel, Lake Buena Vista, tel. 407/827–3425) draws a serious singles crowd of all ages. The music is loud and the dance floor can get very crowded. The bar serves up 99 brands of beer, plus cocktails.

Bennigan's (6324 International Dr., Orlando, tel. 407/351–4436), another young singles spot, draws crowds in the early evening and during happy hours: 2–7 PM and 11 PM–midnight.

J.J. Whispers (5100 Adanson St., Orlando, tel. 407/629–4779), a trendy club complex, draws fashion-conscious locals. It includes: a massive, multilevel, state-of-the-art disco; the Showroom, where the over-30 set listen to music from the '40s, '50s, and '60s; and Bonkerz (tel. 407/629–2665), a comedy club featuring touring local and national comics Thursday–Saturday nights; on Sunday it is transformed into 6 Feet Under, an industrial club that plays hard-core progressive music. Cover charges run $3–$10. J.J.'s is at the end of the Lee Road Shopping Center, 1½ miles west of I–4 (Lee Rd. exit) via Lee Road; watch for a sharp left-hand turn at Adanson Street.

Crocodile Club (118 W. Fairbanks Ave., Winter Park, tel. 407/647–8501), a bar inside a Winter Park restaurant called Bailey's, collects a young, well-dressed crowd from neighboring Rollins College. A DJ plays current dance hits, and the food at Bailey's is fairly good. Cover charge: $2.

Suilivan's Trailways Lounge (1108 S. Orange Blossom Trail (U.S. 441), tel. 407/843–2934) is a Southern country-and-western dance hall where people of all ages come to strut their stuff. Big-name performers entertain on occasion; local bands play Tuesday–Saturday. Cover charge $2 and up.

Big Bang (102 N. Orange Ave., tel. 407/425-9277) is a small Bohemian downtown nightspot. With its mix of music from funk to rave (if you have to ask, you won't like it), it's open Thursday–Saturday until the wee hours for dancing, coffee, mineral water, smart drinks, and more dancing. Cover charge $3.

Mulvaney's Irish Pub (27 W. Church St., tel. 407/872–3296) has seven import beers on tap, including Guinness, and Irish folk singers several nights a week, and it's packed on weekends and on Orlando Magic game nights. The kitchen serves mostly sandwiches, but also has such British staples as shepherd's pie and bangers and mash.

Rockin' Rooster (25 W. Church St., tel. 407/649–4806) is a great place to see a (usually local) band. No ferns or pool tables; just a stage, a few tables, and hordes of occasionally rowdy patrons. Appetizers are the only food served.

Dad's Road Kill Cafe (106 Lake Ave., Maitland , tel. 407/647–5288) is a tiny bar-and-restaurant with an eclectic menu. If the house band is 2EZ (it usually is), demand to hear their rendition of the "Sam I Am" rap. Turn left and go almost 1 mile, and look for the strip mall on the corner of Lake and Orlando.

The Edge (100 W. Livingston, tel. 407/426–9166), *the* current hot dance spot in Orlando, is a multilevel converted warehouse with light shows and smoke machines; the pounding dance music is played just below the pain threshold. Cover charge $4–$5.

Dekko's (46 N. Orange Ave., tel. 407/648–8727) is an Art Deco–theme dance club featuring an extensive light show and a real rainmaker of a sound system. It draws a 30ish crowd most nights. Cover charge $6.

Sports Bars **Coaches Locker Room** (269 W. Rte. 436, Altamonte Springs, tel. 407/869–4446), a two-level sports palace, boasts six big-screen TVs and 12 smaller monitors. Except for blacked-out Tampa Bay Buccaneers games, Coaches shows every pro football contest, plus every other kind of sport imaginable. The food is not the major attraction, but the buffalo wings are worth trying. It's in the strip mall behind the T.G.I.Friday's at the intersection of I–4 and Route 436.

Sports Dimension (3001 Curry Ford Rd., tel. 407/895–0807) has 12 big-screen TVs; more than 75 screens hang from the walls and the ceiling, above the dance floor, and even over the urinals in the men's room.

Dinner Shows Dinner shows are an immensely popular form of nighttime entertainment around Orlando. A fixed price usually buys a theatrical production and a multiple-course dinner (of more or less forgettable food). What the shows lack in substance and depth they make up for in color and enthusiasm; children often love them. Most shows have seatings at 7 and 9:30, and at most you sit with strangers at long tables. Always call and make reservations in advance, especially for weekends.

Arabian Nights looks like an elaborate palace outside; inside it's more like an arena, with seating for more than 1,200. The show features some 25 acts with more than 80 performing horses, music, special effects, and a chariot race; keep your eyes open for a unicorn. The four-course dinners are of prime rib or vegetarian lasagna. *6225 W. Irlo Bronson Memorial Hwy., Kissimmee, tel. 407/396–7400; in Orlando, 407/239–9223; 800/553–6116; in Canada, 800/533–3615. Admission: $29.95 adults, $17.95 children 3–11. AE, D, DC, MC, V.*

Brazil Carnival Dinner Show features the sights and sounds of Brazil. Brazilian dancers bring to life the Bossa Nova and the Lambada, and singers present their renditions of old favorites such as the "Girl from Ipanema." The four-course meal includes broccoli soup, salad, a main course with meat, rice, and a vegetable, plus dessert. *7432 Republic Dr., Orlando, tel. 407/352–8666 or 800/821–4088 for reservations. Admission: $28 adults, $17 children 3–12. MC, V.*

Wild Bill's Wild West Dinner Show at Fort Liberty is a mixed bag of real Indian dances, foot-stompin' singalongs, and acrobatics. The chow, served by a rowdy chorus of cavalry recruits, is beef soup, fried chicken, corn-on-the-cob, and pork and beans. *5260 W. Irlo Bronson Memorial Hwy., Kissimmee, tel. 407/351–5151. Admission: $29.95 adults, $19.95 children 3–11. AE, DC, MC, V. No smoking in the show room.*

King Henry's Feast, set in a Tudor-style building, features jesters, jugglers, dancers, magicians, and singers, ostensibly feting Henry VIII as he celebrates his birthday. Saucy wenches serve forth potato-leek soup, salad, and chicken and ribs. *8984 International Dr., Orlando, tel. 407/351–5151. Admission: $29.95 adults, $19.95 children 3–11. AE, D, DC, MC, V.*

Mardi Gras is an hour-long cabaret that showcases colorful song and dance routines to Dixieland jazz and Latin American and Caribbean beats. The fare is simple and undistinguished—vegetable soup, chicken nuggets, french fries, and Key lime pie.

Mercado Mediterranean Village, 8445 International Dr., Orlando, tel. 407/351-5151. Admission: $29.95 adults, $19.95 children 3-11. AE, D, DC, MC, V.

Mark Two stages complete Broadway musicals—such as *Oklahoma, My Fair Lady, West Side Story,* and *South Pacific*—throughout the year and musical revues chockablock with Broadway tunes during the Christmas holidays. For about two hours before curtain, you can order from the bar and help yourself at buffet tables laden with institutional seafood Newburg, baked whitefish, meats, and salad; dessert arrives during intermission. Unlike other dinner theaters, the Mark Two offers only tables for two and four. *Edgewater Center, 3376 Edgewater Dr., Orlando (from I-4 take Exit 44 and go west), tel. 407/843-6275. Tickets: $28-$32 adults, $23-$27 all children under 13. AE, D, MC, V. Performances Wed.-Sat. at 8; Wed., Thurs., Sat. at 1:15; Sun. at 6:30.*

Medieval Times, in a huge, medieval-style manor house, portrays a two-hour tournament of sword fights, jousting matches, and other games, featuring no less than 30 charging horses and a cast of 75 knights, nobles, and maidens. The bill of fare is heavy on the meat and potatoes. *4510 W. lrlo Bronson Memorial Hwy., Kissimmee, tel. 407/239-0214, 407/396-1518, or 800/239-8300. Tickets: $29.95 adults, $20.95 children 3-12. D, MC, V.*

10 The Tampa Bay Area

By Karen
Feldman Smith
and G. Stuart
Smith

Updated by
Natalie Fairhead

Around Tampa Bay lies a microcosm of those qualities of life most of us appreciate: a semitropical climate, bayside landscapes, barrier islands with white-sand beaches, picturesque settings for pleasure and business, an international community with a proud past and promising future.

Over the last 25 years the region has become fully developed, but at a much slower pace and with a less commercial atmosphere than the East Coast. As a result, this is a community with a varied economic base, not entirely dependent upon tourism, but it also happens to have excellent beaches and several superior hotels and resorts that cater to families. Many hotels offer reasonably priced two-bedroom, two-bath suites with full kitchens and laundry facilities, in addition to supervised children's programs. Taking advantage of the facilities, mom and dad can pursue their own activities, which may include 18 holes of golf, or a couple of tennis matches organized by the property. They might also try their hand at boating or deep-sea fishing, both of which rank among the favorite pastimes here.

As for cities, the closest resemblance to a metropolis you'll find in this region is Tampa, the crown jewel and entertainment hub, with the greatest concentration of restaurants, stores, and nightlife of any Southwest Florida city. Tampa does not have a Gulf beach, however, and Tampa Bay, though lovely to look at, is not suited for swimming. For that, visitors should head to neighboring St. Petersburg, which sits on a peninsula bordered on three sides by bays and the Gulf of Mexico, filled with pleasure and commercial craft.

Inland, to the east of Tampa, is a typical American residential area: suburban sprawl, freeways, shopping malls, and—the main draw—Busch Gardens. The northern coast has been coined "Manatee Country" for its extensive nature preserves and parks, designed to protect these water creatures and other wildlife indigenous to the area.

It's fitting that an area with a thriving international port should also be populated by a wealth of nationalities—Greeks, Scots, Hispanics, and Italians, to name only a few. American Indians were the sole inhabitants of the region for many years (Tampa is an Indian phrase meaning "sticks of fire"). The Spanish explorers Juan Ponce de Léon, Pánfilo de Narváez, and Hernando de Soto passed through in the mid-1500s. The U.S. Army and civilian settlers arrived in 1824; a military presence remains in Tampa in the form of MacDill Air Force Base, where the U.S. Operations Command is located. The Cuban community centers around the east Tampa suburb of Ybor City; north of St. Petersburg, in Dunedin, the heritage is Scottish; and the area north of Dunedin, in Tarpon Springs, has supported a large Greek population for decades.

Essential Information

Important Addresses and Numbers

Tourist
Information

The following offices are open weekdays 9–5 and closed on holidays:

Greater Clearwater Chamber of Commerce (128 N. Osceola Ave., tel. 813/461–0011).

Greater Dunedin Chamber of Commerce (301 Main St., tel. 813/736-5066).

Gulf Beaches on Sand Key Chamber of Commerce (105 5th Ave., Indian Rocks Beach, tel. 813/595-4575 or 813/391-7373).

Pinellas Suncoast Tourist Development Council (4625 E. Bay Dr., Suite 109, Clearwater, tel. 813/530-6452).

St. Petersburg Chamber of Commerce (100 2nd Ave. N, tel. 813/821-4069).

Sarasota Convention and Visitors Bureau (655 N. Tamiami Trail, tel. 813/957-1877 or 800/522-9799).

Greater Tampa Chamber of Commerce (Box 420, tel. 813/228-7777). For information on current area events, call the **Visitors Information Department** (tel. 813/223-1111).

Tampa/Hillsborough Convention and Visitors Association (111 Madison St., Suite 1010, tel. 800/826-8358; information and hotel reservations, tel. 800/448-2672; vacation packages, tel. 800/284-0404).

Tarpon Springs Chamber of Commerce (210 S. Pinellas Ave., Suite 120, tel. 813/937-6109).

Treasure Island Chamber of Commerce (152 108th Ave., tel. 813/367-4529).

Emergencies Dial 911 for **police** or **ambulance** in an emergency.

Hospitals Hospital emergency rooms are open 24 hours. In **Tampa:** University Community Hospital (3100 E. Fletcher Ave.). In **St. Petersburg:** Bayfront Medical Center (701 6th St. S). In **Bradenton:** Manatee Memorial Hospital (206 2nd St. E). In **Sarasota:** Sarasota Memorial Hospital (1700 S. Tamiami Trail, U.S. 41).

24-Hour Pharmacy **Eckerd Drugs** (11613 N. Nebraska Ave., Tampa, tel. 813/978-0775).

Arriving and Departing

By Plane **Tampa International** (tel. 813/870-8700) is 6 miles from downtown. It is served by Air Canada (tel. 800/776-3000), Air Jamaica (tel. 800/523-5585), American (tel. 800/433-7300), Bahamasair (tel. 800/222-4262), British Airways (tel. 800/247-9297), Canadian Holidays (tel. 800/282-4751), Cayman Airlines (tel. 800/422-9626), Continental (tel. 800/525-0280), Delta (tel. 800/221-1212), Mexicana (tel. 800/531-7921), Northwest (tel. 800/225-2525), Transworld (tel. 800/221-2000), United (tel. 800/241-6522), and USAir (tel. 800/428-4322).

Sarasota's Airport is **Sarasota-Bradenton** (tel. 813/359-5200), just north of the city. It is served by American, Continental, Delta, Northwest, Transworld, United, and USAir.

Between the Airport and Hotels In Tampa, major transportation services include **Central Florida Limousine** (tel. 813/276-3730), serving Hillsborough and Polk counties; **The Limo** (tel. 813/572-1111 or 800/282-6817 in St. Petersburg and Clearwater), serving Pinellas County; and **Florida Suncoast Limousines** (tel. 813/620-3597). Expect taxi fares to be about $11-$21 for most of Hillsborough County and about twice that for Pinellas County.

In Sarasota, transportation includes **Airport Limousine** (tel. 813/355-9645) and **Diplomat Taxi** (tel. 813/359-8600). Both deliver to most parts of the county. An average cab fare is $12-$20.

By Car I–75 spans the region from north to south. Once you cross the border into Florida from Georgia, it should take about three hours to reach Tampa, and another hour to reach Sarasota. If you're coming from Orlando, you'll likely drive west into Tampa on I–4.

By Train **Amtrak** (tel. 800/872–7245) connects the Northeast, Midwest, and much of the South to Tampa. In Tampa, the Amtrak station is at 601 N. Nebraska Avenue (tel. 813/221–7600).

By Bus **Greyhound/Trailways** provides service to and throughout the state. Call the nearest office for schedules and fares (St. Petersburg, tel. 813/898–1496; Sarasota, tel. 813/955–5735; and Tampa, tel. 813/229–2112).

Getting Around

By Car I–75 and U.S. 41 run the length of the region; U.S. 41 links the business districts of many communities. It's best to avoid all bridges and U.S. 41 during rush hours, 7–9 AM and 4–6 PM. U.S. 19 is the major north–south artery through St. Petersburg; traffic can be heavy, and there are many lights, so avoid U.S. 19 whenever possible.

I–275 crosses Tampa Bay west from Tampa to St. Petersburg, then swings south to cross the bay again (the Sunshine Skyway) into Bradenton. Route 64 connects I–75 to Bradenton and Anna Maria Island.

Scenic Drives On **I–275 between St. Petersburg** and **Terra Ceia,** motorists get a bird's-eye view of bustling Tampa Bay along the Sunshine Skyway and its bright-yellow suspension bridge.

Head north or south on the **Bayshore Drive Causeway** for a spectacular view of Tampa Bay.

Route 679 takes you along two of St. Petersburg's most pristine islands, Cabbage and Mullet keys.

Route 789 carries you over several of the coast's slender barrier islands, past miles of green-blue Gulf waters, beaches, and waterfront homes. The road does not connect all the islands, however. It runs from Holmes Beach off the Bradenton coast south to Lido Beach in Sarasota, then begins again on Casey Key south of Osprey and runs south to Nokomis Beach.

By Bus Around Tampa, the **Hillsborough Area Regional Transit** (HART) (tel. 813/254–4278) system serves most of the county. In Sarasota, **Sarasota County Area transit** (SCAT) (tel. 813/951–5850) is the public transit company.

Guided Tours

Orientation Tours **Around the Town** (tel. 813/932–7803) conducts tours for groups of 25 or more in the Tampa Bay area, plus Tarpon Springs and Sarasota, the dog tracks, and area theaters. Try to make reservations several weeks in advance.
Gulf Coast Gray Line (tel. 813/822–3577) makes daily trips from Tampa to Disney World, Epcot Center, Sea World, Busch Gardens, and other attractions.
Travel is Fun Tours of St. Petersburg (tel. 813/821–9479) offers day-long tours to area sights from St. Petersburg.

Boat Tours The *Captain Anderson* (tel. 813/367–7804) combines sightseeing with lunch and dinner cruises from the St. Petersburg Causeway (3400 Pasadena Ave., St. Petersburg Beach). It operates from October through May.

The Admiral (tel. 813/462–2628 or 800/444–4814), docked at Clearwater Beach Marina, runs dinner and sightseeing cruises daily, with dinner cruises only December to mid-February.

The *Starlite Princess* (tel. 813/595–1212) is an old-fashioned paddle-wheel excursion boat offering sightseeing and dinner cruises from Hamlin's Landing, Indian Rocks Beach.

The *Miss Cortez* (tel. 813/794–1223) departs from Cortez, just north of Bradenton, every Tuesday, Thursday, and Sunday for Egmont Key, a small abandoned island just north of Anna Maria Island.

Le Barge Tropical Cruises (tel. 813/366–6116) offers a variety of half- and full-day cruises and private charters from Marina Plaza in downtown Sarasota.

Marina Jack II (tel. 813/366–9255), also departing from Sarasota's Marina Plaza, offers lunch and dinner cruises on a stern-wheel paddleboat.

Myakka Wildlife Tours (tel. 813/365–0100) is at Myakka River State Park, east of Sarasota on Route 72. *The Gator Gal*, a large airboat, conducts one-hour tours of the 29,000-acre wildlife and bird sanctuary. There are four trips daily.

By Plane Helicopter tours of the Tampa Bay area and the west coast of Florida are offered by **Suncoast Helicopters** (tel. 813/872–6625), based at Tampa International Airport, and **West Florida Helicopters** (Albert Whitted Airport, tel. 813/823–5200).

Exploring the Tampa Bay Area

Highlights for First-Time Visitors

Crystal River, the Manatee Coast
DeSoto National Memorial, Bradenton
Ringling Museum, Sarasota
Sunshine Skyway, St. Petersburg

Tampa

Numbers in the margin correspond to points of interest on the Tampa/St. Petersburg map.

Tampa is the business and commercial hub of this part of the state, as you'll quickly notice when driving by the busy port. Along the I–4 corridor, at Exit 5 (Orient Rd., east of the city), you'll see a water tower with an arrow sticking through it: this ➊ is **Seminole Indian Village,** which consists of a village and museum displaying artifacts of the Seminole Indians, who inhabited Florida long before white settlers arrived. Tour groups can arrange for alligator wrestling and snake shows. *5221 N. Orient Rd., tel. 813/620–3077. Admission: $4.50 adults, $3.75 children under 12, $3.50 senior citizens. Open Mon.–Sat. 9–5, Sun. 10–5.*

➋ **Ybor City** is Tampa's Cuban melting pot. To get there, take I–4 west to Exit 1 (22nd St.) and go south five blocks to 7th Avenue.

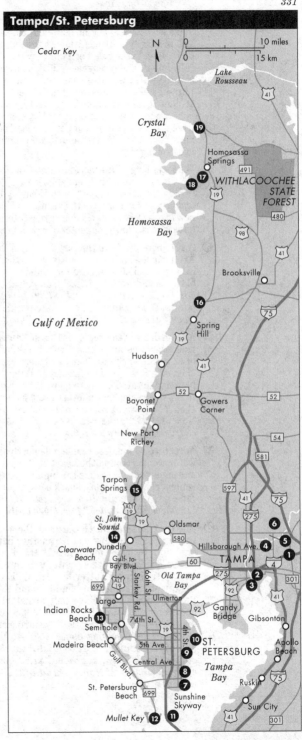

Tampa/St. Petersburg

The Cubans brought their cigar-making industry to Ybor (pronounced EEbor) City in 1866, and this east Tampa suburb is still primarily Cuban. Although the number of cigar makers is dwindling, in the heart of Ybor City the smell of cigars—hand-rolled by Cuban refugees—still drifts around the old-world architecture. Take a stroll past the ornately tiled Columbia Restaurant and the stores lining the street, or step back to the past at **Ybor Square,** a restored cigar factory at 1901 13th Street that is now a mall with boutiques, offices, and several restaurants (free guided walking tours at 1:30 PM Tuesday, Thursday, and Saturday). You can watch as artisans continue the local practice of hand rolling cigars.

For something a little more modern, head for the new skyscrapers downtown. From 7th Avenue, go west to Nebraska Avenue and turn left. That will take you to Kennedy Boulevard; turn right and drive a few blocks to the vicinity of Franklin Street. You are now in one of Tampa's booming growth areas, where there's a pedestrian mall down the center of Franklin Street.

❸ A few more blocks to the east you'll find the **Tampa Museum of Art,** near the Hillsborough River. Particularly strong in classical art, this 35,000-square-foot building houses a fine selection of Greek and Roman artifacts, as well as traveling exhibitions. *601 Doyle Carlton Dr., tel. 813/223–8128. Admission: $3.50 adults, $2.50 students, $2 senior citizens, $1.50 children 6–16. Open Tues.–Sat. 10–5, Wed. 10–9, Sun. 1–5.*

❹ A main draw in the region is **Busch Gardens,** where a monorail ride simulates an African safari, taking in free-roaming zebras, giraffes, rhinos, lions, and more exotic animals. The new "Myombe Reserve: The Great Ape Dome" is a gorilla and chimpanzee habitat. There are many other rides and attractions in this 300-acre park, so allow at least six hours here. *3000 Busch Blvd. (Rte. 580), 2 mi east of I–275, tel. 813/987–5082. Admission: $27.95 adults, $22.95 children 3–9, plus $3 parking charge. Open daily 9:30–6.*

❺ **Adventure Island,** less than a mile north of Busch Gardens, is a water wonderland in the heart of Tampa. Water slides, pools, and man-made waves are the highlights; the park also has convenient changing rooms, snack bars, a gift shop, and a video arcade. *4545 Bougainvillea Ave., tel. 813/987–5660. Admission: $13.95, children under 2 free. Open daily. Closed Dec.–Feb.*

❻ One mile north of Busch Gardens, the **Museum of Science and Industry** could occupy you for another half day. A "hands-on" museum, the MOSI features both traveling and permanent exhibits. The Butterfly Encounter is an interactive garden inhabited by free-flying butterflies; the GTE Challenger Learning Center offers simulated "flights"; and the 100-seat Saunders Planetarium, Tampa Bay's only planetarium, offers afternoon and evening shows daily. A new 110,000-square-foot addition is expected to open in early 1995, featuring an Omni Theatre with a 360-degree revolving dome. *4801 E. Fowler Ave., tel. 813/ 985–5531. Admission: $4.50 adult Florida residents, $5 other adults, $2 children; additional $1.50 for planetarium show; optional admission Mon. Open daily 9–4:30 PM; hours extended in peak season.*

St. Petersburg

St. Petersburg and the Pinellas Suncoast form the thumb of the hand jutting out of the west coast, holding in Tampa Bay. There are two distinct parts of St. Petersburg—the downtown and cultural area, centered around the bay, and the beach area, on a string of barrier islands facing onto the Gulf. Several causeways, many of which charge tolls, link the beach communities to the mainland.

❼ **Great Explorations!** is a museum where you will never be told, "Don't touch!" Everything is designed for a hands-on experience. The museum is divided into theme rooms, such as the Body Shop, which explores health; the Think Tank, which features mind-stretching puzzles and games; the Touch Tunnel, a 90-foot-long, pitch-black maze you crawl through; and Phenomenal Arts, which displays such items as a Moog music synthesizer (which you can play) and neon-filled tubes that glow in vivid colors when touched. *1120 4th St. S, just off Exit 9 of I–275, tel. 813/821–8885. Admission: $5 adults, $4 children 4–17, $4 senior citizens. Open Mon.–Sat. 10–5, Sun. noon–5.*

❽ A few blocks north and one block east, at the **Salvador Dali Museum,** you will find a large collection of paintings of melting watches, colorful landscapes, and thought-provoking works of the late Spanish surrealist. *1000 3rd St. S, tel. 813/823–3767. Admission: $5 adults, $3.50 students and senior citizens. Open Tues.–Sat. 10–5, Sun. noon–5.*

❾ Eight blocks north and two blocks east, the **Museum of Fine Arts** has outstanding examples of European, American, pre-Columbian, and Far Eastern art, as well as photographic exhibits. *255 Beach Dr. NE, tel. 813/896–2667. Suggested donation: $4. Open Tues.–Sat. 10–5, Sun. 1–5.*

A little farther north on Fourth Street lies one of Florida's
❿ most colorful spots, **Sunken Gardens.** Visitors can walk through an aviary with tropical birds, stroll among more than 50,000 exotic plants and flowers, and stop to smell the rare, fragrant orchids. *1825 4th St. N, tel. 813/896–3186. Admission: $8.95 adults, $5 children 3–11. Open daily 9–5:30.*

⓫ There is a $1 toll for the trip over the **Sunshine Skyway,** heading south on I–275, but it's worth it for the bird's-eye view of the islands and Tampa Bay. You can also see what's left of the original twin span that collapsed and killed more than 30 people when a ship hit it in 1980. Turn around and come back north for a view of several small islands that dot the bay, and St. Petersburg Beach. At the north end of the causeway, turn left on 54th Avenue South (Route 682), and cross the water on the Pinellas Bayway. Turn left on Route 679 and you'll cross the islands you saw from the Sunshine Skyway. You'll end up eventually at
⓬ **Fort DeSoto Park** at the mouth of Tampa Bay. This 900-acre park is spread over six small islands, called keys. The fort for which it is named was built on the southern end of Mullet Key to protect sea lanes in the gulf during the Spanish-American War. Roam the fort (admission free) or wander the beaches of any of the islands that make up the park.

The Pinellas Bayway continues over to the barrier islands, beginning with St. Petersburg Beach. Gulf Boulevard (Route 699) runs the length of these islands. When pelicans become entangled in fishing lines, locals sometimes carry them to the

⓭ **Suncoast Seabird Sanctuary,** a nonprofit rehabilitation center that also cares for cormorants, white herons, ospreys, and many other species. *18328 Gulf Blvd., tel. 813/391–6211. Admission free, but donations welcome. Open daily 9–5:30.*

U.S. 19 leads north from St. Petersburg through **Dunedin,** so named by two Scots in the 1880s. If the sound of bagpipes played by men in kilts appeals to you, head to Dunedin in March or April, when the Highland games and the Dunedin Heather and Thistle holidays pay tribute to the Celtic heritage.

⓮ **Caladesi Island State Park** lies 3 miles off Dunedin's coast, across Hurricane Pass. One of the state's few remaining undeveloped barrier islands, this 600-acre park is accessible only by boat. There's a beach on the gulf side, mangroves on the bay side, and a self-guided nature trail winding through the island's interior. Park rangers are available to answer questions. This is a good spot for swimming, fishing, shelling, boating, and nature study. Facilities include boardwalks, picnic shelters, bathhouses, and a concession stand. Take the Dunedin Causeway to Honeymoon Island, to the north, then get on the ferry, which runs hourly from 10–5 (in good weather only) to Caladesi Island. *Ferry tel. 813/734–5263. Ferry admission: $4 adults, $2.50 children 3–12. Park admission: $3.25 per car.*

⓯ Continue on U.S. 19 to **Tarpon Springs,** the region's Greek community. Sponge divers from the Dodecanese Islands of Greece moved here at the turn of the century, and it became the world's largest sponge center by the 1930s. Although a bacterial blight wiped out the sponge beds in the 1940s, the Greeks held on, and the sponge industry has returned, though in lesser force than during its heyday. Today, the Greek influence remains evident in the churches, the restaurants, and, often, the language spoken on the streets.

The Manatee Coast

The coastal area north of Tampa, from Weeki Wachee to Crystal River, can aptly be called the Manatee Coast. Its springs, rivers, and creeks are among the best spots to view manatees, also called sea cows. Only about 1,200 of these curious mammals, related to elephants, are alive today. It's believed that ancient mariners' tales of mermaids were based on sightings of manatees.

U.S. 19 is the prime route through manatee country. Traffic flows freely on this highway once you've left the congestion of St. Petersburg. Most of the sights on this coast are outdoors, so plan for a picnic lunch by picking up provisions before you leave the city.

About 60 miles north of St. Petersburg on U.S. 19, at the junction with Route 50, you'll see **Weeki Wachee Spring.** Here, an underwater theater presents mermaid shows, a nature trail threads through the subtropical wilderness, and a jungle boat cruises to view local wildlife. Allow at least four hours to see everything. *U.S. 19 and Rte. 50, Weeki Wachee, tel. 904/596–2062. Admission: $14.95 adults, $10.95 children 3–11. Open daily 9:30–5:30.*

About 15 miles farther north on U.S. 19 (about 90 minutes north of Tampa), is another of Florida's natural wonders:

⓱ **Homosassa Springs State Wildlife Park.** Turn left on County

Road 490-A and follow the signs to the attraction at Fish Bowl Drive. Here you may see manatees, but the "Spring of 10,000 Fish" is a main attraction, where you seem to mingle with the inhabitants in a floating observatory. A walk along the park's paths will lead you to reptile, alligator, and exotic bird shows. Jungle boat cruises on the Homosassa River are available across Fish Bowl Drive from the park's main entrance. *One mi west of U.S. 19 on Fish Bowl Drive, Homosassa Springs, tel. 904/628–2311. Admission: $6.95 adults, $3.95 children 3–11. Open daily 9–5:30.*

⑱ A great place to stop for a picnic is the **Yulee Sugar Mill State Historic Site,** just a short drive from Homosassa Springs. It's on the site of a ruined sugar plantation built by the state's first U.S. senator. *From Homosassa Springs Park, turn left on C.R. 490-A, tel. 904/795–3817. Admission free. Open daily dawn–dusk.*

⑲ **Crystal River Wildlife Refuge** is a U.S. Fish and Wildlife Service sanctuary for manatees, with wide stretches of the river designated for people to watch and swim with the sea cows. The main spring feeds crystal-clear water into the river at 72 degrees year-round, and during winter months manatees congregate around the spring. Even during the warmer months, when manatees scatter, the main spring is still a fun place for a swim. *Go north on U.S. 19 into town of Crystal River, turn left on C.R. 44, tel. 904/563–2088. Admission: free. Open daily 9–4.*

Time Out   **Charlie's Fish House Restaurant** (224 U.S. 19 N, Crystal River, tel. 904/795–3949) is a popular, no-frills seafood spot featuring locally caught fish, oysters, crab claws, and lobster.

Bradenton and Sarasota

Numbers in the margin correspond to points of interest on the Bradenton/Sarasota map.

The southern end of Tampa Bay is anchored by the two cities of Bradenton and Sarasota, which also have their string of barrier islands with fine beaches. Sarasota is very much a resort town—Sarasota County has no less than 35 miles of Gulf beaches, as well as two state parks, 22 municipal parks, and 46 golf courses, many of them open to the public. But Sarasota also has a thriving cultural scene, thanks mostly to John Ringling, founder of the Ringling Brothers Barnum & Bailey Circus, who chose this area for the winter home of his circus and his family. Bradenton maintains a lower profile than Sarasota, though it also has its share of sugar-sand beaches, golf courses, and historic sites dating back to the mid-1800s. Many of Sarasota County's beaches are located around Venice, a few miles south on the Gulf Coast, which was the actual winter home of the circus; today Venice contains the world's only clown college.

Bradenton   Hernando de Soto, one of the first Spanish explorers, set foot in Florida in 1539 near what is now Bradenton. From I–75, take **①** Route 64 to 75th Street NW, turn north, and drive to **DeSoto National Memorial.** In the high season (late-December–early April), park employees dressed in 16th-century costumes demonstrate various period weapons and show how the European explorers prepared and preserved food for their journeys over

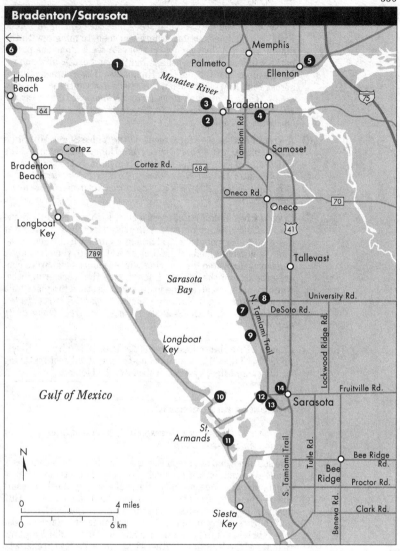

Bradenton/Sarasota

Memphis

Palmetto

Ellenton

5

1

Holmes
Beach

Manatee River

3 Bradenton

2

64

4

Samoset

Cortez

Bradenton
Beach

Cortez Rd. 684

Oneco Rd.

70

Oneco

Longboat
Key

789

41

Tamiami Rd.

Tallevast

*Sarasota
Bay*

N. Tamiami Trail

University Rd.

8

DeSoto Rd.

7

*Longboat
Key*

9

Lockwood Ridge Rd.

Gulf of Mexico

14

Fruitville Rd.

10

12

13 Sarasota

*St.
Armands*

11

Tuttle Rd.

S. Tamiami Trail

Bee Ridge
Rd.

Bee
Ridge

Proctor Rd.

Beneva Rd.

Clark Rd.

N

*Siesta
Key*

| 0 | | 4 miles |
| 0 | | 6 km |

6

Bellm's Cars & Music
of Yesterday, **8**
Bishop Planetarium, **3**
DeSoto National
Memorial, **1**
Downtown Art
District, **14**
Egmont Key, **6**

Gamble Plantation and
Confederate Memorial, **5**
Manatee Village
Historical Park, **4**
Marie Selby Botanical
Gardens, **13**
Marina Plaza, **12**
Mote Marine
Aquarium, **10**

Ringling Museums, **7**
Sarasota Jungle
Gardens, **9**
South Florida
Museum, **2**
South Lido Park, **11**

the untamed land. Films, demonstrations, and a short nature trail are available on the grounds. *75th St. NW, tel. 813/792–0458. Admission: free. Open daily 8–5:30.*

In the center of the city, a few blocks from the Manatee River, ❷ the **South Florida Museum** exhibits artifacts of Florida history, including displays of Indian culture and an excellent collection of Civil War memorabilia. The museum is also home to "Snooty," the oldest living manatee in captivity. Snooty likes to shake hands and perform other tricks at feeding time in his viewing pool in the newManatee Education and Resource Center. *201 10th St., tel. 813/746–4132. Admission: $5 adults, $2.50 children and students. Open Tues.–Sat. 10–5, Sun. noon–6.*

❸ Also part of the museum is the **Bishop Planetarium,** where, inside a domed theater, you can see star shows and special-effects laser light displays. *201 10th St., tel. 813/746–4131. Admission: $5 adults, $2.50 children 5–12. Star show Tues.–Sun. at 1:30 and 3 PM.*

Take Route 64 back east, and 1 mile past U.S. 41 you'll find ❹ **Manatee Village Historical Park,** consisting of an 1860 courthouse, 1887 church, 1903 general store and museum, and 1912 settler's home. The Old Manatee Cemetery, which dates back to 1850, contains the graves of early Manatee County settlers. *Rte. 64, 1 mi east of U.S. 41, tel. 813/749–7165. Admission free. Appointments necessary to tour cemetery. Open Sept.–June, weekdays 9–4:30 and Sun. 2–5; July–Aug., weekdays 9–4:30.*

Cross to the north side of the river on U.S. 41 and turn right when U.S. 301 splits off. On the left, 3 miles ahead, is the ❺ **Gamble Plantation and Confederate Memorial.** The mansion, built in 1850, is the only pre–Civil War plantation house surviving in south Florida. This is where the Confederate secretary of state took refuge when the Confederacy fell to Union forces. Some of the original furnishings are on display in the mansion. *3708 Patten Ave., Ellenton, tel. 813/723–4536. Admission: $2 adults, $1 children 6–12. Open Thurs.–Mon. 8–5; tours at 9:30, 10:30, 1, 2, 3, and 4. Closed Tues. and Wed.*

❻ **Egmont Key** lies just off the northern tip of Anna Maria Island, Bradenton's barrier island to the west. On it is **Fort Dade,** a military fort built in 1900 during the Spanish-American War, and Florida's sixth-brightest lighthouse. The primary inhabitant of the 2-mile-long island is the threatened gopher tortoise. The only way to get to the island is by the *Miss Cortez,* an excursion boat (*see* Boat Tours, *above*). Shellers, in particular, will find the trip rewarding.

Sarasota Long ago, circus tycoon John Ringling found Sarasota an ideal spot to bring his clowns and performers to train and recuperate during the winter. Along Sarasota Bay, Ringling also built himself a fancy home, patterned after the Palace of the Doges ❼ in Venice, Italy. Today, the **Ringling Museums** include that mansion, as well as his art museum (with a world-renowned collection of Rubens paintings) and a museum of circus memorabilia. *½ mi south of Sarasota-Bradenton Airport on U.S. 41, tel. 813/355–5101. Combined admission (good for mansion and museums): $8.50 adults, $7.50 senior citizens, children 12 and under free. Open daily 10–5:30.*

8 Across the road, **Bellm's Cars & Music of Yesterday** displays 130 classic cars, such as Pierce Arrows and Auburns, and 2,000 old-time music makers, such as hurdy-gurdies and calliopes. *5500 N. Tamiami Trail, tel. 813/355-6228. Admission: $7.50 adults, $3.75 children 6-12, under 6 and over 89 free. Open Mon.-Sat. 8:30-6, Sun. 9:30-6.*

9 From the Ringling museums, head south on U.S. 41 about 1½ miles to **Sarasota Jungle Gardens.** It'll take you a couple of hours to stroll through this 10-acre spread of tropical plants. There are bird and reptile shows daily at 10, noon, 2, and 4. *3701 Bayshore Rd., tel. 813/355-5305. Admission: $8 adults, $4 children 3-12. Open daily 9-5.*

Across the water from Sarasota lie the barrier islands of Siesta Key, Longboat Key, and Lido Key, with myriad beaches, shops, hotels, condominiums, and houses. Go south on U.S. 41 to Route 789, turn right, and cross the Ringling Causeway to the small island of **St. Armand's Key,** where you'll find several exclusive restaurants and boutiques at Harding's Circle.

10 Go north on Ringling Boulevard, and before you reach the bridge to Longboat Key, turn right at the sign for City Island and the **Mote Marine Aquarium,** which displays sharks, rays, and other marine creatures native to the area. A huge outdoor shark tank lets you see its inhabitants from above and below the water's surface. *1600 City Island Park, tel. 813/388-2451. Admission: $6 adults, $4 children 6-17. Open daily 10-5.*

11 Heading back south, past the public beach at Lido Key, you'll come to **South Lido Park.** Here you can try your luck at fishing, take a dip in the waters of the bay or Gulf of Mexico, roam the paths of the 130-acre park, or picnic as the sun sets through the Australian pines into the Gulf. *Admission free. Open daily 8-sunset.*

12 You can also go back east across the bay and turn right into **Marina Plaza,** along U.S. 41, where several boats offer waterborne tours of the bay (*see* Boat Tours, *above*).

13 **Marie Selby Botanical Gardens** are near the Island Park yacht basin. Here you can stroll through a world-class display of orchids and wander through 14 garden areas along Sarasota Bay. *800 S. Palm Ave., off U.S. 41, tel. 813/366-5730. Admission: $6 adults, $3 children 6-11. Open daily 10-5 except Christmas.*

14 In the heart of Sarasota, around Palm Avenue and Main Street, you'll discover a **downtown art district,** with such galleries as **Art Uptown** (1367 Main St.), **Corbino Galleries** (1472 Main St.), **Apple & Carpenter Gallery of Fine Arts** (645 N. Palm Ave.), and **J. E. Voorhees Gallery** (1359 Main St.).

Venice Take U.S. 41 south from Sarasota to Venice, the Ringling Brothers Circus's winter headquarters. Named after Venice, Italy, this town is crisscrossed with even more canals than its namesake.

Many of Sarasota County's beaches are in Venice. Shell collecting is quite good on these beaches, but they are best known for the wealth of shark teeth and fossils to be found.

Southwest Florida for Free

Fort De Soto Park (*see* St. Petersburg, *above*).

Heritage Park and Museum consists of several restored pioneer homes and buildings on a 21-acre wooded site. The museum is the park's centerpiece, with exhibits depicting Pinellas County's pioneer lifestyle. Spinning, weaving, and other demonstrations are held regularly. *11909 125th St. N, Largo, tel. 813/462-3474. Donations accepted. Open Tues.–Sat. 10–4, Sun. 1–4.*

Manatee Village Historical Park (*see* Bradenton, *above*).

Shrimp Docks (22nd St. Causeway, Tampa) are the place to watch while the shrimp boats pull in to unload their catches in the late afternoon.

Suncoast Seabird Sanctuary (*see* St. Petersburg, *above*).

University of Tampa administration building, built as a luxury hotel in 1890, served as Theodore Roosevelt's headquarters during the Spanish-American War. Free tours are given Tuesday and Thursday at 1:30 during the school year. *401 W. Kennedy Blvd., tel. 813/253-6220.*

What to See and Do with Children

Adventure Island (*see* Exploring Tampa Bay Area, *above*).

Busch Gardens (*see* Exploring the Tampa Bay Area, *above*).

Circus Galleries, Ringling Museum (*see* Bradenton and Sarasota, *above*).

Great Explorations! (*see* Exploring the Tampa Bay Area, *above*).

Sarasota Jungle Gardens (*see* Bradenton and Sarasota, *above*).

Off the Beaten Track

Up in the area known as the Big Bend, Florida's long, curving coastline north of Tampa, you won't find many beaches. But you will find an idyllic island village tucked in among the marshes and scenic streams feeding the Gulf of Mexico. From U.S. 19, take Route 24 until the highway ends: This is **Cedar Key.** Once a strategic port for the Confederate States of America, Cedar Key today is a commercial fishing center. The **Cedar Key Historical Society Museum** displays historical photographs and exhibits that focus on the development of the area. *Rte. 24 and 2nd St., tel. 904/543-5549. Admission: $1 adults, 50¢ children 6–12. Open daily 11–4.*

Shopping

Special souvenirs from this area include local natural sponges, which can be bought at reasonable prices along Dodecanese Boulevard, the main street in Tarpon Springs. In Tampa's Ybor City, many small cigar shops sell hand-rolled cigars.

Shopping Areas **Hamlin's Landing** (401 2nd St. E), at Indian Rocks Beach, has several shops and restaurants along the Intracoastal Waterway, in a Victorian-style setting.

Harding Circle on St. Armand's Key (just west of downtown Sarasota) is a circular string of exclusive shops and restaurants that cater to consumers seeking out-of-the-ordinary, pricey items.

John's Pass Village and Boardwalk in Madeira Beach (12901 Gulf Blvd.), one of the St. Petersburg beach communities, features a collection of shops and restaurants in an old-style fishing village. Pass the time watching the pelicans cavorting and dive-bombing for food.

Tampa's **Old Hyde Park Village** (tel. 813/251–3500) is an elegant outdoor shopping center that stretches more than seven blocks along Swan Avenue, near Bayshore Boulevard.

The Pier (800 2nd Ave. NE, Tampa), near the Museum of Fine Arts, is a five-story bayfront building that looks like an inverted pyramid. Inside are numerous shops and eating spots.

Flea Markets **Dome** has dozens of stalls under sheltered walkways, where you can buy new and recycled wares. *Rte. 775, west of U.S. 41, Venice, tel. 813/493–6773. Open Fri.–Sun. 9–4. Closed Sept.*

Red Barn has the requisite big red barn, in which vendors operate daily except Mondays. The number of vendors increases to about 1,000 on weekends. *1707 1st St. E, Bradenton, tel. 813/747–3794. Some stores open Tues.–Sun. 10–4; others Wed., Sat., Sun. 8–4.*

Oldsmar Flea Market is a charming place to hunt for bargains. *Off Rte. 580 near Old Tampa Bay, tel. 813/855–5306. Open Fri. 10–3, Sat.–Sun. 9–5.*

Wagonwheel is 100-plus acres containing some 2,000 vendors and a variety of food concessions. There is a tram from the parking lot to the vendor area. *7801 Park Blvd., Pinellas Park, tel. 813/544–5319. Parking: $1. Open weekends 8–4.*

Participant Sports

Biking There aren't many reserved bike paths around these cities and towns, but there are plenty of places to rent bikes, should you want to pedal along the streets. The following stores rent bikes: Bicycle Center (2610 Cortez Rd., Bradenton, tel. 813/756–5480), D & S Bicycle Shop (12073 Seminole Blvd., Largo, tel. 813/393–0300), Mr. CB's (1249 Stickney Point Rd., Sarasota, tel. 813/349–4400), Pedal N Wheels (Merchants Pointe Shopping Center, 2881 Clark Rd., Sarasota, tel. 813/922–0481), The Beach Cyclist (7517 Blindpass Rd., St. Petersburg, tel. 813/367–5001), The Bike Doctor (291 Trott Circle, Venice, tel. 813/426–4807), and Bicycles International (1744 Tamiami Trail S, U.S. 41, Venice, tel. 813/497–1590).

Canoeing Inland, there are several rivers that make for good canoeing. **Canoe Outpost** (18001 U.S. 301 S, Wimauma, just south of Tampa, tel. 813/634–2228) offers half-day, full-day, and overnight canoe-camping trips from a number of southwest Florida locations, including Little Manatee River. At **Myakka River State Park** (tel. 813/361–6511), 15 miles south of Sarasota, near Venice, you can rent canoes, paddles, and life vests.

Fishing Anglers flock to southwest Florida to catch tarpon, kingfish, speckled trout, snapper, grouper, sea trout, snook, sheepshead, and shark in these coastal waters. Avoid fishing in Tampa Bay because the water is polluted. You can charter a fishing boat or join a group on a party boat for full- or half-day outings.

Party boats in the area include **Florida Deep Sea Fishing** (4737 Gulf Blvd., St. Petersburg, tel. 813/360–2082), **Rainbow Party Fishing** (Clearwater Marina, Clearwater Beach, tel. 813/446–7389), **Flying Fish** (Marina Jack's, U.S. 41 on the bay front,

Sarasota, tel. 813/366–3373), and **L-C Marine** (215 Tamiami Trail S, U.S. 41, Venice, tel. 813/484–9044).

Golf The following courses are open to the public.

Bradenton **Manatee County Golf Course** (tel. 813/792–6773).

Crystal River **Plantation Inn Golf Club** (Crystal River, tel. 904/795–7211).

St. Petersburg Area **Clearwater Golf Park** (tel. 813/447–5272), **Largo Golf Course** (tel. 813/587–6724), **Dunedin Country Club** (tel. 813/733–7836), **Innisbrook Resort & Golf Club** (Tarpon Springs, tel. 813/942–2000), **Mangrove Bay Golf Course** (tel. 813/893–7797), **Twin Brooks Golf Course** (tel. 813/893–7445).

Sarasota **Bobby Jones Golf Course** (tel. 813/955–8097), **Forest Lake Golf Course** (tel. 813/922–1312), **Longboat Key** (Longboat Key, tel. 813/383–8821).

Tampa **Apollo Beach Club** (tel. 813/645–6212), **Babe Zaharias Golf Course** (tel. 813/932–4401), **Bloomingdale Golfers Club** (Valrico, tel. 813/685–4105), **The Eagles** (tel. 813/920–6681), **Rocky Point Golf Course** (tel. 813/884–5141), **Saddlebrook Golf Club** (Wesley Chapel, tel. 813/973–1111).

Venice **Bird Bay Executive Golf Course** (tel. 813/485–9333), **Plantation Golf & Country Club** (tel. 813/493–2000).

Motorboating **Florida Charter** (tel. 813/347–SAIL) in South Pasadena has power and sailboats for rent, bareboat or captained.

Don and Mike's Boat and Jet Ski Rental (520 Blackburn Point Rd., Sarasota, tel. 813/966–4000) has water skis, jet skis, pontoon boats, and instruction for all activities.

Sailing You can take sailing lessons and rent boats at **La Gringa Sailing Services** (400 2nd Ave. NE, St. Petersburg, tel. 813/822–4323), **M&M Beach Service & Boat Rental** (5300 Gulf Blvd., St. Petersburg Beach, tel. 813/360–8295), and **O'Leary's Sarasota Sailing School** (near Marina Jack's, U.S. 41 and the bay front, Sarasota, tel. 813/953–7505).

Tennis Most hotels and motels in Florida have outdoor tennis courts, some lighted for night use. If you are serious about tennis, consider staying at **The Colony Beach Resort** (*see* Dining and Lodging, *below*), which offers guests complimentary games on 10 clay hydro courts and 11 hard courts. The resort runs a wide variety of clinics and camps for all levels of players, with scaled-down racquets for children. Guaranteed matchmaking means guests play a pro if another guest is not free to be a partner. Every member of the tennis staff is USPTA certified and a video analysis of your game is available.

If your hotel doesn't have a tennis court, try one of the following public courts: **City of Tampa Courts** (59 Columbia Dr., Davis Islands, Tampa, tel. 813/253–3997), **McMullen Park** (1000 Edenville Ave., Clearwater, tel. 813/462–6144), and **Dunedin Community Center** (Pinehurst and Michigan Sts., Dunedin, tel. 813/734–3950).

Windsurfing For sailboard rentals and lessons try **Gulf Water Sports Center** at the Colony Beach and Tennis Resort (1620 Gulf of Mexico Dr., Longboat Key, tel. 813/383–7692) or **Ocean Boulevard Sailboarding** (1233 Gulf Stream Ave. N, Sarasota, tel. 813/364–9463).

Spectator Sports

Baseball   The season comes early to Florida with the annual convergence of the Grapefruit League—major-league teams that offer exhibitions in March and April during their spring training camps. For information on all the teams, call 904/488–0990. The teams that play in this area are: **Pittsburgh Pirates** (McKechnie Field, 17th Ave. W and 9th St., Bradenton, tel. 813/747–3031), **Philadelphia Phillies** (Jack Russell Stadium, Seminole and Greenwood Ave., Clearwater, tel. 813/442–8496), **Toronto Blue Jays** (Grant Field, 373 Douglas Ave., north of Rte. 88, Dunedin, tel. 813/733–9302), **St. Louis Cardinals** (Al Lang Stadium, 1st St. and 2nd Ave., St. Petersburg, tel. 813/822–3384), and the **Chicago White Sox** (Ed Smith Stadium, 2700 12th St., Sarasota, tel. 813/954–7699).

Dog Racing   Dog races are held somewhere in the region all year: January–June at **Derby Lane** (10490 Gandy Blvd., St. Petersburg, tel. 813/576–1361); July–December at **Tampa Greyhound Track** (8300 N. Nebraska Ave., Tampa, tel. 813/932–4313); late December–June at the **Sarasota Kennel Club** (5400 Bradenton Rd., Sarasota, tel. 813/355–7744).

Football   NFL football comes in the form of the **Tampa Bay Buccaneers,** who play at Tampa Stadium (4201 N. Dale Mabry Hwy.). For information, call 813/461–2700 or 800/282–0683.

Hockey   The **Tampa Lightning** hockey team makes its fall and winter home at the Exposition Hall at Florida State (I–4 and U.S. 301, 7 mi east of downtown Tampa, tel. 813/229–8800).

Horse Racing   **Tampa Bay Downs** (Race Track Rd., off Rte. 580, Oldsmar, tel. 813/855–4401) holds Thoroughbred races from mid-December to early May.

Jai-Alai   **Tampa Jai-Alai Fronton** (S. Dale Mabry Hwy. and Gandy Blvd., Tampa, tel. 813/831–1411) offers jai-alai year-round.

Beaches

The waters of the Gulf of Mexico, fed by rivers and streams originating "up North," vary according to tides and storms. Not all are pristinely clear. The best beaches in the region are in Tampa's Clearwater Beach area—Southwest Florida's version of Daytona Beach. Avoid swimming in any of the bays, however, as the waters are polluted from boaters, marinas, and industry.

Bradenton   **Anna Maria Island,** just west of the Sunshine Skyway Bridge, boasts three public beaches. **Anna Maria Bayfront Park,** at the north end of the municipal pier, is a secluded beach fronting both the Intracoastal Waterway and the Gulf of Mexico. Facilities include picnic grounds, a playground, rest rooms, showers, and lifeguards. At mid-island, in the town of Holmes Beach, is **Manatee County Beach,** popular with all ages. It has picnic facilities, a snack bar, showers, rest rooms, and lifeguards. At the island's southern end is **Coquina Beach,** popular with singles and families. Facilities here include a picnic area, boat ramp, playground, refreshment stand, rest rooms, showers, and lifeguards.

Cortez Beach, on the mainland, is on Gulf Boulevard in the town of Bradenton Beach. This one's popular with those who like their beaches without facilities—nothing but sand, water, and trees.

Palma Sola Causeway, which takes Manatee Avenue on the mainland to Anna Maria Island, also offers beachgoers a long, sandy beach fronting Palma Sola Bay. There are boat ramps, a dock, and picnic tables.

Greer Island Beach is at the northern tip of the next barrier island south, on Longboat Key. It's accessible by boat or via North Shore Boulevard. The secluded peninsula has a wide beach and excellent shelling, but no facilities.

Clearwater   **Clearwater Beach** is a popular hangout for teenagers and college students. On a narrow island between Clearwater Harbor and the Gulf, it is connected to downtown Clearwater by Memorial Causeway. Facilities: marina, concessions, showers, rest rooms, and lifeguards.

St. Petersburg Area   **Bay Beach** (North Shore Dr. and 13th Ave. NE, on Tampa Bay) charges 10¢ admission. It has showers and shelters.

Fort DeSoto Park (*see* St. Petersburg, *above*) consists of the southernmost beaches of St. Petersburg, on five islands totaling some 900 acres. Facilities: two fishing piers, picnic sites overlooking lagoons, a waterskiing and boating area, and miles of beaches for swimming. Open daily until dark. To get there, take the Pinellas Bayway through three toll gates (cost: 85¢).

Indian Rocks Beach (off Rte. 8 south of Clearwater Beach) attracts mostly couples.

Maximo Park Beach (34 St. and Pinellas Point Dr. S) is on Boca Ciega Bay. There is no lifeguard, but there is a picnic area with grills, tables, shelters, and a boat ramp.

North Shore Beach (901 North Shore Dr. NE) charges $1 admission and has a pool, beach umbrellas, cabanas, windbreaks, and lounges.

Pass-a-Grille Beach, on the Gulf, has parking meters, a snack bar, rest rooms, and showers.

St. Petersburg Municipal Beach (11260 Gulf Blvd.) is a free beach on Treasure Island. There are dressing rooms, metered parking, and a snack bar.

Sarasota   **Siesta Beach** is on Beach Road on Siesta Key. The 40-acre park contains nature trails, a concession stand, soccer and softball fields, picnicking facilities, play equipment, rest rooms, and tennis and volleyball courts.

South Lido, at the southern tip of Lido Key, is among the largest and best beaches in the region. The sugar-sand beach offers little for shell collectors, but the interests of virtually all other beach lovers are served on its 100 acres, which attracts a diverse mix of people. Facilities include fishing, nature trails, volleyball, playground, horseshoes, rest rooms, and picnic grounds.

Turtle Beach is on Siesta Key's Midnight Pass Road. Though only 14 acres, it includes boat ramps, horseshoe courts, picnic and play facilities, a recreation building, rest rooms, and a volleyball court.

Tarpon Springs Tarpon Springs has two public beaches: **Howard Park Beach,** where a lifeguard is on duty daily 8:30–6 Easter through Labor Day, and **Sunset Beach,** where there is similar lifeguard duty as well as rest rooms, picnic tables, grills, and a boat ramp.

Venice **Caspersen Beach,** on Beach Drive in South Venice, is the county's largest park. It has a nature trail, fishing, picnicking, rest rooms, plus lots of beach for those who prefer space to a wealth of amenities. Along with a plentiful mix of shells, observant beachcombers are likely to find sharks' teeth on Venice beaches, washed up from the ancient shark burial grounds just offshore.

Manasota Key spans much of the county's southern coast, from south of Venice to Englewood. It has two choice beaches: Manasota, on Manasota Beach Road, with a boat ramp, picnic area, and rest rooms; and Blind Pass, where you can fish and swim but will find no amenities.

Nokomis Beach is just north of North Jetty on Albee Road. Its facilities include rest rooms, a concession stand, picnic equipment, play areas, two boat ramps, a vollyball court, and fishing.

North Jetty Park is at the south end of Casey Key, a slender barrier island. It's a favorite for family outings, and fossil hunters may get lucky here. Amenities include rest rooms, a concession stand, play and picnic equipment, fishing, horseshoes, and a volleyball court.

Dining and Lodging

Dining As in most coastal regions, fresh seafood is plentiful. Raw bars, serving just-plucked-from-the-bay oysters, clams, and mussels, are everywhere. The region's ethnic diversity is also well represented. Tarpon Springs adds a hearty helping of such classic Greek specialties as *moussaka*, a ground meat and eggplant pie, and *baklava*, delicate layers of pastry and nuts soaked in honey. In Tampa, the cuisine is Cuban, and standard menu items include black beans and rice or paella—a seafood, chicken, and saffron rice casserole. In Sarasota, the accent is on Continental fare, both in food and service.

Many restaurants, from family neighborhood spots to the very expensive places, offer "early bird" menus with seating before 6 PM. These are even more prevalent off season, from May through October.

Highly recommended restaurants are indicated by a star ★.

Category	Cost*
Very Expensive	over $50
Expensive	$35–$50
Moderate	$20–$35
Inexpensive	under $20

per person, excluding drinks, service, and 6% sales tax

Lodging There are historic hotels and ultramodern chrome-and-glass high rises, sprawling resorts and cozy inns, luxurious waterfront lodges and just-off-the-highway budget motels. In general, you'll pay more for a water view. Rates are highest mid-December–mid-April; the lowest prices are available May–November. Price categories listed below apply to winter rates; many of these hotels drop to a less expensive category at other times of the year.

Highly recommended lodgings are indicated by a star ★.

Category	Cost*
Very Expensive	over $150
Expensive	$90–$150
Moderate	$60–$90
Inexpensive	under $60

All prices are per person, double occupancy, excluding 6% state sales tax and 1%–3% tourist tax.

Bradenton
Dining

Crab Trap. Rustic decor, ultrafresh seafood, gator tail, and wild pig are among the trademarks of this restaurant. *U.S. 19 at Terra Ceia Bridge, Palmetto, tel. 813/722–6255; 4814 Memphis Rd., Ellenton, tel. 813/729–7777. No reservations. Dress: casual. D, MC, V. Moderate.*

Lodging

Holiday Inn Riverfront. This Spanish Mediterranean–style motor inn near the Manatee River is easily accessible from I–75 and U.S. 41. One-third of the rooms are suites. *100 Riverfront Dr. W, 34205, tel. 813/747–3727, fax 813/746–4289. 153 rooms. Facilities: pool, whirlpool, restaurant, lounge. AE, DC, MC, V. Expensive.*

Cedar Key
Lodging

Historic Island Hotel. Located in the historic district, this bed-and-breakfast hotel features Jamaican-style architecture circa 1850. Gourmet natural foods are served. *Main and B Sts., 32625, tel. 904/543–5111. 10 rooms. Facilities: café, bicycle built for 2. MC, V. Moderate.*

Clearwater
Dining

Bob Heilman's Beachcomber. Southern-fried chicken and mashed potatoes with gravy have long been the Sunday staple at this 40-year-old restaurant. It's also known for its seafood, homemade desserts, and hearty portions. *447 Mandalay Ave., Clearwater Beach, tel. 813/442–4144. Reservations advised. Dress: casual. AE, DC, MC, V. Moderate.*

Lodging

Belleview Mido Resort and Hotel. This 21-acre Victorian resort on Clearwater Bay is listed on the National Register of Historic Places. It has been expanded to offer lots of recreational facilities and restaurants. *25 Belleview Blvd., 34616, tel. 813/442–6171, fax 813/441–4173. 350 rooms. Facilities: 6 pools, whirlpools, saunas, golf, tennis, bicycles, playground, fishing, sailboats, 10 restaurants, lounge. AE, D, DC, MC, V. Very Expensive.*

Sheraton Sand Key Resort. For those who want lots of sun, sand, and surf, this resort is a good choice. Balconies and patios overlook the Gulf and well-manicured grounds. *1160 Gulf Blvd., Clearwater Beach 33515, tel. 813/595–1611, fax 813/596–8488. 390 rooms. Facilities: pool, wading pool, beach, whirlpool, playground, tennis courts, windsurfing, sailboats, restaurant, lounge. AE, DC, MC, V. Expensive.*

New Comfort Inn. This is a comfortable, unpretentious motor inn centrally located near St. Petersburg and Tampa Bay. Recently remodeled, it is built around an atrium courtyard with pool. *3580 Ulmerton Rd. (Rte. 688), 34622, tel. 813/573–1171, fax 813/572–8736. 119 rooms. Facilities: pool, whirlpool, fitness center, restaurant. AE, DC, MC, V. Moderate.*

Crystal River
Lodging

Plantation Golf Resort. Set on the banks of Kings Bay, this recently remodeled 2-story plantation-style resort is set on 175 acres, near several nature preserves and rivers. *C.R. 44, 34423, tel. 904/795–4211, fax 904/795–1368. 136 rooms. Facilities: lounge, pools, golf, saunas, canoes, rental boats, fishing, tennis, scuba rental, restaurant. Pets permitted. AE, DC, MC, V. Moderate.*

Econo Lodge Crystal Resort. This cinder-block roadside motel is close to Kings Bay and its manatee population. There's a marina within steps of the motel, with dive boats departing for scuba and snorkeling excursions. The only rooms that view the water are 114 and 128. *U.S. 19, 32629, tel. 904/795–3171, fax 813/795–3179. 94 rooms. Facilities: pool, waterfront restaurant. AE, DC, MC, V. Inexpensive.*

Homosassa Springs
Dining

K.C. Crump on the River. An 1870 Old Florida residence on the Homosassa River, K.C. Crump was restored in 1986, then opened as a restaurant in 1987. There is a marina on the river, lounge, and outdoor dining, plus large, airy dining rooms serving meat and seafood. *3900 Hall River Rd., tel. 904/628–1500. Reservations advised. Dress: casual but neat. AE, DC, MC, V. Expensive.*

Lodging

Riverside Inn. A rustic little place, this inn boasts an intimate location across from Monkey Island—residence of six such mammals—and beside the Homosassa River. Complete with its own restaurant (The Yard Arm) and lounge (Ship's Lounge), the Riverside is also conveniently situated within walking distance of three local restaurants and near two others accessible by boat. Rent bicycles, canoes, or paddle boats to get a feel for these lovely surroundings. *Box 258, 32687, tel. 904/628–2474, fax 904/628–5208. 76 rooms. Facilities: marina, restaurant, lounge, pool, tennis courts, ship's store, bike and boat rentals. AE, MC, V. Moderate.*

Riverside Inn Downtown. This is a simple motor inn that features queen-size beds in most rooms. It accepts pets and has a playground for the kids; children 14 and under stay for free. *On U.S. 19 at C.R. 490A West, 34448, tel. 904/628–4311, fax 904/628–4311. 104 rooms. Facilities: pool, tennis, restaurant, lounge. AE, D, DC, MC, V. Moderate.*

Homosassa River Resort. Located right on the banks of the Homosassa River, with two boat docks and pontoon rentals, this resort is well situated for outdoor adventuring. *10605 Hall's River Rd., 32646, tel. 904/628–7072. 9 cottages. Facilities: kitchen, laundry. MC, V. Inexpensive.*

St. Petersburg
Dining

King Charles Room. Quiet elegance, attentive service, and soothing harp music are to be found in this restaurant on the fifth floor of the Don CeSar Beach Resort. Continental specialties include beluga caviar on ice and smoked salmon stuffed with crab mousse. *3400 Gulf Blvd., tel. 813/360–1881. Reservations advised. Jacket and tie suggested. AE, DC, MC, V. No lunch. Very Expensive.*

Pepin. The fish is fresh, the beef well-aged, and the wine list broad-ranging. *4125 4th St. N, tel. 813/821–3773. Dress: casual but neat. AE, MC, V. Expensive.*

Peter's Place at the Tower. This established St. Pete chef wants dinner to be an evening's entertainment—hence this restaurant serving Continental fare (breakfast, lunch, and dinner) in Egyptian decor circa 1350 BC. Although the menu changes regularly, you can always expect selections from around the world, including such dishes as Mexican chicken mole and French roast duckling in brandied peaches. *200 Central Ave., tel. 813/ 822–8436. Dress: casual but neat. MC, V. Moderate.*

★ **Hurricane Seafood Restaurant.** Located right on historic Pass-a-Grille Beach (also known as St. Pete Beach), this seafood joint is popular for its grilled, broiled, or blackened grouper; steamed shrimp; and homemade crab cakes. One of the few places in St. Petersburg with live jazz (Wed.–Sun.), it also has an adjacent disco called Stormy's at the Hurricane, so it's well frequented even after mealtime. A sundeck on the third floor attracts crowds who come to see those gorgeous sunsets. *807 Gulf Way, tel. 813/360–9558. Reservations advised. Dress: casual. MC, V. Inexpensive.*

★ **Ted Peters Famous Smoked Fish.** The menu is limited to mackerel and mullet, but both are smoked and seasoned to perfection and served with heaping helpings of German potato salad. All meals are served outdoors. *1350 Pasadena Ave. S, Pasadena, tel. 813/381–7931. No reservations. Dress: casual. No dinner. Closed Tues. No credit cards. Inexpensive.*

Lodging **Don CeSar Beach Resort.** This palatial, pink-rococo resort sprawls along the Gulf front, with bright, airy rooms decorated in pastel shades. It was a favorite of such celebrities as writer F. Scott Fitzgerald and baseball great Babe Ruth in the 1920s and '30s. *3400 Gulf Blvd., St. Petersburg Beach 33706, tel. 813/ 360–1881, fax 813/367–3609. 277 rooms. Facilities: pool, whirlpool, beach, saunas, tennis, children's program, exercise room, sailboats, parasails, jet skis, 3 restaurants, lounge. AE, DC, MC, V. Very Expensive.*

Tradewinds on St. Petersburg Beach. Old Florida ambience is offered here, with white gazebos, gondolas gliding along canals, and hammocks swaying on 13 acres of beachfront property. *5500 Gulf Blvd., St. Petersburg Beach 33706, tel. 813/367– 6461, fax 813/367–4567. 381 rooms. Facilities: kitchens, pools, wading pool, beach, sauna, whirlpools, boating, dock, fishing, tennis, racquetball, bicycles, playground, exercise room, scuba instruction, waterskiing, windsurfing, restaurant, lounge. AE, DC, MC, V. Very Expensive.*

Colonial Gateway Resort Inn. This Gulf-front hotel is family-oriented, with half of its rooms equipped with kitchenettes. The resort was recently remodeled to give it a contemporary look for young families. *6300 Gulf Blvd., St. Petersburg Beach 33706, tel. 800/237–8918 or 813/367–2711, fax 813/362–7068. 200 rooms. Facilities: beach bar, pool, water sports, restaurants, lounge. AE, DC, MC, V. Moderate.*

Sarasota **The Bijou Cafe.** Wood, brass, and sumptuous green carpeting
Dining surround diners in this gas station turned restaurant. Chef
★ Jean Pierre Knaggs's Continental specialties include crispy roast duckling with tangerine brandy sauce or cassis and blackberry sauce, rack of lamb for two, and *crème brûlée,* a custard with a caramelized brown-sugar topping. *1287 1st St., tel. 813/ 366–8111. Reservations advised. Dress: casual but neat. DC, MC, V. Expensive.*

★ **Cafe L'Europe.** Located on fashionable St. Armand's Key, this greenery- and art-filled café specializes in fresh veal and seafood. Menus change frequently, but might include fillet of sole Picasso, Dover sole served with a choice of fruits, or wiener schnitzel sautéed in butter and topped with anchovies, olives, and capers. *431 St. Armand's Circle, tel. 813/388–4415. Reservations advised. Dress: casual but neat. AE, DC, MC, V. Expensive.*

Marina Jack. Have a dinner cruise on the *Marina Jack II* or eat fresh seafood overlooking Sarasota Bay. *2 Marina Plaza, tel. 813/365–4232. Reservations advised. Dress: casual but neat. MC, V. Expensive.*

Ophelia's on the Bay. Sample mussel soup, eggplant crêpes, chicken pot pie, seafood spiedini, or cioppino, among other things, at this waterfront restaurant. *9105 Midnight Pass Rd., Siesta Key, tel. 813/349–2212. Reservations advised. Dress: casual. AE, D, DC, MC, V. Moderate.*

Lodging **The Colony Beach.** If tennis is your game, this is the place to play it—such tennis greats as Bjorn Borg make The Colony their home court, and for good reason. The resort has 10 clay hydro courts and 11 hard courts and a staff of USPTA certified professionals. After the game, or whenever, visit the health spas (separate for men and women), which offer seaweed body packs, facials, licensed shiastu and western massage, whirlpool, steambaths, and too much more to list. The fitness center is run by pros and provides Stairmasters, free weights, yoga, and aerobics classes. All accommodations are suites, some of which sleep as many as eight people. Private beach houses and lanais that open onto sand and sea are also available. The rooms are done in four different styles, from Southwestern to more classic looks. As for dining, the formal Colony Restaurant has held *Wine Spectator*'s Grand Award since 1982 and is one of the "outstanding restaurants of the world," according to *Travel-Holiday* magazine. There's a complimentary children's program with indoor and outdoor activities, and virtually all activities are available, including ecology trips and deep-sea fishing. *1620 Gulf of Mexico Dr., Longboat Key 34228, tel. 813/383–6464, 800/237–9443 outside FL, or 800/282–1138 in FL, fax 813/383–7549. 235 suites, 25 VIP rooms. Facilities: 3 restaurants, bar, health club, tennis clinics, 21 tennis courts, pool, whirlpools, children's activities. AE, D, MC, V. Very Expensive.*

Hyatt Sarasota. The Hyatt is contemporary in design and conveniently located in the heart of the city, across from the Van Wezel Performing Arts Hall, a major cultural attraction. All of the spacious rooms overlook Sarasota Bay or the marina. *1000 Blvd. of the Arts, 34236, tel. 813/366–9000, fax 813/952–1987. 297 rooms. Facilities: pool, sauna, sailing, health club, dock, 2 restaurants, lounge. AE, DC, MC, V. Very Expensive.*

The Resort at Longboat Key Club. This is not simply a refined luxury hotel, it's one of *the* places to golf in the state. All 45 holes of golf on the silver medal courses (most likely ranking gold in the near future) are known as a watery challenge. The par-72 Islandside Course was designed by Billy Mitchell and boasts 5,000 palm trees. The Harbourside Course is a championship layout designed by Willard Byrd. Both have excellent pro shops, lessons, and clinics. Additionally, there are 38 Hartru tennis courts, ranked among the top 50 in the United States, and 1,000 acres of landscaped public areas. The 228 suites, which accommodate up to four people, are decorated in tropical patterns with light wood furnishings. Views of the golf course or beaches are to be had from huge private balconies; one even overlooks a private lagoon, where manatees can be seen from time to time. The deluxe suite sleeps up to six and has a kitchen. Choose from the five restaurants, among them the award-winning Orchids for gourmet dining, the casual poolside Barefoots, and, after a game of golf, Spike and Tees. Hobie Cats, kayaks, Sunfish, deep-sea charters, and ecology trips are all available on the beach. *301 Gulf of Mexico Dr., Box 15000, Longboat Key 34228, tel. 813/383–8821, 800/282–0113 in FL, or 800/237–8821 outside FL, fax 813/383–0359. 228 rooms. Facilities: 4 restaurants, golf courses, meeting rooms, library, 38 tennis courts, water sports and rentals, charters. AE, DC, MC, V. Very Expensive.*

Half Moon Beach Club. Conveniently located just minutes from St. Armand's Circle, this horseshoe-shape hotel offers Lido Key's finest accommodations. Elegance begins with the alabaster-lit lobby, and continues as you pass through the glass doors to the hotel's centerpiece, a tropical garden surrounding the pool. A $3 million renovation begun in 1989, together with inspirational 1950s and 1960s architecture, has returned the Half Moon to its original adored state. Walk past the pool, the tiki huts, and yogurt bar to the spacious beach deck where you can enjoy a cool drink. Continue on to the wide beach where, to the left, the sand meets the forest. Decorated in pink pastels, every asymmetrical room and suite is unique; four have direct Gulf views. Rooms on the inside of the horseshoe overlook the pool and garden. *2050 Ben Franklin Dr., Lido Beach 34236, tel. 813/388–3694 or 800/358–3245, fax 813/388–1938. 74 rooms, 12 suites. Facilities: restaurant, bar, yogurt bar, pool. AE, DC, MC, V. Expensive.*

Days Inn Sarasota–Siesta Key. Modern, built in 1986, with earth-tone rooms, this inn is 1 mile from the beaches and close to many restaurants and shopping centers. *6600 S. Tamiami Trail (U.S. 41), 34231, tel. 813/924-4900, fax 813/924-4900. 132 rooms. Facilities: pool, whirlpool. AE, DC, MC, V. Moderate.*

Gulf Beach Resort Motel. The stylized pink sign, enclosed in teal arching waves, gives new arrivals their first—and accurate—impression of this kitsch cinder block palace. Guests—a number of them young Europeans—sign in, meet others, and return year after year to reacquaint with old friends. Maybe the management draws the clientele: three delightful women show you a choice of rooms, each unit differently furnished from the others. The best—both with sea views—are a modern two-bedroom, done in white, and the one-bedroom below it. Some rooms have balconies, screened-in patios, or small private gardens with lime trees. All have kitchens, private baths, and basic cable TV. It's a 1-mile walk from St. Armand's Circle, through one of Florida's typical '50s residential neighborhoods. Daily, weekly, or monthly (Sept.–Jan.) rates available. *930 Ben Franklin Dr., Sarasota 34236, tel. 813/388–2127 or 800/232-2489 in U.S., 800/331-2489 in Canada, fax 813/388–1312. 48 rooms. Facilities: pool, kitchens, shuffleboard, cable TV. MC, V. Moderate.*

Hampton Inn Sarasota Airport. On the main drag and convenient to beaches and downtown, this motel serves a free Continental breakfast with a complimentary newspaper. Though it has no restaurant, there are four restaurants within walking distance. *N. Tamiami Trail (U.S. 41), 34234, tel. 813/351–*

7734, fax 813/351–7734. 100 rooms. Facilities: pool, exercise room. AE, DC, MC, V. Moderate.

Tampa Dining

★ **Armani's.** Located in the Hyatt Regency Westshore, this northern Italian–style restaurant offers a great view of Old Tampa Bay and the city. For an even closer look, take a seat on the terrace, where you can have dessert and really get a good look around. The interior is appealing, with an elegant almond-and-black color scheme, dim lighting, and many windows. Someone at your table should order the tasty veal Armani—veal sautéed with mushrooms, cream, and cognac in black and white truffle sauce. If it strikes your fancy, give the extensive antipasto bar a try. *6200 Courtney Campbell Causeway, tel. 813/281–9165. Reservations advised. Jacket and tie required. AE, DC, MC, V. Closed lunch and Sun. Very Expensive.*

★ **Bern's Steak House.** Perhaps the best steak house, not just in Tampa but in all of Florida, Bern's offers specialties created with finely aged prime beef. Choose from an extensive wine list—some 7,000 choices, with selections ranging in price from $10 to $10,000 a bottle. The vegetables are grown on owner-chef Bern Lexer's organic farm. Upstairs are the dessert rooms: small, glass-enclosed rooms where sumptuous desserts are served. Each room is equipped with a control panel for TV, radio, or listening in to the live entertainment in the lounge. *1208 S. Howard Ave., tel. 813/251–2421. Reservations advised. Dress: casual but neat. AE, DC, MC, V. No lunch. Very Expensive.*

★ **Bella Trattoria.** Brightly lit and slightly noisy, this restaurant is filled with the smells of such Italian fare as *capelli di l'Angelo*—smoked salmon and caviar tossed with spinach and angel-hair pasta in a vodka and cream sauce—and *Bella! Bella!*, a truffle torte of bittersweet, semisweet, and white chocolates. Crayons and paper tablecloths are provided for frustrated artists. *1413 S. Howard Ave., tel. 813/254–3355. No reservations. Dress: casual. AE, MC, V. Moderate.*

Colonnade. The wharfside location of this popular family restaurant is reflected in its nautical decor. Seafood—particularly grouper, red snapper, and lobster—is a specialty, but steak and chicken are also served. *3401 Bayshore Blvd., tel. 813/839–7558. No reservations. Dress: casual. AE, DC, MC, V. Moderate.*

★ **Columbia.** A Spanish fixture in Tampa's Ybor City for more than 85 years, this restaurant has several airy and spacious dining rooms and a sunny atrium with tile decor. Specialties include the Columbia 1905 salad—lettuce, ham, olives, cheese, and garlic; and paella—saffron rice with chicken, fish, and mussels. Flamenco dancing. *2117 E. 7th Ave., tel. 813/248–4961. Reservations accepted. Dress: casual weekdays, jacket suggested weekends. AE, DC, MC, V. Moderate.*

RG's. Two locations offer imaginative food in sophisticated settings served by a competent staff. Char-grilled duck and chocolate pecan toffee mousse are among the dishes found here. *RG's at City Center: 110 N. Franklin St., tel. 813/229–5536; RG's North: 3807 Northdale Blvd., tel. 813/963–2356. Reservations advised. Dress: casual but neat. AE, MC, V. At City Center, closed Sun. and lunch Sat.; at North, closed lunch. Moderate.*

Selena's. New Orleans Creole food is served here with some Sicilian dishes as well, in antique-filled dining rooms. Shrimp scampi and other fresh seafood are featured. *1623 Snow Ave.,* *tel. 813/251–2116. Dress: casual. Reservations advised. AE, DC, MC, V. Moderate.*

The Cactus Club. Southwestern cuisine such as fajitas is what you'll get at this casual but fashionable restaurant. Also available is a pretty good pizza. *1601 Snow Ave. (in the Old Hyde Park Mall), tel. 813/251–4089. Reservations not needed. Dress: casual. AE, DC, MC, V. Inexpensive.*

Lodging **Hyatt Regency Westshore.** From the marble-accented lobby to the casita villas scattered around the grounds, this large, business-oriented luxury hotel is well placed, right by a waterfront bird sanctuary on Tampa Bay. *6200 Courtney Campbell Causeway, 33607, tel. 813/874–1234, fax 813/281–9168. 445 rooms. Facilities: 3 restaurants, 4 lounges, pool, tennis, racquetball, jogging trails. AE, D, DC, MC, V. Very Expensive.*

Saddlebrook. Arguably one of Florida's premier tennis (42 courts) and golf (36 holes) resorts, Saddlebrook rests on sprawling, heavily wooded grounds situated just 15 miles north of Tampa. A variety of accommodations and amenities are available. Families should find the two-bedroom, two-bath suites (with full kitchens) convenient and comfortable. *100 Saddlebrook Way, Wesley Chapel 34249, tel. 813/973–1111, fax 813/773–4504. 501 rooms. Facilities: kitchenettes, pools, wading pools, whirlpools, saunas, fishing, golf, tennis, bicycles, health club, restaurants, lounge. AE, DC, MC, V. Very Expensive.*

Wyndham Harbour Island Hotel. Elegant ambience, with lots of dark wood paneling, substantial furniture, and attentive service is featured here. The tennis facilities are excellent. *725 S. Harbour Island Blvd., 33602, tel. 813/229–5000, fax 813/229–5322. 300 rooms. Facilities: pool, dock, sailboats, tennis, health club, restaurant, lounge. AE, DC, MC, V. Very Expensive.*

Embassy Suites Hotel–Tampa Airport. This modern all-suite hotel is located midway between Tampa International Airport and downtown Tampa. Each suite has a fully-equipped kitchen, and guests are entitled to a complimentary cooked breakfast. *555 N. Westshore Blvd., 33609, tel. 813/875–1555, fax 813/287–3664. 221 rooms. Facilities: pool, whirlpool, health club, transportation to airport, restaurant, lounge. Pets allowed. AE, DC, MC, V. Expensive.*

Holiday Inn Busch Gardens. Recently renovated, this family-oriented motor inn just 1 mile west of Busch Gardens is located across the street from the University Square Mall, Tampa's largest mall. *2701 E. Fowler Ave., 33612, tel. 813/971–4710, fax 813/977–0155. 399 rooms, including 7 suites. Facilities: pool, exercise room, restaurant, lounge. AE, DC, MC, V. Moderate.*

Tahitian Inn. This family-run motel offers comfortable rooms at budget prices. It's 5 minutes from Tampa Stadium, 20 minutes from Busch Gardens. *601 S. Dale Mabry Hwy., 33609, tel. 813/877–6721, fax 813/877–6218. 79 rooms. Facilities: pool, restaurant. AE, DC, MC, V. Inexpensive.*

Tarpon Springs **Louis Pappas' Riverside Restaurant.** The decor consists mainly
Dining of wall-to-wall people who pour into this waterfront landmark
★ for all manner of Greek fare, especially the Greek salad, made with lettuce, feta cheese chunks, onions, and olive oil. *10 W. Dodecanese Blvd., tel. 813/937–5101. Reservations advised. Dress: casual. AE, DC, MC, V. Moderate.*

Lodging **Innisbrook Hilton Resort.** This get-away-from-it-all resort offers plenty of activities, including superb golfing, on 1,000 wooded acres. There are deluxe suites of all sizes, all with kitchens, some with balconies or patios. *Box 1088, U.S. 19, 34689, tel. 813/942–2000, fax 813/942–5576. 1,200 rooms. Facilities: golf, tennis, racquetball, pools, health club, children's program (May–Sept.), miniature golf, saunas, 3 restaurants, nightclub. AE, DC, MC, V. Very Expensive.*

Venice **Sharky's on the Pier.** Gaze out on the beach and sparkling wa-
Dining ters while dining on grilled fresh seafood. *1600 S. Harbor Dr., tel. 813/488–1456. Reservations advised. Dress: casual. MC, V. Moderate.*

Lodging **Days Inn.** Located on the main business route through town, this recently renovated motor inn has comfortable rooms—and it's only 10 minutes from the beach. *1710 S. Tamiami Trail (U.S. 41), 34293, tel. 813/493–4558, fax 813/493–1593. 72 rooms. Facilities: pool, restaurant, lounge. Pets allowed. AE, MC, V. Moderate.*
Veranda Inn–Venice. A landscaped pool is the focal point of this small but spacious inn. All rooms look out on the pool and courtyard. *625 S. Tamiami Trail (U.S. 41), tel. 813/484–9559, fax 813/484–8235. 37 rooms. Facilities: pool, restaurant. AE, DC, MC, V. Moderate.*

The Arts

Between Tampa and Sarasota, this region hums with cultural activity. It's a good idea to purchase tickets before you arrive, especially during the busy winter tourist season. Most halls and theaters accept credit-card charges by phone. Area chambers of commerce (*see* Important Addresses and Numbers, *above*) can supply schedules of upcoming cultural events.

The **Tampa Performing Arts Center** (1010 W. C. MacInnes Pl., Box 2877, tel. 813/221–1045 or 800/955–1045) occupies 9 acres along the Hillsborough River and is one of the largest such complexes south of the Kennedy Center in Washington, DC. The festival hall, playhouse, and small theater accommodate opera, ballet, drama, and concerts.

Ruth Eckerd Hall (1111 McMullen Booth Rd., Clearwater, tel. 813/791–7400) also plays host to many national performers of ballet, drama, and music—pop, classical, or jazz.

Sarasota's **Van Wezel Performing Arts Hall** (777 N. Tamiami Trail, tel. 813/953–3366) is easy to find—just look for the purple shell rising along the bay front. It offers some 200 performances each year, including Broadway plays, ballet, jazz, rock concerts, symphonies, children's shows, and ice skating. For tickets and information, contact the box office.

Concerts The **Sarasota Concert Band** (Van Wezel Hall, 777 N. Tamiami
Bradenton/Sarasota Trail [U.S. 41], Sarasota, tel. 813/955–6660) includes 50 players, many of whom are full-time musicians. The group performs monthly concerts.
Florida West Coast Symphony Center (709 N. Tamiami Trail, Sarasota, tel. 813/953–4252) consists of a number of area groups that perform in Manatee and Sarasota counties regularly: Florida West Coast Symphony, The Florida String Quartet,

Florida Brass Quintet, Florida Wind Quintet, and New Artists String Quartet.

The **Sarasota Opera** (61 N. Pineapple Ave., tel. 813/953–7030) performs February–March in a historic theater downtown. Internationally known artists sing the principal roles, supported by a professional apprentice chorus—24 young singers studying with the company.

Tampa Bay Area **The Tampa Convention Center** (333 S. Franklin St., tel. 813/223–8511) hosts concerts throughout the year.

Dance The **St. Petersburg Concert Ballet** performs periodically throughout the year, mostly at the Bayfront Center in St. Petersburg (tel. 813/892–5767).

The Tampa Ballet performs at the Tampa Bay Performing Arts Center (tel. 813/221–1045).

Film The **Sarasota Film Society** operates year-round, showing foreign and nonmainstream films daily at 2, 5:45, and 8 at the Cobb Cinema (100 N. Fruitville Rd., tel. 813/388–2441).

Theater The **Asolo Center for the Performing Arts** (Drawer E, Sarasota, *Bradenton/Sarasota* tel. 813/351–8000) is a new $10 million facility that offers productions nearly year-round.

Florida Studio Theatre (1241 N. Palm Ave., Sarasota, tel. 813/366–9796) is a small professional theater that presents contemporary dramas, comedies, and musicals.

Golden Apple Dinner Theatre (25 N. Pineapple Ave., Sarasota, tel. 813/366–5454) combines a buffet dinner with musicals and comedies.

The **Players of Sarasota** (U.S. 41 and 9th St., Sarasota, tel. 813/365–2494), a long-established community theater, has launched such performers as Montgomery Clift, Polly Holiday, and Pee-Wee Herman. The troupe performs comedies, thrillers, and musicals.

Theatre Works (1247 1st St., Venice, tel. 813/952–9170) presents professional, non-Equity productions at the Palm Tree Playhouse.

Venice Little Theatre (corner of Tampa and Nokomis Aves., Venice, tel. 813/488–1115) is a community theater offering comedies, musicals, and a few dramas during its October–May season.

Tampa Area The **Tampa Theater** (711 N. Franklin St., Tampa, tel. 813/223–8981) presents shows, musical performances, and films.

Area dinner theaters include the **Showboat Dinner Theatre** (3405 Ulmerton Rd., Clearwater, tel. 813/223–2545).

Nightlife

Bars and **Blueberry Hill** (Harbour Island, Tampa, tel. 813/221–1157) is a **Nightclubs** nightclub-restaurant with performing disc jockeys and large-screen TV. The crowd is mostly yuppie couples.

Coliseum Ballroom (535 4th Ave. N, St. Petersburg, tel. 813/892–5202) offers ballroom dancing Wednesday and Saturday nights.

Harbour Island Hotel (Harbour Island, Tampa, tel. 813/229–5000) has a bar with a great view of the bay, large-screen TV, and thickly padded, comfortable chairs.

Harp & Thistle (650 Corey Ave., St. Petersburg Beach, tel. 813/

360–4104) presents live Irish music Wednesday through Saturday.

The Patio (Columbia Restaurant, St. Armand's Key, tel. 813/388–3987) is a casual lounge with live music nightly.

Yucatan Liquor Stand (4811 West Cypress, Tampa, tel. 813/289–8454) is a trendy spot with live music, dancing, a performing disc jockey, and a nosh menu that includes seafood, burgers, and Mexican delights.

Comedy Clubs Local venues include **Comedy Works** (3447 W. Kennedy Blvd., Tampa, tel. 813/875–9129); **Coconuts Comedy Club at Barnacle Bill's** (Howard Johnson's, 6110 Gulf Blvd., St. Petersburg, tel. 813/367–NUTS); and **Ron Bennington's Comedy Scene** (Rodeway Inn, 401 U.S. 19 S, Clearwater, tel. 813/799–1181).

Country-and-Western There are four Tampa-area places where you can hear country-and-western music: **Joyland Country Night Club** (11225 U.S. 19, St. Petersburg, tel. 813/573–1919); **Carlie's** (5641 49th St., St. Petersburg, tel. 813/527–5214); **Dallas Bull** (8222 N. Hwy. 301, Tampa, tel. 813/985–6877); and **Maestro's Country Lounge** (14727 N. Florida Ave., Tampa, tel. 813/961–5090).

Discos **Animal House** (1927 Ringling Blvd., Sarasota, tel. 813/366–3830) is a veritable rock-and-roll palace, complete with extensive light show, music videos, a DJ, and several bars. It's especially popular with the younger set.

Jazz Clubs Most of the following clubs offer jazz several nights a week: **Baxters Lounge** (714 S. Dale Mabry Hwy., Tampa, tel. 813/879–1161); **Cha Cha Coconuts** (City Pier, St. Petersburg, tel. 813/822–6655); and **Hurricane Lounge** (807 Gulf Way, Pass-a-Grille Beach, tel. 813/360–9558).

Rock Clubs **The Barn** (13815 Hillsborough Ave., Tampa, tel. 813/855–9818) plays '50s and '60s hits.

Club Yesterdays (2224 S. Tamiami Trail, Venice, tel. 813/493–2900) is a popular club with the under-30 set, playing Top-40 hits.

MacDintons (405 S. Howard Ave., Tampa, tel. 813/254–1661) presents live rock music nightly, starting at 10 PM. There's a full Continental menu for when the munchies strike.

306th Bomb Group (8301 N. Tamiami Trail, Sarasota, tel. 813/355–8591), decorated with World War II gear, features a DJ spinning Top-40 tunes for a generally over-25 clientele.

11 Fort Myers and Naples

By Karen
Feldman Smith
and G. Stuart
Smith

Updated by
Natalie Fairhead

The Lee County coast is often called "Florida's Florida" because its natural tropical environment has become a favorite vacation spot for Floridians as well as for visitors from across the United States and abroad. There's lot to do down here, but most of it has to with beaches and water.

Along the county's western border are the resort islands of Estero, Sanibel, and Captiva; Marco Island lies off the coast just south of Naples. Estero contains Fort Myers Beach, a laidback beach community favored by young singles and those who want to stay on the Gulf without paying the higher prices on Sanibel or Captiva. A few miles farther off the coast are Sanibel and Captiva, connected to the mainland by a mile-long causeway. In recent years development has threatened the charm of the islands. However, island dwellers have staunchly held the line on further development, keeping buildings low and somewhat farther apart than on the majority of Florida's barrier islands. Sanibel has long been a world-class shelling locale, with fine fishing, luxury hotels, and dozens of restaurants. You will not be able to see most of the houses, which are shielded by tall Australian pines, but the beaches and tranquil Gulf waters are readily accessible.

Inland, Fort Myers gets its nickname, the City of Palms, from the hundreds of towering royal palms that inventor Thomas Edison planted along the main residential street, McGregor Boulevard, on which his winter estate stood. Edison's idea caught on, and there are now more than 2,000 royal palms on McGregor Boulevard alone, with countless more throughout the city.

Once a small fishing village, Naples has grown into a thriving and sophisticated city, often likened to Palm Beach for its ambience. Here you can still appreciate the magnificent natural beauty of old Florida while also taking in some of the most lush tropical landscaping in the world. Third Street South and Fifth Avenue South (both in Olde Naples) offer shoppers a chance to make serious inroads in their disposable cash. The number of golf courses per capita in Naples is the highest in the world, a new 1,200-seat performing arts hall attracts world-class performers, and the town is the west coast home of the Miami City Ballet.

Unlike Palm Beach, where public beaches are scarce, the Naples area prides itself on a multitude of access points along its 41 miles of sun-drenched white beach.

East of Naples stretches the wilderness of the Big Cypress National Preserve, and if you take U.S. 41 south from Naples for 35 miles, you'll reach Everglades City, the western gateway to Everglades National Park (see Chapter 5).

Essential Information

Important Addresses and Numbers

Tourist Information
The following offices are open weekdays 9–5 and closed on holidays.

Charlotte County Chamber of Commerce (2702 Tamiami Trail, Port Charlotte, tel. 813/627–2222).

Lee County Visitor and Convention Bureau (2180 W. First St., Fort Myers, tel. 813/338–3500 or 800/533–4753).
Naples Area Chamber of Commerce (3620 N. Tamiami Trail, Naples, tel. 813/262–6141).
Sanibel-Captiva Chamber of Commerce (Causeway Rd., Sanibel, tel. 813/472–1080).

Emergencies Dial 911 for **police** or **ambulance** in an emergency.

Hospitals Hospital emergency rooms are open 24 hours. In Fort Myers: **Lee Memorial Hospital** (2776 Cleveland Ave.). In Naples: **Naples Community** Hospital (350 7th St. N); **North Collier Hospital** (1501 Immokalee Rd.).

24-Hour Pharmacies **Walgreens Pharmacy** (7070-3 College Pkwy., Fort Myers, tel. 813/939–2142; 8965 Tamiami Trail, North Naples, tel. 813/597–8196).

Arriving and Departing

By Plane The Fort Myers/Naples area's airport is **Southwest Florida Regional Airport** (tel. 813/768–1000), about 12 miles south of Fort Myers, 25 miles north of Naples. It is served by Air Canada (tel. 800/776–3000), American (tel. 800/433–7300), Canadian Holidays (tel. 800/282–4751), Continental (tel. 800/525–0280), Delta (tel. 800/221–1212), Northwest (tel. 800/225–2525), Transworld (tel. 800/221–2000), United (tel. 800/241–6522), and USAir (tel. 800/428–4322). A taxi ride from Southwest Florida Regional Airport to downtown Fort Myers or the beaches (Sanibel, Captiva) costs about $30; it's about twice that to Naples. Other transportation companies include **Aristocat Super Mini-Van Service** (tel. 813/275–7228), **Personal Touch Limousines** (tel. 813/549–3643), and **Sanibel Island Limousine** (tel. 813/472–8888).

The **Naples Airport** (tel. 813/643–6875), a small facility just east of downtown Naples, is served by American Eagle (tel. 800/433–7300), ComAir (tel. 813/263–1101), and USAir Express (tel. 800/428–4322).

Commercial shuttle service between Naples Airport and Naples is generally $10 to $25 per person. Call **Naples Taxi** (tel. 813/643–2148) or, to get to nearby Marco Island, try **Marco Transportation, Inc.** (tel. 813/394–2257).

By Car I–75 spans the region from north to south. Once you cross the border into Florida from Georgia, it should take about five hours to reach Fort Myers, and another hour to Naples. Alligator Alley is a two-lane toll road (75¢ at each end) that links up with I–75 at Naples and runs east through the Everglades to Fort Lauderdale, bringing travelers from the east coast. Count on two hours between Naples and Fort Lauderdale.

By Bus **Greyhound/Trailways** provides service to the area. Call the nearest office for schedules and fares (2275 Cleveland Ave. [U.S. 41], Fort Myers, tel. 813/334–1011; 2669 Davis Blvd., Naples, tel. 813/774–5660).

Getting Around

By Car I–75 and U.S. 41 run the length of the region; U.S. 41 goes through downtown Fort Myers and Naples, and is called the

Tamiami Trail. U.S. 41 is also called Cleveland Avenue in Fort Myers and 9th Avenue in Naples.

McGregor Boulevard runs from downtown Fort Myers southwest to Sanibel-Captiva. Summerlin Road runs southwest from Colonial Boulevard in South Fort Myers to Sanibel-Captiva and Fort Myers Beach. Route 78 (Pine Island–Bayshore Rd.) leads from North Fort Myers through north Cape Coral onto Pine Island.

By Bus The **Lee County Transit System** (tel. 813/939–1303) serves most of the county.

Scenic Drives **Route 867 (McGregor Boulevard),** Fort Myers's premier road, passes what were the winter homes of Thomas Edison and Henry Ford and goes southwest toward the beaches. The road is lined with thousands of royal palm trees and many large old homes.

Wildlife Drive is a 5-mile dirt road running through the J.N. "Ding" Darling National Wildlife Refuge on Sanibel Island. Especially at low tide, you may see raccoons, alligators, and birds, such as roseate spoonbills, egrets, ospreys, herons, and anhingas. The refuge is closed on Friday.

Guided Tours

Orientation Tours **Naples Trolley Tours** (tel. 813/262–7300) offers five 1¾-hour narrated tours daily, covering more than 100 points of interest. You can get off and re-board at no extra cost throughout the day.

Boat Tours **Dalis Charter** (tel. 813/262–4545) offers half-day fishing and sightseeing trips and sunset cruises, as well as private cocktail cruises. It's docked at Old Marine Market Place at Tin City (1200 Fifth Ave. S, Naples).

Epicurean Sailing Charters (tel. 813/964–0708) conducts half- and full-day cruises from Boca Grande to Useppa Island, Cabbage Key, and other area islands.

Everglades Jungle Cruises (tel. 813/334–7474) explores the Caloosahatchee and Orange rivers of Lee County. The *Capt. J.P.*, a stern paddle wheeler, offers a variety of cruises on the Caloosahatchee River and environs from mid-November through mid-April. Brunch, lunch, and dinner cruises are available, departing from the Fort Myers Yacht Basin.

The *Island Rover* (tel. 813/765–SHIP) offers morning, afternoon, and sunset sails on a tall ship in the Gulf of Mexico that leave from Gulf Star Marina, Fort Myers Beach.

Jammin' Sailboat Cruises (tel. 813/463–3520) offers day and sunset cruises from Fort Myers Beach. Call for reservations.

King Fisher Cruise Lines (tel. 813/639–0969) offers half-day, full-day, Sunday brunch, and sunset cruises in Charlotte Harbor, Peace River, and the Intracoastal Waterway. Boats depart from Fishermen's Village, Punta Gorda.

Tall Ship Eagle (tel. 813/466–3600), a topsail schooner much like those sailed by pirates in the 1800s, is available for cruising on the Gulf of Mexico. There are also weekend trips to Cabbage Key and a once-monthly trip to Key West. The boat sails from the Getaway Marina on Fort Myers Beach.

Tarpon Bay Recreation Center (tel. 813/472–8900) operates guided canoe tours through the J.N. "Ding" Darling Wildlife Refuge's mangroves.

Tours from the Air **Boca Grande Seaplane Service** (tel. 813/964–0234) operates sightseeing tours in the Charlotte Harbor area, leaving from 4th and Bayou streets, Boca Grande.

Classic Flight (tel. 813/939–7411) flies an open cockpit biplane for sightseeing tours of the Fort Myers area, leaving from the Fort Myers Jet Center (501 Danley Rd.).

North Port Hot-Air Balloon (tel. 813/426–7326) lifts off from North Port at an early hour to watch the sunrise, followed by a leisurely picnic breakfast. The cost is high—$129 per person, with a maximum of four people.

Skyrider Parasailing (tel. 813/463–351) leaves from the Time Square area of Fort Myers Beach.

Exploring Southwest Florida

Highlights for First-Time Visitors

Corkscrew Swamp Sanctuary, Naples
J. N. "Ding" Darling Wildlife Refuge, Sanibel Island
McGregor Boulevard, Fort Myers
Thomas Edison Home, Fort Myers

Fort Myers

Numbers in the margin correspond to points of interest on the Fort Myers/Naples map.

Most vacationers who come to Lee County spend their time on the beach, but if you want some sightseeing, head for downtown **Fort Myers,** the heart of Lee County. Drive along palm-lined **McGregor Boulevard** to reach downtown from the Gulf shore; from College Parkway north into town is the most scenic stretch of this beautiful road.

The city's premier attraction is **Thomas Edison's Winter Home,** containing a laboratory, botanical gardens, and a museum. The property straddles McGregor Boulevard (Rte. 867) about a mile west of U.S. 41 near downtown Fort Myers. The inventor spent his winters on the 14-acre estate, developing the phonograph and teletype, experimenting with rubber, and planting some 6,000 species of plants from those collected throughout the world. A recent addition to the Edison complex is **Mangoes,** the winter home of the inventor's long-time friend, automaker Henry Ford. *2350 McGregor Blvd., tel. 813/334–3614. Combined admission to the Edison house and Mangoes: $10 adults, $5 children 6–12. Tours Mon.–Sat. 9–4, Sun. noon–3:30. Closed Thanksgiving and Christmas.*

Just a few blocks east is the **Fort Myers Historical Museum,** which is housed in a restored railroad depot. Its displays depict the area's history dating back to 1200 BC, with special exhibits about boats and fishing. *2300 Peck St., tel. 813/332–5955. Admission: $2.50 adults, $1 children. Open Mon.–Fri. 9–4:30, Sun. 1–5.*

Fort Myers/Naples

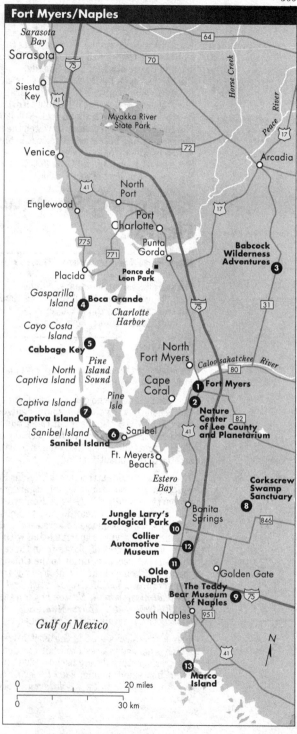

Sarasota Bay

Sarasota

Siesta Key

Venice

Englewood

Placida

Gasparilla Island — **Boca Grande** ④

Cayo Costa Island

Cabbage Key ⑤

North Captiva Island

Captiva Island

Captiva Island ⑦

Sanibel Island

Sanibel Island ⑥

Ft. Meyers Beach

Pine Island Sound

Pine Isle

Sanibel

Estero Bay

Myakka River State Park

North Port

Port Charlotte

Punta Gorda

Ponce de Leon Park

Charlotte Harbor

North Fort Myers

Cape Coral

Horse Creek

Peace River

Arcadia

Babcock Wilderness Adventures ③

Caloosahatchee River

Fort Myers ①

② **Nature Center of Lee County and Planetarium**

Jungle Larry's Zoological Park

⑩

Collier Automotive Museum — ⑫

⑪

Olde Naples

Bonita Springs

Corkscrew Swamp Sanctuary

⑧

Golden Gate

The Teddy Bear Museum of Naples ⑨

South Naples

Gulf of Mexico

⑬ **Marco Island**

N

0   20 miles

0   30 km

Head northwest to Edwards Drive, which borders the Caloosahatchee River. The **Fort Myers Yacht Basin** has tour boats that offer sightseeing and luncheon cruises on the river (*see* Boat Tours, *above*). Alongside Edwards Drive, a string of shuffleboard courts weather heavy use on all but the hottest days. Adjacent to the courts is the **Harborside Convention Center** complex, and one block away is the office where the Greater Fort Myers Chamber of Commerce dispenses information. *2310 Edwards Dr., tel. 813/322–3624.*

Time Out Park and walk a block in from the river to First Street, which runs through the heart of downtown Fort Myers. Stroll past the shops and have lunch at one of several eateries, including **Casa De Guerrero** (2225 First St., tel. 813/332–4674), **French Connection Café** (2282 First St., tel. 813/332–4443), and **April's** (2269 First St., tel. 813/337–4004).

❷ The **Nature Center of Lee County and Planetarium** offers frequently changing exhibits on wildlife, fossils, and Florida's native habitats and animals. You can see a live alligator and bobcat, plus an aviary full of permanently disabled birds, including hawks, owls, and bald eagles. There are 2 miles of nature walks through the cypress swamps. The planetarium offers star shows, laser light shows, and Cinema-360 films. *3450 Ortiz Ave., tel. 813/275–3435. Nature Center admission: $2 adults, $1 children 3–11; Planetarium admission: $3 adults, $2 children under 12. Open Mon–Sat. 9–4, Sun. 11–4:30.*

To see what Florida looked like centuries ago, reserve a place ❸ on **Babcock Wilderness Adventures,** 90-minute swamp buggy excursions through the Telegraph Cypress Swamp on the 90,000-acre Babcock Crescent B Ranch, south of Punta Gorda. Among the inhabitants you are likely to see are turkey, deer, bobcats, alligators, cows, and a herd of bison. From downtown Fort Myers, head east on Route 80 (Palm Beach Blvd.) past the I–75 interchange, then look for Route 31. Make a left and drive until you see the entrance for Babcock Wilderness Adventures on your right. *Rte. 31, tel. 813/656–6104. Reservations required. Admission: $16.91 adults, $8.43 children. Four tours daily, weather permitting; closed Mon., Apr.–Nov.*

The Barrier Islands

Before roads to southwest Florida were even talked about, the wealthy boarded trains to get to the Gasparilla Inn, built in ❹ 1912 in **Boca Grande,** on Gasparilla Island. From U.S. 41 in Murdock (in northern Port Charlotte), head southwest on Route 776, then south on Route 771 into Placida, where a causeway runs out to the island.

While condominiums and other forms of modern sprawl are creeping up on Gasparilla, much of Boca Grande looks as it has for a century or more. The mood is set by the old Florida homes, many made of wood, with wide, inviting verandas and wicker rocking chairs. The island's general sleepy ambience is disrupted only in the spring, when tarpon fishermen descend with a vengeance on Boca Grande Pass, considered among the best tarpon-fishing spots in the world.

At the island's southern end is **Old Lighthouse Beach,** where a historic wooden lighthouse still stands. There's ample parking here, and lots of Gulf-front beach space.

❺ You'll have to board a boat to visit **Cabbage Key,** which sits at Marker 60 on the Intracoastal Waterway. Atop an ancient Calusa Indian shell mound on Cabbage Key is the friendly, 6-room Cabbage Key Inn that novelist and playwright Mary Roberts Rinehart built in 1938. Now the inn also offers several guest cottages, a marina, and a dining room that is papered in thousands of dollar bills, signed and posted by patrons over the years. *Lunch and dinner tours available through Captiva's South Seas Plantation (tel. 813/472–5111), and Fishermen's Village in Punta Gorda (tel. 813/639–0969).*

❻ ❼ About 23 miles from downtown Fort Myers, neighboring **Sanibel Island** and **Captiva Island** are reached via a toll bridge on the Sanibel Causeway. Though there is a $3 round-trip toll, avid shell collectors and nature enthusiasts are apt to get their money's worth, for Sanibel's beaches are rated among the best shelling grounds in the world. For the choicest pickings, get there as the tide is going out or just after a storm.

On the southern end of Sanibel Island, explore the **J. N. "Ding" Darling National Wildlife Refuge**—by car, foot, bicycle, or canoe. The 5,014-acre refuge is home to some 290 species of birds, 50 types of reptiles, and various mammals. A 5-mile dirt road meanders through the sanctuary. An observation tower along the road is a prime bird-watching site, especially in the early morning and just before dusk. *Tel. 813/472–1100. Admission: $3 per car or $15 for a duck stamp (which covers all national wildlife refuges); $1 for pedestrians and bicyclists. Wildlife Drive open Sat.–Thurs. 7–5:45, closed Fri; Visitor Center open daily 9–5.*

The Tarpon Bay Recreation Center operates a specially designed open-air tram with a naturalist on board that tours the J. N. "Ding" Darling Wildlife Refuge daily (tel. 813/472–8900, $6.75 adults, $3.50 children).

An additional treat on Sanibel Island is the new **Bailey-Matthews Shell Museum,** set to open in spring 1994. The centerpiece will be a huge, interactive world globe, where visitors can push buttons to see where in the world the museum's shells are found. More than a million shells are in the museum's archives, as well as thousands of 35-millimeter slides. *2431 Periwinkle Way, tel. 813/395–2233. Admission: $3. Open daily; call for hours.*

Naples

To get a feel for what this part of Florida was like before civil engineers began draining the swamps, take a drive out Route **❽** 846 to the **Corkscrew Swamp Sanctuary.** The National Audubon Society manages the 11,000-acre tract to help protect 500-year-old trees and endangered birds, such as the wood storks that often nest high in the bald cypress. Visitors taking the 1¾-mile self-guided tour along the boardwalk may glimpse alligators, graceful wading birds, and unusual air plants that cling to the sides of trees. *16 mi east of I–75 on Rte. 846, tel. 813/657–3771. Admission: $6.50 adults, $3 children 6–18. Open Dec.–Apr., daily 7AM–5 PM, May–Nov., daily 8–5.*

From Corkscrew Swamp Sanctuary, take Route 846 back to I–75 and head south to the next exit, Pine Ridge Road. Take that

⑨ west to **The Teddy Bear Museum of Naples.** Built by oil heiress and area resident Frances Pew Hayes, the $2 million museum houses more than 1,500 teddy bears. *2511 Pine Ridge Rd., tel. 813/598–2711. Admission: $5 adults, $3 students and senior citizens, $2 children 4–12. Open Wed.–Sat. 10–5, Sun. 1–5.*

⑩ For some real wildlife, head for **Jungle Larry's Zoological Park.** Continue west on Pine Ridge Road to U.S. 41. Turn left and drive south, past Mooring Line Road, until you see the big sign for Jungle Larry's, then turn left. Originally a botanical garden planted in the early 1900s, the 52-acre park now houses exotic wildlife in its jungle-like park. A safari boat trip takes visitors out to the island where the primates live. Kids will enjoy the petting zoo. *1590 Goodlette Rd., tel. 813/262–4053. Admission: $10.95 adults, $6.95 children 3–15. Open Dec.–Apr., daily 9:30–5:30; May–Nov., Tues.–Sun. 9:30–5:30.*

For a look at Naples' impressive residential areas, return to **Mooring Line Drive,** where you turn left, heading west, past some of the most expensive coastline property in the state. Mooring Line Drive turns south and runs into **Gulfshore Boulevard**, which is lined with condominiums, shops, hotels, and a Gulf beach with many public entrances. Just near the end of Gulfshore Boulevard on Broad Avenue, you can pick up 2nd Street South, which becomes **Gordon Drive.** It leads into Port Royale, where million-dollar-plus homes are a dime a dozen. Dazzling architecture, landscaping, and statuary are visible from the road.

Going south on U.S. 41, as the highway curves left to go over a large bridge into East Naples, stay on the street heading south

⑪ and follow signs into **Olde Naples,** the city's historic downtown core. Tree-lined streets and promenades make this an attractive place to get out of your car and walk around. Fifth Avenue South is an upscale shopping street, with potted greenery and seasonal flowers punctuating the route that leads past a minipark to the gulf. Third Street South has lots of little courtyards where you can rest your feet.

Time Out | **Merriman's Wharf** (1200 5th Ave. S, tel. 813/261–1811), in the Old Marine Market Place, is a good bet for a drink or a seafood lunch—either along the dock or indoors in air-conditioned comfort.

⑫ Antique-car enthusiasts should head to the **Collier Automotive Museum,** where you can see 75 antique and classic sports cars, including Gary Cooper's 1935 Duesenberg SSJ. Sometimes a traveling exhibit of Rolls Royces comes to visit. *2500 S. Horseshoe Dr., Collier Park of Commerce, off Airport-Pulling Rd., tel. 813/643–5252. Admission: $6 adults, $3 children 5–12. Open Dec.–Apr., daily 10–5; May–Nov., Tues.–Sat. 10–5.*

Marco Island | South of Naples is yet another resort island, **Marco Island,**
⑬ linked to the mainland by a short causeway. High-rise condominiums and hotels line much of the waterfront, but many natural areas have been preserved, including the tiny fishing village of **Goodland,** where Old Florida lives on.

Southwest Florida for Free

The Naples Fishing Pier (12th Ave. S, Naples), extending 1,000 miles into the Gulf, is said to be the most photographed pier anywhere. It's a perfect spot for viewing spectacular sunsets. Bait, snack bar, rest rooms, and showers are available.

Sun Harvest Citrus offers free guided tours of this citrus packinghouse from November through May. Visitors learn the history of the Florida citrus industry while watching fruit get squeezed into juice at a rate of 500 gallons per hour. *Six Mile Cypress Rd. and Metro Pkwy., Fort Myers, tel. 800/743–1480. Admission free. Tours Mon.–Sat. at 10, 1, and 3.*

Museum of Charlotte County (*see* What to See and Do With Children, *below*).

What to See and Do with Children

Babcock Wilderness Adventures (*see* Fort Myers, *above*).

Children's Science Center is a "please do touch" center, with rotating exhibits that include mazes, optical tricks, mind benders, dinosaurs, brain twisters, and more. *2915 Pine Island Rd., Cape Coral, ½ mi west of U.S. 41, tel. 813/997–0012. Admission: $3 adults, $1 children 3–11. Open Mon.–Fri. 9:30–4:30, Sat. 9–5, Sun. noon–5.*

Everglades Wonder Gardens captures the flavor of untamed Florida with its exhibit of native wildlife and natural surroundings. *U.S. 41, Bonita Springs, tel. 813/992–2591. Admission: $8 adults, $4 children 3–12. Open daily 9–5.*

Jungle Larry's Zoological Park (*see* Naples, *above*).

Nature Center of Lee County and Planetarium (*see* Fort Myers, *above*).

Sun Splash Family Waterpark features more than two dozen wet and dry attractions. *400 Santa Barbara Blvd., Cape Coral, tel. 813/574–0557. Admission: $7.95 for visitors over 54 inches, $5.95 for children 3 and older standing under 54 inches. Open Mon.–Fri. 11–5, Sat.–Sun. 10:30–6.*

The Teddy Bear Museum of Naples (*see* Naples, *above*).

Y Museum of Charlotte County features many animal specimens from Africa and North America, plus dolls and shells. A variety of programs entertain and educate the kids. *260 W. Retta Esplanade, Punta Gorda, tel. 813/639–3777. Donations accepted. Open Tues.–Fri. 10–5, Sat. noon–5.*

Off the Beaten Track

Fort Myers   **Eden Vineyards Winery and Park** opened to the public in late 1989, claiming to be the southernmost bonded winery in the United States. The family-owned winery offers tours, tastings, picnics, and tram rides. *Rte. 80, 10.2 mi east of the I–75 interchange, tel. 813/728–9463. Admission: $2.50 adults, children 12 and under free; complimentary tasting. Reservations needed for groups of 10 or more. Open daily 11–5.*

North Fort Myers   **ECHO** (Educational Concerns for Hunger Organization) is a small, active group striving to solve the world's hunger problems. The group offers tours of its gardens, which feature collections of tropical food plants, simulated rain forests, and fish farming. *17430 Durrance Rd., tel. 813/543–3246. Admission free. Tours Tues., Fri., Sat. 10 AM or by appointment.*

Palmdale You aren't likely to happen upon Palmdale, a speck of a town about 40 minutes east of Punta Gorda, unless you make a point of visiting either of two singular attractions. You know you're approaching the **Cypress Knee Museum** when you see spindly hand-carved signs along Route 27 with such sayings as "Lady, If He Won't Stop, Hit Him on Head with a Shoe." In the museum are thousands of cypress knees, the knotty, gnarled protuberances that sprout mysteriously from the bases of some cypress trees and grow to resemble all manner of persons and things. There are specimens resembling dogs, bears, ballet dancers' feet, an anteater, Joseph Stalin, and Franklin D. Roosevelt. *1 mi south of the junction of U.S. 27 and U.S. 29, tel. 813/675–2951. Admission: $2 adults, $1 children 6–12. Open daily 8AM–dusk.*

Just 2 miles southeast on U.S. 27, **Gatorama's** 1,000 alligators and assorted crocodiles await visitors, smiling toothily. Visitors who want to take a good long gander at gators can get their fill here, where a variety of species and sizes cohabit. It's also a commercial gator farm, so you'll see how the "mink" of the leather trade is raised for profit. *U.S. 27, 3 mi south of junction with U.S. 29, tel. 813/675–0623. Admission: $4.50 adults, $2.50 children 2–11. Open daily 8–6.*

Shopping

Shell items—jewelry, lamps, plant hangers, and such—are among the more kitschy commodities found in abundance in the region. Sanibel Island, one of the world's premier shelling grounds, has numerous shops that sell shell products. **The Shell Factory** (2787 N. Tamiami Trail, U.S. 41) in North Fort Myers claims to have the world's largest display of seashells and coral.

Shopping Areas In Fort Myers, two shopping centers cater to upscale tastes— **Bell Tower** (U.S. 41 and Daniels Rd., South Fort Myers) and **Royal Palm Square** (Colonial Blvd., between McGregor Blvd. and U.S. 41). Both have about 36 shops and restaurants. Both are worth visiting just to look at the elegant tropical landscaping, which includes parrots that stand sentry from perches among the palms. Neither center is enclosed, but both have covered sidewalks.

In **Olde Naples,** shoppers stroll along 3rd Street South, and nearby 5th Avenue South, which offer an intriguing selection of shops.

The **Village on Venetian Bay** on Gulf Shore Boulevard in Naples has several upscale shops built over the water of the bay.

Old Marine Market Place at Tin City (1200 5th Ave. S), in a collection of former fishing shacks along Naples Bay, has 40 boutiques, artisans' studios, and souvenir shops offering everything from scrimshaw to Haitian art.

The **Waterside Shops** at Pelican Bay is an open-air specialty shopping center with elaborate waterscapes in its interior courtyard. Anchored by Saks Fifth Avenue and Jacobson's Department Store, Waterside houses 50 shops and several eating places.

Flea Market **Ortiz** features covered walkways and hundreds of vendors selling new and used items. *Ortiz and Anderson Aves., east of Fort Myers, tel. 813/694–5019. Open Fri.–Sun. 6–4.*

Participant Sports

Biking Boca Grande, an hour's drive from Fort Myers, has good bike paths. The best choice in Fort Myers is the path along Summerlin Road; for rental, try **Trikes & Bikes & Mowers** (3224 Fowler St., tel. 813/936–4301). Sanibel Island's extensive bike path is in good condition and runs throughout the island, keeping bikers safely apart from the traffic and allowing them some time for reflection on the waterways and wildlife they will encounter. Rent bikes at **Finnimore's Cycle Shop** (2353 Periwinkle Way, Sanibel, tel. 813/472–5577), **Tarpon Bay Marina** (900 Tarpon Bay Rd., Sanibel, tel. 813/472–8900), or **Jim's Bike & Scooter Rental** (11534 Andy Rosse La., Captiva, tel. 813/472–1296). In Bonita Springs, rent bicycles at **Pop's Bicycles** (3685 Bonita Beach Rd., Bonita Springs, tel. 813/947–4442). In Naples, try **The Bicycle Shop** (813 Vanderbilt Beach Rd., Naples, tel. 813/566–3646). On Marco Island, rentals are available at **Scootertown** (855 Bald Eagle Dr., tel. 813/394–8400).

Canoeing **Lakes Park** (tel. 813/481–7946) in Fort Myers rents canoes on waterways where you can see the carp swimming, and, if you are quiet enough, some herons and osprey fly overhead. **Canoe Safari** (tel. 813/494–7865), about 25 miles inland up the Peace River at Arcadia, operates half- and full-day trips, plus overnighters including camping equipment. **Tarpon Bay Marina** (Sanibel, tel. 813/472–8900) has canoes and equipment for exploring the waters of the J. N. "Ding" Darling National Wildlife Refuge. **Estero River Tackle and Canoe Outfitters** (20991 Tamiami Trail S, Estero, tel. 813/992–4050) has canoes and equipment for use on the meandering Estero River.

Fishing Tarpon, kingfish, speckled trout, snapper, grouper, sea trout, snook, sheepshead, and shark are among the species to be found in coastal waters. You can charter your own boat or join a group on a party boat for full- or half-day outings.

Party boats in the area include **Kingfisher Charter** (Fishermen's Village, Punta Gorda, tel. 813/639–0969), **Deebold's Marina** (1071 San Carlos Blvd., Fort Myers, tel. 813/466–3525), **Gulf Star Marina** (708 Fisherman's Wharf, Fort Myers Beach, tel. 813/765–1500), **Deep Sea Charter Fishing** (Boat Haven, Naples, tel. 813/263–8171), and **Sunshine Tours** (Marco Island, tel. 813/642–5415).

Golf The following courses are open to the public.

Fort Myers Area **Bay Beach Club Executive Golf Course** (Fort Myers Beach, tel. 813/463–2064), **Cape Coral Golf & Tennis Resort** (Fort Myers, tel. 813/542–7879), **Cypress Pines Country Club** (Lehigh Acres, tel. 813/369–8216), **The Dunes** (Sanibel, tel. 813/472–2535), **Eastwood Country Club** (Fort Myers, tel. 813/275–4848), **Fort Myers Country Club** (Fort Myers, tel. 813/936–2457), **Lochmoor Country Club** (North Fort Myers, tel. 813/995–0501), **Pelican's Nest Golf Course** (Bonita Springs, tel. 813/947–4600), **Wildcat Run** (Estero, tel. 813/936–7222).

Naples Area **Hibiscus Country Club** (Naples, tel. 813/774–3559), **Lely Flamingo Island Club** (Naples, tel. 813/793–2223), **Naples Beach Golf Course** (Naples, tel. 813/261–2222), and **Oxbow** (LaBelle, tel. 813/334–3903).

Port Charlotte Area **Burnt Store** (Punta Gorda, tel. 813/332–7334), **Deep Creek Golf Club** (Charlotte Harbor, tel. 813/625–6911), and **North Port Golf Course** (North Port, tel. 813/426–2804).

Motorboating **Boat House of Sanibel** (Sanibel Marina, tel. 813/472–2531) rents powerboats. **Brookside Marina** (2023 Davis Blvd., Naples, tel. 813/263–7250) rents 16- to 25-foot powerboats. **Getaway Bait and Boat Rental** (1091 San Carlos Blvd., Fort Myers Beach, tel. 813/466–3200) rents powerboats and fishing equipment and sells bait.

Sailing For sailing lessons or charter sail cruises, contact **Fort Myers Yacht Charters** (Port Sanibel Yacht Club, South Fort Myers, tel. 813/466–1800), **Marco Island Sea Excursions** (1281 Jamaica Rd., Marco Island, tel. 813/642–6400), **Southwest Florida Yachts** (3444 Marinatown La. NW, Fort Myers, tel. 813/656–1339 or 800/262–7939).

Tennis Most hotels and motels in Florida have outdoor tennis courts, some lighted for night use. Public courts in this region include:

Bay Beach Racquet Club (120 Lenell St., Fort Myers Beach, tel. 813/463–4473), **Cambier Park** (775 8th Ave. S, Naples, tel. 813/434–4690), **The Dunes** (949 Sand Castle Rd., Sanibel, tel. 813/472–3522), **Forest Hills Racquet Club** (100 Forest Hills Blvd., Naples, tel. 813/774–2442), **Lochmoor Country Club** (3911 Orange Grove Blvd., North Fort Myers, tel. 813/995–0501), and **Port Charlotte Tennis Club** (22400 Gleneagles Terr., Port Charlotte, tel. 813/625–7222).

Spectator Sports

Baseball Major-league teams offer exhibitions in this area in March and April, during their spring training sojourns. For information on all the teams, call 904/488–0990. Teams playing here are the **Minnesota Twins** (Lee County Sports Complex, 1410 Six Mile Cypress Pkwy., Fort Myers, tel. 813/768–4278); the **Boston Red Sox** (2201 Edison Ave., Fort Myers, tel. 813/334-4700); and the **Texas Rangers** (Charlotte County Stadium, Rte. 776, Port Charlotte, tel. 813/625–9500).

Dog Racing There's dog racing year-round at the **Naples–Fort Myers Greyhound Track** (10601 Bonita Beach Rd., Bonita Springs, tel. 813/992–2411).

Beaches

The best beaches in the region are on Sanibel and Captiva islands, and in the Naples area.

Fort Myers Area **Carl E. Johnson Recreation Area** lies on the island south of Fort Myers Beach. Admission is $1.50 per adult, 75¢ per child; this covers a round-trip tram ride from the park entrance in Bonita Beach to Lovers Key, on which the park is situated. Shelling, bird-watching, fishing, canoeing, and nature walks in an unspoiled setting are the main attractions here. There are also rest rooms, picnic tables, a snack bar, and showers.

Estero Island, otherwise known as **Fort Myers Beach,** is 18 miles from downtown Fort Myers. It has numerous public accesses to the beach, which is frequented by families and young singles. You are never far from civilization, with houses, condominiums, and hotels nestled along most of the shore. The island's shores slope gradually into the usually tranquil and warm Gulf waters, affording a safe swimming area for children. From Fort Myers, it is reached via San Carlos Boulevard; from Naples and Bonita Springs, via Hickory Boulevard.

Lynn Hall Memorial Park is on Estero Boulevard, in the more commercial northern part of Fort Myers Beach. Singles can be found playing in the gentle surf or sunning and socializing on shore. A number of night spots and restaurants are within easy walking distance. A free fishing pier adjoins the public beach. Facilities include picnic tables, barbecue grills, playground equipment, and a bathhouse with rest rooms. The beach is open 7 AM–10 PM; lifeguards are on duty 10 AM–5:45 PM.

Naples Area   **Bonita Springs Public Beach** is 10 minutes from the I–75 exit at Bonita Beach Road, on the southern end of Bonita Beach. There are picnic tables, free parking, and nearby refreshment stands and shopping.

Delnor-Wiggins Pass State Recreation Area is at the Gulf end of Bluebill Avenue, off Vanderbilt Drive in North Naples. The well-maintained park offers miles of sandy beaches, lifeguards, barbecue grills, picnic tables, a boat ramp, observation tower, rest rooms with wheelchair access, lots of parking space, bathhouses, and showers. Fishing is best in Wiggins Pass at the north end of the park. *Admission: Florida residents pay $1 for driver, 50¢ per passenger; out-of-state drivers pay $2, $1 per passenger. Boat launching costs $1. No alcoholic beverages allowed.*

Lowdermilk Park stretches along Gulf Shore Boulevard in Naples. There are 1,000 feet of beach plus parking, rest rooms, showers, a pavilion, vending machines, and picnic tables. No alcoholic beverages or fires permitted.

Tigertail Beach is on Hernando Drive at the south end of Marco Island. Singles and families congregate here. Facilities include parking, concession stand, picnic area, sailboat rentals, volleyball, rest rooms, and showers.

Port Charlotte Area   **Englewood Beach,** near the Charlotte-Sarasota county line, is popular with teenagers, although beachgoers of all ages frequent it. In addition to a wide and shell-littered beach, there are barbecue grills, picnic facilities, and a playground.

Sanibel Island   **Bowman's Beach** is mainly a family beach on Sanibel's northwest end.

Gulfside Park, off Casa Ybel Road, is a lesser-known and less-populated beach, ideal for those who seek solitude and do not require facilities.

Lighthouse Park, at Sanibel's southern end, attracts a mix of families, shellers, and singles. Rest rooms are available. One of the draws is a historic lighthouse.

Dining and Lodging

Dining   In Fort Myers and Naples, seafood reigns supreme, especially the succulent claw of the native stone crab, in season from October 15 through May 15. It's usually served with drawn butter or a tangy mustard sauce. Many restaurants offer "early bird" menus with seating before 6 PM.

Highly recommended restaurants are indicated by a star ★.

Category	Cost*
Very Expensive	over $50
Expensive	$35–$50
Moderate	$20–$35
Inexpensive	under $20

per person, excluding drinks, service, and 6% sales tax

Lodging In general, inland rooms are considerably cheaper than those on the islands. The most expensive accommodations are those with waterfront views. Many apartment-motels are springing up in the area, and these can bring great savings for families or groups, especially when you save dining costs by cooking some of your own meals.

Rates are highest mid-December–mid-April. The lowest prices are available May–November. Price categories listed below apply to winter rates.

Highly recommended lodgings are indicated by a star ★.

Category	Cost*
Very Expensive	over $150
Expensive	$90–$150
Moderate	$60–$90
Inexpensive	under $60

All prices are per person, double occupancy, excluding 6% state sales tax and 1%–3% tourist tax.

Cape Coral **Cape Crab House.** Crabs are served Maryland-style—with mal-
Dining let and pliers and heaped on a tablecloth of newspaper—or in the more refined atmosphere of a second dining room with linen tablecloths and a piano player. *Coralwood Mall, Del Prado Blvd., tel. 813/574-2722. Reservations accepted. Dress: casual. AE, MC, V. Moderate.*
Venezia. This small, neighborhood restaurant serves straightforward Italian food including pastas, pizza, chicken, veal, and fresh seafood. *1515 S.E. 47th Terr., tel. 813/542-0027. No reservations. Dress: casual. No lunch. MC, V. Moderate.*
★ **Siam Hut.** Thai music pings and twangs in the background while the dishes do the same to your tastebuds. Get it fiery hot or extra mild. Specialties: *pad thai* (a mixture of noodles, crushed peanuts, chicken, shrimp, egg, bean sprouts, and scallions) and crispy Siam rolls (spring rolls stuffed with ground chicken, bean thread, and vegetables). *1873 Del Prado Blvd., Coral Pointe Shopping Center, tel. 813/772-3131. No reservations. Dress: casual. AE, MC, V. Inexpensive.*

Lodging **Cape Coral Golf & Tennis Resort.** Oriented toward golf and tennis enthusiasts, this resort offers good value. Understated decor reflects the sporty atmosphere. *4003 Palm Tree Blvd., 33904, tel. 813/542-3191, fax 813/542-4694. 100 rooms. Facilities: pool, golf, driving range, tennis, baby-sitting, restaurant, lounge. AE, DC, MC, V. Moderate.*

Quality Inn. Conveniently located in downtown Cape Coral near parks, beaches, restaurants, and malls, this motel offers nonsmoking and handicapped-accessible rooms with complimentary breakfast and newspaper. *1538 Cape Coral Pkwy., 33904, tel. 813/542–2121, fax 813/542–6319. 146 rooms. Facilities: pool. Pets permitted. AE, DC, MC, V. Moderate.*

Fort Myers
Dining
★

Peter's La Cuisine. The quiet elegance of this downtown restaurant blends perfectly with the fine Continental cuisine served within. The menu changes every few weeks but usually includes a fresh salmon dish, chateaubriand, and duck or some other exotic meat. *2224 Bay St., tel. 813/332–2228. Reservations advised. Dress: casual but neat. AE, DC, MC, V. Expensive.*

★ **The Prawnbroker.** Its ads urge you to scratch and sniff. There is no odor, says the ad, because fresh fish does not have one. What there is is an abundance of seafood seemingly just plucked from Gulf waters, plus some selections for landlubbers. This place is almost always crowded, for good reasons. *13451–16 McGregor Blvd., tel. 813/489–2226. Reservations accepted. Dress: casual. AE, MC, V. Closed lunch. Moderate.*

Sangeet of India. Indian melodies waft through the air mingling with fragrant spices used in traditional dishes of India. A buffet lunch is served weekdays. *Villas Plaza, U.S. 41 and Crystal Dr., tel. 813/278–0101. Reservations accepted. Dress: casual. AE, MC, V. Moderate.*

The Veranda. Within a sprawling turn-of-the-century home is served an imaginative assortment of American regional cuisine. This is a popular place for business and governmental bigwigs. *2122 2nd St., tel. 813/332–2065. Reservations accepted. Dress: casual. AE, DC, MC, V. Moderate.*

Miami Connection. If you hunger for choice chopped liver, lean-but-tender corned beef, and a chewy bagel, this kosher-style deli can fill the bill. The sandwiches are huge. It is, as the local restaurant critic aptly said, "the real McCohen." *11506 Cleveland Ave., tel. 813/936–3811. No reservations. Dress: casual. No credit cards. Closed dinner. Inexpensive.*

Woody's Bar-B-Q. A no-frills barbecue pit, Woody's features chicken, ribs, and beef in copious amounts at bargain-basement prices. *13101 N. Cleveland Ave. (U.S. 41), North Fort Myers, tel. 813/997–1424. No reservations. Dress: casual. AE, MC, V. Inexpensive.*

Lodging

Sonesta Sanibel Harbour Resort. This high-rise apartment hotel sits on the east end of the Sanibel Causeway, not quite in Fort Myers, not quite on Sanibel. It overlooks San Carlos Bay, has a full complement of amenities, and was once home to tennis great Jimmy Connors. *17260 Harbour Pointe, 33908, tel. 813/466–4000, fax 813/466–6050. 240 rooms, 100 condominiums. Facilities: pools, health club, tennis, whirlpool, restaurant, lounge. AE, DC, MC, V. Very Expensive.*

Sheraton Harbor Place. This modern high-rise hotel commands a dominant spot on the downtown Fort Myers skyline, rising above the Caloosahatchee River and Fort Myers Yacht Basin. *2500 Edwards Dr., 33901, tel. 813/337–0300, fax 813/337–1530. 437 rooms. Facilities: pool, tennis, a games room, whirlpool, dock, exercise room. AE, DC, MC, V. Expensive.*

Robert E. Lee Motor Best Western. Located 1 mile from downtown Fort Myers and the Edison home, this motel has spacious rooms, with patios or balconies overlooking the Caloosahatchee River. *6611 U.S. 41 N, North Fort Myers 33903, tel. 813/*

997–5511, fax 813/656–6962. 108 rooms. Facilities: pool, dock, lounge. AE, DC, MC, V. Moderate.

Fort Myers Beach
Dining
★ **The Mucky Duck.** There are two restaurants by this name— one a waterfront spot on Captiva Island, the other a slightly more formal restaurant in Fort Myers Beach. Both concentrate on fresh, well-prepared seafood. A popular dish is the bacon-wrapped barbecued shrimp. *2500 Estero Blvd., tel. 813/463–5519; Andy Rosse La., Captiva, tel. 813/472–3434. Reservations for large parties only. Dress: casual. MC, V. Moderate.*

Snug Harbor. A casual, rustic atmosphere is evident at this seafood restaurant on the harbor at Fort Myers Beach. It's a favorite of year-round residents as well as seasonal visitors. *645 San Carlos Blvd., tel. 813/463–8077. No reservations. Dress: casual. AE, MC, V. Moderate.*

Lodging **The Boathouse Beach Resort.** A nautical theme pervades this all-suite time-share resort, with lots of teak and brass throughout. *7630 Estero Blvd., 33931, tel. 813/481–3636 or 800/237–8906. 22 units. Facilities: kitchen, beach, pool, whirlpool, shuffleboard. MC, V. Expensive.*

Lani Kai Island Resort. This resort overlooks nothing but the Gulf of Mexico—many guests simply anchor their boats out front. Rooms are large, and all have water views. The three tiki bars on the beach provide music and entertainment, making this a favorite of locals as well as visitors. *1400 Estero Blvd., 33931, tel. 813/463–3111, fax 813/463–2986. 100 units, 15 condominiums. Facilities: restaurant, pool, 3 bars. D, DC, MC, V. Expensive.*

Sandpiper Gulf Resort. This apartment motel is on the beach. *5550 Estero Blvd., 33931, tel. 813/463–5721. 63 rooms. Facilities: pools, beach, whirlpool, playground, shuffleboard. MC, V. Expensive.*

Marco Island
Dining **Marco Lodge Waterfront Restaurant & Lounge.** Built in 1869, this is Marco's oldest landmark. The tin-roofed, wood building is on the waterfront; boats tie up dockside, and you can dine on a wide veranda overlooking the water. Fresh local seafood and Cajun entrées are featured. One specialty is a wood bowl of blue crabs in rich garlic butter. *1 Papaya St., Goodland, tel. 813/642–7227. Reservations advised. Dress: casual. AE, DC, MC, V. Moderate.*

★ **Island Cafe.** This small, intimate European-style café specializes in seafood and Continental cuisine. Pompano is prepared in a multitude of ways. *918 N. Collier Blvd., tel. 813/394–7578. Reservations accepted. Dress: casual but neat. MC, V. Inexpensive–Moderate.*

Lodging **Eagle's Nest Beach Resort.** This time-share resort contains one- and two-bedroom villas (with French doors opening onto screened patios) clustered around a large tropical garden, and a high rise with two-bedroom suites overlooking the Gulf. *410 S. Collier Blvd., 33937, tel. 813/394–5167 or 800/237–8906. 96 rooms. Facilities: kitchen, beach, pool, whirlpool, sauna, exercise room, tennis, racquetball, sailing, windsurfing. AE, MC, V. Very Expensive.*

★ **The Marco Beach Hilton.** With fewer than 300 rooms and wisely apportioned public areas, the Hilton is smaller than most resorts in the area. For this reason guests typically have no trouble taking advantage of the many recreational facilities available to them, including a brand-new, well-equipped fitness center adjacent to the three tennis courts. All of the rooms in this 11-story beachfront hotel have private balconies with unobstructed Gulf views, a sitting area, wet bar, refrigerator, and plenty of space. Furnishings are cheerful and unobtrusive—the same can be said about the staff. *560 S. Collier Blvd., 33937, tel. 813/394–5000 or 800/443–4550, fax 813/394–5251. 295 rooms. Facilities: restaurant, lounges, beach, pool, whirlpool, tennis, golf nearby, fitness center, sailing, sailboarding. AE, D, DC, MC, V. Very Expensive.*

Marriott's Marco Island Resort and Golf Club. Large rooms with balconies are surrounded by lush, tropical grounds right next to the Gulf. Water sports are a strong point of this resort. *400 S. Collier Blvd., 33937, tel. 813/394–2511, fax 813/394–4645. 735 rooms, 86 suites. Facilities: pools, beach, whirlpool, waterskiing, sailboats, windsurfing, tennis, bicycles, golf, exercise room, 5 restaurants, lounge. AE, DC, MC, V. Very Expensive.*

Radisson Beach Suite Resort. All 214 one- and two-bedroom suites plus 55 rooms in this medium high-rise resort contain kitchens fully equipped with utensils to give a home-away-from-home touch. The casual decor of the suites contrasts sharply with the marble floors and chandelier in the lobby. The resort faces a large beachfront. *600 S. Collier Blvd., 33937, tel. 813/394–4100 or 800/333–3333, fax 813/394–0262. 214 suites, 55 rooms. Facilities: pool, beach, whirlpool, exercise room, games room, water sports equipment, restaurant, lounge. AE, DC, MC, V. Very Expensive.*

Lakeside Inn. This long-time inn on Marco Island houses a four-star restaurant, Busghetti's—which, as you might guess from the name, specializes in Italian cooking. The inn's 24 efficiency units were renovated in 1991, and 12 one-bedroom apartments with views of the lake were added; all units have kitchens. Located about 1 mile from the gulf, the inn has its own swimming pool. *155 1st Ave., 33937, tel. 813/394–1161. 12 1-bedroom apartments, 26 efficiencies. Facilities: pool, lake fishing. AE, MC, V. Moderate.*

Naples
Dining
★

The Chef's Garden. A mixture of Continental, traditional, and California cuisines has consistently won this restaurant awards over the past decade. Some daily specials include Scottish smoked salmon with avocado and caviar, roast rack of lamb, and spinach and fresh mango salad with toasted cashews and honey vinaigrette. The less formal Truffles bistro, upstairs, features sandwiches, pastas, and pastries to take-out or to eat in. *1300 3rd St. S, tel. 813/262–5500. Reservations advised. Jacket required during winter season. AE, D, DC, MC, V. Very Expensive.*

Villa Pescatore. Northern Italian cuisine is the theme of this romantic restaurant with white linen, candlelight, crystal, and wicker furnishings. While half of the vast menu remains constant, the other half is ever changing, to keep up with the chef's creative ideas. Specials might include duck in sage sauce, or saffron and linguine with salmon and tomatoes in a pepper-vodka cream sauce. In another wing is Plum's Café, a bistro-style restaurant serving light fare. *8920 N. Tamiami Trail, tel. 813/597–8119. Reservations advised. Dress: casual but neat. AE, DC, MC, V. Expensive.*

Clyde's Steak & Lobster House. A longtime neighborhood favorite in a small downtown spot, Clyde's is now in a prime location in the Village on Venetian Bay. The restaurant continues to serve U.S. prime beef, fresh Maine lobsters flown in daily, and fresh Gulf fish. *4050 Gulfshore Blvd. N, tel. 813/261-0622. No reservations. Jacket suggested. No lunch May–Nov. AE, MC, V. Moderate.*

★ **St. George and the Dragon.** A long-lived seafood-and-beef restaurant, it has decor reminiscent of an old-fashioned men's club—heavy on brass, dark woods, and deep-red tones. Among the specialties are conch chowder, various cuts of prime rib, and shrimp steamed in beer. *936 5th Ave. S, tel. 813/262-6546. No reservations. Jacket suggested. Closed Sun. and Christmas. AE, DC, MC, V. Moderate.*

Lodging **Edgewater Beach Hotel.** An all-suite Gulf-front hotel on fashionable Gulf Shore Drive, this has long been an elegant address in Naples. It's also close to downtown. *1901 Gulfshore Blvd. N, 33940, tel. 813/262-6511, 800/821-0196, or 800/282-3766 in FL, fax 813/262-1243. 124 rooms. Facilities: beach, pool, exercise room, restaurant. AE, DC, MC, V. Very Expensive.*

The Registry Resort. This modern, luxurious high-rise resort is ½ mile from the beach. It's known for its excellent tennis facilities: there are 15 courts, five of which can be lit for night play. Gourmet diners will enjoy the award winning Lafite restaurant and the Brass Pelican eatery. *475 Seagate Dr., 33940, tel. 813/597-3232, fax 813/597-3147. 50 tennis villas, 29 suites, 395 rooms. Facilities: pools, whirlpools, bicycles, tennis, health club, 2 restaurants, lounge. AE, DC, MC, V. Very Expensive.*

The Ritz-Carlton. Considered by some to be the finest resort in Florida, the Ritz-Carlton justifies its reputation with an almost overwhelming array of creature comforts. Equally fabulous hotel rooms can be had elsewhere, but guests were are treated as Royalty—high tea is better attended than high tide. The extensive network of lavishly appointed public rooms is astounding, with a dozen meeting rooms of varying shapes and sizes and an estimable collection of 19th-century European oils. Though you might feel a little uncomfortable traipsing through the lobby in tennis shoes, you will be graciously welcomed. Even if you are staying elsewhere in the Naples area, at least drive by and admire this marvelous fairy castle. Better yet, shake the sand out of your shoes, press the wrinkles out of your dress-up clothes, and make reservations for High Tea, served each afternoon at 3 PM during season. *280 Vanderbilt Beach Rd., 33941, tel. 813/598-3300, fax 813/598-6690. 463 rooms. Facilities: 4 restaurants, lounge, beach, pool, saunas, whirlpool, 6 tennis courts, access to nearby 27-hole golf course, fitness center, children's programs, sailboarding, sailing. AE, D, DC, MC, V. Very Expensive.*

La Playa Beach & Racquet Inn. At this large Gulf-front motor inn, guests can stay close to the ground or get a gull's-eye view from one of the apartments in the mid-rise tower. *9891 Gulfshore Blvd., 33963, tel. 813/597-3123, fax 813/597-6278. 137 units. Facilities: pool, beach, dock, tennis, restaurant, deli, lounge. AE, MC, V. Expensive.*

Comfort Inn. One of the more attractive chain motels along busy U.S. 41, this four-floor, pink-and-white stucco lodging on the banks of the Gordon River is centrally located—a 20-minute walk from the beaches. Rooms are clean, and a bountiful breakfast (everything but bacon and eggs) is served every morning in a bright and spacious lounge. *1221 5th Ave. S (corner of U.S. 41), 33940, tel. 813/649-5800 or 800/221-2222, fax 813/649-0523. Facilities: pool. AE, D, DC, MC, V. Moderate.*

Port Charlotte/ **Salty's Harborside.** Seafood is served from a dining room that
Punta Gorda looks out on Burnt Store Marina and Charlotte Harbor. *Burnt*
Dining *Store Marina, Burnt Store Rd., Punta Gorda, tel. 813/639–*
3650. Reservations advised. Dress: casual. AE, DC, MC, V.
Moderate.

Mexican Hacienda. Tex-Mex of a high order is presented in
humble surroundings. The building matches its well-worn
neighbors; inside are well-interpreted guacamole dip and tacos
made with tender shredded beef. *Harbour Inn, U.S. 41, Char-*
lotte Harbor, tel. 813/625–4211. Reservations accepted for par-
ties of 6 or more. Dress: casual. MC, V. Inexpensive.

Lodging **Burnt Store Marina Resort.** For golfing, boating, and getting
away from it all, Burnt Store can fill the bill. One- and two-
bedroom modern apartments are situated along a relatively undeveloped stretch of vast Charlotte Harbor. Two-bedroom
units are available only on a weekly or monthly basis. *3150*
Matecumbe Key Rd., Punta Gorda 33955, tel. 813/639–4151. 46
1-bedroom condominiums. Facilities: kitchens, pool, golf, ma-
rina, boats, tennis, restaurant, lounge. AE, DC, MC, V. Ex-
pensive.

Days Inn of Port Charlotte. This modern midrise motel on Charlotte County's major business route is between Fort Myers and
Sarasota and offers free coffee in the lobby, as well as a refrigerator in every room. *1941 Tamiami Trail (U.S. 41), Port*
Charlotte 33948, tel. 813/627–8900, fax 813/743–8503. 126
rooms. Facilities: pool. AE, DC, MC, V. Moderate.

Sanibel and **The Bubble Room.** It's hard to say which is more eclectic here,
Captiva Islands the atmosphere or the menu. Waiters and waitresses wearing
Dining Boy Scout uniforms race amid a dizzying array of Art Deco,
while music from the 1940s sets the mood. The aged prime rib is
ample enough to satisfy two hearty eaters—at least. Chances
are you'll be too full for dessert, but it can be wrapped to go.
Captiva Rd., Captiva, tel. 813/472–5558. No reservations.
Dress: casual. AE, DC, MC, V. Expensive.

The Greenhouse. Though the kitchen is in full view of the diminutive dining area, all is calm and quiet as you wend your way
through the day's specials. Chef-owner Danny Melman changes
his Continental-style menu every four to six weeks. Each menu
features fresh seafood and game among its selections. *Captiva*
Rd., Captiva, tel. 813/472–6066. Reservations advised. Dress:
casual but neat. No lunch. No credit cards. Expensive.

★ **Jean Paul's French Corner.** The French food here is finely seasoned with everything but the highfalutin attitude often dished
up in French establishments. Salmon in a creamy dill sauce,
sautéed soft-shell crabs, and roast duckling in fruit sauce are
among the few but well-prepared choices on the menu. *708 Tar-*
pon Bay Rd., tel. 813/472–1493. Reservations advised. Dress:
casual. No lunch. MC, V. Expensive.

Windows on the Water. Savor a Gulf view and some of Sanibel's
finest food, as Chef Peter Harman concocts cuisine with Continental and Cajun overtones, making the most of fresh seafood.
Try the outstanding bronzed fish special, a take-off on blackened fish, but with garlic. *Sundial Beach & Tennis Resort,*
1451 Middle Gulf Dr., tel. 813/472–4151. Reservations advised.
Dress: casual but neat. AE, DC, MC, V. Expensive.

McT's Shrimphouse and Tavern. Somewhat of a departure from
most Sanibel establishments, McT's is lively and informal, featuring a host of fresh seafood specialties, including all-you-can-
eat shrimp and crab. *1523 Periwinkle Way, Sanibel, tel. 813/*

472–3161. No reservations. Dress: casual. AE, DC, MC, V. Moderate.

Lodging **Casa Ybel Resort.** This time-share property features contemporary one- and two-bedroom Gulf-front condominium villas on 23 acres of tropical grounds, complete with palms, ponds, and a footbridge. *2255 W. Gulf Dr., Sanibel 33957, tel. 813/472–3145 or 800/237–8906, fax 813/472–2109. 40 1-bedroom units, 74 2-bedroom units. Facilities: kitchens, pool, whirlpool, biking, tennis, sailing, playground, shuffleboard, games room, babysitting, restaurant, lounge. AE, DC, MC, V. Very Expensive.*

★ **South Seas Plantation Resort and Yacht Harbour.** This quiet, elegant 330-acre property is more like a neighborhood community than a beach resort, with nine different types of accommodations, among them tennis and harborside villas, Gulf cottages, and private homes. Walk, cycle, or Rollerblade (rentals in town) along the well-paved 1-mile path that runs through the neatly landscaped grounds, fashionably overgrown with exotic vegetation. Better yet, sign up for some of the many outdoor activities, including wave running, sailboarding, waterskiing, tennis, golf, and shelling, to mention a few. From the service in the posh restaurant—The King's Crown Dining Room—to the waterskiing instructors, the staff is five-star. The clientele is a good mix—the endless activities and good nightlife attract singles and couples, while supervised children's programs for *all* ages (including toddlers) draw a good number of families. But somehow, even with all the options, the pace is satisfyingly slow and the atmosphere calm and relaxed. Rates can drop as much as 40% off-season. *South Seas Plantation Rd., Captiva 33924, tel. 813/472–5111 or 800/237–1260, fax 813/472–7541. 600 rooms. Facilities: 4 restaurants, 2 lounges, kitchens, boating docks, fishing, golf, tennis, games room, playground, pools, parasailing, sailboats, wave runners, waterskiing, sailboarding, sailing school, beauty parlor, children's programs. AE, DC, MC, V. Very Expensive.*

Sundial Beach & Tennis Resort. The largest all-suite resort on the island, Sundial has many suites that look out upon the Gulf of Mexico, and all have full kitchens and laundry facilities, making them great for families. *1451 Middle Gulf Dr., Sanibel 33957, tel. 813/472–4151 or 800/237–4184, fax 813/472–1809. 265 suites. Facilities: kitchens, pools, beach, bicycles, tennis, sailboats, recreational program, children's program, baby-sitting, games room, shuffleboard, 2 restaurants, pool bar, lounge. AE, DC, MC, V. Very Expensive.*

The Arts and Nightlife

The Arts

Naples tends to be the cultural capital of this stretch of the coast. The **Naples Philharmonic Center for the Arts** (5833 Pelican Bay Blvd., tel. 813/597–1111) comprises two theaters and two art galleries offering a variety of plays, concerts, and exhibits year-round. The **Naples Dinner Theatre** (Immokalee Rd., halfway between U.S. 41 and the I–75 interchange, tel. 813/597–6031) features professional companies performing a variety of mostly musicals and comedies, October–August; admission includes a buffet. The **Naples Players** (399 Goodlette Rd., tel. 813/263–7990) has winter and summer seasons—winter shows often sell out well in advance.

Nightlife

Bars and Nightclubs
Witch's Brew (4836 N. Tamiami Trail, Naples, tel. 813/261–4261) is a lively location for entertainment nightly. There's a happy hour weekdays 4–6 PM and an excellent menu featuring Continental cuisine. Its sister restaurant, **Seawitch** (179 Commerce St., Vanderbilt Beach, tel. 813/566–1514), overlooks Vanderbilt Bay from the upstairs lounge, a relaxing spot for casual dining.

Comedy Clubs
Comedians entertain at two local spots: **Bijou Comedy Club & Restaurant** (McGregor Point Shopping Center, Fort Myers, tel. 813/481–6666), and **Comedy Cafe** (Island Park shopping Center, U.S. 41 S, Fort Myers, tel. 813/481–1151).

Discos
Club Mirage (4797 U.S. 41, Fort Myers, tel. 813/275–9997) packs in the singles (21 and up) with such events as hot legs and lip-sync contests, hot-tub night, live bands and disc jockeys.

Jazz Clubs
Jazz is featured at least a couple days a week at **Upstairs at Peter's** (2224 Bay St., Fort Myers, tel. 813/332–2223); **Gatsby's** (2840 Tamiami Trail N, Naples, tel. 813/262–2040), **Chef's Garden** (1300 Third St. S, Naples, tel.813/262–5500), and **Key West Fish House** (4947 U.S. 41 N, Naples, tel. 813/263–FISH).

Rock Club
Edison's Electric Lounge (Holiday Inn, 13051 Bell Tower Dr., Fort Myers, tel. 813/482–2900) plays Top-40 tunes, usually with live bands.

12 The Panhandle

By Ann Hughes

Northwest Florida resident Ann Hughes is former editor of Indiana Business magazine and a contributing editor to other travel and trade publications.

Because there are no everglades or palm trees here, some call northwest Florida "the other Florida." Instead, magnolias, live oaks, and loblolly pines flourish, just as they do in other parts of the Deep South. When the season winds down in south Florida, it picks up here (beginning in May). Northwest Florida is even in a different time zone: Crossing the Apalachicola River means an hour's difference between eastern and central times.

Others call this section of the state "Florida's best-kept secret." It was, until World War II when activity at the air bases in the area began to rev up. Also known as the Panhandle—because of the region's long, narrow shape—northwest Florida is nestled between the Gulf of Mexico, just west of Tallahassee, and the Alabama and Georgia state lines.

By the mid-1950s, the 100-mile stretch along the Panhandle coast between Pensacola and Panama City was dubbed the "Miracle Strip" because of the dramatic rise in property values of this beachfront land that in the 1940s sold for less than $100 an acre. Today, property fetches millions. But the movers and shakers of the area felt this sobriquet fell short of conveying the richness of the region, with its white sands and forever-green sparkling waters, swamps, bayous, and flora. And so the term "Emerald Coast" was coined.

This little green corner of Florida that snuggles up to Alabama is a land of superlatives: It has the biggest military installation in the Western Hemisphere (Eglin Air Force Base); the oldest city in the state (Pensacola, claiming a founding date of 1559); and the most prolific fishing village in the world (Destin). Thanks to restrictions against commercial development imposed by Eglin AFB and the Gulf Islands National Seashore, the Emerald Coast has been able to maintain several hundred linear miles of unspoiled beaches. A 1991 study by the University of Maryland's Laboratory for Coastal Research named Grayton Beach, Perdido Key, St. Joseph State Park, and Eastern Perdido Key all among the top 10 beaches in America.

The Panhandle is also an ideal tourist destination. It has resorts that out-glitz the Gold Coast's and campgrounds where possums invite themselves to lunch. Lovers of antiquity can wander the many historic districts or visit archaeological digs. For sports enthusiasts, there's a different golf course or tennis court for each day of the week; and for those who decide to spend time with nature, there's a world of hunting, canoeing, biking, and hiking. And anything that happens on water happens here, from surfboarding and scuba diving to fishing off the end of a pier or casting a line from a deep-sea charter boat.

Essential Information

Important Addresses and Numbers

Tourist Information Apalachicola Chamber of Commerce (128 Market St., tel. 904/653-9419) is open weekdays 9-4; closed noon-1.

Crestview Chamber of Commerce (502 S. Main St., tel. 904/682-3212) is open weekdays 8-5.

Destin Chamber of Commerce (1021 Highway 98E, tel. 800/837-7300) is open weekdays 9-5.

Fort Walton Beach Chamber of Commerce (34 S.E. Miracle Strip Pkwy., tel. 904/244–8191) is open weekdays 8–5.
Niceville/Valparaiso Chamber of Commerce (170 John Sims Pkwy., tel. 904/678–2323) is open weekdays 9–4:30.
Panama City Beach Chamber of Commerce and Information Center (12015 W. Front Beach Rd., tel. 904/234–3193) is open October–April, weekdays 9–5; May–September, daily 9–5.
Pensacola Convention & Visitor Information Center (1401 E. Gregory St., tel. 904/434–1234 or 800/343–4321; 800/874–1234 outside FL) is open daily 8:30–5.
Tallahassee Area Convention and Visitor Bureau (Plaza Level, New Capitol, Duvall St., tel. 904/488–7460 or 800/628–2866) is open weekdays 8–5.
Walton County Chamber of Commerce (200 W. Circle Dr., tel. 904/892–3191) is open weekdays 8–4:30. The chamber operates a Welcome Center on U.S. 331 at U.S. 98 (tel. 904/267–3511), open weekdays 8–4:30, Saturday 9–4.

Emergencies Dial 911 for **police** and **ambulance** in an emergency.

Hospitals Emergency rooms are open 24 hours. In **Destin:** Humana Hospital-Destin (996 Airport Rd., tel. 904/654–7600). In **Fort Walton Beach:** Humana Hospital-Fort Walton Beach (1000 Mar-Walt Dr., tel. 904/862–1111). In **Panama City:** HCA Gulf Coast Hospital (449 W. 23rd St., tel. 904/769–8341). In **Pensacola:** HCA West Florida Regional Medical Center (8383 N. Davis Hwy., tel. 904/494–4000). In **Tallahassee:** Physician Care (tel. 904/385–2222) has three locations, all open daily.

Arriving and Departing

By Plane A new, state-of-the-art terminal opened in 1991 at the **Pensacola Regional Airport,** which is served by American Eagle (tel. 800/433–7300), ASA–The Delta Connection (tel. 800/282–3424), Comair (tel. 800/282–3424), Continental Airlines (tel. 800/525–0280), Delta (tel. 800/221–1212), Northwest Airlink (tel. 800/225–2525), and USAir and USAir Express (tel. 800/428–4322). A trip from Pensacola Regional Airport via **Yellow Cab** (tel. 904/433–1143) costs about $7 to downtown and $15 to Pensacola Beach.

Fort Walton Beach/Eglin AFB Airport/Okaloosa County Air Terminal is served by ASA–The Delta Connection, American Eagle, Northwest (tel. 800/225–2525), and USAir Express. A ride from the Fort Walton Beach airport via **Yellow Cab** (tel. 904/244–3600) costs $11 to Fort Walton Beach, Niceville, or Valparaiso and $18 to Destin. **A-I Taxi** (tel. 904/678–2424) charges $12 to Fort Walton Beach and $16–$18 to Destin.

Panama City–Bay County Airport is served by American Eagle, Comair, ASA–The Delta Connection, Northwest Airlink, and USAir.

From the Panama City airport, **Yellow Cab** (tel. 904/763–4691) taxi service charges about $15 to the beach area, depending on where your hotel is. **DeLuxe Coach Limo Service** (tel. 904/763–0211) provides van service to downtown Panama City for $5.25–$8.25 and to Panama City Beach for $11.25–$16.75.

Tallahassee Regional Airport opened its new terminal in 1990. It is served by American Eagle, ASA–The Delta Connection, Delta, and USAir.

Quick Service (tel. 904/224–1121), **City Taxi** (tel. 904/893–4111), **Tallahassee Cab** (tel. 904/576–2227), and **Yellow Cab** (tel. 904/222–3070) all travel to downtown for about $11. Some Tallahassee hotels provide free shuttle service.

By Car The main east–west arteries across the top of the state are I–10 and U.S. 90. Pensacola is about an hour's drive east from Mobile. Tallahassee is 3½ hours west of Jacksonville.

By Train **Amtrak** (tel. 800/USA–RAIL) plans to begin a Los Angeles-to-Panhandle route in spring of 1993. Among the towns served will be Pensacola, Crestview, and Chipley.

By Bus The principal common carrier throughout the region is the **Greyhound/Trailways Bus Line,** with stations in Crestview (tel. 904/682–6922), DeFuniak Springs (tel. 904/892–5913), Fort Walton Beach (tel. 904/243–1940), Panama City (tel. 904/785–7861), and Pensacola (tel. 904/476–4800).

Getting Around

By Car It takes about four hours to cross this region from Pensacola to Tallahassee. Driving east–west along I–10 tends to be monotonous, but U.S. 90 piques your interest by taking you down the main streets of several county-seat towns. U.S. 98 snakes eastward along the coast, forking (into 98 and 98A) at Inlet Beach before becoming U.S. 98 again at Panama City and continuing down to Port St. Joe and Apalachicola. Major north–south highways that weave through Florida's Panhandle are (from east to west) U.S. 231, U.S. 331, Route 85, and U.S. 29.

Scenic Drives **Route 399** between Pensacola Beach and Navarre Beach takes you down Santa Rosa Island, a spit of duneland that juts out into the turquoise and jade waters of the Gulf of Mexico. It's a scenic drive if the day is clear; otherwise, it's a study in gray.

The view of the Gulf from U.S. 98 can leave you oohing and ahhing, too, if the sun's out to distract you. If not, the fast-food restaurants, sleazy bars, and tacky souvenir stores along the Miracle Strip Parkway are a little too noticeable.

The panorama of barge traffic and cabin cruisers on the twinkling waters of the Intracoastal Waterway will get your attention from U.S. 331, which runs over a causeway at the east end of Choctawhatchee Bay between Route 20 and U.S. 98.

By Boat The Emerald Coast is accessible to yacht captains and sailors from the Intracoastal Waterway, which turns inland at Apalachicola and runs through the bays around Panama City to Choctawhatchee Bay and into Santa Rosa Sound.

Exploring the Panhandle

Pensacola, with its antebellum homes and historic landmarks, is a good place to start your trek through northwest Florida. After a browse through its museums and a stroll through the preservation districts, begin heading east on U.S. 98. Don't overlook the deserted beaches along the Gulf of Mexico, where the sugar-white quartz-crystal sand crunches underfoot like snow on a subzero night. The next point of interest is Fort Walton Beach, the Emerald Coast's largest city and the hub of its vacation activity, and neighboring Destin, where sport fishing is king. From Fort Walton, there are several interesting side trips to smaller towns. A drive along Route 20—a two-laner that twists along Choctawhatchee Bay and through the piney woods past bait shacks and catfish restaurants—is a great way to see the other Florida.

The next resort center along the coast is Panama City Beach, a good base for visiting several state parks. A long drive east on I–10 will bring you to the state capital, Tallahassee. Then swing south and west, skirting the Apalachicola National Forest, to return to the coast at Apalachicola, an important oyster-fishing town.

Highlights For First-Time Visitors

Air Force Armament Museum, Fort Walton/Destin
Capitol Complex, Tallahassee
Eden State Gardens, Fort Walton/Destin
Grayton Beach, Fort Walton/Destin
Pensacola Historic Districts, Pensacola
Seaside, Fort Walton/Destin
Wakulla Springs, Tallahassee

Pensacola

Numbers in the margin correspond to points of interest on the Panhandle map.

❶ The flags of five nations have flown over **Pensacola,** earning this fine, old southern city its nickname: the City of Five Flags. Spanish conquistadors, under the command of Don Tristan de Luna, made landfall on the shores of Pensacola Bay in 1559, but, discouraged by a succession of destructive tropical storms and dissension in the ranks, De Luna abandoned the settlement two years after its founding. In 1698, the Spanish once again established a fort at the site. During the early 18th century, control jockeyed back and forth between the Spanish, the French, and the British and ultimately, in 1819, landed in the hands of the United States. During the Civil War, Pensacola flew yet another flag when it came under the governance of the Confederate States of America.

Today, historic Pensacola consists of three distinct districts—Seville, Palafox, and North Hill—though they are easy to explore as a unit. Stroll down streets mapped out by the British and renamed by the Spanish, such as Cervantes, Palafox, Intendencia, and Tarragona. Be warned, though, that it is best to stick to the beaten path; Pensacola is a port town and can get rough around the edges, especially at night.

The best way to orient yourself is to stop at the **Pensacola Convention & Visitors Information Center** (1401 E. Gregory St., tel. 904/434–1234 or 800/874–1234). Located at the foot of the Three-Mile Bridge over Pensacola Bay, it's easy to find. You can pick up maps of the self-guided historic district tours and other information.

Approaching from the east, the first historic district you reach is **Seville**—the site of Pensacola's first permanent Spanish colonial settlement. Its center is Seville Square, a live oak-shaded

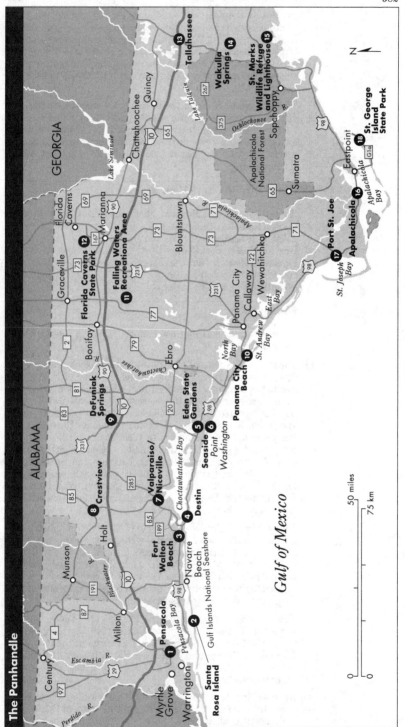

The Panhandle

Gulf of Mexico

50 miles

75 km

park bounded by Alcaniz, Adams, Zaragoza, and Government streets. Park your car and roam these brick streets past honeymoon cottages and bay-front homes. Many of the buildings have been restored and converted into restaurants, commercial offices, and shops where you can buy anything from wind socks to designer clothes.

Continue west to Palafox Street, the main stem of the **Palafox Historic District.** This was the commercial and government hub of old Pensacola. On Palafox Place, note the Spanish Renaissance–style Saenger Theater, Pensacola's old movie palace; and the Bear Block, a former wholesale grocery with wrought-iron balconies that are a legacy from Pensacola's Creole past. Though the San Carlos Hotel has been closed for many years, in its heyday the Mediterranean-style building at Palafox and Garden streets was the proper place for business tycoons and military officers to savor their cigars and brandies and where Pensacola's elite dined after the theater and introduced their daughters to society. Nearby, on Palafox between Government and Zaragoza streets, is a statue of Andrew Jackson that commemorates the formal transfer of Florida from Spain to the United States in 1821.

Palafox Street also funnels into the **North Hill Preservation District,** where Pensacola's affluent families, many made rich during the turn-of-the-century timber boom, built their homes on ground where British and Spanish fortresses once stood. To this day residents occasionally unearth cannonballs while digging in their gardens. North Hill occupies 50 blocks that consist of more than 500 homes in Queen Anne, neoclassical, Tudor Revival, and Mediterranean architectural styles. Take a drive through this community, but remember these are private residences not open to the public. Places of general interest in the district include the 1902 Spanish mission–style Christ Episcopal Church; Lee Square, where a 50-foot-high obelisk stands as Pensacola's tribute to the Old Confederacy; and Fort George, an undeveloped parcel of land at the site of the largest of three forts built by the British in 1778.

From the North Hill district, go south on Palafox Street to Zaragoza Street to reach the **Historic Pensacola Village,** a cluster of museums between Adams and Tarragona. The **Museum of Industry,** housed in a late 19th-century warehouse, hosts permanent exhibits dedicated to the lumber, maritime, and shipping industries—once mainstays of Pensacola's economy. A reproduction of a 19th-century streetscape is displayed in the **Museum of Commerce,** while the city's historical archives are kept in the **Pensacola Historical Museum**—what was once Old Christ Church, one of Florida's oldest churches. Also in the village are the **Julee Cottage Museum of Black History, Dorr House, Lavalle House,** and **Quina House.** *Historic Pensacola Village: tel. 904/444–8905. Open Mon.–Sat. 10–4:30. Pensacola Historical Museum: tel. 904/433–1559. Admission: $2 adults, $1.50 senior citizens and military, $1 children, under 4 free. Open Mon.–Sat. 9–4:30.*

In the days of the horse-drawn paddy wagon the two-story mission revival building housing the **Pensacola Museum of Art** served as the city jail. *407 S. Jefferson St., tel. 904/432–5682. Admission free. Open Tues.–Fri. 10–5, Sat. 10–4.*

Pensacola's 1908 old City Hall has been refurbished and re-opened as the **T. T. Wentworth, Jr. Florida State Museum.** The Wentworth displays some 150,000 artifacts ranging from Civil War weaponry to bottle caps. Representing more than 80 years of collecting, the assemblage is worth over $5 million. *333 S. Jefferson St., tel. 904/444-8905. Admission: $5.50 adults, $4.50 senior citizens, $2.50 children over 4. Open Mon.–Sat. 10–4:30.*

Time Out   **Napoleon Bakery** (101 S. Jefferson St., tel. 904/434-9701) is French-y, right down to the accents of the wait staff. Mingle with workaday Pensacolans over a continental breakfast of just-baked pastries or lunch of quiche, croissants, and, of course, Napoleons served tearoom-style with fresh-brewed, aromatic coffees.

From the port, take Palafox Street to U.S. 98 (Garden St.) to reach the **Pensacola Naval Air Station** (tel. 904/452-2311). Established in 1914, it is the nation's oldest such facility. On display in the **National Museum of Naval Aviation** are more than 100 aircraft that have played an important role in naval aviation history. Among them are the NC-4, which in 1919 became the first plane to cross the Atlantic by air; the famous World War II fighter, the F6F *Hellcat;* and the *Skylab Command Module.* Thirty-minute films on aeronautical topics are shown, June–August. Call for details. The National Park Service–protected **Fort Barrancas,** established during the Civil War, is also located at the NAS. Nearby are picnic tables and a ½-mile woodland nature trail. *Navy Blvd. (off U.S. 98), tel. 904/455-5167. Admission free. Open Oct.–Apr., daily 10:30–4; May–Sept., daily 9:30–5.*

Back on U.S. 98, head south over the 3-mile-long Pensacola Bay ❷ Bridge to **Santa Rosa Island.** This barrier island offers more than seascapes and water sports: It's also a must-see for bird-watchers. Since 1971 more than 280 species of birds, from the common loon to the majestic osprey, have been spotted here. Two caveats for visitors: "Leave nothing behind but your footprints," and "Don't pick the sea oats" (natural grasses that help keep the dunes intact). At Santa Rosa Island's western tip is **Fort Pickens National Park,** where there are a museum, nature exhibits, aquariums, and a large campground. Fort Pickens's most famous resident was imprisoned Apache Indian chief Geronimo, who was reportedly fairly well liked by his captors. *Ranger station at Fort Pickens Rd., tel. 904/934-2635. Admission: $4 per car. Open daily 8:30–4:30.*

Proceed along Route 399 from Fort Pickens to **Navarre Beach,** a small, relaxed community without the traffic and congestion common to most resort areas. To reach Fort Walton Beach, 15 miles farther east, cross over the Navarre Bridge to U.S. 98.

Fort Walton Beach/Destin

❸ **Fort Walton Beach** dates from the Civil War years when patriots loyal to the Confederate cause organized Walton's Guard (named in honor of Colonel George Walton, one-time acting territorial governor of West Florida) and made camp on Santa Rosa Sound, the site that would come later to be known as Camp Walton. In 1940, fewer than 90 people lived in Fort Walton Beach, but thanks to the development of Eglin Field during

World War II and New Deal money spent for new roads and bridges, within a decade the city became a boom town. Today, Greater Fort Walton Beach has more than 78,000 residents, making it the largest urban area on the Emerald Coast. The military is Fort Walton Beach's main source of income, but tourism runs a close second.

Eglin Air Force Base encompasses 728 square miles of land, has 10 auxiliary fields (including Hurlburt and Duke fields), and a total of 21 runways. Jimmie Doolittle's Tokyo Raiders trained here, as did the Son Tay Raiders, a group that made a daring attempt to rescue American POWs from a North Vietnamese prison camp in 1970. The main gate is on U.S. 98 northeast of Fort Walton Beach; tours of the base leave from the officers club. You can pick up free tour tickets at the Niceville/Valparaiso Chamber of Commerce (*see* Important Addresses and Numbers, *above*) or from the Air Force Armament Museum (*see below*). *Tel. 904/678-2323. Tours Jan.–Mar. and June–Aug., Mon., Wed., Fri. 9:30–noon.*

Just outside Eglin's main gate on Rte. 85 is the **Air Force Armament Museum,** with an uncluttered display of more than 5,000 articles of Air Force armaments from World Wars I and II, and the Korean and Vietnam wars. Included are uniforms, engines, weapons, aircraft, and flight simulators; larger craft such as transport planes and swept-wing jets are exhibited on the grounds outside the museum. A 32-minute movie about Eglin's history and its role in the development of armaments is presented continuously throughout the day. *Rte. 85 Eglin Air Force Base, tel. 904/882-4062. Admission free. Open daily 9:30–4:30 except Thanksgiving, Christmas, and New Year's Day.*

Kids especially enjoy the **Indian Temple Mound Museum,** also on U.S. 98, where they can learn all about the prehistoric peoples who inhabited northwest Florida as long as 10,000 years ago. The funerary masks and weaponry on display are particularly fascinating. The museum is adjacent to the 600-year-old **National Historic Landmark Temple Mound,** a large earthwork built over saltwater. *139 Miracle Strip Pkwy. (U.S. 98), tel. 904/243-6521. Admission: 75¢ adults, children 12 and under free. Open Sept.–May, Mon.–Fri. 11–4, Sat. 9–4; June–Aug., Mon.–Sat. 9–4.*

A 2-mile jaunt east on U.S. 98 will bring you to the **Gulfarium**—a great way to spend a few hours when bad weather drives you off the beach. The Gulfarium's main attraction is its "Living Sea" presentation, a 60,000-gallon tank that simulates conditions on the ocean bottom. There are performances by trained porpoises; sea lion shows; and marine life exhibits featuring seals, otters, and penguins. There's also an extensive gift shop where you can buy anything from conch shells and sand-dollar earrings to children's beach toys. *U.S. 98E, tel. 904/244-5169. Admission: $12 adults, $8 children 4–11, children under 3 free. Open May 15–Sept. 15, daily 9–6; Sept. 16–May 14, daily 9–4.*

❹ Destin, Fort Walton Beach's neighbor, lies on the other side of the strait that connects Choctawhatchee Bay with the Gulf of Mexico. Destin takes its name from its founder, Leonard A. Destin, a New London, Connecticut, sea captain who settled his family here sometime in the 1830s. For the next 100 years,

Destin remained a sleepy little fishing village until the strait, or East Pass, was bridged in 1935. Then, recreational anglers discovered its white sands, blue-green waters, and the abundance of some of the most sought-after sport fish in the world. More billfish are hauled in around Destin each year than from all other Gulf fishing ports combined. But you don't have to be the rod-and-reel type to love Destin. There's also plenty to entertain the sand-pail set as well as senior citizens, and there are many gourmet restaurants.

The Destin Fishing Museum has a dry aquarium where lighting and sound effects create the sensation of being underwater. It's a good place for the marine enthusiast to get an overview of aquatic life in the Gulf of Mexico—you can get the feeling of walking on a sandy bottom that's broken by coral reef and dotted with sponges. *35 U.S. 98E, tel. 904/654–1011. Admission: $1 adults, children under 12 free. Open Tues.–Sat. noon–4, Sun. 1–4.*

Drive east on U.S. 98 for about 8 miles to the **Museum of the Sea and Indian,** where cassette players let you set your own pace. This funky tourist attraction, a fixture in Destin for more than 30 years, began with arrowheads and sea shells from a private collection and has since been augmented with child-pleasing stuffed whales, killer sharks, and alligators. A spook house and live zoo add to the fun. *4801 Beach Hwy. (off U.S. 98), tel. 904/ 837–6625. Admission: $3.75 adults, $3.45 senior citizens, $2 children. Open summer, daily 8–7; winter, daily 9–4.*

❺ In the **Eden State Gardens,** 25 miles east of Destin on U.S. 98, an antebellum mansion set amid an arcade of moss-draped live oaks is open to the public. Furnishings in the spacious rooms date from several periods as far back as the 17th century. The surrounding gardens are beautiful year-round, but they're nothing short of spectacular in mid-March when the azaleas and dogwoods are in full bloom. *County Rte. 395, Point Washington, tel. 904/231–4214. Admission to gardens free; mansion tour $1.50. Open daily 8 AM–sunset. Hourly mansion tours Thurs.–Mon. 9–4.*

About 30 miles east of Destin on Route 30A, **Grayton Beach State Recreation Area** (tel. 904/231–4210) is one of the most scenic spots along the Gulf Coast, with blue-green waters, white-sand beaches, salt marshes, and swimming, snorkeling, and campground facilities. Just east of here is the architectural **❻** award-winning village of **Seaside,** where houses with Victorian fretwork, white picket fences, and captain's walks make visitors feel as though they have been magic-carpeted to Cape May or Cape Cod. Seaside is the brainchild of Robert Davis, who dictated certain architectural elements that he felt would promote a neighborly, old-fashioned lifestyle. Built on small lots, no house is more than ¼ mile from the center of town, so residents get about most easily on foot. There isn't enough moss in the brick sidewalks yet for Seaside to have the "historic district" look, but pastel paint jobs, latticework, and rockers on the front porches make this architectural/social experiment a visual stunner.

Farther inland, up Route 85 from Fort Walton Beach, there are several towns worth visiting in "Lower Alabama," as the locals have labeled this region. On the northern side of Choctawhat- **❼** chee Bay are the twin cities of **Valparaiso** and **Niceville,** both relatively young towns, having been granted their charters in 1921 and 1938, respectively. Niceville evolved from a tiny fishing hamlet called Boggy, whose sandy-bottomed bays were rich in mullet. Valparaiso was founded by an entrepreneurial Chicagoan named John B. Perrine, who envisioned it as an ideal city by the sea, or "vale of paradise." Together, the cities have maintained an uncomplicated and serene existence, more or less untouched by the tourist trade farther south. But that may change as word gets out about the water sports here—waterskiing, fishing, and sailing.

In Valparaiso's **Historical Society Museum,** you can take a step back in time among 8,000-year-old stone tools and early-20th-century iron pots and kettles. A rarity on display here is a steam-powered, belt-driven cotton gin. The museum also maintains a reference library of genealogical and historical research materials and official Civil War records. *115 Westview Ave., tel. 904/678–2615. Admission free. Open Tues.–Sat. 11–4.*

East of Niceville, off Route 20 on Rocky Bayou, are 50 excellent picnic areas, nature trails, boat ramps, and uncrowded campsites with electrical and water hookups in the **Fred Gannon Rocky Bayou State Recreation Area.** It's quiet and secluded, yet easy to find, and a great venue for serious bikers. *Rte. 20, tel. 904/833–9144. Admission: $2 for day use; campsites $8.48, or $10.50 with electricity. Open daily 8 AM–sunset.*

When the Louisville & Nashville Railroad Company completed a line through northwest Florida in 1882, its surveyors dubbed the area **Crestview** because, at 235 feet above sea level, it had the highest altitude in the state. There's been a settlement of sorts here since the days of the Conquistadors, when it was a crossroads on the Old Spanish Trail. Crestview is the sort of small town where the mayor rides shotgun with the police patrol on a Saturday night and folks enjoy the simpler pleasures, such as roller skating and playing softball. But it is not without its cultural attributes. The **Robert L. F. Sikes Public Library** and research center, housed in an imposing Greek Revival building, boasts more than 44,000 volumes as well as the private papers of its namesake, a former U.S. congressman.

About 28 miles east of Crestview along I–10, or about 50 miles from Destin (go east on U.S. 98, then north on U.S. 331), **DeFuniak Springs** is another small town that brags about its culture. It was originally the site of the Knox Hill Academy, founded in 1848 and for more than half a century the only institution of higher learning in northwest Florida. The railroad came in 1882, and DeFuniak Springs was so named to flatter a then-prominent railroad official, Frederick de Funiak. In 1885, it was chosen as the location for the New York Chautauqua winter assembly of the educational society. The Chautauqua programs were discontinued in 1928, but DeFuniak Springs attempts to revive them, in spirit at least, with a county-wide Chautauqua Festival it sponsors every May.

Time Out **Chautauqua Winery** (I–10 and U.S. 331, tel. 904/892–5887) opened in 1989, but already its award-winning wines have earned raves from oenophiles nationwide. You can take a free tour of the winery to see how an ancient art blends with modern technology, then retreat to the tasting room. Open Mon.–Sat. 9–5, Sun. noon–5.

Another legacy from the Chautauqua era is the **Walton-DeFuniak Public Library,** by all accounts Florida's oldest library continuously operating in its original building. This tiny facility, measuring 16 feet by 24 feet, opened in 1887 to make reading material available to the Chautauqua crowd. Added to and expanded over the years, at present it contains nearly 30,000 volumes, including rare books, many of which are older than the structure itself. The collection has grown to include antique musical instruments and an impressive display of European armor. *100 Circle Dr., tel. 904/892–3624. Open Mon. 9–7; Tues., Wed., Fri. 9–6; Sat. 9–3.*

Panama City Beach

⑩ A vacation spot with mass appeal, **Panama City Beach** is about 5 miles south and to the west of Panama City proper. In spite of the shoulder-to-shoulder condominiums, motels, and amusement parks that make it seem like one big carnival ground, Panama City Beach has a natural beauty that excuses its over-commercialization. The incredible white sands, navigable waterways, and plentiful marine life that attracted Spanish conquistadors are a lure for today's family-vacation industry.

Time Out **Pineapple Willie's** (Beach Blvd. at Thomas St., tel. 904/235–0928) brings together the best elements of a discotheque and a Wild West saloon, and caters to the 25–40 crowd. If you feel overwhelmed by the live entertainment, you can escape to the serenity of a seaside deck.

At the eastern tip of Panama City Beach is the **St. Andrews State Recreation Area,** which comprises 1,038 acres of beaches, pinewoods, and marshes. There are complete camping facilities here, as well as ample opportunities to swim, pier fish, or hike the dunes along clearly marked nature trails. You can board a ferry to **Shell Island**—a barrier island in the Gulf of Mexico that offers some of the best shelling north of Sanibel Island.

⑪ **Falling Waters State Recreation Area** is about an hour's drive north on Route 77 from Panama City. One of Florida's most recognized geological features is the Falling Waters Sink, a 100-foot-deep cylindrical pit that provides the background for a waterfall. There's an observation deck for viewing this natural phenomenon. *Rte. 77A, tel. 904/638–6130. Admission: $3.25 per vehicle with up to 8 people. Open daily 8 AM–sunset.*

From Panama City, head north for a two-hour drive on U.S. 231 ⑫ to Route 167 to visit the 1,783-acre **Florida Caverns State Park.** Take a ranger-led spelunking tour to see an array of stalactites, stalagmites, and "waterfalls" of solid rock. The park also has hiking trails, campsites, and areas for swimming and canoeing on the Chipola River. *Rte. 167, tel. 904/482–9598. Admission to park: $3.25 per vehicle with up to 8 people, children under 6 free. Admission to caverns: $4 adults, $2 children 6–12. Open daily 8 AM–sunset; cavern tours 9–4.*

Tallahassee

⑬ I–10 rolls over the timid beginnings of the Appalachian foothills and through thick pines into the state capital, **Tallahassee,** with its canopies of ancient oaks and spring bowers of azaleas. Among the best canopied roads are St. Augustine, Miccosukee,

Meridian, Old Bainbridge, and Centerville. Country stores and antebellum plantation houses still dot these roads, much as they did in earlier days.

The downtown Capitol complex is compact enough for walking, though it is also served by a free, continuous shuttle trolley. Stop at the **Tallahassee Area Convention and Visitors Bureau,** on the plaza level of the New Capitol (open weekdays 8–5), to pick up information about the capital and the surrounding area.

On a clear day, you can catch a panoramic view of Tallahassee and its surrounding countryside from the top floor of the **New Capitol,** a modern skyscraper that looms up 22 stories directly behind the low-rise Old Capitol. *Duvall St., tel. 904/488–6167. Admission free. Hourly tours of the New Capitol, weekdays 9–4, weekends 11–3.*

The centerpiece of the Capitol complex is the **Old Capitol,** a pre–Civil War structure that has been added to, and subtracted from, several times over the years. A recent renovation has restored its jaunty red-and-white stripe awnings and combination gas-electric lights to make it look much as it did in 1902. *Monroe St. at Apalachee Pkwy., tel. 904/487–1902. Admission free. Self-guided or guided tours weekdays 9–4:30, Sat. 10–4:30, Sun. noon–4:30.*

Across the street from the Old Capitol is the **Union Bank Building,** built in 1833—Florida's oldest bank building. Since it closed in 1843, it has played many roles, from ballet school to bakery. It's been restored to what is thought to be its original appearance. *Monroe St. at Apalachee Pkwy., tel. 904/487–3803. Admission free. Open Tues.–Fri. 10–1, weekends 1–4.*

Two blocks west of the New Capitol is the **Museum of Florida History**. Here, the long, intriguing story of the state's role in history—from prehistoric times of mastodons to the present, with the launching of space shuttles—is told in lucid and entertaining ways. *500 S. Bronough St., tel. 904/488–1484. Admission free. Open weekdays 9–4:30, Sat. 10–4:30, Sun. and holidays noon–4:30.*

Also a stroll away from the Capitol complex are the **Park Avenue** and **Calhoun Street historic districts,** with many fine examples of Italianate and Greek Revival architecture.

San Luis Archaeological and Historic Site focuses on the archaeology of 17th-century Spanish mission and Apalachee Indian townsites. In its heyday, in 1675, the Apalachee village here had a population of at least 1,400. Threatened by Creek Indians and British forces in 1704, the locals burned the village and fled. *2020 W. Mission Rd., tel. 904/487–3711. 1-hr guided tours weekdays at noon, Sat. at 11 and 3, Sun. at 2.*

Just north of Tallahassee off U.S. 27 is **Lake Jackson,** a resource bass fishermen hold in reverence. Sightseers view, along the shores of the lake, Indian mounds and the ruins of an early-19th-century plantation built by Colonel Robert Butler, adjutant to General Andrew Jackson during the siege of New Orleans. *Indian Mound Rd., off U.S. 27, tel. 904/562–0042. Admission free. Open 8 AM–sunset.*

Five miles north of town on U.S. 319 is the magnificent **Maclay State Gardens.** In springtime the grounds are afire with azaleas, dogwood, and other showy or rare annuals, trees, and shrubs. Allow at least half a day for wandering the paths past the reflecting pool, into the tiny walled garden, and around the lakes and woodlands. The Maclay residence, furnished as it was in the 1920s, as well as picnic grounds, and swimming and boating facilities, are open to the public. *3540 Thomasville Rd. (1 mi north of I-10), tel. 904/487-4556. Admission: $3.50 per vehicle, with up to 8 people. Open daily 8 AM-sunset.*

In 1865, Confederate soldiers stood firm against a Yankee advance on St. Marks. The Rebs held, saving Tallahassee—the only southern capital east of the Mississippi that never fell to the Union. The **Natural Bridge Battlefield State Historic Site,** about 10 miles southeast of the capital, marks the victory, and is a good place for a hike and a picnic. *Natural Bridge Rd. (Rte. 354), off U.S. 363 in Woodville, tel. 904/922-6007. Admission free. Open daily 8 AM-sunset.*

⑭ **Wakulla Springs,** about 15 miles south of Tallahassee on Route 61, is one of the deepest springs in the world. The wilderness remains relatively untouched, retaining the wild and exotic look it had in the 1930s, when Tarzan movies were made here. Aboard glass-bottom boats, visitors probe deep into the lush, jungle-lined waterways to catch glimpses of alligators, snakes, waterfowl, and nesting limpkin. More than 154 bird species can be spotted, as well as raccoon, gray squirrel, and an encyclopedia of southern flora. *1 Springs Dr., Wakulla Springs, tel. 904/ 222-7279. Admission: $3.25 per car. Boat tours $4.50 adults, $2.25 children. Tours daily 9 AM-sunset. Springs open daily 8 AM-sunset.*

Time Out The **Wakulla Springs Lodge and Conference Center** (tel. 904/ 224-5950), located on the grounds, serves three meals a day in a sunny, spartan room that also seems little changed from the 1930s. Schedule lunch here to sample the famous bean soup, home-baked muffins, and a slab of pie.

⑮ About 25 miles south of Tallahassee along the coast is the **St. Marks Wildlife Refuge and Lighthouse.** The once-powerful Fort San Marcos de Apalache was built here in 1639. Stones salvaged from the fort went into building the lighthouse, which is still in operation today. Exhibits are on display at the visitor center. *C.R. 59 (3 mi south of the Newport and U.S. 98 intersection) in St. Marks, tel. 904/925-6121. Admission: $3 per car. Refuge open sunrise-sunset; visitor center open weekdays 8-4:15, weekends 10-5.*

Apalachicola

Spreading west of Tallahassee and north of Apalachicola is the **Apalachicola National Forest,** where you can camp, hike, picnic, fish, or swim. U.S. 98 skirts the forest's eastern border on ⑯ its way to **Apalachicola,** the state's most important oyster fishery, about 90 minutes from Tallahassee. In Apalachicola, drive by the **Raney House,** circa 1850; **Trinity Episcopal Church,** built from prefabricated parts in 1838; and the **John Gorrie State Museum,** honoring the physician who is credited with inventing ice-making and air-conditioning. Exhibits of Apalachicola history are displayed here as well. *John Gorrie State Museum, Ave. C and Sixth St., tel. 904/653-9347. Admission: $1 adults, children under 6 free. Open Thurs.-Mon. 9-5.*

⓱ About 34 miles west of Apalachicola on U.S. 98 at **Port St. Joe** is the spot where Florida's first constitution was drafted in 1838. Most of the old town, including the original hall, is gone— wiped out by hurricanes—but the exhibits in the **Constitution Convention State Museum** recall the event. There are also provisions for camping and picnicking in a small park surrounding the museum. *200 Island Memorial Way, tel. 904/229–8029. Open Thurs.–Mon. 9–5. Closed noon–1. Admission: $1 per person, children under 6 free.*

⓲ **St. George Island State Park** can be reached by a causeway from Eastpoint, where you can drive toward the sea along the narrow spit of land with its dunes, sea oats, and abundant bird life. *Tel. 904/927–2111. Admission: $3.25 per vehicle with up to 8 people. Open 8 AM–sunset.*

What to See and Do with Children

Fort Walton/Destin   **Big Kahuna's Lost Paradise** (U.S. 98, Destin, tel. 904/837–4061) is a water park with miniature golf and an amphitheater. **Island Golf Center** (1306 Miracle Strip Pkwy., Fort Walton Beach, tel. 904/244–1612) has 36 holes of miniature golf, a nine-hole par-three course, pool tables, and video games. **Museum of the Sea and Indian** (*see* Destin, above). **The Track Recreation Center** (1125 U.S. 98, Destin, tel. 904/654–4668) is a special theme park with go-cart tracks and rides.

Panama City Beach   **Gulf World** (15412 Front Beach Rd., Panama City Beach, tel. 904/234–5271) performers include a bottle-nosed dolphin, porpoises, seals, otters, and sea lions. **Miracle Strip Amusement Park** (12000 U.S. 98W, Panama City Beach, tel. 904/234–5810) has 30 rides, including a roller coaster with a 65-foot drop. **Shipwreck Island** (12000 U.S. 98W, Panama City Beach, tel. 904/234–2282) features 6 acres of water rides for kids and adults of all ages.

Pensacola   **Fast Eddie's Fun Center** (W St. at Michigan Ave., Pensacola, tel. 904/433–7735) features kiddie rides, a video room, air hockey, and basketball. **The Zoo** (5701 Gulf Breeze Pkwy., Gulf Breeze, tel. 904/932–2229) is home to plants, animals, and 30 acres of ponds, lakes, and open plains.

Tallahassee   **Tallahassee Museum of History and Natural Science** features a collection of old cars and carriages, a red caboose, nature trails, a snake exhibit, and a restored plantation house. *3945 Museum Dr., Tallahassee, tel. 904/576–1636. Admission: $5 adults, $4 senior citizens, $3 children 4–15, under 4 free. Open Mon.–Sat. 9–5, Sun. 12:30–5.*

Shopping

Cordova Mall (511 N. Ninth Ave., Pensacola, tel. 904/477–7562) is anchored by four department stores in addition to its specialty shops and a food court with 13 fast-food outlets. **Harbourtown Shopping Village** (913 Gulf Breeze Pkwy., Gulf Breeze, no phone) has trendy shops and the ambience of a wharfside New England village. Near Fort Walton Beach, there are four department stores in the **Santa Rosa Mall** (300 Mary Esther Cut-off, Mary Esther, tel. 904/244–2172), as well

as 118 other shops and 15 bistro-style eateries. Stores in the
Manufacturer's Outlet Centers (127 and 225 Miracle Strip
Pkwy., Fort Walton Beach, and 105 W. 23rd St., Panama City,
no phone) offer well-known brands of clothing and accessories
at a substantial discount. **The Market at Sandestin** (5494 U.S.
98E, Destin, tel. 904/267–8092) has 27 upscale shops that ped-
dle such wares as gourmet chocolates and designer clothes in
an elegant minimall with boardwalks. **The Panama City Mall**
(U.S. 231 and Rte. 77, Panama City, tel. 904/785–9587) has a
mix of more than 100 franchise shops and national chain stores.

Participant Sports

Biking
Some of the nation's best bike paths run through northwest
Florida's woods and dunelands, particularly on Santa Rosa Is-
land where you can pedal for 50 miles and never lose sight of the
ocean. Routes through Eglin AFB Reservation present cyclists
with a few challenges. Biking here requires a $3 permit, which
may be obtained at **Jackson Guard Forestry** (tel. 904/882–4164).
Rentals are available from **Bob's Bicycle Center** (Fort Walton
Beach, tel. 904/243–5856) and at **The Wheel Works** (Fort Walton
Beach, tel. 904/244–5252).

Boating
There are niches for boaters of all classes in northwest Florida's sheltered inlets and lazy rivers, as well as in the open waters of its bays and the Gulf of Mexico. You can rent powerboats
for fishing, skiing, and snorkeling at **Baytowne Marina**, 5500
U.S. 98E, Sandestin, tel. 904/267–8123). Pontoon-boat rentals
are available at **Consigned RV's** (101 W. Miracle Strip Pkwy.,
Fort Walton Beach, tel. 904/243–4488).

Canoeing
Both beginners and veterans will get a kick out of canoeing the
Florida Panhandle's abundance of rivers and streams. The
shoals and rapids in the Blackwater River in the **Blackwater
River State Forest**, 40 miles northeast of Pensacola, will challenge even the most seasoned canoeist, while the gentler currents in the sheltered marshes and inlets are less intimidating.
Canoe rentals are readily available from **Blackwater Canoe
Rental** (U.S. 90E., Milton, tel. 904/623–0235) and at **Adventures Unlimited** (12 mi north of Milton on Rte. 87, tel. 904/623–
6197). For a trip down Econfina Creek, "Florida's most beautiful canoe trail," rentals are supplied by **Econfina Creek Canoe
Livery, Inc.** (north of Rte. 20 on Strickland Rd., tel. 904/722–
9032). Contact **TNT Hideway** (St. Marks, tel. 904/925–6412) to
canoe the Wakulla River near Tallahassee.

Diving
In the Panama City Beach area, you can investigate the wreck-
age of sunken tanker ships, tugboats, and cargo vessels. For
snorkelers and beginning divers, the jetties of St. Andrews
State Recreation Area, where there is no boat traffic, are safe.
Wreck dives are offered by **Diver's Den** (3804 Thomas Dr., tel.
904/234–8717) or **Panama City Dive Center** (4823 Thomas Dr.,
tel. 904/235–3390). In the Destin–Fort Walton Beach area, you
can arrange for diving instruction and excursions through
Aquanaut Scuba Center, Inc. (24 U.S. 98W, Destin, tel. 904/
837–0359) or **The Scuba Shop** (348 Miracle Strip Pkwy., Fort
Walton Beach, tel. 904/243–1600).

Fishing
Northwest Florida's fishing options range from fishing for
pompano, snapper, marlin, and grouper—in the saltwater of
the Gulf of Mexico—to angling for bass, catfish, and bluegill in

the freshwaters of the region. You can buy bait and tackle at **Stewart's Outdoor Sports** (4 Eglin Pkwy., Fort Walton Beach, tel. 904/243–9443; 1025 Palm Plaza, Niceville, tel. 904/678–4804), at **Panama City Beach Pier Tackle Shop** (16101 Front Beach Rd., Panama City, tel. 904/235–2576), or at **Penny's Sporting Goods** (1800 Pace Blvd., Pensacola, tel. 904/438–9633). If your idea of fishing is to drop a line off the end of a pier, you can fish from **Old Pensacola Bay Bridge** or from the 3,000-foot-long **Destin Catwalk,** along the East Pass Bridge. For $2 adults, $1.50 children, $1 observer, you can also fish from Panama City Beach's **city pier.**

Deep-Sea Fishing Charters   When planning an excursion, be advised that rates for renting deep-sea fishing boats are usually quoted by the day (about $550) or half day (about $350). This is an immensely popular pastime on the Emerald Coast, so there are boat charters aplenty. Among them are **Miller's Charter Services**/*Barbi-Anne* (off U.S. 98 on the docks next to A.J.'s Restaurant, Destin, tel. 904/837–6059), **East Pass Charters** (at East Pass Marina, U.S. 98E, Destin, tel. 904/654–2022), **Lafitte Cove Marina** (1010 Ft. Pickens Rd., Pensacola Beach, tel. 904/932–9241), **The Moorings Marina** (655 Pensacola Beach Blvd., Pensacola Beach, tel. 904/932–0305), and **Rude Roy's Marina** (6400 U.S. 98W, Panama City Beach, tel. 904/235–2809).

Party boats that carry as many as 100 passengers at $35–$40 per head are the cheapest way to go, offering everything from half-day fishing excursions to dinner cruises. The old standbys are ***Capt. Anderson's*** (Captain Anderson Pier, 5550 N. Lagoon Dr., Panama City Beach, tel. 904/234–3435) and ***Emmanuel*** (U.S. 98E, Destin, tel. 904/837–6313).

Golf   The Gulf is northwest Florida's number-one asset; golf is number two. Courses open to the public include:

Fort Walton/Destin   **Fort Walton Beach Municipal Golf Course** (Rte. 189, Fort Walton Beach, tel. 904/862–3314, 18 holes), **Bluewater Bay** (Rte. 20, 6 mi east of Niceville, tel. 904/897–3241, 36 holes), **Indian Bayou Golf & Country Club** (Airport Rd. off U.S. 98, Destin, tel. 904/837–6192, 18 holes), **Sandestin Beach Resort** (Emerald Coast Pkwy., Destin, tel. 904/267–8155 or 904/267–8144, 36 holes), **Santa Rosa Golf & Beach Club** (C.R. 30A, Santa Rosa Beach, tel. 904/267–2229, 18 holes), **Shalimar Pointe Golf & Country Club** (2 Country Club Dr., Shalimar, tel. 904/651–1416, 18 holes).

Panama City Beach   **Marriott's Bay Point Resort** (100 Delwood Beach Rd., Panama City Beach, tel. 904/234–3307, 36 holes), **St. Joseph's Bay Country Club** (Rte. C-30 S, Port St. Joe, tel. 904/227–1751, 18 holes), **Sunny Hills Country Club** (1150 Country Club Blvd., Sunny Hills, tel. 904/773–3619, 18 holes).

Pensacola   **Perdido Bay Resort** (1 Doug Ford Dr., Pensacola, tel. 904/492–1223, 18 holes), **Tiger Point Golf & Country Club** (1255 Country Club Rd., Gulf Breeze, tel. 904/932–1333, 36 holes), **The Club at Hidden Creek** (3070 PGA Blvd., Gulf Breeze, tel. 904/939–4604, 18 holes).

Tallahassee   **Killearn** (100 Tyron Circle, Tallahassee 32308, tel. 904/893–2144, 18 holes).

Sailing   **Hobie Shop** (12705 Front Beach Rd., Panama City Beach, tel. 904/234–0023) rents Hobie Cats and Windsurfers. Sailing instruction as well as rentals are offered by **Friendship Charter**

Sailing (404 U.S. 98, Destin, tel. 904/837–2694). Sailboat rentals come in a range of classes at **Cove Marina at Bluewater Bay** (300 Yacht Club Dr., Niceville, tel. 904/897–2821). Renting sailboats, jet skis, or catamarans from **Bonifay Water Sports** (460 Pensacola Beach Blvd., Pensacola Beach, tel. 904/932–0633) includes safety and sailing instructions. Hobie Cats, Sunfish, jet skis, Windsurfers, and surfboards are available at **Key Sailing** (400 Quietwater Beach Blvd., Pensacola Beach, tel. 904/932–5520).

Tennis   Tennis courts are available in more than 30 locations in the Pensacola area, among them the **Pensacola Racquet Club** (3450 Wimbledon Dr., Pensacola, tel. 904/434–2434). The **Municipal Tennis Center** (45 W. Audrey, Fort Walton Beach, tel. 904/243–8789) has 12 lighted Laykold courts and four practice walls. You can play tennis day or night on seven Rubico and two hard courts at the **Ft. Walton Racquet Club** (23 Hurlburt Field Rd., Fort Walton Beach, tel. 904/862–2023). There are 21 courts (12 lighted) featuring three different playing surfaces at **Bluewater Bay Resort** (Tennis Center, Bay Dr., Niceville, tel. 904/897–3679). **Sandestin Resort** (U.S. 98E, Destin, tel. 904/267–7110), one of the nation's five-star tennis resorts, has 16 courts with grass, hard, or Rubico surfaces. **Destin Racquet & Fitness Center** (995 Airport Rd., Destin, tel. 904/837–7300) boasts six Rubico courts. At **Marriott's Bay Point Resort**'s (100 Delwood Beach Rd., Panama City Beach, tel. 904/235–6910) tennis center there are 12 Har-Tru clay tennis courts.

Spectator Sports

Auto Racing   Billed as the fastest ½-mile track in the country, **Five Flags Speedway** features action-packed racing with top-name stockcar drivers. Races are every Friday night at 8, from late March through September. *7450 Pine Forest Rd., Pensacola, tel. 904/944–0466. Admission: $8 adults, $3 children 6–12.*

Dog Racing   Rain or shine, year-round, there's racing with pari-mutuel betting Tuesday–Sunday nights and afternoons on Friday, Saturday, and Monday at the **Pensacola Greyhound Track**. Lounge and grandstand areas are fully enclosed, air-conditioned, and have instant-replay televisions throughout. *U.S. 98 at Dog Track Rd., W. Pensacola, tel. 904/455–8598 or 800/345–3997.*

There's pari-mutuel betting year-round, and live greyhound racing six nights a week during the spring and summer, at the **Ebro Greyhound Track**. *Rte. 20 at Rte. 79, Ebro, tel. 904/535–4048. Open nightly, Mon.–Sat., 7:30 PM post time; matinee racing, Wed. and Sat., 11:30 PM and 1:30 AM post times.*

Beaches

Crystal Beach Wayside Park (tel. 904/837–6447) has something to appeal to just about everyone. This Gulf-side sanctuary, located just 5 miles east of Destin, is protected on each side by undeveloped state-owned land.

Eglin Reservation Beach (no phone) is situated on 5 miles of undeveloped military land, about 3 miles west of the Brooks Bridge in Fort Walton Beach. This beach is a favorite haunt of local teenagers and young singles.

Grayton Beach State Recreation Area (tel. 904/231–6447) is sandwiched between Santa Rosa Beach and Grayton Beach, about 30 miles east of Destin. Swimming, snorkeling, and campgrounds are available.

Gulf Island National Seashore (tel. 904/934–2631) is a 150-mile stretch of pristine coastline from Gulfport, Mississippi, to Destin. Managed by the National Park Service, these beach and recreational spots include the **Fort Pickens Area,** at the west end of Santa Rosa Island; the **Santa Rosa Day Use Area,** 10 miles east of Pensacola Beach; and **Johnson's Beach** on Perdido Key, about 20 miles northwest of Pensacola's historic districts. Check with the National Park Service for any restrictions that might apply.

John C. Beasley State Park (no phone) is Fort Walton Beach's seaside playground on Okaloosa Island. A boardwalk leads to the beach where you'll find covered picnic tables, changing rooms, and freshwater showers. Lifeguards are on duty during the summer.

Panama City Beaches (tel. 800/PC–BEACH), public beaches along the Miracle Strip, combine with the plethora of video-game arcades, miniature golf courses, sidewalk cafés, souvenir shops, and shopping centers to lure people of all ages.

Pensacola Beach (tel. 904/932–2258) is 5 miles south of Pensacola—take U.S. 98 to Gulf Breeze, then cross the Bob Sikes Bridge over to Santa Rosa Island. Beachcombers and sunbathers, sailboarders and sailors keep things going at a fever pitch in and out of the water.

St. Andrews State Recreation Area (tel. 904/233–5140), on the eastern tip of Panama City Beach, is Florida's most visited park. An artificial reef creates a calm, shallow play area that is perfect for young children.

Dining and Lodging

Dining Since the Gulf of Mexico is only an hour's drive from any spot in the Panhandle, menus in restaurants from modest diners to elegant cafes feature seafood, most of which will be hauled out of the water and served that same day. Native fish such as grouper, red snapper, amberjack, catfish, and mullet are the regional staples.

Unless otherwise noted, these restaurants are open for lunch and dinner. Highly recommended restaurants are indicated by a star ★.

Category	Cost*
Very Expensive	over $50
Expensive	$35–$50
Moderate	$20–$35
Inexpensive	under $20

per person, excluding drinks, service, and 6% sales tax

Lodging Northwest Florida offers everything from posh seaside resorts to modest roadside motels. The rule of thumb is: The closer you are to the water, the more you can expect to pay. If you're planning a lengthy stay, a condominium rental is a good idea. Most accept walk-ins, but to be on the safe side, reserve a spot through a property management service. Prices vary: During the summer, which is high season for this part of Florida, you can expect to pay a premium, but during the winter months, room rates are a bargain.

Highly recommended lodgings are indicated by a star ★.

Category	Cost*
Very Expensive	over $150
Expensive	$90–$150
Moderate	$60–$90
Inexpensive	under $60

All prices are for a standard double room, excluding service charge.

Crestview
Lodging

Crestview Holiday Inn. Within this simple sandstone stucco motel is typical Florida decor: shell-shape ceramic lamps, seashell-print bedspreads, and oceanic art on the walls. It's right on the main drag and is the "in" place for local wedding receptions and high-school proms. *Rte. 85 and I–10, Box 1355, 32536, tel. 904/682–6111, fax 904/689–1189. 120 rooms. Facilities: pool, restaurant, lounge. AE, D, DC, MC, V. Inexpensive.*

Destin
Dining
★

Marina Cafe. A harbor-view setting, impeccable service, and uptown ambience have earned this establishment a reputation as one of the finest dining experiences on the Emerald Coast. The decor's oceanic motif is expressed in shades of aqua, green, and sand accented with marine tapestries and sea sculptures. An up-to-the-minute menu gives diners a choice of classic Creole, Italian, or Pacific Rim cuisine. Try a regional specialty, such as the award-winning black-pepper crusted yellowfin tuna with braised spinach and spicy soy sauce, or grilled jumbo Gulf shrimp with cilantro chili cream and sweet-pepper salsa. The wine list is extensive. *404 U.S. 98E, tel. 904/837–7960. Reservations suggested. Dress: casual but neat. AE, MC, V. No lunch. Moderate.*

Captain Dave's on the Gulf. This beachfront restaurant comprises three dining rooms: a central room with a glass dome overlooking the Gulf; a sports room filled with bats, helmets, jerseys, autographed baseballs, and photographs of professional atheletes; and finally, a more intimate dining area with dim lights and potted plants. The hearty menu offers seafood entrées such as fillet of snapper sprinkled with crabmeat and covered with shrimp sauce and Parmesan cheese; and a medley of broiled seafood served with celery, onions, bell peppers, tomatoes, and topped with black olives and mozzarella cheese. Children's plates are available. Dancing and live entertainment are featured in the downstairs lounge. *3796 Old Hwy. 98, tel. 904/837–2627. No reservations. Dress: casual. No lunch. AE, MC, V. Inexpensive.*

Flamingo Cafe. Two types of atmosphere are presented at the Flamingo Cafe: the black, white, and pink color scheme, with waiters and waitresses dressed in tuxedos with pink bow ties, shouting nouveau; and the airy, seaside setting embraced by the panoramic view of Destin harbor seen from every seat in the house, or from a table on the full-length porch outside. Chef's specialties include veal Magenta (baby white veal sautéed with lobster and shrimp, finished with raspberry beurre blanc and garlic butter) and grouper Flamingo (broiled with butter, Madeira wine, and bread crumbs, topped off with sautéed mushrooms and artichoke hearts in lemon-butter sauce). *414 U.S. 98E, tel. 904/837–0961. Reservations accepted. Dress: casual. AE, D, DC, MC, V. Inexpensive.*

Lodging
★
Sandestin Beach Resort. This 2,600-acre resort of villas, cottages, condominiums, and an inn seems to be a town unto itself. All rooms have a view, either of the Gulf, Choctawhatchee Bay, a golf course, lagoon, or bird sanctuary. This resort provides something for an assortment of tastes, from simple to extravagant, and offers special rates October–March. *Emerald Coast Pkwy., 32541, tel. 904/267–8000 or 800/277–0800, fax 904/267–8222. 175 rooms, 316 villas. Facilities: private beach, several pools, 2 golf courses, 16 tennis courts, tennis and golf pro shops, marina, 5 restaurants, shopping mall. D, DC, MC, V. Expensive–Very Expensive.*

Summer Breeze. White picket fences and porches or patios outside each unit make this condominium complex look like a summer place out of the Gay Nineties. One-bedroom suites have fully equipped kitchens and can sleep up to six people in queen-size beds, sleeper sofas, or bunks. It's halfway between Destin and Sandestin and is across from a roadside park that gives it the feel of privacy and seclusion. *3884 U.S. 98E, 32541, tel. 904/837–4853, 800/874–8914, or 800/336–4853, fax 904/837–5390. 36 units. Facilities: pool, Jacuzzi, barbecue. MC, V. Moderate–Expensive.*

Village Inn of Destin. This property, only minutes away from the Gulf, was built in 1983 with families in mind. A variety of amenities, including entertainment, are provided to occupy each member of the family in some way. Rooms have serviceable dressers and queen- or king-size beds. Senior citizen discounts are available. *215 U.S. 98E, 32541, tel. 904/837–7413, fax 654–3394. 100 rooms. Facilities: pool. AE, D, DC, MC, V. Inexpensive–Moderate.*

Fort Walton Beach
Dining
★
Seagull. In addition to an unobstructed view of Brooks Bridge and the sound, this waterside restaurant has a 400-foot dock for its cruise-minded customers. Decorated with pictures from Fort Walton in the 1940s, and dimly lit, the Seagull is a comfortable place to dine. Choose between no-frills steak and prime rib or fancier fare, such as fillet of snapper topped with almonds and Dijon mustard sauce. After the family business clears out, things liven up a bit when one of two bands provide live soft rock music. *U.S. 98E, by the Brooks Bridge, tel. 904/243–3413. Dress: casual. Reservations accepted. No lunch. AE, DC, MC, V. Inexpensive–Moderate.*

The Sound. Lean back and watch the action on Santa Rosa Sound from any seat in the house in this easygoing establishment where wood paneling and rattan fixtures make a happy marriage. The grouper del Rio, sauced with Dijon mayonnaise and topped with bread crumbs and Parmesan cheese, is touted, as is the prime rib. Let your appetite determine whether you order a junior or senior cut. A children's menu is available lunch and dinner. Cap off an evening meal with a wedge of Key lime pie, then move over to the adjacent lounge for live jazz and blues. *108 W. U.S. 98, tel. 904/243-7772. Reservations accepted. Dress: casual. AE, DC, MC, V. Inexpensive.*

Lodging **Holiday Inn.** This U-shape hotel consists of a seven-story tower flanked on either side by three-story wings. Rooms feature pastel green-and-peach decor and have flowered bedspreads and complementing striped draperies and face either the Gulf or the pool, but even the poolside rooms have at least some view of the sea. There are four floors of suites in the middle tower, each with a spacious sitting area and access to an extensive veranda overlooking the Gulf. The lobby, with an upscale, contemporary design, boasts glass elevators, colored banners hanging from the ceiling, wicker furniture, and tile floors. *1110 Santa Rosa Blvd., 32548, tel. 904/243-9181, 800/465-4329 outside FL, fax 904/664-7652. 385 rooms. Facilities: 3 pools, 800-foot beach, tennis courts, exercise room, restaurants, lounge. AE, D, DC, MC, V. Moderate-Expensive.*

Ramada Beach Resort. The lobby and entrance presents a slick look: black marble and disco lights—what some locals feel is too much like the Las Vegas strip. Activity here centers around a pool with a five-story grotto and a swim-through waterfall, and along the 800-foot private beach. *U.S. 98E, 32548, tel. 904/243-9161, 800/874-8962, or 800/2-RAMADA, fax 904/1/243-2391. 454 rooms. Facilities: pools, whirlpool, tennis courts, game room, exercise room, 3 restaurants, 2 lounges. AE, D, DC, MC, V. Moderate-Expensive.*

Panama City Beach
Dining

Boar's Head. An exterior that looks like an oversize thatch cottage sets the mood for dining in this ever-popular ersatz-rustic restaurant and tavern. Prime rib has been the number-one people-pleaser since the house opened in 1978, but broiled shrimp with crabmeat and vegetable stuffing, and native seafood sprinkled with spices and blackened in a white-hot skillet, are popular, too. For starters, try escargot in mushroom caps or a shrimp bisque. There's a special menu for the junior appetite. *17290 Front Beach Rd., tel. 904/234-6628. No reservations. Dress: casual. D, MC, V. No lunch. Inexpensive-Moderate.*

Capt. Anderson's. Come early to watch the boats unload the catch of the day, and be among the first to line up for one of the 600 seats in this noted restaurant. The atmosphere is nautical, with tables made of hatch covers. The Greek specialties aren't limited to feta cheese and shriveled olives; charcoal-broiled fish and steaks have a prominent place on the menu, too. *5551 N. Lagoon Dr., tel. 904/234-2225. No reservations. Dress: casual. AE, D, DC, MC, V. No lunch. Closed Nov.-Jan., and Sun. Sept.-May. Inexpensive-Moderate.*

Montego Bay. Queue up with vacationers and natives for a table at any one of the four restaurants in this local chain. Service is swift and the food's good. Some dishes, such as red beans and rice or oysters on the half shell, are no surprise. Others, such as shrimp rolled in coconut and served with a honey mustard and orange marmalade sauce, or steak doused with Kentucky bourbon and presented with a bourbon marinade, are real treats. *4920 Thomas Dr., tel. 904/234-8686; 9949 Thomas Dr., tel. 904/235-3585; The Shoppes at Edgewater, tel. 904/233-6033; 17118 Front Beach Rd., tel. 904/233-2900. No reservations. Dress: casual. AE, D, MC, V. Inexpensive.*

Lodging
★
Edgewater Beach Resort. Luxurious one-, two-, and three-bedroom units in beachside towers or golf-course villas are elegant-

ly furnished with wicker and rattan and done in the seaside colors of peach, aqua, and sand. The centerpiece of this resort is a Polynesian-style lagoon pool with waterfalls, reflecting ponds, footbridges, and more than 20,000 species of tropical plants. *11212 U.S. 98A, 32407, tel. 904/235-4044, 800/874-8686 outside FL, fax 904/233-7599. 530 units. Facilities: golf, 12 tennis courts, games rooms, health club, shuffleboard, 3 restaurants, lounge. AE, D, MC, V. Expensive-Very Expensive.*

★ **Marriott's Bay Point Resort.** Sheer elegance is the hallmark of this pink stucco jewel on the shores of Grand Lagoon. Wing chairs, camel-back sofas, and Oriental-patterned carpets in the common areas re-create the ambience of an English manor house, which is sustained by the Queen Anne furnishings in the guest rooms. Gulf view or golf view—take your pick. Kitchen-equipped villas are a mere tee-shot away from the hotel. *100 Delwood Beach Rd., 32411, tel. 904/234-3307, 800/874-7105 outside FL, fax 904/233-1308. 400 rooms, suites, or villas. Facilities: 5 outdoor pools, 1 indoor pool with Jacuzzi, 2 golf courses, 12 lighted Har-Tru tennis courts, 145-slip marina, sailboat rentals, fishing charters, riverboat cruises, 5 restaurants, lounges. AE, D, DC, MC, V. Moderate-Expensive.*

Miracle Mile Resort. A mile of beachfront is awash with hotels: Miracle Mile Inn, Gulfside, Sands, Barefoot Beach Inn. These older properties target the family and convention trade. *9450 S. Thomas Dr., 32407, tel. 904/234-3484, 800/342-8720 in FL, 800/874-6613 outside FL, fax 904/233-4369. 632 units. Facilities: 4 pools, 2 tennis courts, restaurant, lounge. AE, D, DC, MC, V. Inexpensive-Moderate.*

Pensacola
Dining
★ **Jamie's.** This is one of a handful of Florida restaurants that are members of the prestigious Master Chef's Institute. Dining here is like spending the evening in the antiques-filled parlor of a fine, old southern home. If a visit to Florida has you fished-out, try the pâté du jour, followed by almond-coated breast of chicken accompanied by a champagne cream sauce and seedless grapes. The wine list boasts more than 200 labels. *424 E. Zaragoza St., tel. 904/434-2911. Reservations advised. Dress: casual. AE, MC, V. Closed. Sun. Moderate.*

Cap'n Jim's. Get a table by a picture window and gaze at Pensacola Bay while you savor a house special, such as snapper Chardonnay (served with lobster-based wine and cream sauce, scallions, and mushrooms) or snapper Dean'o (broiled and served with fresh tomatoes, spring onions, and lemon butter sauce). *905 E. Gregory St., tel. 904/433-3562. Reservations accepted. Dress: casual. AE, D, DC, MC, V. Closed Sun. Inexpensive.*

McGuire's Irish Pub. Drink cherry beer brewed right on the premises in copper and oaken casks, and eat your corned beef and cabbage while an Irish tenor croons in the background. Located in an old firehouse, the pub is replete with antiques, moose heads, Irish Tiffany lamps, and Erin-go-bragh memorabilia. More than 36,000 dollar bills signed and dated by the pub's patrons flutter from the ceiling. McGuire's also has a House Mug Club with more than 2,000 personalized mugs. The waitresses are chatty and aim to please. Menu items run from kosher-style sandwiches to chili con carne to Boston cream pie. *600 E. Gregory St., tel. 904/433-6789. No reservations. Dress: casual. AE, D, DC, MC, V. Inexpensive.*

Perry's Seafood House & Gazebo Oyster Bar. This vintage 1858 house, known locally as "the big red house," was a residence, a tollhouse, and a fraternity house before Perry purchased it in 1968 and turned it into a restaurant. Native fish are broiled with Perry's secret sauce and garlic butter, or baked and topped with garlic sauce and lemon juice. The menu varies depending on weather conditions, fishing boat schedules, and what was caught that day. *2140 S. Barrancas Ave., tel. 904/ 434–2995. No reservations. Dress: casual. AE, DC, MC, V. Closed Tues. Inexpensive.*

Lodging **Pensacola Grand Hotel.** The lobby is in the renovated L & N train depot. Ticket and baggage counters are still intact and old railroad signs remind guests of the days when steam locomotives chugged up to these doors. The old train station connects via a canopied two-story galleria to a 15-story tower. Here's where the spittoons and hand trucks give way to upholstered furniture and deep-pile carpet; standard doubles are up-to-date and roomy. Bilevel penthouse suites have snazzy wet bars and whirlpool baths. The hotel is adjacent to the Pensacola Civic Center and only few blocks away from the historic districts. *200 E. Gregory St., 32501, tel. 904/433–3336, fax 904/432–7572. 212 rooms. Facilities: heated pool, 2 restaurants, 3 lounges, complimentary airport limo. AE, D, DC, MC, V. Expensive– Very Expensive.*

Perdido Sun. This high rise is the perfect expression of Gulf-side resort living. After a stay here, you'll know why the Spanish explorers of 300 years ago called the area the "Lost Paradise." One-, two-, or three-bedroom decorator-furnished units all have seaside balconies with spectacular views of the water. You can choose to make this your home away from home—accommodations include fully equipped kitchens—or you can pamper yourself with daily maid service. *13753 Perdido Key Dr., 32507, tel. 904/492–2390, 800/227–2390 outside FL, fax 904/492–4135. 93 units. Facilities: glass-enclosed heated pool, outdoor pool, spa, health club. MC, V. Expensive–Very Expensive.*

Holiday Inn/Pensacola Beach. This property enjoyed its finest hour during the filming of *Jaws II,* when the cast made this its headquarters. Inside, the lobby is simple, with potted plants, floral arrangements, and a coral-color decor. Outside, the Holiday Inn has its own 1,500 feet of private beach. From the ninth-floor Penthouse Lounge, you can watch the goings-on in the Gulf, especially when the setting sun turns the western sky to lavender and orange. *165 Ft. Pickens Rd., Pensacola Beach, 32561, tel. 904/932–5361 or 800/HOLIDAY, fax 904/932–7121. 150 rooms. Facilities: outdoor pool, tennis courts, restaurant, lounge. AE, D, DC, MC, V. Moderate.*

★ **New World Inn.** This is Pensacola's little hotel, where celebrities who visit the city are likely to stay. Photos of dozens of the inn's famous guests (Lucille Ball, Shirley Jones, Charles Kuralt) hang behind the front desk in the lobby. The exquisite furnishings in the guest rooms take their inspiration from the five periods of Pensacola's past: French or Spanish provincial, early American, antebellum, or Queen Anne. The baths are handsomely appointed with brass fixtures and outfitted with oversize towels. *600 S. Palafox St., 32501, tel. 904/432–4111, fax 904/435–8939. 14 rooms, 2 suites. Facilities: restaurant, lounge. AE, D, DC, MC, V. Moderate.*

Ramada Inn North. All the guest rooms at this hotel have been renovated. Suites have game tables and entertainment centers; some have whirlpools. This Ramada is conveniently located close to the airport. *6550 Pensacola Blvd., 32505, tel. 904/477–0711, 800/2–RAMADA outside FL, fax 904/477–0711, ext. 602. 106 rooms. Facilities: pool, restaurant, lounge, courtesy airport transportation. AE, D, DC, MC, V. Inexpensive–Moderate.*

Seaside
Dining
★

Bud & Alley's. This roadside restaurant grows its own herbs—rosemary, thyme, basil, fennel, and mint. The inside room has a unique, down-to-earth feel, with hardwood floors, ceiling fans, and six-foot windows looking out onto the garden. There is also a screened-in porch area with a view of the Gulf. The Gorgonzola salad with sweet peppers is a delightful introduction to one of the entrées, perhaps the seared duck breast with caramelized garlic, wild mushrooms, and Cabernet sauce. *C.R. 30A, tel. 904/231–5900. Dinner reservations accepted. Dress: casual. MC, V. Closed Tues. Sept.–May. Inexpensive.*

Lodging
★

Seaside. Two- to five-bedroom porticoed Victorian cottages are furnished right down to the vacuum cleaners. Although there's no air-conditioning, the Gulf breezes blowing off the water will cool rooms and remind you of the miles of unspoiled beaches so nearby. *C.R. 30A, 32459, tel. 904/231–1320, fax 904/231–2219. 148 units. Facilities: pool, tennis court, croquet, badminton, bicycles, Hobie Cats, and beach equipment rentals. AE, MC, V. Expensive–Very Expensive.*

Tallahassee
Dining
★

Andrew's 2nd Act. Part of a smart complex in the heart of the political district, this is classic cuisine: elegant and understated. If you like pub hopping, there's Andrew's Upstairs, and the Adams Street Cafe (also by Andrew) is next door. For dinner, the veal Oscar is flawless or choose a chef's special from the chalkboard. You can't go wrong. *102 W. Jefferson St., tel. 904/222–2759. Reservations advised. Jacket and tie suggested. AE, DC, MC, V. Expensive.*

Nicholson's Farmhouse. The name says a lot about this friendly, informal country place with an outside kitchen and grill. If you've never tried amberjack, discover this unusual, meaty fish—a specialty of the house. *Turn off Hwy. 27 to Hwy. 12 toward Quincy and follow signs, tel. 904/539–5931. Reservations advised on weekends. BYOB. Dress: casual. MC, V. Closed Sun.–Mon. Moderate.*

Anthony's. Often confused with Andrew's, but a different and equally deserving restaurant, this is the locals' choice for uncompromising Italian classics. Try one of the Italian-style grouper or salmon dishes. *1950 Thomasville Rd., tel. 904/224–1447. Reservations advised. Dress: casual. AE, MC, V. Inexpensive.*

★ **Barnacle Bill's.** Don't be put off by the slummy decor. The seafood selection is whale-size and it's steamed to succulent perfection before your eyes, with fresh vegetables on the side. This popular hangout is famous for pasta dishes and home-smoked fish, too. Choose from complete weight-loss menus and daily chalkboard specials. Children eat for free on Sunday. The full menu is available for carryout. *1830 N. Monroe St., tel. 904/385–8734. Reservations required for large groups. Dress: casual. AE, MC, V. Inexpensive.*

Lodging
★

Governors Inn. Only a block from the Capitol, this plushly restored historic warehouse is abuzz during the week with politicians, press, and lobbyists. It's a perfect location for business travelers involved with the state, and on weekends, for tourists who want to tour the Old Capitol and other downtown sites.

Rooms are a rich blend of mahogany, brass, and classic prints. The VIP treatment includes airport pickup, breakfast, cocktails, robes, shoe shine, and a daily paper. *209 S. Adams St., 32301, tel. 904/681–6855, 800/342–7717 in FL, fax 904/222–3105. 41 units. AE, D, DC, MC, V. Very Expensive.*

Las Casas. The quiet courtyard with its own pool and the darkly welcoming cantina (where a complimentary Continental breakfast and evening cocktail are served) convey the look of old Spain. Rooms are furnished in heavy Mediterranean style. *2801 N. Monroe St., 32303, tel. 904/386–8286, 800/521–0948 in FL, fax 904/422–1074. 112 rooms. Facilities: heated pool. AE, D, DC, MC, V. Moderate.*

Tallahassee Sheraton. Bustling and upscale, the hotel hosts heavy hitters from the worlds of politics and media who can walk from here to the Capitol. *101 S. Adams St., 32301, tel. 904/224–5000 or 800/325–3535, fax 904/224–5000. 246 rooms. Facilities: pool, restaurant, lobby bar, lounge with entertainment, gift shop. AE, D, DC, MC, V. Moderate.*

Valparaiso/Niceville
Dining

Flags. Colorful banners of many nations flutter from the lobby's vaulted ceiling, and don't be surprised if the people at the next table are tête-a-têting in a foreign tongue. But these international vacationers usually want local dishes, so the chef's specialty is grouper Floridian sautéed and dressed with pecans and orange zest, flamed in Grand Marnier and served with citrus. Elegantly set tables on two tiers give diners a view of the dockside action. *300 Yacht Club Dr., Niceville, tel. 904/897–2186. Reservations accepted. Dress: casual. MC, V. Inexpensive–Moderate.*

Lodging
★

Bluewater Bay Resort. This upscale residential resort is carved out of 1,800 acres of pines and oaks on the shores of Choctawhatchee Bay. It's still woodsy around the edges, but showcase homes are surrounded by tenderly manicured gardens. Rentals run the gamut from motel rooms to villas, some with fireplaces and fully equipped kitchens, and patio homes. Check-out information in the rental units is translated into German for the benefit of the international visitors who flock to this golf course–rich region. *Rte. 20E, Box 247, Niceville, 32578, tel. 904/897–3613, 800/874–2128 outside FL, fax 904/897–2424. 134 units. Facilities: 2,000-ft private beach, 3 pools, 36 holes of golf, 21 tennis courts, marina, playground, exercise room, 2 restaurants, lounge. AE, D, DC, MC, V. Moderate–Expensive.*

The Arts and Nightlife

The Arts

Broadway touring shows, top-name entertainers, and concert artists are booked into the **Marina Civic Center** (8 Harrison Ave., Panama City, tel. 904/769–1217), the **Tallahassee-Leon County Civic Center** (505 W. Pensacola St., Tallahassee, tel. 904/487–1691), and the **Saenger Theatre** (118 S. Palafox St., Pensacola, tel. 904/444–7686).

Concerts

Okaloosa Symphony Orchestra (tel. 904/244–3308) performs a series of concerts featuring guest artists at Rita Schaeffer Hall (38 S.W. Robinwood Dr., Fort Walton Beach). **Pensacola Symphony Orchestra** (tel. 904/435–2533) presents a series of five concerts each season at the Saenger Theatre (118 S. Palafox St.).

Florida State University School of Music (tel. 904/644–4774), in Tallahassee, stages 350 concerts and recitals a year.

The **Tallahassee Symphony Orchestra** (tel. 904/224–0461) performs at Florida State University, September–April.

The **Capitol City Band** (tel. 904/893–8303) has been brandishing its brass in Tallahassee since 1924.

Dance **The Northwest Florida Ballet** (101 S.E. Chicago Ave., Fort Walton Beach, tel. 904/664–7787) has a repertoire of the classics and performs in communities throughout the Panhandle.

Opera The **Monticello Opera House** (U.S. 90E, tel. 904/997–4242) presents operas in the restored gaslight-era playhouse, near Tallahassee.

Theater **Florida State University** (tel. 904/644–6500) in Tallahassee presents 15–20 productions a year.

The **Pensacola Little Theatre** (186 N. Palafox St., tel. 904/432–8621) presents plays and musicals during a season that runs from fall through spring.

Stage Crafters Community Theatre (U.S. 98W, tel. 904/243–1102) stages four first-rate amateur productions a year at the Fort Walton Beach Civic Auditorium.

Nightlife

Northwest Florida's nightlife falls on the scale somewhere between uptown Manhattan supper clubs and Las Vegas–style dinner shows. There are places that cater especially to the night owls, but some of the family restaurants also take on a different character when the sun goes down.

Destin **Nightown** (140 Palmetto St., tel. 904/837–6448) has a dance floor with laser lights and a New Orleans–style bar with a live band.

Fort Walton Beach Catch the action at **Cash's Faux Pas Lounge** (106 Santa Rosa Blvd., tel. 904/244–2274), where anything goes. **Jamaica Joe's** (790 Santa Rosa Blvd., tel. 904/244–4137) features a DJ and drink specials that appeal to younger pub crawlers.

Panama City **Pineapple Willie's** (9900 Beach Blvd., tel. 904/235–0928) alter-
Beach nately features big-band and rock music and caters to the post-college crowd.

Pensacola After dark, **McGuire's Irish Pub** (600 E. Gregory St., tel. 904/433–6789) welcomes anyone of legal drinking age, particularly those of Irish descent. If you don't like crowds, stay away from McGuire's on Friday night and nights when Notre Dame games are televised. **Mesquite Charlie's** (5901 N. W St., tel. 904/434–0498) offers good ol' down-home pickin' and grinnin' with live entertainment that keeps the crowd singin' up a storm. **Seville Quarter** (130 E. Government St., tel. 904/434–6211), with five fabulous bars featuring music from disco to Dixieland, is

Pensacola's equivalent to the New Orleans French Quarter. **Tickets** at the Pensacola Hilton (200 E. Gregory St., tel. 904/433–3336) is the spot for those who dip when they dance but still like to boogie.

Tallahassee Stop by **Andrew's Upstairs** (228 S. Adams St., tel. 904/222–3446) to hear contemporary jazz and reggae.

13 Northeast Florida

By Janet and Gordon Groene

Updated by Ann Hughes

In Northeast Florida you'll find some of the oldest settlements in the state—indeed in all of the United States—though this region didn't get much attention from outsiders until Union Army troops came through here during the Civil War. Their rapturous accounts of the mild climate, pristine beaches, and lush vegetation captured the imagination of folks up north. First came the speculators and the curiosity seekers; the advent of the railroads brought more permanent settlers; and finally, with the invention of the automobile, came the snowbirds, seasonal residents escaping from harsh northern winters. They still come, to sop up the sun on the beaches that stretch all along the Atlantic coastline; to tee 'em up in this year-round golfer's paradise; to bass fish and bird watch in the forests and parks; and to party in the cabanas and barrooms of Daytona (which has the dubious honor of replacing Fort Lauderdale as the destination of choice for spring break).

When Orlando's new cinema industry scouts for filming locations, it can find almost any setting it needs in Northeast Florida. Towering, tortured live oaks, plantations, and antebellum-style architecture symbolize the Old South, and the mossy marshes of Silver Springs and the St. Johns River look today as they did generations ago when Tarzan movies were filmed in the jungles here. Jacksonville is a modern metropolis abounding with skyscrapers; Payne's Prairie, near Gainesville, looks like it's a lost prehistoric stomping ground; county seats such as De Land and Green Cove Springs are reminiscent of Thornton Wilder's *Our Town*.

Horse farms around Ocala have a look of Kentucky's bluegrass country or the hunt clubs of Virginia; towns in the Big Bend region along the Gulf resemble ramshackle New England fishing villages. Glamorous resorts along the Atlantic coast outdo hotels in Maui and Oahu for opulence and glitz, while backwoods communities like Cross Creek have the rustic flavor of Appalachian hamlets. St. Augustine's missions are a match for any of southern California's. And the beaches, spreading in shimmering, sandy glory south from Fernandina, vary in likeness from the stony shores of the North Sea to the deep, hot sands of the Caribbean.

Essential Information

Important Addresses and Numbers

Tourist Information

Amelia Island–Fernandina Beach Chamber of Commerce (102 Centre St., tel. 904/261–3248) is open weekdays 9–5.

Cocoa Beach Area Chamber of Commerce (400 Fortenberry Rd., Merritt Island, FL 32952, tel. 407/459–2200) is open weekdays 8:30–5.

Destination Daytona! (126 E. Orange Ave., tel. 904/255–0415 or 800/854–1234) is open weekdays 9–5.

Gainesville Chamber of Commerce (300 E. University Ave., tel. 904/336–7100) is open weekdays 8:30–5.

Jacksonville and Its Beaches Convention & Visitors Bureau (6 E. Bay St., Suite 200, tel. 904/353–9736) is open weekdays 8–5.

Ocala–Marion County Chamber of Commerce (110 E. Silver Springs Blvd., tel. 904/629–8051) is open weekdays 8:30–5.

St. Augustine Visitor Information Center (10 Castillo Dr., tel. 904/825–1000) is open daily 8:30–5:30.

Emergencies Dial 911 for **police** or **ambulance** assistance in life-threatening situations.

Hospitals Emergency rooms are open 24 hours at the following: In **Daytona,** Halifax Medical Center (303 N. Clyde Morris Blvd., tel. 904/254–4100). In **Gainesville,** Alachua General (801 S.W. 2nd Ave., tel. 904/372–4321). In **Jacksonville,** St. Luke's Hospital (4201 Belfort Rd., tel. 904/296–3700). In **Ocala,** Munroe Regional Medical Center (131 S.W. 15th St., tel. 904/351–7200).

24-Hour The only 24-hour pharmacy in the area is **Eckerd Drug** (4397
Pharmacies Roosevelt Blvd., Jacksonville, tel. 904/389–0314).

Arriving and Departing

By Plane The main airport for the region is **Jacksonville International.** It is served by American (tel. 800/433–7300), American Eagle (tel. 800/433–7300), Comair (tel. 800/354–9822), Continental (tel. 800/525–0280), Delta (tel. 800/221–1212), TWA (tel. 800/221–2000), United (tel. 800/241–6522), and USAir (tel. 800/428–4322). Vans from the Jacksonville airport to area hotels cost $16 per person. Taxi fare is about $20 to downtown, $40 to the beaches and Amelia Island. Among the limousine services, which must be booked in advance, is **AAA Limousine Service** (tel. 904/751–4800 or 800/780–1705), which charges $20 for one or two persons to downtown ($8 for each additional person), $40 to the beaches and to Amelia Island.

Daytona Beach Regional Airport is served by American, Continental, Delta, and USAir. Taxi fare to beach hotels is about $8–$10; cab companies include **Yellow Cab** (tel. 904/252–5536), **Checker Cab** (tel. 904/255–8421), **AAA Cab** (tel. 904/253–2522), and **City Cab** (tel. 904/253–0675). **DOTS Transit Service** (tel. 904/257–5411) has scheduled service connecting the Daytona Beach Airport to Orlando International Airport, the Palm Coast Sheraton area, De Land, De Land's Amtrak station, Sanford, and Deltona; fares to the Orlando airport are $26 one way and $46 round-trip from Daytona; $20 one way and $36 round-trip from De Land or Deltona.

Gainesville Regional Airport is served by Delta, USAir, Comair, and ASA (tel. 800/282–3424). Taxi fare to the center of Gainesville is about $10; some hotels provide free airport pickup.

By Car East–west traffic travels the northern part of the state on I–10, which is a cross-country highway stretching from Los Angeles to Jacksonville. Farther south, I–4 rambles east from Tampa to Orlando, then northeast to the sea. Signs indicate this east–west orientation, which can be confusing when you're driving north (signs say east) from Orlando to Daytona Beach.

By Train **Amtrak** (tel. 800/USA–RAIL) schedules stops in Jacksonville, De Land, Waldo (near Gainesville), Ocala, and Palatka. The Auto Train serves Sanford from the Washington, DC, area. Schedules vary depending on the season.

By Bus **Greyhound/Trailways** serves the region, with stations in Jacksonville (tel. 904/356–9976), St. Augustine (tel. 904/829–6401), Gainesville (tel. 904/376–5252), Daytona Beach (tel. 904/255–7076), and De Land (tel. 904/734–2747).

Getting Around

By Car Chief north–south routes are I–95 along the east coast, and I–75, which enters Florida south of Valdosta, Georgia, and joins the Sunshine Parkway toll road at Wildwood. If you want to drive as close to the Atlantic as possible, and are not in a hurry, stick with A1A (although the name changes several times along the way). Where there are no bridges across inlets, cars must return to the mainland. Where there are bridges, openings and closings cause unexpected delays. While I–75 is the fast route from Georgia to Tampa and points south, U.S. 19–98 takes you closer to the Gulf, for quick forays into coastal communities, beaches, and fishing villages.

Scenic Drives The **Buccaneer Trail** (Route A1A) on the Atlantic Coast goes from Mayport (where a ferry is part of the state highway system), through marshlands and beaches into Fort Clinch State Park, with its massive brick fortress, then into the 300-year-old seaport town of Fernandina Beach.

Route 13 takes you up one side of the St. Johns River, through has-been hamlets. **U.S. 17** travels the west side of the river, passing through Green Cove Springs and Palatka, where Ravine State Gardens' mountains of spring azaleas bloom.

State Road 19 runs north and south through the Ocala National Forest, giving a nonstop view of stately pines and bold wildlife. Short side roads lead to parks, springs, picnic areas, and campgrounds.

Riverside Drive, where New Smyrna Beach's grand old homes line the Intracoastal Waterway, is a picturesque throughway.

By Bus Daytona Beach has an excellent bus network, **Votran** (tel. 904/761–7600), that serves the beach area, airport, shopping malls, and major arteries. Exact fare is required.

By Water Taxi Connecting the banks of the St. Johns River to different points of interest in the downtown Jacksonville area, this system puts many attractions within easy reach of one another. Round-trip fare is $3 adults, $2 senior citizens; $1.50 one way. Water taxis run every 15 minutes.

Guided Tours

Daytona Beach Helicopter flights are booked at **Space Coast Helicopter Services** (tel. 904/724–4191) in Palm Bay. **Dixie Queen Riverboat Cruises** (tel. 904/255–1997 or 800/329–6225) runs lunch, brunch, dinner, and specialty cruises throughout the Daytona Beach area.

Jacksonville City tours of Jacksonville are offered by **Jacksonville Historical Society Tours** (tel. 904/396–6307). **Europa Cruise Line Ltd.** (tel. 800/688–7529) has a daily "cruise to nowhere" from Mayport, wowing the entire family with boffo buffets, floor shows, games, dancing, casino gambling (for adults only), and other cruise ship hoopla.

Northeast Florida **Suwannee Country Tours** (White Springs, tel. 904/397–2347), run by the Florida Council of American Youth Hostels, organizes bicycle and canoe trips on some of the state's most unspoiled and unique roads and waters. Stay overnight in country inns, picnic in ghost towns, eat at country churches, and explore forgotten sites.

Exploring Northeast Florida

Much of this region's tourist territory lies along the Atlantic coast, starting just across the Georgia border with Amelia Island and running on down through Jacksonville, St. Augustine, Daytona, and eventually Cocoa Beach. The following tours follow this route, but then swing inland to visit some charming, lesser-known towns, such as Deltona, De Land, De Leon Springs, Barberville, and Crescent City, on the way to the sprawling Ocala National Forest. Stay on this route to the city of Ocala, then head north to Gainesville for the last leg of your trip.

Highlights For First-Time Visitors

Birthplace of Speed Museum (Daytona Beach Area)
Castillo de San Marcos National Monument (St. Augustine)
Fort Clinch State Park (Jacksonville/Jacksonville Beach)
Kingsley Plantation (Jacksonville/Jacksonville Beach)
Lightner Museum (St. Augustine)
Marjorie Kinnan Rawlings Historical Site (Gainesville)
Ocala National Forest (Ocala)
Payne's Prairie State Preserve (Gainesville)
Silver Springs (Ocala)
Spaceport USA, Cocoa Beach

Jacksonville and Jacksonville Beach

Numbers in the margin correspond to points of interest on the Northeast Florida map.

One of the oldest cities in Florida and, in terms of square miles ❶ (730), the largest city in the United States, **Jacksonville** is an underrated tourist destination. Recently, it has had to grapple with a reputation as an unsafe drive-through, but police patrols along I–295 have succeeded in holding highway hooliganism in check. It continues its battle against the stench of the sulfur pulp mill that kept many travelers speeding straight on through. But if you do stop, you'll find handsome, well-established residential neighborhoods, a thriving arts scene, and some of the best beaches in the state. Remnants of the Old South flavor the city, though it also maintains the sense of subtropical paradise for which Florida is famous.

Because Jacksonville was settled around the St. Johns River, many attractions are on or near one riverbank or the other. On the map the twists of the river and its estuaries resemble the cardiovascular system on an anatomical chart. To avoid crossing back and forth, you may want to sit down and plan your trip carefully. Some attractions can be reached by water taxi (*see* Getting Around, *above*), but for most, a car is necessary.

Jacksonville's Museum of Science and History presents hands-on exhibits, live animals, temporary displays, and a planetarium with free astronomy programs. Devote an entire day to this museum, and lunch in the café. Located downtown on the south bank, the museum can be reached by water taxi. *1025 Museum Circle, tel. 904/396–7062. Admission: $5 adults, $3 senior citi-*

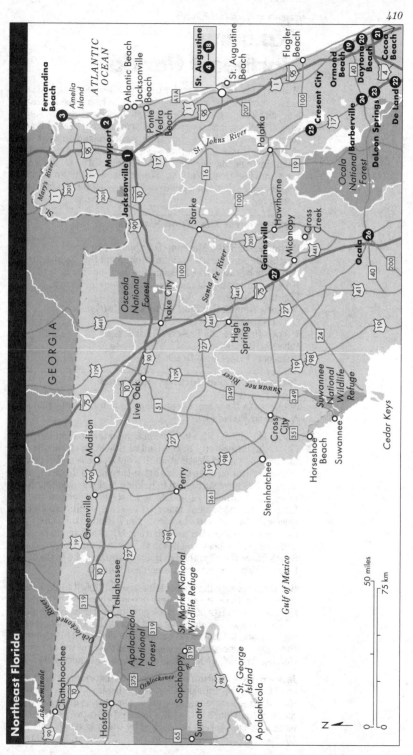

Northeast Florida

zens, $3 children, children under 4 free. Open Mon.–Fri. 10–5, Sat. 10–6, Sun. 1–6.

Also on the south side of the river, though not on the water taxi route, the **Jacksonville Art Museum** brings together contemporary and classic arts. Especially noteworthy are the Koger collection of Oriental porcelains and the pre-Columbian collection of rare artifacts. Special exhibits, film and lecture series, and workshops make this destination worthy of more than one visit. *4160 Boulevard Center Dr., tel. 904/398–8336. Admission free. Open Tues., Wed., Fri. 10–4, Thurs. 10–10, weekends 1–5; closed Mon.*

The **Cummer Gallery of Art,** situated on the northwest side of the river, amidst leafy formal gardens, occupies a former baron's estate home. The permanent collection of more than 2,000 items includes one of the nation's largest troves of early Meissen porcelain as well as the works of some impressive Old Masters. *829 Riverside Ave., tel. 904/356–6857. Admission: $3 adults, $2 senior citizens, $1 students and children. Open Tues.–Fri. 10–4, Sat. noon–5, Sun. 2–5. Closed Mon.*

The **Alexander Brest Museum,** located on the river's east bank, on the campus of Jacksonville University, has a small but important collection of Steuben glass, Boehm porcelain, ivories, and pre-Columbian artifacts. The home of composer Frederick Delius is also on the campus and is open for tours, upon request. *2800 University Blvd. N, tel. 904/744–3950, ext. 3371. Admission free. Open weekdays 9–4:30, Sat. 12–5. Closed school holidays.*

Jacksonville's sensational beaches spread south from Mayport at the mouth of the St. Johns River. They're about a half-hour's drive from downtown, via Routes 10 and 202 or U.S. 90. **Atlantic Beach** was developed (in 1901) by railroad magnate Henry Flagler, as were many others down the Atlantic Coast. Now a condo complex, the once-grand Atlantic Beach Hotel was built here in 1929. Neighboring **Neptune Beach** is a quiet bedroom community. **Jacksonville Beach,** once called Ruby Beach and later Pablo Beach, was a tent city in 1884 when a narrow-gauge railway came through, spurring development; a 350-room hotel was built here then, though it burned down in 1890. Today, it's a solid resort community with several new beach hotels. **Ponte Vedra Beach,** now the home of the Tournament Players Club and American Tennis Professionals, has been popular with golfers since 1922 when the National Lead Company built a nine-hole course for its workers to play.

② For an interesting excursion in the Jacksonville area, start with the ferry to **Mayport** (located 3 miles east of A1A). Dating back more than 300 years, Mayport is one of the oldest fishing villages in the United States. Today it's home to a large commercial shrimp boat fleet and is the Navy's fourth-largest home port. *Ferry tel. 904/246–2922. Ferry admission: $2.50 per car, 50¢ pedestrians. Ferry runs daily 6:20 AM–10 PM, every ½ hour. Naval station tel. 904/270–NAVY. Admission to naval station free. Open Sat. 10–4:30, Sun. 1–4:30.*

Travel south on A1A to Route 10; drive for about 2 miles to Girven Road; follow signs to the replica of **Fort Caroline National Monument.** The original fort was built in the 1560s by French Huguenots who were later slaughtered by the Spanish. The site, which is the scene of the first major clash between European powers for control of what would become the United States, maintains the memory of a brief French presence in this area. Today, it's a sunny place to picnic (bring your own food and drink), stretch your legs, and explore a small museum. *12713 Fort Caroline Rd., tel. 904/641–7111. Admission free. Museum open daily 9–5. Closed Christmas.*

Take Fort Caroline Road west to Route 9A, on which you'll travel for 3 miles, crossing the N.B. Broward Bridge (locally known as Danes Point Bridge). Take the first exit (S.R. 105) and drive northeast for about 12 miles to Fort George Island, where signs will lead you to the **Kingsley Plantation.** Built by an eccentric slave trader, the Kingsley dates to 1792 and is the oldest remaining plantation in the state. Slave quarters, as well as the modest Kingsley home, are open to the public. *Tel. 904/ 251–3537. Admission free. Open daily 9–5. Guided tours Thurs.–Mon. 9:30, 11, 1:30, and 3.*

From the plantation, drive northeast on A1A for about 5 miles to **Little Talbot Island State Park**—a gorgeous stretch of sand dunes, endless beaches, and golden marshes that hum with birds and bugs. Come to picnic, fish, swim, snorkel, or camp. *Tel. 904/251–2320. Admission: $3.25 per vehicle with up to 8 people. Open daily 8 AM–sunset.*

❸ The town of **Fernandina Beach** lies north of Jacksonville on **Amelia Island,** across the border from St. Marys, Georgia. Take A1A east off I–95 or, for a more fun and leisurely approach, drive north on A1A from the Jacksonville beaches; take the Mayport ferry across the St. Johns River, then drive the Buccaneer Trail (A1A). Once an important political and commercial stronghold, now a quaint haven for in-the-know tourists, Fernandina Beach offers a wide range of accommodations from bed-and-breakfasts to Amelia Island Plantation (*see* Dining and Lodging, *below*), a sprawling resort.

The town's 30-block historic district includes the old cemetery where names on gravestones reveal the waves of immigrants who settled here: Spanish, French, Minorcan, Portuguese, and English. In **Old Town** you'll see some of the nation's finest examples of Queen Anne, Victorian, and Italianate mansions dating back to the haven's glory days of the mid-19th century. Begin your self-guided walking or driving tour of the historic district with a visit to the old railroad depot, originally a stopping point on the first cross-state railroad and now the **Amelia Island–Fernandina Beach Chamber of Commerce** (102 Centre St., tel. 904/261–3248; open weekdays 9–5).

Follow Centre Street (which turns into Atlantic Avenue) for about eight blocks to **St. Peter's Episcopal Church.** Founded in 1859, the church once served as a school for freed slaves. Continuing on Atlantic Avenue, you will reach the bridge. From here you can see the **Amelia Lighthouse,** built in 1839. It's a great background for photos, but the inside is not open to the public.

A couple of blocks farther is **Fort Clinch State Park,** home to one of the country's best-preserved and most complete brick forts. Fort Clinch served to protect against further British intrusion after the War of 1812 and was occupied in 1847 by the Confederacy; a year later it was retaken by the north. During the Spanish-American War it was reactivated for a brief time but for the most part was not used. Today the park offers camping, nature trails, carriage rides, swimming, surf fishing, picnicking, and living history reenactments showing life in the garrison at the time of the Civil War. *Tel. 904/261–4212. Admission: $3.25 per vehicle with up to 8 people. Open daily 8 AM–sunset.*

Time Out **The Palace Saloon** (117 Centre St., tel. 904/261–6320) is the state's oldest continuously operating watering hole, still sporting swinging doors straight out of Dodge City. Stop in for a cold drink and a bowl of boiled shrimp. The menu is limited, but the place is unpretentious, comfortable, and as genuine as a silver dollar.

St. Augustine

To reach **St. Augustine,** take U.S. 1 south about 45 minutes from Jacksonville's city limits. Upon arrival, head straight for the **Visitor Information Center** (10 Castillo Dr., tel. 904/825–1000), where you'll find loads of brochures, maps, and information about the nation's oldest city. Once you've visited the historic sites, however, you haven't exhausted this city's charms—it also has 43 miles of wide, white, level Atlantic Ocean beaches.

Numbers in the margin correspond to points of interest on the St. Augustine map.

The massive **Castillo de San Marcos National Monument** hunkers over Matanzas Bay, and looks every century of its 300 years. Park rangers provide an introductory narration, after which you're on your own. This is a wonderful fort to explore, complete with moat, turrets, and 16-foot-thick walls. The fort was constructed of coquina, a soft limestone made of broken shells and coral, and it took 25 years to build it. Garrison rooms depict the life of the era, and special artillery demonstrations are held periodically on the gun deck. *1 Castillo Dr., tel. 904/ 829–6506. Admission: $2 adults, children under 16 and senior citizens over 62 free. Open daily 8:30–5:30; winter months 8:45–4:45.*

The **City Gate,** at the top of St. George Street, is a relic from the days when the Castillo's moat ran westward to the river and the Cubo Defense Line (defensive wall) protected the settlement against approaches from the north. Today it is the entrance to the city's popular restored area.

Stop by the **Museum Theatre** to see one of two historical films shown several times daily: One tells the story of the founding of the city in 1565, and the other depicts life in St. Augustine in 1576. *5 Cordova St., tel. 904/824–0339. Admission: $3 adults, $1.50 children under 15. Open daily 9–5.*

The **Oldest Wooden Schoolhouse** (14 St. George St.) is a tiny, 18th-century structure that, because it was the closest structure to the city gates, served as a guardhouse and sentry shelter during the Seminole Wars.

The **Spanish Quarter** is a state-operated, living-history village with eight sites; you can wander through the narrow streets at your own pace. Along your way you may see a Colonial soldier's wife cooking over an open fire; a blacksmith building his shop (a historic reconstruction); and craftsmen busy at candle dipping, spinning, weaving, and cabinetmaking. They are all making reproductions that will be used within the restored area. *En-*

Basilica Cathedral, **10**
Castillo de San Marcos National Monument, **5**
City Gate, **6**
Flagler College, **15**
Flagler Memorial Church, **16**
Fountain of Youth, **18**
Lightner Museum, **14**
Mission of Nombre de Dios, **17**
Museum Theatre, **7**
Oldest House, **13**
Oldest Wooden Schoolhouse, **8**
Oldest Store Museum, **12**
Spanish Quarter, **9**
Ximenez-Fatio House, **11**

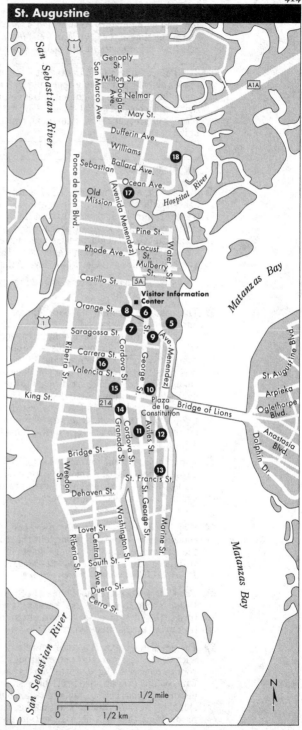

St. Augustine

trance at Triay House, 29 St. George St., near the Old City Gate, tel. 904/825–6830. Admission: $5 adults, $3.75 senior citizens, $2.50 students 6–18; $10 family ticket. Open daily 9–5.

Time Out | **Spanish Bakery,** behind Casa de Calcedo on St. George Street, has meat turnovers, cookies, and fresh-baked bread made from a Colonial recipe.

⑩ Basilica Cathedral of St. Augustine has parish records dating back to 1594, the oldest written records in the country. Following a fire in 1887, extensive changes were made to the current structure, which dates from 1797. It was remodeled in the mid-1960s. *40 Cathedral Pl., tel. 904/824–2806. Admission free, but donations accepted. Open weekdays 5:30–5, weekends 5:30 AM–7 PM.*

Plaza de la Constitution, at St. George Street and Cathedral Place, is the central area of the original settlement. It was laid out in 1598 by decree of King Philip II, and little has changed since. At its center there is a monument to the Spanish constitution of 1812; at the east end is a public market dating from early American days. Just beyond is a statue of Juan Ponce de León, who discovered Florida in 1513.

⑪ The **Ximenez-Fatio House** was built in 1797, and it became a boarding house for tourists in 1885. *20 Aviles St., tel. 904/829–3575. Admission free. Open Mar. 1–Aug. 31, Sun.–Thurs. 1–4.*

⑫ The **Oldest Store Museum** re-creates a turn-of-the-century general store. There are high-button shoes, lace-up corsets, patent drugs, and confectionery specialties. *4 Artillery La., tel. 904/829–9729. Admission: $3.50 adults, $3 senior citizens, $1.50 children 6–12. Open Mon.–Sat. 9–5, Sun. noon–5.*

⑬ Operated by the Historical Society, the **Oldest House** reflects much of the city's history through its changes and additions, from the coquina walls built soon after the town was burned in 1702 to the house's enlargement during the British occupation. *14 St. Francis St., tel. 904/824–2872. Admission: $5 adults, $4.50 senior citizens, $2.50 students, $10 family ticket. Open daily 9–5.*

⑭ The **Lightner Museum** is housed in one of two posh hotels built in 1888 by Henry Flagler, who wanted to turn Florida into an American Riviera. The museum contains a collection of ornate antique music boxes (ask about demonstrations!), and the Lightner Antique Mall perches on three levels of what was the hotel's grandiose indoor pool. *75 King St., tel. 904/824–2874. Admission to museum: $4 adults, $1 students, children under 12 free. Museum open daily 9–5; mall open Tues.–Sun. 10–4.*

⑮ Across from the Lightner Museum, **Flagler College** occupies the second of Flagler's hotels. The riveting structure is replete with towers, turrets, and arcades decorated by Louis Comfort Tiffany. The front courtyard is open to the public.

⑯ At Valencia and Sevilla streets, behind Flagler College, the **Flagler Memorial Presbyterian Church,** which Flagler built in 1889, is a splendid Venetian Renaissance structure. The dome towers more than 100 feet, and it is topped by a 20-foot Greek cross. *Open Mon.–Sat. 9–5.*

⑰ Away from the historic district, the **Mission of Nombre de Dios** commemorates the site where America's first Christian mass was celebrated. A 208-foot stainless-steel cross marks the spot where the mission's first cross was planted. *San Marco Ave. and Old Mission Rd., tel. 904/824–2809. Admission free, but donations requested. Open summer weekdays 8–8, weekends 9–8; winter weekdays 8–5:30, weekends 9–5.*

⑱ The **Fountain of Youth** salutes Ponce de León. In the complex there is a springhouse, an explorer's globe, a planetarium, and an Indian village. *155 Magnolia Ave., tel. 904/829–3168. Admission: $4 adults, $3 senior citizens, $1.50 children 6–12, under 6 free. Open daily 9–5.*

Daytona Beach Area

Numbers in the margin correspond to points of interest on the Northeast Florida map.

Allow a good hour to make the trip from St. Augustine to Daytona on the interstate, an additional 15 minutes if you take the scenic route along A1A. Like most of coastal Florida, Daytona sprang up around the water, so its waterfront offers views of historic homes between expanses of natural marsh. As you venture along the Intracoastal Waterway, take note of the different names assigned to the passage. In the Daytona area, it's called the Halifax River, though it is not actually a river, but a tidal waterway that flows between the mainland and the barrier islands.

A good place to begin touring the Daytona environs is along a segment of Old Dixie Highway. From I–95 north of Ormond Beach, take Exit 90 and travel east. The first left off Old Dixie Highway (Kings Highway) will take you to the entrance of **Bulow Plantation Ruins State Historic Site,** built in 1821. From the entrance, a winding dirt road cuts through tangled vegetation and leads to a picnic area and day-use facilities facing Bulow Creek. All that remains of the plantation are the massive ruins of the sugar mill, which may be reached either by auto or bicycle along a one-way loop road, or on foot via a scenic walking trail from the picnic area. *Tel. 904/439–2219. Admission: $2 per car. Open daily 9–5.*

Continue southeast on Old Dixie Highway through a tunnel of vine-laced oaks and cabbage palms. Next stop is **Tomoka State Park,** site of a Timucuan Indian settlement discovered in 1605 by Spanish explorer Alvaro Mexia. Wooded campsites, bicycle and walking paths, and guided canoe tours on the Tomoka and Halifax rivers are the main attractions. *2099 N. Beach St., Ormond Beach, tel. 904/676–4050. Admission: June 1–Dec. 31, $8 per day; Jan. 1–May 31, $15 per day; electricity, $2 per day. Open daily 8 AM–sunset.*

⑲ Time moves forward and the canopy begins to thin as you travel east on Old Dixie Highway to **Ormond Beach.** Auto racing was born on this hard-packed beach back in 1902, when R. E. Olds and Alexander Winton staged the first race. **Birthplace of Speed Antique Car Show and Swap Meet** is an annual event, attracting enthusiasts from across the nation. Sportsmen and socialites flocked to Ormond Beach each winter and made the massive Ormond Hotel their headquarters. The grand old wooden hotel (built in 1888 to pamper Flagler's East Coast

Railway passengers) still stands watch on the east bank of the Halifax, but it is now vacant and no longer entertains guests.

Across the street from the hotel is **The Casements,** the restored winter retreat of John D. Rockefeller, now serving as a cultural center and museum. The estate and its formal gardens host an annual lineup of special events and exhibits. Tours of the estate also are offered. *25 Riverside Dr., Ormond Beach, tel. 904/673–4701. Admission free, but donations are accepted. Open Mon.–Thurs. 9–9, Fri. 9–5, Sat. 9–noon.*

From the Casements go two blocks east to the **Birthplace of Speed Museum.** Devoted to the most exciting moments in America's long love affair with the automobile, the museum exhibits a replica of the Stanley Steamer, old Model T and Model A Fords, and a wealth of auto racing memorabilia. *160 E. Granada Blvd., Ormond Beach, tel. 904/676–3216. Admission: $1 adults, 50¢ children under 12. Open Tues.–Sat. 1–5.*

㉒ Take A1A about 8 miles south to **Daytona Beach,** driving down Beach Street on the mainland. In the old downtown section is the **Halifax Historical Society Museum.** Photographs, Native American artifacts, and war memorabilia relevant to this area's fascinating, varied past are on display here. You can also shop for gifts and antiques. *252 S. Beach St., Daytona Beach, tel. 904/255–6976. Admission: $2 adults, 50¢ children 12 and under. Open Tues.–Sat. 10–4.*

Pick up Volusia Avenue and drive west to Nova Road. Go two blocks south and follow signs to Museum Boulevard and the **Museum of Arts and Sciences.** This competent little museum has two blockbuster features: One is a large collection of pre-Castro Cuban art; the other is a complete and eye-popping skeleton of a giant sloth. The sloth remains—found near here—are the most complete skeleton of its kind ever found in North America. *1040 Museum Blvd., Daytona Beach, tel. 904/255–0285. Admission: $3 adults, $1 children and students; members free Fri. Open Tues.–Fri. 9–4, weekends noon–5.*

To reach the famous beaches of Daytona Beach, go east to A1A and follow signs to beach ramps, which lie for miles both north and south. During spring break, race weeks, and summer holidays, expect heavy traffic along this strip of garishly painted beach motels and tacky souvenir shops.

Several miles south of the Marriott, on A1A, is **Ponce Inlet,** which is frequented by locals and visitors who are familiar with the area. A manicured drive winds through low-growing shrubs and windblown scrub oaks to parking and picnic areas. Boardwalks traverse the delicate dunes and provide easy access to the wide beach. Marking this prime spot is a bright red century-old **lighthouse,** now a historic monument and museum. *Tel. 904/761–1821 or 904/767–3425. Admission $3 adults, $1 children. Open daily 10–5.*

Time Out   **Lighthouse Landing** (4931 S. Peninsula Dr., tel. 904/761–1821), only yards from the historic light, is a good place for sipping cocktails and watching the sunset.

Cocoa Beach

About 1½ hours down the coast on I–95 (slightly longer if you take the scenic route along U.S. 1), is **Cocoa Beach,** home to the Kennedy Space Center and **Spaceport USA,** perhaps the best entertainment bargain in Florida. There are two narrated bus tours: One passes by some of NASA's office and assembly buildings, including current launch facilities and the Space Shuttle launching and landing sites. The other goes to Cape Canaveral Air Force Station, where early launch pads and unmanned rockets that were later adapted for manned use illuminate the history of the early space program. Even more dramatic is the IMAX film *The Dream is Alive,* shown hourly in the Galaxy Theater. Projected onto a five-and-a-half-story screen, this overwhelming 40-minute film, most shot by the astronauts, takes you from astronaut training through a thundering shuttle launch, into the cabins where the astronauts live while in space and aboard the shuttle during flight. In addition, you can stroll through the Spaceport's outdoor rocket garden, lawns bristling with authentic rockets, and tour a museum filled with spacecraft. For a close-up of how space-related products have affected our daily lives, see "Satellites and You," a free multimedia presentation at Spaceport Central. Hosted by an animatronic crew, it takes visitors through a simulated space station. *Kennedy Space Center, tel. 407/452–2121 or 800/432–2153. Admission free. Bus tours: $7 adults, $4 children 3–11. IMAX film: $4 adults, $2 children 3–11. Complex open daily 9 AM–dark; last tour 2 hrs. before dark. Closed Christmas Day and on certain launch dates (call ahead).*

At the **United States Astronaut Hall of Fame** museum, one block east of U.S. 1, at the entrance to Spaceport USA, you can view videotapes of historical moments in the space program. *Tel. 407/269–6100. Admission: $6.95 adults, $4.95 children 3–11. Open daily 9–5, longer in summer; closed Christmas.*

After leaving the Space Center, going toward Cocoa Beach southbound on A1A, the first traffic light you reach marks the entrance to **Port Canaveral,** a once-bustling commercial fishing area where cruise ships and charter and party fishing boats now dock. A few miles farther south on A1A is Cocoa Beach. **Ron Jon Surf Shop** (4151 N. Atlantic Ave., tel. 407/799–8840) is a local attraction in its own right—a castle that's purple, pink, and glittery as an amusement park, plunked right down in the middle of the beach community. In downtown Cocoa Beach, cobblestone walkways wind through **Olde Cocoa Village,** a cluster of restored turn-of-the-century buildings now occupied by restaurants and specialty shops purveying pottery, macrame, leather and silvercraft, afghans, fine art, and clothing.

Take Route 520 to U.S. 1 and Michigan Avenue, then turn west and follow the signs to the **Brevard Museum of History and Natural Science.** Don't overlook the hands-on discovery rooms, and the Taylor Collection of Victorian-era memorabilia. The museum's nature center has 22 acres of trails encompassing three distinct ecosystems—sand pine hills, lakelands, and marshlands. *2201 Michigan Ave., tel. 407/632–1830. Admission: $3 adults, $1.50 senior citizens and students, children under 3 free. Open Tues.–Sat. 10–4, Sun. 1–4.*

From Cocoa Beach, you can take the wonderfully scenic Bee-line Expressway (Rte. 528; toll up to $2.45 for a car) to Orlando, about an hour's drive away.

Inland to Ocala

From Daytona, leave the Atlantic coast and drive west 20 miles on U.S. 92 (International Speedway) toward the hill and lake region, as the topographers call the country surrounding

㉒ Ocala. The gateway to this region is the little town of **De Land,** home of **Stetson University.** The **Gillespie Museum of Minerals,** on the stately campus, houses one of the largest private collections of gems and minerals in the world. *Michigan and Amelia Ave., tel. 904/822-7330. Admission free. Open weekdays 9–noon and 1–4.*

Drive 4 miles south on U.S. 17 (U.S. 92), toward Orange City. Follow signs to **Blue Spring State Park,** a great place to spot manatees. February is the top month for sightings, but you're likely to see one almost any time. The park, once a river port where paddle wheelers stopped to take on cargos of oranges, also includes a historic homestead that is open to the public. Park facilities include camping, picnicking, and hiking. *2100 W. French Ave., Orange City, tel. 904/775-3663. Admission: $3.25 per vehicle with up to 8 people. Open 8 AM–sunset.*

㉓ North from De Land on U.S. 17 is **De Leon Springs,** promoted as a fountain of youth to 1889 winter tourists. Today, the **De Leon Springs State Recreation Area** lets visitors picnic, swim, fish, and hike the nature trails. *Tel. 904/985-4212. Admission: $3.25 per vehicle with up to 8 people. Open daily 8 AM–sunset.*

Northwest of De Leon Springs, at the crossroads of Route 40

㉔ and U.S. 17, in **Barberville,** is the **Pioneer Settlement for the Creative Arts, Inc.** A bridge house, moved from the St. Johns River at Astor, forms the entrance to the museum. On the grounds are an old-time caboose, a railroad depot, the commissary store of a turpentine camp, and a newly constructed "post-and-beam" barn, built of wood milled on the premises. *U.S. 17 and Rte. 40, Barberville, tel. 904/749-2959. Admission: $2.50 adults, $1 children 3-12. Open weekdays 9-3.*

About 20 miles north of Barberville on U.S. 17 is another 1800s

㉕ steamboat stop, **Crescent City,** where the historic **Sprague House Inn** (125 Central Ave., tel. 904/698-2430) traces steamboat-era history through the inn's collection of stained-glass windows. The three-room bed-and-breakfast inn also features a full-service restaurant.

Just east of Barberville on Route 40, you'll reach the eastern boundary of the **Ocala National Forest,** a 366,000-acre wilderness with lakes, springs, rivers, hiking trails, campgrounds, and historic sites. Area residents recall the filming of *The Yearling* at several locations within the forest. There are three major recreational areas in the national forest, from east to west: **Alexander Springs,** off Route 40 (via Route 445 South), featuring a swimming lake and campground; **Salt Springs,** off Route 40 (via Route 19 North), featuring a natural saltwater spring where Atlantic blue crabs come to spawn each summer; and **Juniper Springs,** off Route 40, featuring a picturesque stone waterwheel house, campground, natural-spring swimming pool, and hiking and canoe trails. **Lake Waldena Resort & Camp-**

ground (tel. 904/625–2851), on Route 40, features a white-sand bathing beach and crystal-clear freshwater lake; noncampers pay day-use fees for picnicking and access to the beach.

At the forest's **Visitor Information Center** (tel. 904/625–7470), just inside the western entrance, you can watch old-fashioned sugarcane grinding and cane-syrup making during the first two weeks of November each year. The syrup is bottled and sold on the premises.

At the western edge of the forest is **Silver Springs,** the state's oldest attraction. Established 1890 and listed on the National Register of Historic Landmarks, it features the world's largest collection of artesian springs. Today, the park presents wild animal displays, glass-bottom boat tours in the Silver River, a jungle cruise on the Fort King Waterway, Jungle Safari, an antique and classic car museum, and walks through natural habitats. *Rte. 40, 1 mi east of Ocala, tel. 904/236–2121. Open daily 9–5:30. Admission to all attractions: $20 adults, $15 children 3–10.*

Next door is Silver Springs's **Wild Waters,** a water theme park with a giant wave pool and seven water-flume rides. *Admission: $9.95 adults, $8.95 children 3–10. Open late Mar.–July daily 10–5; Aug. daily 10–7; Sept. weekends only 10–5.*

㉖ The city of **Ocala** is on Route 40 just east of I–75. Once known only as the home of Silver Springs and the Ocala National Forest, Ocala has become a center for thoroughbred breeding and training. Along with the horses have come a new generation of glitterati, with their private jets and massive estates surrounded by green grazing grasses and white fencing. As Ocala matures from country to gentry, its tourist appeal becomes more upscale. Trendy hotels and inns now dot the city; restaurants serve more innovative, international fare; and the **Appleton Museum of Art** anchors a three-building cultural complex. A marble-and-granite tour de force with a serene esplanade and reflecting pool, the Appleton Museum has a collection of more than 6,000 pre-Columbian, Asian, African, and 19th-century objets d'art. *4222 E. Silver Springs Blvd., tel. 904/236–5050. Admission: $3 adults, $3 students, 17 and under free. Open Tues.–Sat. 10–4:30, Sun. 1–5.*

It's an easy 85-mile jaunt from Ocala on down to Orlando (*see* Chapter 9) on I–75 and the Florida Turnpike.

Gainesville

Travel north from Ocala for about an hour on I–75 to **㉗** **Gainesville,** home of the University of Florida. Visitors to Gainesville are mostly Gators football fans and parents with kids enrolled at the university, so styles and prices are geared primarily to modest budgets.

During the 1600s, the largest cattle ranch in Spanish Florida flourished on these great savannas. The area, written about in Marjorie Kinnan Rawlings's *The Yearling* and shown on film in *Cross Creek*, a movie about Rawlings's life, is a place of great vitality and energy—to be discovered by the diligent hiker. Be warned, though, that the shimmering heat can be stupefying to even the most knowledgeable outdoorsperson.

The **Florida State Museum,** on the campus of the University of Florida, will be of interest to the entire family. Explore a replica Mayan palace, see a typical Timucuan household, and walk through a full-size replica of a Florida cave. There are outstanding collections from throughout Florida's history, so spend at least half a day here. *Museum Rd. at Newell Dr., tel. 904/392–1721. Admission free. Open Tues.–Sat. 10–5, Sun. and holidays 1–5; closed Christmas.*

About 11 miles south of Gainesville on U.S. 441 is the village of **Micanopy** (micka-*no*-pee), where Timucuan Indians settled. There was a Spanish mission here, but little remains from before white settlement, which began in 1821. Today, the streets are lined with antiques shops and live oaks. Browse the shops on the main street, or come in the fall for a major antiques event involving 200 dealers.

Paynes Prairie State Preserve, situated between I–75 and U.S. 441 in Micanopy, is a strangely out-of-context site that attests to Florida's fragile, highly volatile ecology. Evidence of Indian habitation dated as early as 7,000 BC has been found on this 18,000-acre wilderness that was once a vast lake. Only a century ago, the lake drained so abruptly that thousands of beached fish died in the mud. The remains of a ferry, stranded here in the 1880s, can still be seen. In recent years buffalo lived here; today persimmon trees, planted by settlers long ago, flourish, and wild cattle and horses roam. Swimming, boating, picnicking, and camping are permitted in the park. *Tel. 904/466–3397. Admission: $3.25 per vehicle with up to 8 people. Open daily 8 AM–sunset.*

At the **Marjorie Kinnan Rawlings State Historic Site,** Rawlings's readers will feel her presence. A typewriter rusts on the ramshackle porch; the closet where she hid her booze during Prohibition yawns open; and clippings from her scrapbook reveal her legal battles and marital problems. Bring lunch and picnic in the shade of one of Rawlings's trees. Then visit her grave a few miles away at peaceful Island Grove. *S.R. 325 at Hawthorn, southeast of Gainesville, tel. 904/466–3672. Admission: $2 adults, $1 children 6–12. Open daily; tours given on the hour Thurs.–Sun. 10–4; closed Thanksgiving, Christmas, and New Year's Day.*

The **Devil's Millhopper State Geological Site** is a botanical wonderland of exotic, subtropical ferns and trees, with a waterfall. The state geological site is situated in and around an enormous 1,100-foot-deep sinkhole. *Off U.S. 441 north of Gainesville, tel. 904/336–2008. Admission: $2 per vehicle, $1 pedestrians. Open daily 9 AM–sunset.*

To return to Jacksonville, head north on Route 24 and U.S. 301, the most direct route, or I–75 north and then I–10. Either way, the trip takes about two hours.

Off the Beaten Track

About 55 miles south of Jacksonville in Palatka is **Ravine State Gardens,** which began during the depression as a WPA project, and blossomed into one of the area's great azalea gardens. The ravines are atypical in flat Florida. They're steep and deep, threaded with brooks and rocky outcroppings, and floored with little flatlands that make for a perfect intimate picnic. Although any month is a good time to hike the shaded glens here, the azaleas are in full bloom February and March. The gardens can be easily reached from Gainesville or St. Augustine. *Off Twig St., from U.S. 17 S, tel. 904/329–3721. Admission: $3.25 per vehicle with up to 8 people. Open daily 8–sunset.*

What to See and Do with Children

Castle Adventure is a slick update of an old-style family fun park, where you can play miniature golf; wander through a giant maze; and explore waterfalls, caves, and lush tropical landscaping. *200 Hagen Terr., Daytona Beach, on U.S. 92, tel. 904/238–3887. Admission: $7 adults, $6 children and senior citizens. Golf alone or maze alone, $4.50 adults, $3.50 children. Open daily 10–10.*

Jacksonville Zoo is best known for its rare white rhinos and an outstanding collection of rare waterfowl. On a 7-acre veldt, see 10 species of African birds and animals. *I–95 N to Hecksher Dr. E, Jacksonville, tel. 904/757–4463. Admission: $4 adults, $2.50 children 3–12, $3 senior citizens. Open daily 9–5.*

Marineland, one of the first of such attractions in the United States, is still a magic place. Dolphins grin, sea lions bark, and seals slither seductively to everyone's delight. *South of St. Augustine on A1A, tel. 904/471–1111 or in FL 800/824–4218. Admission: $12 adults, $9 students 12–18, $7 children 3–11, under 3 free. Open daily 9–5:30, shows held continuously.*

The Fred Bear Museum displays archery artifacts dating to the Stone Age, and a wealth of natural history exhibits all seeable in a one-hour guided tour. *Fred Bear Dr. at Archer Rd., Gainesville, tel. 904/376–2411. Admission: $2.50 adults, $1.50 children 6–12, $6 family ticket. Open daily 8–6.*

At the **Florida Sports Hall of Fame** children can see mementos of more than 100 of their favorite sports heroes. *601 Hall of Fame Dr., off U.S. 90 W, Lake City, tel. 904/758–1310. Admission: $2 adults, children 12 and under free. Open Mon.–Sat. 9–9, Sun. 10–7.*

Shopping

Souvenirs unique to northeast Florida include stuffed manatees, citrus fruits, gems and minerals from De Land, beach-and surf-theme merchandise from along the coast, and auto racing items from Daytona Beach.

For specialty shops, roam around **Jacksonville Landing,** downtown at the Main Street Bridge.

Brand-name items are sold at discount prices at the **Daytona Beach Outlet Mall** (2400 S. Ridgewood Ave., South Daytona, tel. 904/756–8700). Daytona's **Flea Market** is one of the South's largest (I–4 at U.S. 92).

Beaches

Beaches in northeastern Florida are the most varied in the state, ranging from the rocky moonscape of Washington Oaks State Park, just below St. Augustine, to the slick sands of Daytona.

This area's white sand beaches are much less densely built-up than those in the Daytona area. Those below Satellite Beach—south of Cocoa Beach—tend to be rocky, with uneven bottom.

The 57,000-acre **Canaveral National Seashore** (tel. 904/428–3384), just 8 miles south of New Smyrna Beach on A1A, is the home of more than 250 species of birds and animals. The area is undeveloped and hilly with dunes; a self-guided hiking trail leads to the top of an Indian shell midden at Turtle Mound, where picnic tables are available. There's a Visitor Center on A1A. Remote **Playalinda Beach,** part of the National Seashore (tel. 407/267–1110), is the longest stretch of undeveloped coast on Florida's Atlantic Seaboard; hundreds of giant sea turtles come ashore here from May to August to lay their eggs and the extreme northern area is favored by nude sun worshippers. There are no lifeguards, but park rangers patrol. Take Exit 80 from I–95, follow Route 406 east across the Indian River, then Route 402 east for 12 more miles.

Cocoa Beach on A1A has public dressing facilities, showers, playgrounds, picnic areas with grills, snack shops, and plenty of well-maintained, inexpensive surfisde parking lots. Beach vendors offer a variety of necessities for sunning and swimming, and guards are on duty in summer.

Daytona Area **Daytona,** which bills itself as the "World's Most Famous Beach," permits you to drive your car right up to your beachsite, spread out a blanket, and have all your belongings at hand; this is especially convenient for elderly or handicapped beachgoers.

Flagler Beach is a vast, windswept swath of sand with easy access, about 25 miles north of Ormond Beach.

Jacksonville Area **Amelia Island's** lower half is mostly covered by the Amelia Island Plantation resort. However, on the island's extreme southern tip you can go horseback riding along the wide, almost deserted beaches.

Atlantic Beach is a favored surfing area. Around the popular Sea Turtle Inn, you'll find catamaran rentals and instruction. Five areas have lifeguards on duty in the summer 10–6.

Fort Clinch State Park, on Amelia Island's northern tip, includes a municipal beach and pier; you pay a state-park entrance fee to reach them. The beaches are broad and lovely, and there is parking right on the beach, bathhouses, picnic areas, and all the facilities of the park itself, including the fort.

Jacksonville Beach is the liveliest of the long line of Jacksonville Beaches. Young people flock to the beach, where there are all sorts of games to play and also beach concessions, rental shops, and a fishing pier.

Kathryn Abbey Hanna Park, near Mayport, is the Jacksonville area's showplace park, drawing families and singles alike. It offers beaches, showers, and snack bars that operate April–Labor Day.

Neptune Beach, adjoining Jacksonville Beach to the north, is more residential and offers easy access to quieter beaches. Surfers take to the waves, and consider it one of the area's two best surfing sites (the other is Atlantic Beach, *see above*).

St. Augustine Area The young gravitate toward the public beaches at **St. Augustine Beach** and **Vilano Beach,** while families prefer the **Anastasia State Recreation Area.** All three are accessible via Route A1A: Vilano Beach is to the north, across North River, and Anastasia State Park and St. Augustine Beach are both on Anastasia Island, across the Bridge of Lions.

Participant Sports

Boating Pontoon boats, houseboats, and bass boats for the St. Johns River are available from **Hontoon Landing Marina** (De Land, tel. 904/734–2474, or in FL 800/248–2474). Boats for the Tomoka River are offered by **Daytona Recreational Sales & Rentals** (Ormond Beach, tel. 904/672–5631). **Club Nautico** rents boats to members and nonmembers (St. Augustine, tel. 904/825–4848). Other rentals are available from **The Boat Club** (New Smyrna Beach, tel. 904/258–2991).

Canoeing Float down sparkling clear spring "runs" that may be mere tunnels through tangled jungle growth. Try the 7-mile Juniper Springs run in the Ocala National Forest (tel. 904/625–2808) and the Sante Fe River in the O'Leno State Park at High Springs (tel. 904/454–1853).

Fishing Your options range from cane-pole fishing in a roadside canal or off a fishing pier to luxury charters. On the cheaper end of the scale, **Jacksonville Beach Fishing Pier** extends 1,200 feet into the Atlantic, and the cost for fishing is $3 for adults, $1.50 for children and senior citizens, or 50¢ for watching.

Charters Deep-sea fishing charters are provided by **Critter Fleet Marina,** (Daytona Beach, tel. 904/767–7676 or in FL, 800/338–0850), **First Shot Charters** (Ponce Inlet, tel. 904/788–3469), **Cape Marina** (800 Scallop Dr., Port Canaveral, tel. 407/783–8410), or **Pelican Princess** (655 Glen Cheek Dr., Port Canaveral, tel. 407/784–3473).

For sportfishing, charter the *Sea Love II* (St. Augustine, 904/824–3328) or contact **Critter Fleet Marina** (Daytona Beach, tel. 904/767–7676). One of the savviest guides to St. Johns River bass fishing is **Bob Stonewater** (De Land, tel. 904/736–7120). He'll tow his boat to whichever launch ramp is best for the day's fishing, and meet clients there.

Rentals Rental boats and motors for fishing the St. Johns are available from **Highland Park Fish Camp** (De Land, tel. 904/734–2334), **Blair's Jungle Den Fish Camp** (near Astor, tel. 904/749–2264), **Tropical Apartments & Marina** (De Land, tel. 904/734–3080), and **South Moon Fishing Camp** (near Astor, tel. 904/749–2383).

Golf Top-flight courses in this area that you can arrange to play on include:

Daytona Beach **Indigo Lakes Resort** (2620 Volusia Ave., Daytona Beach 32020, tel. 904/258–6333 or 800/874–9918, 18 holes, headquarters of the Ladies Professional Golf Association) and **Spruce Creek Golf & Country Club** (1900 Country Club Dr., Daytona Beach, tel. 904/756–6114, 18 holes).

Jacksonville Area **Amelia Island Plantation** (Hwy. A1A S., Amelia Island 32034, tel. 904/261–6161 or 800/874–6878, 45 holes), the **Tournament Players Club** (18 holes) at the Marriott at Sawgrass (110 TPC

Blvd., Ponte Vedra Beach 32082, tel. 904/273–3235, 99 holes total at resort, home of the PGA Tour), **Ponte Vedra Inn & Club**
(200 Ponte Vedra Blvd., Ponte Vedra Beach 32082, tel. 904/285–
1111 or 800/234–7842, 36 holes), and **Ravines Golf & Country
Club** (2932 Ravines Rd., Middleburg 32068, tel. 904/282–7888,
18 holes).

Ocala **Golden Ocala Golf Club** (7300 U.S. 27 NW, Ocala 32675, tel.
904/622–0172, 18 holes).

St. Augustine **Ponce de Leon Golf Club** (4000 U.S. 1N, St. Augustine 32085,
tel. 904/829–5314, 18 holes) and **Sheraton Palm Coast** (300
Clubhouse Dr., Palm Coast 32137, tel. 904/445–3000, 72 holes).

Horseback Riding Ocala's bluegrass horse country can be explored during trail
rides organized by **Oakview Stable** (S.W. 27th Ave., behind the
Paddock Mall, tel. 904/237–8844).

Skydiving Anybody who wants to jump out of an airplane when it's thousands of feet up in the air can do so with the help of **Skydive De
Land** (tel. 904/738–3539), open daily 8 AM–sunset.

Tennis Resorts especially well known for their tennis programs include **Amelia Island Plantation** (tel. 904/277–5104), site of the
nationally televised WTA Championships; the **St. Augustine
Beach and Tennis Resort** (tel. 904/471–0909); **Ponce de Leon
Lodge and Country Club** (tel. 904/824–2821); the **Ponte Vedra
Club** (tel. 904/285–3856); and the **Marriott at Sawgrass** (tel. 904/
285–7777).

Water Sports Most larger beachfront hotels offer water-sports equipment
for rent. Other sources for renting sailboards, surfboards, or
boogie boards include **The Surf Station** (1002 Anastasia Blvd.,
St. Augustine Beach, tel. 904/471–9463), **Salty Dog** (700 Broadway, Daytona Beach, tel. 904/258–0457), and **Sandy Point
Sailboards** (1114 Riverside Dr., Holly Hill, near Daytona, tel.
904/255–4977).

For jet-ski rentals, try **J&J** (841 Ballough Rd., Daytona Beach,
tel. 904/255–1917).

Diving and Northeast Florida offers, in addition to ocean diving, a wide
Snorkeling range of cave diving and snorkeling over spring "boils." For information about scuba diving in springs and caves, instruction,
and rental equipment, call **Drive & Tour Inc.** (1403 E. New York
Ave., De Land, tel. 904/736–0571).

Scuba equipment, trips, refills, and lessons are available from
Adventure Diving (3127 S. Ridgewood Ave., South Daytona,
tel. 904/788–8050).

Spectator Sports

Auto Racing The massive **Daytona International Speedway** on U.S. 92 (Daytona Beach's major east–west artery) is home of year-round
auto and motorcycle racing including the annual Daytona 500 in
February and Pepsi 400 in July. Twenty-minute narrated tours
of the historic track are offered daily 9–5 except on race days.
For racing schedules, call 904/254–2700.

The Gatornationals of the **National Hot Rod Association** (tel.
818/914–4761) are held each year in late winter at the
Gainesville Raceway (1121 N. County Rte. 225, Gainesville).

Football The blockbuster event in Northeast Florida is Jacksonville's **Gator Bowl** (tel. 904/396–1800). Other major events include **Florida Gators** games in Gainesville (call 904/375–4683 for tickets).

Golf The Tournament Players Championship is a March event at the **Tournament Players Club** (near Sawgrass in Ponte Vedra Beach, tel. 904/273–3382 or 800/741–3161), which is national headquarters of the PGA Tour.

Greyhound Races Year-round, you can bet on the dogs every night but Sunday at the **Daytona Beach Kennel Club** (on U.S. 92 near the International Speedway, tel. 904/252–6484).

Greyhounds race year-round in the Jacksonville area, with seasons split among three tracks: **Jacksonville Kennel Club**, May–September (1440 N. McDuff Ave., tel. 904/646–0001); **Orange Park Kennel Club**, November–April (U.S. 17, about ½ mi south of I–295, tel. 904/646–0001); and **St. John's Greyhound Park**, March–April (7 miles south of I–95 on U.S. 1, tel. 904/646–0001).

Jai Alai The speediest of sports, jai-alai is played year-round at **Ocala Jai-Alai** (Rte. 318, Orange Lake, tel. 904/591–2345).

Tennis The top-rated Women's Tennis Association Championships is held in April, and the Men's All-American Tennis Championship in September, both at **Amelia Island Plantation** (Amelia Island, tel. 904/277–5145).

Dining and Lodging

Dining Between the Atlantic Ocean, the Intracoastal Waterway, and the numerous lakes and rivers of this region, seafood is prominently featured on local menus. In coastal towns, the catches often come straight from the restaurant's own fleet. Shrimp, oysters, snapper, and grouper are especially popular.

Restaurants are organized geographically. Unless otherwise noted, they serve lunch and dinner. Highly recommended restaurants are indicated by a star ★.

Category	Cost*
Very Expensive	over $50
Expensive	$35–50
Moderate	$20–$35
Inexpensive	under $20

**per person, excluding drinks, service, and 6% sales tax*

Lodging Accommodations range from splashy beachfront resorts and glitzy condominiums to cozy inns and bed-and-breakfasts nestled in historic districts. As a general rule, the closer you are to the center of activity in the coastal resorts, the more you'll pay. You'll save a few dollars if you stay across from the beach rather than on it, and you'll save even more if you select a place that's a bit removed from the action.

Highly recommended lodgings are indicated by a star ★.

Category	Cost*
Very Expensive	over $150
Expensive	$90–$150
Moderate	$60–$90
Inexpensive	under $60

All prices are per double room, excluding 6% state sales tax and nominal tourist tax.

Amelia Island
Lodging
★

Amelia Island Plantation. One of the first "environmentally sensitive" resorts, Amelia Island's grounds ramble through ancient live-oak forests and behind some of the highest dunes in the state. A warm sense of community prevails; some homes are occupied year-round, and accommodations range from home and condo rentals to rooms in a full-service hotel. The resort is best known for its golf and tennis programs, but hiking and biking trails thread through the 1,300 acres. Restaurants range from casual to ultraelegant. *3000 First Coast Hwy., 32034, tel. 904/261–6161 or outside FL 800/874–6878, fax 904/277–5159. 125 rooms in the inn; 475 villa apartments. Facilities: private indoor pools in honeymoon villas, water sports, 25 tennis courts, 2 golf courses, fishing, racquetball, fitness center, pro shops, children's activities, restaurants, shopping, entertainment. D, MC, V. Expensive.*

Cocoa Beach
Dining

Captain Ed's World Famous Seafood Restaurant. From the tables of this local favorite that opened in 1965, diners can watch the arrivals of both glittering cruise ships and working shrimp and scallop boats, and enjoy the aerobatic antics of gulls and pelicans. The menu offers the freshest of the local catch, but you can also order chicken, lobster, and prime rib. A nautical theme prevails, and a gallery displays autographed photographs of astronauts. *700 Scallop Dr., Port Canaveral, tel. 407/783–1580. Reservations required for parties of 8 or more. Dress: casual. AE, D, DC, MC, V. Moderate.*

Pier House Restaurant. In this elegant establishment in a shopping, dining, and entertainment complex on Cocoa Beach Pier, you can enjoy fresh fish in a room with floor-to-ceiling windows that overlook the ocean. Try the mahi mahi, or the grouper, which you can order broiled, blackened, grilled, or fried. *401 Meade Ave., tel. 407/783–7549. Reservations advised. Dress: casual. AE, DC, MC, V. Moderate.*

Herbie K's. This 1950s rock'n'roll diner has become a landmark since it 1987 opening. Servers dress, walk, and talk the '50s—you'll see saddle shoes and revisit expressions such as "Daddy-o" and "doll-face." Famous for its burgers, Herbie K's also serves homestyle blue plate and old-fashioned ice-cream desserts. It's great for families. *2080 N. A1A, tel. 407/783–6740. Reservations not necessary. Dress: informal. AE, D, DC, MC, V. Inexpensive.*

Lone Cabbage Fish Camp. The natural habitat of wildlife and local characters, Lone Cabbage sits on the St. John's River 9 miles north of Cocoa city limits on Route 520 and 4 miles west of I–95. The catfish, frog legs, turtle, country ham, and alligator on the menu make the drive well worthwhile. A fun family outing, this one-of-a-kind spot also has a dock where you can fish, buy your bait here, or rent a canoe for a trip on the St. Johns. *8199 Rte. 520, Cocoa, tel. 407/632–4199. Reservations not required. Dress: casual. No credit cards. Inexpensive.*

Lodging **Radisson Resort at the Port.** This elegant new resort directly across the street from Port Canaveral provides complimentary transportation to the nearest beaches as well as to restaurants and shopping on request. Tame peacocks roam the grounds. Rooms have a Caribbean motif, with wicker appointments, hand-painted wallpaper, and ceiling fans. The pool is lavish in the best central Florida fashion, tropically landscaped and complete with its 95-foot mountain waterfalls and its cascade. *8701 Astronaut Blvd., Cape Canaveral 32920, tel. 407/784-0000 or 800/333-3333. 200 rooms. Facilities: restaurant, pool, children's pool, whirlpool, 2 lighted tennis courts, fitness center, playground, game room. AE, D, DC, MC, V. Expensive.*

Wakulla Motel. This motel has the best occupancy rate on the beach. Its completely furnished five-room suites, designed to sleep six, are great for families; they include two bedrooms, living room, dining room, and fully equipped kitchen. The grounds are landscaped with tropical vegetation. *3550 N. Atlantic Ave., 32931, tel. 407/783-2230. 116 suites. Facilities: 2 heated outdoor pools, shuffleboard court, outdoor grills. Moderate.*

Pelican Landing Resort on the Ocean. This two-story beachfront motel is friendly and warm. Rooms have ocean views, microwaves, and TVs; one even has a screened porch. Boardwalks to the beach, picnic tables, and a gas grill round out the amenities. *1201 S. Atlantic Ave., 32931, tel. 407/783-7197. 11 units. Facilities: beach, afficiencies with fully equipped kitchens. D, MC, V.*

Daytona Beach **Gene's Steak House.** This family-operated restaurant, located
Dining west of town, in the middle of nowhere, has long upheld its reputation as the place for steaks. The wine list is one of the state's most comprehensive, and there are seafood specialties, but it's basically a meat-and-potatoes paradise for power beef-eaters. *U.S. 92, 4.5 mi west of the I-95/I-4 interchange, tel. 904/255-2059. Reservations advised. Dress: casual but neat. Closed Mon. AE, DC, MC, V. Expensive.*

★ **Top of Daytona.** Especially dazzling at sundown, this 29th-floor supper club has a 360° view of the beach, Intracoastal, and the city. It's a project of television personality and cookbook author Sophie Kay, who is famous for her shrimp dishes, chicken inventions, and delicate veal recipes. *2625 S. Atlantic Ave., tel. 904/767-5791. Reservations advised. Dress: casual. AE, DC, MC, V. Moderate.*

Lodging **Daytona Beach Marriott.** The location is a bombshell: The
★ Ocean Center is in one direction and the best of the beach, boardwalk, and band shell is in the other. Fresh and flowery pastels set a buoyant tone for a beach vacation and every room views the ocean. *100 N. Atlantic Ave., 32118, tel. 904/254-8200, fax 904/253-0275. 402 rooms. Facilities: indoor-outdoor pool, 2 whirlpools, children's pool and playground, poolside bar, 3 restaurants, 30 specialty shops. AE, DC, MC, V. Expensive-Very Expensive.*

Captain's Quarters Inn. It may look like just another mid-rise hotel, but inside, this is a home away from home with an antique desk, Victorian love seat, and tropical greenery set in the lobby of this beachfront inn. Fresh-baked goodies and coffee are served in The Galley, which overlooks the ocean and looks like grandma's kitchen with a few extra tables and chairs. Each guest suite features rich oak furnishings, a complete kitchen, and private balcony. *3711 S. Atlantic Ave., Daytona Beach*

Shores 32127, tel. 904/767–3119, fax 904/760–7712. 25 suites. Facilities: heated pool, sunbathing deck. AE, D, MC, V. Expensive.

Daytona Beach Hilton. A towering landmark, this Hilton is situated on a 22-mile beach. Most rooms have balconies; some have a kitchenette, patio, or terrace. Convenient touches include an extra lavatory in every room, hair dryer, lighted makeup mirror, and a bar with refrigerator. *2637 S. Atlantic Ave., 32118, tel. 904/767–7350 or 800/525–7350, fax 904/760–3651. 214 rooms. Facilities: heated outdoor pool, children's pool, Jacuzzi, exercise room, sauna, games room, playground, gift shop, laundry. AE, D, DC, MC, V. Expensive.*

Howard Johnson Hotel. Straight out of the glamour films of the 1930s, this 14-story hotel on the beach is an oldie that has been brought back to the splendor of its Deco years. Kitchenette suites are available. *600 N. Atlantic Ave., 32118, tel. 904/255–4471 or 800/767–4471, fax 904/2253–7543. 324 rooms. Facilities: pool, restaurant, lounge with live entertainment and dancing. AE, D, DC, MC, V. Moderate.*

★ **Indigo Lakes Resort & Conference Center.** Home of the Ladies Professional Golf Association, this sprawling inland resort offers sports galore. The championship golf course measures 7,123 yards and has the largest greens in the state. Rooms are light and lavish in Florida tones. *U.S. 92 and I–95, Box 10859, 32120, tel. 904/258–6333; in FL, 800/223–4161; outside FL, 800/874–9918, fax 904/254–3698. 211 rooms, 64 condo suites. Facilities: Olympic-size pool, racquetball, tennis, golf, archery, pro shops, 2 restaurants, nightclub, courtesy transportation to airport, in-room coffee, nonsmoker and handicapped rooms available. AE, D, DC, MC, V. Moderate.*

Perry's Ocean-Edge. Long regarded as a family resort, Perry's enjoys one of the highest percentages of repeat visitors in the state. Spacious grounds are set with picnic tables. Free homemade doughnuts and coffee—a breakfast ritual here—are served in the lush solarium, a good way to get acquainted. *2209 S. Atlantic Ave., 32118; tel. 904/255–0581, in FL 800/342–0102, outside FL 800/447–0002, fax 904/258–7315. 204 rooms. Facilities: heated indoor pool, 2 outdoor pools, whirlpools, golf privileges, putting green, games room, café. AE, D, DC, MC, V. Moderate.*

Aku Tiki Inn. Located right on the beach, the family-owned inn has a Polynesian theme inside and out. You can bake by the large heated pool or snooze under a shady tree on the spacious grounds. *2225 S. Atlantic Ave., 32118, tel. 904/252–9631 or 800/528–1234, fax 904/252–1198. 132 rooms, some with efficiencies. Facilities: pool, shuffleboard, games room, restaurant, 2 lounges with live entertainment, pool bar. AE, D, DC, MC, V. Inexpensive–Moderate.*

De Land
Dining
★ **Pondo's.** You lose a couple of decades as you step into what was once a romantic hideaway for young pilots who trained in De Land during the war. The owner/chef specializes in whimsical veal dishes, but he also does fish, beef, and chicken—always with fresh vegetables, a platter-size salad, and oven-baked breads. The old-fashioned bar is "Cheers"-y, and a pianist entertains. *1915 Old New York Ave., tel. 904/734–1995. Reservations advised. Dress: casual but neat. AE, MC, V. Moderate.*

★ **Karlings Inn.** A sort of Bavarian Brigadoon, set beside a forgotten highway near De Leon Springs, this restaurant is decorated like a Black Forest inn. Karl Caeners personally oversees the preparation of the sauerbraten, red cabbage, succulent roast duckling, sumptuous soups, and tender schnitzels. Ask to see the dessert tray. *4640 N. U.S. 17, tel. 904/985–5535. Reservations advised. Dress: casual but neat. Closed Mon., lunch Sun. only. AE, MC, V. Inexpensive.*

The Original Holiday House. This, the original of what has become a small chain of buffet restaurants in Florida, is enormously popular with senior citizens, families, and college students. Patrons can choose from three categories: salads only, salads and vegetables only, or the full buffet. *704 N. Woodland Blvd., tel. 904/734–6319. No reservations. Dress: casual but neat. MC, V. Inexpensive.*

Lodging **Holiday Inn De Land.** Picture a snazzy, big-city hotel in a little college town, run by friendly, small-town folks with city savvy. An enormous painting by nationally known local artist Fred Messersmith dominates the plush lobby. Rooms are done in subdued colors and styles; prestige suites have housed the likes of Tom Cruise and the New Kids on the Block. *350 International Speedway Blvd. (U.S. 92), 32724, tel. 904/738–5200 or 800/826–3233, fax 904/734–7552. 150 rooms. Facilities: pool, tennis and golf privileges, restaurant, nightclub, bar. AE, D, MC, V. Moderate.*

De Land Country Inn. This home, replete with spacious verandas and glowing hardwoods, was built in 1903 and is furnished in an eclectic blend of restored antiques and reproductions. Hosts Raisa and Bill Lilley serve a complimentary Continental breakfast to start your day. *228 W. Howry Ave., 32720, tel. 904/736–4244. 5 rooms with bath. Facilities: pool. AE, MC, V. Inexpensive–Moderate.*

University Inn. For years this has been the choice of business travelers and visitors to the university. Located on campus, and across from the popular Holiday House restaurant, this motel is in a convenient location, has clean, comfortable rooms, and offers a Continental breakfast each morning. *644 N. Woodland Blvd., 32720, tel. 904/734–5711 or 800/345–8991, fax 904/734–5716. 60 rooms, some with kitchenette. Facilities: pool. AE, D, DC, MC, V. Inexpensive.*

Flagler Beach **Topaz Café.** An unexpected treasure on a quiet stretch of the
Dining beach highway, this intimate restaurant is operated by two sis-
★ ters who do all their own cooking and baking: vegetables are bright and appealing and meats and fish are artistically presented. The menu changes weekly. Though the selection is limited, there are always enough choices, including a vegetarian entrée. The decor is a whimsical combination of enamel-top tables, unmatched settings and linens, and wildflowers. *1224 S. Ocean Shore Blvd., 32136, tel. 904/439–3275. Dress: casual but neat. Reservations advised. Closed Mon., lunch Fri. only. MC, V. Inexpensive.*

Lodging **Topaz Motel/Hotel.** This lovingly restored 1920s beach house is
★ lavishly furnished in museum-quality Victoriana. It's a popular beachfront honeymoon hideaway—romantic and undiscovered. *1224 S. A1A, 32136, tel. 904/439–3301. 48 units, including efficiencies. Facilities: pool, restaurant, laundry. AE, D, MC, V. Inexpensive–Moderate.*

Flagler Beach Motel. If you yearn for the mom-and-pop motels of old Florida, at 1950s prices, this is it in plain vanilla. It's on a quiet stretch of beach, away from the Daytona crowds, and dressed with old-fashioned informality and friendliness. *1820*

S. Ocean Shore Blvd., 32136, tel. 904/439–2340. 23 units, including efficiencies, cottages, and apartments. Facilities: pool, shuffleboard, cable TV. MC, V. Inexpensive.

Gainesville
Dining

Capriccio. This rooftop restaurant is a celebration spot for locals and a dependable place for travelers who are looking for a good meal. The superb view and classic Italian cuisine make for a relaxing evening. The pastries and breads are home-baked. *University Centre Hotel, 1535 S.W. Archer Rd., tel. 904/371–3333. Reservations advised. Dress: casual but neat. AE, D, DC, MC, V. Inexpensive.*

Sovereign. Crystal, candlelight, and a jazz pianist set a theme of restrained elegance in this 1878 carriage house. The veal specialties are notable, particularly the *saltimbocca* (veal sautéed with spinach and cheese). Duckling and rack of baby lamb are dependable choices as well. *12 S.E. Second Ave., tel. 904/378–6307. Reservations advised. Jacket suggested. AE, D, DC, MC, V. Inexpensive.*

Lodging

Herlong Mansion. Adorned with old relics at every turn, this late-19th-century home trumpets its antiquity. Continental breakfasts and evening cordials with petit fours, provided by caring hosts, strengthens the appeal. Although the nearest restaurants are in Gainesville, this inn has much to offer. There's no street address; just look for the big, brick house on the short main street of Micanopy. *Tel. 904/466–3322. 7 rooms with private baths. Facilities: library, music room with TV. D, MC, V. Moderate.*

Residence Inn by Marriott. Studios and two-bedroom suites with kitchen and fireplace make a cozy pied-à-terre. Cocktails, Continental breakfast, and a daily paper are part of the hospitality. The central location is convenient for the university or business traveler. *4001 S.W. 13th St. (at U.S. 441 and S.R. 331), 32608, tel. 904/371–2101 or 800/331–3131, fax 904/371–2101. 80 suites. Facilities: outdoor pool, whirlpool, exercise equipment, microwave, laundry, complimentary Continental breakfast daily and hospitality hour Mon.–Thurs. AE, D, DC, MC, V. Moderate.*

Cabot Lodge. Included in the room rate is a Continental breakfast and a chummy two-hour cocktail reception. Spacious rooms and a clublike ambience make this a favorite with business and university travelers. *3726 S.W. 40th Blvd., 32608, tel. 904/375–2400 or outside FL 800/843–8735, fax 904/335–2321. Facilities: satellite TV. AE, D, DC, MC, V. Inexpensive.*

Jacksonville and Jacksonville Beach
Dining

Cafe on the Square. This 1920 building, the oldest on San Marco Square, is an unpretentious place for an after-theater meal, tête-à-tête dining, or Sunday brunch. Dine indoors or out and choose from a menu ranging from steak sandwiches to quiche, marinated chicken, or pasta—all choices with a Continental flair. *1974 San Marco Blvd., Jacksonville, tel. 904/399–4848. Reservations accepted Mon.–Thurs. Dress: casual. AE, MC, V. Lunch Mon.–Fri. Moderate.*

Angelo's. At this cozy, inelegant, hospitable family spot, you can dive into mountainous portions of southern Italian standards, including a socko eggplant parmigiana. House specials change daily. *2111 University Blvd. N, Jacksonville, tel. 904/743–3400. Reservations accepted. Dress: casual. AE, DC, MC, V. Inexpensive.*

Beach Road Chicken Dinner. If down-home chicken, potatoes, and biscuits are your comfort food, this is the place. It's the best of basic roadside diner stuff at Depression-era prices. Eat in or take out. *4132 Atlantic Blvd., Jacksonville, tel. 904/398–7980. Reservations accepted. Dress: casual. No credit cards. Inexpensive.*

Crawdaddy's. Take it Cajun or cool, this riverfront fish shack is the place for seafood, jambalaya, and country chicken. Dig into the house specialty, catfish—all you can eat—then dance to a fe-do-do beat. *1643 Prudential Dr. (just off I–10 at I–95), Jacksonville, tel. 904/396–3546. Reservations accepted. Dress: casual. AE, D, DC, MC, V. Inexpensive.*

★ **Homestead.** A down-home place with several dining rooms, a huge fireplace, and country cooking, this restaurant specializes in skillet-fried chicken, which comes with rice and gravy. Chicken and dumplings, deep-fried chicken gizzards, buttermilk biscuits, and strawberry shortcake also draw in the locals. *1712 Beach Blvd., Jacksonville Beach, tel. 904/249–5240. Dress: informal. Reservations accepted for parties of 6 or more. AE, D, MC, V. Inexpensive.*

Ragtime. A New Orleans theme threads through everything from the Sunday jazz brunch to the beignets. It's loud, crowded, and alive with a sophisticated young bunch. If you aren't into Creole and Cajun classics, have a simple po-boy sandwich or fish sizzled on the grill. *207 Atlantic Blvd., Atlantic Beach, tel. 904/241–7877. No reservations. Dress: casual. AE, DC, MC, V. Inexpensive.*

Lodging **Jacksonville Omni Hotel.** This 16-story, ultramodern facility features a splashy lobby atrium and large, stylish guest rooms. All rooms have either a king-size or two double beds. You'll feel pampered anywhere in the hotel, but the extra frills are to be found in the two floors of the concierge level. *245 Water St., Jacksonville 32202, tel. 904/355–6664, fax 904/354–2970. 354 rooms. Facilities: heated pool, restaurant, lounge, exercise room, nonsmoker rooms. AE, D, DC, MC, V. Expensive.*

Marina Hotel at St. Johns Place. This five-story luxury hotel, connected to the Riverwalk complex, has modern rooms with either a king-size or two double beds. It's located right in the center of things, and the hotel bustles with activity inside and out. Rooms overlooking the St. Johns River command the highest prices. *1515 Prudential Dr., Jacksonville 32207, tel. 904/396–5100, fax 904/396–7154. 321 rooms, 18 suites. Facilities: outdoor pool, 2 lighted tennis courts, restaurant, lounge, shopping arcade, nonsmoker rooms, facilities for handicapped persons. AE, DC, MC, V. Moderate–Expensive.*

Comfort Suites Hotel. Located in bustling Baymeadows, central to the currently "in" restaurants, nightclubs, and shops, this all-suites hotel is an unbeatable value. Suites, which are decorated in breezy, radiant Florida hues, include refrigerators, remote control TV, and sofa sleepers. Microwaves and VCRs come with master suites. Daily Continental breakfast and cocktail hour during the week are included in rates. *8333 Dix Ellis Trail, Jacksonville 32256, tel. 904/739–1155, fax 904/731–0752. 128 suites. Facilities: outdoor pool, heated spa, laundry. AE, DC, MC, V. Moderate.*

House on Cherry St. This early 20th-century treasure is furnished with pewter, oriental rugs, woven coverlets, and other remnants of a rich past. Carol Anderson welcomes her guests to her riverside home with wine and hors d'oeuvres and serves full breakfast every morning. Walk to the parks and gardens of the chic Avondale district. *1844 Cherry St., Jacksonville*

32205, tel. 904/384–1999. 4 rooms with private bath. Facilities: bicycles. MC, V. Moderate.

Sea Turtle Inn. Every room in this inn has a view of the Atlantic. Let the staff arrange special outings for you: golf, deep-sea fishing, or a visit to a Nautilus fitness center. You'll be welcomed each evening with a complimentary cocktail reception, and in the morning you'll be awakened with hot coffee and a newspaper. *One Ocean Blvd., Atlantic Beach 32233, tel. 904/ 249–7402, fax 904/241–7439. 198 rooms. Facilities: oceanfront pool with cabana bar, restaurant, lounge with live entertainment, free airport shuttle. AE, D, DC, MC, V. Moderate.*

New Smyrna Beach

Dining

Riverview Charlie's. Look out over the Intracoastal Waterway while you choose from a menu loaded with local and imported fish, all available broiled, blackened, or grilled. The shore platters are piled high; landlubbers can choose steaks and chicken dishes instead. *101 Flagler Ave., tel. 904/428–1865. Reservations advised. Dress: casual but neat. AE, D, DC, MC, V. Inexpensive–Moderate.*

The Skyline. Watch private airplanes land and take off at the New Smyrna Beach airport as you dine on secretly seasoned Tony Barbera steaks, veal, shrimp, chicken, and fish. A tray will be brought for your selection: order steaks by the ounce, cut to order if you wish. House specialties include the *zuppa di pesce*, served in a crock; fresh homemade pastas; and a New England clam chowder that took first place in the 1988 Chowder Debate. The building, once an officers club for American and RAF pilots, is filled with aeronautical nostalgia. *2004 N. Dixie Fwy., tel. 904/428–5325. Reservations advised. Dress: casual but neat. AE, MC, V. No lunch. Inexpensive–Moderate.*

Franco's. Begun as a pizza joint in 1983, Franco's has become a high-voltage Italian specialty house. Light concoctions include spinach or broccoli pies, pasta salads, and what could possibly be the best Greek salad you've ever had. There's a long list of fish, Italian classics, including a captivating zucchini parmigiana, seven styles of veal, and gourmet pizzas. *1518 S. Dixie Fwy. (U.S. 1, ½ mi south of Rte. 44), tel. 904/423–3600. Reservations advised. Dress: casual. No lunch Sun. MC, V. Inexpensive.*

Goodrich Seafood & Restaurant. For those who like mullet, this is a piscatorial Shangri-la. Gorge on steamed oysters, fried fish, hush puppies, clams, shrimp, and chowders. Fresh and frozen seafood is also sold over the counter. *253 River Dr., tel. 904/345–3397. Reservations required for all-you-can-eat buffet (Sept.–May). Dress: casual. No credit cards. Closed Sun. Inexpensive.*

Lodging

Riverview Hotel. A landmark since 1886, this was once a bridge tender's home. Verandas look over the Intracoastal, dunes, and marshes, while inside, Haitian prints and wicker furniture add to the feeling that this is an island getaway. Complimentary Continental breakfast is served in your room. *103 Flagler Ave., 32169, tel. 904/428–5858 or 800/945–7416, fax 904/423–8927. 18 rooms with private bath. Facilities: restaurant, pool, bicycle rentals. AE, D, DC, MC, V. Moderate.*

Sea Woods Resort Community. Get the best of the beach plus 50 acres of rolling dunes and hammocks. A true community of homes, condos, and villas, this has a rhythm of doing, going, and playing. Most people rent by the week, month, or season. *4309 Sea Mist Dr., 32169, tel. 904/423–7796 or 800/826–8614, fax 904/423–1278. 180 units. Facilities: racquetball, tennis,*

Nautilus fitness center, outdoor heated pool, planned activities in winter. No credit cards. Inexpensive–Moderate.

Ocean Air Motel. One of those modest little "finds," this motel is operated by a caring British couple who, in the English manner, groom the grounds as carefully as they do the neat and commodious rooms. It's only a five-minute walk from the beach. *1161 N. Dixie Fwy., 32069, tel. 904/428–5748. 14 rooms. Facilities: pool, picnic tables. AE, DC, MC, V. Inexpensive.*

Ocala **Seven Sisters Inn.** This showplace Queen Anne mansion is now
Lodging an award-winning bed-and-breakfast. Each room has been glowingly furnished with period antiques and has its own bath; some have a fireplace. Rates include a gourmet breakfast. *820 S.E. Fort King St., 32671, tel. 904/867–1170. 7 rooms; wicker-furnished loft sleeps 4. AE, MC, V. Expensive.*

Ocala Hilton. A winding, tree-lined boulevard leads to this nine-story pink tower, nestled in a forested patch of countryside just off I–75. The marble-floor lobby, with piano bar, greets you before you enter your spacious guest room, decorated in deep, tropical hues. *3600 S.W. 36th Ave., 32674, tel. 904/854–1400, fax 904/854–4010. 200 rooms. Facilities: outdoor heated pool and Jacuzzi, tennis courts, restaurant, pub, live entertainment on weekends. AE, D, DC, MC, V. Moderate–Expensive.*

Ormond Beach **Shogun II.** The largest of this area's Japanese steak and sea-
Dining food houses, this is the place for flashy tableside food preparation, a sushi bar, and a tropical bar. It's a fun, family place; call ahead if you want to celebrate a special occasion in traditional Japanese style. The steak and shrimp are stellar, but the lobster and chicken are also tempting. *630 S. Atlantic Ave. (A1A), in the Ellinor Village Shopping Center, tel. 904/673–1110. Reservations accepted. Dress: casual. AE, MC, V. Inexpensive.*

Ponte Vedra Beach **The Lodge at Ponte Vedra Beach.** The look of this plush new re-
Lodging sort is Mediterranean villa grand luxe, aimed at serving an elite clientele whose passions are golf and tennis. The PGA Tour, Tournament Players Club, and Association of Tennis Professionals are based here. Rooms, designed with a country-French flair, have private balconies and cozy window seats. *607 Ponte Vedra Blvd., 32080, tel. 904/273–9500, fax 904/273–0210. 66 rooms, 24 suites, some with private whirlpool and fireplace. Facilities: 54 holes of golf, water sports, deep-sea fishing, horseback riding, two beachside pools with bar and grill, exercise room, restaurant, lounge. AE, D, DC, MC, V. Very Expensive.*

Marriott at Sawgrass. A tropical design is conveyed throughout this luxury hotel. Pick a room with a fireplace or private balcony. Fine details, from the private lounge and special services on the concierge level to the mood set by the lagoon and waterfall in the complex, enhance this resort. *1000 TPC Blvd., 32082, tel. 904/285–7777, fax 904/285–0906. 546 units. Facilities: 2 pools, children's program and pool, lighted tennis courts, 99 holes of golf and complete golf program, bicycling, putting green, horseback riding, boating, exercise facilities, restaurants, valet, private beach privileges. AE, D, DC, MC, V. Very Expensive.*

St. Augustine **La Parisienne.** Tiny and attentive, pleasantly lusty in its ap-
Dining proach to honest bistro cuisine, this little place is a true find— and weekend brunches are available, too. Save room for the pastries. *60 Hypolita St., tel. 904/829–0055. Reservations re-*

quired at dinner. Dress: casual but neat. AE, MC, V. Closed Mon. Moderate.

Le Pavilion. The Continental approach spills over from France to Germany with a wow of a schnitzel with spätzle. Hearty soups and good breads make a budget meal, or you can splurge on the rack of lamb or escargot. *45 San Marco Ave., tel. 904/824–6202. Reservations advised; required for 6 or more. Dress: casual but neat. AE, D, DC, MC, V. Moderate.*

★ **Columbia.** An heir to the cherished reputation of the original Columbia founded in Tampa in 1905, this one serves time-honored dishes including *arroz con pollo* (chicken with rice), filet salteado, shrimp and scallops Marbella, and a fragrant, flagrant paella. The Fiesta Brunch on Sunday is a Spanish gala. *98 St. George St., tel. 904/824–3341 or 800/227–1905 in FL. Dinner reservations advised. Dress: casual but neat. AE, D, MC, V. Inexpensive–Moderate.*

Santa Maria. This ramshackle landmark, run by the same family since the 1950s, perches over the water beside the colorful city marina. Seafood is the focus, but there are also steaks, chicken, prime rib, and a children's menu. Have drinks first in the salty lounge or feed the fish from the open-air porch. *135 Avenida Menendez, tel. 904/829–6578. No reservations. Dress: casual. AE, DC, MC, V. Inexpensive–Moderate.*

★ **Raintree.** The oldest home in this part of the city, this building has been lovingly restored. The buttery breads and pastries are baked on the premises. Try the brandied pepper steak or the Maine lobster special. The Raintree's Madrigal or Champagne dinners are especially fun. The wine list is impressive, and there are two dozen beers to choose from. Courtesy pickup is available from any lodging in the city. *102 San Marco Ave., tel. 904/824–7211. Reservations accepted. Dress: casual but neat. AE, DC, MC, V. No lunch. Inexpensive.*

Zaharias. The room is big, busy, and buzzing with openhanded hospitality. Serve yourself from an enormous buffet instead of, or in addition to, ordering from the menu. Greek and Italian specialties include homemade pizza, a big gyro dinner served with a side order of spaghetti, shish kebab, steaks, seafood, and sandwiches. *3945 Rte. A1A S, tel. 904/471–4799. Reservations accepted. Dress: casual. AE, MC, V. Inexpensive.*

Lodging **Casa Solana.** A hushed air of yesteryear hangs over this gracious, antiques-filled, 225-year-old home where you'll be welcomed like an old friend. Complimentary sherry and chocolates and a breakfast of fresh fruits and homemade specialties further convey the mellow but comfortable tone of this inn. *21 Aviles St., 32084, tel. 904/824–3555. 4 suites with bath. Facilities: bicycles. AE, D, MC, V. Expensive.*

★ **Colony's Ponce de Leon Golf and Conference Resort.** Pick your site to loll in the sun from the 350 lavishly landscaped subtropical acres or seek the shade of century-old live oaks in spacious contrast to the narrow streets and crowding of the old city. Insiders reserve well in advance to stay here for special events occurring around the area. *4000 U.S. 1N, 32095, tel. 904/824–2821 or in FL 800/228–2821, fax 904/824–8254. 200 rooms, 99 condos. Facilities: pool, tennis, 18-hole championship golf course, 18-hole poolside putting course, volleyball, horseshoes, restaurant, lounge. AE, D, DC, MC, V. Expensive.*

★ **Sheraton Palm Coast.** This is a bright, nautical-style resort hotel about a mile inland, facing onto a marina on the Intracoastal Waterway. Rooms have private patios that overlook the Intracoastal. Recreation is its strong point—the four championship golf courses were designed by Arnold Palmer, Tom Fazio, and other top designers, and kids can frolic on an island playground with waterfalls and ponds. *300 Club House Dr., 32137, tel. 904/ 445-3000 or 800/325-3535, fax 904/445-9685. 150 rooms, 2 suites. Facilities: 2 heated pools, children's pool, marina, 16 tennis courts, access to 5 championship golf courses, whirl-pool, exercise equipment, sauna, restaurant, bar, refrigera-tors, free transportation around resort and to beach. AE, D, DC, MC, V. Moderate-Expensive.*

Carriage Way Bed and Breakfast. A Victorian mansion grandly restored in 1984, this B&B is within walking distance of restaurants and historic sites. Innkeepers Diane and Bill Johnson see to such welcoming touches as fresh flowers and home-baked breads. Special-occasion breakfasts, flowers, picnic lunches or romantic dinners, or a simple family supper can be arranged with advance notice. *70 Cuna St., 32084, tel. 904/829-2467. 9 rooms with bath. Facilities: bicycles. D, MC, V. Moderate.*

★ **Kenwood Inn.** For more than a century this stately Victorian inn has been welcoming wayfarers, and the Constant family continues the tradition. Located in the heart of the historic district, the inn is within walking distance of restaurants and sightseeing. A Continental breakfast of home-baked cakes and breads is included. *38 Marine St., 32084, tel. 904/824-2116. 10 rooms, 4 suites. Facilities: walled-in courtyard with pool, fish pond, street parking and off-street parking 1 block away. D, MC, V. Moderate.*

The Old Powder House Inn. Part of an 1899 Flagler development of winter cottages for the rich, this inn stands on the site of an 18th-century Spanish gunpowder magazine. Imaginative decor makes every room, from "Granny's Attic" to "Queen Anne's Lace," unique. *38 Cordova St., 32084, tel. 904/824-4149. 9 rooms with bath. Facilities: bicycles. MC, V. Moderate.*

Beacher's Lodge. An all-suites hotel on the dazzling white beach of Anastasia Island provides complimentary coffee, juice, newspaper, and a glimpse of the sun rising over the Atlantic. *6970 Rte. A1A S, 32086, tel. 904/471-8849 or 800/527-8849, fax 904/471-3002. 132 suites. Facilities: pool, fully equipped kitchen, laundry. D, MC, V. Inexpensive-Moderate.*

St. Francis Inn. If only the walls could whisper, this late-18th-century house would tell tales of slave uprisings, buried doubloons, and Confederate spies. The inn, which was a boarding house a century ago, now offers rooms, suites, an apartment, and a cottage. Rates include Continental breakfast. *279 St. George St., 32084, tel. 904/824-6068. Facilities: pool, bicycles. MC, V. Inexpensive-Moderate.*

The Arts and Nightlife

The Arts Broadway touring shows, top-name entertainers, and other major events are booked at the **Florida Theater Performing Arts Center** (128 E. Forsyth St., Jacksonville, tel. 904/355-5661), the **Jacksonville Civic Auditorium** (300 W. Water St., Jacksonville, tel. 904/630-0701), and **The Ocean Center** (101 N. Atlantic Ave., Daytona Beach, tel. 904/254-4545 or in FL 800/858-6444).

Concerts **Peabody Auditorium** (600 Auditorium Blvd., Daytona Beach, tel. 904/255-1314) is used for many concerts and programs throughout the year.

The **Jacksonville Symphony Orchestra** (tel. 904/354–5479) presents a variety of concerts around town.

Theater **Seaside Music Theater** (Box 2835, Daytona Beach, tel. 904/252–3394) presents professional musicals in two venues, January–March and June–August.

Alhambra Dinner Theater (12000 Beach Blvd., Jacksonville, tel. 904/641–1212) offers professional theater and complete menus that change with each play.

Nightlife **Finky's** (640 N. Grandview, Daytona Beach, tel. 904/255–5059)
Daytona Beach brings in name entertainers you've seen on the Nashville Network and MTV. **Waves,** in the Daytona Beach Marriott (100 N. Atlantic Ave., tel. 904/254–8200), is the area's hot, upscale place to drink, dance, and nosh while you listen to Top-40 and mellow standards. **Ocean Pier** (1200 Main St., Daytona Beach, tel. 904/253–1212), located on the ocean, has four bars and one of the biggest dance floors in town.

St. Augustine **Richard's Jazz Restaurant** (77 San Marco Ave., tel. 904/829–9910), **Scarlett O'Hara's** (70 Hypolita St., tel. 904/824–6535), the **White Lion** (20 Cuna St., tel. 904/829–2388), and **Trade Winds** (124 Charlotte St., tel. 904/829–9336) offer live music from bluegrass to classic rock. Call for information on specific performances.

Index

Escape to ancient cities and exotic

islands  *with CNN Travel Guide, a*

wealth of valuable advice. Host Valerie Voss will take you

to all of your favorite destinations,

including those off the beaten path.

 *Tune into your passport to the world.*

CNN TRAVEL GUIDE
SATURDAY 10:00 PMPT   SUNDAY 8:30 AMET

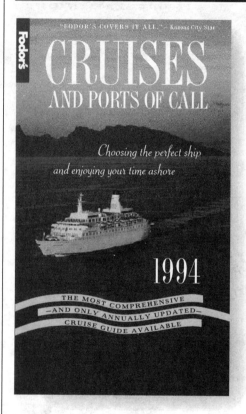

Announcing the only guide to explore a Disney World you've never seen before:

The one for grown-ups.

This terrific new guide is the only one written specifically for the millions of adults who visit Walt Disney World each year <u>without</u> kids. Upscale, sophisticated, packed full of facts and maps, *Walt Disney World for Adults* provides up-to-date information on hotels, restaurants, sports facilities, and health clubs, as well as unique itineraries for adults, including: a Sporting Life Vacation, Day-and-Night Romantic Fantasy, Singles Safari, and Gardens and Natural Wonders Tour. Get essential tips and everything you need to know about reservations, packages, annual events, banking service, rest stops, and much more. With *Walt Disney World for Adults* in hand, you'll get the most out of one of the world's most fascinating, most complex playgrounds.

At bookstores everywhere, or call 1-800-533-6478

WHEREVER YOU TRAVEL, *H*ELP IS NEVER FAR AWAY.

From planning your trip to providing travel assistance along the way, American Express® Travel Service Offices* are always there to help.

FLORIDA

DAYTONA BEACH
Fun Vacations Travel Center
904-258-7774

JACKSONVILLE
Lifeco/American Express
904-642-1701

KEY WEST
Boulevard Travel
305-294-3711

MIAMI/FT. LAUDERDALE
American Express
Ft. Lauderdale
305-565-9481

American Express, Miami
305-358-7350

Adventure Travels, Palm Beach
407-845-8701

ORLANDO
American Express Travelport
Epcot Center
Walt Disney World Resort
407-827-7500

American Express, Orlando
407-843-0004

PENSACOLA
Fillette Green Travel
904-434-2543

SARASOTA
Around the World Travel
813-923-7579

TAMPA/ST. PETERSBURG
American Express, Tampa
813-273-0310

Shouppe Travel, St. Petersburg
813-894-0623

INTRODUCING

Fodor's WORLDVIEW TRAVEL UPDATE

AT LAST, YOUR OWN PERSONALIZED LIST OF WHAT'S GOING ON IN THE CITIES YOU'RE VISITING.

KEYED TO THE DAYS WHEN YOU'RE THERE, CUSTOMIZED FOR YOUR INTERESTS, AND SENT TO YOU BEFORE YOU LEAVE HOME.

EXCLUSIVE FOR PURCHASERS OF FODOR'S GUIDES...

Introducing a revolutionary way to get customized, time-sensitive travel information just before your trip.

Now you can obtain detailed information about what's going on in each city you'll be visiting <u>before</u> you leave home—up-to-the-minute, objective information about the events and activities that interest you most.

This is a special offer for purchasers of Fodor's guides – a customized Travel Update to fit your specific interests and your itinerary.

Travel Updates contain the kind of time-sensitive insider information you can get only from local contacts – or from city magazines and newspapers once you arrive. But now you can have the same information before you leave for your trip.

The choice is yours: current art exhibits, theater, music festivals and special concerts, sporting events, antiques and flower shows, shopping, fitness, and more.

The information comes from hundreds of correspondents and thousands of sources worldwide. Updated continuously, it's like having your own personal concierge or friend in the city.

You specify the cities and when you'll be there. We'll do the rest — personalizing the information for you the way no guidebook can.

It's the perfect extension to your Fodor's guide and the best way to make the most of your valuable travel time.

Your Itinerary:
Customized reports available for 160 destinations

to
990

Regent
The ann
in this a
domain of
tion as Joe
worthwhile.
the perfomanc
Tickets are usual
venue. Alternate
mances are cancelle
given. For more infor.
Open-Air Theatre, Inner
NW1 4NP Open Air Th
Tel: 935-5756. Ends: 9-11-9

International Air Tattoo
Held biennially, the wo
military air displa
demostra
tions, m
ba

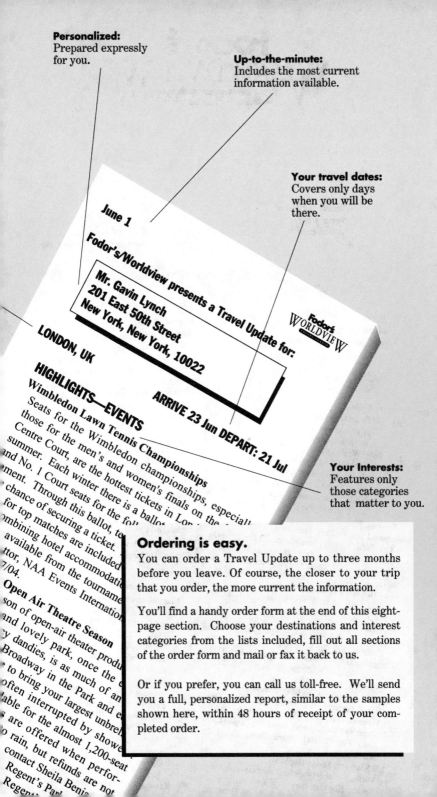

Personalized:
Prepared expressly for you.

Up-to-the-minute:
Includes the most current information available.

Your travel dates:
Covers only days when you will be there.

June 1

Fodor's/Worldview presents a Travel Update for:

Mr. Gavin Lynch
201 East 50th Street
New York, New York, 10022

Fodor's WORLDVIEW

LONDON, UK

ARRIVE 23 Jun DEPART: 21 Jul

HIGHLIGHTS—EVENTS

Wimbledon Lawn Tennis Championships

Seats for the Wimbledon championships, especially those for the men's and women's finals on the Centre Court, are the hottest tickets in Lon summer. Each winter there is a ballot and No. 1 Court seats for the fol ment. Through this ballot, to chance of securing a ticket. for top matches are included ombining hotel accommodati available from the tournam tor, NAA Events Internati 7/04.

Open Air Theatre Season

son of open-air theater produ and lovely park, once the y dandies, is as much of an Broadway in the Park and e to bring your largest unbre often interrupted by showe able for the almost 1,200-seat are offered when perfor o rain, but refunds are not contact Sheila Beni Regent's Par Regen

Your Interests:
Features only those categories that matter to you.

Ordering is easy.

You can order a Travel Update up to three months before you leave. Of course, the closer to your trip that you order, the more current the information.

You'll find a handy order form at the end of this eight-page section. Choose your destinations and interest categories from the lists included, fill out all sections of the order form and mail or fax it back to us.

Or if you prefer, you can call us toll-free. We'll send you a full, personalized report, similar to the samples shown here, within 48 hours of receipt of your completed order.

**Special interest,
in-depth listings**

**Special concerts—
who's performing
what and where**

**One-of-a-kind,
one-time-only events**

Children — Events
Angel Canal Festival
The festivities include a children's funfair, entertainers, a boat rally and displays on the water. Regent's Canal. Islington. N1. Tube: Angel. Tel: 267 9100. 11:30am-5:30pm. 7/04.

Blackheath Summer Kite Festival
Stunt kite displays with parachuting teddy bears and trade stands. Free admission. SE3. BR: Blackheath. 10am. 6/27.

Megabugs
Children will delight in this infestation of giant robotic insects, including a praying mantic 60 times life size. Mon-Sat 10am-6pm; Sun 11am-6pm. Admission 4.50 pounds. Natural History Museum, Cromwell Road. SW7. Tube: South Kensington. Tel: 938 9123. Ends 10/01.

Childminders
This establishment employs only women, providing nurses and qualified nannies to

Music — Jazz & Blues
Tito Puente's Golden Men of Latin Jazz
The father of mambo and Cuban rumba king comes to town. Royal Festival Hall. South Bank. SE1. Tube: Waterloo. Tel: 928 8800. 8pm. 7/15.

Georgie Fame and The New York Band
Riding a popular tide with his latest album, the smoky-voiced Fame and his keyboard are on a tour yet again. The Grand. Clapham Junction. SW11. BR: Clapham Junction. Tel: 738 9000. 7:30pm. 7/07.

Jacques Loussier Play Bach Trio
The French jazz classicist and colleagues. Kenwood Lakeside. Hampstead Lane. Kenwood. NW3. Tube: Golders Green, then bus 210. Tel: 413 1443. 7pm. 7/10.

Tony Bennett and Ronnie Scott
Royal Festival Hall. South Bank. SE1. Tube: Waterloo. Tel: 928 8800. 8pm. 7/11.

Santana
Royal Festival Hall. South Bank. SE1. Tube: Waterloo. Tel: 928 8800. 8pm. 7/12.

Count Basie Orchestra and Nancy Wilson Trio
Royal Festival Hall. South Bank. SE1. Tube: Waterloo. Tel: 928 8800. 8pm. 7/14.

King Pleasure and the Biscuit Boys
Royal Festival Hall. South Bank. SE1. Tube: Waterloo. Tel: 928 8800. 6:30 and 9pm. 7/16.

Al Green and the London Community Gospel Choir
Royal Festival Hall. South Bank. SE1. Tube: Waterloo. Tel: 928 8800. 8pm. 7/13.

BB King and Linda Hopkins
Mother of the blues and successor to Bessie Smith, Hopkins meets up with "Blues Boy" [Smith]. [Royal Festival] Hall. South Bank. SE[1]

Music — Classical
Marylebone Sinfonia
Kenneth Gowen conducts music by Puccini and Rossini. Queen Elizabeth Hall. South Bank. SE1. Tube: Waterloo. Tel: 928 8800. 7:45pm. 7/16.

London Philharmonic
Franz Welser-Moest and George Benjamin conduct selections by Alexander Goehr, Messiaen, and some of Benjamin's own compositions. Queen Elizabeth Hall. South Bank. SE1. Tube: Waterloo. Tel: 928 8800. 8pm.

London Pro Arte Orchestra and Forest Choir
Murray Stewart conducts selections by Rossini, Haydn and Jonathan Willcocks. Queen Elizabeth Hall. South Bank. SE1. Tube: Waterloo. Tel: 928 8800. 7:45pm. 7/

Kensington Symphony Orchestra
[Russell] Keable conducts Dvorak's Dmi[nor]

Here's what you get . . .

Detailed information about what's going on — precisely when you'll be there.

Show openings during your visit

Reviews by local critics

Exhibitions & Shows—Antique & Flower
Westminster Antiques Fair
Over 50 stands with pre-1830 furniture and other Victorian and earlier items. Thu-Fri 11am-8pm; Sat-Sun 11am-6pm. Admission 4 pounds, children free. Old Royal Horticultural Hall. Vincent Square. SW1. Tel: 0444/48 25 14. 6-24 thru 6/27.

Royal Horticultural Society Flower Show
The show includes displays of carnations, summer fruit and vegetables. Tue 11am-7pm; Wed 10am-5pm. Admission Tue 4 pounds, Wed 2 pounds. Royal Horticultural Halls. Greycoat Street and Vincent Square. SW1. Tube: Victoria. 7/20 thru 7/21.

mpton Court Palace International Flower Show
Major international garden and flower show king place in conjunction with the British

Theater — Musical
Sunset Boulevard
In June, the four Andrew Lloyd Webber musicals which dominated London's stages in the 1980s (Cats, Starlight Express, Phantom of the Opera and Aspects of Love) are joined by the composer's latest work, a show rumored to have his best music to date. The 1950 Billy Wilder film about a helpless young writer who is drawn into the world of a possessive, aging silent screen star offers rich opportunities for Webber's evolving style. Soaring, aching melodies, lush technical effects and psychological thrills are all expected. Patti Lupone stars. Mon-Sat at 8pm; matinee Thu-Sat at 3pm. In-person sales only at the box office; credit card bookings, Tel: 344 0055. Admission 15-32.50 pounds. Adelphi Theatre. The Strand. WC2. Tube: Charing Cross. Tel: 836 7611. Starts: 6/21

Leonardo A Portrait of Love
A new musical about the great Renaissance arti and inventor comes in for a London premier tested by a brief run at Oxford's Old Fire Stati autumn. The work explores the relation Vinci and the woman

Alberquerque • Atlanta • Atlantic City • N
Baltimore • Boston • Chicago • Cincinnati
Cleveland • Dallas/Ft.Worth • Denver • De
• Houston • Kansas City • Las Vegas • Los
Angeles • Memphis • Miami • Milwaukee •
New Orleans • New York City • Orlando •
Springs • Philadelphia • Phoenix • Pittsburg
Portland • Salt Lake • San Antonio • San Di
• San Franc   Tamp
Oslo • Wash   St Louis
Hawaii •   Island •
Ex   Bimini
Ber   ntry
Antigua & B   illa

Spectator Sports — Other Sports
Greyhound Racing: Wembley Stadium
This dog track offers good views of greyhound racing held on Mon, Wed and Fri. No credit cards. Stadium Way. Wembley. HA9. Tube: Wembley Park. Tel: 902 8833.

Benson & Hedges Cricket Cup Final
Lord's Cricket Ground. St. John's Wood Road. NW8. Tube: St. John's Wood. Tel: 289 1611. 11am. 7/10.

Business-Fax & Overnight Mail
Post Office, Trafalgar Square Branch
Offers a network of fax services, the Intelpost system, throughout the country and abroad. Mon-Sat 8am-8pm, Sun 9am-5pm. William IV Street. WC2.

Gorda • Barbados • Dominica • Gren
ucia • St. Vincent • Trinidad &Tobago
ymans • Puerto Plata • Santo Doming
Aruba • Bonaire • Curacao • St. Ma
ec City • Montreal • Ottawa • Toron
Vancouver • Guadeloupe • Martiniqu
helemy • St. Martin • Kingston • Ixta
o Bay • Negril • Ocho Rios • Ponce
n • Grand Turk • Providenciales • S
St. John • St. Thomas • Acapulco •
& Isla Mujeres • Cozumel • Guadal
a • Los Cabos • Manzinillo • Mazatl
City • Monterrey • Oaxaca • Puerto
do • Puerto Vallarta • Veracruz • Puerto
dam • Athens

Interest Categories

For your personalized Travel Update, choose the categories you're most interested in from this list. Every Travel Update automatically provides you with *Event Highlights* – the best of what's happening during the dates of your trip.

1.	**Business Services**	Fax & Overnight Mail, Computer Rentals, Photocopying, Secretarial , Messenger, Translation Services
	Dining	
2.	**All Day Dining**	Breakfast & Brunch, Cafes & Tea Rooms, Late-Night Dining
3.	**Local Cuisine**	In Every Price Range—from Budget Restaurants to the Special Splurge
4.	**European Cuisine**	Continental, French, Italian
5.	**Asian Cuisine**	Chinese, Far Eastern, Japanese, Indian
6.	**Americas Cuisine**	American, Mexican & Latin
7.	**Nightlife**	Bars, Dance Clubs, Comedy Clubs, Pubs & Beer Halls
8.	**Entertainment**	Theater—Drama, Musicals, Dance, Ticket Agencies
9.	**Music**	Classical, Traditional & Ethnic, Jazz & Blues, Pop, Rock
10.	**Children's Activities**	Events, Attractions
11.	**Tours**	Local Tours, Day Trips, Overnight Excursions, Cruises
12.	**Exhibitions, Festivals & Shows**	Antiques & Flower, History & Cultural, Art Exhibitions, Fairs & Craft Shows, Music & Art Festivals
13.	**Shopping**	Districts & Malls, Markets, Regional Specialities
14.	**Fitness**	Bicycling, Health Clubs, Hiking, Jogging
15.	**Recreational Sports**	Boating/Sailing, Fishing, Ice Skating, Skiing, Snorkeling/Scuba, Swimming
16.	**Spectator Sports**	Auto Racing, Baseball, Basketball, Football, Horse Racing, Ice Hockey, Soccer

Please note that interest category content will vary by season, destination, and length of stay.

Destinations

The Fodor's/Worldview Travel Update covers more than 160 destinations worldwide. Choose the destinations that match your itinerary from this list. (Choose bulleted destinations only.)

United States (Mainland)
- Albuquerque
- Atlanta
- Atlantic City
- Baltimore
- Boston
- Chicago
- Cincinnati
- Cleveland
- Dallas/Ft. Worth
- Denver
- Detroit
- Houston
- Kansas City
- Las Vegas
- Los Angeles
- Memphis
- Miami
- Milwaukee
- Minneapolis/ St. Paul
- New Orleans
- New York City
- Orlando
- Palm Springs
- Philadelphia
- Phoenix
- Pittsburgh
- Portland
- St. Louis
- Salt Lake City
- San Antonio
- San Diego
- San Francisco
- Seattle
- Tampa
- Washington, DC

Alaska
- Anchorage/Fairbanks/Juneau

Hawaii
- Honolulu
- Island of Hawaii
- Kauai
- Maui

Canada
- Quebec City
- Montreal
- Ottawa
- Toronto
- Vancouver

Bahamas
- Abacos
- Eleuthera/ Harbour Island
- Exumas
- Freeport
- Nassau & Paradise Island

Bermuda
- Bermuda Countryside
- Hamilton

British Leeward Islands
- Anguilla
- Antigua & Barbuda
- Montserrat
- St. Kitts & Nevis

British Virgin Islands
- Tortola & Virgin Gorda

British Windward Islands
- Barbados
- Dominica
- Grenada
- St. Lucia
- St. Vincent
- Trinidad & Tobago

Cayman Islands
- The Caymans

Dominican Republic
- Puerto Plata
- Santo Domingo

Dutch Leeward Islands
- Aruba
- Bonaire
- Curacao

Dutch Windward Islands
- St. Maarten

French West Indies
- Guadeloupe
- Martinique
- St. Barthelemy
- St. Martin

Jamaica
- Kingston
- Montego Bay
- Negril
- Ocho Rios

Puerto Rico
- Ponce
- San Juan

Turks & Caicos
- Grand Turk
- Providenciales

U.S. Virgin Islands
- St. Croix
- St. John
- St. Thomas

Mexico
- Acapulco
- Cancun & Isla Mujeres
- Cozumel
- Guadalajara
- Ixtapa & Zihuatanejo
- Los Cabos
- Manzanillo
- Mazatlan
- Mexico City
- Monterrey
- Oaxaca
- Puerto Escondido
- Puerto Vallarta
- Veracruz

Europe
- Amsterdam
- Athens
- Barcelona
- Berlin
- Brussels
- Budapest
- Copenhagen
- Dublin
- Edinburgh
- Florence
- Frankfurt
- French Riviera
- Geneva
- Glasgow
- Interlaken
- Istanbul
- Lausanne
- Lisbon
- London
- Madrid
- Milan
- Moscow
- Munich
- Oslo
- Paris
- Prague
- Provence
- Rome
- Salzburg
- St. Petersburg
- Stockholm
- Venice
- Vienna
- Zurich

Pacific Rim Australia & New Zealand
- Auckland
- Melbourne
- Sydney

China
- Beijing
- Guangzhou
- Shanghai

Japan
- Kyoto
- Nagoya
- Osaka
- Tokyo
- Yokohama

Other
- Bangkok
- Hong Kong & Macau
- Manila
- Seoul
- Singapore
- Taipei

Fodor's
WORLDVIEW **Order Form**

L. A. O'Tuan

THIS TRAVEL UPDATE IS FOR (Please print):

Name		
Address		
City	State	ZIP
Country	Tel # ( ) -	

Title of this Fodor's guide: _____

Store and location where guide was purchased: _____

INDICATE YOUR DESTINATIONS/DATES: Write in below the destinations you want to order. Then fill in your arrival and departure dates for each destination.

			Month	Day		Month	Day
(Sample)	LONDON	From:	6 /	21	To:	6 /	30
1		From:	/		To:	/	
2		From:	/		To:	/	
3		From:	/		To:	/	

You can order up to three destinations per Travel Update. Only destinations listed on the previous page are applicable. Maximum amount of time covered by a Travel Update cannot exceed 30 days.

CHOOSE YOUR INTERESTS: Select up to eight categories from the list of interest categories shown on the previous page and circle the numbers below:

1   2   3   4   5   6   7   8   9   10   11   12   13   14   15   16

CHOOSE HOW YOU WANT YOUR TRAVEL UPDATE DELIVERED (Check one):

❑ Please mail my Travel Update to the address above **OR**

❑ Fax it to me at **Fax #   (   )   -** _____

DELIVERY CHARGE (Check one)

	Within U.S. & Canada	Outside U.S. & Canada
First Class Mail	❑ $2.50	❑ $5.00
Fax	❑ $5.00	❑ $10.00
Priority Delivery	❑ $15.00	❑ $27.00

All orders will be sent within 48 hours of receipt of a completed order form.

ADD UP YOUR ORDER HERE. *SPECIAL OFFER FOR FODOR'S PURCHASERS ONLY!*

	Suggested Retail Price	Your Price	This Order
First destination ordered	$13.95	$ 7.95	$ 7.95
Second destination (if applicable)	$ 9.95	$ 4.95	+
Third destination (if applicable)	$ 9.95	$ 4.95	+
Plus delivery charge from above			+
		TOTAL:	$

METHOD OF PAYMENT (Check one):   ❑ AmEx   ❑ MC   ❑ Visa   ❑ Discover
                                       ❑ Personal Check   ❑ Money Order

Make check or money order payable to: Fodor's Worldview Travel Update

Credit Card # _____   **Expiration Date:** _____

Authorized Signature _____

SEND THIS COMPLETED FORM TO:
Fodor's Worldview Travel Update, 114 Sansome Street, Suite 700, San Francisco, CA 94104

OR CALL OR FAX US 24-HOURS A DAY
Telephone **1-800-799-9609** • Fax **1-800-799-9619** (From within the U.S. & Canada)
(Outside the U.S. & Canada: Telephone 415-616-9988 • Fax 415-616-9989)

(Please have this guide in front of you when you call so we can verify purchase.)

Offer valid until 12/31/94.